Third Edition

CANADIAN FEDERALISM

Performance, Effectiveness, and Legitimacy

Herman Bakvis • Grace Skogstad

OXFORD
UNIVERSITY PRE

D1113899

OXFORD
UNIVERSITY PRESS

Oxford University Press is a department of the University of Oxford.
It furthers the University's objective of excellence in research, scholarship,
and education by publishing worldwide. Oxford is a registered trade mark of
Oxford University Press in the UK and in certain other countries.

Published in Canada by
Oxford University Press
8 Sampson Mews, Suite 204,
Don Mills, Ontario M3C 0H5 Canada

www.oupcanada.com

Copyright © Oxford University Press Canada 2012

The moral rights of the authors have been asserted

Database right Oxford University Press (maker)

First Edition published in 2002
Second edition published 2008

Library and Archives Canada Cataloguing in Publication

Canadian federalism : performance, effectiveness, and legitimacy / edited by
Herman Bakvis & Grace Skogstad. 3rd ed.

Includes bibliographical references.
ISBN 978–0–19–543979–3

1. Federal government Canada Textbooks.
2. Canada Politics and government 1993-2006 Textbooks.
I. Bakvis, Herman, 1948– II. Skogstad, Grace, 1948–

JL27.C3493 2012   320.471   C2012-900062-0

Cover image © Rolf Hicker Photography / Alamy

Oxford University Press is committed to our environment.

Printed and bound in Canada
4 5 6 — 20 19 18

Contents

Preface

Like Canadian federalism itself, this third edition of *Canadian Federalism: Performance, Effectiveness, and Legitimacy* exhibits both continuity and change relative to the two earlier editions published in 2002 and 2008. As in earlier editions, we raise the same three questions: How well are the institutions and processes of Canadian federalism performing? Are they effective in addressing substantive problems? And are they seen as legitimate by the various communities and constituencies that make up Canada? Most of the policy sectors and institutions that were under scrutiny in earlier editions are also the subjects of the chapters in this edition.

As befits a new edition, however, there are also important innovations that go beyond updating of chapter material to take account of developments in Canadian federalism over the past four years. In response to feedback from instructors who used earlier editions of *Canadian Federalism*, this third edition includes three new additions: a chapter on the political economy of regionalism and federalism by Garth Stevenson, a chapter on Quebec and the Canadian federation by David Cameron, and a chapter on immigration by Keith Banting. With these changes, we believe this text on Canadian federalism offers an even more comprehensive examination of Canadian federalism than earlier editions.

This third edition would not have been possible without the collaboration and assistance of many people. Above all, we thank our contributors: the authors of the chapters that follow. They have been exemplary in their commitment to writing a clear and up-to-date account of developments in Canadian federalism in their chosen subject matter. We have also benefited from the advice of the anonymous reviewers who were commissioned by Oxford University Press to evaluate the prospectus for this third edition and, later, to read the entire manuscript. Finally, we are also grateful to the editors at Oxford University Press for steering this collection through to publication.

Herman Bakvis   Grace Skogstad
(hbakvis@uvic.ca)   (skogstad@chass.utoronto.ca)

Contributors

Gerald Baier
Department of Political Science
University of British Columbia

Herman Bakvis
School of Public Administration
University of Victoria

Keith G. Banting
School of Policy Studies & Department of
  Political Studies
Queen's University

Douglas M. Brown
Department of Political Science
St. Francis Xavier University

David Cameron
Department of Political Science
University of Toronto

Martha Friendly
Childcare Resource and Research Unit
University of Toronto

Rodney Haddow
Department of Political Science
University of Toronto

Douglas Macdonald
Centre for the Environment
University of Toronto

Antonia Maioni
Department of Political Science
McGill University

Amy Nugent
Government of Ontario

Martin Papillon
Department of Political Studies
University of Ottawa

Andrew Sancton
Department of Political Science
University of Western Ontario

Richard Simeon
Department of Political Science
University of Toronto

Julie Simmons
Department of Political Science
University of Guelph

Grace Skogstad
Department of Political Science
University of Toronto

Garth Stevenson
Department of Political Science
Brock University

A. Brian Tanguay
Department of Political Science
Wilfrid Laurier University

Linda A. White
Department of Political Science
University of Toronto

Mark Winfield
Faculty of Environmental Studies
York University

Part I

The History, Institutions, and Processes of Canadian Federalism

Questions for Critical Thought

1. Why is executive federalism such an enduring fixture of Canadian federalism and why does it remain relatively closed to scrutiny by the public?

2. How does the concept of intra- vs. interstate federalism help us identify and understand the critical features of the Canadian federation and the dynamics of intergovernmental relations?

3. How crucial to the evolution of Canadian federalism is the constitutional distribution of powers? Has the constitution impeded necessary change?

4. How has the development of Canada's political economy shaped Canadian federalism and its institutions? Is regionalism as important a factor in determining patterns of conflict and co-operation in the Canadian federation today as it was historically?

5. To what degree are fundamentally different conceptions of federalism in Quebec and the rest of the Canada a fault line in the federation? Can asymmetrical federalism and recognition of Quebec's special status in the federation overcome this fault line?

6. Has the Canadian party system served to knit together the Canadian federation? If not, why not?

1   Canadian Federalism: Performance, Effectiveness, and Legitimacy

Herman Bakvis and Grace Skogstad

Since the latter half of the nineteenth century, Canada has sought to unite a linguistically and regionally diverse citizen body within the confines of a single nation-state. The chosen formula has been federalism: a combination of shared rule, through a central government, on matters common to all citizens, and local self-rule, through provincial governments, on matters involving regionally distinctive identities, within a balanced structure designed to ensure that neither order of government is subordinate to the other (Watts, 1999: 1). From most perspectives, the Canadian federal arrangement has succeeded in striking the requisite balance between unity and diversity. It has also proven to be both flexible and resilient, allowing Canada to adjust its public policies to changing circumstances over time.

Even so, there have always been critics of the way Canadian federalism performs. Some observers have claimed that the federal 'balance' is lopsided, skewed by a tendency to either centralization or decentralization; others, that effective policy-making is hampered by either intergovernmental conflict or elite collusion. And, of course, the legitimacy of the Canadian federal system has been found wanting by groups with a strong sense of their own national identity, notably francophone Quebecers and indigenous peoples.

The purpose of this text is to investigate the state of contemporary Canadian federalism. It does so by asking three questions. How are the institutions of Canadian federalism performing? How do existing patterns of intergovernmental relations help or hinder effective policy-making? And how do Canadians evaluate the legitimacy of the institutions, processes, and outcomes of intergovernmental relations?

The investigation that follows has three dimensions: descriptive, evaluative, and explanatory. To explain the performance, effectiveness, and legitimacy of Canadian federalism it is necessary to look at a number of factors besides the structures of federalism itself. The Canadian federal system, like federal systems elsewhere, is embedded in a broader social, economic, institutional and political context. In other words, the institutions and processes of federalism can be seen as both responding to and shaped by:

1. structural cleavages in Canadian society, of which the most important historically have been ethno-linguistic and territorial differences in identities, values, and material/economic base;
2. the interests and ideas of authoritative political leaders in provincial and national capitals; and

3. extra-federal institutions including, most prominently, the Constitution and the parliamentary system.

These contextual factors, together with others originating in the international political economy, shape the performance of Canadian federalism. Some of them, like the Westminster parliamentary system, are relatively stable over time, and so their effects tend to be stable as well. Others, like the ideas and interests of first ministers, may vary quite widely: as the individuals who hold the highest government offices change, so (to a greater or lesser degree) does the functioning of Canadian federalism. Furthermore, with new personnel and their ideas, traditional institutions and practices may well be put to different uses and take on new meanings. A major objective of this text is to highlight how these institutional and contextual features interact with the structures and processes of federalism to shape the latter's performance, effectiveness, and legitimacy over time.

Performance: Institutions and Processes

Above all, assessing the performance of the Canadian federal system means focusing on the functioning of the institutions and processes of Canadian federalism. These institutions and processes are first, the constitutional division of powers between the two orders of government, along with the process of judicial review to which this division is subject; second, the institutions of intrastate federalism that provide for the representation of constituent units within the central government and the management of conflicts between the two orders of government; and third, the institutions and processes of interstate federalism through which the two orders relate directly to one another. Throughout this book, three criteria are used to assess performance: the consistency of governing arrangements with federal principles; the 'workability' of the institutions in question, both formal and informal; and the capacity of federal institutions to produce results in the form of agreements.

Consistency with Federal Principles

The foremost principle of federalism is that each order of government is autonomous within its sphere of authority: its jurisdictional powers may be altered only in conformity with constitutional provisions, never through unilateral action by the other order of government. Two questions are relevant here. Are the component units recognized by the centre as full members of the federation, with their own powers and the authority to act on them? And do the constituent units recognize the central government as having its own proper and autonomous role? To answer these questions we begin by examining the political economy of regionalism and federalism (Chapter 2, by Garth Stevenson), the place of Quebec in Canada (Chapter 3, by David Cameron) and judicial review of the formal division of powers in the Canadian Constitution (Chapter 5, by Gerry Baier). The chapters demonstrate, respectively, how regionalism in Canada, Quebec's insistence on respect for federal principles, and the courts' interpretation of the formal Constitution have thwarted the centralist vision of the federation of John A. Macdonald and ensured respect for the federal principle.

The second principle of federalism follows from the first and is the purpose that federal systems are created to serve: to provide a balance between unity and diversity. The relevant 'performance' question here is whether the mechanisms of interstate and intrastate federalism in fact secure the balance needed to ensure that the system does not slide into either a confederal arrangement (with the central government subordinate to the constituent units) or a unitary system (with the constituent units subordinate to the central government). Generally, the federal balance is a function of both the pattern of intergovernmental relations (interstate federalism) and the representation of constituent units in the central government (intrastate federalism).

Intrastate federalism is weak in Canada because, unlike most other federations, Canada lacks an effective second chamber of Parliament. The German upper house (Bundesrat), for example, is composed of representatives of the state (Länder) governments, while the Australian and American senates provide direct representation for citizens of the various constituent states. But the Canadian Senate offers no such representation to the provinces. With limited opportunity for formal representation of provincial interests in federal policy-making institutions, provincial governments have acquired over time greater authority to speak on behalf of the people within their borders. One consequence is that in Canada the task of securing the federal balance falls mainly to interstate federalism, since most intergovernmental activity takes place *between* governments rather than *within* an intrastate body such as a senate.

'Workability'

We adopt J.S. Dupré's (1985) definition of well-performing federal institutions and processes as providing forums 'conducive to negotiation, consultation, or simply an exchange of information'. Given a changing policy environment and continually shifting agendas, governments need to interact with each other in order to address mutual problems and manage interdependencies; at a minimum, they need to communicate with one another in order to make adjustments in their respective roles. As policy interdependence increases, so does the need for co-ordination and collaboration.

Capacity to produce results

In a federal system, producing results means reaching agreement on issues. Conflict is inherent in federal systems. Thus a crucial test of their performance is their ability to manage intergovernmental conflict. Simply agreeing to disagree may be one way of managing conflict. However, citizens will normally expect the two orders of government to set aside their differences and deal with the issues upon which citizens' well-being and the integrity of the political community as a whole depend.

In brief, to perform well a federal system must respect federal principles, sustain the balance between unity and diversity, provide a setting for discussion and negotiation between governments, and facilitate agreement, or at least understanding, on major issues in a manner that respects the positions of both levels of government. Given the centrality of interstate federalism to the performance of the Canadian federal system, patterns of intergovernmental relations are a frequent theme in this book.

The chapters that follow make it abundantly clear that there is no single way to describe intergovernmental relations in Canada. Patterns shift not only over time but across

Independent governments	Consultation	Co-ordination	Collaboration	Joint decision-making

Figure 1.1 Models of Canadian Federalism

issues within a single period, and scholars have used a variety of labels to describe them. Figure 1.1, for example, locates several models of federalism along a continuum from independence to interdependence of the two orders of government.

At one end of the continuum, central and provincial/territorial governments are independent of one another. This is the classical form of federalism: the 'watertight compartments' model in which each order of government has exclusive authority in its sphere of jurisdiction, and no attempt is made to consult or co-ordinate activities with the other order (Wheare, 1951). But exclusivity of jurisdiction in itself does not ensure respect for the federal balance. Much depends as well on the distribution of legal authority across the two orders of government: each must have sufficient authority to maintain the unity–diversity balance. Striking that balance in the Constitution Act of 1867 (formerly the British North America Act, 1867) was crucial to the formation of a political and economic union that included Quebec.

Scholars have generally situated the Canadian federal Constitution in the late nineteenth century at the 'watertight compartments' end of the continuum. In contrast to some other federal constitutions, the 1867 Act assigned almost all subject matters to either the federal or the provincial order of government, giving that order the exclusive authority both to make laws in that area and to implement them. The one exception is criminal law: what constitutes criminal activity is defined by the federal government in the Criminal Code, but the provinces are responsible for enforcing that legislation. There are also three areas of shared or concurrent jurisdiction: immigration and agriculture have been shared jurisdictions since 1867, and pensions joined them in the mid-twentieth century.

Thus the federal system created in 1867 was situated near the left-hand end of the continuum—but at the same time it was not entirely consistent with the watertight compartments model. In fact the compartments were far from impermeable (Stevenson, 1993; Watts, 2003), and the central government had various instruments it could use in areas of provincial jurisdiction: the power to appoint lieutenant-governors with the right to reserve provincial legislation, the declaratory power that allowed the federal government to take over provincial undertakings in the national interest, and the power of the governor general to disallow provincial legislation. Federal challenges to provincial legislative authority through these 'quasi-federal' mechanisms were infrequent by the late nineteenth century, but it was not until 1943 that Ottawa used the power of disallowance for the last time.

Since the 1930s Canadian federalism has moved towards the other end of the continuum. As governments at both levels expanded the range of their activities, jurisdictional overlap and policy interdependence intensified. So did the need for consultation and, eventually, co-ordination. 'Consultation' as a model of intergovernmental relations means that governments exchange information and views before acting independently, leaving the other order to make its own arrangements (Watts, 2003). Co-ordination means going beyond consultation to develop mutually acceptable policies and objectives, which each order of government then applies in its own jurisdiction.

Successful intergovernmental co-operation around taxation policies during the Second World War continued after 1945 as the Canadian social welfare state was constructed. A period of federal dominance during the Second World War gave way to an era of '**co-operative federalism**' during the 1950s lasting into the early 1960s (Simeon and Robinson, 1990: Chs. 6, 8, and 9). Together, fiscally and politically strong provincial governments and a national government armed with a potent spending power created social programs in areas of provincial jurisdiction like health care, post-secondary education, and social assistance. (For a more detailed discussion of 'shared-cost federalism', see Keith Banting in Chapter 8.) At least one of these social programs, the Canada Pension Plan, led to a joint-decision model of federalism: not only did the two orders of government work closely to construct the pension plan, but under its decision-making rules any changes to the plan required the agreement of a specified number of provincial governments as well as Ottawa.

Co-operative federalism coexisted with **competitive federalism**. The competitive dynamic is virtually inherent in Canadian federalism, rooted in ideological diversity, genuine differences of interests arising from differences in material/economic base and societal demands, and the electoral imperative to gain credit and avoid blame (Simeon, 1972). Led by different political parties fighting elections at different times over different issues, provincial and national governments inevitably butt heads as each seeks to maximize its autonomy, jurisdiction, and standing with voters. Intergovernmental competition reached a zenith during the 1970s and early 1980s, when province-building ambitions clashed with the unilateral nation-building initiatives of Prime Minister Trudeau, including the 1980 National Energy Program and constitutional patriation and reform. Competition receded somewhat during the Mulroney era (1984–93).

Whether in its co-operative or its competitive form, the pattern of intergovernmental relations that took shape in the 1960s brings elected and appointed officials of the two orders of government into repeated interaction. Labelled 'executive federalism' (Smiley, 1976: 54), this is the defining feature of Canadian federalism. The predominant role of governmental executives (ministers and their officials) in intergovernmental relations is a uniquely Canadian phenomenon that originated in the combination of Canada's jurisdictional federalism and Westminster parliamentary system.

As we noted earlier, Canada's weak intrastate federalism gives provincial governments both the opportunity and the incentive to claim an exclusive right to represent the interests of Canadians within their borders. In Chapter 4, Richard Simeon and Amy Nugent elaborate on how the logics of the parliamentary and federal systems combine to create this effect. The national government lacks effective forums for the representation of 'provincial' interests. At the same time, political authority is concentrated in the executive: the prime minister/premier and cabinet (Savoie, 1999; White, 2005). Executives at both levels thus have considerable latitude to strike bargains on behalf of their governments. And because these executives are relatively few in number—fourteen with the inclusion of territorial governments—the federal–provincial bargaining characteristic of executive federalism is, at least in theory, logistically manageable in a way that it would not be in the United States, for example. Accordingly, inter-provincial disputes are generally resolved through direct negotiations between ministers or senior officials rather than submitted to the upper chamber of the central government (as in Germany or even the United States) for resolution by elected representatives of the people.

As we suggested above, executive federalism is also a response to policy interdependence: the overlap and duplication that are inevitable with two activist orders of government. Since the rise of the modern state in the mid-twentieth century, there have been very few policy areas in which either Ottawa or the provinces can operate without bumping into the jurisdiction of another government. Thus, finding an effective solution to a policy dilemma, even one that lies entirely within the jurisdiction of a single order of government, invariably requires collaboration with the other order. At the very least, the government with the authority to make a decision must take into account its implications for other governments. Executive federalism, with its dual logic of co-operation and competition, is therefore central to any discussion of the performance of Canadian federalism, as well as its effectiveness and legitimacy.

The most important forums of intergovernmental consultation and co-ordination are:

1. first ministers' conferences (FMCs) and first ministers' meetings (FMMs) of premiers and the prime minister;
2. ministerial meetings (i.e., meetings of the various ministers holding a particular portfolio, such as health or the environment);
3. meetings of public servants (officials); and
4. inter-provincial meetings of the provinces and the territories, in which the federal government does not take part.

FMCs were particularly frequent during the constitutional negotiations of the early 1990s, after which they declined in number and were replaced by less formal FMMs. At the same time, the numbers of ministerial and, especially, officials' meetings began to increase, and they have grown steadily ever since.

These forums of executive federalism have often provided opportunities for intergovernmental co-operation, allowing politicians to circumvent constitutional rigidities and respond more directly to societal demands and problems. Co-operation is most likely when the stakes are relatively low and the participants share the same values, typically in a substantive policy domain. When the stakes are higher, political elites may not be so willing to compromise, and the forums of executive federalism can become venues for intergovernmental competition. This dysfunctional feature of executive federalism, J.S. Dupré (1985) has argued, has been promoted by the centralization of intergovernmental relations within first ministers' offices and specialized agencies. It manifests itself in particular at the upper levels: at FMCs or meetings of finance ministers, where the stakes tend to be very high.

Since the mid- to late 1990s, some analysts have identified a new variant that they call '**collaborative federalism**'. For Cameron and Simeon (2002: 49) the distinguishing feature of collaborative federalism is 'co-determination of broad national policies'. This collaboration takes one of two forms: federal and provincial/territorial governments 'working together as equals', or provincial and territorial governments working together to formulate national policy themselves, without the federal government. For

Lazar (1997), collaborative federalism is less hierarchical than the co-operative federalism of the Pearson and Trudeau years (the 1960s and 1970s), when Ottawa alone initiated shared-cost programs and the provinces followed its lead. In some respects collaborative federalism reflects Canada's evolution, since the era of co-operative federalism, into one of the world's most decentralized federations, with federal and provincial governments relatively evenly balanced in their power and status and at the same time highly interdependent (Watts, 1996: 111).

Collaborative federalism represents an effort to formalize the increasingly informal, rules-free relationship that had developed between the two orders of government under executive federalism. Agreements like the 1995 Agreement on Internal Trade (AIT), the 1998 Canada-Wide Accord on Environmental Harmonization, and the 1999 Social Union Framework Agreement (SUFA) sought to clarify and streamline government responsibilities in order to minimize the negative spillover effects for other governments and/or industry. These agreements are not legally binding ('justiciable'), but they do include dispute settlement mechanisms. Whether this rule-based federalism is effective in managing the conflict inherent in federal systems is a question taken up by Gerald Baier in Chapter 5.

Collaborative federalism emerged in response to the circumstances in which Ottawa and the provinces found themselves in the 1990s. Formal efforts to reverse the decline in perceptions of the performance and legitimacy of the federal arrangement through constitutional reform—specifically the Meech Lake Accord (1987–90) and the Charlottetown Agreement (1992)—had failed. When the Liberal government of Jean Chrétien took power in 1993, it turned its back on constitutional reform as a way of correcting perceived deficiencies in the Canadian federal system. The need to demonstrate that the federal system could be renewed and reformed to work in the interests both of Quebec and of the other provinces was only heightened following the razor-thin defeat of the separatist forces in the 1995 Quebec referendum (Lazar, 1997). Collaboration was not the only game in town, however. The referendum result stiffened Ottawa's resolve vis-à-vis Quebec separatists, as well as its determination to demonstrate that the government of Canada was a power to be reckoned with. The *Reference re Quebec Secession* and the subsequent Clarity Bill were two indications of this 'tough love' strategy.

Three other circumstances also promoted collaborative federalism. First was the increasing *regional and global integration* of the Canadian political economy in the 1990s. It exposed Canadian firms to more foreign competition even while it opened new foreign markets for them. It also required Canadian governments to share more of their sovereignty with international rule-making and rule-enforcement institutions, such as the World Trade Organization. These developments highlighted the interdependence of governments, and responding effectively to them, it is argued, demanded greater policy co-ordination and collaboration between governments within Canada. A second factor was the increasing *regionalization* of Canada's national political parties after 1993 with the rise of the Reform and Bloc Québécois parties. (See Chapter 6.) As the governing Liberal party became increasingly vulnerable to charges that it did not represent all parts of the country, provincial governments increasingly became the champions of interests and ideas not represented in Ottawa. A third factor was the ascendancy of *neo-liberalism* and the companion philosophy known as *new public management*. While the former called for governments to play a smaller role in society and the market, the latter called for governments to work more closely with one another in the interest of greater administrative efficiency and clarity. Proponents of New Public Management and collaborative federalism espouse similar values and tenets: decentralization, less emphasis on formal rules, and more flexible and informal arrangements (Simeon, 1997).

At the same time, regional and global economic integration and the new public management philosophy created pressures for extension of the collaborative model to embrace non-state actors. And a shift in the *political culture*, away from elitist and non-transparent executive federalism towards more direct citizen input into decision-making, had a similar effect (Nevitte, 1996). Among the societal cultural changes that have been particularly consequential, as Martin Papillon explains in Chapter 15, is the growing determination of Canada's First Nations to move beyond the legacy of colonialism and take more direct control over their own affairs in many areas.

A number of contextual factors ensured that the competitive dynamic never disappeared from intergovernmental relations in this period, despite the rhetoric of collaborative federalism. *Fiscal deficits* at both levels of government put the two starkly at odds over who would fund costly social programs like health care. And in other policy domains, as the first edition of *Canadian Federalism* (2002) showed, initiatives such as the National Child Benefit (1998) demonstrated that the Chrétien government never entirely abandoned the 'independent governments' model.

As the chapters that follow will make clear, Canadian federalism has taken a variety of forms, sometimes simultaneously: co-operative and competitive, collaborative and independent. Figure 1.1 (p. 5) captured neither the competitive dynamic nor the element of unilateralism in intergovernmental relations. Lazar's (2006) typology of intergovernmental relations in the area of social policy subdivides the 'independent governments' model into **classical federalism** and **unilateral federalism**. In the former, governments act independently and each remains within its own constitutionally assigned jurisdiction; in the latter, one order of government (usually the federal) imposes its views and priorities on the other, usually by attaching conditions to its fiscal transfers. Lazar differentiates unilateral federalism, which he reserves for cases of policy interdependence, from 'beggar-thy-partner federalism', in which governments act independently but the actions of one impose substantial obligations on the other (2006: 29).

Looking ahead to the chapters that follow in this collection, is there reason to expect one or more of various federalism models—classical federalism, independent governments, collaborative federalism, **joint-decision federalism**, unilateral federalism, competitive federalism, shared-cost federalism—to have been at the fore in recent years? More specifically, should we expect to see more of the collaborative federalism that emerged in the late 1990s and early 2000s?

To answer this question, it is helpful to reflect on some features of the context of Canadian federalism in the latter half of the first decade of the twenty-first century that are likely to have shaped the ideas and interests of pivotal actors (in particular, first ministers and their cabinets). Some of these features are similar to those that gave rise to collaborative federalism in the 1990s. First, the integration of the Canadian and American economies has remained important. Writing in the early 2000s, scholars like Lazar et al. (2003) and Simeon (2003) argued that there was no evidence that regional and global integration were undermining the federal bargain or having a discernible impact on Canadian federalism and intergovernmental relations. However, as Grace Skogstad discusses in Chapter 11, the increasing intrusion of international trade agreements into provincial areas of jurisdiction has the potential to reshape intergovernmental relations because provinces alone have the authority to implement provisions of international treaties that fall within their jurisdiction. Second, there has been continuity in the central institutions of intrastate and interstate federalism whose various logics of parliamentary government, federalism, and intergovernmental relations tend to encourage certain patterns of behaviour (see Chapter 4).

At the same time, the context and the individual actors who are pivotal to the performance of the Canadian federalism have changed in some important ways from those that spurred collaborative federalism. First, Canada experienced an extended period of minority government in the House of Commons, beginning in June 2004 with the Paul Martin Liberal government, continuing with the successive Conservative governments elected in January 2006 and October 2008, and ending only in May 2011 when the Conservative Party obtained a majority. As Prime Minister, Stephen Harper publicly espouses a policy of Open Federalism that respects provincial jurisdiction and is less intrusive in provincial affairs. Such a policy, alongside the Conservative governments' 'small government' preference, implied the need for less intergovernmental collaboration. Whereas Liberal governments sought to demonstrate the importance of the national government (and thus garner votes) by expanding the scope of federal activity to include spheres of provincial jurisdiction like health, child care, and cities, the strategy of the Harper Conservative government to achieve these same ends has been to expand the role of the government of Canada in areas of federal jurisdiction like defense and criminal justice (prisons), and to retract it in areas of provincial jurisdiction like child care (see Friendly and White, Chapter 10) and the environment (see Winfield and Macdonald, Chapter 13). That is, while the Liberal government's minority government status and the search for votes lent momentum to collaborative federalism, the Conservatives' philosophy veers towards the independent governments' model.

However, the Conservative government's preference for a lesser government role in the economy was derailed to some considerable degree when it was forced—on real threat of defeat—by opposition parties into stimulus spending to mitigate the effects of the downturn in the American and global economies after September 2008. This stimulus spending has entailed extensive collaboration with provincial/territorial and municipal governments.

Second, since 2003, Quebec has been governed by a Liberal Premier who differs from his Parti Québécois predecessor in his practice of working with his provincial counterparts to achieve his goals. Premier Jean Charest took the lead in the creation of the Council of the Federation, a decision which has provided greater institutional backing to the annual premiers' conference, and potentially made it easier for the 10 provincial premiers and three territorial leaders to develop a common bargaining position vis-à-vis the government of Canada. A high priority for the Charest government has been to correct the perceived 'fiscal imbalance' that opened up as the budgetary situations of the federal and most provincial governments improved and the gap between a wealthy, energy-rich province like Alberta has widened.

Third, there has been an ongoing shift in economic power westward, especially to Alberta. Since 2009, and for the first time in the country's history, the province of Ontario is a recipient of equalization payments. The redistribution of wealth across provinces, and the novel position in which the province of Ontario finds itself, are putting pressure on the equalization program in fiscal federalism, as Doug Brown explains in Chapter 7. This situation also foreshadows a more aggressive Ontario in the federation, one that no longer believes it is a net beneficiary of federalism and so is less inclined to support a national government with strong wealth redistributive powers (Matthews and Mendelsohn, 2010).

Fourth, if the above suggest a more competitive federalism, another development gives room for optimism that the collaborative model of federalism still flourishes. There is evidence that provinces are collaborating more with one another. Some of this collaboration is occurring across all provinces within the Council of the Federation, but other interprovincial collaboration is bilateral or trilateral. For example, Ontario and Quebec have engaged in efforts to remove barriers to movement of labour across their borders, and BC, Alberta, and Saskatchewan have co-operated on removing barriers to the movement of labour, goods, and services across their provincial borders in the form of the New West Partnership Trade Agreement, struck in 2010.

Effectiveness: Policy Outcomes

'Effectiveness' refers explicitly to policy outcomes: the public policies and programs made within and resulting from the web of intergovernmental interactions. How effective are they in dealing with the substantive problems that occasioned intergovernmental bargaining and conflict resolution in the first place? How efficient are the resulting programs in marshalling resources? Do policies allow for asymmetry where it is desired and appears warranted? Do policy outcomes allow international commitments to be met? The fact that two or more governments reach agreement on a particular issue does not necessarily mean that the underlying social or economic issues have been effectively resolved. Focusing on substantive policy typically requires the use of benchmarks or standards to see how policy outcomes measure up. But assessment is easier in some policy areas than in others. In the case of the environment, for example, it is possible to measure quantities of emissions and effluents. In other areas, however, one has to depend on more qualitative assessments. The quality of policy outcomes often lies in the eyes of the beholder. It is also useful to remember that there is a distinction between 'policy outcomes' and 'policy outputs'. Policy outputs—the decisions made regarding programs and policies—may have unintended consequences and, as a result, their actual outcomes may look quite different from the original plan. It is often only with hindsight that the distinction between outputs and outcomes becomes clear.

It is difficult to determine exactly how federalism and intergovernmental relations affect public policy outcomes. First, developments in any policy area are contingent on several factors, of which federalism is only one—though it may be the most important. Studies of federal systems have found no discernible effects of federalism on policy outcomes and have had difficulty identifying any differences between federal and decentralized unitary states in this respect (Braun, 2000; Norris, 2005). Second—and a reason why those studies have yielded few results—the effects of federalism on policy-making are likely to depend on the prevailing model of federalism: independent governments, unilateralism, competitive, collaborative, or joint-decision (McRoberts, 1993).

Any discussion of how different models of federalism shape public policy outcomes in Canada must begin with a discussion of the spending power: the power that allows the Parliament of Canada to make payments to individual Canadians, institutions, or provincial governments for purposes outside its constitutional jurisdiction. Although the spending power can be used in a way consistent with the independent governments model (for example, when the federal government makes payments directly to individual Canadians for child care, or to post-secondary educational institutions), it is more often used as an instrument to increase interdependence across the two orders of government.

The federal spending power has important implications for the performance, effectiveness, and legitimacy of the federation. It breaches the federal principle of exclusive jurisdictions and (as will be discussed further in the next section) undermines the legitimacy of the federal system, particularly in the eyes of many Quebecers. The chapters on social policy in this volume suggest that its impact on the effectiveness of the federation may be more positive. But the impact of its use has generally been judged differently, depending on whether it is used unilaterally (in a model of unilateral federalism, to use Lazar's 2006 term) or constrained by collaborative or joint-decision federalism.

The arm's length or 'independent governments' model of classical federalism preserves autonomy and freedom of action at both levels. It gives each government the opportunity and flexibility to experiment with and innovate in devising solutions to policy problems (Banting, 1995). Indeed, citizens who live outside an innovative state or province may eventually benefit from its experiments. The classic Canadian example is the adoption of universally available and publicly funded hospital and clinical care, following Saskatchewan's pioneering example (see Chapter 9 by Antonia Maioni). A more recent example is child care; Quebec's innovative low-cost, universally available program has provided an attractive model for child-care advocates in other provinces.

Some analysts argue that the 'independent governments' model is likely to be particularly effective in addressing citizens' demands when the competitive dynamic is uppermost (Breton, 1996; Harrison, 1996; Young, 2003). Competition across provinces can create 'a race to the top' when voters press their provincial governments to emulate policies and standards developed somewhere else (Harrison, 2005). In a period of buoyant finances, the competition for voters' support can lead both orders of government to expand public services and take on new state activities, as Banting demonstrates in Chapter 8.

The 'independent governments' model can also work to the advantage of non-state actors with the resources to organize on both federal and provincial fronts. Having two access points, federal and provincial, gives non-state actors two kicks at the can, allowing them to play one order of government off against the other in pursuit of their policy objectives.

There are, of course, downsides when governments act independently of one another and fail to co-ordinate their activities. The risks of policy incoherence and program incompatibility increase. Problems are more likely to be ignored when blame can be shifted to the other order of government. The latter dynamic is especially likely when it is unclear which level of government should be responsible for addressing a problem, or when resolving it will entail significant financial or political costs. Even when intergovernmental competition promotes the development of new programs, the results may not be entirely beneficial. Policies may be designed with more concern for the interests of the sponsoring government than for efficacy in dealing with the problem at hand. A tax benefit or direct payment to parents to help cover child-care costs, for instance, may serve the interests of a government seeking to improve its image among voters, but such a policy will do nothing to create the new daycare spaces that working parents need.

The joint decision-making model is typically associated with ineffective policy-making and poor outcomes (Scharpf, 1988; Pierson, 1995). This model requires joint action of governments at both levels, by virtue of either unanimous or super-majority agreement. Governments lose their autonomy and flexibility, but they do retain the power of veto. With multiple points at which change can be rejected, joint decision-making typically leads to a number of 'traps'. Existing programs become difficult if not impossible to modify. When agreement is reached, the outcome is often less than optimal—a 'lowest common denominator' solution, designed to satisfy the most recalcitrant party.

As with any collaborative model, resolving substantive problems in the most effective and efficient way is likely to take second place to the political and institutional concerns of state actors, the desire for status and recognition, and the desire to gain credit and avoid blame. From the perspective of non-state actors, the multiple 'veto points' offered by a joint-decision model present both opportunities and obstacles. As Banting explains in Chapter 8, those who favour the status quo are likely to welcome the high threshold of agreement for policy change, while those who seek change will be frustrated.

Co-operative and collaborative models fit somewhere between the 'independent governments' and joint-decision models, depending on how formalized they are and how much scope they leave for independent action by governments. Social safety-net programs are a case in point. At first the government of Canada contributed half the costs of hospital care, post-secondary education, and social assistance. Then it reduced its financial contribution for these programs, leaving the provincial level to pay a larger share of the tab, although the shift to block funding gave the provinces more scope to direct the money as they saw fit. More recent forms of collaborative federalism have limited the participating governments' scope for action; SUFA, for example, constrains the federal spending power even while recognizing its legitimacy. The more rule-bound the collaborative model, the greater the likelihood that intergovernmental relations will be hampered by these joint-decision traps. On the other hand, a set of specific rules governing decision-making, such as decision-rules that allow for qualified majority decision-making (as distinct from unanimity), as in the case of the Canada Pension Plan, can help limit to some degree the occurrence of joint-decision-making traps (Bakvis et al 2009).

The ability of Canadian federalism to tackle major policy challenges has varied over time. The Depression of the 1930s is widely seen as a low-water mark, when the Judicial Committee of the Privy Council insisted on a classic interpretation of federalism that prevented the national government from playing a broader role in social and economic programs to address the needs of Canadians. Federalism scored higher points after the Second World War, as governments variously recognized their interdependence, co-operated, and competed with one another for the political affections of Canadians (Simeon, 1972, 2006). If international indices measuring physical and social well-being and overall quality of life are a reliable guide, it appears that federalism has not impeded Canadian federal and provincial governments in their pursuit of effective and coherent policies, either jointly or separately.

Still, the effectiveness of Canadian federalism depends on both the policy area or substantive issue in question and the model of federalism at work. The following chapters cover a wide array of policy areas, from social policy, health care, child care, and immigration to the environment, economic development, skills training, and international trade. They also investigate some subjects that involve multiple policy issues: cities, Aboriginal governance, recognition of Quebec's distinct needs, and the role of non-governmental actors in intergovernmental relations. These policy areas have been chosen for three reasons.

First, they are essential to the integrity of the Canadian social and economic union. In the field of social policy, for example, programs such as child and health care represent principles central to Canadian identity and citizenship: all Canadians, regardless of where they live, share both the obligation to finance these programs and the right to benefit from them. It is the sense of mutual obligations and rights that underpins Canada as a social union (Courchene, 1994). Immigration policies are also central to the Canadian identity, literally defining who we are. Policies in areas such as international trade (Chapter 11 by Grace Skogstad), economic development and skills training (Chapter 12 by Rodney Haddow), and climate change (Chapter 13 by Mark Winfield and Doug Macdonald) have more to do with the productivity and competitiveness of the economic union. At the same time, distinctive provincial needs and tastes in these policy areas reinforce claims for provincial jurisdiction and policy diversity. This policy array therefore provides insight into the balance struck between the rights and duties of membership in the social and economic union, on the one hand, and recognition of the diverse needs and circumstances of the constituent provincial units and communities, on the other.

Second, the policy areas chosen for examination are ones that allow us to assess the resilience and adaptability of Canadian federalism in response to different kinds of challenges. The contextual shift from a period of government deficits to one of fiscal surpluses and then back again to deficits, for instance, has significant implications for social policies (health, child care, and post-secondary education); it also tests the capacity of fiscal federalism to continue playing the role of an east–west 'social railway' ascribed it by Thomas Courchene (1994). Canadians' commitment to income redistribution appears to be threatened as we increasingly trade more with non-Canadians than with each other. Canada's participation in international environmental treaties and protocols tests the capacity of the two orders of government to devise a coherent response to evolving international environmental norms and to implement effective international agreements at home. Similarly, Canada's integration into the North American political economy tests the collaborative capacities of Canadian governments, in this case to develop coherent trade and economic development strategies.

Third, the policy areas and issues examined in this book contain a mix of high- and low-profile issues on which the dynamics of intergovernmental relations, and potentially the models as well, can be expected to differ (Dupré, 1985). To some extent this is also a distinction between 'old' and 'new' issues. Some issues, like economic development strategies, fiscal federalism, immigration, and international trade are of interest to specialized policy communities. Others, like health care, attract the attention of all Canadians. Some fall somewhere in between, engaging the attention of the general public only intermittently. Intergovernmental competition is expected to be greater on high-profile issues, particularly when the issue is an old one with a history of intergovernmental acrimony (e.g., health care), while co-operative or collaborative models are more likely to come to the fore on issues of interest mainly to those citizens with a direct stake in the policy. International trade and climate change are examples here. Issues that touch deeply on provincial areas of jurisdiction, or that are associated with a history of intergovernmental acrimony, are likely to prove especially difficult tests. Policy interdependence itself is not necessarily a barrier to effective policy-making; whether it becomes a problem will depend on the public salience of the policy area and the historic legacy of intergovernmental relations attached to it.

Even though the focus of this text is on the role of federalism in policy development, it is important not to exaggerate federalism's impact. Developments in any one policy area are contingent on a number of factors, and (as we observed earlier) federalism's impact in that area may be minimal at a particular point in time. At other times federalism may well be the crucial factor determining success or failure. Furthermore, neither competition nor co-operation should be automatically equated with positive outcomes. Competition can be associated with either innovation or stalemate, co-operation with either problem resolution or elite collusion.

Legitimacy

Governments must be perceived as legitimate if they are to count on the unequivocal support of citizens. Legitimacy is a reflection of the public's perceptions of the appropriateness of governing arrangements and their outcomes. In federal systems, the cleavages of region, culture, language, and the division between first peoples and immigrant settlers (to name the most obvious case), raise the real possibility that some citizens may view the governing arrangements associated with federalism as legitimate and others may not. To appraise the legitimacy of Canadian federalism, therefore, we view it through the separate lenses of the various communities and constituencies that make up Canada.

One highly relevant question for appraising the legitimacy of Canadian federalism is whether the governing federal arrangements incorporate the various constituent units' understandings of their own roles and status in the federal system. As David Cameron explains (Chapter 3), Quebec's political elite (if not most of its population) has had a different understanding of federalism from its counterparts in other provincial capitals and in Ottawa. For Quebec's political elite, the federal union represents the union of two political communities, 'peoples', or 'nations': one English-speaking and located mostly outside Quebec, the other overwhelmingly francophone and based in Quebec. In the words of Claude Ryan (2003), 'Quebec is the seat of a national community. Its legislature and government are national institutions, at least in their jurisdictions.' English-speaking Canada, in contrast, sees the country as a union of territorial units (provinces), all of which are equal in legal status. In other words, the distinction is between Canada as a multinational federation (of which Quebec is one of two or more constituent nations) versus Canada as a territorial federation (Tully, 1995).

The understanding that Quebec constitutes a distinct political community within Canada has led Quebec's political elite to demand two things of the federal system: (1) formal recognition of Quebec's distinct status within the federation and, consistent with such recognition, (2) preservation and expansion of the province's legal authority and autonomy so as to safeguard the unique cultural and linguistic character of the Quebec national community. For Quebec's political elite, the legitimacy of the federal system depends overwhelmingly on the degree to which it provides for asymmetry between Quebec's status in the federation and that of the other provinces (Gagnon, 2001).

There has always been some asymmetry in the autonomy and power of different provinces within the Canadian federation (Watts, 2005). Some asymmetrical features were embedded in the Constitution Act of 1867; others have been introduced over time. Two examples are the administrative arrangement under which Quebec runs its own version of the Canada Pension Plan and immigration policy. While only Quebec administers its own pension plan, Banting documents in Chapter 14 extension of the principle of asymmetry to several provinces when it comes to immigration policy.

Quebec's quest for formal recognition of its distinct status within the federation has been less successful than its pursuit of asymmetry. The Constitution Act 1982 represented an outright rejection of its aspirations, and the failure of subsequent efforts at constitutional reform (the Meech Lake Accord and the Charlottetown Agreement) almost proved deadly for Canadian federalism. The 1995 referendum on Quebec's secession from Canada was defeated by the slimmest of margins.

Quebec is not the only political community to question the legitimacy of Canada's federal Constitution: so do Canada's Aboriginal peoples. Martin Papillon (Chapter 15) reminds us that Aboriginal peoples also seek recognition and greater control over their own communities, often through a third order of self-governing communities. Papillon explores the progress that has been made towards Aboriginal self-government and the obstacles that still lie in the way of reconciling the federal system and Aboriginal self-government.

A different sort of pressure on the federal system comes from one order of government that has been excluded from the federal arrangement. Advocates for the municipal level argue that changes in the global economy have put cities at the heart of provincial and national competitiveness strategies, and therefore that cities urgently need greater political autonomy and more fiscal resources. Andrew Sancton weighs the case for city-states against that for better co-ordination of federal and provincial policies with respect to cities in Chapter 16.

For many Canadians, including executives of most of the English-speaking provinces, assessing the legitimacy of the Canadian federal system means examining the appropriateness of the procedures and processes followed in policy-making and the substantive features of policy outcomes. Are the rules of the game by which governments interact and negotiate to arrive at policy decisions accepted by governments themselves? How well do existing federal institutions and intergovernmental processes conform to citizens' expectations regarding their own roles as participants in decision-making? Are these processes consistent with norms of accountability and transparency? Do they meet the expectations of the relevant policy community? Do the outcomes of intergovernmental policy-making reflect the distinct values and preferences of the communities concerned? Are they consistent with those communities' standards of effectiveness, efficiency, and fairness?

The three criteria—performance, effectiveness and legitimacy—are closely linked. Weak performance, in the form of gridlock in executive federalism, for instance, will normally lead to policy ineffectiveness. Problems will go unresolved where effective action requires intergovernmental co-operation. Yet intergovernmental consensus in itself does not necessarily yield effective policies. It may simply mean that the two orders of government have agreed to ignore politically difficult issues. Repeated over time, policy ineffectiveness will only lead citizens to give failing marks to the system as a whole. Similarly, a federal system that under-performs by failing to provide sufficient scope for the expression of regional particularities will also undermine the legitimacy of the system. Because legitimacy is appraised in both substantive and procedural terms, the links between effectiveness and legitimacy are somewhat complex. One would ordinarily expect citizens to support federal practices that yield effective policies by addressing problems in a timely and efficient manner. If the political culture places a high priority on democratic processes, however, policies arrived at through closed, non-transparent, and unaccountable processes may still be viewed as illegitimate, even if they are highly effective in delivering certain outcomes.

When individual Canadians are asked to appraise the legitimacy of Canadian federalism, they appear to be much more interested in outcomes than in respect for federal principles. Cutler and Mendelsohn (2001a) found that Canadians outside Quebec show little concern for whether governments respect the constitutional division of powers. In their words,

> Canadians have no deep commitment to the principle of federalism, have little knowledge of the existing division of powers, and care little about which government exercises which power. In important policy areas, they care about results, and they see co-operation between governments as best able to achieve this (Cutler and Mendelsohn, 2001b).

Even so, individual Canadians' perceptions of the legitimacy of Canadian federalism are likely to be based on both the results of executive federalism (output legitimacy) and its procedures (input legitimacy). Certainly, Jennifer Smith (2004) argues that Canadian federalism falls short when it comes to promoting democratic participation in the policy-making process.

Two chapters in this collection focus directly on the democratic quality of intergovernmental processes. First, in Chapter 4, Richard Simeon and Amy Nugent examine how executive federalism undermines democratic norms of citizen participation and accountability through chambers of representative democracy. Later, in Chapter 17, Julie Simmons takes a careful look at the roles played by non-state actors in a variety of intergovernmental policy initiatives as she examines three different models of democracy at work in intergovernmental relations: representative, consultative, and deliberative participatory democracy. Several other chapters also examine the roles of non-state actors in policies related to the social and economic union.

In the second decade of the twenty-first century, federalism continues to provide the essential framework for governance in Canada. How effectively and legitimately it does so, and how it is changing as political elites within both orders of government grapple with contemporary challenges, is the subject of the chapters that follow.

References

Bakvis, H., G. Baier, and D. Brown. 2009. *Contested Federalism: Certainty and Ambiguity in the Canadian Federation*. Don Mills, ON: Oxford University Press.

Banting, K. 1995. 'The Welfare State as Statecraft: Territorial Politics and Canadian Social Policy'. In *European Social Policy*, ed. S. Leibfried and P. Pierson. Washington: Brookings Institution.

Braun, D. 2000. 'Territorial Division of Power and Public Policy-Making: An Overview'. In *Public Policy and Federalism*, ed. D. Braun. Aldershot: Ashgate.

Breton, A. 1996. *Competitive Governments: An Economic Theory of Politics and Public Finance*. New York: Cambridge University Press.

Cameron, D., and R. Simeon. 2002. 'Intergovernmental Relations in Canada: The Emergence of Collaborative Federalism', *Publius* 32, 2: 49–71.

Courchene, T.J. 1994. *Social Canada in the Millennium: Reform Imperatives and Restructuring Principles*. Toronto: C.D. Howe Institute.

Cutler, F., and M. Mendelsohn. 2001a. 'What Kind of Federalism Do Canadians (outside Quebec) Want?' *Policy Options* 22, 8: 23–9.

——— and ———. 2001b. Op-Ed. *Globe and Mail*, 31 Jul.: A11.

Dupré, J.S. 1985. 'Reflections on the Workability of Executive Federalism'. In *Intergovernmental Relations*, ed. R. Simeon. Toronto: University of Toronto Press.

Gagnon, A.-G. 2001. 'The Moral Foundations of Asymmetrical Federalism'. In *Multinational Democracies*, ed. A.-G. Gagnon and J. Tully. Cambridge: Cambridge University Press.

Harrison, K. 1996. *Passing the Buck: Federalism and Canadian Environmental Policy*. Vancouver: University of British Columbia Press.

———, ed. 2005. *Racing to the Bottom? Provincial Interdependence in the Canadian Federation*. Vancouver: University of British Columbia Press.

Lazar, H. 1997. 'Non-Constitutional Renewal: Toward a New Equilibrium in the Federation'. In *The State of the Federation 1997: Non-Constitutional Renewal*, ed. H. Lazar. Kingston: Institute of Intergovernmental Relations, Queen's University.

———. 2006. 'The Intergovernmental Dimensions of the Social Union: A Sectoral Analysis', *Canadian Public Administration* 49, 1: 23–45.

———, H. Telford, and R.L. Watts. 2003. 'Diverse Trajectories: The Impact of Global and Regional Integration on Federal Systems'. In *The Impact of Global and Regional Integration on Federal Systems: A Comparative Analysis*, ed. H. Lazar, H. Telford, and R.L. Watts. Kingston and Montreal: McGill–Queen's University Press.

Matthews, J. Scott, and M. Mendelsohn. 2010. 'The New Ontario: The Shifting Attitudes of Ontarians toward the Federation'. Toronto: Mowat Centre for Policy Innovation. Available at: http://www.mowatcentre.ca/pdfs/mowatResearch/8.pdf.

McRoberts, K. 1993. 'Federal Structures and the Policy Process'. In *Governing Canada: Institutions and Public Policy*, ed. M.M. Atkinson. Toronto: Harcourt Brace Janovich.

Nevitte, N. 1996. *The Decline of Deference: Canadian Value Change in Cross-national Perspective*. Peterborough, Ont.: Broadview.

Norris, P. 2005. 'Stable Democracy and Good Governance in Divided Societies: Do Powersharing Institutions Work?' Faculty Research Working Paper RWP05-014. John F. Kennedy School of Government, Harvard University.

Pierson, P. 1995. 'Fragmented Welfare States: Federal Institutions and the Development of Social Policy', *Governance* 8, 4: 449–78.

Rice, J.J., and M.J. Prince. 2000. *Changing Politics of Canadian Social Policy*. Toronto: University of Toronto Press.

Ryan, C. 2005. 'Quebec and Interprovincial Discussion and Consultation'. Kingston: Queen's Institute of Intergovernmental Relations. Available online at: www.iigr.ca/iigr.php/site/pdf/publications/316QuebecandInterprovinci.pdf.

Savoie, D.J. 1999. *Governing from the Centre: The*

Concentration of Power in Canadian Politics. Toronto: University of Toronto Press.

Scharpf, F. 1988. 'The Joint-Decision Trap: Lessons from German Federalism and European Integration', *Public Administration 66*, 3: 239–78.

———. 1999. *Governing in Europe: Effective and Democratic?* Oxford: Oxford University Press.

Simeon, R. 2006 [1972]. *Federal–Provincial Diplomacy: The Making of Recent Policy in Canada.* Toronto: University of Toronto Press.

———. 1997. 'Rethinking Government, Rethinking Federalism'. In *The New Public Management and Public Administration in Canada*, ed. M. Charih and A. Daniels. Toronto: Institute of Public Administration.

———. 2003. 'Important? Yes. Transformative? No. North American Integration and Canadian Federalism'. In *The Impact of Global and Regional Integration on Federal Systems: A Comparative Analysis*, ed. H. Lazar, H. Telford, and R.L. Watts. Kingston and Montreal: McGill–Queen's University Press.

———. 2006. *Federal–Provincial Diplomacy: The Making of Recent Policy in Canada.* Toronto: University of Toronto Press. (With a new preface and postscript.)

——— and I. Robinson. 1990. *State, Society, and the Development of Canadian Federalism.* Toronto: University of Toronto Press.

Smiley, D.V. 1976. *Canada in Question: Federalism in the Seventies.* 2nd edn. Toronto: McGraw Hill-Ryerson.

Smith, J. 2004. *Federalism.* Vancouver: University of British Columbia Press.

Stevenson, G. 1993. *Ex Uno Plures: Federal–Provincial Relations 1867–1896.* Montreal and Kingston: McGill–Queen's University Press.

Tully, J. 1995. *Strange Multiplicity: Constitutionalism in an Age of Diversity.* Cambridge: Cambridge University Press.

Watts, R.L. 1996. *Comparing Federalism in the 1990s.* Kingston: Institute of Intergovernmental Relations, Queen's University.

———. 1999. *The Spending Power in Federal Systems: A Comparative Study.* Kingston: Institute of Intergovernmental Relations, Queen's University.

———. 2003. 'Managing Interdependence in a Federal Political System'. In *The Art of the State: Governance in a World without Frontiers*, ed. T.J. Courchene and D.J. Savoie. Montreal: Institute for Research on Public Policy.

———. 2005. 'A Comparative Perspective on Asymmetry in Federations'. Kingston: Institute of Intergovernmental Relations. Available at: www.iigr.ca/pdf/publications/359_A_Comparative_Perspectiv.pdf.

Wheare, K.C. 1951. *Federal Government.* London: Oxford University Press.

White, G. 2005. *Cabinets and First Ministers.* Vancouver: University of British Columbia Press.

Young, R. 2003. 'Managing Interdependence in a Federal Political System: Comments'. In *The Art of the State: Governance in a World Without Frontiers*, ed. T.J. Courchene and D.J. Savoie. Montreal: Institute for Research on Public Policy.

2 The Political Economy of Regionalism and Federalism

Garth Stevenson

This chapter begins by defining the terms 'region' and 'regionalism', with particular reference to ways in which they have been used in Canada. It then discusses how the **National Policy** introduced in 1879 contributed to the development of specialized regional economies and thus to the intensification of regionalism. The chapter continues with a discussion of changes in the political economy of Canada from the 1960s onwards, particularly the growing importance of oil and natural gas, and the influence of these developments on regionalism, which continued to exist despite the transformation of the economy. A short section that follows inquires whether regionalism is likely to decline and disappear in Canada. The chapter concludes with an assessment of how regionalism affects the performance, effectiveness, and legitimacy of Canadian federalism.

'Regionalism' is a term frequently used in Canada and elsewhere, but rarely defined with much precision. Regionalism in the Canadian sense, which Americans usually refer to as **sectionalism**, is found in all large or medium-sized countries, although perhaps to varying degrees, whether or not they have federal institutions with two distinct orders of government. India, the world's most populous democracy, is a country of many regions whose unity has sometimes been considered precarious. New England and the South are two historically defined regions in the United States, and the Midwest is often referred to although its boundaries are less clearly defined. The northern and southern parts of England, Italy, and France have distinct cultural, social, and political characteristics, as do the eastern and western parts of Germany and the highlands and lowlands in Scotland. Even in homogeneous Australia, people in the outlying states of Queensland, Tasmania, and Western Australia see themselves as different from those in the more thickly populated southeast. A majority of Western Australians even voted to separate from the rest of Australia in 1933 (Stevenson, 1981).

Peter McCormick (1989) distinguishes four 'dimensions' of Canadian regionalism which he calls distributional, economic, perceptual, and political. The first includes demographic variables like ethnicity, language, religion, or age distribution in spatially differentiated populations. The second refers to the relative importance of different industries in different parts of the country, and to differences in average income, public and private expenditure, unemployment, and similar variables. Perceptual regionalism means the way in which regions are defined, perceived, and identified with by Canadians in different parts of the country. Political regionalism measures attachment to regional political institutions.

Assuming that regionalism exists, what are its consequences and implications? Goldwin Smith asserted more than a century ago that Canada was an artificial union of four regions or 'blocks of territory' that had more in common with nearby regions of the United States than with one another. He posed what he called 'the Canadian question', namely whether Canada's regions could remain both politically united among themselves and politically separated from the United States, and he was not hopeful that they could (Smith, 1971: 5). Harold A. Innis (1970: 386–92), on the other hand, argued that the transcontinental dimensions of Canada and the boundary between Canada and the United States were not artificial but rather the logical and natural consequences of geography, which had oriented the northern half of the continent towards the fur trade and towards an east–west network of transportation, finance, and eventually politics.

Canada's preoccupation with regionalism has been blamed for the lack of creativity and ideological clarity in Canadian politics (Porter, 1965: 368–9). It has also been suggested as an explanation for the fact that the provincial governments are stronger and more autonomous than John A. Macdonald intended them to be or than a reading of the formal constitution would suggest (Rogers, 1933). Alan Cairns (1977) has suggested, on the other hand, that what appears to be regionalism is really an artefact of the provincial governments themselves and has little or no independent significance.

Region is primarily a geographical term, and a discussion of the concept should logically begin with geography, a field of study that is often neglected by Canadian social science. Canada's geographical features—the Arctic north, the pre-Cambrian or Laurentian shield, the Rocky Mountains, the prairies, the St. Lawrence River and the Great Lakes, and the collection of islands and peninsulas that comprise Atlantic Canada—obviously existed before humans inhabited the country. Long before Europeans arrived, the aboriginal peoples of North America adapted successfully to these different environments by developing different economies and styles of life, such as the settled agricultural communities of the Iroquois near the Great Lakes, the semi-nomadic life of the buffalo hunt on the prairies, or the importance of fishing on both the Atlantic and Pacific coasts. Geographical barriers to transportation and communication reinforced the cultural and linguistic, as well as economic and political, differences among these various peoples, who had no sense of comprising a single collectivity until very recent times. While all 'Indians' may appear the same to European settlers and their descendants, their cultures are really as distinct from one another as the English are from the French or the French from the Germans.

European settlers faced the same geographical barriers as the aboriginal peoples, although they possessed more sophisticated technology for overcoming them, and their arrival reinforced both the cultural and economic differences among regions. On the Atlantic coast and the offshore islands various European nations competed to gain control of the fisheries, with the British eventually emerging victorious. The French established an agricultural economy in the St. Lawrence valley and used it as a base for the western fur trade, in which they competed against English and Scottish fur traders who entered the continent by way of Hudson Bay. United Empire Loyalists founded what is now southern Ontario, where they encountered a physical environment very similar to the northern parts of the United States from which they had come. With the disappearance of the buffalo and the arrival of the railway, the prairies became an agricultural frontier that attracted a different mixture of ethnic groups than the older provinces of central and eastern Canada. The Pacific coast, where the British had established a foothold between the Russians to the north and the Spanish (subsequently replaced by Americans) to the south, remained almost totally isolated from the rest of the continent until the railway age. The Arctic north, even today, is occupied mainly by the Inuit and is no more familiar to the majority of Canadians than the surface of the moon.

The boundaries of colonies, or provinces, were superimposed over these geographical features in ways that were sometimes arbitrary and sometimes logical. In the east, as Innis (1956) suggested, the geography was conducive to political decentralization and the emergence of several small provinces. In the centre, the boundary between Upper and Lower Canada was designed to separate the French from the Loyalists, and was thus primarily cultural rather than economic. On the prairies, lines were drawn arbitrarily on a map to designate districts, territories, and then provinces, leading eventually to three provinces approximately equal in size. British Columbia, because of its geographical isolation and an economy in which agriculture played only a small part, was inevitably a separate region and province. Portions of the northern territories were given to Quebec, Ontario and Manitoba in 1898 and 1912. Yukon Territory was created in 1898 to deal with the administrative implications of the gold rush, while Nunavut, the most recent addition to Canada's political map, corresponds roughly with the boundaries of the Inuit culture. The Judicial Committee of the Privy Council in 1927 ruled that a large mainland area claimed by Quebec actually belonged to Newfoundland, which was thereby more than doubled in size. The latter province changed its name in 2001 to 'Newfoundland and Labrador' in an effort to reinforce the legitimacy of its present boundaries.

As this history suggests, institutional provinces or territories and natural regions are by no means the same. Newfoundland and Labrador, as its new name suggests, is a combination of two distinct regions. So, in effect, is Ontario, where the huge but thinly populated region north of Lake Nipissing and the French River has more in common, geographically, culturally, and economically, with Manitoba than it has with the 'old Ontario' settled by the Loyalists. (Part, although not all, of this region was actually claimed by Manitoba for nearly two decades after Confederation.) Quebec still officially refers to the territory it acquired in 1912, which is mainly populated by aboriginal peoples, as Nouveau Québec, and it recognizes other distinct regions such as l'Outouais (the Ottawa Valley) and l'Estrie (the Eastern Townships) within its 'national' territory. The northeastern corner of New Brunswick, sometimes called 'the republic of Madawaska', has strong affinities with Quebec, from which a large part of its population migrated during the nineteenth century.

On the other hand, the 'perceptual' regions referred to by Peter McCormick may, for some Canadians at least, be larger than a single province. Nova Scotia, New Brunswick, and Prince Edward Island, which for a short time in the eighteenth century comprised a single colony, have enough geographical, cultural, and historical affinities to constitute a meaningful region known as 'the Maritimes'. In fact 'Maritime Union' was the original objective of the Charlottetown Conference of 1864, to which the central Canadians invited themselves in an effort to place their more extensive project of British North American union on the agenda. The term 'Atlantic Canada', on the other hand, has only been used since Newfoundland became a Canadian province in 1949. The people of Newfoundland

and Labrador quite rightly insist that the four-province 'region' to which the term 'Atlantic Canada' ostensibly refers exists only in the imagination of federal bureaucrats and other central Canadians.

The available data on how Canadians envisage regions are somewhat dated but still of interest, and have been reproduced in a recent study of political culture (Clarke, Pammett, and Stewart, 2002). The Canadian National Election Studies in 1974 and 1979 included a question on what region, if any, respondents considered that they lived in. A large number (41 per cent in the first survey and 47 per cent in the second) said that they did not know or did not think in terms of regions, and in Newfoundland this group accounted for more than half the sample. People in the three largest provinces were the most likely to say that their own province was a region, while Quebec was the only province in which a significant number (20 and 18 per cent) referred to a smaller area within their province as a region. The concept of a Maritime region was popular in Nova Scotia and Prince Edward Island, but less so in New Brunswick. The most striking result was the strong identification with Western Canada as a region in all four of the western provinces, particularly in 1979, which was a time of considerable conflict between the western provincial governments and the federal government. The biggest increase in support for 'Western Canada' between the two surveys was in Saskatchewan, where identification with the prairies as a region declined sharply. In British Columbia, whose people had been the Canadians most likely to consider their own province as a region in 1974, that option suffered a significant loss of popularity by 1979. In the other three western provinces the concept of one's own province as a region had insignificant support in both surveys. Identification with 'Western Canada' was consistently high in Alberta.

The concept of multi-province regions has been recognized in Canada's constitution since 1867, when Ontario, Quebec, and the Maritimes were treated as three regions with equal representation (24 seats for each) in the Senate. This contrasted with the American (and later Australian) practice of equal representation for each state. In 1915 Western Canada was given the status of a fourth region, also with 24 seats. In more recent times six seats have been added for Newfoundland and one for each of the territories, making a total of 105. Prime Minister Trudeau tried unsuccessfully in 1971 and again in 1980 to build the concept of four regions into the constitutional amending formula. The idea was revived in 1996, when Parliament adopted legislation providing that no amendment pertaining to the entire country would be proposed unless it had the support of Ontario, Quebec, at least two Atlantic provinces, and at least two Western provinces, comprising a majority of the region's population in each case.

Regionalism and the National Policy

The tendency of some Canadians to see themselves as part of a multi-province region may result in part from the constitutional recognition of the concept. It may also owe something to a sense of geographical proximity and common physical features, although neither the proximity of nor the physical similarity between British Columbia and Saskatchewan, or between British Columbia and Manitoba, is immediately obvious. However, a much more likely explanation is the interaction between federal public policy and the economy. Thus we are led to the concept of regionalism as a *relationship* between two spatial entities. This relationship may be, or at least may be viewed as, one of conflict and also as one of inequality. The dominant centre in such a relationship is sometimes described as the **metropolis** and the subordinate region as the **hinterland** (Gras, 1922: 184–5). This concept of a region has parallels with the Marxist concept of class, in which a class is viewed not just as a collection of people with similar characteristics, but as a self-conscious collectivity experiencing domination or subordination, and conflict, in relation to another class.

When the four original provinces were united in 1867, they all had somewhat similar economies, with between 40 and 50 per cent of the labour force employed in agriculture. Ontario was actually the most agricultural province with 49.3 per cent of its labour force in agriculture as of 1871, and Nova Scotia the least, at 41.9 per cent. The national average was 47.5 per cent.

By 1881 there were seven provinces but the percentage of the labour force in agriculture for the four original provinces had changed hardly at all, rising slightly in New Brunswick and Nova Scotia but falling slightly in Ontario and Quebec. All four were close to the national average, which was practically unchanged at 47.7 per cent. Two of the new provinces, Manitoba and Prince Edward Island, had more than half of their labour force in agriculture, at 58.3 and 60.1 per cent respectively. British Columbia was the outlier, economically as well as spatially, with an economy based on forestry, fishing and mining, and with only 14.5 per cent in agriculture (Stevenson, 1993: 27). However, British Columbia at that time was the smallest province in terms of population and thus had little influence on the national average.

Two years before that census, however, John A. Macdonald's government had introduced the National Policy, which would remain the basis of Canada's economic strategy for almost a century (Easterbrook and Aitken, 1956: 383). Its purpose was to stimulate economic growth and provide jobs for Canadians, and at the same time to make Canada less dependent on the United States. The strategy had three parts. The first was protective tariffs to encourage manufacturing, to provide jobs for Canadians who might otherwise have to move to the United States, and to reduce the need for manufactured imports. The second part was completion of the transcontinental railway that had been promised to British Columbia in 1871 but on which little progress had been made in eight years, and which would also open the thinly populated prairies to settlement. The third part was the promotion of immigration, which would help to populate western Canada and provide both freight and passenger traffic for the Canadian Pacific Railway.

Previous to the National Policy the provinces had similar economies, as noted above, and thus little reason to trade with one another. Poor transportation links, except between Ontario and Quebec, had also given them little opportunity to do so, although the Intercolonial Railway connecting Quebec, New Brunswick, and Nova Scotia had been completed just before the National Policy was announced. Most products were consumed locally, although there were modest exports, mainly of farm products, to the United Kingdom and the United States. The National Policy, however, encouraged provincial interdependence and also provincial specialization, although the latter was really a by-product of the policy rather than a conscious choice. Tariff-protected manufacturers chose to locate mainly in Quebec and Ontario, and to some extent Nova Scotia. Prince Edward Island, Manitoba, and the territories that later became Saskatchewan and Alberta specialized in agriculture. British Columbia concentrated, even more than before, on producing fish, lumber, and minerals. The whole economy was tied together by the railways, which by 1885 extended continuously from Halifax to Vancouver by way of Montreal, a distance of about 6000 kilometres entirely on Canadian soil. By 1911, in just under 40 years, Canada's population had doubled in size, two additional railways were under construction from the St. Lawrence to the Pacific, enough settlers had arrived on the prairies to make possible the creation of two new provinces—Saskatchewan and Alberta—in 1905, and the prairie economy was providing a large surplus of grain for export, mainly to the United Kingdom.

Despite these achievements, a feeling developed in the western and Maritime provinces that the benefits of the National Policy were going disproportionately to the metropolitan region of central Canada (Ontario and Quebec) while the western and eastern hinterlands were bearing a disproportionate share of the costs. This perception of the National Policy had emerged on the prairies as early as the 1890s, when the allegedly high freight rates of the Montreal-based Canadian Pacific Railway and its near-monopoly of transportation in much of the west were the targets of resentment (Innis, 1971: 172–96). Somewhat later, animosity was directed towards the banks, mainly based in Montreal, Toronto, and Halifax, whose allegedly high interest rates were a burden on heavily indebted farmers and other entrepreneurs in western Canada. The most important and lasting western grievance was the protective tariff, which raised the price of manufactured goods used by western farmers, miners, and forest workers in order to provide jobs for industrial workers in Ontario and Quebec. At the same time, western farmers and resource industries received no tariff protection but had to compete in world markets where prices were unstable, as well as paying the transportation costs to get their products to market.

These grievances contributed to regional solidarity in the west, particularly since the federal government, which imposed the tariffs and regulated the banks and railways, was considered to be largely responsible for them. Although the Liberal Party had criticized the National Policy while in opposition, Wilfrid Laurier's Liberal government between 1896 and 1911 continued it with little modification. Admittedly the Liberals proposed a limited free trade agreement with the United States, known as **Reciprocity**, in the latter year, but they lost the election because of an overwhelming Conservative vote in tariff-protected Ontario, as well as considerable Liberal losses in Quebec. Six years later most English-speaking Liberals joined with the Conservatives in a coalition government led by the Conservative prime minister, so that the Liberal Party temporarily ceased to exist as an independent force in western Canada. This event persuaded many western Canadians that the two traditional parties were essentially similar in their outlook and in the interests that they represented (Morton, 1950: 49 and 106). This perception led westerners to form a series of new parties over the next several decades: the Progressives, United Farmers, Co-operative Commonwealth Federation (CCF), Social Credit, and more recently the Reform Party. These parties argued that the real enemies of western voters were located in central Canada and that there were no significant differences among westerners themselves. The logical conclusion of this view was that a competitive party system within the region was unnecessary and counterproductive. Manitoba was governed by a coalition with virtually no opposition from 1928 until 1945. Alberta developed what has been termed a **quasi-party system**, in which there was no significant opposition to the single dominant party (Macpherson, 1962: 215–49).

The new parties reinforced the sense that Western Canada was a distinct region that had little in common with Ontario or Quebec, where the traditional two-party system largely held sway. In the 1920s the Progressives held the balance of power in Ottawa and were able to win two significant gains for prairie interests. First, lower freight rates for western grain, originally conceded by the Canadian Pacific in 1897 in return for a subsidy to build its second main line through the Crowsnest Pass, were embodied in a statute and made applicable to the government-owned Canadian National as well (Morton, 1950: 156–7). The second gain, which proved to be far more important in the long run, occurred at the end of the decade when Manitoba, Saskatchewan, and Alberta were given control over their public lands and natural resources, which the federal government had retained when those provinces were established. (Martin, 1973: 204–26). Western attitudes towards central Canada and the federal government did not noticeably improve, however, as a result of these events.

The depression of the 1930s hit the western provinces hard because of their dependence on foreign markets, while the protective tariff helped to lessen the damage in Ontario, Quebec, and even the Maritimes. At the same time southern Saskatchewan experienced a drought that made farming virtually impossible. Many prairie farmers went bankrupt and lost their mortgaged farms to the banks. In 1933 per capita money incomes in Saskatchewan and Alberta were only 25.7 per cent and 37.6 per cent, respectively, of what they had been five years earlier. In all other provinces per capita incomes in 1933 were more than 50 per cent of what they had been in 1928 (Mackintosh, 1964: 137). These circumstances helped to elect in 1935 the most radical provincial government in Canadian history, Social Credit in Alberta, which attempted to take control of banking and monetary policy but was frustrated when the federal government unexpectedly resorted to using its power of disallowance (Mallory, 1976). In Saskatchewan the CCF gained rapidly in strength and formed the government in 1944 (Lipset, 1968).

Events took a somewhat different course in British Columbia. The resource interests that dominated that province were just as vulnerable to the instability of global markets as the prairie farmers but were different in that their labour was performed by wage earners who neither owned nor controlled the means of production. The result was strong labour unions and a high level of industrial conflict, which helped to create a party system polarized between left and right, similar to the party systems of the United Kingdom and Australia. The British Columbia CCF, the successor to various labour and socialist parties that had existed since the first decade of the twentieth century, was a party of industrial workers, in contrast to its agrarian namesake in Saskatchewan. Class conflict in British Columbia politics contrasted with Ontario, where both business and labour supported protective tariffs, and with the prairies, where political discourse was dominated by self-employed farmers and their grievances against the National Policy.

British Columbia's distinct economy, and the physical barriers between the Pacific coast and the prairies, contributed to the perception that it was a region in itself, and not part of 'Western Canada', a perception that was encouraged by the provincial government. The federal government also employed a five-region model of Canada (Atlantic, Quebec, Ontario, Prairies, and Pacific) for organizing statistical data and for certain other purposes. In the 1960s this sense of isolation on the west coast began to break down when the Trans-Canada Highway was completed through Rogers Pass and when jet aircraft made air travel across the mountains safer and more comfortable. British Columbia experienced a large influx of migrants from the prairies and other parts of Canada, doubling the size of its population between 1951 and 1971. The exploitation of natural gas in British Columbia also gave it a common interest with Alberta that had not previously existed. The Trade, Investment and Labour Mobility Agreement (TILMA) signed by British Columbia and Alberta in 2009 indicates that British Columbia no longer sees itself as a region distinct from western Canada.

Anti-National Policy sentiment in the Maritime provinces was somewhat different in character and perhaps less intense than in the west, although it was far from negligible. Unlike the western provinces, the Maritime provinces, particularly Nova Scotia, had been mature and reasonably successful societies before Confederation. Nova Scotia also had most of Canada's coal, which was as important in the age of steam as oil became later. For a while the Maritimes seemed to share in the benefits of the National Policy, at least to some extent, and to enjoy considerable influence over the country. However, as Canada's centre of gravity shifted to the west, the Maritimes began to decline economically, and the percentage of Canada's population who lived there declined even faster, reducing their representation in Parliament and their influence in federal politics.

By the 1920s it was obvious that the Maritimes were in trouble, although the science of economics, at that time anyway, suggested no obvious remedy. Maritime manufacturing firms were too small, and too far from most Canadian consumers, to compete against those based in central Canada. Tariffs, which seemed to benefit mainly Ontario and Quebec, and freight rates, which increased suddenly after the Intercolonial Railway was absorbed into Canadian National in 1919, became targets of resentment, just as they were in the west. The Halifax-based banks moved their headquarters to Montreal and Toronto. Some Maritimers recalled that their region had been more prosperous, relatively speaking, before the National Policy began and even before it became part of Canada. Their discontent was expressed not through new parties, as in the western provinces, but through a regional pressure group, the **Maritime Rights Movement**, which was largely organized by local businessmen and which flourished in the 1920s (Forbes, 1979). The federal government responded by providing small subsidies to the provincial governments and making incremental changes in tariffs and freight rates. More systematic and substantial efforts to combat economic underdevelopment in the region did not begin until the 1960s. Thus by the early decades of the twentieth century the National Policy had created strong regional identities, and strong regional grievances, in the hinterlands of both east and west. Ontario and Quebec, which between them had well over half the population, most of the manufacturing, and the headquarters of the major banks, railways, and insurance companies as well as the headquarters of the federal government itself, appeared to dominate the country, although it should be noted that a disproportionate share of the benefits of Quebec's metropolitan position went to its Anglophone minority.

The Second World War, postwar prosperity, the beginnings of the welfare state, and equalization payments from the federal government to the poorer provinces beginning in 1957 helped to dull the edge of discontent but by no means ended it. (Unemployment insurance and family allowances, both introduced during the war, also helped to lure Newfoundland into Confederation, from which it had stood aloof for eighty years.)

The pronounced economic specialization and resulting differences among the provinces that the National Policy had created survived to a large extent in the postwar period. The 1961 census showed that Saskatchewan still had 36.6 per cent of its labour force in agriculture and only 4.7 per cent in manufacturing, while Ontario had only 7.0 per cent in agriculture and 26.9 per cent in manufacturing. The next most agricultural provinces after Saskatchewan were Prince Edward Island at 26.9 per cent, Alberta at 21.2 per cent, and Manitoba at 17.3 per cent, while all other provinces were below the national average of 9.9 per cent. Apart from Ontario, the only province with a larger than average share of its labour force in manufacturing was Quebec at 26.4 per cent. The national average was 21.7 per cent. Newfoundland, New Brunswick, British Columbia, and Quebec, in that order, were the only provinces with larger shares of their labour force in forestry than the national average, while Nova Scotia was practically at the national average in this regard. All four Atlantic provinces were well above the national average in terms of the shares of their labour force devoted to fishing and trapping (which were not separated in the data), with Newfoundland leading at 7.4 per cent. In all of the other six provinces less than 1 per cent of the labour force worked in these industries. Above average employment in mining, oil, and gas (also combined in the data) was found in Nova Scotia, Newfoundland, and Alberta, in that order, while Prince Edward Island had no employment at all in those industries (Canada, 1961).

Another indicator of economic differences among the regions was per capita income. In 1961 average personal income in Newfoundland and in Prince Edward Island was about half what it was in Ontario. Ontario and British Columbia were significantly above the national average, Alberta almost exactly at the national average, Quebec and Manitoba somewhat below average, and the remaining provinces considerably below average (Polèse, 1985: 1560). When equalization payments began in 1957, they were paid to every province except Ontario. After 1962, when resource revenues began to be factored into the equation, British Columbia and Alberta ceased to be eligible.

Regionalism in a Changing Nation

Canada underwent massive economic, social, and political changes in the 1960s and 1970s. New social programs vastly expanded the scope (and expense) of the welfare state. Equalization payments became increasingly generous at the same time as provincial government revenues from their own sources grew faster than the revenues of the federal government. Province-building, including extensive use of state-owned enterprises, transformed the political economy of federalism, with especially noticeable consequences in Quebec and in the western provinces. The federal government established regional development programs in an effort to stimulate the economies of poorer provinces and regions, particularly in Atlantic Canada. Disparities in personal income between the provinces narrowed considerably, with Alberta moving into first place and Saskatchewan approaching the national average. All provinces became increasingly urbanized and employment in agriculture steadily decreased. Trade barriers, in North America and around the world, were gradually reduced, making the traditional preoccupation with tariffs less relevant. Ontario's (and Canada's) most important manufacturing sector, the automobile industry, was fully integrated with that of the United States by the **Auto Pact** of 1965, resulting in huge increases in Canadian employment, productivity, and exports. Freight rates also declined in importance as truck transport increasingly competed with the railways. Despite all of these developments, regionalism and the associated anti-federal sentiment (often referred to in the western provinces as 'western alienation') did not decrease and in fact was expressed more stridently by provincial politicians and provincially based media in the 1970s and early 1980s than at any time since the depression of the 1930s.

Quebec's Quiet Revolution, and resentment in other provinces at the federal government's preoccupation with that province, contributed to this paradoxical result. An even more significant reason for it was the so-called 'energy crisis' of the 1970s. Events in the Middle East drastically increased the prices of oil and natural gas and the revenues from taxes and royalties that producing provinces (principally Alberta, but also British Columbia and Saskatchewan to some extent) could potentially derive from those commodities, which generally belong to the provinces under Canada's constitution. Alberta had been a major producer of oil since 1947 and began to export natural gas to other provinces and to the United States in the 1950s, but oil and gas had little impact on federal–provincial relations as long as their prices remained low, as they did through the 1960s.

As it happened, a vigorous new Conservative government with close ties to the Calgary business community replaced the long-established Social Credit dynasty of Alberta in 1971, just in time to enjoy the fiscal and economic benefits of the energy crisis (Richards and Pratt, 1979: 148–76). However, Pierre Trudeau's federal Liberal government, with its electoral base mainly in Quebec and Ontario, had other plans. As well as fearing the impact of higher energy prices on central Canada's industrial economy, the federal government was troubled by the impact of Alberta's resource wealth on its own obligation to top up the revenues of the less fortunate provinces through equalization payments. The equalization formula had included a portion of natural resource revenues since 1962, and virtually all of them since 1967, meaning that every increase in Alberta's revenue from royalties increased federal obligations to subsidize the other provinces, potentially including Ontario.

Trudeau's government responded to the sudden increase in global energy prices in ways that were bitterly resented in Alberta and the other energy-rich provinces of the west. Using its constitutional authority to regulate trade and commerce and beginning in 1973, it kept the domestic price of oil at an artificially low level to protect central Canadian consumers. Almost simultaneously, it established a state-owned oil company, Petro-Canada, which over the next few years absorbed a number of foreign-controlled enterprises to become one of Canada's largest producers and refiners of oil. Although its headquarters were placed in Calgary rather than in Ottawa, Petro-Canada was for many Albertans a symbol of unwanted federal interference in 'their' economy, and revived memories of the fact that the federal government had retained its ownership of western resources and public lands until 1930. Trudeau's government also curtailed oil and gas exports to the United States and imposed various taxes on those commodities, as well as declaring in 1974 that corporations could no longer deduct royalties paid to the provinces from their taxable income. Finally, in 1980, it unveiled a series of measures which it called the **National Energy Program**, designed to increase the level of Canadian ownership in the oil and gas industries and also to redirect oil and gas exploration away from

Alberta and towards federally owned lands in the northern territories and on the continental shelf (Milne, 1986, 69–116).

These federal initiatives were supported by the government of Ontario and, with certain reservations, by that of Quebec. They were also welcomed by most voters in the central provinces. In the oil- and gas-producing provinces, on the other hand, they were so unpopular that the Liberals elected no members west of Winnipeg in the federal general election of 1980, forcing Trudeau to select three members of the appointed Senate as the representatives of the three westernmost provinces in his cabinet. A 'western separatist' movement also emerged, and even elected one member to the Alberta Legislative Assembly in a by-election in 1982. By that time, however, the crisis had passed its peak, with the federal and Alberta governments reaching a compromise agreement on the domestic price of oil just as the world price began to decline. (A photograph of Trudeau and the Alberta premier toasting this agreement with champagne was used in the election leaflets of the western separatist party, which argued that the premier had failed to defend Alberta's interests). After 1984 the new federal Conservative government led by Brian Mulroney dismantled what remained of the National Energy Program and also handed over the resources of the continental shelf to the adjacent provinces, a measure from which Newfoundland and Nova Scotia would reap considerable benefits in later years.

Meanwhile, the Trudeau government had appointed, in November 1982, the Royal Commission on the Economic Union and Development Prospects for Canada, usually known as the Macdonald Commission. As the Commission's chairman, Donald Macdonald, aptly observed three years later in his foreword to the final report, the Royal Commission was established 'in the aftermath of one of the most turbulent periods of Canadian history' (Canada, 1985: Volume One, xi). Although it occupied less than a hundred pages in a massive three-volume report, the Macdonald Commission's most significant, and least expected, recommendation was that Canada should seek a bilateral free trade agreement with the United States, an option that would end the last vestiges of the National Policy (Canada, 1985, Volume One: 299–385). In justifying this choice, the report referred briefly to the traditional unpopularity of protective tariffs in the western and eastern hinterlands of Canada, and the support for them in Ontario and Quebec, but suggested that the issue might no longer be as divisive along regional lines as it had been in the past, since some hinterland industries were protected and some central Canadian industries were not. It concluded, somewhat tentatively, that all regions of Canada would benefit from continental free trade and would probably support it. This forecast was belied, however, by the fact that when the Mulroney government actually negotiated a free trade agreement with the United States a few years later, it was vigorously opposed by the government of Ontario despite, or perhaps because of, that province's favourable experience with the Auto Pact. On the other hand, Quebec supported the free trade agreement and Prince Edward Island opposed it, both contrary to what the traditional interpretation of the National Policy would suggest.

One of the most interesting comments on regionalism to emerge from the Macdonald Commission's massive output of research came from an economist at the University of New Brunswick, who admitted that Atlantic Canada had 'a strong sentimental attachment to the idea of free trade with the United States' (Earl, 1985: 371) even though he was not personally convinced that the region would benefit economically. He observed that

[t]he formation of a free trade area with the United States would do much to redress a histor-ical grievance and at the same time remove a major obstacle to intelligent discussion of the economic difficulties of the Atlantic provinces. ... If trade barriers were eliminated, rational analysis could be substituted for central Canada 'bashing' and the economic problems and potential of the Atlantic provinces could be assessed in realistic terms, to the benefit of all concerned. (Earl, 1985: 370)

His conclusion, in other words, was that the 'issue' of protective tariffs had become more symbolic than real, which was not to deny its continuing importance in the minds of Atlantic Canadians. A similar conclusion regarding the other traditional issue of Canadian regionalism, railway freight rates, had already appeared in a book whose au-thor had worked as a transportation economist in both the public and private sectors (Darling, 1980).

In the early 1980s the so-called Crowsnest Pass freight rate legislation, which had been introduced at the behest of prairie farmers in 1925, was finally abolished after lengthy ne-gotiations between the federal government, farm organizations, and the railways (Milne, 1986: 147). Long viewed as the *Magna Carta* of western Canadian farmers, the legislation had fixed the freight rates on export grain at an artificially low level, which in later years caused the railways to lose money on grain traffic but at the same time discouraged any diversion of it to the highways. A dense network of railway branch lines, with grain ele-vators located every few miles, existed only to serve this unprofitable traffic. When the railways understandably refused to buy freight cars to carry grain at a loss, the federal government, through the Canadian Wheat Board, purchased the necessary rolling stock. By 1983, however, westerners were no longer unanimous in support of this arrangement, and in the end Saskatchewan was the only provincial government that resisted its aboli-tion. Many western Canadians realized by this time that, by subsidizing the export of raw grain from the prairies, the Crowsnest rate benefited the livestock, flour milling, and beverage industries outside of their region and discouraged those industries from locat-ing in the west. While 'western alienation' still existed, the diversification of the western Canadian economy had eroded much of the consensus on substantive issues.

This was demonstrated once again when western Conservatives, including the govern-ment of Alberta, began in the 1980s to call for the abolition of compulsory marketing of wheat and barley through the Canadian Wheat Board, an agency that had been estab-lished in 1935 and kept in effect afterwards to protect prairie farmers from the instability of the market. Stephen Harper's Conservative government, after it took office in 2006, began the process of ending compulsory marketing, despite the opposition of the National Farmers' Union, the more left-wing of the two major farm organizations. Once it acquired a parliamentary majority in the spring 2011 election, the Harper Conservative govern-ment introduced legislation in the fall of 2011 to end the monopoly of the Canadian Wheat Board over export barley and wheat marketing.

One sector of the economy that still tends to unite the residents of certain provinces, and to generate strong differences of opinion between Canada's provinces and regions, is the production of oil and natural gas. The most significant change in this industry in recent years has been that the traditional producing provinces, Alberta, Saskatchewan, and British Columbia, have been joined by Newfoundland and Labrador and, to a much lesser extent (so far), by Nova Scotia. Newfoundland and Labrador's conventional crude oil reserves (a category that excludes the potential of the Alberta tar sands) are now estimated to exceed those of Alberta, and the east coast now accounts for about one-seventh of Canada's production (*Canada Year Book 2008*: 137–8, 146). As Ontario and Quebec, where more than half of Canada's people live, are still the major consumers, the clash between central Canadian and hinterland interests continues, with the difference that the eastern hinterland is beginning to rival the western hinterland in economic power and wealth for the first time in a hundred years. Newfoundland and Labrador, traditionally the poorest province, ceased to be eligible for equalization payments in 2009–10. Ontario, traditionally the richest province until it was overtaken by Alberta in the 1970s, became eligible for a small equalization payment at the same time.

The conflict-producing potential of petroleum resources is not a uniquely Canadian phenomenon, as suggested by their contribution to the hostilities between the United States, Iran, and Iraq in recent years, the Nigerian civil war in the 1960s, and even the resurgence of Scottish nationalism in the 1970s. In Canada, unlike the United States, the conflict between regions is reinforced by the common law doctrine that mineral resources belong to the Crown, even if they are under privately owned land, and by the fact that the prerogatives of the Crown, under our federal constitution, belong to the provincial level of government where natural resources are concerned. The governments of provinces that possess oil and gas are the main stakeholders in those resources, and understandably seek to protect what they have from any effort by outsiders, including the federal government, to share the wealth or to restrict their own ability to enjoy it. It is not hard for those provincial governments to mobilize their own populations, whose standard of living may be affected, against external threats to their resources. Peter Lougheed, Alberta's premier from 1971 until 1985, was highly successful in this regard as was Danny Williams, premier of Newfoundland and Labrador (2003–10). Such leaders are particularly effective because they can draw on memories of a regional history of poverty, powerlessness, and exploitation by outside interests prior to the development of oil and gas. The fear of returning to the unhappy circumstances of the past is a powerful incentive to believe the premier when he says that the province must maintain control over its resources.

A relatively recent addition to the agenda of disputes between regions or provinces that produce oil and gas and those that do not is the concern over global warming. (See Chapter 13 by Winfield and Macdonald.) Provinces and regions that produce carbon fuels benefit from higher consumption of such fuels, which appears to be a principal cause of greenhouse gases and global warning, so they may suffer economically from efforts to curb consumption. In the case of Alberta's tar sands, on which the province's future as a major producer of oil largely rests, there is the additional problem that not only the consumption but the production of the commodity is a major source of greenhouse gases and global warming, meaning that the cost of protecting the environment will fall disproportionately on Alberta's economy.

Another source of oil and gas-related conflict is fiscal equalization, a program that was designed to lessen regional resentments and conflicts but has paradoxically contributed to exacerbating them. (See Chapter 7 on fiscal federalism.) This is not to say that equalization, which since 1982 is an obligation entrenched in the constitution, is a bad idea or that it should be abolished. It does indicate, however, that the details of the program should be reexamined and perhaps modified, and that the federal government should do a better job of explaining to all Canadians how equalization works and what it is intended to do.

Producing provinces argue, with some justification, that revenue from royalties, which are really payments for the sale of a diminishing asset that belongs to the Crown, is not the same as revenue from taxation. When it is included in the equalization formula, the argument that equalization represents a theft of their resources, although inaccurate, becomes somewhat more plausible in provinces like Alberta or Saskatchewan. Conversely, when provinces like Newfoundland and Labrador or Nova Scotia stand to lose all or part of their equalization payment because they have discovered and exploited deposits of oil or gas, it seems unfair. Regional animosity would probably be lessened if non-renewable resource revenues were totally excluded from the formula, in the same way that revenue from winning a lottery is excluded from an individual's income tax calculations. It would also be considerably cheaper for the federal government, since it would lessen the amount of equalization that must be paid to recipient provinces, particularly those that do not produce oil or natural gas.

The End of Regionalism?

The entrenchment of the *Canadian Charter of Rights and Freedoms* in the constitution since 1982 has focused more attention on elements of Canadian diversity, such as religion, race, gender, and even sexual orientation, that have little or no relationship to geography. In addition, the strong preference of recent immigrants to settle in a few large metropolitan centres like Montreal, Toronto, Calgary, and Vancouver has made those urban areas very different in terms of culture and ethnicity from the provinces of which they form a part, but increasingly similar to one another, tendencies that may weaken regional (and provincial) identities in the long run. Also, NAFTA has ended the traditional situation in which the hinterland regions exported their products to foreign countries while central Canada's manufacturing industries served domestic markets. All provinces now send more goods and commodities to the United States than to other parts of Canada.

Finally, the economic and occupational characteristics that distinguish one province or region from another are diminishing. In all provinces the sectors of the economy that produce physical goods and commodities (agriculture, fishing, manufacturing, and the resource industries) have declined in relative importance as sources of employment. While manufacturing was still the main source of employment in Quebec and Ontario in 2006, the largest source of employment in every other province was either retail trade or health care and social assistance. Agriculture, forestry, fishing and hunting (now combined as a single category) accounted for only 12.8 per cent of employment in Saskatchewan in 2006, compared to 36.6 per cent for agriculture alone in 1961. In Prince Edward Island, where agriculture employed 26.9 per cent of the labour force and fishing and trapping employed 6.1 per cent in 1961, agriculture, forestry, fishing, and hunting together employed only 9.5 per cent in 2006, while in Alberta the comparable numbers were 21.2 per cent in 1961 and 4.3 per cent in 2006. On the other hand, the percentage of the labour force employed in manufacturing actually increased after 1961 in both Saskatchewan and Prince Edward Island and was practically unchanged in Alberta and Nova Scotia, while it declined sharply in Quebec, Ontario, and British Columbia. In 1961 the difference between the highest and lowest province in the percentage of employment in manufacturing (Ontario and Saskatchewan) was 21.7 percentage points. In 2006 the difference between the highest and the lowest (Quebec and Saskatchewan) was only 9.3 percentage points. Retail trade and health care and social services each accounted for more than one fifth of the labour force in every province (Canada, 2006).

Thus if a Canadian who died a generation ago could return to see the Canada of today, he or she would find a very different country in which regional economic differences are much less conspicuous than in the past. Newfoundland's cod fishery has collapsed, Cape Breton's coal mines have closed, many of Ontario's and Quebec's manufacturing industries have disappeared, and the network of railway branch lines and local grain elevators that still dotted the prairies when Pierre Trudeau retired has gone the way of the steam locomotive. In Hamilton, where two Canadian-owned steel companies dominated the city's economy for most of the twentieth century, what remains of the steel industry is now foreign-owned and employs fewer people than the city's hospitals. Services of all kinds increasingly dominate the economies of every province and region and are increasingly concentrated in the larger urban areas of each province, so that the typical employed person in Ontario and her counterpart in Saskatchewan are probably doing the same kind of work in the same kind of setting.

However, it would be premature to say that regionalism is dead, even though it may gradually decline. Historical memories and grievances, once established, do not die easily, as shown by the number of white southern Americans who still fly the Confederate flag and cherish the traditions of the Civil War, which they persist in calling 'the war between the states'. Although the National Policy is dead and the lives of Canadians in the sprawling suburbs of our great cities seem increasingly similar, some sense of regional identity can be expected to linger on. Despite the cliché that air travel, the long-distance telephone, and the internet have brought people closer together, it still makes a difference whether Ottawa is in a different time zone or just a few hours' drive down the road.

One indicator of regionalism that seems remarkably durable is voting behaviour in both federal and provincial elections. Although the Liberals governed Canada for most of the twentieth century, they have not won a majority of western ridings since 1949. The last time they won a majority of Alberta ridings was in 1911, when the province was only six years old and Sir Wilfrid Laurier was leader of the party. Conversely, Liberals have usually won a majority of Newfoundland and Labrador's ridings since it joined Canada in 1949. In 2008 Premier Danny Williams, although nominally a Conservative, advised the people of Newfoundland and Labrador to vote 'ABC' (anything but Conservative) in the federal election to protest against the partial inclusion of offshore oil revenues in the equalization formula. Most of them took his advice and the federal Conservative candidates in the province were all defeated. At the time of writing Saskatchewan is governed by the Saskatchewan Party, which has replaced both the Liberals and Conservatives as the only serious alternative to the NDP. The newly formed Wild Rose Party (named for Alberta's floral emblem) is a serious contender to defeat the long-entrenched Conservatives in Alberta, who are lagging in the polls. The Bloc Québécois held most of Quebec's federal ridings from 1993 until 2011, when the NDP unexpectedly swept the province. The Parti Québécois is still one of the two major parties in the National Assembly.

Performance, Effectiveness, and Legitimacy

How does regionalism influence the performance, effectiveness and legitimacy of Canadian federalism? As explained in the introductory chapter of this book, performance refers to the functioning of political institutions, effectiveness refers to policy outcomes, and legitimacy is a measure of how positive Canadians feel about Canada and its political regime.

In terms of performance perhaps the greatest failure of Canadian institutions is the appointed Senate. This is significant because in most federations the principal function of the upper house is precisely to represent regional interests and points of view, something that the Senate of the United States and the **Bundesrat** in Germany do reasonably well. In Canada, however, the Senate cannot represent regional interests effectively because its members are appointed by the federal government and because they may serve for several decades, until they reach the age of 75, without any accountability to the people or to the regions which they ostensibly represent. Western Canada, which arguably has the most distinctive regional interests, is also under-represented, with only 24 senators out of 105. Thus support for senate reform, and particularly for the idea of an elected senate with an equal number of members from each province, is stronger in western Canada than elsewhere.

To some extent the cabinet has had to replace the Senate as the major institution for accommodating regional interests. It did so quite well in the early and middle years of Canadian federalism, when ministers controlled the party machines in their provinces and distributed the patronage. Even as recently as the Trudeau era some ministers like Lloyd Axworthy of Manitoba and Allan MacEachen of Nova Scotia were important and influential spokesmen for their regions (Bakvis, 1988). However, regional variations in voting behaviour and the 'first past the post' electoral system sometimes make it difficult or impossible for the governing party to elect potential ministers from certain provinces. In addition, the growing influence of central agencies, especially the Privy Council Office and the Prime Minister's Office, as well as the greater use of cabinet committees and the disappearance of most patronage, have eroded much of the influence that ministers formerly enjoyed.

Conferences and meetings of provincial premiers, with or without the prime minister of Canada, are another way of representing regional interests. From about 1960 to 1993 the First Ministers' Conference (FMC), including the heads of all provincial governments as well as the federal government, met frequently and was an important forum for dealing with certain kinds of issues, especially constitutional change and fiscal federalism. Recently the meetings have been less frequent since prime ministers Chrétien and Harper have preferred to have as few as possible, and the term First Ministers' Meeting (FMM) has been adopted to downgrade their importance. The presence of territorial leaders has also lessened the influence of the premiers. A recent study of the institution suggests that it is lacking in effectiveness and even refers to it as 'the weakest link' of Canadian federalism

(Papillon and Simeon, 2004). On the other hand, the Council of the Federation, in which the federal government is not represented, was formed in 2003 at the initiative of Quebec and provides a continuous forum for the brokerage of regional interests. There is also a Council of Atlantic Premiers which meets twice a year and a Western Premiers' Conference meeting annually. None of these institutions, of course, can influence the federal government as much as an effective upper house, on either the American or the German model, would be able to do.

Despite the mediocre performance of its institutions in representing regional interests, Canadian federalism arguably has been reasonably effective in producing public policies satisfactory to most regions, at least in the long run. The economic issues on which regional interests clash are usually difficult and complex, but they often seem to be amenable to some sort of compromise that leaves no region completely dissatisfied. The National Energy Program, which was viewed as regionally discriminatory, did not last long, and the federal and Alberta governments eventually reached an agreement over energy prices. Provinces with offshore oil resources were given a role in administering them in 1985, even though such resources legally belong to the federal government, and have been able to reap most of the financial benefits. Free trade with the United States, and later with Mexico, was a victory for most regions, and arguably benefited even those that were sceptical about it. The abolition of the Crowsnest freight rate and deregulation of other freight rates have made the railways much more vigorous and competitive, and the Canadian Pacific moved its headquarters from Montreal to Calgary in 1996. The equalization program, although almost by definition it can never be equally beneficial to every province, seems in its present (post-2007) form to be close to a **Pareto optimum** solution.

Legitimacy, finally, is influenced by both performance and effectiveness. In assessing it, one may conclude either that the glass is half full or half empty. Low rates of participation in federal elections, the constant complaining about federal politicians on open-line radio and other vehicles of public sentiment, occasional expressions of resentment by provincial premiers, and the low repute of both houses of Parliament, might suggest that the Canadian federal state lacks legitimacy. However, it is unclear what standards it should be compared with or whether the political institutions of other countries, including the United States, would rank any higher. Furthermore, the sovereignty movement in Quebec seems to have subsided, at least for the time being, and 'separatism' in other parts of Canada exists only on the lunatic fringes of political discourse. Most Canadians appear to be proud of their country, as the Vancouver Olympic Games suggested, regardless of where they live. Despite the scepticism of Goldwin Smith and many subsequent observers, Canadian unity seems reasonably secure.

References

Bakvis, H. 1988. 'Regional Ministers, National Policies and the Administrative State in Canada: The Regional Dimension in Cabinet Decision-Making, 1980–1984', *Canadian Journal of Political Science*, 12: 539–67.

Cairns, A.C. 1977. 'The Governments and Societies of Canadian Federalism', *Canadian Journal of Political Science*, 10: 695–725.

Canada, 1961. Census, catalogue no. 94-518.

Canada. 1985. *Report of the Royal Commission on*

the Economic Union and Development Prospects for Canada, Volume One. Ottawa: Minister of Supply and Services.

Canada, 2006. Census, catalogue no. 97-561.

Canada Year Book 2008. 2008. Ottawa: Statistics Canada.

Clarke, H.D., J.H. Pammett, and M.C. Stewart. 2002. 'The Forest for the Trees: Regional (Dis) Similarities in Canadian Political Culture'. In Regionalism and Party Politics in Canada, eds. L. Young and K. Archer. Toronto: Oxford University Press.

Darling, H. 1980. The Politics of Freight Rates: The Railway Freight Rate Issue in Canada. Toronto: McClelland and Stewart.

Earl, J.F. 1985. 'U.S.–Canada Free Trade: A View from the East'. In Canada–United States Free Trade, ed. J. Whalley. Toronto: University of Toronto Press.

Easterbrook, W.T., and H. G. J. Aitken. 1956. Canadian Economic History. Toronto: Macmillan.

Forbes, E.R. 1979. The Maritime Rights Movement, 1919–1927: A Study in Canadian Regionalism. Montreal: McGill-Queen's University Press.

Gras, N.S.B. 1922. An Introduction to Economic History. New York and London: Harper and Brothers.

Innis, H.A. 1956. 'An Introduction to the Economic History of the Maritimes, including Newfoundland and New England'. In Essays in Canadian Economic History. Toronto: University of Toronto Press.

Innis, H.A. 1970. The Fur Trade in Canada: An Introduction to Canadian Economic History. Toronto: University of Toronto Press.

Innis, H.A. 1971. A History of the Canadian Pacific Railway. Toronto: University of Toronto Press.

Lipset, S.M. 1968. Agrarian Socialism: The Cooperative Commonwealth Federation in Saskatchewan, A Study in Political Sociology. New York: Anchor Books.

Mackintosh, W.A. 1964. The Economic Background

of Dominion–Provincial Relations. Toronto: McClelland and Stewart.

Macpherson, C.B. 1962. Democracy in Alberta: Social Credit and the Party System. 2nd ed., Toronto: University of Toronto Press.

Mallory, J.R. 1976. Social Credit and the Federal Power in Canada. 2nd ed. Toronto: University of Toronto Press.

Martin, C. 1973. 'Dominion Lands' Policy. Toronto: McClelland and Stewart.

McCormick, P. 1989. 'Regionalism in Canada: Disentangling the Threads', Journal of Canadian Studies 24, 2: 5–21.

Milne, D. 1986. Tug of War: Ottawa and the Provinces Under Trudeau and Mulroney. Toronto: James Lorimer and Company.

Morton, W.L. 1950. The Progressive Party in Canada. Toronto: University of Toronto Press.

Papillon, M., and R. Simeon. 2004. 'The Weakest Link? First Ministers' Conferences in Canadian Intergovernmental Relations'. In Reconsidering the Institutions of Canadian Federalism, eds. J. P. Meekison, H. Telford and H. Lazar. Kingston: Institute of Intergovernmental Relations.

Polèse, M. 1985. 'Regional Economics,' The Canadian Encyclopedia. Edmonton: Hurtig.

Porter, J. 1965. The Vertical Mosaic. Toronto: University of Toronto Press.

Richards, J., and L. Pratt. 1979. Prairie Capitalism: Power and Influence in the New West. Toronto: McClelland and Stewart.

Rogers, N.M. 1933. 'The Genesis of Provincial Rights', Canadian Historical Review 14: 9–23.

Smith, G. 1971 (1891). Canada and the Canadian Question. Toronto: University of Toronto Press.

Stevenson, G. 1981. 'Western Alienation in Australia and Canada'. In Western Separatism: The Myths, Realities and Dangers, eds. L. Pratt and G. Stevenson. Edmonton: Hurtig.

Stevenson, G. 1993. Ex Uno Plures: Federal-Provincial Relations in Canada 1867–1896. Montreal and Kingston: McGill-Queen's University Press.

3 Quebec and the Canadian Federation

David Cameron

Evaluating Canadian federalism according to the three criteria of performance, effectiveness, and legitimacy is a challenging exercise: the judgments inevitably carry a good dose of subjectivity, depending on the perspective and frame of reference one brings to bear on the subject. In the midst of the bloody American Civil War, it would have been hard to argue that American federalism was a success. When the state of Western Australia voted strongly to secede from the union in the early 1930s, 'success' would not likely have been the term used to describe the Australian federation. Austrian federalism would have been hard to discover and applaud in 1938–45, when Nazi Germany took over the country and incorporated it into the Third Reich. So when, in the life of a country, you make your assessment is important.

But there is also the question of *what* you are assessing. What is success and how will you recognize it? Is it simple survival, endurance, living from one year to another? Or is it meeting the purposes for which the federation was created in the first place? Is it the capacity of that political community to suppress violence and unmanageable conflict? To act as a barrier to tyranny? Or is it the measures many federalism scholars often use—the fostering of local experimentation, the alleged fact that the states or regions in a federal system are schools for democracy, and federalism's capacity to bring government closer to the people? Is it simply good government? Or, finally, is it a federation's apparent utility in managing ethno-cultural, religious and other forms of diversity within the country?

Questions of this magnitude arise when one is seeking to evaluate the Canadian federation in relation to Quebec and Canada's francophone population, because French–English relations go to the existential heart of the Canadian political community. How you assess Canada's performance in this domain depends radically on your foundational values and preferences. Lord Durham would no doubt have judged the evolution of the country on the basis of whether it was leading effectively to the assimilation of French Canadians into English-speaking North America (Durham, 1982; Cameron, 1990). John A. Macdonald would have assessed the issue differently; to the extent that Quebec and French Canada did not get in the way of building a strong national (meaning Canadian) government and a strong national economy, he would have pronounced the arrangements successful (Ajzenstat et al., 2003). A.A. Dorion, however, as one of the most eloquent exponents of the French-Canadian view in the Confederation debates, took a very different position: the purpose of the new federal arrangement, and the single most important criterion of its success, would be the degree to which it protected the survival of French Canada (Waite, 1963).

Evaluative differences almost as great exist today, although few contemporary Canadians would seriously adhere to the Durham view. Nevertheless, the assessment of the performance, effectiveness, and legitimacy of the Canadian federation as it relates to Quebec engenders widely different opinions. Some—and I would place myself in this camp—regard the operation of Canadian federalism vis-à-vis Quebec as a success. Despite many failures, setbacks, and injustices, the federal framework has permitted the francophone community in Quebec not simply to survive, but to develop, to transform itself according to its lights. French-speaking Canadians have used their majority status in Quebec to shape the provincial government and public policy very substantially to suit their needs, and Quebec as a federal actor has profoundly influenced the character and operation of Canadian federalism. What is more, with the Supreme Court's judgment on the Secession Reference in 1998, Canadians now know that the country rests ultimately on the consent of the people in its federal units, and that it is possible for a province to secede constitutionally from Confederation if there is a clear and authoritative withdrawal of that consent.

A large number of Quebec citizens and many, perhaps most, of the Québécois political elite, on the other hand, would likely regard the Canadian federal experience as deeply flawed, a story of continuing failure so far as Quebec is concerned.[1] The English-speaking majority in Canada, in this view, has consistently used its power and control over the federal government to ensure that its vital interests are protected, and to resist the continuing efforts of members of the francophone community to secure their rights, advance their interests and establish a standing in the federation that they themselves would recognize as just and appropriate. Through the aggressive use of the spending power and the passage of the 1982 Constitution, the federal government has sought to trump the constitutional distribution of authority between it and the provinces, centralizing power in Ottawa. Quebec is subject to the 1982 Constitution, but not a consenting party to it, leading to the perverse situation that the jurisdiction which, far more than any other, pressed for constitutional reform, is the only jurisdiction whose aspirations were not met.

There is no way that I know of to establish a federal balance sheet on this matter that could be agreed on by everyone. The differences are not rooted in miscalculation but rather in different worldviews. François Rocher (2009: 81) points out that 'even the least attentive observer would note that the interpretation of the evolution of Canadian federalism differs greatly depending on the origin of the author'. And compelling evidence can be advanced on both sides. Just as I would acknowledge that the fact that Quebec has never signed on to the 1982 Constitution raises a grave question about the legitimacy of Canada's constitutional arrangements, so, I imagine, would Québécois colleagues acknowledge that the experience of French-speakers and of Quebec within Canada since Confederation could have been a whole lot worse.

It is helpful to make these widely diverse understandings of the situation clear at the beginning of this chapter, so that the reader will have a sense of the larger context within which the narrative is placed. It is, then, not so much a matter of establishing an uncontested truth, as it is a matter of appreciating the angle of vision from which one gazes on the Canadian federal experience.

In what follows I suggest that there were a number of reasons why a federal structure of government for Canada seemed, if not inevitable, at least highly logical, and I argue that French Canada and Quebec were critical in establishing a vibrant federal system in this country.

Federations and Unitary States: The Logic of Federal Government in Canada

Federations are not at their inception the naturally emerging product of long historical experience, but 'artificial' constructs, created by explicit agreement at a certain historical moment. The English could take the Burkean view that England's constitutional order was the natural historical outcome of centuries of people living together on the same piece of ground, gradually developing a sense of themselves, and, through trial and error, presiding over the emergence of the political institutions that have shaped English life and culture. The common law and the unwritten character of the British Constitution express this traditional emergence of a political community.

It is quite otherwise with federations. These political regimes are self-consciously willed into being by an agreement or compact, usually a federal constitution, which establishes a new political order. When was the USA and its federal constitution created? 1789. The Swiss federal system? 1848. The Canadian? 1867. The Australian Commonwealth? 1901. What year was England and the English Constitution created? That is an inappropriate question.

If a political regime is the product of a formal founding moment or social compact, then it is possible to give reasons for why the deed was done. What are the characteristic reasons for creating federal structures? Some of the most obvious are:

- large size of the territory;
- defense and common security;
- creation of a larger, stronger economic union;
- the accommodation of history, tradition and local loyalties as new states are formed;
- the accommodation of significant, territorially concentrated ethnic, cultural, linguistic or religious differences in existing states; and
- the protection of liberty by the dispersion and limiting of state power.

In the case of Canada in 1867, two of the key reasons that several of the colonies of British North America chose to establish a new political association were: first, the need to create a strong, common security zone for all the colonies, faced with a retreating Britain and a powerful and bellicose American North, flushed with its recent victory over the South in the Civil War; and second, the desire to create an integrated economy and transportation system in the top half of North America, and to settle, develop and control the central and western part of the continent north of the 49th parallel. These were reasons to form a new, larger political association, but they were not, in themselves, reasons for federalism; in principle, a new, large unitary state would have done these tasks just as well or better, which is in fact what John A. Macdonald believed.

However, a unitary state was not in the cards for a number of reasons, and these offer us the more powerful justifications for specifically choosing a federal form of government. One obvious factor was the sheer size of the territory under consideration, particularly given the available communications technologies of the day; without a railway link, it took days to get from Halifax to Quebec City, and weeks to sail to Europe. The idea that, in the huge territory of British North America, a single, unitary state could effectively perform all the necessary duties of an emergent modern democratic state was not plausible; dispersing the powers and responsibilities of the state in a decentralized form of government made good sense.

Equally important were two elements in the socio-political situation confronting the founders at the time of Confederation. British North Americans in large numbers felt a strong loyalty to their own colonial governments and to the political communities of which they were already members. They were not prepared to abandon these local governments in favour of an untried experiment in a new, larger and more distant political realm. The strength of local loyalties, and the suspicion of the new arrangements can be seen in the fact that two of the colonies that had been party to the discussions declined to join Confederation in 1867; Prince Edward Island did not enter Confederation until 1873, and Newfoundland stood apart until 1949. Further evidence of local loyalty and suspicion of the new arrangements may be seen in the fact that one of the original signatories, Nova Scotia, had second thoughts soon after coming on board, and tried unsuccessfully to get out of the deal to which it had just signed on.

The second socio-political element was French Canada. It would be no exaggeration to say that a larger political association that failed to make substantial provision for the protection and self-government of the French community in North America would have been impossible. The preservation of a coherent French community and the re-establishment of a significant capacity for that community to govern itself after the experience of the United Province of Canada were unconditional objectives during the Confederation debates.

That covers five of the items on our list above—size, security, the economy, local loyalties, and ethnocultural diversity. The sixth—the protection of liberty—was not really a concern for the colonial politicians who put the Confederation bargain together. Britain's North American colonies had all been granted responsible government by the time the discussion of these new arrangements occurred. There was simply an assumption that the benefits of self-government and the protection of liberties that the colonial societies were enjoying would be carried forward into whatever new institutional framework was created.

The two spoilers, then—the two requirements that had absolutely to be met if the new Canadian association were to be accomplished—were the preservation of the colonial units and their governance capacity, and the preservation and self-government of French Canada: both drove the Fathers of Confederation to federalism. It would be difficult to say that one was more essential than the other; both were necessary for the Confederation bargain to be consummated, and from then on both echo through the Canadian federal story. Our focus in this chapter, however, is on the place of French Canada and Quebec in the Canadian federal system.

Federal Pressures before Federalism: The French Fact Prior to 1867

The association of distinct communities, then, is a principle buried deep in our history. The encounter of European settler societies with Aboriginal communities and governments brought two radically different civilizations in contact with one another. Until the power of Native people was reduced, the British Crown took care to recognize and treat Native communities as pre-existing autonomous entities. The federalizing potential of this reality was submerged for well over a century, not to rise again until the latter half of the twentieth century. For close to two generations now, the country has been engaged in the effort to right some deep historic wrongs, and to recognize and accommodate the Aboriginal component of Canadian society within the country and its Constitution (Royal Commission on Aboriginal Peoples, 1996: vol. 1).

The French were the first to confront this challenge in what was ultimately to become British North America. The arrival of French explorers and settlers in the sixteenth and seventeenth centuries raised the question of intercultural, and indeed, inter-civilizational relationships. The English inherited the issue when they assumed control of this part of North America in 1759, but they faced another, even more fateful, challenge: how were they to deal with the 65,000-strong French community they encountered on the banks of the St. Lawrence? Acadian-style expulsion proved not to be an option; forced integration or assimilation was not feasible and—for some of the early imperial representatives—not desirable. Accommodation in some form or other was the chief remaining alternative.

It would be wrong to leave the impression that this was a clear policy choice, taken self-consciously at one point in time, after careful discussion and analysis in Great Britain's Whitehall. Rather, the choice was made in fits and starts over decades, largely by dint of geopolitical events to which the British imperial authorities had to respond. A policy direction could be set in Whitehall, but it had to be implemented a couple of thousand miles across the sea in British North America, and both distance and local exigencies offered an opportunity to local British officials in North America to adapt policies and develop actual arrangements that could be implemented in the practical circumstances they faced.

One can get a sense of the movement of policy in the early years by reviewing some of the critical documents of the period. The Royal Proclamation of 1763 enunciated the basis on which relations with Aboriginal peoples would be carried on: it sought to limit the westward expansion of the American colonies; it provided for representative institutions; and it outlined a policy of assimilation for the French who had stayed on in British North America after the Conquest or Cession. The Quebec Act of 1774 has often been called the charter of French Canada. Passed in anticipation of the pending American Revolution of 1775–81, the Quebec Act offered French Canada, and especially its elites, much of what they sought: toleration of French Canada's way of life, the establishment of the Roman Catholic church and its power to collect tithes, a special oath to permit Catholics to hold civil office, an acceptance of the seigneurial land-holding system, and recognition of the French civil law. All these provisions were made in the hope of securing the loyalty of the French Canadian community in the face of the pending American rebellion. The Quebec Act placed political authority in the hands of the governor and an appointed council, again giving reassurance to the French Canadian elites that their interests would not be trampled by an unruly English assembly.

The Constitutional Act, passed in 1791 after the American Revolution had successfully delivered independence to the United States, recognized the loss of territory to the US, and attempted to cope with the heavy influx of Loyalist immigration to British North America by dividing Quebec into Upper and Lower Canada, implicitly acknowledging Lower Canada as the homeland of the French Canadians. It retained French civil law and the establishment of the Roman Catholic church in Lower Canada, and supported the introduction of representative government in both Canadas, with French Canadians enjoying political rights to vote and run for office in the Lower Canada Assembly.

The **Durham Report** of 1839, prepared in the aftermath of the 1837 rebellions in Upper and Lower Canada, proposed a return to the assimilation strategy of earlier years. Dismissing French Canadians as an `uninstructed, inactive, unprogressive people', Lord Durham believed North America belonged to the English, that 'great race which must, in the lapse of no long period of time, be predominant over the whole North American Continent' (Durham, 1982: 27, 146). Durham believed that by reuniting Upper and Lower Canada in a new United Province of Canada, the continuous immigration of English-speaking peoples would swamp the French Canadians over time and lead to their assimilation into English-speaking North America. He also proposed the introduction of responsible government, making the British representative subject to the will of the colonial assembly, bringing a substantial measure of self-government to the British colony.

The British government proceeded with part of Durham's proposals, passing the Act of Union in 1840, which created the United Province of Canada, but declined to institute responsible government, which did not come to the British North American colonies until 1848. English and French Canadians worked within the United Province system until it was dismantled by Confederation in 1867, but it did not have the hoped-for effect. Instead of leading to the assimilation of French Canadians into an English majoritarian political system, leaders from the two communities turned this expectation on its head, paying scrupulous attention to the needs and prerogatives of the two linguistic communities, and instituting a practice of double majorities and other consociational arrangements for the conduct of the business of the Province. What was meant to lead to assimilation in reality confirmed the significant dualism of Canadian society, and the need to find means to accommodate that dualism in our national politics.

By the time the Confederation bargain was negotiated in the mid-1860s, the continued existence of the French-Catholic community on the shores of the St. Lawrence was a given and an unquestioned fact; finding the means of accommodating that fact appropriately in the new constitutional arrangements was one of the key challenges of the negotiations that led to the establishment of Canada.

Confederation: Irresolution at the Heart of the 1867 Deal

The British North America Act, now known as the Constitution Act, 1867, responds to this central element of Canadian diversity in a number of ways.

- It established Canada as a federation, thus responding to both the regional and the bi-national features of British North America.
- It severed the United Province of Canada, which had amalgamated Upper and Lower Canada in 1840, thereby giving provincial status, with government power and constitutionally defined jurisdictions, to Quebec, where the vast majority of French Canadians lived. Thus, Confederation's country-building aspiration had an element of separation embedded in it.
- The jurisdictions allocated to provinces—and therefore to Quebec—were the matters of greatest concern to French Canadians seeking to protect and control their own community: health, education, social assistance, municipal institutions, the solemnization of marriage, and property and civil rights in the province.
- The French system of civil law was recognized in Quebec for civil matters.
- The French and English languages were accorded a limited degree of constitutional status. Either could (and still can) be used in the debates and proceedings of the Parliament of Canada and the Legislature of Quebec, and in the Courts of the two jurisdictions.
- The Catholic and Protestant school systems existing at the time of Confederation or established afterwards were given constitutional protection.

Unresolved at the country's inception, however, and still unresolved today, are two competing conceptions of Canada's federal association and the meaning of 1867. Is Confederation best understood as a constitutional agreement among the four original provinces, now grown to 10, or as a compact between two founding peoples? An act or a pact (Stanley, 1956; Royal Commission on Bilingualism and Biculturalism, 1965; Paquin, 1999)? Most English-speaking Canadians would incline to the first view; the vast majority of French-speaking Canadians would argue it is the second. The Fathers of Confederation were able to agree on the formal terms of the new political association, but not on its deeper meaning. Each side was able to preserve its own view of itself and its own view of the federal association. The debate over 'act or pact' was in reality a debate over the nature of the social units that composed the society of which the federal system was the expression. Were there two peoples coming together in an historic compact, each pre-existing and each pursuing the protection and advancement of its own identity in the new configuration? Or was it an act bringing into a new association a group of British colonies, populated predominantly by British colonists, where the question of people or peoples did not seriously enter into the equation?

Thus was created the greatest fault line in the Canadian political order—a disagreement about the very meaning of Canada, which lay, for the most part unacknowledged, at the deepest foundation of the Canadian state. Both sides, for the sake of getting agreement and creating the new political regime, came to terms on what they could agree on, and were complicit in pushing this cleavage so far as possible beneath the realm of normal political discourse.

The issue of the constitutive status of Canadian federalism was not resolved, therefore, but covered over in the 1867 Constitution. The Canadian federation is formally an association of provinces, not a union of peoples, but there was enough of the latter in the agreement to permit Quebec to participate and to allow that other conception of the association to establish itself and endure. Far from disappearing or being rendered power-less by inattention, this cleavage has had the power to unleash political earthquakes and to shake the very foundations of the constitutional order. And it has done so, regularly, in our history. Canada's moments of deepest conflict have invariably led Canadians to the edge of this existential chasm between political worldviews. The **Riel Rebellions** of 1869 and 1885, the **Manitoba Schools Crisis** in the latter part of the 19th century, the **Conscription Crises in World War I** and **World War II**—all have drawn their destructive energy from this underlying and virtually unbridgeable cleavage. The terms of reference of Quebec's renowned Tremblay Commission, established by Premier Maurice Duplessis in 1953, left no doubt about the Quebec Government's view of the salience of this issue nor about the Government's position: the first article of the Commission's terms of reference states that 'the Canadian confederation, born of an agreement between the four pioneer provinces, is first and above all a pact of honour between the two great races which founded it. . .'. (Kwavnick, 1973) As we shall see below, that divergence of view continues unabated, although in a modern idiom.

Until the 1960s, there was a further ambiguity. On the francophone side of the equation, how was one to understand the French fact in Canada? Was it to be under-stood as French Canadians wherever they found themselves across the country or as Quebec (or, yet again, the French in Quebec)? Quebec was always recognized as the *foyer principal* of French Canada, but the first, more expansive view included as well the francophones of New Brunswick, who today compose around one-third of that province's population, as well as the 500,000 or so *franco-ontariens* and the smaller groups scattered elsewhere in the country. In this more expansive view, these were understood as integral parts of the French-Canadian community in North America. For much of our political existence, both conceptualizations of francophone identity had currency and were a vital part of public debate. The status and prospects of French Canada writ large was clearly at the centre of the 19th-century Riel and Schools con-troversies in Manitoba: would the western part of the country be French and English, or was it to be the preserve of English speakers? At one point this was thought by many French Canadians to be an open question, although by the end of the 19th century, English Canadians in the other provinces had made it pretty clear that the West would be Anglophone (Heintzman, 1971).

This ambiguity over how to understand the French fact in Canada was dissolved dur-ing the 1960s with the fragmentation and provincialization of French Canada. French Canadians in Quebec adopted a statist nationalism very different in its character and implications from the more religiously based French Canadian nationalism of the previ-ous century. Their central preoccupation became the fortunes of the French-speaking community within Quebec—the Québécois; this focus undermined the broader multi-province understanding of French Canada. Over time, the French minorities in the other provinces drew the lesson from the new situation, and began to redefine themselves in provincial terms—as Acadiens, Franco-Ontariens, Franco-Manitobains, Fransaskois, etc., realizing that they could not rely on the leadership of the French Canadians in Quebec for their survival, but would have to deal directly with their own provincial gov-ernment, often with the assistance of a concerned federal government.

How did this shift in perspective and positioning occur?

French Canada and Quebec in the Federation prior to 1960

Much has been written about the nature of French Canada and Quebec in the generations after Confederation. Over time, a defining myth grew up in French Canada depicting the character of that community and the way in which it saw itself differentiated from the rest of North American society. French Canada was understood to be defined by its Catholicism, its rural, agrarian economy and social structure, and the French language.[2] Life was thought to revolve around the parish church, with the church rivalling the state as the central institution of French Canada. This depiction was not only a way of describing what French Canada was, but also what it was not: it was not urban, or secular, or commercial, or anglicized. As a minority community, it was natural that there was a serious effort to articulate what was distinctive and of special value about the community and what was potentially under threat.

The myth was not without substance, but the reality of French Canada was always richer and more diverse than allowed for (McRoberts, 1993: Chs. 2–4). Yet the myth was powerful in shaping the attitudes, assumptions, and behaviour of people both within and outside Quebec. The virtue of the federal system was that it created a sub-national government with special responsibility for the protection of the heart of the French Canadian community in North America, the territory where a decisive majority of French Canadians lived. The job of that government was to help preserve a way of life and to shield the community from the corrosive impact of a huge and growing English majority in North America.

The **Tremblay Report** (1956) was the most elaborate and philosophically sophisticated statement of this general world view and remains influential today (Laforest, 2010). Yet it described a society that was already in the process of disappearing. By the time the Tremblay Commissioners reported, Quebec was long since more urban than rural, more industrial than agricultural, more embedded in, than standing apart from, the commercial society of English North America. Despite this, and despite earlier efforts in the 1930s to launch serious political and social reform (Dirks, 1991), the Quebec provincial government under Premier Maurice Duplessis functioned largely within the framework of this myth, and did relatively little to assist Quebec and Quebecers to adjust to the modern realities with which their society was increasingly infused.

What role did Quebec play in the evolution of the Canadian federal system during this period? It was something like a sheet anchor that imposed a constraint or a drag on what might otherwise have been a powerful drift in the development of the federal system. The existence of the Province of Quebec in Canada's federal order meant that there was a federal constraint on English-speaking Canada, limiting the extent to which the processes of modernization and the centralizing effects of world wars and economic depression were able to trump the forces of decentralization in the country.[3]

The Quiet Revolution: Intergovernmental Relations Transformed

With the death of Duplessis in 1958, and the untimely demise of his successor, Paul Sauvé, in 1960, the rudderless party was defeated by the Quebec Liberals in the 1960 provincial election, and the Quiet Revolution began. Much has been written about this period of Quebec's history, and some have argued that it does not really qualify as a 'revolution', quiet or noisy, because, for example, there were no radical structural changes in the institutions and governing processes of the Province (McRoberts, 1993: Ch. 5). Quebec was less different from the rest of North America in its political economy than it might appear on the surface; it was more a matter of evolution than revolution. The transformative forces of urbanization and industrialization had been working their magic in Quebec for generations; Quebec society had been changing throughout the earlier part of the 20th century, as had the rest of Canada. Like elsewhere, French Canadians were moving off the farms and villages of the provinces into the factory towns and cities of the region; some, as the availability of arable land declined, were moving right out of Quebec, to states south of the border (Brault, 1986). So it is not as if French Canada had stood utterly apart from the forces transforming North America in the first half of the 20th century.

The Quiet Revolution may be best understood as a period of ideological and political, rather than material, transformation, in which the conservative nationalism of the previous era was rapidly replaced by a positive, liberal nationalism: the provincial state assumed pride of place in the institutions of the French-speaking community, quickly pushing the Catholic Church into the background; the government assumed responsibility for education and for establishing some of the basic institutions of the modern welfare state. In addition, the government became far more active in the development of the provincial economy. The Quiet Revolution was, therefore, not simply a sudden shift at the level of ideology, but a period of significant policy and institutional innovation as well. There were significant changes at the level of society, too. Perhaps the most eloquent testimony of this is found in the precipitous decline in Quebec's birthrate. As Kenneth McRoberts points out, in 1956 Quebec's fertility rate was close to four children per couple. 'Yet, over the years 1959–72, it plummeted 56 per cent, falling below the rate of 2.1 needed to maintain population size' (McRoberts, 1993: 139). In a few short years, Quebec's birthrate fell from the highest to the lowest in Canada.[4] This extraordinary decline symbolizes a remarkably rapid shift in social norms and practices within the French-speaking community, as well as the breathtaking decline in the role of the Catholic Church in the life of Quebec.

The impact of the Quiet Revolution on the federal government and intergovernmental relations was immediate. Where traditionally Quebec had adopted a protective posture in intergovernmental relations, seeking to defend its position and its people's way of life, it became in the 1960s an agenda-setting government, demanding changes in the way in which the federation worked and actively pursuing policy goals that would invest Quebec with a greater capacity to determine its own social and economic development. The challenge to Canadian federalism was of two sorts: the quest for increased autonomy and greater jurisdictional control for Quebec, and the demand for greater fiscal resources, both through a decentralization of tax space from Ottawa to the Province and increased federal fiscal transfers. Quebec's desire for greater tax room was shared by a number of provinces seeking to reverse the fiscal centralization that had occurred during the war years, but, unlike the other provinces, it placed its demands in the context of nation building.

Faced with a reformist government in Ottawa under Lester Pearson (1963–8), Premier Jean Lesage and his colleagues acted adroitly on the intergovernmental front to ensure that progressive social and economic policy was executed within Quebec by Quebec, rather than the federal government. A good example of this can be seen in Ottawa's effort to establish a national pension plan. Through stormy intergovernmental negotiations, Quebec succeeded in opting out of the Canadian plan, introducing its own version and using the capital it generated to establish the *Caisse de dépôt et placement*, which became in time a powerful provincial investment and economic development vehicle. The Quebec government's reformist zeal was demonstrated by the nationalization of a number of private hydroelectric companies in 1962 and their incorporation into Hydro-Québec.

The period of the Quiet Revolution, from 1960 to around 1966, then, marked a profound shift in Quebec's self-conception, its development strategies, and thus its approach to federalism and intergovernmental relations. Quebecers increasingly wanted to see themselves as members of a modern national community, and expected their government to help them build a set of institutions and the social, educational and economic capacities appropriate to a modern state—but *en français*. The government's desire to respond and to find the resources needed to do the job set it on a collision course with Ottawa. Quebec's goals produced not only acute intergovernmental conflict but also a deepening cleavage in identities and in perceptions of the roles of the two orders of government. Earlier French Canadian nationalists had been inclined to argue that the problem was that the constitutional order was not respected by Ottawa; increasingly, Québécois nationalists contended that the problem was that the constitution needed to be transformed.

Thirty Years of Travail: 1965–95

The Quiet Revolution marked the onset of an extended period of nation-building in Quebec, which ripened into demands for constitutional reform, and ultimately spawned a powerful sovereignist movement. How was the nation understood? The essentially binary view of the federation did not change, but the idiom through which it was expressed was different, as was the sense of collective identity. French Canadians in Quebec identified themselves as Québécois and the distinctive features of their national community narrowed and sharpened. Where once the dimensions of identity were understood to be multiple—French, Catholic, rural—they were reduced effectively to one. The Québécois were defined by language, by the singular fact that they spoke French. In his 1968 manifesto for **sovereignty-association**, *An Option for Quebec*, René Lévesque wrote: 'At the core of this [Québécois] personality is the fact that we speak French. Everything else depends on this one essential element and follows from it or leads us infallibly back to it' (Lévesque, 1968: 4). This reshaping of identity was inevitable, once Quebecers became more like the rest of North American society in their lifestyle and aspirations and the markers of religion and rurality were discarded. Until the 1960s, no Quebec government had established a language policy; it was not seen to be necessary (Gagnon and Montcalm, 1989). By the end of the decade, this had changed: a succession of governments passed language legislation, culminating in the Parti Québécois **Bill 101** in 1977. Language has been a central policy preoccupation ever since.

The cleavage noted earlier resurfaced with a bang at the start of this long period of nation building, but it was different because the perception of national identity and the economic and political circumstances were different. French-speaking Canadians were still inclined to view the federal relationship in dualistic or binary terms, at least so far as the principled meaning of Confederation was concerned, if not in constitutional fact. A central part of their constitutional ambitions was in fact to bring the terms of the foundational document into line with reality as they perceived it. Two-nations theory, special status for Quebec, the distinct-society concept, the notion of sovereignty-association—these ideas were all ways of representing the constitutional implications of the French fact within the context of the binary relationship that, in the view of the Québécois, lay at the heart of the Confederation bargain. These concepts were at bottom constitutional in character; they implied a particular understanding of the Canadian federal system, not just of Quebec, and they fostered a different style of intergovernmental relations.

Much of the next 30 years of intergovernmental discussion was devoted to an often heated debate about the validity of these concepts and whether or not they were to receive constitutional expression. Most of the normal intergovernmental business of the federation—relating, for example, to fiscal arrangements, federal support of health care, social assistance, higher education, pension policy, the free trade agreements, international relations, and so forth—was mediated through Quebec's nation-building aspirations. The pressure for change was relentless, no matter what party or political leader was in office in Quebec City. For three decades Quebec put Canada to the question in an unrelenting effort to transform the relationship.

The debate was played out on several fronts. First of all, there was a vigorous and often rancorous discussion 'within the family'—both among Quebecers themselves and their political leaders within the province, and between francophone political elites in Quebec City and Ottawa. At times it seemed as if the rest of the country were onlookers, so intense was the contestation between and among francophone citizens and their political leaders. Pierre Elliott Trudeau led the federal Liberal Party during much of this period (1968–79 and 1980–84), and the conflict between him and René Lévesque invested the discussion about Quebec's place within or outside Canada with a highly personal dimension, most in evidence publicly during the 1980 referendum campaign and in the constitutional talks which followed. This was the heyday of executive federalism and numerous First Ministers' Conferences, many of them televised, convened to tackle the large questions of the day.

These conferences became the forum within which not just the conflict between Ottawa and Quebec City could be played out, but within which the differences between Quebec and the rest of the country, and latterly between many of the other provinces and the federal government, were given expression, often personified by compelling provincial premiers. Intergovernmental relations at this time tended to be more public, more aggressively conflictual, and more obviously 'zero-sum' in character. The stakes were seen to be higher than usual, having to do with collective identities, membership in the federation, and the 'architectural' features of the Canadian political community, such as constitutional reform and control over energy policy (Russell, 2004).

Québécois saw themselves as a nation, and there was a tendency within French-speaking Canada to view the other partner in similar terms. Just as there was a French-speaking national community, so, it was believed, there was the equivalent in English-speaking Canada—a national community that lay behind the superstructure of the other provincial governments, and which had the singular advantage of being able to count, not only on its many provincial governments, but on the federal government as well, to see to its interests. That was not for the most part how the rest of the country understood itself, and it seemed less and less true as the 1960s and 1970s wore on.

It was not just Quebec, but the rest of the country that was changing, and many of the other provinces during this period embarked on a process of province-building, seeking to strengthen provincial institutions and policy capacity, and challenging the federal government for control and resources. Some of this was learned from observing Quebec. Unintentionally, Quebec broke trail for the other provinces and inadvertently encouraged them to pursue their own processes of redefinition and regional development. The hierarchical model of the federal–provincial relationship was gradually set aside by many of the provinces and replaced with a more egalitarian and less paternalistic assumption about the respective roles of the federal and provincial governments. This change helped to further fragment whatever understanding of an English-Canadian national community there may have been and reinforced the belief that the Canadian federation was an association of provinces, not a partnership of two nations.

The thirty years of travail or mega-constitutional politics (Russell, 2004), are bracketed by Quebec's Quiet Revolution at the beginning and by the second Quebec referendum on sovereignty at the end. In between, there was the passage of Canada's Official Languages Act, the October Crisis, the election of the PQ, the passage of Bill 101, the first referendum on sovereignty-association in 1980, the debate over the constitution and its patriation in 1982 with the introduction of an amending formula and a Charter of Rights and Freedoms, the negotiation of the Meech Lake Accord in 1987 and its demise in 1990, the intergovernmental agreement on the Charlottetown Accord and its referendum defeat in 1993, and the razor-thin victory for the federalist forces in the second Quebec referendum in 1995. All of these bore directly on the effort to find a way of accommodating the new Quebec in the Canadian federation. Alongside these, there were major intergovernmental issues, such as the successive adjustment of the fiscal arrangements between the federal government and the provinces and the establishment of some of the key components of the Canadian welfare state—pensions; support for health, post-secondary education, and social assistance; the adjustment of employment insurance programs; the National Energy Program; and the free-trade agreements. Each issue had Quebec-sensitive dimensions to it, and all issues involved Quebec directly as a participating government in the federal–provincial forums that tackled them.

These were unusually stressful and significant decades for the Canadian federation and for intergovernmental affairs. Why did Canada experience these acute federal and national-unity pressures? Why did they burst out when they did and in the way they did? It is not every day that the very existence of a modern democratic state is called into question.

I would suggest that three factors help us in some measure to understand what brought on these existential pressures. The first and most obvious is the rapid transformation of Quebec and Quebec society, which put Canada dramatically to the test. What might be understood as the increasingly acute contradictions between what was happening on the ground in French Canada, socially and economically, and the formal belief system that framed its culture, came to a head after the death of Duplessis, unleashing a wave of political reform and attitudinal change. It soon became apparent that Quebecers increasingly wanted many of the same things as their English-speaking compatriots, but they wanted them in a French-language universe. Whereas the divergence of aspirations in the previous era had reduced head-to-head competition between the two linguistic communities, Quebec and French Quebecers after the Quiet Revolution began to share the same ambitions as other Canadians—educational achievement, economic and commercial opportunity, a secular, urban life, the nuclear family. Prior to the Quiet Revolution, the two societies were well positioned to minimize conflict except in moments of crisis, in the sense that each community thought of itself as espousing different values and pursuing distinguishable social and economic objectives. In normal times, members from each side could get on with their lives without directly confronting one another, because the relationship was not understood to be directly competitive. This was always less true in practical reality than it was at the level of myth and opinion; but there was, nevertheless, a significant shift with the transformation of Quebec starting in the 1960s. Now, values and aspirations began to converge, with the result that there was more direct competition between members of the two groups; if francophones in Quebec were to fulfill their ambitions, anglophones would need to give way, linguistically and economically.

The stress arising from change was felt at the federal level as well. French-speaking Canadians challenged their subordinate status in the country's common institutions, and demanded its correction—in Parliament and in the Cabinet, in the public service, and in the general operations and agencies of the federal government. A new flag for Canada was adopted in 1965, as part of the effort to respond to these pressures, just as the country's currency had been 'bilingualized' about a decade before; the symbolic apparatus of the state was gradually altered, with the removal over time of outward manifestations of the British link, and their replacement with indigenous forms of representation.

The shift was most evident in the regulation of language. The Government of Canada, while struggling to block or limit Quebec's drive for special status, also attempted to broaden the recognition of the French fact, not only in Quebec but across Canada. The Official Languages Act, passed under the leadership of then Prime Minister Trudeau in 1969, made French and English official languages for all matters pertaining to the institutions of the Parliament and Government of Canada, and provided for services to citizens in either official language, where the numbers warranted. In addition, the federal government began supporting second-language and minority-language education in the provinces across the country, with the hope that increasing numbers of young Canadians would grow up with a reasonable knowledge of the second language.

In Quebec, language rapidly took centre stage politically. The disappearance of other markers of identity increased the sense that the residual, thinned-down identity was fragile and at risk. Given that the French language had become the critical identifier of the Québécois, its health and status became an obsessive preoccupation of opinion leaders and politicians. A draft of Bill 101 was the first piece of legislation the newly elected Parti Québécois placed before the National Assembly in 1977 (Fraser, 1984: 91–112). French also assumed a central place in Quebec's nation-building strategy because it would prove to be the instrument for altering the relationship and relative status of the two language communities within the province. The various pieces of language legislation, passed over a decade from 1969 to 1977, were designed to do several things. Most importantly, they aimed to ensure that immigrants to Quebec would integrate themselves into the franco-phone community, not the anglophone. This became critical as the French-speaking Canadian birthrate plummeted; it was believed that, depending on whether immigrants integrated into the French-language or the English-language community in Quebec, im-migration would either be a boon to the survival of the Québécois in North America or the instrument of their collective demise. The language legislation was also designed to guarantee that the language of business and commercial life, and, more generally, the normal language of the province, would be French. The *minorisation* of the English-speaking community in Quebec was necessary if French were to become the dominant language in its *foyer principal* in North America.

A second factor that explains why the country entered into this difficult period as and when it did is the evolution of English-speaking society in Canada. In the decades following WWII, English-speaking Canada was changing, too, partly as a result of the general post-war modernization processes most societies were experiencing and, more specifically, because of a reform of immigration policy in the 1960s to allow easier access for immigrants from Asia, Africa, Latin America, and the Caribbean. This reform sharply increased the racial, cultural, linguistic, and religious diversity of Canada's immigrants and contributed to the reconceptualization of Canada from a British North American community with a large French minority to a multicultural society composed of two major language groups. Thus, while Quebec was rapidly and demonstratively changing, the rest of the country was going through its own even quieter quiet revolution, partly in response to the Quebec challenge and partly as a result of the significantly different immigration patterns that began to transform Canada's cities. Some of the stress on the federation arose, then, out of the effort to accommodate and reconcile these two overlap-ping but distinctive processes of change.

A third factor in explaining the charged character of our politics and intergovernmental relations during much of this period had to do with leadership. In René Lévesque, the sovereignty movement found a political leader who was trusted and held in high regard by the Quebec people, enabling the Parti Québécois over time to become a highly suc-cessful political party and provincial government. Lévesque offered reassurance to the many people who thought at the time that the sovereignty of Quebec was a radical and dangerous proposition. Fatefully, he was confronted in Ottawa with another Quebec pol-itician who was highly regarded and trusted, but who took a position aggressively contra-dictory to that of Lévesque. Pierre Trudeau was the unusual sort of political leader who argued his position from first principles and, at least on the national question, wished to make things clear. Given his passionate anti-nationalism, together with the fact that he was a French-speaking Quebecer, it is no surprise that the debate over Quebec's status took on an air of even higher drama than it otherwise would have.

More generally, the fact that the majority of the key federal political players during this whole period were Quebecers made the debate, among many other things, a passionate in-house struggle between members of the Quebec family. The period starts with Lester Pearson in charge in Ottawa (1963–8), and came to an end during Jean Chrétien's rule from 1993–2003. Quebecers held the office of prime minister for 35 of the 40 years between 1963 and 2003. Consider how different things might have been had Robert

Stanfield defeated Pierre Trudeau in the 1968 election. Instead of confrontation and inter-necine contestation within the Quebec family, one would have had a continuation of the pragmatic, low-key, accommodative style that marked the leadership of Mike Pearson; though none of us can say what the result would have been, the tone would clearly have been very different from that set by Trudeau. The importance of the conjunction of leader-ship with circumstance and opportunity is often underestimated in assessing the reasons for the unfolding of political events.

The Return of Normal Politics

Although it was not evident at the time, the 1995 Quebec referendum on sovereignty marked a turning point in Canada's long period of intergovernmental travail. The close referendum result might have suggested that 1995 set the stage for the final contest be-tween sovereignists and federalists in Quebec. But the outcome set the stage for some-thing very different: the gradual return of normal politics in Canada. With the narrow defeat of the referendum, it was as if Quebecers—francophone and anglophone, sover-eignist and federalist—had had enough. The heat went out of the nationalist debate, both within and outside Quebec, and it appeared that Canadians—whether out of boredom, fatigue or frustration—simply turned their minds to other things.

In Quebec, Lucien Bouchard, who had succeeded Jacques Parizeau as premier of Quebec in January 1996, declared that he had no intention of holding another referen-dum on sovereignty until 'winning conditions' presented themselves. None did prior to his retirement from politics in March 2001 and the defeat of the PQ under Bernard Landry in 2003.

Not even the passage of the federal **Clarity Act** in 2000, in response to the 1998 **Supreme Court Reference on Secession** (Schneiderman, 1999), was enough to deter the Québécois and other Canadians from their determination to set aside the *sturm und drang* of high-wire constitutional politics for the pursuit of a quieter life. Citizens, it seemed, had no stomach to continue the bruising national debate they had carried on for the previous 35 years.

The politicians followed suit. The warriors of the national-unity battles were replaced by politicians of less heroic stripe, who viewed politics more prosaically as a means of regulating conflict and pursuing common public purposes in a democratic society, rather than as a glorious field of conflict in which battles are lost and won before an anxious and admiring audience of citizens. Both the Prime Minister, Jean Chrétien, and Quebec's first minister, PQ Premier Bernard Landry, left office in 2003, to be replaced by Paul Martin and Jean Charest respectively.

The salience of summit federalism decreased dramatically, and intergovernmental rela-tions returned to pretty much what they had been historically: a game politicians play with one another, generally out of the public eye. Federal–provincial disputes—whether about the fiscal imbalance, equalization, or Ottawa's transfers to the provinces to sup-port social programs—ceased to be heavily burdened with national-unity implications and began to look more like the normal, ongoing conflicts that arise in any functioning federal system.

Jean Charest actively sought to establish normal intergovernmental relations, and to 'de-dramatize' the conflicts which inevitably arose between Quebec City and Ottawa. 'Acting from a resolutely federalist perspective', his government 'champions the affirmation of Quebec, both within Canada and on the international scene' (Pelletier, 2009: 471). Premier Charest has worked actively with the other provinces in developing collective positions vis-à-vis the federal government. He took the leadership in setting up the Council of the Federation, composed of the Canadian provinces and territories, which was the institutional expression of this approach to federal affairs. Quebec began to put more emphasis on working co-operatively with other provinces, refining common priorities and approaches, and seeking to develop alliances of provinces, which together could put pressure on the Government of Canada.

By the time Stephen Harper assumed office as the leader of a minority Conservative government in 2006, the shift to normal politics had conclusively been made. In that year, consistent with what was then his Quebec strategy, Harper brought a resolution to the House of Commons recognizing Quebec as a nation within Canada. Despite the fact that he sprang the idea on the opposition parties with only a few hours' notice, the resolution passed with massive support from all parties—265 members to 16. The resolution declared that 'the Québécois form a nation within a united Canada'. During the debate, the Prime Minister stated that the rationale for the motion was simple: 'Quebecers want recognition, respect and reconciliation. ... [T]hey do not want another referendum' (House of Commons, *Debates*, 27 November 2006, 2035). Three days later, Quebec's National Assembly in a vote of 107 to 0 recognized 'the positive nature of the motion' (*Votes and Proceedings*, 30 November 2006, 697–8). If there were any doubt that Canadians had no wish to re-enter the national-unity fray, the public reception of this initiative surely put the matter to rest. In acknowledging that Quebec is a nation, the House of Commons resolution went further than granting special status to Quebec or recognizing it as a distinct society. While it is true that the recognition took the form of a Parliamentary resolution rather than a constitutional amendment, it was striking how little public debate or reaction it occasioned, despite the federal minister of intergovernmental affairs of the day resigning in protest.

While the federal landscape appears tranquil in 2011, it is possible to imagine that circumstances may change, putting the Quebec question back on the country's agenda. Jean Charest is in his third term as Premier of Quebec. In contemporary Canadian politics, it is very difficult for a political leader to win a fourth consecutive term. In Quebec, Maurice Duplessis had four consecutive terms of office from 1944 to 1959, plus an extra one for good measure from 1936 to 1939. Robert Bourassa led the provincial Liberals to power on four occasions, but they were not consecutive; his first two terms (1970–76) were separated from the second two (1985–94) by almost a decade of PQ rule. It will be an uphill battle for the Liberals, whether under Jean Charest or someone else, to win a fourth consecutive election, which must be held before the end of 2013.

Were the Parti Québécois to take office, still formally committed to sovereignty, the issue would be forced back on to the table, whatever the preferences of Quebec voters may be.[5] Should this happen, it will likely be more the result of the functioning of the two-party system in Quebec rather than a change in the mood of Quebecers. To vote the Liberal rascals out is to vote in the sovereignist PQ, along with their independence agenda.

This scenario assumes that no significant third party emerges in Quebec in the interim to challenge the old-line parties. In the 2007 provincial election, many Quebec voters turned to Mario Dumont's Action démocratique du Québec (ADQ), rather than support the PQ and invite the resurgence of referendum politics. But the ADQ has since faded, and the two-party system has again become dominant. Until the Parti Québécois abandons its sovereignty platform or a new, competitive, non-sovereignist third party appears on the scene, the normal cycle of democratic politics in Quebec risks spawning periodic nationalist controversy. Yet, as the fate of the Bloc Québécois in the 2011 federal election indicates, given the current political and attitudinal environment of Quebec, it will be a challenge for the sovereignty movement to gain traction among the population.

Conclusion

Performance. Effectiveness. Legitimacy. How does one evaluate Canadian federalism's performance in relation to Quebec? How does one assess Quebec's contribution to Canadian federalism?

Let me take the second question first. How does one assess Quebec's contribution to Canadian federalism? If one regards the structure and processes that compose governance in Canada to be in part a learning system, then it may be said that a great deal of growth and democratic learning has arisen out of the often frictional relationship between the French and English in Canada. The experience of more than two centuries of cross-cultural accommodation within the frame of a single political order teaches people something about the political arts of compromise, tolerance, and respect for the position of the other. Painfully, Canadians have learned that winner-take-all politics is not a recipe for success or community amity north of the 49th parallel. We learn that there are some social cleavages that cannot be overcome without doing violence to one's deepest values, but that they can only be lived with, generation after generation. Our internationally recognized capacity for multiculturalism, as well as our belated efforts to make things right between Aboriginal and other Canadians, owe something to our experience of living within a political community inhabited by two large linguistic and cultural groups.

Let me turn now from political culture to constitutional and political structure. Here Quebec's contribution is somewhat clearer. In the absence of French Canada and Quebec, our federal system would have been very different. Earlier I described the conservative, reclusive French Canadian nationalism prior to the 1960s as a kind of sheet anchor, restraining Canada from drifting more and more towards a centralized federal system. From the 1960s to the 1990s, Quebec became much more than simply a drag on the ambitions of the federal government, instead directly challenging it and claiming—in many cases, successfully—that political power and policy authority should flow away from Ottawa and towards Quebec. Indeed, it wanted an actual reconstitution of the system along these more decentralized lines. For at least a hundred years until the dawn of the 21st century, most of the dominant economic, social and political forces seemed to have favoured the increase and concentration of power in central governments. One of the most powerful corrective mechanisms in federations, constantly making the case for decentralization and the dispersion of power, has been territorially concentrated ethnocultural diversity.

In this respect, Quebec has been a faithful, steady counterweight to the forces of centralization in the Canadian federation.

This line of reasoning doesn't quite complete this very limited exercise in evaluation, because one would still have to sort out whether constraining the forces of centralization in Canada is a good or a bad thing. People are entitled to hold different opinions on the matter, but it certainly seems to be the case that Quebec was instrumental in the preservation of a vital, functioning federal system in Canada.

What of the second question? How does one evaluate the Canadian federation's performance in relation to Quebec? Has Canada's federal system been good for Quebec? Here it is necessary to emphasize once again the fact that there are radically different opinions on this matter, symbolized by the fact that the Parti Québécois and a good portion of the Quebec population want to wind up the federal experiment, while many other Quebecers and a great majority in the rest of Canada believe that that would be a disaster. In my view the Canadian federation and political system have been good for Quebec, for French Canadians and for the Québécois. It has been the framework within which French Canada has survived, within which it has changed, and within which Quebec is now flourishing. Canadian federalism has largely accommodated Quebec's evolving conception of itself and its developing expectations for self-government. Canada has not responded as fully or as quickly to Quebec's declared needs as many in Quebec would like, but the country has listened and changed. The language barrier and the social distance between the two societies remains in place and, despite efforts to increase second-language capacity, relatively few surmount it comfortably, but this arguably is not a reasonable criterion of assessment in a large, decentralized federal country, especially on a continent in which the world's lingua franca is dominant.[6] Indeed, some degree of linguistic separation may be beneficial to the preservation of Quebec's French-language society. On balance, then, I would say that Quebec has benefited from its association with the rest of Canada. The Canadian federal system has performed fairly effectively over the years in relation to the Quebec question.

But what of legitimacy in the eyes of Quebecers? Here I would acknowledge a serious deficiency. Legitimacy cannot be commanded, but must be won. A leader's right to rule, or the rightness of a leader's policy or political program, is granted by others. A political system is awarded legitimacy by its citizens, not ordered into existence by its rulers. That being so, there is surely a problem of legitimacy in the Canadian federation. A significant portion of the Quebec population believe the 1982 Constitution is illegitimate in that it is not based on the consent of the Quebec people. All other provinces agreed to the passage of the 1982 constitutional amendments; Quebec did not. The Government of Quebec and the National Assembly both opposed the passage of the Constitution Act. It can be argued that Quebec did not possess a veto, and that the fact that nine provinces and the vast majority of the Canadian population plus the federal government supported its passage means the act was not only legal, but legitimate. One can add, as Pierre Trudeau did, that his Liberal government in Ottawa had recently been elected (1980), winning 74 out of 75 seats in Quebec; its support of the Constitution Act, therefore, must reflect the perceived legitimacy of the amendments on the part of the province's federal representatives.

But these arguments do not cut much ice with a great many Quebecers, and the reason goes back to the competing conceptions of the federal association that lie unresolved at the heart of Confederation. Is it an association of provinces or of French and English peoples? If one takes the latter view, and we have seen how widely accepted that view is in French-speaking Canada, then the constitutional amendments of 1982 are—even if formally legal—illegitimate in that they proceeded despite the opposition of one of the country's two founding peoples (Laforest, 1992). And the voice of the people of Quebec speaks through the National Assembly and the Government of Quebec, not through Parliament and its Quebec representatives, even if the Prime Minister is a Québécois. You can accept that view of the country as valid or not, but it is difficult to deny that Quebec as a jurisdiction plus a substantial proportion of the French-speaking citizens of Canada have withheld recognition of the patriation of Canada's constitution as a legitimate act. This is a serious deficiency in our constitutional arrangements, which it would be highly desirable, were it possible, to repair. While I share the view that re-opening the constitutional file at this point is inadvisable, I nevertheless am of the view that this situation leaves the Canadian federation more vulnerable than it ought to be and that until it is corrected—until the Québécois consent to the 1982 Constitution—there is something awry in our constitutional and federal arrangements.[7]

Notes

1. Public opinion polls consistently find a large minority of Québécois to be in favour of the sovereignty of Quebec. According to Alain-G. Gagnon (2009): 'As it is practiced in Canada, federalism has never been popular in Quebec. It is not that the Québécois are opposed to federalism in itself but rather that they refuse to accept the way it is implemented by Ottawa.'
2. Michel Brunet identifies three themes in traditional French-Canadian thinking: agriculturalism, anti-statism, and messianism. (Brunet, 1957)
3. This is not something that Quebec achieved all on its own. The local loyalties of other parts of the country also had a role to play. Oliver Mowat, Premier of Ontario from 1872-96, was in fact the first defender of provincial rights, battling John A. Macdonald in a series of legal and political disputes to enhance the power and authority of Ontario.
4. Jean Chrétien reflects this transformation. He was the eighteenth of nineteen children, nine of whom perished in infancy. He and Aline Chrétien have three children, one of them adopted.
5. Guy Laforest (2010) explores the extent to which a significant shift in thinking about federalism, unfavourable to the PQ project, is underway in Quebec.
6. *Language Matters: How Canadian Voluntary Associations Manage French and English* (Cameron and Simeon, 2009) explores linguistic practices at the level of civil society organizations, and finds that bilingualism is a feature of head offices and leadership actors, but not of members.
7. I have explored elsewhere, with Jacqueline Krikorian, a possible way in which this issue might be tackled (Cameron and Krikorian, 2008).

References

Ajzenstat, J., P. Romney, I. Gentles, and W. Gairdner eds., 2003. *Canada's Founding Debates*. Toronto: University of Toronto Press.

Brault, G. 1986. *The French-Canadian Heritage in New England*. Hanover: University Press of New England.

Brunet, M. 1957. 'Trois dominantes de la pensée canadienne-française: l'agriculturisme, l'anti-étatisme, et le messianisme. Essai d'histoire intellectuelle'. *Écrits du Canada français* III, 33–117.

Cameron, D. 1990. 'Lord Durham Then and

Now'. *Journal of Canadian Studies* 25,1: 5–38.

Cameron, D., and J. Krikorian 2008. 'Recognizing Quebec in the Constitution of Canada: Using the Bilateral Amending Formula'. *University of Toronto Law Journal*, 58,4: 389–420.

Cameron, D., and R. Simeon eds. 2009. *Language Matters: How Canadian Voluntary Associations Manage French and English*. Vancouver: UBC Press.

Caron, J.-F. 2006. 'L'Héritage républicain du fédéralisme: une théorie de l'identité nationale dans les federations multinationales'. *Politique et Sociétés*, 25, 2–3: 121–46.

Commission royale d'enquête sur les problèmes constitutionnels 1956. (Rapport Tremblay) 4 vols.

Dirks, P. 1991. *The Failure of L'Action libérale nationale*. Montreal: McGill-Queen's University Press.

Durham, Lord 1982. *Lord Durham's Report: An Abridgement*, ed. G.M. Craig. Ottawa: Carleton University Press.

Fraser, G. 1984. PQ: *René Lévesque and the Parti Québécois in Power*. Toronto: Macmillan.

Gagnon, A.-G. ed. 2009. *Contemporary Canadian Federalism: Foundations, Traditions, Institutions*. Toronto: University of Toronto Press.

Gagnon, A.-G., and M.B. Montcalm 1990. *Quebec: Beyond the Quiet Revolution*. Scarborough: Nelson Canada.

Heintzman, R. 1971. 'The spirit of Confederation: Professor Creighton, Biculturalism, and the Use of History'. *Canadian Historical Review* 52: 245–75.

House of Commons, *Debates*, No. 087 (27 November 2006), 2035.

Hueglin, T., and A. Fenna 2006. *Comparative Federalism; A Systematic Inquiry*. Peterborough: Broadview Press.

Kent, T. 2009. 'When Minority Government Worked: The Pearson Legacy'. *Policy Options*. October 2009.

Kwavnick, D. ed. 1973. *The Tremblay Report*. Toronto: McClelland and Stewart.

Laforest, G. 1992. *Trudeau et la fin d'un rêve canadien*. Sillery: Editions du Septentrion.

Laforest, G., 2010. 'The Meaning of Canadian Federalism in Québec: Critical Reflections'. *REAF* 11(October 2010): 10–55.

Lévesque, R. 1968. *An Option for Quebec*. Toronto: McClelland and Stewart.

McRoberts, K. 1993. *Quebec: Social Change and Political Crisis*. 3rd ed. McClelland and Steward.

Paquin, S. 1999. *L'invention d'un mythe: le pacte entre deux peoples fondateurs*. Montreal: VLB.

Pelletier, B. 2009. 'The Future of Quebec within the Canadian Confederation'. *Contemporary Canadian Federalism: Foundations, Traditions, Institutions*. Ed. A-G Gagnon. Toronto: University of Toronto Press.

Quebec National Assembly. 2006. *Votes and Proceedings*, No. 065 (30 November, 697–8.

Rocher, F. 2009. 'The Quebec-Canada Dynamic or the Negation of the Ideal of Federalism'. *Contemporary Canadian Federalism: Foundations, Traditions, Institutions*. Ed. A-G Gagnon. Toronto: University of Toronto Press.

Royal Commission on Aboriginal Peoples 1996. Volume 1.

Royal Commission on Bilingualism and Biculturalism 1965. A Preliminary Report of the Royal Commission on Bilingualism and Biculturalism. Ottawa.

Russell, P. 2004. *Constitutional Odyssey: Can Canadians Become a Sovereign People?* 3rd ed. Toronto: University of Toronto Press.

Schneiderman, D. ed. 1999. *The Quebec Decision: Perspectives on the Supreme Court Ruling on Secession*. Toronto: James Lorimer and Company.

Stanley, G.F.G. 1956. 'Act or Pact: Another Look at Confederation.' *Report of the Annual Meeting of the Canadian Historical Association* 35, 1: 1–25.

Waite, P.B. ed. 1963. *The Confederation Debates in the Province of Canada/ 1865*. Toronto: McClelland and Stewart.

Watts, R. 2008. *Comparing Federal Systems* 3rd ed. Kingston: McGill-Queen's University Press.

4 Parliamentary Canada and Intergovernmental Canada: Exploring the Tensions

Richard Simeon and Amy Nugent

The three principal pillars of Canada's institutional architecture are Westminster-style parliamentary government, federalism, and the Charter of Rights and Freedoms. A fourth pillar, derived from the first two, might be labelled intergovernmental relations. In many ways these four pillars are part of a coherent whole: one that balances majority rule against minority rights, and national interests against interests and identities that are defined by territory and language.

But each of these pillars also embodies values—including fundamental conceptions of democracy, federalism and effective government—that may be in deep tension with each other. In this chapter we will explore some of these tensions as they relate to the fundamental purpose of this volume: to understand federalism in terms of its 'performance, effectiveness, and legitimacy'. To that end, we will investigate the development of what we might call '**intergovernmental Canada**', and the ways in which this conception interacts with what we might call 'parliamentary Canada'. Responsible government, a foundational principle of Canadian parliamentary democracy, is at the heart of this tension. It says that each government (first minister and cabinet) is responsible to its own legislature for legislation, regulation, and the raising and spending of revenue. In a federal system, however, many policy responsibilities are shared; both orders of government have broad taxing powers; there are extensive transfers of funds between orders of government; and much of the intergovernmental relationship is managed through intergovernmental accords and agreements. As a consequence, another level of accountability arises: that of the responsibility of governments to each other for the shared management of the federal system.

So long as Canadian governance remains executive-centred, with the executive fully in control of legislative majorities, it is possible to overcome these difficulties through 'elite accommodation': informal, high-level intergovernmental negotiations that make intergovernmental decision-making possible (Watts, 1989: abstract). Yet measures to further institutionalize 'intergovernmental Canada' through more binding and enforceable intergovernmental agreements may well run afoul of a more robust 'legislative Canada'. We will conclude our discussion by asking whether these two conceptions can be effectively blended, either through greater legislative involvement in intergovernmental relationships or through more flexible mechanisms for transparency, accountability, citizen participation, and deliberation.

From this discussion a reform agenda emerges. Indeed, there are two reform agendas at play here. One is about reforming the institutions and practices of federalism and inter-governmental relations (IGR) in order to make them more open, accountable, transparent, legitimate, and effective. The other is about legislative reform, designed to mitigate the executive dominance—excessive even in comparison with other Westminster-style dem-ocracies—that characterizes the Canadian system at both federal and provincial levels.

But readers should not hold their breath. The institutions of Canadian governance, with their built-in incentives and constraints, are remarkably resistant to change. For example, despite the massive changes that have occurred in the Canadian society and economy—globalization, multiculturalism, the mobilization of Aboriginal peoples, and the rise of non-territorially-defined social movements—the dynamics of **executive fed-eralism** or 'federal-provincial diplomacy' today look remarkably like those that existed in the 1960s (Simeon, 2006b: 314–32). There have been important changes in IGR, to be discussed below, but they are limited and incremental. Similarly, in recent years there has been much discussion of parliamentary reform, generally designed to check the domin-ance of the executive ('First Minister Government') through an enhanced role for back-bench Members of Parliament (MPs) (Baier et al., 2005). But the dynamics of 'government from the centre' suggest limited prospects for change. The contrast between the com-mitment to restoring the role of Parliament in the Conservatives' 2006 election platform and the reassertion of central control immediately upon their forming the government that year makes the point (Doyle, 2006). Nevertheless, in the hopes of better policy and more legitimate, democratic relations, it is worth exploring the possibilities for change and innovation.

The Logic of Parliamentary Government

The Westminster model of parliamentary government that Canada inherited from Britain has, as part of its 'unwritten' constitution, a number of central features in both the federal parliament and provincial legislatures. First, responsible government requires that the government (prime minister/premier and cabinet) remain in office only so long as it holds the confidence of the House of Commons or legislature. Accountability in its most fun-damental sense, therefore, runs from the government to the elected members of the legis-lature and from those members to the electorate. As is well known, in all Westminster systems this logic has been turned around as a result of party discipline and many other forces that (at least in times of majority government) strengthen the hand of the executive vis-à-vis ordinary members (White, 2004: 64–101). (Prime Minister Trudeau once fam-ously described MPs as 'nobodies' once they left Parliament Hill.) Except in their party caucus, backbench members have little opportunity to express either their own views or those of their constituents when doing so would challenge the government and party leadership. Second, parliamentary government places virtually all power in the hands of the majority; 'Her Majesty's Loyal Opposition' has little opportunity to influence govern-ment policies. During the era of minority federal governments (June 2004–May 2011), however, the role of individual MPs within Parliament did not become considerably more influential. This was due, at least in part, to all party leaders' (and their professional advisors') careful management of electoral cycles and chances, necessitating carefully managed legislative behaviour. Third, Westminster systems are typically (though some changes have been made recently in Australia, New Zealand, and the Scottish Parliament) based on single-member, simple-plurality electoral systems, which have the potential to produce large discrepancies between votes received and seats won.

All these characteristics have recently created their own reform agendas. They include a greater role for backbench members, more free votes in the legislature, stronger committees, and more direct reporting to the legislature by independent agencies like the Auditor-General, the Privacy Commissioner, and the newly created Parliamentary Budget Officer (MacKinnon, 2003; Docherty, 2004; Savoie, 1999). Many commentators also appear to wish that adversarial and combative legislatures could become more collegial, deliberative, and consensus-oriented, though the logic of the institutional design makes such a transformation unlikely. Many also worry about the 'wasted' votes and unfair representation associated with the first-past-the-post system and call for reform of the electoral system to inject a substantial measure of proportionality into the system (Law Commission of Canada, 2004; Kent, 2003).

These characteristics of the parliamentary system also have important implications for federalism and the capacity of the federal legislature to represent fairly all regions of the country. A significant part of the problem is the interaction of Canada's regional society and economy with the electoral system. The result is that parties with regionally concentrated support (such as the Bloc Québécois from 1993 to 2011) are strongly rewarded while those whose support is distributed across the country (such as the NDP) are penalized. This effect artificially reinforces the perception of deep regional divisions in our national Parliament. Moreover, as Chapter 6, on political parties, demonstrates, the discrepancy between seats and votes has typically meant that one or more parties have often found it impossible to win substantial numbers of seats in some regions, even if they have significant voter support in them. The result is, again, to enhance the perception that regional divisions are insurmountable. When power is concentrated in the hands of a government that has little or no representation from important regions of the country, those regions are likely to feel excluded and marginalized. And this effect is exacerbated by the inability of the appointed Senate to give effective voice to smaller provinces or those not adequately represented in the cabinet. This analysis should not be pushed too far: regional interests are often strongly expressed in party caucuses, and convention demands full regional representation in the cabinet (even if the prime minister needs to reach into the Senate to find suitable representatives). Nevertheless, in addition to a widely perceived 'democratic deficit' in the operations of the national Parliament, there is what we might call a '**federalism deficit**' as well. Canadian federalism manifests itself primarily as 'inter-state' federalism; 'intra-state' federalism, or power sharing at the centre, is weak.

The consequence of this federalism deficit in the national government is that the national Parliament is not well equipped to represent all regions of the country effectively, much less to be the primary arena for accommodation among competing regional interests. This failure is perhaps the chief reason intergovernmental relations are so critical in the Canadian system. Citizens who feel excluded from the federal table are likely to turn to their provincial governments, both to take responsibility for issues important to them and to provide them with a stronger voice in dealing with Ottawa. This effect is reinforced by yet another characteristic of the parliamentary system: the concentration of power in the hands of executives who exercise authority not only by virtue of controlling legislative majorities, but also by virtue of the fact that they exercise many of the prerogatives once exercised by the British Crown. This situation is what permits executive federalism: first ministers can claim to speak with one voice for their constituents and to make commitments that they will be able to enforce. Contrast this situation with that in the United States, where the separation of powers sharply limits the power of executives at both federal and state levels. Westminster-style parliamentary government explains why the Canadian pattern of intergovernmental relations leans towards the inter-state rather than the intra-state model.

Tom Kent (2003) sees this failure of effective representation of regional diversity in national institutions as a fundamental reason for the weakening of federal authority and legitimacy. 'The obstacle', he says, is 'not in the provinces' or in the 'diversities of our regions. It lies in the poverty of democratic involvement in our national politics' (2003: 5).

The Logic of Federalism

In Canada both federal and provincial governments follow the parliamentary model of 'First Minister' government. In principle, therefore, there should be no conflict on this score. In the classical federal model of 'watertight compartments'—in which each order of government has both a clear list of powers and responsibilities, and the financial and bureaucratic resources to carry them out—there is little need to interact or overlap. The federal principle would require only that each government be autonomous within its own jurisdiction, that there be no hierarchy or subordination between them—hence that each order respects the jurisdiction of the others—and that each government be responsible to its own legislators and citizens for its assigned tasks.

But of course hierarchy has never been lacking in Canadian federalism. The Constitution Act of 1867 gave the federal government draconian powers with respect to the (then) major areas of public policy; sweeping responsibility for the 'peace, order, and good government' of Canada; the power to 'disallow' any provincial legislation of which it disapproved, to declare provincial 'works and undertakings' national responsibilities, and so on. The result was what the noted British scholar K.C. Wheare called 'quasi-federalism' (1953). By the 1930s a combination of political events and judicial decisions (the relative weight of these factors remains in dispute) had curbed the dominance of the federal government and enhanced provincial autonomy (Simeon and Robinson, 1990). But then the tables turned again. With the Great Depression of the 1930s, which drove several provinces close to bankruptcy, followed by the need for massive centralization to fight the Second World War, and then the post-war commitment, in Canada and all other western democracies, to the building of the welfare state, the pendulum shifted once again towards federal leadership. The new policy agenda engaged issues—health, education, welfare—that were largely within provincial jurisdiction. But Ottawa had the resources and the public support to take the lead by engineering the transfer of responsibility for employment insurance and pensions to Ottawa through constitutional amendment, and by using its 'spending power' to influence provincial priorities and programs with 'fifty-cent dollars'. In this period, commitment to the 'federal principle' mostly took a back seat to 'co-operative federalism': the need to work together on collective goals, whatever the Constitution said.

More recently, the pendulum has swung again, and the federal principle, along with the power of the provinces, has returned to the forefront. While it is extremely difficult to measure, the 'presence' of the federal government in the national policy agenda, or in the minds of citizens, has seemed to be in retreat. The reasons are complex and little understood. They range from globalization and North American integration, which both undermines the economic linkages among Canadians and weakens the capacity of the central government, to an extended period of minority government (June 2004–May 2011) in Ottawa, to the presence in power of a government with a strong western base and philosophy of limited government.

In the modern period, the substantial completion of the welfare state, together with the increasing political, bureaucratic, and fiscal weight of the provinces, has brought the federal principle back to the forefront. Now most provinces are unwilling to defer to federal leadership. They wish to exercise their full autonomy in their assigned areas of jurisdiction; they ask what right entitles the federal piper, whose share of spending in areas like health and welfare has dropped precipitately in recent decades, to call the provincial tune. Hence the pressure to limit the spending power, to oppose federal 'intrusions' into provincial jurisdiction, and to ensure that federal transfers come with minimal conditions attached. Hence recent debates and efforts to remedy the 'fiscal imbalance': that is, the mismatch provinces have seen between the responsibilities that governments face and the revenues available to finance them.

In a complex, interdependent, multicultural country like Canada, the very idea of the primacy of the 'federal principle' is problematic. It suggests that federalism is a value in itself, to be sustained even if it contradicts other widely held values. Yet a quick survey of federal systems around the world suggests that there are few common 'federal' values, beyond the classic formulation of Daniel Elazar (1994) that federalism must find the right balance between 'self-rule' and 'shared rule', between pan-Canadian and provincial identities; and between unity, homogeneity, 'national standards,' and common purposes on the one hand, and autonomy, diversity, and difference on the other. Another way of thinking about federalism is as a set of institutions and practices that should be judged and evaluated in terms of whether they serve or frustrate other, more fundamental values, such as democracy, social justice, national unity, and the meeting of citizen needs and concerns (Simeon, 2006a, 18–43). In this case, questions of 'national standards' versus 'provincial variation' become matters of ongoing debate rather than principled fiats. This is where a more malleable federalism and a stricter parliamentary–legislative accountability diverge.

Indeed, though the Constitution Act, 1867 notes that Canadians are to be 'federally united', it has been up to governments, courts, and citizens to express the changing meaning of federal union over time. For the Supreme Court of Canada, in the 1998 *Reference re: Secession of Quebec,*

[t]he principle of federalism recognizes the diversity of the component parts of Confederation, and the autonomy of provincial governments to develop their societies within their respective spheres of jurisdiction. The federal structure of our country also facilitates democratic participation by distributing power to the government thought to be most suited to achieving the particular societal objective having regard to this diversity (para. 58).

The relationship between democracy and federalism means, for example, that in Canada there may be different and equally legitimate majorities in different provinces and territories and at the federal level. . . . No one majority is more or less 'legitimate' than the others as an expression of democratic opinion, although, of course, the consequences will vary with the subject matter. A federal system of government enables different provinces to pursue policies responsive to the particular concerns and interests of people in that province (para. 66).

In accordance with the autonomy of governments, the court tells us that each legislature has the authority to enact its own policies. Yet the co-ordinated policy development that takes place between governments in our federal system creates a deep tension between democratic, responsible government, and effective policy-making.

The Logic of Intergovernmental Relations

The classical 'watertight compartments' model of federalism no longer exists, if indeed it ever did in reality. The pattern common to all federal systems, Canada included, is one of interdependence, overlapping, and shared responsibilities—hence 'Intergovernmental Canada'. Virtually all important problems cut across jurisdictional lines—local, provincial, national, international. This interdependence necessitates intergovernmental machinery to assist in 'multilevel governance' or achieve co-ordination on matters of common concern. As with federalism itself, there is no single model of 'right' intergovernmental relations. In Canada we have seen the shift from federal dominance, in which the disallowance power was wielded aggressively, to a more classical model, to the more paternalistic federally-led model of 'co-operative federalism' in the post-war period. Other federations range from some in which the provinces are subordinate to the central government (South Africa or Australia) to some in which the relationship is much more equal (Watts, 1999; Hueglin and Fenna, 2006).[1] These differences appear to be a result of the interaction of federal states and federal societies. Jan Erk (2003, 2006) nicely demonstrates that culturally homogenous federations, such as Germany, tend to centralization; culturally diverse ones tend to decentralization, whatever their constitutions say.

There is also a debate about the preferred model of intergovernmental relations. On the one hand is the view that the primary goal is to achieve intergovernmental harmony, accommodation, and consensus: intergovernmental 'success' is intergovernmental agreement and mitigation of conflict. In a country as deeply divided on regional and linguistic grounds as Canada this is an important objective.

The alternative view holds that one of the primary virtues of federalism is that it creates alternative governments that will compete for citizen support; and that public policy is likely to be more responsive to public needs as a result of this competition (Breton, 1996;

Harrison, 1996; Kenyon, 1997). In this view, competitive' federalism is more creative than co-operative or consensus federalism.

Intergovernmental relations in Canada today are a complex mixture of collaboration and competition carried out in a wide array of institutions. Some innovations in these institutions and processes have recently been achieved. At the federal–provincial and territorial level (FPT) the apex is the first ministers' conference or meeting. Then there are various ministerial councils covering most of the main areas of public policy. These are backed up by a host of officials' meetings. Informal contacts at all levels play a role in the work of officials and politicians almost every day.

Much intergovernmental discussion consists of debate, argument, persuasion, and information-exchange. But increasingly the results of executive federalism have taken the form of intergovernmental accords and agreements. Many of these—the 1995 Agreement on Internal Trade (AIT), the 1999 Social Union Framework Agreement (SUFA), various health accords and others—are discussed elsewhere in this volume. Typically, these accords contain broad statements of common purposes, commitments to collaboration, co-operation, and information exchange, mechanisms for the resolution of disputes, and commitments to transparency and accountability. It is increasingly common for governments to negotiate a broad multilateral agreement, including common principles and goals and a broad funding structure, supplemented by separate bilateral agreements between the federal government and individual provinces. This development opens the door to more flexibility and to a greater measure of *de facto* asymmetry. These agreements, particularly at the bilateral level, strongly reflect the language and rhetoric of the New Public Management (Savoie, 1995, 2003).

The focus on responsiveness and 'results' in NPM implies a very different idea of accountability than that embedded in the parliamentary system. In a parliamentary sense, accountability means holding the government responsible for actions or decisions: the executive is accountable to the legislature and the legislature to the public. With New Public Management, governments must account to citizens as 'stakeholders' or 'clients' for the responsiveness and efficiency of their actions. Public reports on health-care wait lists, agreed to by first ministers in 2004, remain the pre-eminent example of this kind of accountability (Federal, Provincial, and Territorial Communiqué, 2004).

Most agreements also include provisions for financial transfers from Ottawa to the provinces. In the post-war period of federally led 'co-operative federalism', clear and explicit conditions were attached to significant federal payments: the spending power was used to buy federal policy influence. Today, with some important exceptions such as the Canada Health Act, most intergovernmental transfers have very few, and very general, conditions. Agreements contain language that makes funding contingent on parliamentary approval and asserts that nothing in them alters the legislative powers of any government or its rights under the Constitution. The former clause is effectively more significant, allowing Parliament to withdraw funds from intergovernmental programs with little or no notice to provinces.

Despite their format of clauses, sections, subsections, appendices, indemnity provisions, and signature blocks, these intergovernmental agreements exist in a legal limbo. They are not legally enforceable contracts. Nor are they equivalent to statutes. They do not trump the fundamental parliamentary principle that each government should be responsible to its own legislature. In the *Reference re Canada Assistance Plan (B.C.)* (1991) the Supreme Court made it clear that the doctrine of parliamentary sovereignty trumps intergovernmental agreements, and that any 'legitimate expectations' on the part of the provinces that such agreements could not be altered unilaterally had no legal effect. As Gerald Baier concludes, 'the court abdicated any role in the supervision of the federal spending power even if the stability of an intergovernmental compromise was at stake' (2002: 31). Nor do individual citizens have standing to challenge governmental conduct under the agreements. A challenge to the federal government for failing to enforce provisions of the Canada Health Act and report to Parliament on provincial compliance was rejected by the Federal Court of Appeal (*CUPE*, 2004). In sum, commitments made by governments to each other are fundamentally ambiguous. This poses a serious problem for policy planning and delivery.

An increasingly important element of intergovernmental relations is the Provincial–Territorial (PT) network. Annual Premiers' Conferences (APCs) have been held since the 1960s and have played a steadily growing role both in encouraging the sharing of experience in common policy areas, and in shaping provincial strategies for dealing with Ottawa. On a regional level, collaboration also takes place at annual Atlantic and Western Premiers' Conferences.

The most important recent institutional innovation in intergovernmental relations was the transformation of the APC into the **Council of the Federation** in 2003. Like its predecessor, the Council is made up of the 10 premiers and three territorial leaders, with the chair rotating among provincial premiers and the host acting as the lead provincial/territorial spokesperson for the year. It is to meet twice a year, and has a small permanent secretariat based in Ottawa. According to its Founding Agreement, the Council is intended to strengthen provincial–territorial co-operation, 'provide an integrated coordinated approach to federal–provincial relations', assess federal actions with a major impact on the provinces, 'develop a common vision of how intergovernmental relations should be conducted in keeping with the fundamental values and principles of federalism', and work with 'the greatest respect for transparency and better communication with Canadians' (Council of the Federation, Founding Agreement, 2006: 2–3). Decisions are to be reached by 'consensus'.

An early assessment of the Council of the Federation's transformative potential for intergovernmental relations has to be largely pessimistic. Structural differences and interests between provinces (large/small, rich/poor, resource-intensive/-diversified economies) are the dominant order of the day on many major policy issues before the Council—environment, energy, federal transfer payments. The Council is as yet unproven in reconciling such differences among a hugely diverse membership. This is evidenced in provinces striking individual agreements with Ottawa when it is to their advantage, rather than acting as a group; there is little evidence that provinces are willing to temper their individual interests in favour of inter-provincial consensus. For example, Newfoundland and Labrador as well as Nova Scotia abandoned the united inter-provincial approach to federal–provincial fiscal relations when offered the chance to sign the 2005 Atlantic Accord with Ottawa. Similarly, Ontario Premier Dalton McGuinty wasted no time breaking ranks in response to the report of the Council of the Federation's Advisory Panel on Fiscal Imbalance. The capacity of the Council to resolve inter-provincial differences, and hence to serve as an independent arena for regional accommodation, is thus mainly unproven. There is no getting around the fundamental structure of incentives: provincial politicians are rewarded or penalized by their own voters, not by voters elsewhere in Canada. As a result, provinces seek autonomy not just from Ottawa but also from their governmental peers.

The most expansive possible interpretation of the role of the Council is that it hints at a more 'confederal' Canada, one in which provinces and territories make collective national decisions, at least in those broad areas lying primarily in provincial jurisdiction (Burelle, 2003; Courchene, 1999). This possibility is underlined by the absence of the government of Canada from the Council. Alternatively, the Council of the Federation could become little more than a minor formalization of existing provincial–territorial consultative processes and mechanisms (Brown, 2003).

Complex, elaborate, and pervasive, the institutions and practices of intergovernmental relations nonetheless remain weakly institutionalized. They are awkwardly 'added on' to our parliamentary system, rather than integrated with it (Papillon and Simeon, 2004). There is no reference to mechanisms of IGR in the Constitution; none of the institutions—FMC, ministerial councils, or Council of the Federation—has a statutory basis. FMCs are held at the discretion of the prime minister, according to the prime minister's political needs. There is no regular schedule of meetings. Nor are there any voting procedures or binding decisions.

Some change has taken place in recent years. Intergovernmental accords have become more detailed and precise and, with the use of bilateral agreements, more tailored to the needs of individual provinces. Several ministerial councils have become more formally established, with regular meetings, rotating chairs, and bureaucratic support (Simmons, 2004). In democratic terms, the meetings are largely restricted to ministers and high-level advisers. Although some intergovernmental forums do allow for participation by others—for example, the two meetings of first ministers and Aboriginal leaders in November 2005 that produced the so-called Kelowna Accord—they are infrequent and the non-governmental involvement in them tends to be ad hoc and informal. Furthermore, the products of such forums may not carry sufficient weight to be respected; this was certainly the case with the Kelowna Accord, as Papillon notes in Chapter 15.

The Council of the Federation represents a deepening of the provincial–territorial relationship and a strengthening of the capacity to co-ordinate action. But even here, a recent comparative analysis of horizontal co-ordinating capacity among states and provinces concludes that, of six modern federations, Canada has the least institutionalized machinery (Thorlaksen, 2003.). Two factors seem to account for this situation. First is the principle of parliamentary government, which overrides any inclination to establish intergovernmental mechanisms that would make decisions binding on legislatures. Second is the great variation among provinces, and the resulting diversity of their interests and priorities, which strongly inhibits their capacity for collective decision-making.

Assessing Intergovernmental Canada

Performance

As the various policy-oriented chapters in this book demonstrate, there can be no single answer to the question of whether the intergovernmental system generates or facilitates policy choices that meet the needs and preferences of Canadians in either the federal or the provincial context. We see relative harmony, collaboration, healthy competition, and effectiveness in some areas; conflict and paralysis in others. It is possible to tell a good-news story: despite the rigidities of the Constitution, Canadian governments have managed to work out agreements that permit federal and provincial governments, sometimes on their own, sometimes together, to address many issues effectively; for example, specific outcomes in the area of health care or education. It is also possible to tell a bad-news story about policy overlap, contradictions, and dropped balls; examples here might include climate change or the treatment of urban Aboriginal people.

Such assessments will also vary depending on the perspective of the assessor. Policy activists tend to ask not whether outcomes are consistent with the federal principle or the division of powers in the Constitution, but whether they advance or hinder their particular policy goals. Advocates of a more unitary or centralist vision of Canada will ask whether the system has strengthened or weakened 'national standards' and common policies across the country; provincialists will ask whether the system has blocked or recognized their desire for distinctive provincial variation. Politicians will ask their own questions: have my autonomy, discretion, and ability to win support among my voters been enhanced or constrained? Thus provinces continue to object to federal 'intrusions' and to the fact that, as in the 2006 termination of carefully constructed agreements on support for child care by a newly elected government (see Chapter 10 by Friendly and White), intergovernmental transfers remain subject to the vagaries of federal policy and therefore lack permanence and predictability.

A few general observations about this process are possible. First, the overall dynamic of intergovernmental relations is competitive and adversarial, despite frequent promises of co-operation. Second, this dynamic tends to emphasize turf protection, the claiming of personal credit, and avoidance of blame. This is due in part to the political and electoral cycles of fourteen governments. The substance of public policy often takes second place to such considerations; institutional interests often trump substance (although some would argue that this is a false dichotomy). Third, policy debates in the intergovernmental arena quickly become transmuted into questions of fiscal federalism; money usually trumps policy—just as in an earlier period the Constitution trumped substance. Fourth, the preoccupation of federal and provincial policy-makers with federal–provincial relations diverts their attention from larger questions about Canada's economic and political roles in the world. We are directed inwards rather than outwards. Managing intergovernmental relationships consumes an excessive proportion of the time, attention, and energy of senior politicians and public servants, possibly to the detriment of other considerations. Fifth, all these factors have contributed to a decline in trust among intergovernmental actors, especially between federal and provincial governments.[2] Trust relationships obviously vary between different policy areas and ministries, but at the centre—in the premiers' offices, Privy Council Office (PCO), and Prime Minister's Office (PMO), from which intergovernmental relations are increasingly directed—strategic considerations, institutional protection, and local political calculations (whether federal or provincial) take precedence (Dupré, 1985).

Nothing in this portrait is surprising. These features are built into the political structure of parliamentary federalism and the incentives and constraints that it provides.

Two conditions could overcome these tendencies. The first is a relatively clear hierarchy among governments, as there was in the early years of the federation, before the provinces came to see themselves as equal partners, in no way subordinate to the federal government. The second is a clear national project to which all governments are committed, as with the commitment to building the post-war welfare state. Neither of these conditions holds today, even despite the significant co-ordinated response of governments to the global economic downturn that began in 2008.

Nowhere are the difficulties of competitive intergovernmentalism more evident than in fiscal federalism, where the relationships between money and power have been particularly tumultuous since the federal government made dramatic cuts to the Canada Health and Social Transfer in its 1995 budget. (See Chapter 7 by Douglas Brown.) In 2006, after extensive study and consultation, both the federal government and the Council of the Federation released reports on the health of fiscal relations. *Reconciling the Irreconcilable* is the pessimistic title given by the Council of the Federation Advisory Panel on Fiscal Imbalance to its report. The system of fiscal federalism, the panel said, 'has fallen into disrepair' (Council of the Federation, 2006: 9). Intergovernmental relationships are 'corrosive' (17). The panel's interviews with provincial governments identified a 'decline in trust' attributed to 'irregular federal-provincial meetings, called on an ad hoc basis'; 'last minute negotiations on major issues'; 'wedge strategies' used by the federal government to divide and rule; intergovernmental agreements such as the Social Union Framework Agreement ignored at will; and 'squabbling, ad hoc tinkering, and short-term thinking'. Few if any principles or rules govern the process. There is little permanency, predictability, or consistency when intergovernmental agreements, many of which are achieved only with great difficulty, can be cancelled or altered unilaterally. Provincial policy-making is hostage to federal fiscal decisions; federal policy-making hostage to the need for provincial co-operation. A dramatic example, as Friendly and White note in Chapter 10, is the Harper government's cancellation (contingent on parliamentary approval) in 2006 of the agreements on child care negotiated with all provinces by Paul Martin's government. 'We have a governance problem,' said the Council of the Federation Panel; 'the institutions and processes we use to manage the fiscal arrangements of the Canadian federation are inadequate to the task' (89). The same observation could be applied to several other policy areas.

Democracy

Donald Smiley delivered one of the earliest and most devastating critiques of executive federalism in his article 'An Outsider's Observations of Federal-Provincial Relations among Consenting Adults' (1979: 105–13). First, he wrote, executive federalism

> contributes to undue secrecy in the conduct of the public's business. Second, it contributes to an unduly low level of citizen-participation in public affairs. Third, it weakens and dilutes the accountability of governments to their respective legislatures and the wider public. Fourth, it frustrates a number of matters of crucial public concern from coming on the public agenda. . . . Sixth, it leads to continuous and often unresolved conflicts among governments, conflicts which serve no purpose broader than the political and bureaucratic interests of those involved in them. (1979: 105–6)

'My argument, then,' he concluded, 'is that executive federalism contributes to secret, non-participatory and non-accountable processes of government' (107). Smiley's powerful critique still resonates today.

Most intergovernmental relations continue to take place behind closed doors. The language of intergovernmental relations continues to be arcane and obtuse, especially where fiscal issues are involved. Citizens have little access to the process. Popular mobilization led to the defeat of the Meech Lake Accord in 1990 and the Charlottetown Accord in 1992; more recently, however, there has been no popular mobilization against either the Agreement on Internal Trade or the Social Union Framework Agreement, both of which were negotiated in the traditional closed-door way, with little public input. More specific agreements on topics such as environmental assessments have attracted criticism only from the groups immediately affected. The broad lesson here seems to be that when intergovernmental relations touch on issues of fundamental symbolic importance, such as the Constitution, citizens will mobilize to challenge the process. But public opinion surveys also suggest that citizens do not support one level of government over the other or seek any fundamental shift in the division of powers; above all, what they want is for governments to co-operate and collaborate (Centre for Research and Information on Canada, 2005; Leonard et al., 2006: 6).

How well do contemporary intergovernmental relations meet democratic criteria of transparency, accountability, and participation? With respect to transparency, not well. Despite intensive media coverage of high-profile intergovernmental conflicts over issues such as health-care funding, the process is still largely closed. Intergovernmental relations, like national security issues, remain outside the Freedom of Information Act. Sectoral intergovernmental cultures do vary with respect to levels of citizen responsiveness, opportunities for participation, and degrees of transparency and accountability. But in general the record on these counts is weak (DiGiacomo, 2005).

Accountability is a complex matter in a federal system. Multiple accountabilities co-exist. Fundamental, of course, is the accountability of each government to its own legislature. But when there are large intergovernmental transfers, as in Canada, then the complications begin. If the federal government is to be accountable to Parliament for these expenditures, one would expect recipient provinces to be subject to strict reporting requirements, if not strict conditions, as to how the funds are used. But such a requirement conflicts directly with provincial autonomy, since most transfers are directed to areas in which provincial legislatures and governments make the basic policy choices. Similarly, it is reasonable to assume that the federal government should be accountable for stability in its funding commitments. Yet the federal government is reluctant to curtail in any way its spending power, and provinces have long resisted the attachment of conditions to federal payments. Reconciling these multiple and competing accountabilities is no easy task.

Conditionality in federal transfers has diminished over time, to the point that intergovernmental transfers in Canada have fewer conditions attached to them than is the case in most other federations (Lazar, 1999). In recent years provincial governments have committed themselves to sharing information, developing common indicators of success, and the like. Such reporting and monitoring of program outcomes is increasingly framed not as accountability to the federal government, but as accountability to the provinces' own citizens for how the funds are used (Laurent and Vaillancourt, 2004). The Social Union Framework Agreement (SUFA) established this wording, now invariably included in intergovernmental agreements: 'enhancing each government's transparency and accountability to its citizens', by monitoring and measuring outcomes, and 'reporting regularly' to its citizens.

In terms of participation, the intergovernmental arena is not entirely closed to citizen or civil-society influences. As Julie Simmons demonstrates in Chapter 17, some ministerial councils have been highly effective in involving interest groups in conferences, workshops, and round tables. But even here, when the political and financial stakes for governments increase, the doors tend to close. As Jennifer Smith (2004) concludes, '[t]he general public, mostly, can only watch from the bleachers.' Only when 'there is sharp, deep conflict between the governments' does the public get 'to see through the cracks' (2004: 108).

Whether all this adds up to a serious democratic deficit is debatable. It might be argued that if each government fully represents its citizens and remains responsible to its legislature for its actions in the intergovernmental arena there is little problem: ours is, after all, a representative democracy. There are three problems with this perspective. First, it neglects the central role played by intergovernmental processes in Canadian policy-making; second, executive dominance poses a clear challenge to fully responsible government; and third, recent years have seen calls for a more robust conception of citizen involvement or 'deliberative democracy' than is captured in the traditional model.

Legislative Federalism

The vagaries of electoral and party politics as they play out in federal and provincial parliaments do indeed have important consequences for the intergovernmental agenda, and for the dynamics of intergovernmental relations at any time. The ideology of parties in power, a regionalized federal party system, or whether a government has a majority or minority rule, will all affect the way a government acts, with the immediate pressures and constraints of a domestic political situation weighing more heavily on governments' minds than the one-step-removed intergovernmental arena. The Paul Martin government's pre-election use of its spending power and large surpluses to increase funding in areas of provincial jurisdiction, such as health care and early childhood education, and its 'one-off' deals on equalization with Newfoundland and Labrador and Nova Scotia are examples of intergovernmental politics driven by political need. (See Brown on fiscal federalism in Chapter 7.) So are the Harper government's promises of 'Open Federalism', an end to 'fiscal imbalance', and other efforts to build bases of electoral support outsides its core areas of support.[3] Similarly, provincial strategies in intergovernmental relations are shaped by local circumstances and personalities. This is another example of the tension between parliamentary government and federalism.

The tension is clearest with respect to accountability. The parliamentary principle is that governments are responsible to their own legislatures for laws, regulations, and the raising and spending of money. The federal idea is that each government is autonomous in its own sphere, not subject to monitoring or control from others. These two ideas clash when there are significant transfers among governments, as in Canada.[4] The parliamentary principle suggests that it is legitimate for the federal Parliament to attach clear conditions and rules for reporting to all transfers. If not, how can the legislators hold the government accountable? The more carefully Parliament scrutinizes spending programs such as the Canada Health Transfer, Canada Social Transfer, or federal infrastructure funds (under the 2009 Economic Action Plan), the more provincial autonomy is infringed.

Amy Nugent (2006) illustrates this point in her analysis of the role of the Office of the Auditor General (OAG). It is an agency of Parliament, charged with 'following the money'. Its recent approach has been to move beyond simply counting dollars and investigate more policy-related issues, based on criteria such as 'value for money', effectiveness, and performance. In its 2002 report, *Placing the Public's Money beyond Parliament's Reach*, the OAG recommended that the Treasury Board Secretariat and the Privy Council Office ensure better reporting, more ministerial oversight, and auditing of a large number of major intergovernmental agreements. Nugent concludes: 'The overwhelming thrust of the OAG's recommendations is to treat duly elected and constitutionally autonomous provincial legislatures and governments as an alternative service delivery agent of the federal government (Nugent, 2006: 9).

The debate here touches not only on appropriate mechanisms of accountability, but also on the potential tension between the conditions necessary for government accountability to legislatures and the need for co-operation and trust between orders of government. Even more broadly, the issue is whether the federation is to be an equal partnership or a more paternalistic, hierarchical, top-down system, and whether the primary gains from a federal system are seen to lie in co-operative or in competitive relationships (Smith, 2004: 127–8).

The public is not the only body largely frozen out of the intergovernmental area: so are legislators. Legislatures have on occasion been arenas for fundamental debates about federalism. One thinks of the parliamentary committee that considered Prime Minister Trudeau's proposed constitutional amendments in 1981, or the Bélanger-Campeau Commission that explored constitutional options for Quebec, or the two federal parliamentary committees that explored constitutional options following the failure of the Meech Lake Accord. In general, however, parliaments have little voice. Typically, governments do not consult the legislature at the stage when intergovernmental strategies are being formed. Nor do they typically report back to Parliament on intergovernmental relations unless legislative or budgetary change is involved. Intergovernmental accords and agreements are not normally ratified or approved by legislatures. No government, federal or provincial, has a standing committee on intergovernmental relations, and intergovernmental issues are seldom discussed in sectoral portfolio committees. And the opposition parties, needless to say, have little influence, even though they may well hold the preponderance of seats from particular regions.

It could be argued that openness, responsiveness, and accountability would be enhanced by giving legislatures a stronger role in monitoring and scrutinizing governments' conduct of intergovernmental affairs. Further, a more conversational and deliberative style of parliamentary debate might improve the national Parliament's capacity to act as an arena for the accommodation of regional differences, thus reducing the accommodative burden that now falls on the intergovernmental process. Such reforms would also be consistent with the larger project, advocated by many observers (and promised by opposition parties, but usually abandoned once they gain office), of restoring influence to Parliament.

But here again the tension arises between parliamentary and intergovernmental Canada, and between popular participation and politics as elite accommodation. Assume, for example, that governments agree on a carefully crafted compromise that balances regional and national concerns and is sensitive to the federal principle. Assume then that it must be ratified by 11 (or 14, including the territories) legislatures. In some of those legislatures it is rejected or amended substantially. It falls apart, and there is no effective mechanism to rescue it. This is what happened to the Victoria Charter of 1971. It was agreed to by Quebec Premier Robert Bourassa in the intergovernmental forum, but was soon repudiated when the premier was unable to win caucus and cabinet support at home. A similar process scuttled the Meech Lake Accord, and a referendum—rather than parliamentary process—did the same to Charlottetown. It can be argued that these agreements failed because they did not deserve to succeed (or 'did not meet a democratic standard of legislative or popular support'). But the larger question of governance is how to reconcile these two quite different patterns of decision-making.

It is impossible to predict how a fundamentally reformed federal government would behave. Much would depend on the specific reforms implemented. A mildly enhanced role for MPs and committees, a more proportional electoral system, Senate reform that did (or did not) approach the Triple-E—all would have major implications. On the one hand, Parliament could become a much more majoritarian body (a worry to smaller provinces and, for different reasons, to Quebec); on the other hand, it could become much more regionally fragmented, with regional parties and MPs cultivating local and regional constituencies through log-rolling and coalition-building.[5]

But such fundamental reform is unlikely. We have seen how visceral executives' distaste is for giving up power. We have a constitutional amendment process that requires broad provincial consent; reforms that would weaken their influence will therefore be blocked. If basic legislative reform is achieved, it is much more likely to be at the provincial level, where there are fewer interests to balance and fewer constitutional constraints, than at the federal level.

Thus we are likely to see the difficult and complex dance between federal, intergovernmental Canada, and parliamentary Canada continue. Such tension has not served us too badly in the past, and may continue to serve in the future, even if the aspirations of more radical democrats will be frustrated. But a number of more modest reforms might be possible, both at the level of intergovernmental relations and at the level of parliamentary practice. What might such a reform agenda look like?

In terms of the intergovernmental process, the most serious dysfunctions are a result of the perverse incentives of fiscal federalism. The spending power, especially when there are large federal surpluses, creates a constant incentive for Ottawa to intervene in areas of provincial jurisdiction, often in capricious and uninformed ways. The same dynamic places the provinces in the role of *demandeurs,* always asking for more while resisting stronger conditions and reporting requirements. The transfer system also blurs accountability to citizens: if child-care spaces are inadequate, or support for universities and research too low, who is to blame? Thus there is much to be said for resolving the 'fiscal imbalance', moving towards a closer fit between each government's responsibilities and resources, and reducing the role of federal–provincial transfers outside the Equalization program. Similarly, while interdependence and overlapping responsibilities (and hence the need for intergovernmentalism) will never disappear, there is much to be said for clarifying as far as possible which level of government is responsible for what. In some ways, the remedy for the dysfunctions of intergovernmentalism is to have less of it (Simeon and Cameron, 2002: 291; DiGiacomo, 2005: 36). This approach resonates in the Conservative government's 2006 election platform and subsequent budget documents (Finance Canada, 2006b). Here the emphasis is on re-centring federal spending on core responsibilities such as defense, immigration, justice and law enforcement, and Aboriginal peoples. There is some lack of clarity, however, as to what will happen to investments in intergovernmental initiatives already up-and-running. Some of these envelopes have or are set to simply expire without further federal commitments, leaving provinces with the decision about whether to continue funding to the same level, for example, early childhood development, health wait-times guarantees, or infrastructure. Good policy will not result from overnight withdrawal of federal funds, as with child care agreements. Such a shift requires consultation and joint planning, just as new initiatives would.

Even with a degree of clarifying and disentangling, governments will have to work together to effectively manage economic, social, and cultural aspects of the federation. As has often been suggested (most recently by the Council of the Federation's Advisory Panel), first ministers' conferences should become a regular part of our institutional landscape. They should not be hostage to the political needs of an incumbent prime minister anxious to cobble together some last-minute compromise over dinner at 24 Sussex Drive. Rather, they should be the forum for general and strategic discussion of the policy agenda that faces Canadians everywhere, held largely in public, with follow-up activities delegated to ministerial councils and to individual governments. After four years in office, Prime Minister Stephen Harper, like his predecessors, has avoided making any commitment to such scheduled meetings.

To move away from public perceptions of bickering and blaming, intergovernmental Canada needs greater levels of trust not just between governments but between governments and the public. A step in this direction would be to address the ambiguous status of intergovernmental agreements. Johanne Poirier (2002: 455) suggests that 'an explicit legal framework governing the conclusion, ratification, modification, publicity and archiving of IGAs' would go some way towards making IGAs more formal and reliable.

More formal change could also provide increased permanence and predictability to intergovernmental agreements so that all governments know what the rules are and can trust that they will not be changed unilaterally. The Social Union Framework Agreement pointed in this direction, but had little effect on future government actions. The more these agreements impinge on the rights and concerns of citizens, however, the more important citizen access to their decision-making procedures and their dispute settlement processes becomes (as with the Agreement on Internal Trade). Therefore, the more such agreements take on the form and commitments we associate with legislation or with treaties, the more legislative scrutiny and legitimation is required.

Modest recommendations may be made in terms of **legislative federalism**, including a fuller discussion of intergovernmental issues both before and after major conferences, thus complementing the process as it already works within the bureaucracy and government. Standing committees on intergovernmental relations in federal and provincial legislatures might scrutinize and report to the legislature on the state of intergovernmental relations and agreements in specific policy areas. Meekison, Telford, and Lazar (2004: 11) concluded that 'citizen participation could be effectively channelled through legislative committees in Ottawa and the provincial capitals'. Perhaps legislatures could also ratify major intergovernmental agreements (Simeon and Cameron, 2002: 292). The monopoly that executive federalism currently exercises over intergovernmental relations could be somewhat attenuated by the development of forums in which federal, provincial, and indeed local elected members could informally exchange ideas about development needs in each province.

None of this is to deny the desirability of a much more dramatic reform agenda that addresses the role of municipal and local governments (see Sancton in Chapter 16) and Aboriginal governments (see Papillon in Chapter 15) in our federal system. There is also the matter of how our system should be adapted to the reality of a country in which territorially defined differences, privileged in our existing Constitution and political practice, co-exist with other bases of identity and interest. (See Cameron in Chapter 3.) Adapting federalism to the global imperatives of productivity, competitiveness, and innovation is also critical. Historical legacies and institutional inertia explain why it is so difficult to address these profoundly important questions. Every country carries its inherited burdens. From the beginning, ours has been the need to balance federalism and parliamentary government. We will continue working to figure out how to do so in ways responsive both to democratic participation and to the ever-evolving policy agenda.

Notes

1. Watts (1999) uses several indices to measure the degree of decentralization of a federal system, including the intrastate involvement of sub-national units; scope of jurisdictional and fiscal responsibility and autonomy; and the mobility of people, goods, services, and capital. In aggregate terms, Watts concludes that Canada is one of the world's most decentralized federations.

2. Veterans of intergovernmental relations suggest that in earlier periods, despite occasionally profound policy differences, a network of intergovernmental professionals worked to keep lines of communication open. These links appear to have weakened, partly because of increased control from premiers' offices and the PMO, partly because of more rapid turnover to deputies in intergovernmental affairs units. See Inwood et al. (2004).

3. As explained in the Conservative Party's 2006 federal election platform, 'Open Federalism' will 'facilitate provincial involvement in areas of federal jurisdiction where provincial jurisdiction is affected, and enshrine these practices in a Charter of Open Federalism'. Open Federalism includes inviting Quebec to play a role at UNESCO.

4. However, these transfers are smaller as a proportion of both federal and provincial spending than in most other federations (Courchene, 2004, Watts, 1999, 46–9).

5. This scenario would be similar to the situation in the United States, which comes closer than any other modern federation to full legislative federalism.

References

Arrangement between the Government of Canada and the Government of Nova Scotia on Offshore Revenues. 2005. Available online at: www.fin.gc.ca/FEDPROV05/OffshoreResAcc/novascotiaarr-e.html.

Arrangement between the Government of Canada and the Government of Newfoundland and Labrador on Offshore Revenues. 2005. Available online at: www.fin.gc.ca/FEDPROV05/OffshoreResAcc/nfldarr-e.html.

Baier, G. 2002. 'Judicial Review and Canadian Federalism'. In *Canadian Federalism: Performance, Effectiveness and Legitimacy*, ed. H. Bakvis and G. Skogstad. Toronto: Oxford University Press.

———— H. Bakvis, and D. Brown. 2005. 'Executive Federalism, the Democratic Deficit and Parliamentary Reform'. In *How Ottawa Spends, 2005–2006: Managing the Minority*, ed. G.B. Doern. Montreal-Kingston: McGill–Queen's University Press.

Breton, A. 1996. *Competitive Governments: An Economic Theory of Politics and Public Finance.* Cambridge: Cambridge University Press.

Brock, K. 'The End of Executive Federalism'. In *New Trends in Canadian Federalism,* ed. F. Rocher and M. Smith. Peterborough: Broadview.

Brown, D.M., ed. 2003. *Constructive and Co-operative Federalism?* A Series of Commentaries on the Council of the Federation, Institute of Intergovernmental Relations, Queen's University, Kingston. Available online at: www.iigr.ca/igr.php/site/browse_publications?Section=39.

Burelle, A. 2003. *The Council of the Federation: From a Defensive to a Partnership Approach.* A Series of Commentaries on the Council of the Federation, Institute of Intergovernmental Relations, Queen's University, Kingston.

Cameron, B. 2004. 'The Social Union, Executive Power and Social Rights', *Canadian Woman Studies* 23, 3, 4: 49–56.

Centre for Research and Information on Canada (CRIC). 2005. 'Portrait of Canada 2005, Priorities, Making the Country Work Better'. Ottawa. Available online at: www.cric.ca/pdf/cric_poll/portraits/portraits_2005/en_priorities_tb.pdf.

Conference Board of Canada. 2006. *Death by a Thousand Paper Cuts: The Effect of Barriers to Competition on Canadian Productivity.* Ottawa.

Council of the Federation, Advisory Panel on Fiscal Imbalance. 2006. *Reconciling the Irreconcilable.* Available online at: www.councilofthefederation.ca.

Courchene, T.J. 1996. 'Access: A Convention on the Canadian Economic and Social Systems. Report prepared for the Ontario Ministry of Intergovernmental Affairs'. In *Canadian Business Economics* 4: 3–26.

————. 2004. 'Intergovernmental Transfers and Societal Values'. *Policy Options* 25 6: 83.

DiGiacomo, G. 2005. 'The Democratic Content of Intergovernmental Agreements in Canada'. Public Policy Paper 38. Regina: Saskatchewan Institute of Public Policy.

Docherty, D. 2004. *Legislatures.* Canadian Democratic Audit, Vancouver: University of British Columbia Press.

Doyle, S. 2006. 'Full Cabinet Meeting Irregularly, Every Two Weeks to a Month', *The Hill Times* 26 Jun.: 5.

Dupré, J.S. 1985. 'Reflections on the Workability of Executive Federalism'. In *Intergovernmental Relations,* ed. R. Simeon. Toronto: University of Toronto Press.

Elazar, D. 2006. *Federal Systems of the World.* Harlow: Longman Group Limited.

Erk, J. 2003. 'Federal Germany and its Non-federal Society: Emergence of an All-German Educational Policy in a System of Exclusive Provincial Jurisdiction', *Canadian Journal of Political Science* 36, 1: 295–317.

————. 2006. 'Uncodified Workings and Unworkable Codes', *Comparative Political Studies* 39, 4: 441–62.

Federal, Provincial, and Territorial Communiqué, 'A Ten-Year Plan to Strengthen Health Care'. 2004. First Ministers' Meeting, Ottawa, 13–16 Sept. Available online at: www.hc-sc.gc.ca/hcs-sss/delivery-prestation/fptcollab/2004-fmm-rpm/index_e.html

Federal, Provincial, and Territorial Governments (not Quebec), An Agreement to Improve the Social Union for Canadian (Social Union Framework Agreement). 1999. News release, 4 Feb. Available online at: socialunion.ca/

news/020499_e.html.

Finance Canada. 2006a. *Achieving a National Purpose: Putting Equalization Back on Track*. Ottawa: Department of Finance Canada: 39. Available online at: www.eqtff-pfft.ca/english/EQTreasury/index.asp.

———. 2006b. 'Restoring Fiscal Balance in Canada: Focusing on Priorities', *Turning a New Leaf, Budget 2006*, Ottawa: Department of Finance. Available online at: www.fin.gc.ca/budtoce/2006/budliste.htm.

Gibbins, R., L. Youngman, and K. Harmsworth. 2000. *Following the Cash: Exploring the Expanding Role of Canada's Auditor General*. Calgary: Canada West Foundation.

Globe and Mail. 2006. 'The Bedrock Need to Let Ministers Be Ministers'. Editorial. 22 Mar.: A18.

Harrison, K. 1996 *Passing the Buck: Federalism and Canadian Environmental Policy*. Vancouver: University of British Columbia Press.

Harrison, K. 2004. 'Races to the Bottom? Provincial Interdependence in the Canadian Federation'. Paper presented at the Annual Meeting of the Canadian Political Science Association, Winnipeg.

Hueglin, T., and A. Fenna. 2006. *Comparative Federalism: A Systematic Inquiry*, Peterborough, ON: Broadview Press.

Inwood, G.C., C. Johns, and P. O'Reilly. 2004. 'Intergovernmental Officials in Canada'. In *Canada: The State of the Federation 2002, Reconsidering the Institutions of Canadian Federalism*, ed. J.P. Meekison, H. Telford, and H. Lazar. Montreal and Kingston, McGill–Queen's University Press.

Kent, T. 1999. 'How to Renew Canadian Democracy: PR for the Commons, FPTP Elections for the Senate, and Political Financing for Individuals Only'. In *Making Every Vote Count: Reassessing Canada's Electoral System*, ed. H. Milner. Peterborough, ON: Broadview Press.

———. 2003. *A Short Path to Revitalized Federalism*. A Series of Commentaries on the Council of the Federation, Institute of Intergovernmental Relations, Queen's University, Kingston.

Kenyon, D. 1997. 'Theories of Interjurisdictional Competition', *New England Economic Review* Mar./Apr.: 13–35.

Laurent, S., and F. Vaillancourt. 2004. 'Federal-Provincial Transfers for Social Programs in Canada: Their Status in May 2004'. Institute for Research on Public Policy Working Paper Series, no. 2004–07. Montreal: Institute for Research on Public Policy.

Law Commission of Canada. 2004. *Voting Counts: Electoral Reform for Canada*, Ottawa, ON. Available online at: www.lcc.gc.ca/research_project/gr/er/report/ER_Report_en.pdf.

Lazar, H., ed. 1999. *Canadian Fiscal Arrangements: What Works, What Might Work Better*. Kingston, ON: Institute of Intergovernmental Relations.

Leonard, J., C. Ragan, and F. St. Hilaire. 2006. 'The Canadian Priorities Agenda', *Policy Options* 27: 4–11.

MacKinnon, J. 2003. *Minding the Public Purse: The Fiscal Crisis, Political Trade-offs and Canada's Future*. Montreal–Kingston: McGill–Queen's University Press.

Meekison, J.P., H. Telford, and H. Lazar. 2004. 'Introduction', *Canada: The State of the Federation 2002*. Montreal and Kingston: McGill–Queen's University Press.

Nugent, A. 2006. 'Intergovernmental Accountability and the Office of the Auditor General of Canada', unpublished paper, 31 Mar.

Office of the Auditor General of Canada (OAG). 2002. *Placing the Public's Money Beyond the Public's Reach: Report of the Auditor General to the House of Commons*.

Papillon, M., and R. Simeon. 2004. 'The Weakest Link? First Ministers Conferences in Canadian Intergovernmental Relations'. In *Canada: The State of the Federation 2002, Reconsidering the Institutions of Canadian Federalism*, ed. J.P. Meekison, H. Telford, and H. Lazar. Montreal and Kingston: McGill–Queen's University Press.

Poirier, J. 2004. 'Intergovernmental Agreements in Canada: At the Crossroads Between Law and Politics'. In *Canada: The State of the Federation 2002, Reconsidering the Institutions of Canadian Federalism*, ed. J.P. Meekison, H. Telford, and H. Lazar. Montreal and Kingston: McGill–Queen's University Press.

Savoie, D. 1995. 'What is Wrong with the New Public Management?' Debate in *Canadian Public Administration* 38, 1: 112–21.

————. 1999. *Governing from the Centre: The Concentration of Power in Canadian Politics*, Toronto: University of Toronto Press.

————. 2003. *Breaking the Bargain*. Toronto: University of Toronto Press.

Simeon, R. 2006a. 'Federalism and Social Justice: Thinking Through the Tangle'. In *Territory, Democracy and Justice: Regionalism and Federalism in Western Democracies*, ed. S.L. Greer. Basingstoke: Palgrave Macmillan: 18–43.

————. 2006b. [1972] 'Postscript'. In *Federal-Provincial Diplomacy: The Making of Recent Policy in Canada*. Re-issued with a new postscript. Toronto: University of Toronto Press.

———— and D. Cameron. 2002. 'Intergovernmental Relations and Democracy: An Oxymoron if Ever There Was One?' In *Canadian Federalism: Performance, Effectiveness, and Legitimacy*, ed. H. Bakvis and G. Skogstad. Toronto: Oxford University Press.

———— and I. Robinson. 1990. *State, Society and the Development of Canadian Federalism*. Toronto: University of Toronto Press.

Simmons, J. 2004. 'Securing the Threads of Cooperation in the Tapestry of Inter-governmental Relations: Does the Institutionalization of Ministerial Conferences Matter?' In *Canada: The State of the Federation 2002: Reconsidering the Institutions of Executive Federalism*, ed. J.P. Meekison, H. Telford, and H. Lazar. Montreal and Kingston: McGill–Queen's University Press.

Smiley, D.V. 1979. 'An Outsider's Observations of Intergovernmental Relations Among Consenting Adults'. In *Confrontation or Collaboration: Intergovernmental Relations in Canada Today*, ed. R. Simeon. Toronto: Institute of Public Administration of Canada.

Smith, J. 2004. *Federalism*. Canadian Democratic Audit. Vancouver: University of British Columbia Press.

Thorlakson, L. 2003. 'Comparing Federal Institutions: Power and Representation in Six Federations', *West European Politics* 26: 1–22.

Watts, R.L. 1989. *Executive Federalism: A Comparative Analysis*, Research Paper No. 26, Institute of Intergovernmental Relations.

————. 1999. *Comparing Federal Systems*, 2nd ed. Kingston, Ont.: Institute of Intergovernmental Relations.

Wheare, K.C. 1953. *Federal Government*, 3rd edn. Oxford University Press.

White, G. 2004. *Cabinets and First Ministers*. Canadian Democratic Audit. Vancouver: University of British Columbia Press.

Cases

CUPE v. Canada (Minister of Health), 2004 FC 1334, 244 D.L.R. (4th) 175 (T.D.).

Reference re Canada Assistance Plan (B.C.), [1991] 2 S.C.R. 525.

Reference re Secession of Quebec, [1998] 2 S.C.R. 217.

5 The Courts, the Constitution, and Dispute Resolution

Gerald Baier

Canada's federal system features a rather large gap between the jurisdictional map of the written constitution and the actual activities of its governments. Overlapping jurisdictional responsibilities and the dominance of federal financial powers make the formal division of powers a poor guide to 'who does what?' in Canadian federalism. This gap between the constitution and reality shows no signs of closing. As the other chapters in this volume show, in the almost twenty years since major constitutional change was last attempted, the primary agent of evolution in the federation has been intergovernmental negotiation, not rationalization of constitutional roles. This informal evolution has been a trademark of Canadian federalism since the 1960s. Canada's governments have committed themselves for decades to increased collaboration, administration, and priority setting, further blurring the answer to 'who does what?' In a more classical federal system where there are bright line divisions between national and sub-unit jurisdiction, courts would play a central role patrolling boundaries and keeping governments to their constitutionally assigned tasks. In a federal system characterized by the blurring of responsibilities, the role of courts is less immediately clear. Given all the overlap and collaboration between governments in the Canadian federal system, conflict and disputes are inevitable. This chapter examines the place of courts, particularly the Supreme Court of Canada, in the collaborative federal model. Although there is an almost ever-present need for dispute resolution in a federation like Canada, its courts are increasingly not the institutions called on to settle intergovernmental disputes. The Supreme Court has not been completely relegated to bystander status; its role as interpreter and defender of rights protections has had a measurable effect on federalism, and the Court has still been a key actor in a few intergovernmental disputes; but generally its job as umpire has been overshadowed by the dominance of intergovernmental negotiation and compromise.

One prominent feature of the collaborative model of federalism is increased reliance on sector-specific accords and agreements, often directed by Ministerial councils and assisted by institutionalized secretariats responsible for fulfilling the logistical and reporting requirements necessary to implement the agreements. These regimes profess to increase intergovernmental accountability by increasing the transparency of intergovernmental relations and obliging governments to report to each other and their citizenry on outcomes. These regimes are also often called upon to organize mechanisms for the settlement of intergovernmental disputes related to the specific topics covered by their accord or agreement. These mechanisms generally feature a similar spirit of compromise, prioritizing consultative processes among governments to resolve conflicts informally (a kind of dispute avoidance), but also employing some forms of alternative dispute resolution should they be necessary. Their mere existence is meant to avoid conflicts by creating mutual dependency in goal setting and policy design; however, conflict does not go away that easily. In the most high-profile conflicts between the federal and provincial governments, the Supreme Court still appears to retain a role.

The chapter begins with a brief description of how judicial review of the constitution has historically shaped Canadian federalism. It then looks at recent instances of Supreme Court intervention on federalism. These examples illustrate the more traditional role of the Supreme Court in intergovernmental relations. The chapter then turns to examples of institutions that have emerged to replace the Supreme Court as umpire of intergovernmental conflict. These examples, drawn from the post-Charlottetown generation of intergovernmental agreements, are the mechanisms for intergovernmental dispute resolution incorporated in the *Agreement on Internal Trade* (AIT) and the *Social Union Framework Agreement* (SUFA). The role of judicial power in intergovernmental relations is then discussed and analyzed alongside these new developments. These dispute settlement institutions may be a response to the democratic critique of judicial review, but they are not without transparency and legitimacy problems of their own. They disperse and muddy responsibility for unpopular or unwanted government action and leave those seeking constitutional challenges, including the weaker governments of the federation, with few avenues to pursue. The trend in Canada to settle intergovernmental disputes away from the courts is minimizing the oversight role of the constitution and the courts and, in effect, prioritizing the sovereignty and manoeuvrability of governments over the guarantees of the federal constitution.

Courts and the Division of Powers Cases

There is something of a chicken-and-egg debate about the origins of Canada's decentralized federalism. Historically, judicial review was often pointed to as a primary culprit in the expansion of provincial power. If not for the permissive interpretation of provincial powers by the Law Lords of the Judicial Committee of the Privy Council (JCPC), went the argument, the strong central government envisioned by the Fathers of Confederation would have been realized. Prior to the 1960s, disputes between the provinces and the federal government gave a more prominent role to the judiciary as an umpire. Much of the content of judicial review in that period was the result of corporations, citizens and provincial governments challenging the legislative authority of the national parliament. Individuals and corporations subject to federal regulation would contest the constitutionality of regimes under whose thumb they had found themselves. These individual challenges, as well as challenges originating in reference cases from governments, profoundly altered the map of the nominal division of powers. The origins of these cases are easy to overlook, as little suggests that where they come from influences outcomes. However, the fact that governments or individuals have to initiate a challenge that slowly or quickly finds its way to the Supreme Court tells us something important about judicial power in federalism. If courts are important actors as umpires of the division of powers, it is because governments choose to make them powerful by leaving decision-making to the courts.

The provinces certainly chose to rely on the courts in the early years of the Canadian federation and, with good reason, they were happy with the results. The provinces successfully challenged the scope of the federal parliament's power to make laws for the 'peace, order, and good government' (POGG) of Canada granted by the preamble to section 91 of the *Constitution Act, 1867*. At Confederation, this clause was generally believed to represent a grant of residual or plenary power. Combined with the federal government's assumption of the seemingly most important legislative and taxing powers, as well as its powers to reserve or disallow provincial legislation, the POGG clause seemed to ensure that Canadian federalism would take a centralized form. However, the scope of the POGG clause was profoundly influenced by those early challenges and the interpretation of the JCPC.

Rather than read the clause generously as the centralist Fathers of Confederation had hoped, the JCPC chose to restrict the scope of the clause. It categorized POGG largely as an emergency provision—to be resorted to only on rare occasions. The emergency interpretation of POGG was distinguished early on from an alternative conception which extended POGG to cover matters of a national concern. This interpretation was rarely granted. When POGG was successfully invoked, it was usually for emergency circumstances. In contrast, the JCPC favoured the enumerated powers of the provinces, especially the power over property and civil rights granted by section 92 (13). Portions of the federal parliament's so-called New Deal legislation were ruled *ultra vires* according to this pattern, thus raising the considerable ire of legal and political observers in Canada.

The Canadian critics of the JCPC took it as gospel that a Canadian court would not interpret the federal Parliament's POGG power so restrictively (Laskin, 1951). After the abolition of appeals to the JCPC in 1949, the early years of the autonomous Supreme Court seemingly proved the critics right. In one of its last decisions on Canadian federalism, the *Canada Temperance Federation* case, the JCPC offered up the possibility that POGG could be more generously interpreted in areas of national concern. The Supreme Court took full advantage of this possible interpretation and began to define a broader scope for the POGG power under the national concern branch. This led the court to include under the rubric of POGG the national control of aeronautics (*Johannesson* 1952), atomic energy (*Pronto Uranium Mines* 1956), a national capital region (*Munro* 1966), and seabed natural resources (*Offshore Minerals* 1967).

This cautious run of centralization was essentially brought to a halt by the *Anti- Inflation Reference* case of 1976. The Supreme Court, led by one of the most outspoken critics of previous POGG jurisprudence, Chief Justice Bora Laskin, was asked to consider the constitutionality of the federal government's inflation control legislation. If ever the debate between an emergency and national concern justification for the use of the POGG power was to be resolved, this case presented amenable facts for consideration. The decision of the court, however, offered no clear interpretation of POGG as a justification for the exercise of federal power in matters of national concern. The court left unresolved the potential of a federal plenary power and in the process ushered in a period of 'balanced' federalism which has seemed to favour neither level of government (Hogg, 1979; Russell, 1985).

Recent years have seen sporadic attention paid to questions of constitutional juris-diction. Governments on the whole are not inclined to challenge each other's constitu-tional jurisdiction except as a tactic of last resort. Since the *Anti-Inflation Reference*, the Supreme Court has opened up some possibilities for the extension of federal power under POGG, but it has also seemed to maintain the balanced approach identified by Hogg and Russell (Baier, 2006). Federal power over the environment as a matter of national concern was first justified under the POGG clause in *Crown Zellerbach* (1988), but the court backed away from too generous an interpretation of the national concern branch. In *Hydro-Québec* (1997) and the *Firearms Reference* (2000) the Supreme Court opted for a more generous interpretation of the federal power over criminal law instead of a generous interpretation of the POGG power.

The Court has recently readdressed the scope of the criminal law heading in *Reference Re: Assisted Human Reproduction Act* (2010). The federal parliament passed legislation in 2004 regulating assisted reproduction technology in response to a comprehensive Royal Commission. The legislation set up detailed rules on practices ranging from human clon-ing to paid surrogacy. The Act could nominally be based on a variety of jurisdictional headings, some federal, some provincial. The Royal Commission recommended parlia-ment pass legislation on the basis of the POGG power. Alternatively, health, as a primarily provincial jurisdiction, would also seem to be a likely rubric. On that logic, the govern-ment of Quebec challenged the legislation as *ultra vires* the federal parliament. Given the recent expansion of the criminal law power, Quebec and other provinces were particu-larly keen to challenge the criminal prohibitions that form the core of the regulatory ap-paratus set up by the act. When challenged, the federal government assumed an enduring distaste for POGG from the Supreme Court and defended the law without reference to the power. A divided court saved some of the regulations under the criminal law power and dismissed others. A core group of four judges was prepared to allow all the regulations to continue under a criminal law justification, an equally adamant four were found that the regulations were for health and would have struck down the legislation. Each side found an ally in the newest member of the court, Justice Cromwell, who was ready to accept some regulations and not others. His reasons split the difference between the two sides and left the potential scope of the criminal law's power no more clear than it was going into the case.

POGG jurisprudence is only one part of the history of how the division of powers has been interpreted by Canada's highest courts. The federal trade and commerce power has been interpreted in an equally restrictive way, particularly when compared to the broadly construed commerce power in the United States. Perhaps as a result of its lack of success in the courts, the federal government has tried to assert itself less with legislation and more with its spending power and subsequent agreements with the provinces. Recent events have highlighted one big exception: the trade and commerce power has been the main hook that the present federal government has used to justify its plans for creat-ing a national securities regulator. At present, public incorporation and the issuance of shares in those companies is regulated by the individual provinces. In order to confirm the federal government's belief that it has the necessary jurisdiction to create a national regulator, the question has been referred to the Supreme Court in a reference, but plans are well underway for the development of a national regulator. A number of provinces are vehemently opposed to the idea of a national regulator and have sought to challenge the federal role. The Supreme Court's ruling will likely be necessary to definitively settle this dispute. The case is probably the exception that proves the rule. Judicial review of the division of powers or other federalism issues has not disappeared from the politics of federalism, but it is less prominent since the shift to co-operative federalism in the 1960s.

Alan Cairns' (1971) assessment of the critics of the Judicial Committee downplayed the direct role of the court in shaping the nature of the federation. If Canada was decentralized, argued Cairns, it could not solely be because old men across the pond (the JCPC) generously interpreted provincial powers in the constitution. Arguments that wholly blamed the interpretation of the division of powers erred in being too formal and legalistic about the nature of a federation. Courts, it has since been argued, can never be the sole movers of such societal change (Rosenberg, 1991). Judicial review is only one of several forces influencing relationships between the two levels of government. The nature of the federation, and especially the strength of provincial identities and governments, contributed to decentralization. Further proof of the limited role of judicial review could be found in the fact that Canada did not radically re-centralize when the Supreme Court began to favour the federal government in jurisdictional disputes.

While constitutional jurisdiction is often cited as a resource in intergovernmental relations, it is one among many resources that federal and provincial governments bring to the process of negotiation. Peter Russell (1985) recognized the strategic place that jurisdiction played in intergovernmental relations and the incentives that exist for governments to pursue jurisdictional claims, or to defend jurisdictional ground, as a subset of the broader intergovernmental relations process. If the federal government is affirmed in its belief that it has jurisdiction in a field that provinces claim as their own, negotiating with the provinces to co-operate in the delivery or provision of services in that field becomes easier. Resource strategies do not have to be restricted exclusively to litigating the division of powers, as the **Patriation Reference**, **Quebec Veto Reference** and **Secession Reference** indicate.[1] In these three cases, questions about the process and conventions for changing the constitution were put to the Supreme Court for clarification, with the answers serving as something of a road map for future negotiations and process. (For a discussion of the impact of these cases on Canada–Quebec relations, see Chapter 3 by David Cameron.)

The *Secession reference*, and its impact on the tone of Canada–Quebec relations, has certainly demonstrated the resources game that governments play in the litigation of federal elements of the constitution. As part of its response to the 1995 referendum on Quebec sovereignty, the federal government used the constitutional reference procedure to query the Court on the legality of a unilateral declaration of independence. The Court's unanimous ruling found that Quebec lacked the formal power to separate unilaterally from Canada. It also found that a substantial informal obligation exists in Canada's constitutional culture to address assertions of independence, especially those based on a popular demonstration of that wish. The Court conceded that it was not easy to determine what exactly a popular demonstration of support for sovereignty was. The federal *Clarity Act*, passed in 2000, sought to give the federal parliament some role in determining what constituted a clear question for a sovereignty referendum and what would be a clear result. While the government of Quebec contested federal intervention, the ruling in the *Secession* reference provided some justification for the federal government to entertain such questions, particularly if it were to meet the Court's mandated obligation to negotiate sovereignty or new constitutional arrangements. Dealing as it does with the structure of intergovernmental decision-making on critical constitutional change, the *Secession* reference demonstrates that the judicial role is important, but supplemental to intergovernmental co-operation and negotiation. The Court can weigh in on questions that will affect relative resources and standing, but ultimately the actors of the federal system will work out the specifics. The Supreme Court is not an umpire definitively settling specific disputes so much as it is one setting the stage for intergovernmental compromises to be reached.

The Supreme Court's indirect role in intergovernmental relations can also be seen in another pair of examples. In *Chaoulli*, the Court brought itself into federal–provincial policy-making on health care by way of interpreting the guarantees of the Quebec Charter of Rights. In the *Employment Insurance Reference*, the Court's ruling on a more traditional division of powers question had demonstrable consequences for an eventual intergovernmental agreement on the delivery of maternity and parental benefits.

Chaoulli v Quebec (Attorney General)

In *Chaoulli v Quebec (Attorney General)*, Dr. Jacques Chaoulli, a physician activist who has contested regulations in the Quebec health care system for more than a decade, challenged restrictions in Quebec's *Health Insurance Act* and *Hospital Insurance Act* that prevent residents in the province from purchasing private health insurance or private services in a hospital. He argued that the excessive delays experienced in the Quebec health system, combined with the lack of private options for patients that result from legislative prohibitions against private insurance and care, amounted to violations of federal and provincial Charter rights to security of the person. Chaoulli's argument did not challenge the constitutionality of provincial jurisdiction over health care; in that sense it is not a typical division of powers controversy. However, health care has become the premier issue in intergovernmental relations and a battleground for differing visions of federal and provincial roles in service provision to Canadians, so the results of the case were bound to have an impact on the tone of intergovernmental relations at the very least. The Supreme Court of Canada agreed that the undue wait times experienced in the Quebec public system and the lack of private alternatives amounted to a violation of rights under the Quebec (but not the Canadian) Charter. Finding a violation under the Quebec Charter, but not the federal Charter, limited the application of the decision solely to the province of Quebec. Had the Court found a violation of federal guarantees, legislation in other provinces similar to that in Quebec would also have been found to be unconstitutional.

The main issues highlighted in the *Chaoulli* case, namely waiting times and bans on private insurance and provision of health care services, have become key debating points in intergovernmental discussions, as Antonia Maioni discusses in Chapter 9. Although the ruling only applied to Quebec, a number of provinces have made efforts to respond to the general thrust of the findings in the case. The other important lesson of the *Chaoulli* case is the opportunity that litigation provides for ordinary citizens to become involved in intergovernmental relations. Dr. Chaoulli's activism on health care issues had taken a variety of forms prior to his constitutional challenge. He has long petitioned Quebec regulators and policy makers to change their rules about the delivery of health care. By challenging the constitutionality of legislation, Chaoulli was able to affect an area otherwise dominated by intergovernmental negotiations. While it has become increasingly fashionable for Canadian politicians to pledge their support for the health care system or to promise fixes to the system for future generations, there are serious accountability flaws in a policy field so dominated by intergovernmental interaction. Most Canadians have difficulty identifying who is responsible for the delivery of health care, making it hard for them to influence policy or to hold anyone accountable (Cutler, 2004). Resorting to constitutional challenges may be a last hope, but it is an opportunity nonetheless to infiltrate some of the closed circles of intergovernmental policy making, and to make governments respond.

Employment Insurance Reference

The agenda setting role of the Supreme Court in intergovernmental relations is also illustrated in the *Reference Re: Employment Insurance Act* which forced the Court to revisit questions about unemployment insurance and pension schemes first considered in the 1930s.[2] Ultimately, constitutional amendments were necessary to provide the federal government with adequate constitutional jurisdiction to deliver services in some of those fields. The federal government has since used its assigned heading of employment insurance to design a number of different benefit programs including plans for maternity and parental leave from regular employment.

Quebec has long sought greater control over social and economic policy matters in which the federal government exercises jurisdiction. At Quebec's behest, the Meech Lake and Charlottetown Accords both contemplated limits on federal jurisdiction in provincial labour market development. Since those failed attempts at constitutional change, Quebec has sought more control over areas of social welfare related to employment including the provision of parental leave. Because the parental benefit program is somewhat outside the original rationale of unemployment insurance, there seemed a case to be made that provinces could provide such programs under their own social welfare jurisdiction. Most provinces have demurred from the expense and been happy to let the federal government fill the ensuing vacuum. However, during the Liberal government of Jean Chrétien, federal parental benefits were reduced, giving the Quebec government added incentive to implement its own, more generous program. Quebec sought to retain federal transfers for parental leave benefits to Quebecers, but to have them administered by the provincial, rather than the federal, government.

Negotiations between Quebec and Ottawa through the late 1990s failed to produce an agreement. In 1999, the Chrétien government reversed its original policy and increased the federal benefits substantially. It also suspended efforts to negotiate an opt-out version of the parental leave program with Quebec. Quebec went ahead with its own enhanced program but initiated a challenge to the constitutionality of the federal government's program. The Quebec government argued that the employment insurance power was intended to cover only people who were involuntarily unemployed but able to work, and that the parental leave provisions of the federal program were *ultra vires*. The Quebec Court of Appeal agreed. It offered a fairly narrow reading of the federal power and found that parental benefits more appropriately belonged under the provincial constitutional headings of 'property and civil rights' or 'matters of a merely local nature'.

The federal government appealed the ruling to the Supreme Court because it jeopard-ized not only the parental leave program delivered by the Employment Insurance legisla-tion, but also programs for sickness and compassionate leave. The federal government also renewed negotiations with Quebec for some shared delivery of the enhanced Quebec plan. In October of 2005, the Supreme Court ruled unanimously that parental benefits were legitimately part of the federal power for employment insurance in the amended Section 91(2a) of the *Constitution Act, 1867*. The ruling was almost moot, as the negotia-tions between Quebec and the federal government had been settled earlier that year. The federal ministers involved in the negotiations repeatedly hailed the agreement as evidence that co-operative federalism works. One might be sceptical about how well the negotia-tions would have gone without the spectre of an adverse constitutional ruling hanging over both parties.

New Umpires: Intergovernmental Agreements and Dispute Resolution

If federal judicial review is simply a mechanism of resolving intergovernmental disputes, the main candidates to replace it would be the numerous other forms of intergovernmental co-operation and dispute settlement found in the products of executive federalism. These methods usually find their expression in the accords, frameworks and communiqués that emerge from intergovernmental consultation and bargaining. But such intergovernmental agreements have long been notorious for their weak degree of legal enforceability. As Katherine Swinton notes, 'the method for resolving disputes about obligations between governments tends to lie in the political, rather than the legal, arena. Indeed, some inter-governmental agreements are designed not to be enforceable in any other forum' (1992: 140). This claim is bolstered by the unwillingness of the Supreme Court to interfere when disputes have arisen about such agreements.

The leading example and illustrative case is the *Reference Re: Canada Assistance Plan* (CAP) in which a unanimous Supreme Court refused to limit Parliament's power to unilat-erally alter its obligations to the 'have' provinces under long-standing federal–provincial cost sharing agreements.[3] Parliament was able to limit the increases in CAP grants to the richer provinces, despite a history of 50/50 cost sharing, and the provinces had no legal recourse to force the continuation of equal cost sharing, even if departure from this for-mula would have a negative impact on the delivery of services. The CAP case is generally interpreted as a warning to the provinces about the risks they take in dealing with the federal government in the strictly non-constitutional realm (Barker, 2000; Baier, 2002). But the CAP reference only touches on what might be called the *external enforceability* of intergovernmental agreements. Since the Canada Assistance Plan never took a consti-tutional form, altering Parliament's obligations was as simple as passing new legislation and, as the Court ruled, the provinces had few grounds on which to appeal. Any federal or provincial legislation has a duty to abide by constitutional guarantees, whether of federalism jurisdiction or of rights. These are matters of external enforceability—courts must ensure that legislation, including legislation that enacts intergovernmental agree-ments, still abides by rules like the division of powers. When agreements go unaltered, but remain unimplemented or are not respected by one party or another there is a dimension of *internal enforceability*. The court essentially argued in the CAP case that no external guarantee existed to stop the federal government from changing the internal terms of its agreement with the provinces.

Doubts about the external enforceability of intergovernmental agreements have always been present (Sossin, 1999),[4] but increasingly the possibility that intergovernmental agreements have some internal enforceability seems headed for the same fate. In the *Finlay* cases, a recipient of social benefits tried to ensure that the government of Manitoba lived up to what she argued were its obligations under the Canada Assistance Plan. While initially successful at the lower court level, a narrow majority of the Supreme Court in *Finlay* (1993) did not support the argument and refused to directly patrol the program and its funding levels, leaving it to the province to achieve 'substantial compliance' with the objectives of the CAP. This ruling dashed hope that courts would recognize that 'intergovernmental agreements are not the preserve of the signatory governments' and that courts would give 'the citizen status to patrol the intergovernmental relations process and to enforce obligations between governments' (Swinton, 1992: 145).

Courts have kept out of the business because of a lack of genuine justiciability, but it is unclear whether the structures built into intergovernmental agreements to compel the behaviour of governments are working to fill the void. The *Agreement on Internal Trade* (AIT) and the benchmark *Social Union Framework Agreement*, both much heralded as triumphs of flexible federalism, demonstrate how intergovernmental commitments are likely to be enforced. These agreements consciously added internal mechanisms for dispute resolution, essentially replacing the courts as the arbiter of conflict. Both favour the informal adjustment typical of contemporary executive federalism over the legalistic and more rigid constitutional model of judicial review. They place a premium on negotiation and compromise. Superficially at least, they appear to be a giant leap forward in making federalism more responsive, collaborative, and workable.

The Agreement on Internal Trade

Canada's governments were stung by the defeat of the Charlottetown Accord in 1992 and were understandably loath to go near the wasps' nest of constitutional change with any speed. However, governments (except Quebec) were still eager to make progress on the issues left outstanding by the Accord's defeat, but strictly outside of constitutional change. The Agreement on Internal Trade (AIT), signed in July of 1994, was just such a case. The AIT is in many ways a model for post-Charlottetown intergovernmental relations. Its primary goal is the elimination of barriers to trade and economic mobility between the provinces. The Agreement commits its signatories to the removal of economic barriers under a number of sectoral chapters on issues such as government procurement, labour mobility, or environmental protection. In the event that either a government or person wishes to challenge government policies as being in conflict with the commitments of the Agreement, there are provisions for dispute settlement.

These mechanisms are contained in Chapter 17 of the AIT. From the start, co-operation is signalled as the overriding principle to guide the process. The chapter provides for the general mechanism of dispute resolution, but refers all conflicts initially to chapter-specific methods of dispute avoidance. Before a government or person can engage the general mechanism, the relevant governments must first exhaust the negotiation, consultation and alternative dispute resolution mechanisms embodied in the sector specific chapters. These processes provide the government(s) involved with the opportunity to adjust policies or legislation to keep in tune with the commitments of the AIT. In this initial stage, a premium is placed on working out differences with a minimum of conflict and publicity. To that end, the sector chapters include fairly rigid deadlines meant to move claims through the process reasonably quickly. If disputes remain unresolved after the chapter specific processes, they may proceed to a more formal Chapter 17 resolution.

Disputes under the AIT are administered by the Internal Trade Secretariat, with the actual resolution process being overseen first by the Committee on Internal Trade (made up of ministers from the provinces and federal government) and then with appointed panels drawn from a roster maintained by the governments. Person-to-government disputes have an additional initial hurdle in the form of a pre-panel screening conducted by a roster-appointed screener who determines whether or not claims are simply vexatious or harassing. If the dispute cannot be settled by confidential consultation, a panel is struck. It follows procedures fairly analogous to those of a court, hearing briefs from both sides and releasing a written decision. The enforcement of panel rulings is voluntary. In the case of government-to-government conflicts, retaliatory actions are permitted.

The relatively weak enforcement mechanisms and the ad hoc nature of the panel process were necessitated by the provinces' objection to an independent 'third tier' institution or to the courts settling disputes under the AIT. Doern and Macdonald (1999: 140) associate this objection with the belief that the 'provinces were sovereign entities within a system of federalism and that no enforcement mechanism should be ceded'. The dispute resolution mechanism was structured to be 'clearly government driven and controlled rather than private-sector-access driven' (Ibid: 141). The Internal Trade Secretariat has tallied 49 disputes under the AIT as of January 2011. Less than 20 per cent of those disputes have proceeded to a formal panel resolution and only two non-government parties have initiated complaints (Internal Trade Secretariat, 2011). Anecdotally, the business press has labelled the dispute resolution mechanisms 'complex, inaccessible, expensive [and] time consuming' and 'frighteningly vulnerable to bureaucratic inertia' (Wahl, 2000: 62).

Given the initial onus in the AIT on negotiation and conciliation of disputes (really dispute avoidance), courts are probably not the best institution to perform such oversight. One provincial official described a mechanism for the federal government or the courts to get involved as 'thermonuclear' (Silcoff, 2000: C9). Since interpretation of the agreement is likely to involve trade-offs between permitted 'legitimate objectives' of governments and unduly restrictive barriers, governments are unwilling to trust the courts to make those trade-offs and, according to Swinton (1995: 203), 'remain reluctant to surrender their sovereignty to such a politically unaccountable body'. Douglas Brown (2002) notes similar hesitation on the part of governments to surrender too much authority to an independent secretariat or dispute resolution process, particularly by Ontario and Quebec. Alberta and the federal government, on the other hand, were enthusiastic about a more independent arbiter of such disputes and greater external enforceability of the agreement in general. In fact, the government of Alberta has been the AIT's biggest booster, unique among the provinces in publicly touting its benefits (Alberta, 2006). Alberta is involved in a disproportionate number of AIT complaints, and even touts a winning record of complaints resolved in favour of Albertans, which of course it claims as evidence that 'the dispute resolution process under the AIT has been effective in addressing trade-related complaints of Albertans'.

The quick and quiet resolution of disputes, with a 0.765 batting average, might seem cause for celebration, but it is not clear that Alberta is judging by the right measures. The 34 complaints that Alberta counts did not all engage AIT procedures. The Internal Trade Secretariat (2011) reports do not include all those enumerated by Alberta. Of the 49 disputes it reports, since 1995, 11 are listed as unresolved and inactive—some of those dating nearly to the agreement's conception. It may be the unresolved or difficult cases that are the truest test of the AIT's dispute resolution processes. One must look beyond Alberta's seemingly rosy experience to find such cases.

Unilever, a British multinational with Canadian operations based in Ontario, has actively challenged one of the more pernicious trade barriers in Canadian history, the ban on yellow margarine in Quebec. Justified as a measure to reduce consumer confusion between margarine and butter, the regulations have largely been designed to protect Quebec dairy products from inter-provincial competition. The ban on yellow margarine is exactly the kind of regulation and trade discrimination that the AIT was meant to get rid of. In 1997, Unilever sold several cases of yellow margarine to a Quebec distributor in violation of the act in order to test the legality of Quebec government regulations under the AIT. Under the dispute resolution provisions, the margarine producer must go through its home government to initiate a dispute against another province. While the company received some initial support from the province, Ontario was ultimately unwilling to pursue the case against its neighbour.

Faced with the unwillingness of the provincial government to do anything to engage the AIT process, Unilever sought redress in the regular court system, challenging the government of Quebec's constitutional authority to enact such regulations. It argued the regulations were inconsistent with both the AIT and freedom of expression guarantees in the Quebec Charter of Rights. Unilever lost at both the Quebec Court of Appeal and the Supreme Court of Canada. In a terse oral decision delivered within weeks of hearing arguments, the Supreme Court upheld the Quebec regulations as entirely within the legislative authority of the province. Further, it rejected Unilever's argument that the AIT precluded such a regulation, finding that 'provincial and international trade agreements have no effect on the validity of this provision'. Quebecers can now buy yellow margarine, as the legislature quietly changed the rule in the summer of 2008. Dairy producers consented to the change, citing the increased popularity of butter, which has made margarine less of a threat to the butter business, as well as a general decline in consumer confusion between the two products.

The case demonstrates the limits of internal enforceability of intergovernmental agreements. An inter-provincial agreement cannot supersede the authority that a province has under the constitution. The case also stands as the premier example of the lengths to which companies and individuals may have to go to assert their rights under the AIT should their provincial government prove a reluctant ally. As a large multinational, Unilever had the resources and incentive to launch such a challenge; for the smaller producer or manufacturer adversely affected by these kinds of barriers, the protections that they might seek are even more illusory under the AIT's structure. It should be no surprise, then, that the provinces, under the rubric of the Council of the Federation, agreed to a declaration enhancing the government to government dispute resolution chapter of the AIT in 2009 (Council of the Federation, 2009).

Social Union Framework Agreement

The Social Union Framework Agreement (SUFA) is the benchmark of post-Charlottetown intergovernmentalism. While it already seems passé among dedicated students of intergovernmental relations and is withering as governments seem less and less committed to its promises, the format and spirit of the agreement are still important signifiers of how intergovernmental relations get done in Canada. For example, section 6 of the Accord calls for new efforts to avoid and resolve disputes between governments. It commits governments 'to working collaboratively to avoid and resolve intergovernmental disputes' with 'maximum flexibility' to do so 'in a non-adversarial way'. Governments have differed strongly about how to implement the commitments of the section (Lazar, 2003). SUFA outlines no specific mechanism or approach for the settlement of disputes. Instead section 6 promotes a 'spirit' of dispute resolution marked by intense collaboration and avoidance of formal processes and third parties. Preference is given to quiet consultation and negotiation rather than reference to courts or tribunals as the means to resolve disputes. The Accord underwent an internally mandated three-year review in 2003 during which stakeholders from the policy community as well as provincial and territorial governments had the opportunity to report on its effectiveness. On dispute avoidance and resolution, the review's report points to the process initiated by governments in 2001–2 to deal with disputes under the *Canada Health Act* as the model for future mechanisms to implement section 6 (Federal/Provincial/Territorial Ministerial Council, 2003).

The Canada Health Act process

Despite its imperfections, the model of dispute resolution found in the AIT seems to be replicating itself in SUFA processes. In April of 2002, then federal Health minister Anne McLellan wrote to her provincial counterpart in Alberta, Gary Mar, outlining a dispute avoidance and resolution process for potential violations of the federal *Canada Health Act*. The act provides for financial penalties in the form of reduced federal transfer payments for provinces that fail to abide by the five principles of universal public health care outlined within it. Withholding funds for violations of the principles in the act is a unilateral federal decision. Funds are forthcoming to the provinces that abide by the conditions of the act, and funds are withheld from those who, in the federal Minister's opinion, have violated the conditions of the federal transfer.

Minister McLellan's letter outlined a process strikingly similar to the AIT dispute mechanisms. As in the AIT provisions, the initial emphasis is placed on dispute avoidance, facilitating information exchange and discussion in order to avoid the need for a formal resolution. If the dispute remains, the more formalized process begins with a letter from either Minister of Health to his/her counterpart. Panels are composed of one provincial representative and one federal representative who jointly choose a chairperson. The panel will undertake 'fact-finding and provide advice and recommendations' (McLellan, 2002). The final authority for the interpretation of the act and the implementation of penalties for non-compliance remains with the federal Minister, who may abide by or ignore the panel's interpretation of the facts, advice, or recommendations. The Minister pledges that governments will report publicly on any dispute, including the release of panel reports. There are presently no disputes reported by Health Canada, so the potential of the SUFA dispute settlement procedures remains theoretical. Nevertheless, Annual Reports on the Canada Health Act since 2006 have included an appendix outlining this process and seemingly committing the federal government to its use should it be necessary.

The panel provisions outlined in the McLellan/Mar correspondence nod toward the need for 'objective' decision-making in federal–provincial controversies, or the need for some third party to look at the details of a dispute. Ultimately the procedures contemplated in McLellan's promises undermine that objectivity. Panels might provide the political credibility that a federal minister needs to deny funding to provinces under the CHA, a practice that it has not rigorously engaged despite numerous provincial violations of the act (Flood and Choudhry, 2002; Choudhry, 1996). The extra ounce of credibility that a panel finding might give to a federal government interested in enforcing its own legislation seems little justification for the creation of an *ad hoc* process with minimal procedural guidance and permanent expertise in the resolution of such conflicts.

Conclusion: The Devil You Know

The judicial review of federalism is a difficult practice to defend. This volume's benchmarks of performance, effectiveness, and legitimacy provide some grounds for doing so. While judicial reasoning is not always as consistent or as objective as its practitioners may profess (and hence may lack legitimacy), the use of a judicial umpire is a relatively efficient and final (and thereby effective) mechanism for the resolution of intergovernmental disputes. Judicial power has become increasingly scrutinized by Canadians since the enactment of the Charter of Rights, but the practice of federal judicial review in Canada has a more muted political character than is generally true of other federal high courts (Baier, 2002), and engages seemingly less controversial issues than rights litigation. It is controversial, however, as the Supreme Court's power in the federation runs up against the incrementalist, pragmatic style favoured by intergovernmental relations.

Even if judicial review has a limited direct role in shaping the federation, the resources it assigns are still important to the settlement of intergovernmental issues. Judicial settlement of disputes is by its nature much more zero-sum than negotiation and compromise. For the most part only one party wins in any given constitutional litigation. While negotiation can overcome those results, judicial determinations have some influence on the bargaining power that participants have in the negotiations.

Hence, the effectiveness of judicial review has probably led governments to opt out of judicial settlement of disputes. Here we encounter a question of overall performance.

While judicial review is seen as generally legitimate and is effective, overall dispute resolution suffers from weak performance. The provinces, according to this thinking, are
right to be suspicious of the new umpires created in intergovernmental agreements or
leaving those agreements to the enforcement of the courts. But the creeping informal-
ism of Canadian federalism may not ultimately be to the advantage of the provinces or
of democracy. Federalism litigation is not as zero-sum as the participants may think. In
the recent cases discussed above, the Supreme Court's traditional role as an arbiter of the
division of powers only plays a part in the eventual outcome of an intergovernmental
policy dispute. If the Supreme Court cannot settle the dispute, what particular advantage
does it offer?

Its advantages are procedural ones. Judicial review, unlike the new mechanisms of
intergovernmental dispute resolution, offers actors other than governments an opportunity to be engaged and influential in the politics of intergovernmental relations. It also
reinforces the constitutional character of the federal order. It reminds governments that
the constitution, not intergovernmental compromise, is meant to be supreme. If intergovernmental agreements are all that holds the federation together, the federal order will
begin to be much more confederal, dependent upon the goodwill of governments rather
than the guarantees of the constitution.

Students of executive federalism have increasingly questioned the weak accountability and transparency of intergovernmental relations, and the undemocratic character of
executive federalism. As more and more of the business of Canadian federalism is done at
the executive level, the critique rings truer and truer. The emphasis on settling, avoiding
or amicably resolving disputes in the new collaborative federalism is certainly about pursuing noble goals of co-operation, but it is also about keeping the business of governing
and policy making strictly in the preserve of governments. This is poor performance for
the intergovernmental system. As Harvey Lazar (2003) has noted, 'differences among governments are normal and intergovernmental conflict can be constructive when it exposes
competing ideas to public deliberation'. Collaborative federalism, as it has been practised
in Canada, often tries to erase that advantage from the intergovernmental process.

Federalism litigation, we should not forget, is routinely commenced by individuals or
societal actors who disagreed with the enacting government's constitutional authority
to proceed as it had. Whether one agrees or disagrees with the position of Dr. Chaoulli,
his efforts to break into the closed club of health care policy making that is the intergovernmental protocol are a reminder of the limited opportunities for some parties to
get a hearing in a collaborative federalism world. More judicial review would improve
the performance of the intergovernmental dispute settlement system by truly opening up
intergovernmental relations to outsiders, that is to say, to actors other than governments.
Such opportunities to avail oneself of constitutional guarantees against governments
have all but disappeared in the dispute resolution mechanisms of contemporary federalism. Certainly the Charter of Rights provides an opportunity to hold intergovernmental
agreements to an individual rights standard, but the courts have proven fairly resistant,
Chaoulli notwithstanding, to second-guess the policy choices of legislatures in issues of
intergovernmental cooperation. Governments seem to prefer this limited oversight. The
Agreement on Internal Trade puts numerous hurdles in the way of individuals or interests who want to seek redress. Individuals find the process stacked against them, and the

agreement works efficiently to stop disputes before they happen. The bulk of the consultation and alteration that takes place stays confidential. How are interested publics to stay aware of what those negotiations sacrificed or committed? Dispute resolution in the AIT has simply exaggerated the already negative tendencies of executive federalism.

The SUFA is even less encouraging. SUFA provisions do not have nearly the detail of their AIT cousins or their relative institutionalization. The supposed annual reporting of dispute resolution is uneven to non-existent and may be nearly impossible to realize. As a public service primer on the SUFA notes, 'there is no formula for deciding that a dispute has occurred or been resolved' (CCMD Roundtable, 2002). The same primer tells managers to use prudence to determine when a dispute has been identified and settled and to report accordingly. Reference to third parties is possible, but not required, and governments determined to keep conflicts to themselves will be able to do so.

The genuine advantages of judicial review, whatever its faults, are lost in the new dispute resolution mechanisms. Perhaps what is most troubling to the defender of judicial involvement in federalism disputes is that some of these mechanisms resemble courts themselves. The panel decisions of the AIT have included dissenting opinions. While there is no basis for precedent, they do use legalistic language and encourage participants to present their cases in adversarial proceedings. Essentially these mechanisms trade on the seeming objectivity of courts.[5] Public opinion tells us that judges are still reasonably revered as impartial and independent. These new dispute settlement mechanisms give the appearance of being courts, but are without any of the strictures that condition the judicial mind. Nor are their decisions legally binding on the parties before them. One of the defining features of a federal constitution is the existence of a sovereignty that is neither wholly national nor regional. The constitution and its judicial umpires are meant to enforce the enshrined promises of the constitution, even when governments collectively seek to ignore or circumvent them. Both the AIT and the dispute resolution process under the *Canada Health Act* make a point of preserving governmental and ministerial discretion, respectively.

We have come full circle. Judicial review of federalism is avoided whenever possible because judges are depicted as either political or unpredictable, yet the institutional replacements seem most legitimate when they look most like courts. These pseudo-judicial institutions are effective for governments, but they perpetuate the legitimacy problems of executive federalism that are a perennial theme of Canadian federalism.

Notes

The author wishes to thank the editors for their enormously helpful comments and suggestions, and the Social Sciences and Humanities Research Council of Canada for financial support.

1. *Reference re: Amendment of the Constitution of Canada* (Patriation Reference) (1981), 125 D.L.R. 3rd; Re: A.G. Quebec and A.G. Canada (Quebec Veto Reference) (1982), 2 S.C.R. 793 and *Reference Re: Secession of Quebec* (1998), 2 S.C.R. 217.
2. *Employment and Social Insurance Reference* (1937), A.C. 355.
3. *Reference Re: Canada Assistance Plan* (1991), 83 D.L.R.(4th).
4. Sossin includes 'disputes involving intergovernmental relations' among the settings that stand outside the reach of judicial inquiry.

5. The offshore 'boundary' between Newfoundland and Labrador and Nova Scotia for the purposes of oil and gas development was essentially determined by a non-judicial tribunal which, while not a court, conducted a judicial-style proceeding to determine its recommendations to the federal Minister of Natural Resources. For a criticism of this process see (Baier and Groarke, 2003).h.

References

Alberta. 2006. 'Agreement on Internal Trade: Benefits for Albertans'. Available online at http://www.iir.gov.ab.ca/trade_policy/pdfs/5.3.2.1-Benefits_for_Albertans_Resolved_Complaints.pdf.

Baier, G. 2006. *Courts and Federalism: Judicial Doctrine in the United States, Australia and Canada*. Vancouver: UBC Press.

———. 2002. 'New Judicial Thinking on Sovereignty and Federalism: American and Canadian Comparisons', *Justice System Journal*, 23(1): 1–24.

———. 2002. 'Judicial Review and Federalism'. In *Canadian Federalism: Performance, Effectiveness and Legitimacy*, ed. H. Bakvis and G. Skogstad. Don Mills: Oxford.

——— and P. Groarke. 2003. 'Arbitrating a Fiction: The Nova Scotia/ Newfoundland and Labrador Boundary Dispute and Canadian Federalism', *Canadian Public Administration*, 46(3): 315–38.

Barker, P. 2000. 'Acceptable Law, Questionable Politics: The Canada Assistance Plan Reference'. In *Political Dispute and Judicial Review: Assessing the Work of the Supreme Court of Canada*, ed. H. Mellon and M. Westmacott. Scarborough: Nelson.

Brown, D.M. 2002. *Market Rules: Economic Union Reform and Intergovernmental Policy Making in Australia and Canada*. Kingston and Montreal: McGill–Queen's University Press.

Cairns, A. 1971. 'The Judicial Committee and Its Critics', *Canadian Journal of Political Science*, 4(3): 301–45.

Canada. 1994. *Agreement on Internal Trade*. Ottawa: Industry Canada.

———. 2000. *Social Union Framework Agreement*. Available online at http://www.socialunion.gc.ca.

CCMD Roundtable on the Implementation of the Social Union Framework Agreement. 2002. *Implementing the Social Union Framework Agreement: A Learning and Reference Tool*. Ottawa: Canadian Centre for Management Development.

Choudhry, S. 1996. 'The Enforcement of the Canada Health Act', *McGill Law Journal*, 41(2): 462–509.

Council of the Federation. 2009. *A Declaration regarding the Agreement on Internal Trade*. http://www.councilofthefederation.ca.

Cutler, F. 2004. 'Government Responsibility and Electoral Accountability in Federations', *Publius: The Journal of Federalism*, 34(2): 19–38.

Doern, G.B., and M. MacDonald. 1999. *Free-Trade Federalism: Negotiating the Agreement on Internal Trade*. Toronto: University of Toronto Press.

Federal/Provincial/Territorial Ministerial Council on Social Policy Renewal. 2003. *Three Year Review Social Union Framework Agreement*.

Flood, C., and S. Choudhry. 2002. Strengthening the Foundations: Modernizing the Canada Health Act. Discussion Paper No. 13, Royal Commission on the Future of Health Care in Canada.

Government of Quebec. 2006. Guaranteeing Access: Meeting the Challenges of Equity, Efficiency and Equality.

Hogg, P. 1979. 'Is the Supreme Court of Canada Biased in Constitutional Cases?', *Canadian Bar Review*, 57: 721–39.

Internal Trade Secretariat. 2005. *AIT Disputes-Summary Statistics*. Available online at http://ait-aci.ca/index_en/dispute.htm.

Laskin, B. 1951. 'The Supreme Court of Canada: A Final Court of and for Canadians?' *Canadian Bar Review*, 29: 1038–79.

Lazar, H. 2003. 'Managing Interdependencies in the Canadian Federation: Lessons from the Social Union Framework Agreement'. In *Constructive and Co-operative Federalism?* Kingston and Montreal: IIGR/ IRPP.

McLellan, A. 2002. 'Letter to Gary Mar' 2 Apr. Available online at http://www.gov.bc.ca/igrs/down/gary_mar_e.pdf.

Monahan, P. 1995. "To the Extent Possible': A Comment on Dispute Settlement in the Agreement on Internal Trade'. In *Getting There:*

An Assessment of the Agreement on Internal Trade, ed. M. Trebilcock and D. Schwanen. Toronto: CD Howe Institute.

Rosenberg, G. 1991. *The Hollow Hope: Can Courts Bring About Social Change?* Chicago: University of Chicago Press.

Russell, P. 1985. 'The Supreme Court and Federal Provincial Relations: The Political Use of Legal Resources', *Canadian Public Policy*, 11(2): 161–70.

Silcoff, S. 2000. 'Trade among provinces badly flawed, official says: internal trade deal. Ottawa urged to step in and end disputes'. *Financial Post*, 17 Oct., C1, C9.

Sossin, L.M. 1999. *Boundaries of Judicial Review: The Law of Justiciability in Canada*. Scarborough: Carswell.

Swinton, K. 1995. 'Law, Politics and the Enforcement of the Agreement on Internal Trade'. In *Getting There: An Assessment of the Agreement on Internal Trade*, ed. M. Trebilcock and D. Schwanen. Toronto: CD Howe Institute.

———. 1992. 'Federalism Under Fire: The Role of the Supreme Court of Canada', *Law and Contemporary Problems*, 55(1): 121–45.

Wahl, A. 2000. 'Trade Secrets: Why is nothing being done about interprovincial barriers', *Canadian Business*, 29 May, 73(10): 61–2.

Cases

Chaoulli v. Quebec (Attorney General), [2005] 1 S.C.R. 791.

Employment and Social Insurance Act Reference, [1937] A.C. 355.

Finlay v. Canada (Minister of Finance), [1986] 2 S.C.R. 607.

Finlay v. Canada (Minister of Finance) (1990), 71 D.L.R. (4th) 422 (Fed. C.A.).

Finlay v. Canada (Minister of Finance), [1993] 1 S.C.R. 1080.

Johannesson v. Municipality of West St. Paul, [1952] 1 S.C.R. 292.

Munro v. National Capital Commission, [1966] S.C.R. 663.

Pronto Uranium Mines Ltd. v. Ontario Labour Relations Board (1956), 5 D.L.R. (2nd) 342 (Ont. S.C.).

R. v. Crown Zellerbach Canada Ltd. (1988), 49 D.L.R. (4th) 161 (S.C.C.).

R. v. Hydro-Québec (1997), 151 D.L.R. (4th) 32 (S.C.C.).

Re Attorney General of Quebec and Attorney General of Canada (Quebec Veto Reference), [1982], 2 S.C.R. 793.

Re Resolution to amend the Constitution (Patriation Reference) (1981), 125 D.L.R. (3rd) 1 (S.C.C.).

Re Anti-Inflation Act (1976), 68 D.L.R. (3rd) 452 (S.C.C.).

Reference re Assisted Human Reproduction Act, 2010 SCC 61, [2010] 3 S.C.R. 457.

Reference re Canada Assistance Plan (B.C.) (1991), 83 D.L.R. (4th) 297 (S.C.C.).

Reference re Employment Insurance Act (Can.), ss. 22 and 23, [2005] 2 S.C.R. 669.

Reference re Firearms Act (Can.), [2000] 1 S.C.R. 783.

Reference re Offshore Mineral Rights, [1967] S.C.R. 792.

Reference re Secession of Quebec (1998), 161 D.L.R. (4th) 385 (S.C.C.).

UL Canada Inc. v. Quebec (Attorney General), [2005] 1 S.C.R. 143.

6 Federalism, Political Parties, and the Burden of National Unity: Still Making Federalism Do the Heavy Lifting?

Herman Bakvis and A. Brian Tanguay

Political parties perform a number of essential functions in liberal democratic societies: organizing electoral choices for citizens, representing interests, channelling political participation, and recruiting decision-makers for government are among the most important (King, 1969; Covell, 1991). In federal systems, parties are frequently called upon to perform another task, namely to unify the nation. In Canada, broad-based **brokerage parties** have long played a crucial nation-building role, constituting what David Smith called the 'sinews of a healthy federalism' (1985: 1). From Confederation right up to the Diefenbaker landslide of 1958, and despite the repeated emergence of regional protest parties from 1921 onward, the two main national parties continued to play this pivotal role, although with less success from the late 1950s onward. Voters in the western provinces, in particular, chafed under a series of governments—those of Pierre Trudeau, Brian Mulroney, and Jean Chrétien—seemingly dominated by central Canada. The election in 1993 of a Liberal government with close to two-thirds of its seats drawn from Ontario only served to heighten this perception. The rise of the Bloc Québécois in Quebec and the Reform party in the West constituted strong evidence that the party system had become both regionalized and fragmented. By 2011, when the bulk of the Liberal Party's elected members were drawn disproportionately from Ontario, and the Liberal party had ceased to play its historic role of a significant, if not dominant, centrist party, political parties no longer appear to constitute the 'sinews of a healthy federalism'.

Yet, between 2000 and 2011, the party system appeared to be taking a different turn. First, despite being discredited by scandal (quite likely the product of one-party dominance) and reduced to minority government status in 2004, the Liberal minority government led by Paul Martin appeared responsive to regional and other forces. Second, in 2004 the Canadian Alliance and Progressive Conservative parties merged, with Stephen Harper becoming leader of the new organization. Third, in 2006 the new Conservative party replaced the Liberal government, forming a minority government with a number of seats in Quebec and Ontario and a solid base in Western Canada. The Conservative Party held on to its Quebec seats in the 2008 federal election to form a second minority government. Finally, the Conservative party leadership had taken initiatives to recognize Quebec's unique place in Canada, including by advancing a 2006 parliamentary resolution that 'the Québécois form a nation within a united Canada'.

Optimism that minority government, by requiring inter-party bargaining and compromise, would see the federal parties playing a more prominent and unifying role in fostering agreement on federal–provincial issues (Baier, et al., 2005; Russell, 2008), had faded by the end of 2008. Prime Minister Harper jettisoned the 'Quebec strategy' on which his party's hopes for achieving a majority had initially depended. While the Conservatives held on to 10 seats in Quebec in the 2008 federal election, they were unable to extend their foothold much beyond their regional base in the Beauce and around Quebec City—precisely the same areas in which the *Action démocratique du Québec* (ADQ) once did so well provincially. Nor was this situation likely to change, given Harper's repeated demonization of the Bloc Québécois as separatists in the fall of 2008 as he manoeuvred to delegitimize the abortive Liberal–NDP coalition that formed in the wake of his government's budget update. Moreover, Harper's government exhibited an extreme version of control from the centre, limiting the scope of ministers from different parts of the country to impart a regional dimension to national policy-making. While the Conservatives have links with what remains of the old Mike Harris political machine in Ontario, Alberta Progressive Conservatives and elements of the provincial Liberal party in BC, these links are tenuous at best. The current Conservative government, in the lead up to the 2011 election, used the pork-barrel (e.g., infrastructure spending) in the best tradition of Liberal and Progressive Conservative governments past to target areas within key provinces. However, this practice has not been used by regional figures to bolster their power base. Finally, Harper's ideological rigidity on certain issues—law and order, for example, or the long-form census—has also undoubtedly limited the Conservative government's capacity to compromise.

The federal party system in the Harper era has not, however, been impervious to regional pressures. The Conservative government's rejection of the proposed hostile takeover of the Potash Corporation of Saskatchewan by an Australian firm, BHP Billiton Ltd, in November 2010 illustrated just how effective informal channels of federal–provincial bargaining could be in exerting pressure on a regional caucus within a federal party, and ultimately on governmental decision-makers themselves.

In 2011 support for the Liberals did indeed collapse, but so too did support for the Bloc Quebecois. Rather than further fragmentation, a majority Conservative government now faces a 103 seat official opposition in the form of the NDP, with more than half its seats from Quebec. In the space of a decade the party system appears to have shifted from one-party dominance to fragmentation to something akin to the two-and-a-half party system last seen in the 1980s. Could this new state of affairs since the 2011 election also mean that parties may once again constitute the 'sinews of a healthy federalism'?

This chapter poses three questions: Is there a renewed prospect of parties playing a more active role in carrying the burden of national unity, particularly now that we have two national parties and a less fragmented system? What can one reasonably expect of the two main parties in this respect, one of which, the NDP, has more than half its caucus in Quebec and is essentially new to the job both as a true national party and in the role of official opposition, and the other which has a clear majority but, for the first time in Canadian history, has a majority without support from Quebec? And, by extension, is the 'knitting' function of political parties in federal systems, as displayed in the 1960s and 1970s, once again relevant? The first part of the chapter examines some mechanisms through which parties perform 'knitting' functions and where they appear to fall short. The second part of the chapter discusses how the party system has performed in the past, its putative decline in the final decades of the last century, and now its possible revival. The concluding section addresses the performance, effectiveness, and legitimacy of the party system in relation to the Canadian federation and its future prospects.

A Parties-Based Theory of Federalism

As Campbell Sharman (1994) notes, there are three aspects to a 'parties-based theory of federalism', beginning with William Riker's concept of 'the federal bargain' (Riker, 1964). Riker argued that the degree of partisan symmetry–asymmetry in a federation determined the nature of the federal bargain and whether the federation was centralized or decentralized. A symmetrical party system, with the same parties operating at the national and state or provincial levels, would lead to a more centralized federation, especially if the link between the state and national parties was strong. A strong federal–provincial/state linkage was indicated if a party had a strong presence at both state and national levels, if the two levels shared many members in common, and if local elected officials typically moved up to the national level through the medium of the party. Most of Riker's work in this area was based on evidence from the United States, where the party system is in many ways more flexible and open than its Canadian counterpart.

The second aspect of parties-based federalism is the **intrastate dimension**: the representation of local and regional interests directly in national governance. The thinking here is that parties facilitate the representation of local and regional interests in national political institutions by providing conduits not only for communication but for flows of power, influence, and, above all, people: elected officials from the local and provincial/state arenas who move up to the national arena while maintaining their links with the former. This pattern has several advantages. Politicians starting their careers at the state level and aspiring to higher office at the national level know they must not appear too parochial: they must keep broader national perspectives in mind, and national ambitions reduce politicians' inclination to focus purely on local issues. At the same time, politicians at the national level who have local and regional experience under their belts are likely to be more understanding of the issues faced by local and regional governments (Barrie and Gibbins, 1989). Finally, although this does not bear directly on federalism, regional governments and parties can help national governments perform better by serving as talent pools from which national parties can recruit candidates for national office who have actual government experience.

Examining the degree of alignment between provincial and federal levels of Canadian parties in partisan support, party ideology, nominating procedures, and financial linkages, Donald Smiley argued that on Riker's integrated versus confederal dimension 'the Canadian party system is significantly more confederal than that of any other federation with which I am familiar' (1987: 117). He concluded that there was a disjunction between the federal and provincial party systems; for all intents and purposes the two party systems operated in two separate realms (see also Dyck, 1996). Nonetheless, Smiley and Ronald Watts (1985) argued that the federal cabinet, the most important manifestation of party government under the Westminster model, remains the only significant intrastate institution: that is, the only institution within the government of Canada capable of representing regional interests. Since the parties remain the primary source for the recruitment of cabinet ministers, they remain an important part of the equation, if only by default.

The third dimension of parties consists of the structure of party systems and the norms governing competition between them. William Chandler (1987) identified three types of party system: single party majority; multiparty with one party dominant; and coalition, where no single party has a majority and two or more parties constituting a majority of parliamentary seats form a coalition in order to make government work. The importance of these distinctions, according to Chandler, lies in the type of competition and relations between the parties. In the single party majority system, Chandler claims, highly adversarial relations are often the norm, especially in parliamentary systems. Multiparty systems with one party dominant can also be highly adversarial; the difference is that the dominant party may have a rather narrow base. Coalition-style systems are the least likely to be adversarial. For Chandler, the single-party majority system is the most problematic for federalism because adversarial norms are likely to undermine the collaborative norms necessary for the smooth functioning of the federation. The parties under this model would likely exacerbate rather than alleviate conflict between the national government and the constituent units. Chandler's point—that the combativeness between parties is essentially transplanted to the federal–provincial arena when 'federal and parliamentary traditions are combined within one regime' (1987: 156)—may help explain conflict between federal and provincial governments. Carty and Wolinetz (2004), also focusing on the 'coalition' model, concede that Canadian parties have long eschewed inter-party coalitions of the type typically found in European systems; yet 'their leaders regularly actively engage in bargaining and accommodative coalition-style politics in the federal–provincial decision-making arena' (Carty and Wolinetz, 2004: 67–8). They suggest that competitive behaviour at the level of parties is not necessarily transplanted directly into the federal–provincial arena.

Although the Canadian party system falls short on the three dimensions noted above, it does help to link regions to the centre and promote collaboration, though not necessarily in ways consistent with the standard theories of parties-based federalism.

Canada's Party System from 1867 to 2000: The Triumph of Regionalism

Since Canada's birth as a nation, regionalism has played a prominent role in federal politics. Until the middle of the First World War, however, these regional tensions were effectively contained within a competitive two-party system in which the governing party—the Conservatives, largely under John A. Macdonald, from 1867 to 1896 and the Liberals under Wilfrid Laurier from 1896 to 1911—forged a winning electoral coalition based on solid pluralities (often outright majorities) of the vote in the two most populous provinces, Ontario and Quebec. Together these two provinces accounted for between 60 and 75 per cent of the seats in the House of Commons, and no party was able to win national office without attracting the support of a solid core of moderate nationalist voters in Quebec. This pattern was not broken until the election of the pro-conscription Unionist government in 1917.

The compromises and concessions needed to make Canada a viable political and economic entity—fostering industrialization behind high tariff barriers, opening up the west to settlement, and providing the Maritimes with their own railroad and favourable freight rates, for example—smoothed over the fundamental divisions within the country. But regional economic grievances, coupled with rapid industrialization and urbanization in the early part of the twentieth century, shattered the two-party system and led to the development of a second national party system (English, 1977; Carty, 1988). Between 1921 and 1925 the balance of power was held by the Progressives, the first in a long line of regional protest parties—including the Co-operative Commonwealth Federation (CCF) and Social Credit in the 1930s—that challenged the dominant parties' monopoly on representation. Although these newer minor parties did not necessarily hold the balance of power, they nonetheless articulated the economic, political, and cultural grievances of particular regions and social classes within Confederation (Gagnon and Tanguay, 1996; Mallory, 1954).

The two most successful prime ministers in this second party system, Mackenzie King and Louis St Laurent, contained the challenge to the established political and economic order posed by the regional protest parties. Both party leaders—but King in particular—were astute practitioners of the art of **brokerage** politics, the pragmatic cobbling together of party programs designed to appeal to a broad coalition of diverse interests. King, for instance, limited the effectiveness of the Progressives as the voice of agrarian protest by buying off some of the movement's leaders (most notably T.A. Crerar) with cabinet posts and implementing relatively minor reforms of federal tariff and freight rate policies. By the late 1920s the Progressives were a spent force in federal politics.

King and St Laurent also moderated regional conflict within the party system by stocking their respective cabinets with influential regional chieftains—men like J.G. (Jimmy) Gardiner (former premier of Saskatchewan), C.D. Howe (Ontario), and Ernest Lapointe (Quebec). These figures gave direct representation to broader provincial and regional interests in the Canadian cabinet. King frequently paid heed to the views and advice of these ministers on regional matters, and was particularly dependent on Lapointe for counsel on virtually all matters relating to Quebec. This brokerage system of party politics was far from complete, however, since some provinces, such as Alberta, were simply frozen out of the arrangement. The Maritimes were represented in cabinet by figures such as J.-E. Michaud from New Brunswick, and J.L. Ilsley and Angus L. Macdonald from Nova Scotia, the latter a former premier of his province. However, these maritime ministers carried very little weight in cabinet; Macdonald, for example, was continually out-manoeuvred by C.D. Howe on matters affecting Nova Scotia (Bakvis, 1991). Nonetheless, the system worked—in large part because the ministers in question were able to deliver votes and seats at election time. Two changes were afoot, however. First, while the patronage system declined following the Civil Service Reform Act of 1918, it was replaced in good part by the pork-barrel in the form of large-scale government contracts awarded to favoured regions (Noel, 2001). The new regional barons allowed the Liberal party's connections with the constituencies to atrophy (Whitaker, 1977).

Second, in the post-war period regional brokering was largely displaced by the 'pan-Canadian' approach of John Diefenbaker and, later, Pierre Elliott Trudeau (Smith, 1985). The arrival of television in the mid-1950s sharpened the focus on national leaders and helped make regional power brokers less critical in the conduct of election campaigns and delivery of the vote.

The electoral defeats suffered by the federal Liberals in 1957 and 1958 laid the groundwork for this third, 'pan-Canadian' system. It was less accommodating of regional interests than its two predecessors. The policies pursued by each successive prime minister were shaped by a centralizing vision of the country, even if some leaders (Diefenbaker) were more sensitive to regional concerns than others (Trudeau). Diefenbaker's concept of 'One Canada' and his Bill of Rights drew attention to the formal equality of all citizens and 'appealed to Canadians as Canadians regardless of where they lived or what language they spoke' (Smith, 1985: 27). Lester B. Pearson's national medicare program, the Canada Pension Plan, and the Royal Commission on Bilingualism and Biculturalism, along with Trudeau's Official Languages Act, National Energy Program (NEP), and Charter of Rights and Freedoms were even more centralizing in nature. Trudeau's pan-Canadian policies in many ways failed to unite the country, leaving a significant proportion of Quebec feeling betrayed and creating animosity towards Ottawa in many other regions (McRoberts, 1997). Official bilingualism and the National Energy Program antagonized the western provinces, and though Trudeau's constitutional reforms may have struck a responsive chord in some parts of English Canada, they alienated Quebec and provided fertile soil for the later growth of the sovereignist movement.

The pan-Canadian thrust of federal economic and social policy from 1957 to 1984 was paralleled by the development of an increasingly regionalized party system. The two main parties drew the bulk of their electoral support from one or two regional strongholds, as did the CCF–NDP. None of these organizations was actually a national party with solid cross-country support. Except in 1968, the Liberals in this period managed to win elections mainly because of their pre-eminence in Quebec, where they typically won between 75 and 99 per cent of the available seats. However, the Liberals were virtually shut out in the west: in 1980 they won only 2.5 per cent of the region's seats, which accounted for 1.4 per cent of the governing caucus. The Liberals' woes in the west were mirrored by the Conservatives' failure to make any electoral headway in Quebec. In 1979 Joe Clark formed a minority government with only 1.5 per cent of his caucus drawn from Quebec.

This regional fragmentation was exaggerated by the well-known effects of Canada's **first-past-the-post electoral system**. For example, even though the Progressive Conservatives managed to win at least 13 per cent of the popular vote in Quebec in the five elections held between 1968 and 1980, this electoral support consistently translated into 2 or 3 seats at most (Tanguay, 1999). The problems thereby created were compounded by conscious party electoral strategy. Party officials tended to direct the bulk of their limited organizational and financial resources to those regions in which they stood the best chance of winning. In the case of the Liberals after their crushing defeat in 1958, when Diefenbaker's Conservatives won the biggest landslide in Canadian history, the party's structures were centralized; new candidates were attracted into the fold; new campaign techniques modelled on American practices were adopted (improved use of television and opinion polling, for example); and the focus of the party's electoral appeal was shifted to the urban ridings in British Columbia, Ontario, and Quebec, rural voters being more or less conceded to the populist Diefenbaker (Wearing, 1981).

Thus it is commonplace to depict the evolution of the Canadian party system in linear fashion—from patronage to brokerage to pan-Canadianism and then into a spiral of ever-increasing regionalization—and to see the Mackenzie King period in particular as the heyday of a cohesive Canadian federation brought together through a well-integrated Liberal party. Yet this depiction is not entirely accurate. First, the integration was far from complete. As R.K. Carty (2002: 726) has noted, success in bringing all regions into the fold can be a dangerous thing: major crises affecting the Canadian party system 'have typically arisen when an overreaching national party collapsed under the strain of trying to accommodate the conflicting demands of too many interests gathered into a political omnibus'. Carty points to the eventual collapse of the all-encompassing coalitions constructed by Robert Borden, John Diefenbaker, and Brian Mulroney as a warning that 'successful brokerage parties . . . have to be careful not to actually catch all the interests' (ibid.). The Mackenzie King coalition was successful precisely because it was more limited in scope. In brief, the construction of all-encompassing coalitions *within* national parties was a rare occurrence and often fatal over time.

The Mulroney government also illustrates that change was far from linear. The cabinet formed in 1984 was a throwback to an earlier era, centred on ministers with a strong presence in key regions: John Crosbie from Newfoundland, who dominated the Atlantic region; Donald Mazankowski from Alberta; and (for a while) Lucien Bouchard as Mulroney's Quebec lieutenant. Furthermore, Mulroney's style was more reminiscent of Mackenzie King than of Diefenbaker or Trudeau. Even during the Trudeau period, however, regional representation in cabinet—the intrastate dimension—was far from absent. Though mere shadows of the old regional barons under King and St Laurent, regional ministers continued to perform, and arguably still perform, important representational functions. After the Liberals suffered near-defeat in the federal election of 1972, for example, the party resurrected the role of 'political ministers', one for each province, and gave them responsibility for allocating pork-barrel type funding as well as patronage and party organizational matters in their respective provinces. In the 1980s even unelected ministers, such as senators Hazen Argue in Saskatchewan and H.A. (Bud) Olson in Alberta, exercised considerable influence over the disbursement of infrastructure and regional development funds (Bakvis, 1991).

In addition to dealing with party matters, however, these new-style regional ministers were critical conduits for provincial governments. In the Maritimes, Trudeau-era figures such as Roméo LeBlanc and Allan J. MacEachen interacted on a regular basis with the premiers of New Brunswick and Nova Scotia respectively. In effect this interaction came through necessity. Many of the projects promoted by political ministers (and their colleagues)—new roads, bridges, educational institutions, and the like—fall under provincial jurisdiction. Persuading a provincial government to construct a new bridge in a regional minister's federal riding, for example, usually involved some kind of quid quo pro, such as federal funding for a project high on the list of provincial priorities.

Prime Minister Chrétien continued the practice of appointing regional ministers; Brian Tobin was an especially adroit and influential minister for Atlantic Canada. And by the fall of 2006 it appeared that the cabinet system set up by the new Harper government, with the operations committee playing a central role in handling sensitive political issues and political ministers designated for each of the provinces, essentially replicated the Mulroney-era model. However, over the intervening five years, while there have been some ministers with more public visibility than others, such as Finance Minister James Flaherty, John Baird, Jason Kenney, and Tony Clement, none has had the stature or autonomy of a Donald Mazankowski or John Crosbie in the Mulroney cabinet or a Brian Tobin in the Chrétien cabinet.

Ministers in the Harper cabinet have, however, helped to manage and promote the visibility of the flow of funds from the 2009 $60 billion Economic Action Plan stimulus package launched in 2009 and through the earlier Building Canada infrastructure program (Curry, 2011; Bakvis et al., 2009). A joint investigative report by the Halifax *Chronicle-Herald* and the Ottawa *Citizen* found that infrastructure projects were directed disproportionately to Conservative ridings both in terms of numbers and size of the projects, particularly in Quebec and the Maritimes. In Ontario there was less of an imbalance between Conservative and other ridings, though infrastructure project funds were targeted to the 905 ridings in the Greater Toronto Area where the Conservatives hoped to make gains in the next election (Maher and McGregor, 2009). In Nova Scotia regional minister Peter MacKay played the role of interlocutor between Ottawa and the provincial government. However, much of the strategic decision-making about the 'clustering' of federal spending in different parts of the country is orchestrated primarily out of Ottawa, suggesting that the regional minister system has been supplanted in part by the relentless concentration of executive power under Harper, facilitated by newer technologies, that bypass regional notables (Taber, 2010).

The regional caucuses of the parties constitute another dimension of intrastate activity. All parties with more than one MP per province or region have a regional caucus, which tends to be dominated by the regional or political minister. Paul Thomas, in a study conducted in the 1980s, noted that these regional parliamentary party caucuses tended to be skewed in the direction of 'allocation responsiveness' (i.e., 'generalized benefits for their constituencies'), as opposed to 'symbolic' or 'policy responsiveness' (Thomas, 1985: 74). Nonetheless, regional caucuses will weigh in on broader issues. One flaw with this kind of regional representation at the centre is its focus on the pork-barrel. Another is that not only allocational activities but also broader representational activities tend to take place under the cloak of caucus secrecy (Thomas, 1985). As a result—even though it is a fundamental principle of political representation that politicians must be seen to be working in the interests of their constituents—the efforts of MPs and ministers on behalf of their provinces will often not be known or visible to the public. Even so, party discipline and caucus secrecy have not prevented either ministers or MPs from publicly voicing concerns if they feel important provincial interests are at stake. John Crosbie, the Atlantic regional minister in the Mulroney cabinet, famously rebuked the prime minister and extracted a public apology from the deputy prime minister over a proposed Canada–France fisheries treaty that, in the eyes of Crosbie and the government of his province, would have compromised the cod stocks and other species off Newfoundland (Crosbie, 1997: 261–6). And in the summer of 2006 the Chair of the Saskatchewan Conservative party caucus publicly warned his leader, Prime Minister Stephen Harper, that the Conservative party would face significant damage if the government did 'not stick to the initial promise to exclude non-renewable resources such as oil and gas from the equalization formula' (*Globe and Mail*, 2006). In the fall of 2010, when BHP Billiton made a take-over bid for Saskatchewan-based Potash Corporation, the 13 government MPs were reportedly very nervous about having to explain a possible decision to approve the take-over to their constituents (Chase and McCarthy, 2010). While the prime minister may have been more anxious about the wrath of the premier of Saskatchewan and its effect on Saskatchewan voters, particularly with respect to the proposed takeover of the Potash Corporation, than pressure from his MPs in that province, there is no doubt that caucus still provides an important channel in exerting regional pressure on the centre.

In summary, the basic system of regional ministers and caucuses has evolved and changed, and to some extent it is still in place though under Stephen Harper it has become attenuated. Yet, even in the present era of 'governing from the centre' (Savoie, 1999), regional representation still has some meaning. When a governing party's regional representation in Parliament is uneven, it will tend to be much more balanced in cabinet. Thus, while Quebec currently provides only 3.0 per cent of the Conservatives' seats in Parliament (5 out of 166), just over 10 per cent of Harper's ministers come from that province.

Table 6.1 presents data on regional representation in both Parliament and cabinet since 1867. Note that where regional representation is lacking in Parliament, the difference is almost always compensated for in cabinet. The quality and impact of that representation

Table 6.1 Regional Representation in Government Caucus and Federal Cabinet

General election	Governing party[1]	% of seats from (# of seats)					% of cabinet positions from (# of cabinet positions)			
		West[2]	Ont.	Que.	Atl.	Total[3]	West	Ont.	Que.	Atl.
1867	Liberal-Cons	—	47.0 (47)	45.0 (45)	8.0 (8)	13	—	38.5 (5)	30.8 (4)	30.8 (4)
1872	Conservative	7.1 (7)	38.4 (38)	39.4 (39)	15.2 (15)	13	7.7 (1)	38.5 (5)	23.1 (3)	30.8 (4)
1874	Liberal	1.5 (2)	47.8 (65)	25.7 (35)	25.0 (34)	14	—	35.7 (5)	28.6 (4)	35.7 (5)
1878	Conservative	5.1 (7)	44.6 (62)	33.8 (47)	16.5 (23)	14	—	35.7 (5)	28.6 (4)	35.7 (5)
1882	Conservative	6.5 (9)	40.3 (56)	36.7 (51)	16.5 (23)	14	—	42.9 (6)	28.6 (4)	28.6 (4)
1887	Conservative	10.3 (13)	43.7 (55)	26.2 (33)	19.8 (25)	15	—	33.3 (5)	33.3 (5)	33.3 (5)
1891	Conservative	11.1 (13)	38.9 (46)	23.7 (28)	26.3 (31)	14	7.1 (1)	35.7 (5)	28.6 (4)	28.6 (4)
1896	Liberal	7.6 (9)	36.9 (44)	41.2 (49)	14.3 (17)	14	7.1 (1)	28.6 (4)	35.7 (5)	28.6 (4)
1900	Liberal	7.7 (10)	27.7 (36)	44.6 (58)	20.0 (26)	16	6.3 (1)	37.5 (6)	31.3 (5)	25.1 (4)

Table 6.1 (continued)

General election	Governing party[1]	% of seats from (# of seats)				Total[3]	% of cabinet positions from (# of cabinet positions)			
		West[2]	Ont.	Que.	Atl.		West	Ont.	Que.	Atl.
1904	Liberal	14.6 (20)	27.7 (38)	38.7 (53)	19.0 (26)	16	12.5 (2)	37.5 (6)	31.3 (5)	18.8 (3)
1908	Liberal	13.5 (18)	27.8 (37)	39.1 (52)	19.6 (26)	14	14.3 (2)	35.7 (5)	28.6 (4)	21.4 (3)
1911	Conservative	13.6 (18)	54.6 (72)	19.7 (26)	12.1 (16)	18	22.2 (4)	38.9 (7)	27.8 (5)	11.1 (2)
1917	Unionist	36.0 (54)	48.0 (72)	2.0 (3)	14.0 (21)	22	27.3 (6)	40.9 (9)	18.2 (4)	13.6 (3)
1921	Liberal	5.2 (6)	17.2 (20)	56.0 65)	21.6 (25)	19	15.8 (3)	31.6 (6)	31.6 (6)	21.1(4)
1925	Conservative	18.4 (21)	58.8 (67)	2.6 (3)	20.2 (23)	14	21.4 (3)	14.3 (2)	57.1 (8)	7.1 (1)
1926	Liberal	21.4 (25)	18.8 (22)	52.1 (61)	7.7 (9)	18	27.8 (5)	22.2 (4)	38.9 (7)	11.1 (2)
1930	Conservative	22.6 (31)	43.1 (59)	17.5 (24)	16.8 (23)	19	21.1 (4)	36.8 (7)	26.3 (5)	15.8 (3)
1935	Liberal	20.3 (35)	32.6 (56)	32.6 (56)	14.5 (25)	16	25.0 (4)	25.0 (4)	31.3 (5)	18.7 (3)
1940	Liberal	23.9 (43)	31.1 (56)	34.4 (62)	10.6 (19)	18	27.8 (5)	27.8 (5)	27.8 (5)	16.6 (3)
1945	Liberal	15.6 (19)	27.9 (34)	40.9 (50)	15.6 (19)	20	20.0 (4)	35.0 (7)	30.0 (6)	15.0 (3)
1949	Liberal	22.0 (42)	28.8 (55)	35.6 (68)	13.6 (26)	21	19.0 (4)	33.3 (7)	28.6 (6)	19.0 (4)
1953	Liberal	15.9 (27)	29.4 (50)	38.8 (66)	15.9 (27)	20	25.0 (5)	30.0 (6)	30.0 (6)	15.0 (3)
1957	Pcon	20.3 (23)	54.0(61)	7.1 (8)	18.6 (21)	22	36.4 (8)	31.8 (7)	13.6 (3)	18.2 (4)
1958	Pcon	31.6 (66)	32.5 (68)	23.9 (50)	12.0 (25)	23	30.4 (7)	30.4 (7)	21.8 (5)	17.4 (4)
1962	Pcon	42.2 (49)	30.2 (35)	12.1 (14)	15.5 (18)	21	33.3 (7)	33.3 (7)	19.0 (4)	14.3 (3)
1963	Liberal	7.8 (10)	39.8 (51)	36.7 (47)	15.6 (20)	26	15.4 (4)	38.4 (10)	30.8 (8)	15.4 (4)
1965	Liberal	6.9 (9)	38.9 (51)	42.7 (56)	11.5 (15)	26	11.5 (3)	34.6 (9)	34.6 (9)	11.5 (3)
1968	Liberal	18.2 (28)	40.9 (63)	36.4 (56)	4.5 (7)	29	20.7 (6)	34.5 (10)	34.5 (10)	10.3 (3)
1972	Liberal	6.4 (7)	33.0 (36)	51.4 (56)	9.2 (10)	30	13.3 (4)	40.0 (12)	33.3 (10)	13.3 (4)

Table 6.1 (continued)

General election	Governing party[1]	% of seats from (# of seats)					% of cabinet positions from (# of cabinet positions)			
		West[2]	Ont.	Que.	Atl.	Total[3]	West	Ont.	Que.	Atl.
1974	Liberal	9.2 (13)	39.0 (55)	42.6 (60)	9.2 (13)	29	13.8 (4)	34.5 (10)	37.9 (11)	13.8 (4)
1979	Pcon	43.4 (59)	41.9 (57)	1.5 (2)	13.2 (18)	30	30.0 (9)	40.0 (12)	13.3 (4)	16.7 (5)
1980	Liberal	1.4 (2)	35.4 (52)	50.3 (74)	12.9 (19)	33	12.1 (4)	36.4 (12)	36.4 (12)	15.1 (5)
1984	Pcon	28.9 (61)	31.8 (67)	27.5 (58)	11.8 (25)	40	32.5 (13)	27.5 (11)	27.5 (11)	12.5 (5)
1988	Pcon	28.4 (48)	27.2 (46)	37.3 (63)	7.1 (12)	33	24.2 (8)	33.3 (11)	30.3 (10)	12.1 (4)
1993	Liberal	16.4 (29)	55.4 (98)	10.7 (19)	17.5 (31)	23	21.7 (5)	43.5 (10)	21.7 (5)	13.1 (3)
1997	Liberal	11.0 (17)	65.2 (101)	16.7 (26)	7.1 (11)	28	17.6 (5)	42.9 (12)	25.0 (7)	14.3 (4)
2000	Liberal	9.4 (16)	58.5 (100)	21.1 (36)	11.1 (19)	28	17.6 (5)	42.9 (12)	25.0 (7)	14.3 (4)
2004	Liberal	11.9 (16)	55.2 (74)	15.6 (21)	17.1 (23)	38	23.6 (9)	39.4 (15)	21.0 (8)	15.7 (6)
2006	Con	53.2 (66)	31.4 (39)	8.0 (10)	7.3 (9)	27	40.7 (11)	33.3 (9)	18.5 (5)	11.1 (3)
2008	Con	48.2 (69)	35.7 (51)	7.7 (11)	7.7 (11)	38	42.1 (16)	31.6 (12)	13.1 (5)	10.5 (4)
2011	Con	44.6 (74)	44.0 (73)	3.0 (5)	8.4 (14)	39	38.5 (15)	38.5 (15)	10.3 (4)	12.8 (5)

1. Upper-case = majority government; lower-case = minority government.
2. 'West' includes NWT, Yukon, and Nunavut.
3. Size of cabinet for the year of each general election includes changes occurring up to and including 31 December of that year (i.e., includes the last ministerial shuffles for each portfolio but does not include portfolios terminated in that year).

Source: Guide to Canadian Ministries since Confederation (Canada: Privy Council Office, 2009); Senators and Members—Historical Information (Canada: Library of Parliament, 2006). http://webinfo.parl.gc.ca/MembersOfParliament/CustomizableReports.aspx?Subject=1&Language=E; The Canadian Ministry (Canada: Privy Council, May 18, 2011).

can vary considerably, depending on the ministers, including the prime minister, in question. However, even the supposedly centralized cabinet of Jean Chrétien included some powerful regional personalities. In the Canadian context, cabinet government also means party government, and the political parties are still the primary source of recruits for the cabinet. In short, cabinet and party are inextricably linked.

From Chrétien to Harper: From One-Party Dominance to Hyper-Regionalism to Two-and-a-Half Party System

The 1993 election was a watershed. The collapse of the Progressive Conservative government was unprecedented in Canadian electoral history. The rise of the **Reform Party** in the West and the Bloc Québécois in Quebec, with both parties vying for the mantle of her majesty's official opposition, and the fact that the Liberals drew the bulk of their seats from Ontario with only spotty representation from other regions of the country, suggested that the regionalization of the party system had entered a new and dangerous phase. While the Liberals could claim representation from all regions of the country, most of their 19 Quebec seats came from Montreal ridings with heavy concentrations of anglophones and non-francophone minorities; the BQ, overwhelmingly, was the voice of francophone Quebec. As well, the Reform Party was clearly the first choice of voters in the two most disaffected western provinces, Alberta and British Columbia.

The Parti Québécois returned to power in Quebec City in 1994, and when it held the second referendum in 15 years in the fall of 1995, the No side won with only the slimmest of margins. After the crisis of the referendum, the Chrétien government governed much as previous Liberal governments had: from the centre, finding informal ways to accommodate Quebec's demands. Especially after Chrétien's third victory in 2000, when the Liberals made gains in Quebec at the expense of the Bloc (Tanguay, 2006), it appeared that Canada's '**government party**' had successfully revived its traditional formula and was now poised to extend its benign dictatorship (Simpson, 2001) indefinitely into the twenty-first century (Tanguay, 2003).

There were some crucial differences from the past, however. The regional coalitions under King, St Laurent, and Mulroney had had three components: Quebec, Ontario, and the West (usually a single province such as Alberta or Saskatchewan). In the Chrétien era Ontario for the first time became the Liberals' single stronghold. Aside from the fact that the principal voices from Quebec and the West represented not a competing national party but two distinct regional parties (Reform in the West and the nationalist Bloc in Quebec), there were two other features serving to undermine the role of the Liberal party as a broker of regional interests.

First, the Liberals' total dominance in Ontario and, in turn, the domination of the parliamentary party by the Ontario Liberal caucus, proved in many ways a good illustration of Chandler's thesis that party competition in a single-party majority (i.e., Westminster) system can exacerbate conflict in a federal system. Essentially, the 100-plus members of the Ontario federal Liberal caucus took it on themselves to do battle with the controversial Conservative provincial government of Mike Harris. Federal ministers such as Sheila Copps at times undermined negotiations between Ottawa and the Ontario government on issues such as labour-market development because they were unwilling to see federal dollars transferred to, and spent by, a provincial government with a reputation for slashing social programs. As a result, Ontario was the only province with which Ottawa was unable to negotiate a labour-market development agreement in 1997 (Bakvis, 2002).

Two other factors that ultimately undermined the Liberal party were directly related to its dominance and the absence of an effective opposition. First, when a single party is so dominant that it represents the only route to political power, factions begin to form within it. In the Liberal party factionalism took the form of a bitter conflict between Chrétien loyalists and supporters of his Finance minister, Paul Martin, who had lost the race for the party leadership to Chrétien in 1990.

Second, a dominant party facing a weak or fragmented opposition is almost certain to develop pockets of corruption. In the Liberal case the corruption manifested itself in what has become known as the sponsorship scandal. It involved inflated contracts for government advertising, primarily in Quebec, as part of the national unity campaign that Ottawa launched in the aftermath of the 1995 referendum. Allegations that some of the money attached to these contracts was being kicked back to members of the federal Liberal party in Quebec were subsequently upheld by the Auditor General and the results of a full-scale judicial inquiry under Justice John Gomery. The Gomery inquiry was just beginning its work at the time of the 2004 election, but the scandal likely cost the new Liberal leader, Paul Martin, his majority. The crisis only deepened as Quebecers—outraged to learn that the Liberals had thought they could win support for the federalist option with a few Canadian flags—watched the proceedings of the Gomery Inquiry unfold on television.

The election of January 2006 saw the Conservatives not only break through in Ontario but win 10 seats in Quebec. The Bloc failed to make significant gains, falling short of the high-water mark of 54 seats won in 1993. With the Liberals at 102 seats and the Conservatives at 125, Paul Martin, following the peculiarly Canadian convention on minority governments, turned in his mandate to the governor general, who duly invited Stephen Harper to form a minority government. In addition to signifying that one-party dominance was not necessarily a permanent feature of the Canadian party system, the election of 2006 demonstrated that it was still possible for a second national party to gain a significant foothold in the province of Quebec.

There were some other noteworthy features to the new 2006 Conservative minority government. No fewer than seven of Harper's 27 ministers had served in provincial cabinets—one of the highest proportions ever, not seen since the days of Macdonald and Laurier. In addition to bringing some of their provincial sensibilities to the cabinet table, they also brought the new government hands-on and recent experience in elected office. This feature clearly fits the Riker model of an integrated party system, in which personnel moving from the regional to the national level bring with them a number of positive attributes. It is also a feature that, as Smiley (1987) and Barrie and Gibbins (1989) have argued, has been largely absent from the Canadian party system.

Also notable was the presence in cabinet of no fewer than five representatives from Quebec, including Lawrence Cannon, who had served in the Liberal cabinet of Robert Bourassa, and Josée Verner, who was also closely associated with the Bourassa government as an adviser in the 1980s. Half (14) of Harper's ministers came from Ontario and Quebec, a proportion that reflected the weight of central Canada electorally and in the federal system and the Conservatives' desire to consolidate their electoral gains in those two provinces. The electoral result of 2006 seemed to offer the Conservatives an opportunity to both broaden their base and make further inroads into the key provinces of Ontario and Quebec. Subsequent developments, whether through deliberate design, poor judgment, or an unfortunate series of events, prevented the Conservatives from capitalizing on their 2006 results.

When the Conservatives were returned with a minority in the fall 2008 election, they retained 10 seats in Quebec in 2008 but failed to make their hoped-for breakthrough into the voter-rich suburbs around Montreal. Relations with the province deteriorated following the 2008 election and the events around Finance Minister Jim Flaherty's budget update. The update ignored the need for stimulus spending to counteract the deepening global financial crisis and also proposed to eliminate the $1.95 per vote public subsidy to federal political parties winning at least 2 per cent of the popular vote (or 5 per cent in those ridings in which they fielded candidates). Had such a proposal been implemented, it would likely have crippled the three main opposition parties (and the nascent Green Party as well), leaving the Conservatives, which have been much more successful than their competitors in raising money from modest individual donations, with an enormous strategic advantage over their competitors (Johnson, 2009: 29). This provocative move galvanized the opposition. High-level negotiations among the Liberals, NDP, and the Bloc lead to an agreement among the three parties to defeat the Harper government in the House of Commons in the budget vote and to replace it with a coalition government between the Liberals and the NDP, supported by the Bloc.

Faced with the prospect of being defeated in the House of Commons by a vote of non-confidence in November, 2008, and the possibility of being replaced by a Liberal–NDP coalition led by Stéphane Dion, Harper employed what was seen at the time as a desperate political manoeuvre (Russell and Sossin, 2009): he requested that Governor-General Michaëlle Jean prorogue Parliament, even though the session had barely begun. Jean acceded to his demand. During the 'timeout' provided by **prorogation**, Harper, his advisers, and prominent cabinet ministers worked tirelessly to convince public opinion that the coalition, by virtue of being contingent on the support of the Bloc, would put the separatists directly in the seat of power in Ottawa. While public opinion in English Canada was more or less swayed by Conservative arguments, this was not true within Quebec where the potential role of the Bloc with respect to a possible Liberal–NDP coalition was seen in quite a different light.

In brief, the 2008 election and the prorogation that followed later that year brought to a standstill the Conservatives' foray in Quebec and their longer term strategy of building a sufficiently large base in the province to form a majority government. The prorogation also resulted in a further deterioration of trust within the House of Commons and heightened what was already a highly charged partisan atmosphere.

In one respect the loss by the Conservatives of five of its 10 seats in the 2011 election was not surprising. Nor was the collapse of the Liberals in Ontario. What was surprising was the collapse of the Bloc Québécois and the meteoritic rise of the NDP in that province so that in addition to obtaining 103 seats overall, more than half of the NDP's tally came from Quebec. With the majority Conservative government and the NDP as official opposition together constituting over 87 per cent of the seats in the House, the system appears, in a single election, to have reverted back to something akin to the two-and-a-half party system of years gone by. In this new state of affairs arising out of the 2011 election, could the parties once again constitute the 'sinews of a healthy federalism'?

Performance, Effectiveness, and Legitimacy

Before turning to our three thematic criteria and the above question, let us briefly review our conclusions so far. First, the party system of the past may not always, indeed may never, have performed the role attributed to it. The party omnibus was far from all-encompassing, and when all regions of the country have been represented within a single major party, the results are often calamitous, as Carty (2002) has argued. Party government appeared to work best when it took the form of a minimum winning coalition with three anchors in critical regions of the country.

In the absence of an elected or provincially appointed second chamber, with an electoral system that routinely produces wide discrepancies between popular votes and seats, the institution that makes the system work has always been the federal cabinet. Regional representation in cabinet was the critical link in the eras of both Macdonald and King. When a governing party's regional representation in Parliament is uneven, that imbalance can be compensated for in cabinet.

At a minimum it would be unwise to assume there was ever a halcyon period when parties played a more critical role in linking regions to the centre. Federal and provincial party systems were already bifurcated in the 1920s and 1930s, ostensibly the heyday of regional brokerage; and parties in general have always been limited in terms of the regional interests they accommodate at any one time. In short, it may be unrealistic to use the past either as a standard by which to judge the current party system or as a model we might wish to recreate in order to relieve the present system of executive federalism of some of the burden of national unity. A not unreasonable assessment might be that the Canadian party system was never all that critical to the function of federalism; the Canadian federation survived despite the limited integrative capacity of Canadian parties.

In applying the assessment criteria of performance, effectiveness, and legitimacy, we should include not only the integrative dimension of parties but also the extent to which they help foster flexibility and responsiveness. These three elements are related; for instance, integrative capacity may be improved when the party system demonstrates flexibility. In assessing performance, for example, we likely have in mind the capacity of the system to facilitate upward mobility by channelling politicians from the provincial level to the federal, thereby helping to foster informal linkages, trust, and understanding between the two levels.

The Canadian system has never fared very well in this regard. Barrie and Gibbins note 'that career mobility from provincial to national office is the exception rather than the rule' (1989: 138) and that mobility has declined over time. Even during the King era, the number of provincial figures moving to Ottawa was actually quite limited, and some of those moves involved crossing party lines. On the other hand, the crossing of party lines does suggest flexibility. The appointment of figures closely associated with the Liberal government of Robert Bourassa in Quebec to the Harper cabinet was noted earlier. Jean Charest's transformation from leader of the federal Progressive Conservative party to that of the Quebec Liberal party can be seen as a successful move in the other direction. And Paul Martin recruited Ujjal Dosanjh, former NDP premier of British Columbia, as his minister of Health.

Thus the low overall mobility between provincial and federal parliaments and the weak links between federal and provincial parties have not prevented close interaction between individual ministers in the federal and provincial governments in the past. Even if their attention is often focused on what Thomas (1985) calls allocational issues, the more astute ministers will take their regional roles seriously and use them to convey broader regional concerns directly into cabinet; meanwhile, other ministers and their staffs, as well as the prime minister, will often consult regional ministers to get a sense of the way various issues might play out in their particular regions or provinces. In brief, while it can be argued that the Canadian federation would perform better if the career path of federal politicians were to incorporate a stint in a provincial legislature, and ideally as a member of the same party, the Canadian federation and party system have been able to overcome this obstacle.

At the same time, simply having the same party in power at both the federal and provincial levels is no guarantee that relations will be closer, friendlier, or more effective. The pitched battles between Lester Pearson and Premier Ross Thatcher of Saskatchewan, or Mackenzie King and Mitch Hepburn of Ontario—all of them Liberals—are legendary. Robert Bourassa, as the Liberal premier of Quebec, supported Progressive Conservative Prime Minister Brian Mulroney in the 1988 federal election campaign, to the chagrin of federal Liberal leader John Turner. These examples suggest that common partisan ties are not likely to be terribly helpful when it comes to bridging major divisions between governments; conversely, partisan differences are not likely to be a major hindrance when it comes to forging partnerships when there is a common interest.

At this stage it may be useful to recall the coalition model of parties and federalism. Carty and Wolinetz (2004) note that inter-party coalitions in federal systems are much more common in Europe than in Canada. It can argued, however, that Canada, at least in the past, has had its own unique practice of inter-party coalition-building, though it is not formally labelled as such. It is found primarily in the context of minority government. While there have been no formal agreements between parliamentary parties, extensive consultation and negotiation on an issue-by-issue basis is a hallmark of Canadian-style minority government. Some minority governments have been famously short-lived—notably the Conservative governments of Meighen (1926) and Clark (1979–80) but others, such as the Pearson government of 1963–8, have survived for longer periods. The 1963–8 period coincidentally saw the introduction of most of the major federal–provincial social programs, such as medicare and the Canada and Quebec pension plans, as well as a major expansion of the equalization system (see Chapters 7 and 8 by Brown and Banting respectively).

In the most recent period of minority government, beginning in 2004 with Martin and continuing with Harper until 2011, we saw a familiar pattern emerge: the NDP supporting the Martin government budget in 2005 on the understanding that more money would be devoted to post-secondary education; the Conservatives counting on the support of the NDP when they clamped down on income trusts; and the NDP offering to support the Harper government's 2011 budget (and thereby avoid an election), in exchange for the elimination of the GST on home heating fuel and increases in Canada Pension Plan and Guaranteed Income Supplement payouts (Bryden, 2011). NDP promises of support for the Conservative minority government, however, did not necessarily mean an enhanced role for Parliament as an arena for debate or for individual parliamentarians (Flanagan, 2009). This kind of inter-party bargaining tended to be centred on party leaders and likely contributed to greater centralization within parties and concomitantly greater reliance on instruments such as party discipline. Furthermore, these kinds of understandings and informal horse-trading have been more difficult to come by in the Harper era.

Minority governments raise the prospect that substantial issues of a federal–provincial nature will be raised, discussed, and perhaps even resolved among political parties rather than in the context of executive federalism (e.g., Baier et al. 2005). They also raise the hope that regional voices are able to express themselves directly and openly through regionally based parties, rather than be subsumed in traditional brokerage-style national parties, and that accommodation can occur in the context of open debate in Parliament and parliamentary committees rather than via traditional elite accommodation either in the federal–provincial arena or within traditional parties.

Unfortunately, these prospects were not realized under the minority governments from 2004–11. In the twenty-first century, Canadian parties are engaged in a permanent election campaign, acting on the assumption that an election may be just around the corner (Martin, 2010). The primary feature of the permanent election campaign is the relentless use of attack ads on radio and television, focusing on the leaders of the opposing parties. The Conservatives, with their much greater capacity for fund-raising, have outspent their opponents by a considerable margin in this respect. This spending is not captured by the limits in the Canada Elections Act since it falls outside the formal election period. The prorogation crisis of 2008 can be seen as a direct outcome of the ruthless focus on crippling one's opponents. While parliamentary committees did indeed play a more active role in the 40th parliament and while the executive had to be much more careful in how it moved its legislative agenda forward, parliament and its committees still failed to play a constructive role of providing oversight of how the federal government conducted its relations with other Canadian governments. The more than six years of minority government failed to demonstrate the capacity of Canadian parties, and the party system as a whole, to deal with substantial issues of a federal–provincial nature any more effectively under a minority government than under majority government. Coupled with its traditional weakness in facilitating upward mobility from the provincial to the federal level or encouraging inter-party coalition building, the Canadian party system falls well short in the three dimensions of performance, effectiveness, and legitimacy when it comes to facilitating bargaining and collaboration among the constituent units and integrating the federation.

The final question, or set of questions, revolves around the future prospects of the current party system and the implications for the Canadian federation. As of the May 2011 election, the House of Commons is composed of 166 Conservatives, 103 NDP, 34 Liberals, 4 Bloc Québécois, and 1 Green MP. Aside from the collapse of the Bloc, two features stand out. First, the Conservatives obtained a majority without support from Quebec, demonstrating that Quebec no longer plays a pivotal role in making or breaking governments, or at least that it can be by-passed in this respect. Second, the NDP now has the status of a major national party but its support is heavily skewed towards one province, Quebec, from where it draws more than 57 per cent of its seats. Will the relative absence of Quebec representation in the Conservative caucus, coupled with the virtual disappearance of the Bloc from the House, lead to Quebec's isolation and could this contribute to further tensions between Quebec and the rest of Canada? Will the NDP under Jack Layton's successor be able to construct a workable coalition between its Quebec contingent and its members from other parts of the country?

In the case of the Conservatives, Prime Minister Harper did appoint four of the five MPs from Quebec to cabinet to compensate for the shrunken size of the Quebec caucus.

So far the Harper government has taken a firm but fair approach to Quebec, for example, including provisions in its June 2011 budget for payments of more than $2 billion to Quebec for having harmonized its provincial sales tax with the GST back in the 1990s, essentially making good on a commitment it made during the 2011 election campaign. However, the Conservative party's diminished electoral standings in Quebec will lead to more emphasis on **interstate federalism** in its dealings with that province. It may also raise questions about the legitimacy of the federal government's actions, at least in the eyes of Quebecers, should Ottawa take a position that appears contrary to that of the Quebec government or other significant groups.

With respect to the NDP, its new leader is now faced with the herculean task of bridging two contingents of MPs representing two different political cultures. His task of finding issues on which there is common ground between the two groups is comparable to that previously faced by Mackenzie King and Brian Mulroney. Some expectations raised by Layton, opening up the constitutional question, for example, may make this bridging task not only difficult within the caucus but also across the Canadian electorate. Within Quebec the vote for the NDP cannot be construed as a vote for federalism or as evidence that Quebec voters see the NDP as a federalist party (Gagnon, 2011). Rather than serving as an omnibus along the lines of a traditional brokerage party, within which different interests are reconciled in the name of national unity, the NDP is probably more akin to a parking lot where many Quebec voters have found a temporary spot after tiring from their affair with the Bloc, and before moving on to a new party that better fits with their nationalist aspirations. In brief, it is very likely unrealistic to expect the party system in its current configuration to start doing some of the 'heavy lifting' in keeping the Canadian federation intact and functioning.

Note

The data in Table 6.1 were originally compiled by Shannon Wells in 2004 and updated by the authors in 2011. Financial support provided by the Social Sciences and Humanities Research Council is gratefully acknowledged.

References

Baier, G., H. Bakvis, and D. Brown. 2005. 'Executive Federalism, the Democratic Deficit and Parliamentary Reform', in G.B. Doern (ed.) *How Ottawa Spends, 2005–06* Don Mills: Oxford University Press, 163–182.

Bakvis, H. 1991. *Regional Ministers: Power and Influence in the Canadian Cabinet.* Toronto: University of Toronto Press.

———. 2002. 'Checkerboard Federalism? Labour Market Development Policy in Canada', in *Canadian Federalism: Performance, Effectiveness, and Legitimacy.* Eds. H. Bakvis and G. Skogstad. Toronto: Oxford University Press.

Bakvis, H., G. Baier, and D. Brown. 2009. *Contested Federalism: Certainty and Ambiguity in the Canadian Federation.* Don Mills: Oxford University Press.

Barrie, D., and R. Gibbins. 1989. 'Parliamentary Careers in the Canadian Federal State', *Canadian Journal of Political Science* 22, 1: 137–45.

Bryden, J. 2011. 'Layton meets Harper over budget, says election now in PM's hands', *Winnipeg Free Press* [online edition], February 18. http://stage.www.winnipegfreepress.com/breakingnews/mobile/

harper-layton-in-pre-budget-meeting-that-could-help-avert-spring-election-116499108.html

Carty, R.K. 1988. 'Three Canadian Party Systems: An Interpretation of the Development of National Politics'. In *Party Democracy in Canada*, ed. G. Perlin. Scarborough: Prentice-Hall.

———. 2002. 'The Politics of Tecumseh Corners: Canadian Political Parties as Franchise Organizations', *Canadian Journal of Political Science* 35, 4: 723–45.

——— and S. Wolinetz. 2004. 'Political Parties and the Canadian Federation's Coalition Politics' In *Canada: The State of the Federation 2002: Reconsidering the Institutions of Canadian Federalism*, ed. J.P. Meekison, H. Telford, and H. Lazar. Kingston: Institute of Intergovernmental Relations.

Chase, S., and S. McCarthy. 2010. 'Potash politics put Tories on spot'. *Globe and Mail*. October 22.

Clarkson, S. 2001. 'The Liberal Threepeat: The Multi-System Party in the Multi-Party System'. In *The Canadian General Election of 2000*, ed. J. Pammett and C. Dornan. Toronto: Dundurn.

Covell, M. 1991. 'Parties as Institutions of National Governance'. In *Representation, Integration and Political Parties in Canada*, ed. H. Bakvis. Toronto: Dundurn Press.

Crosbie, J. 1997. *No Holds Barred: My Life In Politics*. Toronto: McClelland and Stewart.

Curry, B. 2011. 'Harper government opens wallet to hype its stimulus package'. *Globe and Mail*. February 24.

Dyck, R. 1996. 'Relations Between Federal and Provincial Parties'. In *Canadian Parties in Transition*, ed. A.B. Tanguay and A.-G. Gagnon. 2nd edn. Scarborough, Ont.: Nelson.

English, J. 1977. *The Decline of Politics: The Conservatives and the Party System, 1901–1920*. Toronto: University of Toronto Press.

Flanagan, T. 2009. 'Coming to terms with minority government', *Globe and Mail* June 22.

Gagnon, A.-G., and A.B. Tanguay. 1996. 'Minor Parties in the Canadian Political System: Origins, Functions, Impact'. In *Canadian Parties in Transition*, ed. A.B. Tanguay and A.-G. Gagnon. 2nd edn. Scarborough, Ont.: Nelson.

Gangon, L. 2011. 'Quebeckers have a mental Bloc'. *Globe and Mail*. May 15.

Globe and Mail. 2006. 'Saskatchewan Tory MPs warn Harper on equalization'. August 15.

Johnson, W. 2009. 'The Outsider: How Stephen Harper brought Canada to conservatism, and the Conservatives to Crisis', *The Walrus* (March): 22–9.

King, A. 1969. 'Political Parties in Western Democracies: Some Sceptical Reflections', *Polity* 2, 2: 111–41.

Maher, S., and G. McGregor. 2009. 'Carving up the pork'. *Chronicle Herald*. October 20.

Mallory, J.R. 1954. *Social Credit and the Federal Power in Canada*. Toronto: University of Toronto Press.

Martin, L. 2010. *Harperland: The Politics of Control*. Toronto: Viking Canada.

McRoberts, K. 1997. *Misconceiving Canada: The Struggle for National Unity*. Toronto: Oxford University Press.

Noel, S.J.R. 1996. 'Patronage and Entourages, Action-Sets, Networks'. In *Canadian Parties in Transition*, ed. A.B. Tanguay and A-G. Gagnon. 2nd edn. Scarborough, Ont.: Nelson.

Riker, W.H. 1964. *Federalism: Origin, Operation, Significance*. Boston: Little, Brown.

Russell, P. 2008. *Two Cheers for Minority Government: The Evolution of Canadian Parliamentary Democracy*. Toronto: Emond Montgomery.

Russell, P., and L. Sossin. (eds.). 2009. *Parliamentary Democracy in Crisis*. Toronto: University of Toronto Press.

Savoie, D.J. 1999. *Governing from the Centre: The Concentration of Power in Canadian Politics*. Toronto: University of Toronto Press.

Sharman, C. 1994. 'Discipline and Disharmony: Party and the Operation of the Australian Federal System'. In *Parties and Federalism in Australia and Canada*, ed. C. Sharman. Canberra: Federalism Research Centre, The Australian National University.

Simpson, J. 2001. *The Friendly Dictatorship*. Toronto: McClelland and Stewart.

Smiley, D.V. 1987. *The Federal Condition in Canada*. Toronto: McGraw-Hill Ryerson.

Smith, D.E. 1985. 'Party Government, Representation and National Integration in Canada'. In *Party Government and Regional Representation in Canada*, ed. P. Aucoin. Toronto: University of Toronto Press.

Taber, J. 2010. "'Cluster' strategy puts Tories on track for majority, poll suggests'. *Globe and*

Mail. December 6.

Tanguay, A.B. 1999. 'Canada's Political Parties in the 1990s: The Fraying of the Ties that Bind'. In *Canada: The State of the Federation 1998/99*, ed. H. Lazar and T. McIntosh. Montreal and Kingston: McGill–Queen's University Press, published for the School of Policy Studies, Queen's University.

———. 2003. 'Canada's Quasi-Party System: the Causes and Consequences of Liberal Hegemony', *Inroads* 12 (Winter/Spring): 136–41.

———. 2006. 'Quebec and the Canadian Federal Election of 2000: Putting the Sovereignty Movement on the Ropes?' In *The Elections of 2000: Politics, Culture and Economics in North America*, ed. M.K. Kirtz, M.J. Kasoff, R. Farmer, and J.C. Green. Akron, Ohio: University of Akron Press.

Thomas, P.G. 1985. 'The Role of National Party Caucuses'. In *Party Government and Regional Representation in Canada*, ed. P. Aucoin. Toronto: University of Toronto Press.

Wearing, J. 1981. *The L-Shaped Party: The Liberal Party of Canada, 1958–1980*. Toronto: McGraw-Hill Ryerson.

Whitaker, R. 1977. *The Government Party: Organizing and Financing the Liberal Party of Canada, 1930–58*. Toronto: University of Toronto Press.

Part II

The Social and Economic Union

Questions for Critical Thought

1. What are the basic principles that can be used to assess the nature of fiscal balance in a federation? How easily can these principles be reconciled?

2. How much importance should we attach to the Social Union Framework Agreement between Ottawa and the provinces as an underpinning of Canada's social safety net?

3. What is unique about the health care field in terms of intergovernmental decision-making relative to other social policy fields such as social assistance, child care, pensions, and post-secondary education?

4. Why does the pattern of intergovernmental relations look so different across policy fields?

5. What explains the relatively high level of federal–provincial co-operation in the international trade policy area in contrast to the lack of co-operation in other areas such as economic development and securities regulation?

6. Are the provinces or the government of Canada leaders or laggards with respect to the climate change file? What explains their leadership/laggard role and changes in it over time?

7 Fiscal Federalism: Maintaining a Balance?

Douglas M. Brown

It is often said that fiscal federalism is the glue that keeps Canada together. But issues about those arrangements are highly political and controversial. Does each province or region get its fair share in transfer payments or **tax allocation**? What does 'fair' mean? Can the federal government afford to fund increasing transfer costs? Is Ontario really a 'have-not' province? Should Alberta share its oil wealth? How do we deal with upheavals in public finance such as the deep recession in 2008–9? These are some of the questions governments have to face in the next few years.

Fiscal federalism is the evolving system of financial arrangements between the federal and provincial orders of government. It is essential to how Canada's federal system works. This chapter begins by outlining the structure of Canadian fiscal federalism: constitutional powers, tax structure and harmonization, intergovernmental transfers, and the fiscal relations process. Then it surveys the evolution of fiscal federalism over the past sixty years, emphasizing the important role played by fiscal relations in building Canada's welfare state, and how the balance, both between the two orders of government and between the values of equity and efficiency, has shifted in the past fifteen years. The chapter concludes with a review of the issues that have emerged in the past decade as federalism seeks a new balance.

Fiscal federalism has a role to play in all three of the areas that are the focus of this book: the performance of the federation, policy effectiveness, and political legitimacy. First, the federation's performance depends in no small part on its ability to be flexible and to adapt to changing conditions. Fiscal relationships provide a key means to achieve such change, as well as to maintain the integrity of federal principles. Second, fiscal federalism contributes to policy effectiveness by underpinning two key economic goals: equity and efficiency. The balance between these two has shifted over time. Fiscal relations are also a means to more specific policy ends involving such fields as health care, post-secondary education, labour mobility or economic development. Finally, with respect to political legitimacy, intergovernmental fiscal relations are marked by secrecy, complexity and, sometimes, muddled accountability. But even if the technical discussions involved in fiscal federalism continue to take place behind closed doors, the underlying issues are well aired in public.

The Structure of Canadian Fiscal Federalism

Fiscal relations among governments in Canada are shaped by the rules and practices that make up the Canadian constitution. The allocation of expenditure and revenue functions is among the more important of these constitutional features. In this respect, it is fiscal federalism that gives shape to the constitution, not vice versa. Formal constitutional powers would have little relevance if revenues could not be collected and expenditures made. And Canada's constitution would have been obsolete long ago if not for the flexible instruments of fiscal federalism. For example, governments used intergovernmental fiscal arrangements to respond to the rise of the modern welfare state—and more recently to its partial retrenchment and adaptation to global economic integration. Federal constitutions are notoriously difficult to amend, and ours is no exception. However, fiscal arrangements change frequently and thus provide opportunities for system-wide adaptation.

Four features of the structure of Canadian fiscal federalism are important. They are (1) the constitutional division of legislative, taxation, and expenditure powers; (2) the evolved pattern of tax allocation, sharing, and harmonization; (3) the system of intergovernmental transfers to bridge the gap between revenue and expenditure responsibilities; and (4) the process through which fiscal arrangements are made by the federal and provincial governments.

Constitutional Powers

The constitutional allocation of powers affects fiscal relations in the Canadian federation in three ways. First, the Canadian constitution emphasizes exclusive fields of jurisdiction, as opposed to the scheme of concurrent, or legally shared powers typical of other federations such as Australia, Germany, and the United States. Exclusivity of jurisdiction, the hallmark of what Keith Banting in Chapter 8 calls the classic model of federalism is that the central government has relatively little opportunity to legislate specific conditions and funding formulae for programs to be delivered by the provinces (Watts, 1999). In Canada fiscal mechanisms must respect the jurisdictional autonomy of the provinces in major expenditure fields. This characteristic has taken on greater significance since the mid-twentieth century because most of the fields central to the welfare state (e.g., social assistance, health care, and education) are under provincial jurisdiction. Moreover, the fiscal transfer program called **equalization** is specifically designed to ensure that all provinces have a similar **fiscal capacity** to exercise their autonomy, and thus reinforce their exercise of exclusive jurisdictions under the Constitution.

The second important feature of this country's constitutional arrangements is that, unlike other federations, Canada gives the two senior levels of government full access to the most important and most broadly based sources of taxation. Both orders of government can levy not only income taxes (personal and corporate) but general sales or consumption taxes, as well as payroll taxes for specific purposes such as unemployment insurance, health care, and pensions. The constituent units of other federal systems are more restricted in their ability to pay for their expenditure responsibilities from their own revenue sources. Thus the **vertical fiscal gap** (defined more fully below) has been considerably less in Canada than in Germany or Australia, for example. On the other hand, governments at both levels must pay attention to **tax harmonization** to ensure that taxpayers are not subjected to conflicting demands and overwhelming tax burdens.

The third important feature is the constitutional allocation of what is known as 'the spending power': the constitutional right of the federal parliament to spend its revenues in any field, as it sees fit. This power has been controversial, particularly among those Canadians, especially in Quebec, who insist on strict adherence to the principle of the provinces' autonomy in their exclusive jurisdictions. Nonetheless, the spending power has been the means by which the federal government has promoted a national (pan-Canadian) approach to social programs, including direct payments to individuals and organizations, for redistributive purposes. The courts have upheld the spending power, so long as the granting of money does not constitute regulation by other means. And in 1999 the federal government and nine provinces (all but Quebec) signed the Social Union Framework Agreement, establishing some general principles for the use of the federal spending power where provincial jurisdiction is concerned. These rules, in general, have affected the shape not only of such major transfers as the Canada Health Transfer (CHT) and the Canada Social Transfer (CST) but also of new intergovernmental initiatives in the social policy field. Finally, although there is no provincial 'spending power' per se, the provinces have a residual power to spend wherever they see fit, including in areas outside their formal field of legislative power, such as the funding of international trade offices (Hogg, 1996: 151–2), provided, again, that such spending is not a backdoor attempt to regulate a federal area of jurisdiction.

These three sets of constitutional powers—in the areas of regulation, taxation, and expenditure—have interacted over the course of Canada's history to produce dramatically different responses to the needs of the day.

Tax Structure and Harmonization

As we have just noted, Ottawa and the provinces share the most important and broadly based sources of revenue (see Table 7.1), including income taxes; in 2010 the federal government took 61 per cent of personal income tax (PIT) and 63 per cent of corporate income tax (CIT) (Treff and Ort, 2010: Table A1). In addition, all provinces except Alberta collect a retail sales tax, and the federal government levies the Goods and Services Tax (GST), a general consumption tax that is fully harmonized with the sales tax in some provinces (Newfoundland and Labrador, Nova Scotia, New Brunswick, and Ontario), and nearly so in Quebec (see Bird, 2001). Overall, federal and provincial shares of these general sales taxes in 2010 were 49 per cent and 51 per cent respectively (Treff and Ort, 2010). The federal and provincial governments also share revenues from taxes on gasoline and other motive fuels, as well as taxes on alcohol and tobacco.

The remaining tax sources of the federal and provincial governments are more exclusive. Only the federal government can impose customs and excise duties, and since the provinces own almost all the natural resources, they levy almost all of the resource royalties and related rents. Resource revenues have been especially important to Alberta because of high prices for its large petroleum reserves, but they are also important to a number of other provinces.

The past sixty years have seen a steady trend towards decentralization in the overall revenue split between the federal and provincial governments. In 1950, when Ottawa

Table 7.1 Federal and Provincial Own Source Revenues/$ millions

	1997			2005		
	Federal	**Prov-local**	**Total**	**Federal**	**Prov-local**	**Total**
Income Taxes	88,223	55,356	143,579	132,668	72,467	205,135
Consumption Taxes	32,007	37,366	69,373	47,126	56,932	104,058
Payroll Taxes	22,658	9,437	32,093	21,102	12,580	33,682
Property Taxes		36,935	36,935		46,784	46,784
Other Revenues	11,930	57,945	69,175	15,149	98,871	104,020
Total	154,818	197,039	351,855	216,045	277,634	493,679

Source: Statistics Canada: Adapted from Treff & Perry (2005: Table A.1, p. A:2)

exercised strong central control over revenue generation, the federal government levied about 65 per cent of total taxes. By 2010 this figure had declined by over one-third to 40 per cent. The main reason for this change was the provinces' need for a greater share of tax revenues to meet their spending responsibilities in areas (e.g., health) where costs were rising much more quickly than they were in areas of federal responsibility (e.g., defense). To help meet provinces' revenue needs, the federal government ceded considerable '**tax room**' on corporate and personal income to the provinces in the 1950s, 1960s and 1970s. At the same time, tax sources—both big and small—have proliferated at the provincial level.

In any federal system, decentralized tax allocation can erode the goals of economic integration (i.e., the creation of a common market) by placing different burdens on individuals and companies depending on where they are located. Moreover, decentralized revenue generation creates a gap between those provinces with lucrative sources of tax revenues and those provinces whose yield from tax sources is far less. It is to address this type of fiscal imbalance, or inequity, resulting from such decentralization that equalization programs become necessary (see discussion below). Harmonization of taxes is also important to ensure that similarly situated taxpayers are treated similarly, and to facilitate the movement between provinces of capital, labour, goods, and services. One of the most successful means of ensuring harmonization has been the Tax Collection Agreements (TCAs), under which the federal government agrees to collect taxes on behalf of any province or territory. TCAs are in place for federal PIT collection in all provinces and territories except Quebec, and for CIT in all except Ontario, Alberta, and Quebec. Under these arrangements the federal government absorbs the collection costs, and in return the provinces agree to a common definition of the **tax base** and a common approach to tax enforcement and allocation. Harmonization through unified collection is somewhat less advanced for consumption taxes. On July 1, 2010 the two large provinces of Ontario and British Columbia harmonized their sales tax with the federal sales tax for the first time (to create a combined Harmonized Sales Tax, or HST). British Columbia has subsequently had to repeal its HST after its citizens voted overwhelmingly to reject it in a binding referendum. Economists claim that this will contribute to more efficient business conditions and smoother economic integration within Canada (see the discussion later in this chapter). In Quebec the GST is collected by the province on behalf of the federal government, not vice versa.

Intergovernmental Transfers

Public finance analysts refer to two kinds of fiscal relationships: vertical and horizontal (Boadway, 2005; Anderson, 2010; Boadway and Shah, 2009). Vertical relations are those between different levels or orders of government: not only federal–provincial or federal–territorial, but also provincial–local, federal–Aboriginal, even federal–local. In all federations there is a natural gap between the central or federal government and the constituent governments or provinces. Central governments, by virtue of their authority over the entire country, are able to tax economic resources—wealth, profits, income, consumption—wherever they occur. Thus from an efficiency perspective it makes sense that the federal government has a greater fiscal capacity than the federation's constituent parts. States or provinces usually have neither the full legal power nor the practical means to tax national wealth in order to fund their expenditures.

The result is a gap between federal revenues and provincial expenditure that should be closed. There are four ways to close this gap. The first and most common way is to transfer cash, on an annual basis, from the federal government to the provinces. A second way is to reallocate or transfer a share of taxes from the federal to the provincial level, which the province would then levy on its citizens. Yet a third way is to shift an entire tax field to the provinces, permanently reducing the federal government's fiscal capacity. And a fourth way is simply to transfer the spending responsibility upwards from the provincial to the federal level. All four methods have been used in Canada at one time or another, with cash transfers being the most common.

A **vertical fiscal imbalance** (compared to a gap) is said to exist when a province's revenues are still not sufficient to meet its needs, even after federal transfers are taken into account. How does one determine what those expenditure needs are, whether provincial revenues (or the ability to raise revenues) are in fact inadequate, and exactly how insufficient the federal transfers? The answers to these questions involve significant differences in interpretation and not a small amount of political posturing. Suffice it to say that 'vertical fiscal imbalance' (VFI) is a loaded term (Lazar, St-Hilaire, and Tremblay, 2004). We return to this issue below in the discussion of the Harper Conservative government's approach to fiscal federalism.

The term 'horizontal imbalance' refers to distinctions at the provincial or territorial level: more specifically, the differing fiscal capacities of the various provinces and territories to fund their own expenditure responsibilities. These differences are primarily due to regional economic disparities: differences in economic activity and accrued wealth among the constituent units—in other words, the Albertan economy is richer than New Brunswick's. In virtually all federations, some way is found to even out these horizontal imbalances, for two reasons. One is a matter of general equity, to ensure a measure of

Table 7.2 Major Federal Cash Transfers To Provinces And Territories Estimated Entitlements, 2011–12 $Millions

	CHT	CST	Equalization	TFF	Offshore Accords	Transfer Protection	Total
NF & Lab.	452	170			473		1,095
PEI	115	48	329				491
NS	759	315	1,167		168	158	2,566
NB	606	251	1,483			150	2,490
Que.	6,408	2,660	7,815			369	17,252
Ont.	10,746	4,461	2,200				17,406
Man.	1,002	416	1,666			276	3,360
Sask.	866	360					1,226
Alta	2,114	1,266					3,380
BC	3,799	1,537					5,336
Nun.	30	11		1,175			1,216
NWT	26	15		996			1,037
YK	29	12		705			745
All provs & terrs	26,952	11,522	14,659	2,876	641	952	57,601

Source: Compiled from Government of Canada Department of Finance website, tables on Major Transfers, updated to May 2011, accessed June 2, 2011. Reproduced with the permission of the Minister of Public Works and Government Services Canada, 2011.

Note: Totals may not add due to rounding.

fiscal equality across the country; the other has a constitutional purpose, to ensure that every unit within the federation can manage the responsibilities allocated to it.

In some federations such as Germany the richer provinces make direct payments to the poorer ones, but more commonly the federal government uses its fiscal capacity to redistribute wealth regionally, through intergovernmental grants and, in some cases, transfers to individual persons through programs such as employment insurance. Since transfers from the federal level are the chief means of bridging horizontal gaps, the federal level would still need to have a larger revenue capacity than the provinces even if, on average, provincial expenditure responsibility and revenue capacity were evenly matched (no VFI).

Intergovernmental transfer payments are also an important means through which the federal government can build national programs while leaving their delivery to the provincial governments. In so doing, the federal government can choose to require that the provinces follow central policy objectives and program design, or it can leave those decisions to the provinces. Thus transfers come in two basic types: conditional and unconditional. Conditional transfers are payments made for specific purposes, often to introduce new social programs with similar entitlements across the country. Unconditional transfers have no strings attached, but are still guided by specific formulae determining which provinces get what proportions of funds.

Transfers from the federal government to the provinces and territories are now largely unconditional with, it can be argued, fewer conditions imposed on federal monies than in any other federal system. The two largest programs, accounting for about 80 per cent of all federal transfers in recent years, are the Equalization Program, funded in 2010–11 at $14.3 billion, and the Canada Health and Social Transfers (CHT and CST), funded in 2010–11 at $36.6 billion (see Table 7.2). The equalization program is wholly unconditional, while the CHT and CST come with only a few general conditions. The conditions on the CST and CHT are discussed in Chapters 8 and 9, respectively. They amount to national principles and leave considerable room for provincial interpretation.

Moreover, both the CHT and CST are **block grants**, intended to cover a broad range of program expenditures in areas from health to social assistance to post-secondary education. Block grants are the amalgamation of previously more specific cost-shared programs. In the former, funds are transferred without reference to explicit provincial expenditures; in the latter, federal funds are matched to actual expenditures according to a formula (e.g., 50–50). Canadian governments still maintain some cost-shared programs, including economic and regional development agreements, and federal–provincial–municipal infrastructure agreements (Vaillancourt, 2000). But in dollar terms they are much less important than the big two transfers—although the infrastructure and related **conditional** funding programs were increased significantly from 2008–9 to 2010–11 as a means to stimulate the economy during the major recession (see discussion below). Canada is notable among federations in the percentage (about 80 per cent) of its intergovernmental transfers that take the form of block payments.

The most unconditional of the transfer programs, equalization, is intended to sustain the provinces' constitutional autonomy by ensuring that each province has the capacity to deliver comparable services at comparable rates of taxation. Initiated in 1957, equalization brings provinces with a fiscal capacity below the national average up to a national standard. Except indirectly, through the redistributive effects of the federal tax system, equalization does not take funds from the richer provinces: the latter are not equalized *down* to the national level, it is only the poorer provinces that are equalized *up*. The funds for this purpose come wholly from the consolidated revenue fund of the federal government. The latter is collected throughout the country and individual taxpayers in the poorer provinces contribute, according to their income, the same as individual taxpayers in the richer provinces. There are no direct transfers between provincial governments.

Provincial fiscal capacity is measured using a national standard based on tax yield from five different categories of revenue sources, an approach referred to as the 'representative tax system'. Each province's actual fiscal capacity is measured against this standard to determine the extent of its entitlement. Currently six of the 10 provinces receive funds to bring them up to the national standard of fiscal capacity. Unlike equalization schemes in some other countries (e.g., Australia, South Africa), the Canadian system is designed only to determine differences in fiscal capacity; it does not attempt to measure differences in the costs of providing provincial services or in the need for specific program expenditures (see Brown, 1996).

For a brief period in 2004–07, following a decision of Paul Martin's Liberal government, all of this complex determination of equalization entitlements was essentially abandoned. Instead the federal government made payments based on the recent past with an incremental increase each year. That approach came under considerable criticism for departing from rational principles and a transparent formula. In 2007 Stephen Harper's Conservative government restored the program to a principles-based formula but, as discussed below, it revised those principles significantly to limit the future growth of the program.

The federal government also transfers funds to the governments of the Northwest Territories, Yukon, and Nunavut. These territorial governments are responsible for nearly the same range of expenditures as the provinces. Yet their needs and per capita costs are greater because of their huge land mass, northern isolation, and sparse populations; furthermore, they lack the full range of provincial taxing powers (resource revenues are shared with the federal government) and their fiscal capacity is much less than that of even the poorest province. Thus the territorial governments depend on federal transfers for well over half of their revenues; the figures have ranged from roughly 65 per cent to 81 per cent, depending on the territory and yearly fluctuations in economic activity (Canada, 2006b: 1). These transfers are provided mainly by the Territorial Funding Formula (TFF); in addition, territorial governments receive the CHT and CST, but these payments are deducted from their TFF entitlements. From 1985 to 2004, TFF amounts were determined according to an expenditure-based formula, adjusted for population, which reflected the special expenditure needs of the territories. The TFF did not escape fiscal restraint; the grants were frozen in 1995–6, and further reduced by 5 per cent in 1996–7. In 1998 a ceiling on future increases was imposed, and since 2004 the actual payments have been de-linked from the need-based formula. In 2010–11 the three northern territories will receive a combined total of $2.67 billion from the TFF (see Table 7.2).

Finally, intergovernmental transfers play a crucial role in funding First Nations governments (the more than 600 Indian Band Councils) and other Aboriginal governments and organizations. These governments are not part of regular fiscal federalism (Federal–Provincial–Territorial) arrangements, and do not receive either equalization or CHT and CST payments. Instead, their funding comes from a specialized federal agency (Indian and Northern Affairs Canada [INAC]) and other specific federal programs. According to federal estimates for 2010–11, the two largest federal sources for funding to Aboriginal people are INAC, which will transfer $5.1 billion to Aboriginal governments and organizations, and Health Canada, which will spend $ 2.15 billion on First Nations and Inuit health programs; approximately $1.04 billion of the Health Canada amount consists of transfers to Aboriginal governments and organizations (Canada, 2010).

Aboriginal governments differ from the other governments in the federation constitutionally, economically, and fiscally (see Chapter 15). Some Aboriginal governments have limited taxing power, but few have much fiscal capacity (i.e., ability to obtain revenues from economic activity as opposed to the legal power to levy taxes), and none has the broad-based fiscal powers of the provinces. Also, the politics and policy discussions surrounding Aboriginal finances tend to take place on a separate track and under the auspices of different executive institutions than discussions at the federal–provincial–territorial level (Prince and Abele, 2005).

In recent years many First Nations have sought modifications in the funding system, including multi-year and more loosely conditional comprehensive arrangements. In late 2005 the Martin government, together with the provinces and territories, agreed in principle with Aboriginal leaders on the 'Kelowna Accord' (CICS, 2005), which was to provide a $5-billion, 10-year framework for significant increases in program funding to Aboriginal governments. However, shortly after its election in January 2006, the Conservative government of Stephen Harper declared that it was not bound by the Accord.

The Fiscal Relations Process

The preceding structural outline may seem bloodless and technical, but the decision-making process through which Canadian fiscal arrangements are made is anything but. As W.A.C. Bennett, the long-time BC premier, used to tell his fellow first ministers, 'Let's get down to the real business of Canada and divvy up the cash.' Almost everything governments do requires money and it seems that there is never enough—policy issues and decisions very often come down to financial requirements. Thus fiscal arrangements are at the heart not only of federal–provincial (and provincial–municipal and federal–Aboriginal) relations, but also the budget-making process in every government. They are among the most hotly contested issues in politics, reflecting real ideological differences and regional interests.

Intergovernmental relations on financial matters suffer from all the defects of other executive federalism processes—and more. Although the fiscal battles between Ottawa and the provinces, and among the provinces themselves, have become highly public, the details of fiscal arrangements are so complex that governments leave them to a handful of technical experts who meet in private. The resulting lack of transparency makes accountability difficult to trace—a characteristic often exploited by governments eager to avoid taking the blame for cutbacks in funding or program entitlements.

Decisions about fiscal arrangements, particularly the final amounts to be transferred to the provinces, are rarely made jointly. Rather, the different levels of government tend to hold frequent meetings, argue their positions, agree on some general approaches and principles, and then leave the final decisions to their own cabinets. The most dramatic change in fiscal arrangements in recent times, the introduction of the CHST in 1995 and the major changes announced in the federal budget of 2007, were made by the federal government alone, following consultation with the provinces (Greenspan and Wilson-Smith, 1997). So too were many, if not all, of the major turns in the fiscal road over the past seventy years (Burns, 1980). Negotiations with the provinces shape the options facing the federal government, and a decision taken against the wishes of all of the provinces can backfire politically. In the end, though, Ottawa's allocation of the cash is a political act, and considerations other than the interests of the provinces can have a big say, particularly when the money is to be directed at social programs.

Finally, the tendency to leave the big budgetary decisions to individual governments is reinforced by two institutional features. First, both the federal parliament and the provincial legislatures want to protect their power to appropriate funds every year (even if budgetary decisions are initially made by the Finance minister or the cabinet). Thus no legislature will consent to be bound by multi-year intergovernmental agreements. Second, Canada's intergovernmental machinery does not function well when it comes to taking final, substantive and binding decisions (Painter, 1991; Brown, 2002). It is simply too cumbersome for governments to have to agree collectively, at least on a regular basis, on financial matters. Nonetheless, issues of accountability, transparency, and decision-making are all of current concern to Canadian citizens and their governments.

Fiscal Federalism 1950–2010: The Balance Shifts

Fiscal relationships in Canada are subject to frequent change, but the changes themselves are usually incremental. Therefore a long sweep of time is required to understand and evaluate the effect of fiscal federalism in Canada. Before turning to the current issues facing fiscal relationships, it is vital to see where we have been. Harvey Lazar wrote in 2000 that

> [u]ntil the late 1970s or early 1980s, Canadian fiscal federalism had a 'mission statement'. Its sense of purpose mirrored the post-war consensus about the role that the state could play, through programs of redistribution and macroeconomic stabilization, in building a fair and compassionate society and a prosperous and stable economy. [Since then] the golden age of consensus had eroded badly. . . . Fiscal federalism has also lacked a strong sense of purpose. (Lazar, 2000: 4)

The post-war consensus was that fiscal policy should strike a balance between social and regional equity on one hand, and the efficiency of the national economy on the other. Interpersonal or social equity was pursued through a progressive income tax system, the social security system, and other universal social programs such as health care and education. Inter-regional equity was pursued through fiscal equalization, unemployment insurance, and regional development programs.

As Banting documents in Chapter 8, key aspects of the welfare state in Canada could be delivered effectively (and constitutionally) only by the provinces. Thus, beginning in the 1950s, the federal government used **cost-shared** programs to induce provincial spending in the areas of social assistance, vocational training, universities, social services, and hospital and medical insurance plans, among others. And after 1957, Ottawa began making separate payments to poorer provinces for fiscal **equalization**. This era was the pinnacle of what Banting calls shared-cost federalism.

The era of shared-cost, co-operative federalism came to an end by 1976, as economic growth and thus federal revenues slowed and the federal government entered a period of chronic budgetary deficits that did not end until 1998. In response to its tighter fiscal position, Ottawa decided it would no longer match whatever the provinces spent, and thus have its spending driven by rising provincial costs and commitments. Instead, in 1977 federal legislation combined transfers for health and post-secondary education into a block grant called the Established Programs Financing (EPF). And in 1990 it put a ceiling on payments to the richer provinces from the Canada Assistance Plan (the transfer for social assistance, i.e., welfare). As a result of these and other changes, the provinces were obliged to fund an ever-larger proportion of social programs from their own revenues.

Federal transfers to the provinces as a share of total government spending peaked around 1982. In that year, as part of the effort to patriate and amend the Constitution, Canadian governments and legislatures made a commitment to the equality of regional economic opportunity and to the principle of equalization payments in Section 36 of the *Constitution Act 1982*. This constitutional commitment has been crucial in sustaining the political commitment to equalization. Equalization payments were spared the relentless cuts in either the growth rate or the actual cash of intergovernmental transfers after 1981 (see Brown, 2007) (see Table 7.3).

Table 7.3 Major Federal Cash Transfers to Provinces and Territories Selected Years 1982–3 to 2007–8/$ millions[1]

	1982–3	1987–8	1992–3	1997–8	2002–3	2007–8
Social Program Transfers[2]	10,271	14,437	18,396	12,500	19,100	31,065
Equalization	4,865	6,605	7,784	9,738	8,859	12,925
Territorial Funding Formula	362	730	1,076	1,229	1,616	2,313
Total	15,498	21,772	27,256	23,467	29,575	46,303

Source: For 1982–3 to 2002–3 Finance Canada, 2006, Annex 3, Tables A3.1–A3.3; for 2007–8, Finance Canada 2008. Reproduced with the permission of the Minister of Public Works and Government Services Canada, 2011.

The 1990s saw even more dramatic changes as fiscal relations in Canada responded to economic and political upheavals. In this decade of globalization and market liberalization, governments reformed the welfare state to suit the more competitive international economy. All governments eliminated their budgetary deficits and began to reduce their accumulated debts; they balanced their budgets, and many were eventually able to accumulate substantial surpluses. Tax reform and tax cuts were responses to Canadian taxpayers, of whom the majority now expected less of government and trusted government less when it came to spending their money wisely.

The key milestone occurred in 1995 with the introduction of the CHST as part of the federal budget and its dramatic plan to restore federal fiscal budgetary balance. The CHST began as a way cutting provincial transfers; then, after 1998, it was the way for the federal government to restore those cuts. Since 2004 the government of Canada has treated the CHST as two programs: the Canada Health Transfer and the Canada Social Transfer (the latter being earmarked for both social assistance and post-secondary education). The CHT and CST inherited two sets of conditions from the CAP and EPF programs (which the original CHST combined): that no province restrict the eligibility for welfare of residents arriving from other provinces, and that all provinces meet the five broad principles of the *Canada Health Act* (see discussion in Chapter 9 on health care) in the design and delivery of their health services. The federal government invited the provinces to work with it to develop shared principles and objectives for the new transfer. But the most important intergovernmental discussions revolved solely around the money: how much there would be and how it would be allocated among the provinces and territories.

For a decade the federal government and the provinces engaged in a tug of war over the CHT and CST, culminating in the 2004 health care accord signed by all the First Ministers, which largely restored the 1995 cuts to provincial transfers (Lazar and St-Hilaire, 2004). In the meantime, however, the provinces and territories squeezed their budgets, especially in education and welfare programs, to pay for ever-increasing health care costs. The issue of the allocation of CHST funds across provinces was even more complicated. The historic patterns of cost-sharing under previous, pre-CHST programs treated each province differently depending on its needs or expenditure record. After the 1995 cuts, however, the richer provinces began demanding equal per capita shares of the CHT and CST funds.[3] The federal 1996 budget reduced the disparity by 10 per cent per year, cutting it in half over five years. The issue of 'equal shares' of health care and other federal payments have continued to vex the Conservative government.

The Harper Era: Achieving Balance?

Since its election in 2006 the Conservative federal government has sought to find a new equilibrium between the competing pressures of equity and efficiency, as well as between decentralization and local initiative on the one hand and national (federal) objectives and control on the other. There have been a number of fiscal conflicts among governments, but on the whole the scene has been much calmer than in the decade of 1995–2005. This reduced conflict has been fortunate given the difficult fiscal challenges forced by the global recession of 2008–9. Here I assess the current issues in the three main areas of the fiscal federalism system: the tax structure, major social transfers, and the equalization program, followed by a brief assessment of the response to the recession.

The Future of the Tax Structure

As noted above, the Canadian tax system is already considerably decentralized, especially compared with other federal systems. Ottawa has significantly reduced its taxation of corporate and personal income tax (PIT) in the past decade, and the GST by two percentage points. These tax changes, amidst new spending commitments, have limited the ability of the federal government to reduce vertical or horizontal imbalances to the extent that some provinces may wish. Tax reform has been important for the provinces as well. Provincial taxes have been cut and tax systems redesigned. Alberta introduced its 'single rate' PIT, and other provinces collapsed rate and bracket structures to a lesser degree. Moreover, most provinces, led by Quebec, increasingly use the tax structure to pursue social policy objectives, including integration of tax treatment with social assistance and related family and social security issues (Lachance and Vaillancourt, 2001). The nine provinces with Tax Collection Agreements (TCAs) have advocated more flexible arrangements to allow the provinces to vary their **tax rate** and bracket structure. The federal government has accommodated many different tax credit and deduction schemes and since 1998 has allowed direct provincial 'tax on income' to replace a formula based simply on a percentage of federal tax. These changes have not posed a significant threat to the harmony of the Canadian tax system, although economists and tax experts worry that a more fragmented tax base will erode the benefits of economic union and increase transaction costs (Brown, 2001). Meanwhile, the Harper government has been strengthening the tax collection system by bringing key provinces into the harmonized sales tax regime and by encouraging more harmonization of corporate income tax (Canada, 2006c: 70; Canada, 2007: 44). Most notable are the agreements with Ontario and British Columbia to harmonize their provincial retail sales taxes with the federal GST[4] on July 1, 2010. As noted earlier, British Columbia later had to retract on its agreement with Ottawa, following the rejection of the HST in a province-wide referendum.

The objective of harmonization is to combine and to treat uniformly the federal and provincial tax bases, so that businesses have only one tax to pay and differing sectors of the economy are treated equitably (both goods and service-producers). Even where the new HST is revenue neutral, the estimated economic gains are said to be significant (Tremblay, 2009). Nonetheless, the impact on the consumer can be large for certain goods or services where the tax has not been previously levied, such as on real estate trans-actions. The public rarely likes new taxes and bringing in the HST just as the economy was recovering from the recession has proven to be politically unpopular in the two provinces. In British Columbia a public initiative succeeded in placing the future of the HST in a provincial referendum to be conducted in September 2011, which saw voters rejecting the new harmonized tax by a significant margin. In response to criticisms, the federal government made concessions to trim some aspects of the harmonized tax base, reducing the overall potential gain for the national economy (McFarland, 2010). Still, the extension of HST regimes to Ontario leaves only one large province, BC, and Manitoba, Saskatchewan, and Prince Edward Island outside the HST system (since Alberta has no retail sales tax, harmonization is not required). Thus the HST system would cover 85 per cent of the national economy—a major policy achievement.

Steady-state on Social Program Transfers

In the 1990s Ottawa largely abandoned the sharing of social policy functions and with it shared-cost federalism (Hobson and St-Hilaire, 2000). Intergovernmental transfers continued to grow faster than direct federal payments to individuals, but Ottawa under Prime Minister Chrétien tended to see new federal–provincial programs as the last re-sort. The Martin government, in contrast, was willing to renew co-operative funding ap-proaches with the provinces, notably in the 10-year health care accord reached in 2004.

The Conservative government under Prime Minister Harper has rejected expensive new federal social programs, whether delivered by it or by the provinces. For example, the Conservatives cancelled the Martin government's 2005 child-care agreements (see Chapter 10 in this volume, by Martha Friendly and Linda White). Nonetheless, the Harper government honoured the 2004 accord on health care; put equalization and TFF back on a more predictable, formula-driven track; and renewed funding for cities and infrastructure (the latter accelerated significantly by its anti-recession economic stimulus program of 2008–11). One issue that has dropped off its agenda is reaching agreement on 'equitable and predictable' support for post-secondary education and training.

At the beginning of Prime Minister Harper's term in office, the terms 'fiscal balance' and 'fiscal imbalance' had clearly entered the Canadian political discourse. The provinces argued that the strong federal surplus combined with the net provincial deficit would only get worse unless corrected. Their view was substantiated by an independent panel (Gagné and Stein, 2006: 62–8) and, more significantly, was generally acknowledged by the Harper government. The solutions proposed to tackle the VFI included: transferring all proceeds of the GST to the provinces (Séguin, 2002); further transfer of income tax points to the provinces (Séguin, 2002); significant increases to the CHT for health care (Romanow, 2002; Gagné and Stein, 2006); and increases in federal equalization and TFF payments, even if these do not benefit all provinces (Canada (Senate), 2002; Gagné and Stein, 2006; O'Brien, 2006a; O'Brien, 2006b).

While the provinces as a whole were clearly in favour of reducing the VFI, they differed sharply on the best solution. The only unambiguous proponent of tax transfers was Alberta. Quebec supported tax transfers until it became clear that it could not afford them without some form of 'associated equalization': either equalized tax points, as in 1977, or an enhanced general equalization program. The idea of equalized tax points was opposed by the richer provinces. The other provinces have also been open to a combination of tax and cash solutions, and most of them have also shared Quebec's position regarding equalization. Ontario took a hard line against enhanced equalization at the expense of correcting its own particular VFI.[5] In sum, the point at issue was balance, with the appropriate point of equilibrium being in the eye of the beholder. The March 2007 budget tabled by Finance Minister Jim Flaherty made significant strides towards fiscal balance, as the Conservative government defined the problem. It re-engineered virtually every aspect of the fiscal arrangements (excepting the 2004 healthcare accord). The Conservatives put the equalization and territorial funding formulae back on a long-term, transparent and principled basis. It responded to concerns about fiscal balance by broadening the standard for equalization, yielding an initial increase of $1 billion in entitlements. It also increased social program spending under the CST and put that transfer on a long-term legislated basis, as well as extending funding for municipalities from the federal gasoline tax and for infrastructure, among others.

Moreover, the 2007 Budget provided further substance to the Harper commitment to an 'open federalism'—essentially a more decentralized and classical approach to intergovernmental arrangements. The Conservatives continued in general to support a more limited use of the federal spending power, avoiding new direct federal programs in areas of provincial jurisdiction. On the other hand, for any new spending initiatives the Budget called for measures to 'ensure appropriate reporting and accountability to Canadians' (Canada, 2007: 23, 26, 31).

In summary, the Conservatives have tried to maintain a relatively steady state when it comes to transfers to social programs. Their efforts to provide more fiscal balance were achieved mainly through changes in the equalization program, discussed next, but as a quid pro quo for the richer provinces who do not receive equalization, it has continued to accelerate the movement in the CST formula for equal per capita shares. This move has stripped some built in equalization features in place for over 30 years, and pushes the system as a whole farther away from the concepts of differential need and regional redistribution.

Controversy over Equalization

The equalization program remains the bottom-line component of Canadian fiscal federalism: it tends to be a residual device for smoothing out the effects of tax allocation and other transfer decisions. Of all the intergovernmental arrangements, it is probably the best understood and the most broadly supported (Gagné and Stein, 2006; O'Brien, 2006a). It is also a constitutional commitment. Equalization makes fiscal and program decentralization possible by ensuring a basic level of comparable services at comparable tax rates across provinces. Without equalization, most provinces could not contemplate the degree of autonomy they enjoy now.

Although it fared reasonably well in the 1990s compared with other federal programs, equalization has been undermined to some degree since 2000 as payments have become more volatile. The (then) eight recipient provinces formed a common front on the VFI and have all benefited from increased cash transfers for health care. But provinces like Newfoundland and Labrador, Nova Scotia, and Saskatchewan did not benefit when equalization was clawed back because of their oil and gas revenues. And the benefits to other provinces were limited by the fact that the formula inadequately reflected real revenue differences. Under the 'five province standard' used until 2004, Alberta's petroleum royalties were left out of the formula.

In partial response to these concerns the Martin government reached agreements with Nova Scotia and Newfoundland and Labrador on protecting their revenues from offshore resources. Other provinces, notably Ontario and Quebec, criticized these bilateral arrangements as subverting the logic and purpose of the existing equalization program. These provinces also opposed any general measure to enhance the equalization program, which essentially has a redistributive or even zero-sum character to it.

The challenge facing the Harper government since 2006 has been to achieve an acceptable trade-off between fixing the vertical imbalance and fixing the horizontal one. Common ground was achievable on health care in 2004 because all provinces and territories got the same share of a growing fiscal pie. This increase made more acceptable, in the short term, the Martin government's decision, a few weeks after the health accord, to de-link equalization and TFF payments from any kind of formula. However, governments and observers alike were concerned about the fairness, predictability, and lack of transparency of the arrangements. In 2006 two major independent panels, one appointed by the provinces, the other by the federal government, proposed ways to return the horizontal equity programs to a firmer foundation. Both reports called for a 10-province standard—i.e., one that includes Alberta—and for either all resource revenues (Gagné-Stein, 2006) or 50 per cent of them (O'Brien, 2006a) to be included in equalization. Both also acknowledged that the level of entitlements that such a new formula would create might be more than the federal government could afford.

Clearly Finance Minister Flaherty hoped, with the 2007 Budget, to restore intergovernmental harmony on the equalization issue. Yet as always the detailed allocation of funds from the application of new policy generated a sense of winners and losers, reflecting also the lack of consensus among provinces and territories about how best to reform fiscal arrangements (Harding, 2006). While all provinces and territories were better off financially, some benefited more than others. Largely by virtue of its population size, Quebec received the lion's share of total cash in the improved equalization program. Ontario and Alberta benefited the most from social program transfer improvements because of the significant policy change to make cash entitlements equal per capita. Provinces that are both recipients of equalization and enjoy increasing non-renewable resource revenues from oil and gas—i.e., Saskatchewan, Nova Scotia, and Newfoundland and Labrador—lost ground as the new principles imposed a more punitive approach.[6]

At a meeting of Finance Ministers in November 2008, federal Finance Minister Flaherty announced two historic firsts: for the first time since the program was inaugurated in 1957, Ontario would receive equalization payments in the next fiscal year; and also for the first time Newfoundland and Labrador would not. Of course in theory and principle, equalization is designed so that provinces can be recipients one year and not the next, depending on their relative fiscal capacity. There should be no political impact, let alone moral lessons, attached. But in reality it is very politically significant for one of Canada's largest and richer provinces (in overall income and wealth terms, if not government revenues) to be perceived as a 'have-not' province (Howlett, 2008). In Newfoundland and Labrador, meanwhile, the milestone of coming off equalization was celebrated as a major and long-sought achievement (Antle, 2008). Ontario's status as a recipient province does create concerns, including about the affordability and volatility of the overall program (in 2011–12 Ontario's equalization payments are estimated to be $2.2 billion, the second highest payment among the recipient provinces). The political optics and possibly even support for equalization may change now that the majority of the Canadian population lives in recipient provinces.[7]

The last major development on equalization, announced in the November 2008 Fiscal and Economic Update, was the unilateral federal decision to depart from a number of the principles of its much heralded 2007 budget—only 18 months earlier—to rein in the growth of equalization in light of revenue shortfalls and new expenditure commitments related to the recession (see below). While not entirely a return to the Martin government's incremental approach unguided by objective principles, the new measures effectively put both a ceiling and a floor on payments for the foreseeable future. In effect the federal measures provide greater expenditure stability and predictability for both the federal government and for each of the recipient provinces. Such stability became an important consideration in the midst of a serious recession, and may explain why the changes received relatively little criticism. What these measures do not do, however, is to advance the cause of **horizontal fiscal** equity in the federation. In this sense, they are a departure from the high ground of Harper's 'open federalism' (Smart, 2009).

Responding to the 2008-09 Recession

The deep recession of 2008–9 played havoc with public finances in Canada, and is forcing what may yet be major changes in fiscal federalism. Indeed the recession can be seen as a test of our intergovernmental and fiscal systems. Was there sufficient intergovernmental co-ordination of macroeconomic policy? Did all of the debt and deficit cutting of the previous two decades put us in a better position? Have the short-term and longer-term economic effects of the recession changed the intergovernmental balance of power in Canada?[8]

Our economy is heavily integrated globally and continentally, so we could hardly avoid the effects of the financial crisis of 2008 even if its main causes were external to Canada. Canadian governments and the business sector did have some initial concern about financial sector liquidity and the effects of a credit crunch on business large and small. However, the major impact was on international commodity prices and international trade (especially with the USA), which drove down employment, profits, investment and, of course, government revenues (Cross, 2010). The overall economy declined by 3.6 per cent over three quarters, the lowest drop among G-8 countries, and unemployment rose from 5.5 per cent in late 2007 to 8.1 per cent in late 2010, over half in the manufacturing sector. While all parts of Canada felt the effects, the downturn was most severe in Alberta (due in part to a sharp drop in oil prices) and in Ontario, particularly in the automobile manufacturing sector (Cross, 2010; Canada, 2009). And of course, the recession had an immediate impact on public finances due to declining revenues and rising costs related to unemployment and welfare, an overall loss of about $20 billion (TD Economics, 2009).

The federal government did most of the heavy lifting in the Canadian response to the international crisis, such as its efforts to sustain financial sector liquidity and to grant loans to the automobile industry. However, it became clear very quickly that all governments would have to be involved in economic stimulus—the spending of funds to halt growing unemployment and to maintain some degree of consumer demand. Even so, when added to the $20 billion hole the recession had already punched into public finances, such expenditures contributed to a substantial deterioration in budget balances. Thus short-term economic stability is purchased by long-term fiscal pain.

In national political terms, the Harper government's initial fiscal response to the international crisis and ensuing recession came in the ill-fated November 2008 statement soon after the general election in October. The political crisis that followed—the claims that the statement did not meet the needs of the economic crisis, the threatened fall of the minority government, the proposed coalition of opposition parties, the proroguing of Parliament, and the delivery of a new budget in January 2009—while fascinating and significant, overshadowed intergovernmental and regional issues. The details of the political controversy are beyond our story here.[9] However, from the events during the recession and in the difficult recovery since, one can make four observations to summarize their impact and interaction with fiscal federalism.

First, as noted, the recession reversed a hard-won position of all governments from financial surplus to budgetary deficits. In August 2010 TD Economics forecasted that the federal budgetary position has deteriorated in just two years from +$9.5 billion in 2007–8 to -$53.8 billion in 2009–10, and the net position of all the provinces and territories from +$11.3 billion to -$26.8 billion, in the same period (TD Economics, 2010). Among the provinces, historic debt legacies combined with the recession to produce significant differences, from Quebec with a debt of nearly 50 per cent of GDP to Alberta with no debt at all, and in terms of budgetary deficit with Ontario having the most serious ongoing budgetary position (the highest annual deficit as a percentage of GDP, approaching 3.5 per cent). While it is perhaps cold comfort to Canadians, international comparisons demonstrate that our deficit and debt hangover from 2008–9 is among the least burdensome among OECD countries. Clearly the difficult choices made in the 1990s contributed to a stronger fiscal position going into the recession (IMF, 2010; TD Economics, 2010). All governments have indicated that their position is to restore their budgets to a balanced position within 2–4 years.

Second, the restoration of a budgetary surplus will mean at least a substantial degree of program expenditure restraint at all levels: in some respects, a return to the difficult years of the early 1990s. Thus far the axe has barely fallen on intergovernmental transfers, and in fact when one considers the extra funds put into infrastructure programs, transfers were still increasing overall in 2010–11. The federal budget of 2009 did place a new ceiling on equalization payments, as noted above. During the 2011 election campaign the Conservatives promised to maintain the 6 per cent annual growth in health transfers for at least two years past the expiry of the 10-year accord in 2014 (CBC News, April 28, 2011). Whether all the transfers to the provinces will be saved from expenditure cuts in the next few years to balance the federal budget remains to be seen.

Third, and on a happier note, the recession demonstrated a generally co-operative and functional relationship among the governments. Perhaps because all regional economies were impacted by the down-turn, there was no evidence of discord on the overall macroeconomic stance to be taken. All provinces undertook a similar degree of counter-cyclical budgeting in synch with the federal position; all participated readily in a major acceleration of existing infrastructure programs to stimulate the construction and related sectors. The provinces may not have been thrilled with the conditional nature of the federal funds, but seemed to swallow their objections (Young, 2009).

Still, old and new regional fault lines can be expected to appear in the federation as a result of changes generated by the crisis. The only massive bailout of the private sector from public funds occurred for General Motors and Chrysler, auto firms based in Ontario, while other sectors had to fend for themselves. Urban and industrial workers, concentrated in central Canada, found the unemployment insurance system to be inequitable and ineffective, and called for fundamental reforms. The western resource economy meanwhile has re-emerged in a stronger position as commodity prices rise. And, existing regional tensions over the speed and depth of reducing greenhouse gas emissions may have been worsened by concern over jobs and economic growth. In sum, as the dust settles slowly from the economic upheaval, the perceived balance of benefits and costs in the Canadian economy will underpin the politics, not only of fiscal federalism, but of other intergovernmental issues.

Evaluating Canadian Fiscal Federalism

We may now come to some judgments about fiscal federalism as a whole, as determined by the three criteria set out at the beginning of this chapter. On the *performance of the federation*, fiscal federalism gets good grades. Its flexibility has enabled the system to transform gradually (though not without conflict) from the heavily centralized framework of the 1940s to the markedly decentralized framework of the late 1990s. The transfer of tax points, the removal of conditions on grant programs, and the maintenance of equalization payments have enabled Canada to sustain an emphasis on provincial autonomy that most other federal systems have abandoned.

Since the 1950s fiscal federalism has been generally consistent with federal principles, including respect for unity and diversity and provincial autonomy, although Quebec's concerns about the use of the federal spending power remains an important and occasionally serious problem. As noted, the arrangements have shown considerable flexibility, contributing in turn to workable intergovernmental relations. The major exception, even if it is part of the pattern, came with the unilateral cuts of 1995, which undermined intergovernmental trust for many years (Inwood, Johns, and O'Reilly, 2004).

The Harper government's approach to long-term, predictable, transparent, and principled funding is, in our view, consistent with federal principles and with a more classical view of federal–provincial responsibilities (which they apparently encompass in the concept of 'open federalism'). The working out of those principles also means a more co-operative ethos than the unilateral federalism of the 1980s and 1990s.

On *policy effectiveness,* the system's remarkable flexibility is also an asset, although judgment on outcomes depends on the beholder and the specific policy program in question. After all, fiscal relations are usually a means to an end, not an end in themselves. The discussions of social program funding elsewhere in this book provide fuller answers on policy effectiveness. As for equalization and territorial financing, there remains some debate about the economic effects of alleged dependency on such transfers,[10] but both programs have worked effectively to achieve their stated purposes of closing the fiscal capacity gap across the provinces and territories:

> Without Equalization payments, the fiscal capacity of the least well-off province was between 58 and 68 per cent of the national average. With Equalization, the fiscal capacity of that province was raised to between 91 and almost 100 per cent of the national average. (O'Brien, 2006a: 30)

The Territorial Funding program is also clearly effective in terms of its simple objective to close the gap between expenditure needs and own-source revenues, although the full adequacy of that funding has been debatable (O'Brien, 2006b: 32–3).

The recent focus on correcting the fiscal balance does not necessarily imply abandoning the emphasis, since the early 2000s, on equity considerations. But the size and distribution of the increased equalization payments announced in the 2007 budget (and scaled back barely two years later) must be measured against other changes such as the relentless move to equal per capita cash shares (and thus less interregional redistribution) in all other federal transfers.

Finally, on the criterion of *political legitimacy*, the most significant trend in the past decade has been the erosion of mutual trust among the governments. As a recent independent report on its fiscal relations with the provinces found, the government of Canada has too often been perceived as a 'rule-breaker, non-negotiator, [and] unapologetic unilateralist' —the very traits that the federal government itself condemns in international contexts (Gagné and Stein, 2006: 90). Thus the provinces and territories have been calling for more formal, deliberate, and predictable fiscal relations.

While it would be unfair to characterize fiscal relations under the Harper government as unilateral, the Conservatives have had to impose solutions in the absence of an intergovernmental consensus. Mutual trust has likely been improved in the more stable, predictable, fair, and transparent arrangements. Also, the 10-year agreement on health care funding has clearly reduced intergovernmental conflict in that area. As the expiry of that agreement in 2014 approaches, one can expect increasing tensions.

A second set of legitimacy considerations relates to accountability. Here the focus is more on citizens' expectations than on governments' needs, although the trend in public management to greater transparency and simpler, more direct and quantifiable accountability structures, has permeated government agendas as well. Being notoriously complex, fiscal federalism is not especially transparent. Yet policy effectiveness often requires complex responses to the widely varying circumstances across a diverse federation, and flexible rather than rigid formulas for responding to often rapidly changing economic, social, and fiscal conditions. In other words, good policy in this area probably should be complex. That said, the very complexity of fiscal federalism has made it easy for governments at both levels to avoid direct accountability, each often blaming the other for perceived failings.

Issues of legitimacy and accountability turn in part on changing norms of democratic input and deliberation. Some Canadians have asked why momentous fiscal federalism issues should be decided behind closed doors by first ministers, finance ministers, and technocrats when other major intergovernmental policy issues are decided in forums that are open to the media and hence to the public. One partial answer, as noted already, is that they are not. Most of the broad issues surrounding fiscal relations are debated in the media and are matters for question period in the House of Commons and the broader political community. Even when tied into budgetary planning, the discussion of fiscal federalism is becoming more open and transparent. As we look forward to the renewal of major intergovernmental transfer programs by March 2014, a broad public debate is inevitable, one in which public opinion and electoral support will go a long way towards determining what can and cannot be achieved.

Notes

1. Dollar amounts are nominal and reflect actual transfer amounts in the years indicated.
2. Social program transfers, 1982–3 to 1992–3, consist of the EPF and CAP cash transfers; since 1997–8 they consist of the CHT/EST cash transfer.
3. During the inaugural year of the CHST, 1996–7, per capita entitlement ranged from $825 for Alberta to $993 for Quebec and $1018 for the Northwest Territories.
4. As an illustration of the difficulties in negotiating a series of bilateral deals for tax harmonization, the terms of the new agreements with BC and Ontario have led to demands for similar funding compensation to Quebec for its harmonization in place since the 1990s.
5. Ontario increasingly made a special case (MacKinnon, 2005A and 2005B; Ontario, 2006; Canada, 2006C: 118–22). It claimed a chronic shortfall of at least $23 billion (in 2005) from the federal government (without accounting for the still enormous net economic advantages it reaps from the Canadian economic union; see Page, 2002).
6. Two new measures, both recommended by the O'Brien report of 2006, placed brakes on fiscal improvement in these provinces. These were the inclusion of 50 per cent of natural resource revenues in the formula for calculating fiscal capacity, and the cap on entitlements if they exceed the fiscal capacity of a non-recipient province (i.e., Ontario). While the new policy claims to respect the Offshore Accords signed in 2005 with the Nova Scotia and Newfoundland and Labrador governments, the new rules sought to quarantine such bilateral arrangements by making their continued operation more difficult.
7. Michael Smart (2009) makes a number of important observations, which are best left out of the main narrative for this chapter. These include the effect of higher energy resource revenues on equalization entitlements. In 2007 the federal government had introduced a fiscal cap on recipient provinces if their entitlements, due to the only 50 per cent inclusion of resource revenues in the formula, meant that their fiscal capacity would exceed that of a non-recipient province (this was a provision that would and did penalize Saskatchewan and Newfoundland and Labrador). Rising energy revenues since 2008 have put Ontario into the recipient group, making British Columbia the next in line as the standard for drawing the fiscal cap. In other words, a much higher bar, which to date has not been reached, therefore helps protect the fiscal position of Saskatchewan and Newfoundland and Labrador.
8. For an overview of how Canadian federalism affects macroeconomic management, see Bakvis, Baier and Brown, 2009: 190–93.
9. For two balanced accounts see MacKinnon, 2009 and Malloy, 2010.
10. See Courchene, 1995; Boessenkool, 1996; PTMF, 1998; Banting, 1995; Milne, 1998.

References

Anderson, G. 2010. *Fiscal Federalism: A Comparative Introduction*. Don Mills: Oxford University Press.

Antle, R. 2008. 'Have Not No More: This is a Good Day, Premier says', *Telegram* (St. John's) 4 November.

Bakvis, H., G. Baier, and D. Brown, 2009. *Contested Federalism: Certainty and Ambiguity in the Canadian Federation*. Don Mills: Oxford University Press.

Banting, K.G. 1995. 'Who 'R' Us?' In *The 1995 Federal Budget: Retrospect and Prospect*, ed. J. Courchene and T.A. Wilson. Kingston: John Deutsch Institute for the Study of Economic Policy, Queen's University: 173–81.

Bird, R.M. 2001. 'Sales Tax Harmonization Issues'. In *Tax Competition and the Fiscal Union in Canada (Conference Proceedings / Working Paper Series)*, ed. D. Brown. Kingston: Institute of Intergovernmental Relations, Queen's University.

Boadway, R. 2005. 'The Vertical Fiscal Gap: Conceptions and Misconceptions'. In *Canadian Fiscal Arrangements: What Works, What Might Work Better*, ed. H. Lazar. Kingston: Institute of Intergovernmental Relations, Queen's University: 51–80.

———— and A. Shah, 2009. *Fiscal Federalism: Principles and Practice of Multiorder Governance*. Cambridge: Cambridge University Press.

Boessenkool, K. 1996. *The Illusion of Equality: Provincial Distribution of the Canada Health and Social Transfer*. Toronto: C.D. Howe Institute.

Brown, D.M. 1996. *Equalization on the Basis of Need in Canada (Reflections Series No. 15)*. Kingston: Institute of Intergovernmental Relations, Queen's University.

————, ed. 2001. *Tax Competition and the Fiscal Union in Canada (Conference Proceedings / Working Paper Series)*. Kingston: Institute of Intergovernmental Relations, Queen's University.

————. 2002. *Market Rules: Economic Union Reform and Intergovernmental Policy-Making in Australia and Canada*. Montreal: McGill-Queen's University Press.

———— 2007. 'Integration, Equity and Section 36', *Supreme Court Law Review*, Vol 37: 285-315.

Burns, R.M. 1980. *The Acceptable Mean: The Tax Rental Agreements, 1941–62*. Toronto: Canadian Tax Foundation.

Canada. 2006a. *The Budget in Brief 2006*. Ottawa: Department of Finance.

————. 2006b. *The Estimates, 2006–07*. Ottawa: Treasury Board Secretariat.

————. 2006c. *Restoring Fiscal Balance in Canada Budget Paper, 2006*. Ottawa: Department of Finance.

————. 2007. *Restoring Fiscal Balance for a Stronger Federation, Budget 2007*. Ottawa: Department of Finance.

————. 2008. *Responsible Leadership, Budget 2008*. 26 February. Ottawa: Department of Finance.

————. 2009. *Canada's Economic Action Plan, Budget 2009*. 27 January. Ottawa: Department of Finance.

————. 2010. *The Government Expense Plan and Main Estimates*, 2010–11. Treasury Board Secretariat, available online at http://www.tbs-sct.gc.ca/est-pre/20102011/me-bpd/toc-tdm-eng.asp, accessed 5 November, 2010.

————. Senate. 2002. *The Effectiveness and Possible Improvements to the Present Equalization Policy, Report of the Standing Committee on National Finance*. Ottawa: Senate of Canada.

CBC News. 2011. 'Reality Check'. 28 April. Accessed 1 June, 2011 at: http://www.cbc.ca/news/politics/canadavotes2011/reality-check/2011/04/surgical-wait-times-how-much-progress-have-we-really-made.htmlsource.

CICS (Canadian Intergovernmental Conference Secretariat). 2005. 'First Ministers and National Aboriginal Leaders Strengthening Relationships and Closing the Gap', 24–5 November. Kelowna, B.C., text at www.scsis.gc.ca. Accessed 1 June, 2006.

Courchene, T.J. 1995. *Redistributing Money and Power: A Guide to the Canada Health and Social Transfer (Observation No. 39)*. Toronto: C.D. Howe Institute.

Cross, P. 2010. 'Year End Review of 2009' *Canadian Economic Observer*. Statistics Canada. 23:4 (April): 3.1–3.13

Gagné, R., and J. Stein (co-chairs). 2006. *Reconciling the Irreconcilable: Addressing Canada's Fiscal Imbalance, Report of the Advisory Panel on Fiscal Imbalance*. Ottawa: The Council of the Federation.

Greenspan, E., and A. Wilson-Smith. 1997. *Double Vision: The Inside Story of the Liberals in Power*. Toronto: McClelland and Stewart / Seal Books.

Harding, K. 2006. 'Premiers' bid for unity turns to acrimony: No deal achieved on equalization plan', *Globe and Mail*, 9 Jun.

Hobson, P., and F. St-Hilaire. 2000. 'The Evolution of Federal–Provincial Fiscal

Arrangements: Putting Humpty Together Again'. In *Search of A New Mission Statement for Fiscal Federalism: Canada: the State of the Federation, 2000*, ed. H. Lazar. Kingston: Institute of Intergovernmental Relations, Queen's University: 159–88.

Hogg, P.W. 1996. *Constitutional Law of Canada (Fourth Student Edition)*. Toronto: Carswell.

Howlett, K. 2008. 'Quebec demands 'fair treatment' as Harper compensates Ontario', *Globe and Mail*, 28 March.

Inwood, G., C.M. Johns, and P.L. O'Reilly. 2004. 'Intergovernmental Officials in Canada'. In *Reconsidering the Institutions of Canadian Federalism: Canada, the State of the Federation, 2002*, ed. J.P. Meekison, H. Telford and H. Lazar. Kingston: Institute of Intergovernmental Relations, Queen's University: 249–84.

Lachance, R., and F. Vaillancourt. 2001. 'Quebec's Tax on Income: Evolution, Status and Evaluation'. In *Tax Competition and the Fiscal Union in Canada (Conference Proceedings / Working Paper Series)*, ed. D.M. Brown. Kingston: Institute of Intergovernmental Relations, Queen's University.

Lazar, H., ed. 2000. *In Search of A New Mission Statement for Fiscal Federalism: Canada: the State of the Federation, 2000*. Kingston: Institute of Intergovernmental Relations, Queen's University.

————. 2000. 'In Search of a New Mission Statement for Canadian Fiscal Federalism'. In *In Search of A New Mission Statement for Fiscal Federalism: Canada: the State of the Federation, 2000*. Kingston: Institute of Intergovernmental Relations, Queen's University: 3–39.

———— and F. St-Hilaire ed. 2004. *Money, Politics and Health Care: Reconstructing the Federal–provincial Partnership*. Montreal: Institute for Research on Public Policy.

———— F. St-Hilaire, and J.-F. Tremblay. 2004. 'Vertical Fiscal Imbalance: Myth or Reality?' In *Money, Politics and Health Care: Reconstructing the Federal–provincial Partnership*, ed. H. Lazar. Montreal: Institute for Research on Public Policy: 135–87.

MacKinnon, D. 2005a. *Fairness in Confederation: Fiscal Imbalance, Driving Ontario to 'Have-Not' Status, Phase One Report for the Ontario Chamber of Commerce*. Toronto: Ontario Chamber of Commerce.

————. 2005b. *Fairness in Confederation: Fiscal Imbalance, A Roadmap to Recovery, Phase Two Report for the Ontario Chamber of Commerce*. Toronto: Ontario Chamber of Commerce.

MacKinnon, J. 2010. 'The Prospect of Hanging? The Political Context for the 2009 Federal Budget'. In *The 2009 Federal Budget: Challenge, Response and Retrospect*, ed. C. Beach et al. Montreal: McGill-Queen's University Press.

Malloy, J. 2010. 'The Drama of Parliament under Minority Government' in G. B. Doern and C. Stoney (eds.): *How Ottawa Spends, 2010–2011, Recession, Realignment and the New Deficit Era* (Montreal: McGill-Queen's University Press): 31–47.

McFarland, J. 2010. 'Two provinces, two sets of rules' *Globe and Mail* 1 July, 2010.

Milne, D. 1998. 'Equalization and the Politics of Restraint'. In *Equalization: Its Contribution to Canada's Economic and Fiscal Progress Policy Forum (Series No. 36)*, ed. R. Boadway and P. Hobson. Kingston: John Deutsch Institute for the Study of Economic Policy, Queen's University: 175–203.

O'Brien, A. (chair). 2006a. *Achieving a National Purpose: Putting Equalization Back on Track, Report of the Expert Panel on Equalization and Territorial Formula Financing*. Ottawa: Department of Finance.

————(chair). 2006b. *Achieving a National Purpose: Improving Territorial Formula Financing and Strengthening Canada's Territories, Report of the Expert Panel on Equalization and Territorial Formula Financing*. Ottawa: Department of Finance.

Ontario. 2006. '*Strong Ontario: Seeking Fairness for Canadians Living in Ontario*'. Available on-line at http://www.strongontario.ca/english/ — accessed June 23, 2006.

Page, M. 2002. *Provincial Trade Patterns (Statistics Canada, Agricultural and Rural Working Paper Series No. 58*. Ottawa: Statistics Canada.

Painter, M. 1991. 'Intergovernmental Relations: An Institutional Analysis', *Canadian Journal of Political Science*, 24: 269–88.

Prince, M., and F. Abele. 2005. 'Paying for Self-Determination: Aboriginal Peoples, Self-Government and Fiscal Relations in Canada'. In *Reconfiguring Aboriginal–State Relations in Canada (Canada: The State of the Federation, 2003)*, ed. M. Murphy. Kingston: Institute of Intergovernmental Relations, Queen's University.

PTMF—Provincial/Territorial Ministers of Finance. 1998. *Report to Premiers: Redesigning Fiscal Federalism—Issues and Options (mimeo).*

Romanow, R. 2002. *Final Report of the Commission on the Future of Health Care in Canada.* Ottawa: Health Canada.

Séguin, Y. 2002. *Report: A New Division of Canada's Fiscal Resources, Commission on Fiscal Imbalance.* Quebec: Commission sur le déséquilibre fiscal.

Smart, M. 2009. 'The Evolution of Federal Transfers since the O'Brien Report'. In *The 2009 Federal Budget: Challenge, Response and Retrospect*, ed. C. Beach et al. Montreal: McGill-Queen's University Press.

TD Economics. 2009. 'Priming the Fiscal Pump,' *TD Economics Special Report*, 28 April.

TD Economics. 2010. 'Canada's Fiscal Exit Strategy', *TD Economics Special Report*, 3 August.

Treff, K., and D. Perry. 2005. *Finances of the Nation 2005.* Toronto : Canadian Tax Foundation.

Treff, K., and D. Ort. 2010. *Finances of the Nation 2010.* Toronto: Canadian Tax Foundation.

Tremblay, J.-F. 2009. 'Implications of the Shifting Fiscal and Economic Position of Ontario within the Canadian Economic Union' Paper presented at Conference: 'The 2009 Federal Budget: Challenge, Response and Retrospect', John Deutsch Institute for Economic Policy, Queen's University, Kingston, May 2009. http://jdi.econ.queensu.ca/content/2009-federal-budget-challenge-response-and-retrospect-may-7-8-2009, accessed 6 June 2011.

Vaillancourt, F. 2000. 'Federal–provincial Small Transfer Programs in Canada, 1957–1998: Importance, Composition and Evaluation'. In *In Search of A New Mission Statement for Fiscal Federalism: Canada: the State of the Federation, 2000*, ed. H. Lazar. Kingston: Institute of Intergovernmental Relations, Queen's University: 189–212.

Young, R. 2009. 'Panel comments on 'Subnational Governments and the Stimulus Packages in Canada and the United States''. American Political Science Association, Toronto, September.

8 The Three Federalisms Revisited: Social Policy and Intergovernmental Decision-Making

Keith G. Banting

Canadians develop their social programs in the context of a vibrant federal state, with strong governments at both the federal and provincial level. Does this structure of political institutions matter for the nature of the social programs that governments adopt at the end of the day? Or do the primary factors that influence social programs emerge from the wider social and political environment?

Answering these questions turns out to be rather difficult. One approach is to compare federal states with unitary states, but such comparisons tend to generate rather broad generalizations and cannot resolve the issue for any specific country such as Canada. An alternative approach is to try to compare Canadian experience with what might have happened if Canada had been a unitary state, but such hypothetical exercises seem unconvincing. Fortunately, there is an alternative strategy. We can examine the policy implications of the three federalisms that co-exist within the country.

Canada has never adopted a single approach to federalism. Rather, we have chosen to live with three distinct models of federalism—three federalisms in one country, each with its own decision rules and intergovernmental processes. Social policy reflects all three models particularly well. Throughout the history of the Canadian welfare state, federal and provincial governments have designed different social programs according to different intergovernmental rules and processes. More precisely, at critical historical junctures, exactly the same federal and provincial governments were shaping different social programs according to different models of federalism, with differing policy outcomes.

Canada therefore constitutes a natural laboratory in which to analyze the implications of different models of federalism. As we shall see, the distinctive incentives and constraints inherent in the different models help explain a number of puzzles about the Canadian welfare state, including the striking contrast between the limited nature of the country's income security programs and the more universalist character of its health care. Moreover, in recent decades, the three models help explain the highly uneven impact of retrenchment on different social programs.

This chapter develops these themes in four sections. The first section describes the federal–provincial division of jurisdiction in social policy and the three models of federalism. The second section examines the impact of the three federalisms on the expansion of the welfare state in the middle decades of the twentieth century, while the third section examines their impact on the politics of retrenchment in recent decades. A final section then pulls together the threads of the argument.

The Three Federalisms and Social Policy

In formal terms, authority over social policy is divided between the federal and provincial governments in ways that make Canada one of the most decentralized welfare states among OECD countries (Banting, 2006). From the outset, the Constitution Act, 1867 gave the provinces a central role in social policy, with specific sections granting them authority over education, hospitals, and related charitable institutions. In addition, the courts extended the provincial role by subsuming social policy under provincial powers over 'property and civil rights' and 'matters of a local or private nature'. In a key decision in 1937, the courts struck down a federal **social insurance program** as intruding on these provincial powers.

Despite the centrality of provincial jurisdiction, the federal government also has a significant presence in social policy. Amendments to the Constitution in the middle of the twentieth century gave federal authorities full jurisdiction over unemployment insurance and substantial jurisdiction over **contributory pensions**. Federal tax powers also constitute a powerful tool of social redistribution, especially with the development of refundable tax credits. The final cornerstone of the federal role has been implicit rather than explicit in the Constitution. According to constitutional convention, 'the federal Parliament may spend or lend its funds to any government or institution or individual it chooses, for any purpose it chooses; and it may attach to any grant or loan any conditions it chooses, including conditions it could not directly legislate' (Hogg, 2001: 6.8a). This convention, known as the doctrine of the spending power, has been challenged both politically and judicially. In the mid-1950s, for example, a Quebec Royal Commission asked, 'What would be the use of a careful description of legislative powers if one of the governments could get around it and, to some extent, annul it by its taxation methods and its fashion of spending?' (Quebec, 1956, vol. 2: 217). Nevertheless, court decisions repeatedly sustained the federal position, and historically the spending power provided the constitutional footing for a number of central pillars of the welfare state. It has helped sustain federal benefits paid directly to citizens, such as Family Allowances; it provides a constitutional basis for shared-cost programs through which the federal government supports provincial social programs; and at the outset it provided authority for equalization grants, which are federal transfers to the poorer provinces designed to enable them to provide average levels of public services without having to resort to above-average levels of taxation.[1]

With federal and provincial governments both engaged in social policy, much depends on the mechanisms through which they manage their interdependence. It is here that the three models of federalism emerge sharply. Each of these models posits a different set of relationships between federal and provincial governments. Each model generates its own decision rules, altering the range of governments in the process, the power of different governments at the table, and the level of intergovernmental consensus required for a decision. And each model has different implications for policy outcomes.

- *Classical federalism*: Some programs are delivered by the federal or provincial governments acting independently within their own jurisdiction: unemployment benefits, child benefits, and non-contributory old-age pensions at the federal level; workers' compensation at the provincial level. This model involves unilateral decisions by both levels of government, with minimal efforts at co-ordination even when decisions at one level have a serious impact on programs at the other level.

- In the classical model, the federal and provincial governments behave in their own domain much as unitary governments would do. Decisions are more flexible, requiring no elaborate intergovernmental consensus, and policy can shift dramatically with changes in the government in power, interest-group pressures, or public opinion. At the federal level, policy-makers are still sensitive to different regional interests in a program such as unemployment benefits, but provincial governments have no formal role in the decisions.

- *Shared-cost federalism*: Under this model, the federal government offers financial support to provinces that operate specific social programs that meet basic conditions or broad principles established by the federal government. This instrument underpinned the development of major sectors of the welfare state, including health care, post-secondary education, social assistance, and social services. The shared-cost model generates an intermediate level of constraint on government action. In formal terms, each government makes separate decisions: the federal government decides when and how to support provincial programs; and each provincial government must decide whether to accept the money and the federal terms. In practice, however, the substance of new programs has tended to be hammered out in intergovernmental negotiations. This process increases the range of governments at the table, and opens more channels for new ideas to be injected into the decision process. But because there are no formal decision rules for this process, agreements depend on a broad intergovernmental consensus or—in some cases—acquiescence.

- The pressures for consensus in this model, however, fall between the other two models. In comparison with joint-decision, which is discussed next, the pressures for consensus in shared-cost federalism are not absolute. Governments retain the right to act unilaterally, as became clear when the federal government began to cut its financial commitments to provincial programs in the 1980s and 1990s. But the political scope for unilateralism is still more constrained than in the classical model. As long as the two levels of government remain committed to the policy sector, they both have stakes in the programs and are held accountable by the electorate. Governments tend to push back politically against unilateralism at the other level, generating pressures over time for a return to consensus decision-making. Over the decades, as a result, the pattern has been a fluctuating one of co-operation, followed by unilateralism, followed by uneasy co-operation, all of which inclines the sector towards a more incremental, evolutionary pattern of policy change than is possible in the classical model.

- *Joint-decision federalism*: In this model, the formal agreement of both levels of government is required before any action is possible. Unilateralism is not an option here. The major example is the Canada Pension Plan, which is operated by the federal government but can be changed only on the basis of an elaborate inter-governmental agreement. The essential feature of this model is that nothing happens unless formal approval is given by both levels of government.

- As in the case of shared-cost federalism, this model increases the range of governments and ideologies at the table. But the formal requirement for a strong intergovernmental majority sets the bar especially high in terms of intergovernmental consensus and reduces the probability of change. As a result, the joint-decision model creates buffers against the shifting currents of democratic politics.

With three distinct models of federalism in operation, the politics of Canadian social policy represent a natural laboratory in which to dissect the impact of institutions on public policy. During the mid-1960s, the same federal government expanded different social programs at the same time and in the same political context, but according to different decision rules. As we shall see, the outcomes differed. Similarly, in the late 1980s and 1990s, the federal government restructured different programs at the same time and in the same political context, but according to different decision rules. Again, the rules mattered to the outcomes. The following two sections highlight these consequences during the development of the welfare state and during its subsequent restructuring in the era of retrenchment.

The Three Federalisms and the Development of the Welfare State

Canada laid down the basic planks of its version of the welfare state between the 1940s and the mid-1970s. As in other countries, the primary pressures for social reform came from changes in the political economy of the country: the emergence of an industrial economy; the steady urbanization of the population; the unionization of the labour force; the mobilization of left-wing political parties in the form of the CCF–NDP; the ideological conversion of policy elites to Keynesian economics; and a widely shared faith in the capacity of state action to solve important economic and social problems.

In Canada, however, reformist pressures were refracted through federal institutions. The early post-war years were a period of unparalleled political dominance by the federal government. The war centralized power dramatically, bequeathing federal authorities with a highly professional bureaucracy and—most importantly—dominance of the primary tax fields. After the war, Ottawa was anxious to retain enough of the tax fields to expand shared-cost programs with all provinces and to provide equalization payments to poorer provinces. Provincial governments, however, fought to recapture tax room to finance education, health, and social services on their own terms. In effect, the struggle was for control over the Canadian welfare state. Federal dominance was to erode over time, as Figure 8.1 indicates, but in the early days Ottawa controlled the purse strings.

In addition, linguistic and regional tensions, while never absent, were at a historic low tide in the 1940s and 1950s. The provinces accepted constitutional amendments to strengthen federal jurisdiction, and many English-speaking provinces lobbied for broader federal engagement. In these early stages, only Quebec complained about

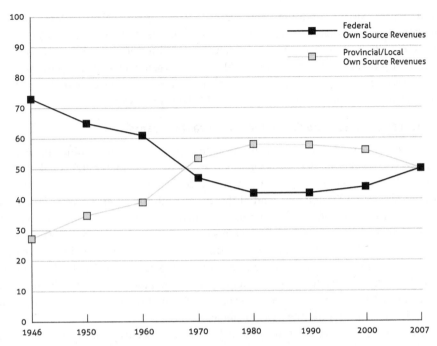

Figure 8.1 Federal and Provincial/Local Government's Share of Government Revenue (excluding Intergovernmental Transfers)

Notes: Data for 1946-1960 not entirely comparable due to break in National Accounts. Excludes C/QPP
Source: Karin Treff and Deborah Ort, *Finances of the Nation 2008* (Toronto: Canadian Tax Foundation, 2009).

federal pre-emption of social policy terrain, but it was not in a strong position to resist. Dominated by a conservative, clerical tradition, the province was not committed to building its own social programs and was therefore vulnerable to federal initiatives that proved popular with the Quebec electorate.

The federal government capitalized on its early strength, introducing several programs during the war years and announcing a sweeping package of proposals as part of post-war reconstruction before the 1945 election. The package collapsed at a federal–provincial conference later that year, when the two largest provinces rejected the associated proposals on intergovernmental finances. Nevertheless, the federal proposals represented a coherent agenda that the federal government pursued on an incremental basis over the next two decades.

The high tide of federal dominance turned out to be short-lived. By the 1960s, provincial resistance was beginning to grow. With the resurgence of Quebec nationalism and the Quiet Revolution, Quebec was increasingly determined to build a *provincial* welfare state, one reflecting a Québécois sensibility. The province declared an end to new jurisdictional concessions and launched a campaign to recapture ground lost in earlier decades. In 1965, Quebec won the right to **'opt out'** of a number of national shared-cost programs, receiving additional tax room from the federal government so that it could operate the programs on its own. The victory was partly symbolic, since the province agreed to meet existing conditions associated with the programs. Nevertheless, symbolic asymmetry signalled that the era of easy centralization was over. In time, other provinces also came to resent the detailed controls and financial tensions implicit in traditional shared-cost programs, and by the mid-1970s provinces generally began to push back.

These swings of the pendulum of power left their imprint on the design of new social programs, but much depended on the model of federalism at work.

Classical Federalism and Exclusively Federal Programs

In comparison with the need for consensus among governments of different political ideologies in the other models, decisions about exclusively federal programs reflected the ideological orientation of the governing party. Since the Liberals formed the government continuously from 1935 until the end of the 1970s, with the exception of a short interregnum from 1957 to 1963, the programs were shaped by the centrist orientation of the Liberal Party, which favoured social programs but ones of relatively modest proportions. The more social democratic perspective of the CCF–NDP was articulated by the party's representatives in Parliament, but theirs was only one voice in the political cacophony of the day. The NDP did have more influence when the Liberals were in a minority in Parliament in 1963–8 and 1972–4, but even then the party's influence was indirect, affecting choices made within the Liberal cabinet.

These dynamics proved critical in the field of income security. In contrast to health care, the programs that emerged were relatively modest compared to the programs developed in many other Western democracies. The first step came in 1940 when a constitutional amendment gave the federal government full authority over unemployment insurance. The Unemployment Insurance (UI) program, which followed that same year, was the first major social insurance program in the country. By comparative standards, however, the Liberals' plan was limited. While it covered most of the industrial workforce, it excluded workers in agriculture, fishing, and private domestic service, as well as public employees and high-income earners. Moreover, the benefit replacement rate was only 50 per cent of wages, with a small supplement for married claimants.

Family Allowances came next. In 1944, the federal government introduced a universal, flat-rate benefit funded from general tax revenues. By the standards of similar programs in Europe, the benefits were modest, providing an average monthly payment of $14.18 per family (Guest, 1997: 132). There was little federal–provincial conflict over the program. Quebec did object, and passed a short bill authorizing a provincial plan if the federal government would withdraw. However, the province had no formal role in the process, and its attack 'was launched too late and soon decreased as the political danger of fighting such a popular measure became clear' (Jean, 1992: 403).

Pensions represented the final step. In 1951, another constitutional amendment gave the federal government authority to provide old-age pensions directly to citizens. At the time, the Quebec government was not interested in launching its own program, but it did preserve its options for the future, insisting that the constitutional amendment retain provincial paramountcy by stipulating that no federal pension plan should affect the operation of any future provincial legislation. The Old Age Security (OAS) enacted the next year was a universal, flat-rate pension of $40 per month for elderly citizens funded through general tax revenues. In 1966, the benefit was extended by the Guaranteed

Income Supplement (GIS), an **income-tested** supplement added to the OAS payment for elderly citizens with low and middle incomes.

These exclusively federal programs, unencumbered by intergovernmental constraints, remained responsive to the shifting currents of national politics in the years that followed. During the post-war era, these currents were largely expansionist, and political parties entered election campaigns armed with promises to raise benefits. From the 1950s until the 1980s, promises to increase the pensions featured in virtually every federal election. After its introduction in 1965, the GIS emerged as a particular favourite in this process, and the program was repeatedly enriched in real terms, usually just before or after an election.

Similarly, the federal government was free to expand UI on its own terms. In 1971, legislation broadened the program to include all employees, increased the replacement ratio to 66 per cent of wages, introduced extended benefits in regions with high levels of unemployment, and covered unemployment resulting from sickness and temporary disability. The legislation also introduced maternity benefits. All of this came with remarkably little consultation with provincial governments; even the regional features of the plan represented 'the federal government's own policy priorities in regional development' and 'were not pressed upon Ottawa by the provinces' (Pal, 1988: 161).

The freedom to act was perhaps best illustrated by Family Allowances, where Liberal governments zigzagged with abandon. In 1970, the Liberals proposed transforming the universal benefit into an income-tested Family Income Supplement, analogous to the GIS, in order to target resources on low-income families. However, Liberal MPs encountered resistance to the idea of taking the Family Allowance away from middle-income families during the 1972 election and the government promptly changed direction after the election, maintaining the universal program and tripling the payment, thereby restoring most of its original purchasing power. In 1978, however, the Liberals returned to income testing in an incremental way, introducing a refundable Child Tax Credit, financed in part through a reduction in the universal Family Allowance.

All of these shifts had major implications for provincial social assistance programs, but the provinces had no role in the decisions.

Joint-Decision Federalism

Joint-decision federalism represented the other extreme. The introduction of contributory pensions in 1965 and their subsequent evolution were governed by a complex intergovernmental process requiring a high level of consensus for change.

The legal origins of joint decision-making lay in the provincial paramountcy embedded in the 1951 constitutional amendment on pensions. When the issue of a contributory pension plan came to the fore in the mid-1960s, Quebec announced that it would operate its own plan. As a consequence, the Quebec Pension Plan (QPP) operates in that province, and the Canada Pension Plan (CPP) operates generally throughout the rest of the country. Although the other provinces were content with a federally delivered plan, they wanted control over it, and the limitations of the 1951 constitutional amendment gave them leverage. An additional constitutional amendment was required to include survivor and disability benefits in the plan, and the provinces insisted on joint decision-making in return for agreeing to the amendment. As a result, changes in the CPP require a super majority: change requires the consent of the federal government and two-thirds of the provinces representing two-thirds of the population of the country, a requirement more demanding than the amending formula for most parts of the Canadian Constitution.

Asymmetry and joint decision-making create complex **veto points**. First, to avoid the administrative and political headaches that would emerge if the two plans diverged sharply, pension planners in Ottawa and Quebec City accept that the Canada and Quebec plans should remain broadly parallel, with neither side making significant changes alone. Second, the formula for provincial consent to changes in the CPP means that Ontario alone, or a variety of possible combinations of other provinces, has a veto. In effect, then, the CPP rules and the pressure for parallelism between CPP and QPP create a system of multiple vetoes: Ottawa, Ontario, Quebec, or several combinations of other provinces can all stop change.

The introduction of the plans illustrates the dynamics well. Federal leadership was critical to catapulting contributory pensions to the top of the national agenda in the 1960s. Had contributory pensions remained an exclusively provincial jurisdiction, 'it is most unlikely that a plan comparable to CPP would have been enacted' (Simeon, 2006[1972]: 270). Pensions were not a provincial priority, and many provinces would have followed the private-sector approach advocated by the Conservative government of Ontario, which planned to require employers above a certain size to provide occupational pensions. However, the federal proposal for a public plan was popular with the electorate, and the Ontario government accepted that contributory pensions of some sort were inevitable. But it held out for a limited plan that left ample scope for private pensions and minimized redistribution by relating individual contributions and benefits closely.

Initially, federal officials assumed Ontario was their major obstacle and trimmed their sails accordingly, for example, reducing the proposed benefits from a replacement rate of 30 per cent to 20 per cent of average wages. But during a 1963 federal–provincial conference, the Quebec government created a sensation by outlining its own plan, which included more generous benefit levels and a more redistributive funding formula. Moreover, Quebec called for partial pre-funding, with the fund purchasing provincial government bonds, effectively loaning capital to the provincial government on favourable terms, an idea that attracted other provinces as well. At that point, the federal proposal was dead. A final round of secret negotiations between Ontario and Quebec City produced a compromise plan: Ottawa accepted partial funding, and the replacement rate was set at 25 per cent of average monthly earnings, lower than Ottawa's initial preference but higher than its Ontario-focused version. The Ontario government and the insurance industry were not happy and felt that Ottawa 'had used Quebec to turn the tables on them' (Kent, 1988: 286). But Ontario, too, was attracted by the funding model, and in the end accepted the need for parallelism with Quebec.

In subsequent decades, multiple vetoes slowed the pace of expansion and helped deflect electoral promises away from the C/QPP. The 1970s did witness one major effort to expand the C/QPP. In 1975 the Canadian Labour Congress and social groups launched a 'Great Pension Debate', urging a doubling of CPP benefits. The federal Liberals were initially sympathetic to some expansion, and an advisory commission in Quebec was also supportive. Wider provincial support, however, was lacking. As the CPP Advisory Committee noted in 1975, 'the CPP has become the backbone of provincial debt financing', contributing more than 30 per cent of total provincial borrowing and even more in periods of stress in capital markets (Canada, 1975: 7–8). In this situation, provinces had a vested interest in opposing any liberalization of benefits that would erode the size of the fund. The campaign's momentum was slowed and the historic moment passed. By the time an intergovernmental consensus emerged 10 years later, economic recession and an increasingly conservative political climate had shifted the currents of Canadian politics: by then, all governments opposed expansion of the C/QPP and focused instead on encouraging private pension plans and personal retirement savings in tax-sheltered accounts. The 1985 changes in the contributory plans were limited to division of credits on divorce and remarriage, and a schedule of increases in the contribution rates.

These institutional dynamics help explain the relatively limited nature of Canadian pensions. The original contributory pensions were modest, more modest even than the federal government's initial intentions, and subsequent expansions were largely forestalled. In combination, the OAS and the maximum C/QPP benefit replace approximately 40 per cent of earnings for the average wage earner, a low rate by European and even US standards. The average Canadian retiree receives a larger portion of his or her income from private occupational pensions, personal retirement accounts, and other forms of savings than in most other Western countries (Béland and Myles, 2005).

Shared-Cost Federalism

The third model, shared-cost federalism, structured federal–provincial relations in the fields of health care and social assistance. In contrast to the classical model, the shared-cost model broadens the range of governments and ideologies influencing policies; but in contrast to the joint-decision rules, this model does not give a veto to any particular province. These differences in decision rules reshuffled the opportunities and constraints facing individual governments at the table, with significant implications for the ideological balances struck in the emerging policies.

Health care

In the early days, federalism slowed progress towards public health insurance. As noted earlier, the courts invalidated the federal government's social insurance legislation in 1937 and the provinces rejected the Green Book proposals in 1945, both of which included health insurance. In the wake of paralysis at the federal level, however, federalism created opportunities for innovation at the provincial level, which the political left used to establish a universal system as the leading option for the country as a whole. In 1947, the social-democratic CCF government of Saskatchewan implemented universal hospital insurance, the first jurisdiction in North America to do so. Two other western provinces—British Columbia and Alberta—followed in quick succession. At that point, the spread across the country stalled, and provinces looked to the federal government to build a national approach. The Liberal prime minister of the day, Louis St Laurent, was initially reluctant to act, insisting that his government would support provincial health insurance programs only when a majority of the provinces representing a majority of the population were ready to join a national scheme. By the mid-1950s, however, this condition was met when Ontario and Newfoundland joined the list of provinces supporting federal action. In 1957, the federal government introduced a universal hospital insurance program, which shared the costs of provincial programs, and all of the provinces had joined within four years.

A similar cycle extended health insurance to physician services. In 1962, the NDP government of Saskatchewan again took the lead, introducing a medicare plan, despite a bitter three-week doctors' strike, the first organized withdrawal of services by medical professionals in North America. Key elements in the settlement that ended the strike—universal and comprehensive coverage, the right of patients to choose their own doctors, and the preservation of fee-for-service payment for physicians—became the starting point for national debate. The Saskatchewan experience demonstrated that a universal approach was feasible in administrative and political terms. Doctors no longer had to provide uncompensated care, and their incomes actually rose in the early years of the program, easing the danger of militant opposition elsewhere. This early success gave ammunition to reformist forces in national politics, and their opportunity came in 1963 with the return to power of the federal Liberal Party. The Liberals were committed to a national program of some sort, and their minority government depended on the support of third parties, including the NDP.

Conservative political forces mounted fierce resistance to the universal model. The Canadian Medical Association and the insurance industry were opposed, and ideological conflict coursed through intergovernmental channels. Conservative governments in Ontario, Alberta, and British Columbia were committed to private coverage for the majority of the population, with public programs limited to the 'hard to insure', such as the elderly and the poor. Without federal action, this position would probably have prevailed in large parts of the country, and health insurance in Canada would have more closely resembled the system emerging at the same time in the US. However, after the Royal Commission on Health Services, chaired by Justice Emmett Hall, recommended in 1964 a universal program, the federal government came down on that side of the debate. The conservative provincial governments were caught in a vice. The federal proposal was popular with their electorates; and if they refused to join, their residents would still have to pay federal taxes to support the program in other provinces. The long-serving health minister in Alberta resigned in protest. The premier of Ontario denounced medicare as 'one of the greatest frauds that has ever been perpetrated on the people of this country' (Taylor, 1987: 375). In this case, however, Ontario lacked the veto that had given it leverage in the pension debate. By 1971, all provinces had medicare programs in place.

Federalism thus played a distinctive role in the politics of health insurance. Although jurisdictional issues delayed action in the early years, federalism created room for a reformist province to implement health insurance on social democratic principles. In the end, federal action was required to transform this regional initiative into a national program. But federal–provincial interaction launched health insurance on a social democratic trajectory that contrasts sharply with the contributory pensions being developed at the same time by the same governments. While the pension reforms carefully left substantial room for private pensions and personal retirement accounts, health insurance displaced the private insurance industry completely from core hospital and medical services. Decision rules were not the only difference between the sectors. But they were critical.

Social assistance

The same dynamics did not shape **social assistance**. The federal government assumed social assistance would shrink to a residual role after the new income security programs matured, and it never sought to establish a powerful national framework for provincial welfare programs. As a result, the CCF–NDP provinces were deprived of the leverage they were able to exert in health care.

Over the years, the federal government had established a number of small shared-cost programs to support provincial benefits for specific categories of needy people, and in 1966 it consolidated these initiatives into a broader program called the Canada Assistance Plan (CAP). Despite the funding, however, the federal policy role in social assistance was tepid. Under CAP, provinces were required to support all persons 'in need', to establish a formal appeal machinery, and to abolish provincial residency requirements for social assistance. Otherwise, they had complete control. The federal government never gave serious thought to establishing national standards for benefit levels, and even a proposal to require provinces to report annually on their policies was squashed within the federal government by the Department of Finance.

Federal financial support did trigger 'a major restructuring of social assistance across Canada on a scale unseen since the Depression' (Struthers, 1994: 190). Spending on social assistance and services rose strongly as a percentage of total provincial expenditures. Although it is impossible to know how much provincial spending would have risen in the absence of federal transfers, the increase was larger in programs eligible for cost-sharing than in non-shareable services; and federal and provincial officials certainly believed the federal transfers were critical, especially in poorer provinces (Canada, 1991). Within this overall pattern, however, the federal approach left lots of room for provincial programs to evolve along distinctive trajectories, and benefits have gone through cycles of convergence and divergence over the years (Boychuk, 1998).

Summary

Three models of federalism thus left their imprint on the new Canadian welfare state. Exclusively federal programs, unconstrained by the need for any formal intergovernmental agreement, were shaped by largely by centrist politics of the Liberal Party, emerging on relatively modest premises. Joint decision-making, with its requirement of a high level of intergovernmental consensus, constrained the role of contributory pensions in the retirement income system. Finally, the shared-cost model gave opportunities to social-democratic forces in health care, although not in social assistance where the federal government did not try to define a comprehensive national approach.

The Three Federalisms and the Politics of Restructuring

The mid-1970s represented the high-water mark of the post-war version of the welfare state. A new politics came to dominate during the last quarter of the twentieth century, as governments focused on retrenchment and restructuring. Restructuring in Canada was driven by the same economic and political changes reshaping the welfare state in other countries: the slowing of economic growth, the acceleration of technological innovation, the globalization of international trade, and the growing strength of conservative political parties and philosophies. In the Canadian case, the fiscal problems of governments were particularly acute. The ratio of public debt to GDP rose steadily from the late 1970s until the mid-1990s, by which time 35 per cent of all federal revenues was pre-empted by interest payments on federal debt and several provinces faced problems placing their bonds in financial markets. In this context, public opinion stiffened. Universal programs such as health care and pensions retained strong support, but opinion polls recorded more resistance to unemployment and social assistance benefits and greater support for tax cuts, a pattern that peaked in the mid-1990s.

The new politics of social policy was reinforced by the politics of federalism, which generated increasing challenges to the social role of the federal government. In 1976 the Parti Québécois won power in the province of Quebec, confirming its status as a major political force. In 1980 and 1995, the country was to live through emotionally wrenching referenda on the separation of Quebec, with the separatist option losing in 1995 by less than 1 per cent of the vote. Regional economic conflicts also deepened, with the energy crisis of the 1970s and free trade in the 1980s pitting region against region. These tensions plunged the country into protracted federal–provincial negotiations over constitutional reform. Throughout this constitutional odyssey, Quebec, supported in varying degrees by other provinces, pressed for restrictions on the federal spending power. In the end, the country failed to coalesce around a new constitutional model, and the spending power was not formally limited. But the social role of the federal government was constantly on the defensive.

The result was an era of retrenchment and restructuring. During the 1980s, change came in relatively incremental steps, but the 1990s saw deep cuts in some programs and complex restructuring in others. This was Canada's neoliberal moment, and the social architecture inherited from the postwar era was redesigned in important ways. As it turned out, the political window for dramatic retrenchment remained open for only a few years. By the late 1990s and early 2000s, the federal budget had moved back into surplus, public opposition to welfare was softening again, and governments at both levels were beginning to reinvest in the social sector. However, the new trajectory established in the 1990s has proven reasonably durable. The recession which began in late 2008 represented a stress test, placing a spotlight on larger gaps in the safety net. But the recession did not lead to a significant U-turn. Governments have contented themselves with marginal and temporary adjustments in response to greater unemployment, and have otherwise stayed the course set in the 1990s.

The impact of restructuring and subsequent reinvestments varied enormously from one program to another. Some programs were better insulated than others from the chill winds of the 1990s and better positioned for the reinvestments of the 2000s. Federalism was part of the buffering process, constraining retrenchment where it had constrained expansion in earlier days. Once again, however, much depended on the model of federalism in play.

Classical Federalism and Exclusively Federal Programs

Classical federalism offered no buffers against the winds of change. Federal decision-makers were unconstrained by intergovernmental relations in restructuring programs in their own jurisdiction, and the outcomes faithfully reflected the electoral importance of different client groups. Pensioners and children were relatively protected; the unemployed were hit hard.

Pensions escaped virtually unscathed. In 1985, the Conservatives proposed partial **deindexation** of OAS, but backed down quickly in the face of angry elderly voters. A decade later, the Liberal government sought to replace the OAS and GIS with an integrated income-tested Seniors' Benefit, but abandoned the idea in the face of attacks from the left by women's groups and the NDP and from the right by investment brokers worried about eroding the incentive to save for retirement. The only change that survived was a more stealthy measure to 'claw back' OAS from high-income seniors through the tax system. However, the measure affects barely 5 per cent of the elderly.

Child benefits actually expanded during the restructuring era. In a long, tortuous series of moves during the 1980s and 1990s, the universal Family Allowance was eliminated, in favour of the Child Tax Benefit, an income-tested payment delivered to low- and middle-income families with children. The Liberal government then gave priority to increases in the benefit as its fiscal positioned improved late in the late 1990s. During this process, the government did depart temporarily from unilateralism, co-ordinating increases in its benefit with related changes in provincial social assistance and social services. However, co-ordination efforts had largely run out of steam by the end of the decade. With a change in government at the federal level, unilateralism quickly reasserted itself. In 2006, the newly elected Conservative government reversed course, reintroducing a universal allowance for all families with young children as part of its approach to child care. As in times of old, there was no advance consultation with provinces.

It was UI, however, that suffered the largest cuts, which came relentlessly, one slice after another. The replacement rate was reduced from the peak of 66 per cent established in 1971 to 60 per cent in 1978, 57 per cent in 1993, 55 per cent for some workers in 1994, and 50 per cent for repeat beneficiaries in 1996 (although offset in part for some recipients by a slightly increased family supplement). By 1996, the replacement rate for the now renamed Employment Insurance (EI) resembled that in 1940. In addition, increasingly restrictive eligibility requirements contributed to a dramatic decline in the proportion of beneficiaries actually receiving benefits.[2] During the recession that began in 2008, the federal government did shift course a little, temporarily extending the maximum duration of benefits by five weeks. The extension, in combination with other features of the program, slightly strengthened income protection for victims of the recession. But even during the recession year of 2009, fewer than half of unemployed Canadians were receiving unemployment benefits, as Figure 8.2 indicates.

The primary constraint on federal discretion over this program was the politics of regionalism. In many countries, proposals to reduce unemployment benefits pit politicians against organized labour; in Canada, the most effective opponents of cutbacks are politicians from poor regions. A ritualized political dance was repeated many times: both Conservative and Liberal governments proposed reductions; backbench MPs from Atlantic Canada and Quebec mounted fierce resistance; provincial governments from those regions supported their protests; and the government compromised in ways that softened the impact in poor areas. When governments did not compromise enough, they paid a political price. In the 1997 election, the Liberal Party suffered significant losses

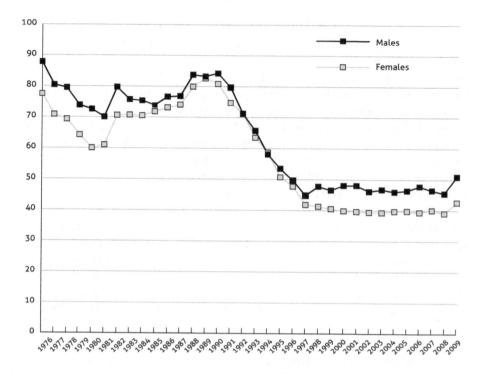

Figure 8.2 Percentage of Unemployed Receiving Regular EI Benefits, 1976–2009

Source: Data from CANSIM. Calculations by Caledon Institute of Social Policy.

in Atlantic Canada and eastern Quebec, in large part because of cuts in unemployment benefits. The government learned its lesson: just before the 2000 election, it reversed aspects of the new rules that hit eastern Canada. In contrast, the unemployed in more affluent provinces such as Ontario and British Columbia received less political protection. The result is growing regional variation in both qualification requirements and benefit duration. Figure 8.3 captures the extent of the variation during the depth of the recession in 2009.[3]

All of these changes in exclusively federal programs had important implications for provincial social assistance programs. With the exception of brief efforts at co-ordination in the case of child benefits, change proceeded with little provincial engagement.

Joint-Decision Federalism

At the other extreme, the consensus-driven, incremental logic inherent in joint decision-making helped constrain change in the C/QPP, cushioning the program from serious retrenchment in the 1990s but also blocking expansionist efforts in the 2000s.

During the 1990s, actuarial reports raised questions about the long-term financial status of the plans, triggering extensive rhetoric about unsustainability. Yet the final adjustments largely served to stabilize the program. Joint decision-making was not the only

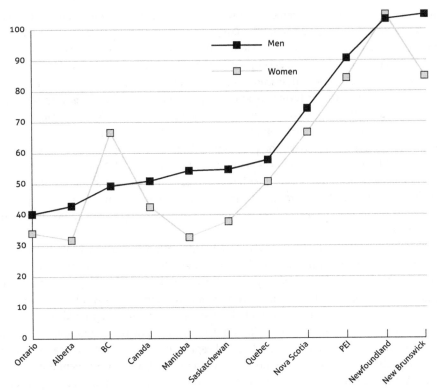

Figure 8.3 Percentage of Unemployed Canadians Receiving Regular EI Benefits, by Province, 2009

Note: See footnote 4 for an explanation of why numbers occasionally exceed 100%.

Source: Data from CANSIM. Calculations by the Caledon Institute of Social Policy.

factor at work. The electoral sensitivity of pensions, evident in the OAS case, was undoubtedly important here as well. Yet contributory pensions create opportunities for subtle adjustments that are largely invisible to the electorate in the short term but have major effects in the long term (Myles and Pierson, 2001). The fact that these opportunities were exploited primarily to reinforce rather than weaken the program was due in part to the need for intergovernmental consensus.

An intergovernmental review was launched in 1996, with the release of a joint discussion paper on reform options (Canada, 1996). From the outset, however, negotiations focused on a narrow range of options, and radical changes were never considered seriously. The province of Quebec announced that it would not consider significant reductions in benefits, a position supported by NDP governments in Saskatchewan and British Columbia. Advocates of an increase in the retirement age, privatization or a shift to personalized accounts within the C/QPP found little resonance for their ideas. In the end, the federal and provincial governments agreed to accelerate increases in contribution rates from 5.5 per cent to 9.9 per cent of earnings over a 10-year period, and to invest the enhanced revenues in equities in the hope of further strengthening the long-term funding of the plan. There was a modest trimming of some benefits, and the two NDP governments refused to sign the final agreement. However, governments did not even try for more dramatic retrenchment, and the final changes largely stabilized the role of contributory pensions in the retirement income system (Little, 2008; Béland and Myles, 2005).

By 2009–10, the cycle of pension politics turned again in an expansionist direction. New evidence made it clear that middle-income Canadians were not saving enough for their retirement, and that private pensions and personal savings, which governments had hoped would fill the gap, were not doing so; if anything, their role was shrinking. The response was another drive to expand C/QPP to strengthen retirement income protection for average Canadians. Initially, the proposal had the support of the federal government and a sizeable number of provinces. However, the province of Alberta adamantly opposed expansion from the outset. Just before the key intergovernmental meeting on the issue in December 2010, six provinces issued a joint statement supporting the expansion of CPP expansion, but two other provinces joined Alberta in opposing action (Curry and Howlett, 2010).

The outcome reflected the unique decision rules of joint-decision federalism. If CPP had been governed according to the classical model, the federal government could have acted on its own. If CPP had been governed by the norms established for shared-cost programs, the support of the federal government and six provinces would have been sufficient for action. Under joint-decision federalism, however, an exceptional level of intergovernmental agreement is required, and it was lacking. The day before the conference, the federal finance minister 'surprised his colleagues' by abandoning 'an idea that he had personally championed for six months', citing the lack of intergovernmental consensus (ibid.). At the conference, the governments agreed to try once again to encourage a voluntary savings approach. Thus, within a decade, joint-decision federalism had worked its magic twice, helping to constrain both retrenchment and expansion of the C/QPP.

Shared-Cost Federalism

The most intense federal–provincial politics in recent years centred on shared-cost programs, which provided ample opportunity for off-loading, blame avoidance, and mutual recrimination. The overall pattern was one of unilateralism at the federal level, relentless push-back from the provinces, and eventual reinvestment by the federal government. These intergovernmental dynamics contributed to relative stability in the basic policy model in the core sectors of health care.

The stage for these conflicts was actually set as far back as 1977, when block funding was introduced in response to frustrations with the traditional form of cost-sharing. The federal government became concerned that its open-ended commitment to pay half the cost of expensive provincial programs reduced its control over its own budget. Provincial governments complained that shared-cost programs distorted provincial priorities and locked them into endless arguments about whether specific projects qualified for federal support. After extensive negotiations, the two levels agreed to shift to a **block grant** for health and post-secondary education. The federal government gained greater control over its finances and provincial governments gained greater freedom. Although the formal conditions attached to the federal health programs remained in place, provinces were able to allocate federal funding as they saw fit. Indeed, there was no explicit requirement that the funding actually be devoted to health and post-secondary education.

Over time, however, provinces were to pay a high price for the additional flexibility, as the federal government was no longer committed to paying half the costs of provincial programs. At the outset, increases in federal support were tied to the rate of growth in the economy as a whole. But as federal deficits grew, Ottawa repeatedly made unilateral cuts: in 1986, indexation of the transfer was limited to the increase in GDP less two percentage points; in 1990, the transfer was frozen in absolute terms for four years; and the 1995 budget folded CAP into a broader block fund known as the Canada Health and Social Transfer (CHST) and cut the cash payment to provinces dramatically. These changes, conceived in secrecy and imposed without warning, provoked a bitter reaction among provinces and seriously eroded the legitimacy of the federal role in their eyes. In the aftermath, the provincial governments pressed for a stronger set of decision rules and a dispute resolution mechanism, an effort in effect to shift closer to a joint-decision model.[4] After lengthy negotiations, the federal government and all of the provincial governments except Quebec agreed to a Social Union Framework Agreement, which contained a set of principles and procedures to guide intergovernmental relations in social policy. But the agreement failed to fully meet provincial concerns, and had little long term effect. As a result, the role of shared-cost federalism remains contested (Bakvis et al., 2009: ch.10).

The impact of these tensions varied from program to program. As in the expansionist period, the key difference was the extent to which the federal government remained committed to a policy role, as the contrast between health care and social assistance again illustrates.

Health insurance

In the case of health care, shared-cost federalism helped to buffer the universal model from pressures for change. The federal government, especially when the Liberals were in power, defined itself as the guarantor of equality of access to health care and resisted efforts by conservative provincial governments to introduce user fees or increase the role of the private sector in core health services. Poll after poll showed that Canadians strongly supported the existing health-care system, and the federal Liberals could mobilize that opinion in conflicts with the provinces. The ability of federal health ministers to play Sir Galahad also reflected the dry realities of intergovernmental finances. Under the block grant system, the federal treasury was not directly affected by changes in provincial health expenditures and therefore did not bear the financial costs associated with the defense of universal health care. As a result, federal health ministers were freer to defend the principles of universality and equality of access. Indeed, they did so even as their colleague, the minister of Finance, was reducing transfers to the provinces.

This drama unfolded in several acts. Just before the 1984 election, the federal Liberals nailed their colours to the mast with the passage of the Canada Health Act (CHA). During the early 1980s, a growing number of doctors began charging patients a supplementary fee in addition to the payment they received from the provincial medical plan, a practice known as 'extra-billing'. At the same time, a number of provinces began to flirt with the idea of hospital fees for patients. The federal Liberals opposed both practices as inhibiting equal access to health care, and the CHA prohibited user fees and all charges at the point of service. The CHA was opposed by all provincial governments. But it was immensely popular with the electorate and passed unanimously in both the House of Commons and Senate.

Table 8.1 Federal Transfers for Health Care as a Percentage of Provincial Health Expenditures, 1975–2010

Year	Cash	Tax	Total
1975	41.3	na	41.3
1977	25.2	17.1	42.3
1980	25.3	17.7	43.7
1985	23.8	15.6	39.7
1990	17.9	16.0	33.9
1995	16.4	15.8	32.1
2000	12.8	16.5	29.3
2005	22.4	13.2	35.6
2010	20.3	10.4	30.7

Source: Calculated on the basis of transfer data provided by Finance Canada and data on provincial health expenditure from Canadian Institute for Health Information 2010.

The federal government proceeded with penalties, withholding a total of $247 million from provinces that allowed charges. However, the financial penalties were not large enough to have induced provincial compliance on their own. The real sanctions were political. Provincial electorates supported the principles of the CHA, and they were upset when their provincial governments were declared to be in violation of its terms. In moving to comply, provinces faced difficult negotiations with the medical profession, which demanded compensation for the banning of extra-billing. Ontario endured a 25-day strike by a majority of doctors, and Saskatchewan doctors held rotating one-day strikes. The doctors made important financial gains in a number of provinces, costs that the provinces alone had to absorb. But by the late 1980s, all provinces were largely in compliance (Tuohy, 1994). The mid-1990s witnessed a repeat of this cycle, this time focused on private clinics providing specialized medical services, such as cataract surgery, and charging a 'facility fee'. The federal Liberal government challenged such fees in 1995, and in the end the provinces grudgingly moved largely into compliance by banning them.

In contrast to this forceful policy role, the federal financial role declined steadily in the 1980s and 1990s. The extent of the erosion depends on how one defines the 'real' federal contribution. At the time of the introduction of block funding in 1977, the federal transfer was split into an annual cash payment and a transfer of tax points (which involved the federal government lowering its taxes and the provinces raising their taxes by the same amount). The result was a bitter dispute over the size of the federal share. Ottawa insisted that its contribution included both the cash payment and the revenue derived from the tax points transferred in 1977. Provinces replied that the tax points were now simply part of the provincial tax base, and the federal contribution was limited to the cash. Table 8.1 demonstrates the dramatic difference: provinces looked only at the first column; Ottawa focused on the final column. On either accounting, however, the federal share of health spending declined in the 1980s and 1990s, bottoming out at the turn of the century.

Provincial governments were squeezed between growing health costs and declining federal transfers. They, in turn, squeezed health spending, reducing expenditures by an average of 2 per cent each year between 1992 and 1997 (Fierlbeck, 2001). However, such intense restraint was difficult to sustain. Beginning in the late 1990s, newspaper reports increasingly described a system in decline: the closing of hospital wards; the slow acquisition of new technologies; declining staffing levels; controversy about waiting times for non-emergency surgical procedures; and crowded emergency departments. Moreover, polls suggested that public faith in the health-care system had fallen more rapidly in Canada than in other Western nations (Schoen et al., 2002). The political limits of retrenchment had been reached.

Not surprisingly, the provincial governments pushed back. They mounted protracted public campaigns blaming Ottawa for the erosion of health care and demanding federal reinvestment. With the return of federal fiscal health in the late 1990s, Ottawa did reinvest, significantly increasing its funding in 1999, 2000, 2002, and 2004. The 2004 agreement was particularly important, providing a major injection of cash immediately and establishing a 10-year plan with an agreed formula for increasing the federal transfer for the duration of the agreement.

In effect, the federal cuts of the 1990s were partially reversed, slice by slice. (See Table 8.1) These increases did not resolve the intergovernmental tensions, and provincial governments rebuffed federal efforts to give priority to specific reforms or attach conditions to the new money. Not until 2004 were provinces prepared to sign a joint plan. Even then, Quebec insisted on a separate agreement, and the other provinces insisted that their only accountability was to report on progress, not to Ottawa, but to their own citizens.

Despite the tensions, the two levels of government have remained locked in an embrace that has tended to protect the core of health care from pressures for change. On the surface, the stability of the basic parameters of the Canadian system is striking. Canada has experienced nothing like the revolution wrought south of the border by HMOs and for-profit hospital chains, or by experiments with internal markets in the UK. Whether these buffering effects will persist is unclear, as challenges to the shared-cost model are growing. Quebec has long advocated a shift to classical federalism, with the transfer of additional tax room to the provinces in exchange for the elimination of the federal cash transfer. Some analysts in English-speaking Canada agree. For example, conservatives tend to complain that federal cash transfers cushion provincial governments from having to make tough choices about health care, forestalling the introduction of a greater role for the private sector and for prices in rationing access to care (Boessenkool, 2010). Such attacks on the shared-cost mechanism are likely to come to a head during negotiations over the renewal of the existing intergovernmental agreement which expires in 2014.

The buffering effects of shared-cost federalism are never absolute. The role of the private sector re-emerged in 2004 with the opening of private clinics offering MRI diagnostic services in Quebec and elsewhere (Laghi, 2004), and the federal government did not charge into the breach as of old, even before the election of a more decentralist Conservative government in 2006. It is possible that Canada will eventually move to a new mix of the public and private sectors in health care. But shared-cost federalism tends to incline the country towards a more evolutionary process, requiring a higher level of consensus for change in the country as a whole for major change.

Social assistance

In contrast with health care, social assistance saw a much more straightforward decentralization, triggering a transition from shared-cost federalism to classical federalism and eliminating the buffering effects of intergovernmentalism. Although CAP was not included in block funding in 1977, full cost-sharing fell victim in the 1990s to the battle against the federal deficit. In 1990, the Conservative federal government unilaterally imposed a 'cap on CAP' for the three richest provinces, limiting growth in the federal contribution to 5 per cent a year. With the onset of a serious recession shortly afterwards, the federal share of welfare costs in these provinces fell sharply; within a few years the Ontario government reported that Ottawa was contributing only 28 per cent of its welfare costs (Courchene with Telmer, 1998). The final step came in 1995, when the subsequent Liberal government abolished CAP altogether, rolling its support for social assistance into the CHST. This change significantly increased provincial discretion, as the federal funding no longer had to be devoted to social assistance. Ottawa also took the opportunity to eliminate the requirements that provincial programs respond to all persons in need and maintain appeals procedures. Only the prohibition on provincial residency requirements remained, and even this modest provision was difficult to enforce.

In contrast with health care, where the federal government accepted a continuing responsibility, the virtually total abandonment of social assistance by the federal government made it harder for provinces to push back. Many social policy advocates predicted that decentralization would trigger a speedy race to the bottom. Although CAP had never set national benefit rates, they argued that cost-sharing had protected social assistance, since provincial treasurers would reap only half of any savings generated by cuts. They also argued that the CAP requirement that provincial programs assist all persons 'in need' precluded the more draconian forms of workfare and term limits that had emerged in the US.

In fact, benefits did decline. In 1996, for example, a newly elected Conservative government in Ontario cut benefits by 20 per cent, and benefits declined more incrementally elsewhere. As always, it is hard to isolate the impact of decentralization. At the national level, the downward trend in benefits began in 1992, between the cap on CAP and CAP's final elimination, and a careful study of the trends concludes that benefits were 'slouching', not racing, towards a bottom (Boychuk, 2006). Moreover, benefits levels tended to stabilize, albeit at the lower levels, in the 2000s (National Council of Welfare, 2010). The consequences for eligibility for benefits were clearer, however. Beneficiaries were under increasing compulsion to participate in employability programs, and liens on home equity were introduced in Ontario. The harshest step came in 2002, when British Columbia introduced time limits, restricting employable people without children to two years of support in any five-year period. Subsequent revisions reduced the numbers affected significantly. But all of these provisions would have been prohibited by CAP.

Summary

As in the postwar era, the new politics of social policy had to flow through the three distinctive institutional filters, which help explain the uneven impact of retrenchment on different social programs. Exclusively federal programs were fully exposed to the shifting currents of centrist politics, with the elderly, children, and the unemployed enduring different fates. At the same time, joint-decision federalism helped protect contributory pensions. Shared-cost federalism helped buffer the basic model of health care, but the mild protection afforded social assistance collapsed with the abolition of CAP, exposing recipients more fully to political pressures in the provinces. Interestingly, the cumulative impact of these changes was to deepen a disjunction at the heart of Canadian social policy. Income security shifted more firmly into the limited, **selectivist** mould, as unemployment benefits and social assistance were weakened and children's benefits shifted towards income testing. In contrast, the universal model of health care has endured, if in somewhat battered form, in hospital and physician services. The two worlds of Canadian welfare have moved further apart.

Conclusions

The Canadian federation embraces three distinct models of federalism, each of which alters the range of governments at the table, redistributes power among the governments that get there, and requires different levels of intergovernmental consensus for action. At any point in time, during both the years of expansion and the years of retrenchment, the same federal and provincial governments operating in the same political environment were shaping different programs according to different rules. These models have left their imprint on the Canadian welfare state. Because they act as institutional filters through which wider political and economic pressures flow, it is difficult to isolate precisely their independent influence on policy outcomes. It is, however, possible to identify the incentives and constraints embedded in each model and determine the direction of its influence. At a minimum, the three models of federalism remain an essential part of explanations of a number of puzzles about Canadian social policy, including the different ideological trajectories of income security and health care and the uneven impact of restructuring in recent decades.

Evaluating the three federalisms in light of the normative criteria adopted in this volume—performance, effectiveness, and legitimacy—produces a mixed report. The classical model, almost by definition, comes closest to meeting traditional federal principles. It presumably scores highest on issues of effectiveness in responding to regional diversities. The issue has always been whether this model establishes the right balance between the claims of social citizenship—the belief that all Canadians should be entitled to a comparable set of social rights and benefits irrespective of where they live—and the belief that a federation should enhance the scope for regional variation in social benefits. In comparative terms, the Canadian welfare state leans towards giving greater scope to regional variation; virtually all other federal states among advanced democracies give more weight to the equal treatment of citizens (Banting, 2006; Obinger et al., 2005). Greater regional variation results primarily because the federal government plays a smaller role in social policy, and more programs fall in the exclusive purview of provincial governments. But regional variation in benefits reflects the tendency for regionalism to creep into the design of some federal programs. The most troublesome failure of the classical model is undoubtedly the federal Employment Insurance program. A basic rationale for central delivery of a program in any federation is to ensure that citizens in similar circumstances are treated similarly, irrespective of where they live. By that standard, the federal unemployment program fails spectacularly.

At the other extreme, the joint-decision model can also be seen as a strong version of another model of federalism. As we have seen, the effect has been to buffer the C/QPP from the pressures for change inherent in democratic politics. Defenders of the model might note that over time the frustrations generated by joint decision-making have been visited equally on advocates and opponents of the welfare state. In the post-war decades, advocates of expansion regarded the formula with despair; in the era of retrenchment, advocates of privatization have faced similar disappointments; in the 2000s, the frustrations are visited on expansionists once again. Defenders of joint decision-making might also argue that privileging stability makes sense in the field of pensions, where policies require long-term horizons. The actual formula is undoubtedly too exacting; there is no reason that contributory pensions should be more difficult to change than most sections of the Constitution. Nevertheless, the model does generate intergovernmental legitimacy, and the plans governed by it enjoy strong public support.

Our greatest difficulties haunt the domain of shared-cost federalism. The legitimacy of this model has been under growing challenge, particularly in health care. Federal intervention in health care is less pervasive and less detailed in Canada than in any other advanced federation, including the United States and Switzerland, yet its intervention generates more intergovernmental resentment (Banting and Corbett, 2002). The country is paying a high price for the lack of agreed federal–provincial decision rules and for the unilateralism and ruptures of the 1990s. As we have seen, the Social Union Framework Agreement failed to meet the provincial concerns, disappointing those who saw it as a mechanism for rebuilding trust between governments.

Undoubtedly, the balance among the three models of federalism will evolve in the future, as it has in the past. The shared-cost model may play a smaller role in the years to come. But as long as Canadians look to both levels of government to respond to the social problems they confront, it is difficult to envisage any of the three models disappearing completely from the world of social policy. It seems likely that pressures for change in the Canadian welfare state will continue to flow through three distinctive institutional filters, each with its own implications for the future.

Notes

1. With the inclusion of section 36 in the Constitution Act, 1982, equalization grants have specific constitutional footing and no longer depend on the federal spending power.
2. The decline in the proportion of unemployed receiving benefits also reflected changes in forms of employment, which decrease eligibility for the program.
3. Throughout the negotiations over the Social Union Framework Agreement, Quebec took a different position from the other provinces, favouring the autonomy of the classical approach rather than an elaborate system of joint decision-making. It briefly joined the provincial consensus on the condition that any province would have the right to opt out fully from any intergovernmental agreement with full fiscal compensation. When this provision was qualified in the final accord, Quebec declined to sign.
4. Numbers occasionally exceed 100% in Atlantic Canada because of the way in which the Labour Force Survey calculates the number of unemployed persons. Some recipients of regular EI payments work a few hours and are considered employed rather than unemployed in the LFS; and

some recipients are considered to be out of the labour force rather than unemployed because of the criteria used in the LFS to determine if they were actively looking for work in the previous weeks and the reasons not.

References

Bakvis, H., G. Baier, and D. Brown. 2009. *Contested Federalism: Certainty and Ambiguity in the Canadian Federation*. Don Mills: Oxford University Press.

Banting, K. 2005. 'Canada: Nation-building in a Federal Welfare State'. In *Federalism and the Welfare State: New World and European Experiences*, ed. H. Obinger, S. Leibfried, and F. Castles. Cambridge: Cambridge University Press.

———. 2006. 'Is a Federal Welfare State a Contradiction in Terms?' In *Democracy and Devolution*, ed. S. Greer. London: Palgrave/ Macmillan.

——— and R. Boadway. 2004. 'Defining the Sharing Community: The Federal Role in Health Care'. In *Money, Politics and Health Care: Reconstructing the Federal–Provincial Partnership*, ed. H. Lazar and F. St-Hilaire. Montreal: Institute for Research on Public Policy.

——— and S. Corbett. 2002. 'Health Policy and Federalism: An Introduction'. In *Health Policy and Federalism: A Comparative Perspective on Multi-Level Governance*, ed. K. Banting and S. Corbett. Montreal and Kingston: McGill– Queen's University Press.

Béland, D., and J. Myles. 2005. 'Stasis Amidst Change: Canadian Pension Reform in an Age of Retrenchment'. In *Ageing and Pension Reform Around the World: Evidence from Eleven Countries*, ed. G. Bonoli and T. Shinkawa. Cheltenham: Edward Elgar.

Boessenkool, K. 2010. 'Fixing the Fiscal Imbalance: Turning GST revenues over to the provinces in exchange for lower transfers'. SPP Research Papers, vol. 3, Issue 10. December. Calgary: University of Calgary, School of Public Policy.

Boychuk, G. 1998. *Patchworks of Purpose: The Development of Provincial Social Assistance Regimes in Canada*. Montreal and Kingston: McGill–Queen's University Press.

———. 2006. 'Slouching Toward the Bottom? Provincial Social Assistance Provision in Canada, 1980–2000'. In *Racing to the Bottom? Provincial Interdependence in the Canadian Federation*, ed. K. Harrison. Vancouver: University of British Columbia Press.

Canada. 1975. Canada Pension Plan Advisory Committee, *The Rate of Return on the Investment Fund of the Canada Pension Plan*. Ottawa: Minister of Supply and Services Canada.

———. 1991. Health and Welfare Canada, Program Audit and Review Directorate, *Evaluation of the Canada Assistance Plan*. Ottawa: Health and Welfare Canada.

———. 1996. *An Information Paper for Consultations on the Canada Pension Plan Released by the Federal, Provincial and Territorial Governments*. Ottawa: Department of Finance.

Canadian Institute for Health Information. 2010. *National Health Expenditure Trends, 1977 to 2010*. Ottawa.

Courchene, T., with C. Telmer. 1998. *From Heartland to North American Region State: The Social, Fiscal and Federal Evolution of Ontario*. Toronto: Faculty of Management, University of Toronto.

Curry, B., and K. Howlett. 2010. 'Pensions dominate summit agenda', Toronto: *Globe and Mail*, 20 December, p. A1.

Fierlbeck, K. 2001. 'Cost Containment in Health Care: The Federalism Context'. In *Federalism, Democracy and Health Policy in Canada*, ed. D. Adams. Montreal and Kingston: McGill– Queen's University Press.

Guest, D. 1997. *Emergence of Social Security in Canada*, 3rd edn. Vancouver: University of British Columbia Press,

Hogg, P. 2001. *Constitutional Law in Canada*. Toronto: Carswell.

Jean, D. 1992. 'Family Allowances and Family Autonomy'. In *Canadian Family History*, ed. B. Bradbury. Toronto: Copp Clark Pitman.

Kent, T. 1988. *A Public Purpose: An Experience of Liberal Opposition and Canadian Government*. Montreal and Kingston: McGill–Queen's University Press.

Langhi, B. 2004. 'Stop Clinics from Billing their Patients, Quebec Told', *Globe and Mail*, 10 Feb.: A4

Lazar, H., F. St-Hilaire, and J.-F. Tremblay. 2004. 'Vertical Fiscal Imbalance: Myth or Reality?' In *Money, Politics and Health Care: Reconstructing the Federal–Provincial Partnership*, ed. H. Lazar and F. St-Hilaire. Montreal and Kingston: Institute for Research on Public Policy and Institute for Intergovernmental Relations, Queen's University.

Little, B. 2008. *Fixing the Future: How Canada's Usually Fractious Governments Worked Together to Rescue the Canada Pension Plan*. Toronto: University of Toronto Press.

Myles, J., and P. Pierson. 2001. 'The Comparative Political Economy of Pension Reform'. In *The New Politics of the Welfare State*, ed. P. Pierson. Oxford: Oxford University Press.

National Council of Welfare. 2010. *Welfare Incomes 2009*. Ottawa.

Obinger, H., S. Leibried, and F. Castles, eds. 2005. *Federalism and the Welfare State: New World and European Experiences*. Cambridge: Cambridge University Press.

Pal, L. 1988. *State, Class, and Bureaucracy: Canadian Unemployment Insurance and Public Policy*. Montreal: McGill–Queen's University Press.

Quebec. 1956. Royal Commission of Inquiry on Constitutional Problems in the Province of Quebec, *Report* (The Tremblay Report), 5 vols. Quebec: Province of Quebec.

Schoen, C., R. Blendon, C. DesRoches, and R. Osborn. 2002. *Comparison of Health Care System Views and Experiences in Five Nations, 2001*. New York: Commonwealth Fund.

Simeon, R. 2006[1972]. *Federal–Provincial Diplomacy: The Making of Recent Policy in Canada*. Toronto: University of Toronto Press.

Statistics Canada, 2011. Canadian Socioeconomic Database (CANSIM). Ottawa. Data accessed on January 13, 2011 from http://www5.statcan. gc.ca/cansim/home-accueil?lang=eng

Struthers, J. 1994. *Limits of Affluence: Welfare in Ontario, 1920–1970*. Toronto: University of Toronto Press.

Taylor, M. 1987. *Health Insurance and Public Policy in Canada*, 2nd edn. Montreal and Kingston: McGill–Queen's University Press.

Tuohy, C. 1994. 'Health Policy and Fiscal Federalism'. In *The Future of Fiscal Federalism*, ed. K. Banting, D. Brown, and T. Courchene. Kingston: Queen's University, School of Policy Studies.

9 Health Care

Antonia Maioni

Federalism and health care are a powerful mix in Canadian politics. For one thing, debates about health care—the most important budget item for provincial governments and the most salient issue for a majority of Canadians—involve larger struggles over economic resources and political jurisdiction in the federation. For another, even though disputes in this arena are often framed around funding formulas and dispute resolution, it is the larger discussions of the future direction of provincial health care systems and the political sustainability of the Canadian health care model that are of more concern these days.

Health care is of central importance to discussions about the future of Canadian federalism. For federal governments in the past, the Canadian health care model captured the essence of the successful model of Canadian federalism: decentralized jurisdictional responsibility (that allows provinces extensive policy-making capacity) combined with flexible federal intervention (that ensures equity across political boundaries). The election of successive Conservative minority governments since 2006 has yet to change this delicate balance. For their part, provincial governments have varying degrees of enthusiasm for the existing model of health care delivery, but all recognize the extent to which disputes about health care involve larger struggles over economic and political space in the federation.

Federalism and Health Policy

Federalism, as a political institution, is a significant element in Canadian health policy development. Federalism, in interaction with the Westminster parliamentary systems, has encouraged health policy innovation and diffusion at some points in time (Gray, 1991) and discouraged policy innovation at other times.

The division of powers in health care, on paper, makes Canada look like the most decentralized of all federations. Instead of a 'national' health care system or a single 'medicare' programme, Canada has a mosaic of 10 provincial and three territorial health care systems. In contrast to national health systems, the Government of Canada does not administer health insurance plans, nor does it allocate health care budgets or stipulate how much money should be spent. Under the division of powers, it is the provinces that have primary responsibility for health care. Section 92(7) of the *Constitution Act* of 1867 gives provincial legislatures exclusive jurisdiction to enact laws for the 'Establishment, Maintenance, and Management of Hospitals, Asylums, Charities and Eleemosynary Institutions'. Section 92(13) gives provinces legal authority over 'Property and Civil Rights in the Province', and section 92(16) gives them jurisdiction over 'Generally all Matters of a merely local or private Nature in the Province'. The federal government does have constitutional responsibilities in public health matters under Section 91(11) and for the general welfare of specific classes of people: 'Indians' and 'aliens', as well as federal inmates and members of the armed forces. However, it is the federal spending power that opened up an important role for the central government to bolster the fiscal capacity of provinces and facilitate the diffusion of health benefits across the country.

The 'Canadian' health care model can be thought of as a system of 10 provincial and three territorial health insurance plans, bound together by certain norms (Maioni, 1999). Some of these norms are incorporated into reciprocal ententes between the provinces, for example, in inter-provincial agreements on medical training or on coverage for out-of-province services. The most important norms, however, are those described in a federal statute, the *Canada Health Act* (CHA). The CHA includes five principles that the provinces must respect in the functioning of their health care systems: **public administration** of health insurance, **comprehensiveness** of benefits, **universality** of coverage, **portability** across provinces, and **accessibility** to services.

The standards derived from these principles that tie provincial health care systems together are at once more fragile and more robust than in other countries: more fragile because they rest on a federal statute rather than constitutional principles; and more robust because they have, until now, limited experimentation with private market mechanisms. Although the CHA arguably leaves considerable room for provincial innovation and experimentation with health care delivery, the health care principles are explicit in banning certain mechanisms, for example, those that impinge on equal access to care or the private financing of health care services under provincial plans. These constraints are unique to Canada. Unlike in virtually every other country in the industrialized world— not just the US, but other publicly financed health care systems as well—most necessary medical services available under provincial health plans cannot be privately insured in Canada. Although supplementary health insurance does exist, it is limited to non-essential care, or various diagnostic testing. And Canadians can, and do, purchase out of their own pockets some medical goods and services.

Some argue that the CHA gives the federal government the moral suasion to ensure that provinces will follow certain rules in the design of their health care systems. But because the CHA's principles derive from a federal statute (not a formal constitutional requirement), the federal government's role is technically one of financial contribution to provincial systems, and imposed remedies in the case of non-compliance. To date, these have included dollar-for-dollar deductions in the cash portion of federal transfers to the province when user fees of extra-billing have been allowed by the provinces.

The role of federalism as a political institution that gives rise to this innovation/diffusion dynamic in health policy can be considered against the backdrop of two other components of policy change. These two components are the logic of policy feedback and the power of political ideas. Policy legacies, in the form of past policy choices at a critical historical juncture, become part of a self-reinforcing positive feedback that shapes the politics of future policy reform (Pierson, 2000). Embarking on a certain 'path' in health care, therefore, creates preferences and expectations about government involvement. The chosen path also shapes the strategies and interests of political and societal actors in the policy process, and narrows the range of feasible policy alternatives. As Tuohy (1999) argues, the logic of the Canadian health care model may have been 'accidental' in that it emerged at a particular moment in which there existed 'windows of opportunity' for co-operation between governments and between the state and health care providers. The timing and sequence of the chosen path is of obvious importance, particularly since the Canadian health care model has since then shut out widespread use of private market alternatives. Public health insurance may be something most Canadians want, but at the same time alternative ideas about health care financing and organization have gathered considerable economic and legal clout and an increasing measure of interest from policy-makers and the public alike.

It is important not only to understand institutions in health policy, but also to con-sider how ideas are embedded in political institutions. Political ideas, when mobilized by influential actors and institutionalized through policy outcomes, can affect political behaviour and perceptions about the boundaries of change. Federal systems by definition should allow innovative ideas to flourish, for such ideas naturally seek out laboratories for experimentation.

The unfolding history of health policy in Canada offers a persuasive example of the connection between ideas and institutions in political life. The presence of a social-demo-cratic party, the Co-operative Commonwealth Federation, and its charismatic leader, Tommy Douglas, were profoundly important in transmitting ideas about the need for public health insurance. Likewise, the Saskatchewan government's initiatives in hospi-tal and then medical insurance provided examples from which other provinces set up their own systems based on these ideas. More recently, the recent Supreme Court of Canada's decision in *Chaoulli v. Québec* (2005) offers a good illustration of this dynamic but in a different direction. In this controversial case, the Supreme Court of Canada ruled that Quebec's ban on private insurance contravened the Quebec Charter of Rights and Freedoms. In a divided ruling penned by Chief Justice Beverley McLachlin on whether the Quebec legislation also contravened the Canadian Charter, ideas about equal access to care in the public system were challenged by alternative ideas about the private provi-sion of insurance, and of health care itself. These alternate ideas to the current health care system have found a powerful transmission belt through the legal system as courts have become important actors in health reform (Manfredi and Maioni, 2002).

Federalism and the Development of Health Insurance in Canada

The development of health insurance in Canada, and the pattern of intergovernmental re-lations that surrounds it, can be divided into three periods. The first period, when prov-incial health plans were put into place, was an era of federal leadership and co-operative federalism. This period lasted from the late 1940s through to the late 1970s. The second period, which began with the passage of the Canada Health Act in 1984, was marked by greater intergovernmental conflict, principally around federal–provincial shares of health care costs. This period lasted through to the late 1990s and is characterized by what some have called 'unilateral federalism' as Ottawa cut its contribution to health care costs. The third era dates from 2000 and is marked by more collaborative intergovernmental relations. The federal government's increase in health care spending and its longer-term funding commitments have helped to ease some of the intergovernmental tensions.

Co-operative Federalism and Shared Cost Federalism 1947–77

The emergence of public health insurance coincided with what has been termed an era of co-operative federalism (Robinson and Simeon, 1994). This co-operative relationship and the federal spending power led to a pattern of shared cost federalism (see Banting in Chapter 8 in this volume) in health care.

Although there were no formal rules about intergovernmental co-operation in policy making, the 1940 Rowell-Sirois Report interpreted the federal spending power as a necessary instrument in building social programs in Canada but conceded that major funding initiatives would necessitate consultation with the provinces. Throughout his long tenure as Prime Minister, Mackenzie King resisted encroaching on provincial jurisdiction in health care matters, although Paul Martin, Sr. did convince him to support the 1948 National Health Grants Program. When it was announced, King referred to the program as one of the 'fundamental prerequisites of a nation-wide system of health insurance' (Quoted in Taylor, 1987: 164).

In the absence of federal initiative, Saskatchewan's CCF government chose to 'go it alone' (Taylor, 1987: 69) in setting up the first public hospital insurance plan in North America in 1947. The demonstration effect of Saskatchewan, in tandem with some of the political pressure applied by the province of Ontario contributed to the Liberal government of Louis St Laurent passing the *Hospital Insurance and Diagnostic Services Act* of 1957. It set up an open-ended cost-sharing arrangement, in which the federal government reimbursed about half of the costs of provincial hospital insurance plans, on condition that coverage was comprehensive and universal. By 1961, all the provinces had implemented hospital insurance plans that conformed to this new arrangement. Quebec was the last province to join; the Union Nationale regime of Maurice Duplessis had railed against the federal intrusion but when the St Laurent's former protégé, Liberal Jean Lesage, came to power in 1960, one of his first legislative actions was to pass and implement hospital insurance, effectively shutting out religious communities from the administration of health services in Quebec (Maioni, 2010b).

Federal involvement also provided the diffusion mechanism for provincial innovation in medical insurance. Against the backdrop of a bitter political battle over the policy proposals, and a doctors' strike against their implementation, Saskatchewan introduced public medical insurance in 1962. Then, after extensive study, a federally appointed Royal Commission (the Hall Commission) recommended in 1964 that the federal government develop legislation for public medical insurance (Canada Royal Commission on Health Services, 1964). At the 1965 Federal–Provincial conference, Liberal Prime Minister Lester Pearson announced a new open-ended arrangement, in which the federal government would cover half the costs of provincial medical insurance plans. To ensure a measure of uniformity across the country, the *Medical Care Insurance Act* of 1966 stipulated that provincial programs would have to be universal, portable, publicly administered, and cover all services provided by physicians. Again, the political support for such innovation was not entirely unanimous. There was considerable debate within the federal cabinet on the fiscal commitment such a move entailed. And, certain provinces had other ideas about medical insurance. The government of Alberta, for instance, was more inclined toward a voluntary plan known as 'Manningcare' (after the Social Credit premier, Ernest Manning).

Nevertheless, by 1971, every province had such a plan in operation. Three specific ideas were embedded in these provincial health plans. The first idea is that health care is a public good and should be subject to extensive regulation. The second idea is that the state must ensure universal coverage and equitable access. The third idea is that the federal (central) government belongs in the health policy arena as a guardian of the 'right' to health care. These ideas are consistent with a social-democratic world-view of the public sector and contributed to the rapid expansion of social protection throughout the industrialized world. In Canada, this world-view was most strongly transmitted by political leaders in the CCF/NDP and institutionalized through the Saskatchewan experiments in public hospital and medical insurance. Once these innovations captured the health policy agenda, federalism was the agent through which these ideas were diffused to other provinces. In some cases, the social-democratic impetus was already strengthening (e.g., the Lesage administration in Quebec); in other cases (e.g., Alberta), the federal purse was able to trump contending ideas and alternatives.

With the help of shared funds from the federal government, each province designed its own health care system to address the specific needs and concerns of its residents. Quebec's health insurance legislation, for example, does not explicitly refer to any federal principles and it was distinctive in several respects. Part of a broader expansion of the role of the state into economic and social affairs begun during the Quiet Revolution in the 1960s, medical insurance was designed as part of an integrated system of health and social services, and included such innovations as the network of CLSCs (health and social services clinics) (White, 1999). From the start, Quebec governments demonstrated a more aggressive stance toward professional stakeholders than in the other provinces. Many reforms that were diffused to the other provinces, such as the ban on extra-billing, salary caps on physicians, wide mandates for regional boards, and a pharmacare program, were first implemented in Quebec.

Although this early era was infused with a spirit of negotiation and compromise, intergovernmental health policy-making in the 1960s was not without conflict. Provincial leaders in Alberta and Ontario objected to the diffusion of universal public health insurance. Conservative premier John Robarts in Ontario referred to the federal policy as 'political fraud' (Taylor, 1987). Successive Quebec governments in the 1960s attempted unsuccessfully to change the cost-sharing funding formula to allow opting-out with compensation.

The rapid expansion of the state into the health care sector contributed to state building by both provincial and federal governments and exacerbated conflict in intergovernmental relations to some extent (Young, Faucher, and Blais, 1984). At the same time, a series of fiscal crises almost immediately placed the two levels of government at loggerheads over health care financing. By 1977, cost sharing was replaced by block grants to provinces for health and post-secondary education. With the introduction of block grants, decisions that affected health care funding were no longer in the realm of intergovernmental relations, but rather were tied to calculations about public expenditures in annual budgets. Known as the Established Programs Financial Arrangements, or EPF, this funding arrangement signalled a major change in the rules of the game in fiscal federalism and the way the government of Canada contributed to health and post-secondary education.

1984–99: Federal Unilateralism and Intergovernmental Conflict

Although the provinces became fully responsible for health care cost increases after the introduction of the EPF, the federal government continued to exert an influence in health policy through the conditions attached to the cash component of fiscal transfers. In a dramatic gesture, Liberal Prime Minister Pierre Trudeau reinforced the federal government's political stake in health care by passing the Canada Health Act in 1984. There had been considerable concern on the part of the federal government that some provinces were allowing user fees to be imposed by health facilities and 'extra-billing' by physicians (i.e., charging above the negotiated fee for service). While Quebec and British Columbia already had banned the practice of extra-billing, it was still in practice in other provinces. Despite the chorus of opposition against the 'arbitrary' nature of the law on the part of the medical profession and some provincial leaders, the 1984 Act amalgamated hospital and medical legislation into a single, visible and highly symbolic federal statute. Although the Liberal party went down to defeat shortly after its passage, the CHA retained both its legislative force and its symbolic appeal. As provincial governments in Manitoba, Saskatchewan, and Nova Scotia introduced new legislation to conform to the CHA, the most politically explosive reaction was in Ontario. In 1985, the Liberal–NDP accord included a ban on extra-billing as a top priority, but after David Peterson's government passed the measure a strike response from specialist physicians ensued (Tuohy, 1988).

After the Progressive Conservative government attempted to scale back social programs with mixed results, Prime Minister Brian Mulroney stated publicly that health care remained a 'sacred trust' of the Canadian government. Following the Liberal party's return to power in Ottawa in 1993, the CHA became a focus of dispute between a federal government with a centralist vision and a tight purse, and provincial governments with increasing financial burdens in health care (Smith and Maioni, 2003). The federal government could more easily disengage itself from the consequences of these cost considerations, while provincial governments remained 'on the "front line" of public displeasure' (Fierlbeck, 1999).

The change in funding with the implementation of the Established Programs Financing (EPF) arrangement in 1977 meant that federal money to each province included both cash transfers and tax points. The EPF formula was initially calculated on a per capita basis but this formula was replaced with one based on growth in GNP—2 per cent in 1986 and essentially frozen after 1990. As each change in the funding formula led to decreases in federal health transfers to the provinces, critics pointed out that the federal government was 'off-loading' its deficit problems by reducing its health care funds to the provinces (Boothe and Johnson, 1993).

More precipitous changes were yet to come. In 1995, Liberal Finance Minister, Paul Martin, introduced the Canada Health and Social Transfer to replace the EPF arrangement and the Canada Assistance Plan. The CHST amalgamated federal funds for health, social assistance and post-secondary education into a single grant, and considerably reduced the cash portion of the transfer (Phillips, 1995). The cash transfer to the provinces declined from $18.5 billion to $12.5 billion. The tax point portion was largely unaffected. In consequence, by the mid-1990s, federal transfers represented only one-third of provincial outlays in health as compared to 40 per cent of provincial health expenditures in the mid-1970s (Canadian Institute for Health Information, 1999).

Intergovernmental relations in health care took a significant turn for the worse with the implementation of the CHST. Strapped for cash, provinces responded by moving rapidly to stench the growth in health care costs, often with dramatic results such as the closure of hospitals and problems of timely access to care on the part of some patients. They also launched their own intergovernmental initiative: to create a 'social union' in which provincial governments would set the agenda rather than the federal government (Courchene, 1996). At the centre of the health agenda were attempts to build an effective partnership between the federal and provincial governments that would entail 'adequate, predictable and stable cash transfers' and new, formal mechanisms to ensure more transparency and less ambiguity in dispute resolution. The federal government eventually captured this process with the signature of all provinces but Quebec to the Social Union Framework Agreement (SUFA) in February 1999. Although broad in scope and not specific to health care, the provisions of SUFA were directly relevant to health policy (Choudhry, 2000). The agreement acknowledged the need for more transparency and consultation in intergovernmental policy-making, including dispute resolutions. Nevertheless, these initiatives were overshadowed by the pressing issue of the day in intergovernmental politics of social policy: money.

1999–Present: A New Kind of Collaborative Federalism?

As the federal government's coffers replenished, the pressure for reinvestment in health care also increased. The 1999 federal budget finally changed the tide. It earmarked additional funds to the CHST (including the injection of $11.5 billion over five years to health transfers to the provinces) and introduced measures to eliminate inter-provincial disparities (Canada, Department of Finance, 1999). In 2000, a health care funding agreement readjusted the increase in provinces' transfers to $23.4B, including an $800-million Primary Health Care Transition Fund. In 2003, the Canada Health Transfer (CHT) came into effect, adjusting these figures upward to $36.8 billion, including a Health Reform Fund intended for targeted initiatives (Primary Health Care, Home Care, Catastrophic Drugs, and Diagnostic/Medical Equipment).

Nevertheless, despite the considerable electoral mileage Jean Chrétien's Liberal government derived from these measures, provincial leaders remained concerned about their fiscal capacity to meet increasing health care costs. The 2002 Romanow report (directed by the former NDP premier of Saskatchewan) identified an outstanding 'gap' in funding, and insisted on more stable financing arrangements for the provinces. When Paul Martin became Prime Minister, observers noticed efforts to change the tenor and practice of intergovernmental affairs—especially in the area of health care. After extensive negotiations at a high-profile First Minister's Meeting in 2004, the premiers reached an historic agreement on health care funding. The federal government committed to a 10-year plan for increased health care transfers, including a $4.5-billion fund to reduce waiting times, a matter that had become a thorny political issue. In addition to immediate increases in cash transfers to the provinces, there was also the promise of an annual 6 per cent escalator from 2006–14. In all, the federal government estimated this would inject $41 billion into health care across Canada. Although this new money ostensibly allowed the provinces not only to increase overall spending, but also to tackle long-overdue primary care reform and to address the waiting-times issue, some critics deplored the 'buying-off' of intergovernmental peace.

There are currently several ways in which the federal government provides money for provincial health care. First, and the largest, is the contribution through the CHT. It consists of both a direct cash and tax-point transfer that is 'tied' to provinces respecting the five principles of the *Canada Health Act*. Second, the federal government has entered into specific funding arrangements with the provinces for targeted initiatives (for example, the recent Health Reform Transfer, the Diagnostic/Medical Equipment Fund, and the Primary Health Care Transition Fund). Third, the federal government also indirectly contributes to health care through equalization payments to certain provinces. These payments are intended to ensure that provinces can deliver comparable levels of services regardless of their revenue situation. Fourth, there are the direct federal government contributions for subject matters that fall under federal authority, like aboriginal peoples and military personnel. These funds also have an impact on provincial health care systems and provincial residents. And finally, although the provinces spend money on public health, health promotion and disease prevention, and health research, the federal government invests very heavily in all provinces in these areas as well.

Health Care: A Poorly Performing Federal System?

How has the federal system performed when it comes to health care in Canada? This question directs us to an examination of whether the institutions and processes of intergovernmental relations have: functioned so as to ensure respect for each order's jurisdiction; maintained a federal balance between unity and diversity; and facilitated communication, negotiation and sometimes agreement across the two orders of government.

By the above measures, the federal system performed poorly over the 1990s when it comes to health care. Throughout the decade, provincial governments were locked in a political battle with the federal government over *who* pays *how much* in health care. The federal government's reduction in its direct transfers to the provinces for health care had an obvious negative impact on provinces' budgets. The Liberal government's zero-sum attitude in dealing with the provinces after 1995 further added to provincial perceptions of Ottawa's perceived intransigence in recognizing provincial concerns in health care. At least part of the resentment on the part of provincial governments had to do with the sense of the ground shifting under their feet. Provinces had agreed to set up health insurance systems that conformed to federal principles, only to have the federal government change the rules of the game. To the provinces, the federal government seemed content to occupy the high ground on health care reform while leaving the provinces with the political fallout over the details of cost containment and access to care. Tensions between provincial and federal governments, from first ministers down through officials in health care bureaucracies, were palpable.

In this rocky intergovernmental landscape, the provinces and the government of Canada acted independently to search for new policy direction in health care. Beginning in the early 1990s, almost every province commissioned reports and studies that could address the political concerns and fiscal pressures of health reform (Angus, 1992). The federal government was also conscious of the political repercussions of a perceived lack of leadership in health care and launched the National Forum on Health in 1994. The Forum met with provincial reluctance, and in some cases, hostility; provinces perceived it to be an instance of federal meddling in a sector of provincial responsibility. However, there was some room for common ground. Both the report of the National Forum on Health (1997) and the report of the Conference of Provincial/Territorial Ministers of Health (1997) concluded that predictable funding was essential for the functioning of provincial health systems and that the federal government should guarantee a minimum cash transfer to the provinces in order to ensure this outcome.

In a healthier financial state by the end of the decade, the federal government was able to respond to the political fallout of its cost control initiatives, and to increase its contributions to the provinces for health care services. And, as health care intensified as a political issue and became increasingly salient in general elections, Prime Minister Jean Chrétien set up a Commission on the Future of Health Care in Canada in 2000. Like the Hall Commission in 1961, it was led by a prominent figure from Saskatchewan; unlike Justice Emmett Hall, however, Roy Romanow had served as the provincial premier in an NDP government that had been faced with major cost-cutting in health care.

While Hall had heard the reasons why public health insurance was needed, Romanow instead was faced with the challenge of reconciling Canadians' evident support for this outcome with preoccupations about the quality of care and the sustainability of health care financing. His report, issued in 2002, was intended to shore up confidence in the public system. But it also included important insights about intergovernmental relations. Romanow said that the 'long-distance hollering' between premiers and the prime minister had to stop, and that the federal government had to re-invest serious money in health care (including in specific targeted areas) (Commission on the Future of Health Care, 2002). Even though several of the Romanow Commission recommendations regarding where to target funds (such as for primary care) were high on provincial reform agendas, the very recommendation to target funds, rather than increase direct transfers, did not sit well with some of the premiers. And some provinces interpreted the Commission's recommendation to set up a Health Council, as a mechanism to ensure accountability in health care spending, as jeopardizing provincial autonomy in health care matters.

Although the recommendations in the Romanow report have had an impact on federal funding of health care, the real contours of health reform in the provinces have been set by provincial health care commissions, many of which were highly critical of the federal government. Provinces have been at the forefront of health care restructuring because the Canadian health care system is not one national health care system but rather 10 provincial and three territorial health insurance plans that are united only by overarching norms.

Subsequent political changes have also affected intergovernmental relations in the health care arena. For example, the transfer of power to Paul Martin, Jr. as prime minister served to mute, at least temporarily, the mutual bashing and led to a more amicable, although not entirely consensual, first minister's meeting and health care accord in 2004.

Health care issues remained salient in the 2006 election, with the major federal political parties reaffirming the importance of public health insurance and emphasizing the need to reduce waiting lists and restore confidence. The arrival in power of a Conservative heralded a potential new day in intergovernmental relations, since the new prime minister, Stephen Harper, was known to be a staunch supporter of provincial autonomy in areas of jurisdiction such as health care. Still, by keeping federal largesse in play, Mr. Harper has been able to reap the political rewards of the 2004 accords, both with the general public and provincial leaders. Even with the economic downturn after 2008, subsequent federal budgets have not reduced health care transfers to the provinces: indeed, finance minister Jim Flaherty stated last year that '[w]e will not balance the budget by cutting transfer payments for health care.' As the 2014 expiry date of the 10-year accords draw near, however, provincial governments are concerned about the future of federal payments.

Provinces are also concerned about the financial sustainability of their health care systems, still the biggest budget item and projected to feel the effects of increased costs, population aging, and the pressures of new technology. Doomsday scenarios about the costs of health care are not new, but the context of economic recession and the uneasiness of the future of federal transfers have sharply increased the political rhetoric surrounding the policy issues. Recent provincial budgets have indicated the growing pressures of health care spending on program funding, yet provincial governments have not turned to drastic cost-cutting as a consequence.

At least one province, Quebec, has turned its attention to another strategy: increasing revenues by other means. The cumulative impact of an economic downturn and strapped government spending led Jean Charest's Liberal government to introduce a new *contribution santé* or health care premium in the 2010 budget; by 2012 it will collect $200 from every taxpayer in the province. While there are some concessions for the lowest-income earners, the premium resembles more of a 'poll tax' than the premiums in place in British Columbia and Ontario, even though the amounts are much more modest (just under $1 billion in annual revenues). More provocative still was the proposal for a *franchise santé*—a retroactive fee assessed on an individual's income tax, based on the number and type of 'medical visits' during the year (Maioni, 2010b). The Quebec government stipulated that these are deductibles and not co-payments or user fees, since the $25 fee per visit would be countered by a threshold spending of 1 or 2 per cent of household income. Within Quebec, negative reaction was largely about the political consequences of imposing yet another burden on taxpayers, while physicians suggested it was a sub-optimal tax on care. Outside of Quebec, the reaction has been about how provincial initiatives might impinge on the Canada Health Act. The potential for a showdown was mooted by the Quebec government's decision to forgo the fee, but the potential for another political showdown has been raised.

Federalism and Health Care Policy: Effectiveness and Legitimacy

Evaluations of the impacts of federalism and intergovernmental relations on the effectiveness of health care policies vary depending upon the observer. Four criteria are used here with respect to the impact of intergovernmental relations on health care: first, its contribution to equitable treatment of all Canadians regardless of their province/economic circumstances and consistent with shared membership in a social union; second, its impact on cost-effective delivery of health care; third, its capacity to facilitate adjustment of health care policies consistent with the fiscal capacities of governments; and fourth, its capacity to respond effectively when new health care issues and crises arise.

Looking at the first indicator of policy effectiveness, goals of inter-personal equity constituted the rationale from the outset for the federal involvement in the health care sector. In using its spending power to assist provinces in financing health care services, the federal government attempted to ensure that all Canadians, regardless of province of residence, could enjoy comparable levels of health care. Reliance on federal transfers plus the use of equalization payments has tended to put provinces on an equal footing in terms of money spent. Today, health care costs show some variation among the provinces but federal transfers and equalization payments tend to minimize these differences. More significant differences in levels of care have to do with regional and economic disparities, both within and between provinces.

A second indicator of policy effectiveness is whether Canadians get good value for money spent on health care. Health care has become an expensive proposition for governments. Overall, Canada is considered a 'big spender' among industrialized countries, with about 10 per cent of the gross domestic product (GDP) going to health care, and about 70 per cent of that figure being spent by the public purse. In 1975, relatively soon after the full implementation of hospital and medical insurance, health care spending accounted for 7 per cent of the GDP. That figure grew to 10 per cent by the early 1990s, and declined over the decade as spending cuts were implemented. In 2005, health care spending represented 10.4 per cent of GDP, or almost $142 billion dollars; by 2010 it reached 11.7 per cent or $191 billion (CIHI, 2010).

Per capita health care spending has also increased substantially since the late 1990s and now averages about $5600 across Canada. Alberta is the highest spender at $6200 per capita and Quebec is the lowest at $5100 per capita. Health care costs are substantially higher in the three territories, which average over well over $7000 per capita in health care spending. Richer provinces tend to spend more per capita on health care, although spending also reflects a government's political priorities as well as the organizational details of the health care system. In Quebec, for example, costs are lower due in part to the distinct organizational features of the system, including the presence of community clinics and lower physician reimbursement rates. The percentage of provincial GDP devoted to health care also varies from one province to another, with about 7 per cent of a province's total wealth now devoted to health care. In some provinces and territories health care has become the largest single item of program expenditure: as a percentage of program expenditures, Ontario spends the most on health care (46 per cent), Newfoundland and Labrador, the least (34 per cent) (CIHI, 2010).

A third indicator of policy effectiveness is the capacity to adjust policies as circumstances warrant. Have intergovernmental relations in health care facilitated the search for cost-containment strategies? Even while it reduced transfers to the provinces, the federal government insisted that the principles of the CHA be respected. In contrast to private insurance plans and most public health insurance systems in other countries, provincial health care services in Canada must provide services without co-payments or any kind of user fees. And, unlike the situation in many other countries, equal access provisions became a rampart against the development of a 'two-tier' health care system in which public and private services co-exist, usually to the detriment of the public system. Essentially, equal access provisions prevented 'excess' demand for health care being channelled toward a parallel private system in which ability (or willingness) to pay could override the need for care. Up to now, by insisting on 'equal access' and 'uniform terms and conditions' in the delivery of health care to individual patients, the federal government has upheld the ideal that all Canadians should receive the same benefits regardless of where they live or their economic situation.

This stance, combined with financial incentives in the form of fiscal transfers, served as a brake on widespread provincial experimentation with other forms of health insurance. But it left the provinces, as the 'single-payers' in the health care system, with the brunt of responsibility—and blame from patients and providers—for cost control. To some extent, the federal system helped provinces learn from one another about how to contain costs. Following the release of the Barer-Stoddart report in 1990, most provinces attempted to reduce costs by reducing the numbers of foreign physicians and the number of medical school enrolments (Sullivan et al., 1996). Other measures to deal with inflationary costs were diffused across the provinces through demonstration effects. Quebec was the first province to regulate physicians directly, imposing income ceilings, regulating the ratio of generalists to specialists, and assigning physician quotas by region (Demers, 1994). British Columbia was the first to attempt to control the number of physicians in the province through differential fees for new physicians, although these measures subsequently came under legal challenge in that province (Barer, 1988; Manfredi and Maioni, 2002).

In the 1990s, provincial governments reduced beds and closed hospitals—a development that would have seemed unthinkable a decade earlier. Although many hospital closures were bitterly opposed by local communities (and several challenged in courts), this practice did not attract a response from the federal government (except in the case of Jean Chrétien's protest of the closure of the Montfort Hospital in Ottawa, on the basis of minority language rights). As cost containment strategies multiplied, however, public and provider discontent fuelled concerns that the reduction of services was jeopardizing access to care, particularly through longer waiting lists for certain procedures and overcrowding in emergency rooms.

Indeed, the very success of provincial health care systems impeded their reform. Canadians consider timely access to expensive, sophisticated, and high-quality health services an entitlement, making provincial attempts at reining in costs and reorganizing delivery politically unpopular. Still, within the explicit constraints of the Canada Health Act and the policy grooves set by past experience, and with some inter-provincial borrowing of tools and instruments, most provinces attempted to 'rationalize' their health care systems. Rationalization meant extensively restructuring the hospital sector and attempting to impose limits on health care providers (Deber, Mhatre, and Baker, 1994). Restructuring was facilitated by 'regionalization'. Newly created regional health boards (some elected, others appointed) were made responsible for making decisions about the allocation of global budgets to health institutions. Regionalization rationalized budget making to some extent, but it raised the problem of passing the burden of accountability from provincial health ministries. In Ontario, the approach was more direct: the Conservative government passed legislation to empower it to close or merge hospitals through the auspices of a temporary Health Services Restructuring Commission (Tuohy, 1999).

In Alberta, following the 1994 Deficit Reduction Act, major hospital cuts were made in Edmonton and Calgary, salary rollbacks were imposed on public sector employees (including hospital workers), and health insurance premiums were raised (Fierlbeck, 1999). By the end of the 1990s, Alberta had one of the lowest rates of growth in public health care expenditures across the provinces, while private spending was among the highest in Canada. But the constraints of the federal conditions imposed on provincial health plans by the CHA frustrated the Klein government's efforts to encourage the expansion of private clinics. In 1996, the Alberta government finally backed down on facility fees after the federal government docked its transfers to the province. Another federal–provincial standoff emerged with the passage of legislation (Bill 11) in early 2000 to allow regional health authorities to contract with private clinics for surgical facilities as a way to deal with excess demand (Choudhry, 2000). The Mazankowski report (Alberta, 2001), highly critical of the federal government and of the 'public monopoly' imposed by the Canada Health Act, provided an alternative roadmap health reform in Alberta, and pushed the boundaries of the debate about private financing in health care. In 2005, the government proposed a plan for health care reform 'that follows neither the American nor the purely Canadian systems of health care' (Alberta, 2005). In 2006, however, reacting to public opinion within the province, the government retreated from some of the more controversial aspects of its 'third way' plan, such as allowing for physicians to be compensated both through the public sector and through private sector arrangements.

A final way to measure the effectiveness of IGR in health care is the capacity of governments to co-ordinate their actions when crises make it necessary. Intergovernmental co-ordination and collaboration are required in areas in which health has no borders: namely, public health, infectious disease, and pandemics. During the spring of 2003, SARS, a highly contagious viral illness, spread quickly through Toronto-area hospitals. Attempts to track and contain it had a ripple effect throughout the provinces and led to calls for a more co-ordinated approach to planning for and dealing with such problems. The taskforce set up to investigate the epidemic zeroed in on the need for better intergovernmental co-ordination, and a 'truly collaborative framework and ethos among different levels of government' (Naylor, 2003). The Canadian Public Health Agency was put into place by the federal government in 2004, and part of its mandate was to ensure federal leadership in this area.

In summary, intergovernmental relations in health care—unilateral reductions in funding while maintaining federal conditions on how the fewer dollars should be spent—have narrowed provinces' scope for reform. But equally, the high value that Canadians put on the existing system has also acted as a break to innovative cost-containment strategies. That said, the challenge of controlling public spending in health care and intergovernmental discord over health care costs has undermined the legitimacy of health care systems. The three ideas that underpinned the original Canadian health care model—state regulation, equitable access, and a federal role in health care—are all under question today. Political and social actors who believe in less state intervention question the legitimacy of federal standards and argue the need to explore other options for financing health care, including private market alternatives.

Although the attachment of Canadians to the principles of universal health care remains robust across the provinces, there are some regional differences in the openness to privatization options (Mendelsohn, 2002). Canadians are nonetheless generally concerned about the long-term sustainability of the existing public model, anxious about its cost and timely access to specific services (Blendon et al., 2002). Changes in ambulatory practice and controls on providers increased the numbers of waiting lists and wait times for some elective procedures and for access to specialist care in some provinces. Waiting lists are also a form of implicit rationing of services in order to contain health care costs. (Unlike user fees or extra-billing, which require patients to contribute directly to the cost of health care, waiting lists are compatible with the principle of equal access in the sense that they ensure that services are dispensed on the criteria of medical need rather than ability to pay.) For consumers of health care, the availability of physicians, the ratio of generalists to specialists, and the distribution of generalists/specialists across urban and rural/remote areas are all matters that affect perceptions of the legitimacy of existing health care systems (CIHI, 2006a).

Ideas that support privatization in health care, while not new in Canada, are pushing the frontiers of public debate about health reform. Although Canadian federalism has so far prevented the widespread implementation of private alternatives, conflicts over what level of government is responsible for cost control and the extent to which provincial health policy choices can be constrained by federal government preferences, have created political room for these alternatives to gather political momentum.

The basic challenges that affect provincial health care systems are ones that directly impact upon the role that the federal government has carved out for itself in health care. What should be covered by a provincial health plan? Who should pay for services? When can equal access be provided? How can the provinces address demographic and technological pressures? And, as the recent court battles over health care suggest, constitutional debates in health care are not only about the division of powers, but also about rights of Canadians under the Charter. For example, in *Auton v. British Columbia*, a group of BC parents claimed a specific treatment for their autistic children under the equality rights provisions (s. 15) of the Canadian Charter of Rights and Freedoms. Although their victory at the provincial court level was overturned by the Supreme Court of Canada, which ruled that the contents of the health care basket were a 'matter for Parliament and the legislature' (Manfredi and Maioni, 2005), the issue lingers.

In 2005, the Supreme Court of Canada invalidated prohibitions against private insurance for core medical services provided through Quebec's public health care system (Manfredi and Maioni, 2006). The decision, known as *Chaoulli v. Québec*, was a divided and controversial one involving three separate judgments. The majority decision overturned rulings by provincial courts, and found Quebec's hospital and health insurance legislation to be in violation of the Québec Charter of Rights and Freedoms (the right to life and inviolability of the person). The Quebec government's legislative response in 2006, Bill 33, opened the provision of core services in the Quebec health care system to private insurance, but only in three specific areas: hip, knee, and cataract surgery (Quebec, 2006). Its wording also suggested the possibility of an eventual extension of private insurance to other procedures and introduced a new instrument for the provision of services through the establishment of 'affiliated medical clinics' through public–private partnerships, a central theme of the Liberal government's attempts to 're-engineer' the Quebec state. At the same time, however, the proposal retained the 'wall' between physicians who remain in the public system and those who opt out of it. It thus differed from Alberta's ill-fated proposals, and introduced a wait-time guarantee akin to what the federal Conservative party had promised in the January 2006 election.

The Chaoulli court case involved the federal government and five other provinces as intervenors on behalf of Quebec. Interestingly, the plaintiffs had the support of a group of Senators who had signed a 2002 Senate committee report claiming that waiting times for certain medical services were unacceptable and suggested a better mix of private and public delivery. Regardless of this interest at the federal level, the case has driven home the fact that health care is governed primarily by provincial laws rather than federal regulations. Because the majority decision was reached on the basis of the Quebec Charter, there was no direct or immediate impact on other provincial health care legislation. But other provinces are facing similar kinds of pressures that led to this legal saga.

Perceptions of legitimacy clearly differ depending upon whether one is a recipient of health care or whether one is a provider. At times, physicians have had a turbulent relationship with Canada's health care system. At the outset of publicly funded health insurance, medical interests came into conflict with the provinces over issues of financial and professional autonomy (Evans et al., 1989). Physicians opposed the introduction of medical insurance legislation in Saskatchewan in 1962; Quebec specialists went on strike in 1970; Ontario doctors opposed the ban on extra-billing in Ontario in 1986; and, more recently, there were limited work stoppages in Ontario to protest funding cuts. Doctors have accepted the bargain of the state monopoly on health care: that is, fee schedules in return for the freedom to practise on a fee-for-service basis. The majority of doctors are reimbursed for their services on a fee schedule negotiated between provincial governments (or their public agency) and the provincial medical association. (In Quebec, there are separate negotiations for specialists, general practitioners, and residents). These fee schedules are roughly similar across the provinces, although they are set separately in each province, and there is some variation in the definition of billing codes and reimbursement rates tend to be lower in Quebec. Across the provinces, most doctors continue to be paid on a fee-for-service basis, although salaried doctors that staff community clinics and hospitals are more common in Quebec, Manitoba, and New Brunswick.

Conclusion

The politics of intergovernmental relations in the health sector point to the strength of federalism in helping to build a coherent health care model across the provinces. Health care has long been touted as a success story of what federalism can achieve, and provincial health care systems are vaunted as the success story of public sector involvement in the health sector. Since the passage of initial health legislation, the health care system has occupied an influential symbolic role in Canadian federalism, and federalism continues to exert a significant influence on health policy. The scope for provincial experimentation in health reform is considerably narrowed by the institutional levers of intergovernmental relations and policy legacies that characterize the health care system in Canada. Health 'reformers' have had to work within the relatively limited boundaries of provincial health statutes and the stipulations of the CHA. In this sense, policy legacies have had powerful resonance in maintaining the logic of a single-payer model.

But this model has hardly survived unscathed from the economic and political turbulence of the past decade. Sustained cost controls, limits on providers, and extensive hospital restructuring have put enormous pressure on provincial health care systems and frayed public confidence in the public sector. Meanwhile, federal–provincial relations in the health policy sector deteriorated, as health ministers and first ministers skirmished publicly over money and rules. And the emergence of the courts in health care has further muddied the health policy playing field. The CHA, which insists that the principle of 'equal access' be maintained by provinces receiving federal monies for health care, is seen by its supporters as a firewall against private health care services. The Act cannot, however, impel provinces to prohibit such services. So far, apart from the attempts of the Quebec government, and the discussions emanating from Alberta, there has been little concrete change in the status quo ante of provincial-federal relations with respect to these principles of the CHA. As the health care accords wind down, however, and money becomes tight, the conflicts between jurisdictional responsibilities and fiscal capacities are likely to re-surface.

Not surprisingly, the conflicts over money did not abate entirely with the return of better economic scenarios in the early 2000s. Although the 2004 10-year plan offered financial security to provinces in need of steady funding for health care, the politics of surplus budgets exacerbated tensions about money and jurisdiction, and about regional disparities. With the return of recession, some provinces may be thinking of 'pushing the envelope' in health reform. The enduring debate over the fiscal imbalance is directly related to health care, since the questions of costs and responsibility remains at the heart of fiscal federalism.

Besides representing a growing share of fiscal resources, health care is also seen by many as the most important service funded by government. The Liberal Party of Canada, throughout the 1990s, seized upon its historical role in promoting and diffusing the public model and carving a political space in the health sector despite a limited jurisdictional role. In so doing, it reinforced Ottawa's role in health care as both symbolic and practical. In symbolic terms, Liberal governments claimed to have 'nationalized' health care, promoted 'equal citizenship' among Canadians, and guaranteed health benefits to all. This discourse is of enormous significance in debates about provincial autonomy, national unity, or constitutional renewal. It has also allowed federal governments to defend the 'integrity' of the features that reflect 'Canadian values' without the headache of administering and budgeting for health care services. In practical terms, the federal government was able to use the CHA as a way to minimize asymmetry in health provision among the provinces and to contribute toward regional equity. In doing so, federalism served as an instrument for narrowing reform alternatives and, ironically, constrained the principle of policy diversity inherent in the Canadian federal principle.

The successive minority Conservative governments in Ottawa may have a different perception and appreciation of federal roles and responsibilities in health care. Nevertheless, federal transfers to the provinces continue to increase and are likely to remain in place through 2013. Still, provincial autonomy and innovation are central principles in Prime

Minister Stephen Harper's worldview. It remains to be seen whether these principles will come into conflict with existing federal statutes, such as the CHA, and how the intergovernmental relations in health care will be played out in a new era of institutional change and against a changing backdrop of political ideas in Canada.

References

Alberta. 2001. Report of the Premier's Advisory Council on Health for Albertans (The Mazankowski Report). Edmonton. Available at: http://www.health.gov.ab.ca/resources/publications/PACH_report_final.pdf.

Alberta, Health and Wellness. 2005. *Getting On With Better Health Care*. Edmonton. Available at: http://www.health.gov.ab.ca/key/AHW_WebFinal_REV.pdf.

Angus, D.E. 1992. 'A Great Canadian Prescription: Take Two Commissioned Studies and Call Me in the Morning'. In *Restructuring Canada's Health System: How Do We Get There From Here?*, ed. R. Deber and G. Thompson. Toronto: University of Toronto Press.

Barer, M.L. 1988. 'Regulating Physician Supply: The Evolution of British Columbia's Bill 41', *Journal of Health Politics, Policy and Law*, 13: 1–25

Blendon, R.J., et al. 2002. 'Inequalities in health care: A five-country study', *Health Affairs*, 21(3): 182–91.

Boothe, P. and B. Johnston. 1993. 'Stealing the Emperor's Clothes: Deficit Offloading and National Standards in Health Care'. *Commentary*, C.D. Howe Institute, 41 (March).

Canada, Department of Finance. 1999. *Federal Transfers to Provinces and Territories*, October.

Canada, National Forum on Health. 1997. *Canada Health Action: Building on the Legacy*. Ottawa: Minister of Public Works and Government Services.

Canada, Royal Commission on Health Services. 1964. *Final Report: Volume I*. Ottawa: Queen's Printer.

Canadian Institute for Health Information (CIHI). 1999. *National Health Expenditure Trends, 1975–1998*. Ottawa.

———. 2006a. *Geographic Distribution of Physicians in Canada: Beyond How Many and Where*. Ottawa.

———. 2010. *National Health Expenditure Trends, 1975 to 2010*. Ottawa.

Choudhry, S. 2000. 'Bill 11, the *Canada Health Act* and the Social Union: The Need for Institutions', *Osgoode Hall Law Journal*, 38: 40–99.

Commission on the Future of Health Care. 2002. *Building on Values: The Future of Health Care in Canada*. Final Report of the Commission. Ottawa.

Conference of Provincial/Territorial Ministers of Health. 1997. *A Renewed Vision for Canada's Health System*.

Courchene, T.J. 1996. 'ACCESS: *A Convention on the Canadian Economic and Social Systems*'. Working Paper prepared for the Ministry of Intergovernmental Affairs, Government of Ontario.

Deber, R., B. Sharmila, L. Mhatre and G.R. Baker. 1994. 'A Review of Provincial Initiatives'. In *Limits to Care: Reforming Canada's Health System in an Age of Restraint*, ed. A. Blomqvist and D.M. Brown. Toronto: C.D. Howe.

Demers, L. 1994. 'La profession médicale'. In Le système de santé québécois: organisations, acteurs et enjeux, ed. Vincent Lemieux et al. Québec: Presses de l'Université Laval.

Desruisseaux, A., and S. Fortin. 1999. 'The Making of the Welfare State'. In *As I Recall/Si je me souviens bien*, ed. Institute for Research in Public Policy. Montreal: IRPP.

Evans, R.G., et al. 1989. 'Controlling health expenditures—the Canadian reality', *New England Journal of Medicine* 320(9): 571–7.

Fierlbeck, K. 1999. 'Cost Containment in Health Care: The Federal Context'. In *The Canadian Social Union: Case Studies from the Health Sector*, ed. H. Lazar and D. Adams. Montreal and Kingston: McGill–Queen's University Press.

Gray, G. 1991. *Federalism and Health Policy: The Development of Health Systems in Canada and Australia*. Toronto: University of Toronto Press.

Maioni, A. 1999. 'Les normes centrales et les politiques de la santé'. In *Le Système de santé québécois: Un modèle en transformation*, ed. C.

Bégin et al. Montreal: Presses de l'Université de Montréal.

Maioni, A. 2010a. 'Health Care Funding: Needs and Realities,' *Policy Options/Options politiques* (May 2010), pp. 69–72.

Maioni, A. 2010b. 'Health Care in Quebec', in *Quebec Questions: Quebec Studies for the Twenty-First Century*, ed. J. Rudy et al. (Oxford University Press, 2010).

Manfredi, C.P.. and A. Maioni. 2002. 'Courts and Health Policy: Judicial Policy Making and Publicly Funded Health Care in Canada', *Journal of Health Politics, Policy and Law*, 27: 213–40.

————— and —————. 2005. 'Reversal of Fortune: Litigating Health Care Reform in *Auton v. British Columbia*', *Supreme Court Law Review (2d)*, 29: 111–36.

————— and —————. 2006. 'The Last Line of Defence for Citizens: Litigating Private Health Insurance in *Chaoulli v. Quebec*', *Osgoode Hall Law Journal*, 44(1) .

Mendelsohn, M. 2002. 'Canadians' Thoughts on their Health Care System: Preserving the Canadian Model through Innovation'. *Royal Commission on the Future of Health Care*. Ottawa: Government of Canada.

Naylor, D.C. 2003. *Learning from SARS - Renewal of Public Health in Canada*. A report of the National Advisory Committee on SARS and Public Health. Ottawa: Health Canada.

Phillips, S.D. 1995. 'The Canada Health and Social Transfer: Fiscal Federalism in Search of a Vision'. In *Canada: The State of the Federation 1995*, ed. D.M. Brown and J. Rose. Kingston: Institute of Intergovernmental Affairs, Queen's University.

Pierson, P. 2000. 'Not Just What, but When: Timing and Sequence in Political Processes', *Studies in American Political Development*, 14: 72–92.

Québec. Assemblée nationale. 2006. *Projet de loi no 33 : Loi modifiant la Loi sur les services de santé et les services sociaux et d'autres dispositions législatives*. Québec : Éditeur officiel du Québec.

Robinson, I. and R. Simeon. 1994. 'The Dynamics of Canadian Federalism'. In *Canadian Politics: 2nd Edition*, ed. J. Bickerton and A.-G. Gagnon. Peterborough: Broadview Press.

Smith, M., and A. Maioni. 2003. 'Health Care and Canadian Federalism'. In *New Trends in Canadian Federalism*, 2nd edn. ed. F. Rocher and M. Smith. Peterborough: Broadview Press.

Sullivan, R.B., et al. 1996. 'The Evolution Of Divergences In Physician Supply Policy in Canada and the United States', *Journal of the American Medical Association*, 276(9): 704–9.

Taylor, M.G. 1987. *Health Insurance and Canadian Public Policy: The Seven Decisions that Created the Canadian Health Insurance System and Their Outcomes*, 2nd edn. Montreal and Kingston: McGill–Queen's University Press.

Tuohy, C.H. 1999. *Accidental Logics: The Dynamics of Change in the Health Care Arena in the United States, Britain and Canada*. New York: Oxford University Press.

Watts, R.L. 1999. *Comparing Federal Systems. Second Edition*. Kingston: Institute of Intergovernmental Relations, Queen's University.

White, D. 1999. 'La santé et les services sociaux: réforme et remise en question'. In *Le Québec en jeu: comprendre les grands défis*, ed. G. Daigle, and G. Rocher. Montréal: Les presses de l'Université de Montréal.

Young, R.A., P. Faucher and A. Blais. 1984. 'The Concept of Province-Building: A Critique', *Canadian Journal of Political Science*, 17(4): 783–818

Cases

Auton (Guardian ad litem of) v. British Columbia (Attorney General), [2004] 3 S.C.R. 657.

Chaoulli v. Quebec (Attorney General), [2005] 1 S.C.R. 791.

10 'No-lateralism': Paradoxes in Early Childhood Education and Care Policy in the Canadian Federation

Martha Friendly and Linda A. White

'Paradoxical' describes trends in Canadian **early childhood education and care** (ECEC) in recent years.[1] On the one hand, increased recognition of the importance of early childhood education (ECE) has spurred major provincial early education initiatives (CRRU, 2009), and provincial and territorial ministers of education have identified 'early childhood learning and development' as the first of four pillars of lifelong learning in their *Learn Canada 2020* declaration (CMEC, 2008). There has also been an emerging recognition on the part of national political parties and provincial governments such as Ontario and PEI (Pascal, 2009; Government of Prince Edward Island, 2010) that ECEC should be designed as a coherent set of policies and programs. At the same time, policy disinterest at the federal government level under the guise of '**open federalism**' (Canada, House of Commons, 2007), and ideological opposition to organized child care services[2] has created a policy vacuum and challenging funding gaps. Thus, policy initiatives that conceive of ECEC as a comprehensive set of programs providing the foundation for early learning and social development for all children have been impeded by the absence of public funds and political will.

Paradoxically, this transformation in thinking about ECEC has occurred just at the time that expansion of child care services and public funding has slowed across Canada (Beach et al., 2009: xvii). At the same time, demand for child care—as mothers' labour force participation has continued unabated—has led to the expansion of for-profit ECEC markets and, increasingly, corporate child care operators (Ladurantaye, 2010). This development is especially paradoxical in light of strong evidence about the importance of high quality ECEC programs for child development (e.g., Shonkoff and Phillips, 2000: 303), together with the consistent finding that for-profit child care provision is considerably less likely to be high quality (Cleveland et al., 2008; Japel, Tremblay, and Côté, 2005).

This chapter charts these trends in the hit-and-miss development of ECEC in Canada, offering an assessment of the ability of the Canadian federation to lead, shape, or even respond to policy initiatives in this area. We first document shifts in conceptions of ECEC and trends in ECEC policy and program delivery. Second, we document what is happening at the intergovernmental level. We label this era of intergovernmental relations '**no-lateralism**' to signal that, since the change in federal government in January 2006, there has been little governance of the federation with regard to social policy for children and families and little action on the federal-provincial-territorial (FPT) front. Thus, as compared to earlier periods of **multilateralism** and **bilateralism** (Friendly and White, 2008; McRoberts, 1985), ECEC is in a new era of even more limited governance and communication among the orders of government. Hence, the term 'no-lateralism'.

The third part of the paper provides more of a 'blue sky' analysis of the future. In speculating about the role of Canadian federal and provincial governments in ECEC, we ask whether a federal government 'should', 'could', and 'would' play a key role. This 'blue sky' analysis challenges certain myths about the role of the federal government.

In terms of whether a federal government *should* play a role, we point out that cross-national indicators reveal that an open federalism model of policy and program delivery is not serving the Canadian population well in a variety of areas of national concern. Referring to several different rationales, we also argue that a federal government *could* play a role in the shaping and funding of ECEC provision in Canada if it so chose. Finally, as provinces across Canada have begun to indicate new interest in ECEC policy, and national political parties in Opposition keep ECEC on their own agendas as part of their challenge to the Conservative government, we suggest that there might be interest in a pan-Canadian approach that *would* see the federal government 'cross the threshold of the school', at least where younger children are concerned. Doing so would allow the federal government to provide significant ongoing funding for ECEC services, as it does for higher education and as it once did for eligible child care services under the Canada Assistance Plan (CAP).

Given the fluidity of child care policy under different federalism regimes, there is no reason to think that the federation is static and could not shift again to see a more pan-Canadian ECEC policy emerge. The chapter concludes, therefore, by exploring possibilities for approaches to ECEC that respect the Canadian constitution, but that also acknowledge the now-considerable evidence of the need for cross-Canada action on ECEC policy as well as fiscal and political realities.

Canadian Trends in ECEC Policy

Relatively well-organized systems of ECEC are now the norm in many industrialized countries (OECD, 2006; UNESCO, 2006; Kaga, Bennett, and Moss, 2010; Bennett, 2010). In most Western European countries, most three- to six-year-olds attend ECEC programs for a full school day. These programs are primarily publicly delivered and publicly funded, although parents usually pay some fees for younger children and after school hours (OECD, 2006). Their main purpose is 'early childhood education', broadly construed, although there are usually provisions—albeit not always adequate—to meet parents' labour force needs for child care. The quality of programs for three- to six-year-olds in most countries is reasonably high (or at least acceptable) by most standards, with educational goals, early childhood teacher training, and curricula in place in most countries (ibid.).

In reviewing Canada as part of a 20-nation study, the Organisation for Economic Co-operation and Development (OECD) commented that 'national and provincial policy for the early education and care of young children in Canada is still in its initial stages. Care and education are still treated separately and coverage is low compared to other OECD countries' (OECD, 2004a: 6). In the study's summary report, the OECD (2006) listed Canada as a country with 'negligible' coverage, remaining a laggard compared not only with Western

Europe but even with other Anglo-American nations (OECD, 2006; UNESCO, 2006; UNICEF, 2008). Public ECEC spending remains extremely low in Canada; the OECD's (2006) analysis shows Canada as the lowest spender in the OECD at 0.25 per cent of GDP (Denmark spends 2 per cent of GDP). UNICEF (2008) ranks Canada at the bottom (tied with Ireland) of 25 OECD countries in terms of 10 benchmarks of ECEC services.

Each province/territory has its own approach to ECEC. Each province/territory has regulated child care centres, part-day nursery schools, family daycare (in private homes), and public kindergarten. The range and quality of, and access to, ECEC programs vary considerably by region and circumstance but 'care' and early childhood education for children younger than five years is largely a private responsibility. The public funding model in all provinces except Quebec[3] relies heavily on fee subsidies targeted to eligible low-income families and, in some provinces, notably Ontario, many eligible families cannot obtain a subsidy. This welfare—rather than universal—approach means that the high user fees for regulated child care that are levied to support most of the cost of program operations are a major barrier to access for low- and middle-income parents. The supply of child care spaces covers only a minority of children, and public kindergarten schedules do not meet the needs of working parents. Across Canada, even regulated child care is more likely to be poor to mediocre than excellent (Goelman et al., 2000; Japel et al., 2005). No province/territory provides sufficient high quality ECEC programs to serve a majority of children.

In addition, no Canadian jurisdiction meets the UNICEF benchmarks for quality, access, and financing (Friendly and Prentice, in press). But recent trends in Canadian ECEC suggest that a number of provincial governments do recognize the importance of the early years as a foundation for for subsequent developmental, social, and economic success. In Quebec the political discourse has shifted from 'care' for children of working mothers to a more holistic approach to early childhood education and care for all young children (e.g., Gouvernement du Québec, Ministère de la Famille et des Aînés, 2007). In September 2010, British Columbia, Ontario, and Prince Edward Island all joined New Brunswick, Nova Scotia, and Quebec in offering full-day ECEC programs in the year before compulsory schooling (CRRU, 2010). While Ontario is the sole province to have embarked on a multi-year plan to extend full-day kindergarten to all four-year-olds, British Columbia announced in early 2010 that it will explore the idea of extending ECEC programs for three- and four-year-olds (Government of British Columbia, 2010: 20).

There has even been a switch in the governing federal Conservative Party's language about ECEC. In the 2006 federal election, the federal Conservatives argued for 'freedom of choice in childcare' (Conservative Party of Canada, 2006: 31). Before they were elected in 2006, as well as after the election and the Conservative government's cancellation of the previous Liberal Government's nascent ECEC program, members of the Conservative government typically called ECEC 'institutionalized day care'. In 2005, the Social Development critic in the Conservative Party, Rona Ambrose, argued in the House of Commons that 'only 23 per cent of parents in Canada choose to place their children into the "institutional" daycare supported by the Liberals' (CTV News, 2005). In a CBC interview in 2006, Human Resources Minister Diane Finley (CBC News, 2006) noted that 'childcare doesn't have to be institutionalized. It might be staying at home. It might be grandma. It might be the next door neighbour. But we believe that parents are the best ones to choose who raises their children.'

In contrast, defending his government's record on child poverty in the House of Commons in 2009, Prime Minister Stephen Harper (2009: 1430) noted that his government spent money on 'early childhood learning, childcare and education.' The 2007 federal budget plan claimed that 'the Government of Canada will provide nearly $5.6 billion in 2007–08 in support of early learning and childcare through transfers, direct spending and tax measures' (Canada, Department of Finance, 2007: 156). It is a rather bold statement for an 'open federalist' to brag about spending money in ostensibly provincial areas of jurisdiction such as education.

From the perspective of policy and program delivery, the shift in language is consistent with best practices and certainly reflects trends in other countries (OECD, 2006) and the multi-faceted, complex needs of Canadian families. The proportion of Canadian mothers in the paid labour force with young children has continuously increased over the last three decades. Between 1995 and 2007, labour force participation rates rose from 61 per cent to 69 per cent for mothers whose youngest child was 0–2 years; to 77 per cent for those whose youngest was 3–5 years; and 84 per cent for those with a child 6–15 years (Beach et al., 2009: Table 21). Between the 1980s and 2006, the proportion of children aged six months to five years who were in child care arrangements outside the nuclear family increased significantly. Cleveland et al. (2008: 7, 27) report that almost 80 per cent of pre-school age children with employed or studying mothers are in some form of non-parental care or early childhood program on a regular basis, almost 50 per cent of them in an organized ECEC program. Low income families may qualify for fee subsidies to cover some or all of the high cost of regulated child care but modest- and middle-income families usually do not qualify (Beach et al., 2009: xiii). Most children with one or both parents in the labour force are assumed to be in unregulated[4] child care (a relative, an unregulated family child care provider or in-home caregiver) (Beach et al., 2009: xi)[5] but there are few concrete data about unregulated child care arrangements.

The idea that good child care and 'early learning' are closely linked is increasingly accepted by the public. A 2002 poll found that 90 per cent of 1,200 Canadians polled agreed that child care is very (64 per cent) or somewhat (26 per cent) important in furthering a child's education and development (Espey and Good Co., 2003: 10). A 2005 survey found that 75 per cent of 1,002 Ontarians polled agreed strongly (37 per cent) or somewhat (38 per cent) that 'licensed daycare programs should share information and co-ordinate programs with public kindergartens' (Livingstone and Hart, 2005: 7). An Environics Research Group (2006: 9) report found that 81 per cent of Canadians polled felt that child care prepares children for school and 79 per cent felt that it promotes early learning and child development. In addition, public opinion data show strong support for a national universally accessible child care system.[6]

ECEC Policy-Making under Federalism: An Overview of Five Federalism Regimes

Federal Leadership Phase

From the 1970s to 1995, the federal government had no qualms about exercising its federal spending power in the development of child care, albeit of limited policy scope. The

Canada Assistance Plan (CAP) provided provinces and territories with cost-shared funds to support the cost of eligible child care services for low-income families. Eligibility was defined by a set of federal conditions that applied to both service providers and parents. However, the federal government did not see itself as responsible for expanding child care services beyond this narrow framework of social assistance—for example, for treating it as part of employment support for all families.

In 1984, the Trudeau government agreed to strike a ministerial-level Task Force to explore child care. In response, even before the Liberal Task Force reported after the 1984 federal election, the new Mulroney Conservative government set up its own special parliamentary committee that held cross-Canada hearings on child care, issued recommendations, and tabled Bill C-144, the *Canada Child Care Act* (Canada, House of Commons, 1988). The federal recommendations were quite intrusive by today's standards, specifying the financing explicitly: 'Operating grants for all spaces in the amount of $3 per day for infants, $2 per day for children age 3–5, $.50 per day for children aged 6–12' (Canada, House of Commons, 1988: 87). The tabled (but not passed) *Canada Child Care Act* specified financial and other record keeping 'by the province' and required the Minister of National Health and Welfare to carry out 'examination and audit' (ibid., 4). Bill C-144 died with the 1988 federal election and was not revived.

In 1993, the federal Liberals under Jean Chrétien campaigned on the Red Book platform, pledging $720 million for child care over three years to create 50,000 new regulated spaces each year. There were two caveats, however: first, spaces would be created only following a year of 3 per cent economic growth; second, expansion would occur only with the agreement of the provinces (Liberal Party of Canada, 1993: 38–40). Although a number of provinces signified their willingness to participate, the Chrétien government failed to fulfill this promise (Timpson, 2001; Friendly, 2001). Instead, in the 1995 federal budget, CAP, the sole federal child care funding scheme, was amalgamated into the Canada Health and Social Transfer (CHST), a block fund replacing specific transfer payment mechanisms for social welfare, post-secondary education, and health. At the same time, federal program expenditures were massively reduced.

By the late 1990s, the federal government looked to be getting out of the business of funding service delivery and providing income supplements to individual Canadians instead via, for example, the 1997 National Child Benefit (Cameron, 2005). It also appeared to tie its hands with the 1999 Social Union Framework Agreement (SUFA). It formalized a more collaborative provincial/executive decision-making model that was intended to preclude unilateral federal action in areas of provincial jurisdiction without provincial consent (Government of Canada and Governments of the Provinces and Territories, 1999).

At the same time, however, the federal government's books showed budget surpluses and it seemed willing to commit federal funds to some kind of national early childhood development program (Canada, House of Commons, 1999; Canada, Department of Finance, 2000). Public and expert opinion showed support for high quality ECEC programs as a means to improve human development and help reconcile work and family life (Cleveland and Krashinsky, 1998; McCain and Mustard, 1999; Michalski, 1999). While the collaborative federalism regime under SUFA seemed to render policy-making increasingly complicated, SUFA's requirement of collaborative intergovernmental relations did not hinder achieving substantive child care policy agreements, as the succeeding half-decade demonstrated.

The Multilateral Phase

Late in its second term in office, the Chrétien government negotiated the Federal–Provincial–Territorial Agreement on Early Childhood Development (ECDA). Signed by all provinces except Quebec in September 2000, the Agreement provided federal transfer funds in program areas deemed to be part of a 'child development' agenda. The Government of Canada committed $2.2 billion over five years, beginning in 2001–2, to enable provincial/territorial governments to improve and expand early childhood development programs in four areas: healthy pregnancy, birth, and infancy; parenting and family supports; early childhood development, learning, and care; and community supports (CICS, 2000; Canada, Social Union, 2010a).

Child care was considered to be part of early childhood development, learning, and care even though child care was not high on government policy agendas in this period and, indeed, lost ground in some provinces (Ontario and Alberta) (Friendly et al., 2002). Under the ECDA, some provinces chose to spend money on child care or ECEC and other provinces focused on parent-based programs. Provincial/territorial spending on regulated child care under the ECDA varied considerably (CRRU, 2001). While some provinces (Newfoundland and Labrador and Nova Scotia) spent much of their allocation on child care, others (Ontario) spent no ECDA funds on regulated child care.

In an effort to direct funds more explicitly to child care programs, the Chrétien government reached an agreement with provincial/territorial ministers responsible for social services (except Quebec) in March 2003 on the Multilateral Framework Agreement on Early Learning and Child Care (MFA). Under the MFA, the federal government agreed to transfer $900 million over five years to support specific provincial/territorial investments in child care (CICS, 2003; Canada, Social Union, 2010b). The programs could be delivered in a variety of regulated settings such as child care centres, family child care homes, and nursery schools. The list of allowed investments was quite broad: capital and operating funding, subsidies for parents, wage enhancements for workers, training, professional development, and parent information and referral services.

The MFA was noteworthy because it had the support of all the provinces (except Quebec, which even so declared support for the principles). Even the child-care-cutting Ontario government of Mike Harris signed on (CRRU, 2002). The MFA specified that the federal funds would only be used for regulated ECEC programs *outside school systems*; it set principles for childcare (available and accessible, affordable, quality, inclusive, parental choice); and it committed governments to annual reporting on 'descriptive and expenditure information', specifying indicators of availability, affordability, and quality (CICS, 2003).

Prior to winning the 2004 election with a minority, Paul Martin, as leader of the Liberal Party, pledged to spend $5 billion over five years (beyond funds already committed through the MFA) to build a national program in collaboration with the provinces/territories. His program was based on four principles, referred to as the 'QUAD': quality, universality, accessibility, and developmentally focused programming (Liberal Party of Canada, 2004: 29). Then, for an 18-month period in 2004–5, federal and provincial/

territorial governments seemed poised to establish the foundations of what was then called a new national early learning and child care (ELCC) system.

The Bilateral Phase

Getting agreement from the provinces to spend the $5 billion on building a national early learning and child care system became one of the defining issues of the Martin government. The extended negotiation process began shortly after Ken Dryden became Social Development minister in July 2004 and lasted almost until the government fell in a non-confidence vote in December 2005. In contrast to the MFA negotiations only two years earlier, this time all the provinces, *including* Quebec, entered into agreements to spend federal government funds.[7] However, although provinces had previously agreed to the similar (and quite limited) conditions in the MFA process and to the QUAD principles at a social services ministers' meeting in November 2004, a public attempt to show-case a multilateral agreement in February 2005 was unsuccessful. The Alberta and New Brunswick governments resisted the requirement that the funds be spent on regulated child care (CBC News, 2005a); the PEI and territorial governments campaigned for an enriched funding formula for smaller jurisdictions (CBC News, 2005b; Laghi, 2005); the Quebec government was, as usual, reluctant to accept any federal conditions at all in an area of contested responsibility (De Souza, 2005).

Turning away from a multilateral approach, Dryden managed to execute arrangements with all provinces through a series of bilateral agreements. The final agreement, signed in November 2005 with the New Brunswick government, came just before the Martin government's defeat on a non-confidence motion. The protocols and overarching scheme for the bilateral agreement fell under the national umbrella of the agreed-upon QUAD principles and a common national format for each (except Quebec's) (Mahon, 2006). Each province and the federal government signed an agreement-in-principle (AIP) that included a general outline of how funds were to be used (CRRU, 2006). Each province was to develop a more specific Action Plan for the five-year phase, with a five-year funding agreement to come next. However, when the government fell at the end of 2005, only Manitoba and Ontario had finished the process, with the other agreements in various stages of progress.

By the time of the 2006 federal election, Canada was close to achieving at least the foundations of a national system.[8] The Liberal Party's 2006 election platform pledged to make the federal commitment to the program permanent (Liberal Party of Canada, 2006). A switch in government, however, ended the federal–provincial agreements and the accompanying development plans, ushering in a new approach to federalism.

The Unilateral Phase

The federal Conservative Party did not include child care in its 2004 federal election campaign. Instead, it committed to a $2,000 per child income tax deduction for all families with dependent children under age 16 (Conservative Party of Canada, 2004: 18). In the 2006 election campaign, the Party took a different approach, however. The Conservatives pledged to end the Liberal Party's bilateral ELCC agreements, introduce a $1,200 taxable allowance for each child under age six, and provide $250 million in tax credits to employ-ers and associations to create 125,000 child care spaces (Conservative Party of Canada,

2006: 31). The Conservative Party explicitly countered the idea of a national early learning and child care system in its election platform by calling its own proposal a 'Choice in Child Care Allowance'. The platform stated:

> The Liberals and the NDP believe that the only answer to expanding childcare in Canada is their one-size-fits-all plan to build a massive childcare bureaucracy which will benefit only a small percentage of Canadians. Only the Conservatives believe in freedom of choice in childcare. The best role for government is to let parents choose what's best for their children, and provide parents with the resources to balance work and family life as they see fit—whether that means formal childcare, informal care through neighbours or relatives, or a parent staying at home. (ibid., 31)

Once in office in early 2006, the minority Conservative government quickly announced—and then notified the provinces—that they were cancelling the intergovernmental agreements negotiated by Ken Dryden with each province. The terms of the agreements had provided one year of funding to each province/territory. In place of a national program focused on provinces/territories developing ECEC systems, the Harper government opted for a straight cash payment to parents, as well as a fund to create new child care spaces (Conservative Party of Canada, 2006: 31). The child allowance was included in the May 2006 budget (Canada, Department of Finance, 2006: 99–103) and cheques to parents began to flow in July. The cash payment, known as the Universal Child Care Benefit (UCCB), cost almost $1.8 billion in the 2007/2008 fiscal year (Beach et al., 2009: xxii).

The second part of the Conservative child care platform, the Child Care Spaces Initiative, was a rather odd policy plank for an 'open federalism' government. The Harper government had intended to offer financial incentives directly to employers and child care operators to encourage them to create child care spaces. Leaving aside the question of whether providing capital incentives in the absence of funds to operate programs has an impact on accessibility or quality for families (CCAAC, 2006b), the initiative had serious jurisdictional implications. One provincial official described the 'space creation' plan as 'bad federalism' and went so far as to say that the decision 'makes me shake my head and wonder if we have not learned anything over the past 30 years . . . . It is one thing to say to provincial governments, we plan to add to provincial coffers in order to create spaces. But if the feds approach a local YMCA, for example, with capital money, it is an entirely different matter and contrary to getting out of the provinces' faces.'

In its 2007 budget, the Conservative government followed through on its pledge to encourage employers and organizations to create child care spaces, introducing a 25 per cent investment tax credit to a maximum of $10,000 per space. It also provided a transfer of $250 million to provinces/territories, also intended to support the creation of child care spaces (this would become part of the Canada Social Transfer) (Canada, Department of Finance, 2007: 124–5). This move marked a change for a government that had earlier refused to provide any money to provinces/territories for child care, although the amount is far less than what the Liberal government had promised.

Following the cancellation of the national child care program, the 'space creation' transfer, together with the annual $350 million that remained in the CST from the

2003 Multilateral Framework Agreement (MFA) (extended to 2013–14 in the 2007 federal budget), made up $600 million federal transfer dollars earmarked for child care in 2008 (Beach et al., 2009: xxii). Unlike the Liberal program that had come before, the Conservative plan does not require conditions or reporting (Greenaway, 2007: A4), so whether the funds have been used for 'space creation', subsidies, or wage grants is unknown. Nor does it offer funding for Aboriginal communities or provide for federal–provincial collaboration on data and accountability, as the Martin program did.

The Harper government claims that its endorsement of 'open federalism'—meaning that the federal government will 'place formal limits on the use of the federal spending power for new shared-cost programs in areas of exclusive provincial jurisdiction'—respects provincial autonomy in areas of exclusive provincial jurisdiction (Canada, House of Commons, 2007: 8). With regard to children's policy, there has been very little participation in intergovernmental activities in which past federal governments had been involved, such as the FPT Council on Social Policy Renewal or FPT First Ministers' meetings. Thus, the federal government's actions since its election in 2006 reflect elements of both **unilateralism** and no-lateralism.

The No-lateralism Phase

It may seem odd to characterize the current federalism regime as 'no-lateralism', given that, according to one former intergovernmental official, approximately 2,900 intergovernmental meetings occur annually across the span of policy sectors (personal communication, 15 October 2010). However, since the change in government federally in January 2006, there has been little governance of the federation with regard to ECEC policy[9] particularly when compared to the intense period of executive policy-making from the late 1990s to 2006.

Not surprisingly, following the Conservatives' cancellation of the bilateral agreements, child care was on the agenda at the May 2006 meeting of the FPT social services ministers responsible for child care (Brown, 2006). Since then, though, while there have been intergovernmental meetings of ministers with other portfolios—Finance, Forestry, Justice and Agriculture, and so on—there have been almost no FPT social services ministers' meetings, and certainly not a meeting at which ECEC has been on the agenda (Québec, Secrétariat aux Affaires Intergouvernementales Canadiennes, 2010). Deputy Ministers of social services have held a number of FPT meetings in the last five years. At one meeting, the importance of the early years (ECD) was the focus, though ECEC was not on the agenda (personal communication, October 26, 2010). Status of Women Ministers—who had been very active with regard to child care in the 1980s—also participated in several FPT meetings in the 2006–10 period but child care was not on their agendas either (telephone interview, October 27, 2010). The Council of Ministers of Education's (CMEC) busy Provincial–Territorial meeting agenda did not include ECEC, although ECEC was identified as the first pillar of lifelong learning in its *Learn Canada 2020 Declaration* in 2008 (personal communication, October 26, 2010). There have been no joint communiqués and no press conferences on ECEC, as there were in the ECDA, MFA, and bi- and multilateral periods. Mid-level ECEC officials with direct responsibility for child care, who are more and more likely to find themselves located in ministries of education, continue to meet twice a year.

At the same time, the civil society groups and activities that kept ECEC a vital public policy subject from the early 1980s to the present time have withered, as groups have lost long-standing public funds and their ability to monitor developments and sustain democratic involvement with policy-makers. This loss of resources has affected not only child care and women's groups but also NGOs working in social policy generally, international development, and health. As journalist Brian Stewart (2010) notes in a CBC News report:

> In Canada's 'marketplace of ideas,' it's amazing how many stalls are being slammed shut these days and how many attendants are trembling for their very existence.
>
> In the fields of justice, human rights and foreign aid, it seems that one non-governmental agency after another is being 'de-funded' into non-existence or near paralysis by the Harper government.

Harper's 'open federalism' thus means not just a return to watertight compartments in terms of federal/provincial jurisdictional responsibilities but also little action on the federal government's part, and shrinkage in the overall activity of the state.

'Blue Skies' Thinking on ECEC Policy Making: They Should, They Could, But Would They?

Much has changed vis-à-vis ECEC and federalism—not only since the 1970s and 1980s, but also since 2006. Certainly, the election of a majority Conservative government in 2011 makes it likely that the post-2006 approaches to social policy may very well continue. Even with very little intergovernmental interaction, provincial/territorial interest and activity have been high.[10] A key question, however, is whether, and how, a future federal government will still be able to play a role on this policy file.

We believe that a federal role in ECEC is not only desirable but also necessary. Historically, institutional and constitutional impediments did not prevent the federal government from taking leadership when the political will existed (e.g., Boismenu and Graefe, 2004) and they should not now. The vertical fiscal imbalance also compels the federal government to continue to exercise its spending power in social policy matters. The best policy practice of blending of care and early childhood education programs in fact requires even greater federal involvement in ways we document below. This third section thus tackles the issues of *should, could,* and *would*.

We first deal with why we *should* see not only government involvement in what some critics complain is purely a market and family matter (Cool, 2004), but also why a *federal* presence is required on this policy file. While child care in Canada is still predominantly financed by parents and delivered by private organizations (Beach et al., 2009: xii), early childhood education and care is more and more considered to be a public good— a human, or children's, right (Bennett, 2010). There is also convincing evidence that unco-ordinated markets, together with limited and sporadic government funding, fail to establish high quality, universally accessible ECEC programs (Cleveland et al., 2008; Penn, 2010; Prentice, 2006). Indeed, while some governments (e.g., Australia), have spent considerable public funds in loosely controlled child care markets, these markets have resulted in massive profits accruing to shareholders while children and parents have been poorly served, as well as spectacular market and business failure (Brennan, 2007). Such cases of market failure comprise part of the policy evidence that supports re-conceiving of ECEC as a collective good, as it is considered to be in many other countries (Friendly and Prentice, 2009); that is, financed, managed, and, indeed, delivered by government, or quasi-government institutions, just as public and post-secondary education are currently delivered in Canada.

We root our *could* analysis in the national dimensions logic of the Peace, Order, and Good Government clause in section 91 of the Constitution Act, 1867, particularly the provincial inabilities test that courts have recognized as granting the federal Parliament the authority to legislate or regulate on matters that are local and provincial in their origins, but that attain such national importance so as to affect the body politic as a whole and to justify federal action. Here we are replicating Sujit Choudhry's (2008: 377) argument that

> the incoherence of granting the federal government fiscal jurisdiction in areas where it lacks regulatory jurisdiction—does not necessarily lead to the conclusion that it should not be able to make conditional transfers to underwrite provincial social programs. Rather, in light of the modern Supreme Court of Canada's expansive conception of federal jurisdiction, an argument could be crafted under the Peace, Order and Good Government (POGG) power for federal jurisdiction over social policy.

We deal with each of these arguments in turn below, turning to 'would' at the end.

Why the Federal Government Should Play a Role in Early Childhood Education and Care

A number of indicators reveal that, in some ways, Canada serves parts of its population poorly, especially children and families. These indicators include poor results on basic measures of child health, such as low birth weight, infant mortality, and childhood immunizations (UNICEF, 2008). Canada's gender equality ranking is fairly poor (Hausman et al., 2010) and the wealth gap—one of the best predictors of poor educational outcomes and poor health outcomes—has grown dramatically in Canada (OECD, 2008). In addition, child poverty rates have been stubbornly high for years, with Canada's figures consistently considerably higher than UNICEF's benchmark of less than 10 per cent of children living in poverty (UNICEF, 2008). Finally, high school completion rates for some populations (especially rural and small-town males and First Nations children) are worryingly low (Canadian Educational Statistics Council/Statistics Canada, 2010). These indicators may be linked to Canada's status as a comparatively low spender on child and family benefits and programs overall (Bennett, 2010).

These are all areas of national concern, as is Canada's laggard status in international analyses of ECEC provision over the past decade or so. The most recent of these, prepared for UNESCO (Bennett, 2010: xi) notes that Canada's comparatively low public investment rates in early childhood services have negative consequences; the resulting high costs to parents lead to unequal access and the segregation of children in child care by income. Many have argued that Canada's limited support for families, women, and children has negative implications for our future as a nation, as birth rates have slowed, the working-age population is aging, and women, immigrants, and Aboriginal Canadians are still impeded in participation in education, training, and the labour force (e.g., McCain and Mustard, 1999; Friendly and Prentice, 2009).

Since 2006, however, there has been a significant shift as Canada's sub-national governments have begun to recognize the value of ECEC in meeting these challenges. Currently, six provinces/territories, following international trends, have moved child care into education ministries; six provinces have now introduced full-day kindergarten; and several—Ontario and PEI—have begun to blend child care and kindergarten better, as least at the policy level (Beach et al., 2009).

While these developments are encouraging and generally acknowledge ECEC as a public good, what is absent is the Government of Canada as a facilitator, a leader, a partner, or significant resource provider; therefore, financing, co-ordination, and resources continue to be lacking. In this hit-and-miss kind of regime, it is hard to imagine that Canada's historical patchwork of ECEC access and quality will not be deepened.

Paradoxically, as Canadian policy thinking about ECEC is shifting amongst provincial governments, there is currently only a limited architecture in place to facilitate and share best practices. In contrast, in health care, a federal department, national data, intergovernmental meetings and institutions such as the Health Council of Canada and the Canadian Institutes of Health Information convene and develop the 13 health care systems that make up Medicare (see chapter 9 in this text). Similarly, in the area of education, the Council of Ministers of Education creates at least a conversational meeting place for education ministers, although to date this has not included extensive interest in ECEC.

Arguments for a more defined federal role in education generally have been put forward by David Johnston, previously President of the University of Waterloo, now Governor-General of Canada. Johnston champions a Canada Learning and Innovation Act with the aim of making 'appropriate learning opportunities available to Canadians of all ages, no matter where in the country they live', proposing a first ministers' meeting on the subject to lead to enactment of a national Act similar in content and purpose to the Canada Health Act (Daily Bulletin, 2005).

Some federalism scholars, as well as some provincial governments, assert that a key role of sub-national governments in a federal system is to serve as laboratories of policy innovation (e.g., Mintrom, 1997; Noël, 1998). Compelling examples are the province of Saskatchewan's innovation in health care in the 1960s and the Quebec government's in child care and maternity/parental leave in the 1990s. Overall, though, the record of provincial/territorial policy innovation with regard to child care has not been outstanding. Even in the CAP era, when the federal government provided open-ended matching funds to provinces to develop social assistance programs, including money for child care for low-income families, provinces were remarkably uncreative and uninspired in developing comprehensive programs such as those found in Europe. Certainly, no province has moved decisively to develop policy and funding schemes to support national objectives (as per the National Children's Agenda), such as promoting the development of all children.

Thus, without a federal role to provide the glue and substantial financing to scale up these efforts, we are not optimistic about the future of ECEC as a portable, equitable, high quality program for all Canadian families. As far back as 1998, Doherty, Oloman and Friendly (1998: 51), analyzing various options for FPT collaboration on child care, described having each province/territory develop its own approach without federal involvement as 'an option that [appears] not to have any strengths. . .' They noted that it was incompatible with the development of services that could support national objectives (such as healthy child development) and that it was unlikely—given the range of provincial ideologies and available resources—that the various jurisdictions would develop comparable principles or programs.

What Could a Federal Government Do?

From a practical perspective, a re-conceptualization of federal authority over social policy requires an acknowledgement that much of what is outlined in the Constitution Act, 1867 bears little resemblance to the pressing policy concerns of the twenty-first century or, indeed, much of the twentieth century (Choudhry, 2008: 378). Early childhood education and/or child care are not among the items specifically assigned to either s. 91 or s. 92 of the Constitution Act, 1867. Thus, ECEC has generally been classified as a matter of social policy, and therefore considered to fall under provincial jurisdiction under s. 92(13), as a matter of 'property and civil rights.' However, traditionally, the federal spending power has allowed the federal government to shape social policy indirectly through the use of financial incentives, something it chose to do quite extensively until the 1990s.

Even if child care is treated as an educational matter, the constitutional jurisdiction still lies with provincial governments under s. 93. But here too there have been shifts—even in a relatively short span of time—in how federal governments choose to exercise the spending power. Although in the negotiations leading up to the Multilateral Framework Agreement around ECEC in 2003, the federal government stipulated that its funds could not be used in an education jurisdiction, just two years later, the bilateral agreements that two provinces (Saskatchewan and British Columbia) made with Paul Martin's government specified that they could spend their funds under an education auspice (CRRU, 2006).

By the mid-1990s and, more specifically, with the watershed 1995 federal budget, the use of the federal spending power as an instrument of federal policy leadership was increasingly contested as a result of federal spending cutbacks and a near-victory for Quebec separatists in the 1995 sovereignty referendum (Boismenu and Graefe, 2004: 72–3; Doherty et al., 1998). SUFA formalized a more collaborative federalism regime that required the co-operation of the provinces in the launch of any new federal social policy initiatives. But scholars such as Noël (2000) have pointed out that the federal government had not shaken its habit of unilaterally involving itself in social programs. Thus, while the federal government continued to use SUFA to justify its failure to take more prescriptive action—for example, by introducing national standards similar to those found in the Canada Health Act—the experience of that period suggests that Ottawa could work with the provinces to forge national programs, if it has the political will to do so. We currently see that the federal government choosing to act even in policy areas that have been the traditional purview of provincial governments—e.g., securities regulation. The idea of a common securities regulator has proven to be quite controversial; some provincial governments view it as usurpation (MacIntosh, 2010). However, the federal government has exhibited few qualms about taking over this traditional area of provincial responsibility. In essence, if there's a will, there seems to be a way.

Would They? Or, 'Blue Sky' Thinking on Where We Go from Here

In the first edition of this book, White (2002: 115) wrote:

> Provincial transfers, either in a shared-cost or block-funded way, may be the more efficient and effective way to deliver monies for child care. However, it will be difficult for all governments to agree on Canada-wide priorities and objectives. . . . Thus, it is possible that the federal government . . . could provide more child care funds via direct transfers to individuals. . . . It would be ironic were ministers to search out ways to 'get around' the SUFA in order to deliver child care monies. If this occurs, it will provide further evidence of the limitations of the collaborative federalism regime.

The Harper government's 'universal child care' policy appears to reflect exactly those sentiments. But while this tactic allows the federal government to spend money without encountering jurisdictional problems, there is evidence that giving parents cash, even through targeted vouchers and tax breaks in a childcare 'market', is not best practice if the goal is to ensure that 'care' and 'early childhood education' become blended, provide quality, and become accessible to families (OECD, 2006).

We have argued they *should* and *could* act. So, what *would* a committed federal government do? That is, what does a national ECEC policy mean? Friendly and Prentice (2009) have described a national ECEC program that would work to meet a range of objectives, following best policy practices as well as keeping within the conventions of Canadian federalism.

First, all three levels of government should be involved in ECEC systems; that is, not only federal and provincial governments, but also local government bodies, either municipalities, or school authorities, or both, as well as educators, parents, and the community. The federal government needs to provide the bulk of the public funding through planned, sustained mechanisms and play a leadership, convening role in a Canada-wide policy framework, as it has done with the Canada Health Act. As with health care, ECEC needs its own branch or secretariat in the federal government. An agency or branch dedicated to ECEC would be able to convene FPT meetings; facilitate work on common policy and program development among the provinces and territories; develop best practices, such as quality improvement, pedagogical frameworks, and human resource issues; and deal with ECEC topics of common interest to all Canadians, such as ways to provide ECEC to children with special needs and Aboriginal Canadians The secretariat also should take a lead role in research and evaluation, ensuring that good data collection, ongoing evaluation and assessment, and a long-term research agenda—all absent from the current environment—become a key part of the ECEC system.

Provinces, territories and First Nations should be responsible for designing, shaping, and maintaining the system(s), including establishing and maintaining standards for service provision. At the provincial level, ECEC should be located in one government department, preferably education, supported by infrastructure, planning, and a critical mass of knowledgeable officials. System-wide provincial planning can ensure targets and timetables for expansion and ongoing quality improvement. Different provinces might opt for somewhat different ECEC options but there should be Canada-wide goals and principles, just as there are for medicare under the *Canada Health Act*. Thus, there should be comparable—not identical—ECEC systems in each province along with local flexibility in determining priorities and program specifics, for example, to meet the needs of a rural community or provide French language programs for francophone families outside Quebec.

ECEC primarily must be publicly financed, with programs receiving operating budgets from provincial governments. Similar to other wealthy countries with high quality ECEC systems, Canada should use the international benchmark of at least 1 per cent of GDP on ECEC as a minimum spending target. Demand-side mechanisms such as vouchers, child care allowances, fee subsidies, or other funding paid to individuals should not be employed. Instead, services should be funded through the supply side, as public schools are financed today. While there might be parent fees for portions of ECEC programs or for certain age groups, costs need to be affordable for all and free for low-income parents. Local government and education authorities should have direct responsibility for local program design, local infrastructure and planning, and service delivery. Finally, publicly managed ECEC programs should be shaped through collaboration that includes educators, parents and community. Programs should be responsive to and involve parents at the local community level.

Developing a full ECEC program in any Canadian jurisdiction is a long-term proposition, taking, conservatively, at least a decade, even with adequate resources and political will. How such systems would be phased in needs to take political and resource issues into account—but, as we have demonstrated above, such long-term planning has been conducted in other policy areas and thus is possible here as well.

Conclusion

The paradox we highlighted at the beginning of this chapter remains: decades of intergovernmental negotiations dominated by different federalism regimes have left us exactly where we were before with no national ECEC system but with nascent programs emerging for four- to five-year-olds in some provinces and an emerging political will to continue to expand these programs. The case thus provides a graphic example of the centrality of political executives—in particular, their interests and their ideological beliefs—to the development of social policy in intergovernmental Canada. Strong executives with political will can enact sweeping changes within their area of jurisdiction, should they be willing to pay the fiscal and political price.

At the same time, the requirement of unanimity and joint agreement among orders of government can allow the strategic interests of ideologically driven political executives opposed to ECEC policy development to act as veto players. As the ECEC case shows, at worst this leads to policy inertia; at best, to lowest-common-denominator policies. Finally, the ECEC case demonstrates that opportunities for agreement can occur when one level of government possesses substantial fiscal resources to leverage agreements with recalcitrant provinces and territories: hence, the need for continued federal leadership on this policy file.

Notes

1. Some interviewees requested that their comments not be attributed by name or by position. Information from interviews has been incorporated into the text without attribution unless there was explicit consent to be quoted.
2. The 2006 election campaign sparked public debate and newspaper commentary regarding the desirability of non-parental care. See Geddes (2005), Leblanc (2005), Sokoloff (2005), MacCharles (2006) and the Conservative Party of Canada's (2006: 31) election platform for a statement on the party's position on child care.
3. In 1997, Quebec began phasing in $5-a-day child care (raised to $7 in 2003) for all 0- to four-year-olds and full-day kindergarten for five-year-olds. See Friendly and Beach (2005: 64–5). In 2006, Quebec also improved its expanded maternity/parental leave program.
4. 'Regulated child care' refers to facilities and homes regulated by provincial/territorial standards specifying physical, health, and safety requirements; child/staff ratios; and staff training.
5. This number is 'assumed' based on the gap between the number of children 0–5 years with a mother in the paid labour force and the number of regulated child care spaces; more specific data are unavailable.
6. A 1999 Angus Reid/*Globe and Mail* survey found that 78 per cent of polled Canadians supported the federal government 'setting up an inexpensive day care system for all families who want it' (Angus Reid/*Globe and Mail*, 1999: 6). The 2006 Environics report found that 77 per cent believed that 'lack of affordable child care is a serious problem in Canada today' (Environics Research Group, 2006: 4). Eighty-two per cent felt 'that government should play a role in helping parents meet their child care needs' (ibid., 5). Seventy-six per cent of those polled believed in the national child care program proposed in 2004 (ibid.) with 50 per cent of those polled favouring funding new child care spaces over the Conservative government's $1,200 taxable allowance (ibid., 7). In a 2008 Nanos telephone poll, 58 per cent of 1201 respondents expressed a preference for 'setting up a national early childhood education and child care system' rather than a '$100 a month cheque' (31 per cent) (CUPE/Nanos, 2008).
7. Quebec and the federal government never signed an agreement-in-principle but went right to a five-year funding agreement, the rationale being that Quebec was already more advanced in its ELCC program than other Canadian jurisdictions.
8. See the Child Care Advocacy Association of Canada (CCAAC) regarding the federal government's budget announcement (CCAAC, 2006a) and the Canadian Child Care Federation's (CCCF) statement after the election of the Harper government (CCCF, 2006).
9. Deborah Coyne, in a 2010 article on the New Brunswick-Quebec hydro deal, echoes this idea, calling it `absentee federalism'. See http://canadianswithoutborders.ca/articlescommentary/absentee-federalism-who%E2%80%99s-looking-after-the-national-interest-in-quebec-new-brunswick-hydro-deal.
10. One individual with long-time FPT experience, interviewed on 30 October, 2010 by telephone, suggested that the FPT negotiations in the 2003–6 period helped generate this interest, and that interest among the provinces remained high, even after the agreements were cancelled in 2006.

References

Angus Reid/*Globe and Mail*. 1999. *Family Matters: A Look at Issues Concerning Families and Raising Children in Canada Today*. Toronto: Angus Reid Group.

Beach, J., M. Friendly, C. Ferns, N. Brabhu, and B. Forer. 2009. *Early Childhood Education and Care in Canada 2008*. Toronto: CRRU.

Bennett, J. 2010. *Early Childhood Education and Care Report: Europe and North America*. 2010/ED/BAS/ECCE/RP/3. Prepared for the UNESCO World Conference on Early Childhood Education and Care, 22–24 September,

Moscow. At: http://unesdoc.UNESCO.org/ images/0018/001892/189211E.pdf

Boismenu, G., and P. Graefe. 2004. 'The New Federal Tool Belt: Attempts to Rebuild Social Policy Leadership', *Canadian Public Policy* 30, 1: 71–89.

Brennan, D. 2007. 'The ABC of Child Care Politics,' *Australian Journal of Social Issues* 42, 2: 213–24.

Brown, J. 2006. 'Child Care Funding Heads Agenda as Federal, Provincial Ministers Meet', *Canadian Press*, 29 May.

Bushnik, T. 2006. *Child Care in Canada*. Cat. no. 89-599-MIE2006003. Ottawa: Statistics Canada.

Cameron, B. 2005. Personal interview, Ottawa, 1 April.

Canada. 2006. *Canada's Universal Child Care Plan: Choice, Support, Spaces*. At: www.universal-childcare.ca/.

———. Department of Finance. 2000. *Budget 2000*. Ottawa: Department of Finance.

———. Department of Finance. 2006. *The Budget Plan 2006: Focusing on Priorities: Canada's New Government Turning a New Leaf*. Ottawa: Department of Finance.

———. Department of Finance. 2007. *The Budget Plan 2007: Aspire to a Stronger, Safer, Better Canada*. Ottawa: Department of Finance.

———. House of Commons. 1988. Bill C-144. An Act to authorize payments by Canada toward the provision of child care services, and to amend the Canada Assistance Plan in consequence thereof. Second Session, Thirty-Third Parliament. Ottawa: Minister of National Health and Welfare.

———. 1999. Speech from the Throne to Open the Second Session, Thirty-Sixth Parliament of Canada. *Debates of the House of Commons of Canada* (Hansard), 12 October.

———. 2007. *Strong Leadership. A Better Canada*. Speech from the Throne 39th Parliament, 2nd Session (16 October). At: http://www.cacp.ca/media/news/download/165/sftddte1.pdf.

———. Standing Committee on the Status of Women. 2005. *Interim Report on the Maternity and Parental Benefits under Employment Insurance: The Exclusion of Self-Employed Workers*. Ottawa: Communication Canada.

———. Social Union. 2010a. *Early Childhood Development Agreement*. At: http://www.socialunion.gc.ca/ecd_e.html.

———. Social Union. 2010b. *Multilateral Framework on Early Learning and Child Care*. At: http://www.socialunion.gc.ca/ecd-framework_e.htm.

Canadian Child Care Federation (CCCF). 2006. 'CCCF Urges New Government to Work Together to Solve Child Care Crisis in Canada' (24 Jan.). At: www.cccf-fcsge.ca/pressroom/pr_32_en.htm.

Canadian Intergovernmental Conference Secretariat (CICS). 2000. 'First Ministers' Meeting Communiqué on Early Childhood Development', Ref. 800-038/005 (11 Sep.). At: www.scics.gc.ca.

———. 2003. 'Multilateral Framework on Early Learning and Child Care'. Ref. 830-779/005 (13 Mar.). At: www.scics.gc.ca.

Canadian Union of Public Employees (CUPE)/ Nanos Research. 2008. 'Most Prefer Child Care to Cheques'. (9 Oct.) At: http://cupe.ca/child-care/Canadians-prefer-chi.

CBC News. 2005a. 'Alberta Says It Won't Participate in National Day-care Program', *CBC News* website (7 Feb.). At: action.web.ca/home/crru/rsrcs_crru_full.shtml?x=72081.

———. 2005b. 'Northern Territories Looking for Extra Childcare Funding', CBC News website (5 Nov.). At: action.web.ca/home/crru/rsrcs_crru_full.shtml?x=83071.

Child Care Advocacy Association of Canada (CCAAC). 2006a. 'No Child Care in Today's Budget' (2 May). At: action.web.ca/home/ccaac/alerts.shtml?x=87322&AA_EX_Session=4ae4a55a585d54d2bc268edb060999a9.

———. 2006b. *The Community Child Care Investment Program: Does the Evidence Support the Claims?* Ottawa: Child Care Advocacy Association of Canada.

Childcare Resource and Research Unit (CRRU). 2001. *The Early Childhood Development Agreement: Provincial Initiatives and Spending Allocations, 2001–2002*. At: circ.web.ca/resources/crrupubs/factsheets/ecd_chart/.

———. 2002. 'Ontario's Spending for Regulated Child Care, 1942–2001', CRRU Briefing Note. Toronto.

———. 2006. 'The State of the National Child Care Program and Provincial/Territorial Contexts', CRRU briefing note (Mar.). At: www.childcarecanada.org/pubs/bn/statenatprogram.html.

————. 2009. *Early Childhood Education and Care in Canada* 2008: Highlights. At: http://www.childcarecanada.org/ECEC2008/ECEC08_highlights_mediarelease.pdf.

————. 2010. *Back to School with Full-day Early Learning.* Online: http://action.web.ca/home/crru/rsrcs_crru_full.shtml?x=130177.

Choudhry, S. 2008. 'Constitutional Change in the 21st Century: A New Debate over the Spending Power', *Queen's Law Journal* 34, 1-2: 375–90.

Cleveland, G., and M. Krashinsky. 1998. 'The Benefits and Costs of Good Child Care: The Economic Rationale for Public Investment in Young Children'. Toronto: University of Toronto Centre for Urban and Community Studies, Childcare Resource and Research Unit.

Cleveland, G., B. Forer, D. Hyatt, C. Japel, and M. Krashinsky. 2008. 'New Evidence about Child Care in Canada: Use Patterns, Affordability and Quality.' *IRPP Choices* 14, 2.

Conservative Party of Canada. 2004. *Demanding Better: Federal Election Platform, 2004.* Ottawa: Conservative Party of Canada.

————. 2006. *Stand Up for Canada: Federal Election Platform, 2006.* Ottawa: Conservative Party of Canada.

Cool, J. 2004. *Child Care in Canada: Regulated, Unregulated, Private or Public.* Ottawa: Library of Parliament, Political and Social Affairs Division.

Council of Ministers of Education, Canada. (CMEC) 2008. *Learn Canada 2020.* Joint Declaration of the Provincial and Territorial Ministers of Education (15 April). Online: http://www.cmec.ca/Publications/Lists/Publications/Attachments/187/CMEC-2020-DECLARATION.en.pdf.

Coyne, D. 2010. 'Absentee Federalism: Who's looking after the national interest in Quebec–New Brunswick hydro deal?' *The Mark News.* 30 January.

CTV News. 2005. 'Liberals Offer an Extra $6 Billion for Day Care'. CTV News website. 6 December. At: http://www.ctv.ca/servlet/ArticleNews/story/CTVNews/20051206/liberals_elexn_update_051206/20051206?s_name=election2006.

Daily Bulletin, University of Waterloo. 2005. *Johnston seeks federal learning law.* 14 September. Online at http://www.bulletin.uwaterloo.

ca/2005/sep/14we.html

De Souza, M. 2005. 'Quebec Isn't Rushing into Day-care Talks', *Montreal Gazette,* 27 Apr. At: action.web.ca/home/crru/rsrcs_crru_full.shtml?x=75910.

Doherty, G., M. Friendly, and M. Oloman. 1998. *Women's Support, Women's Work. Child Care in an Era of Deficit Reduction, Devolution, Downsizing, and Deregulation.* Ottawa: Status of Women Canada.

Environics Research Group. 2006. *Canadians' Attitudes toward National Child Care Policy.* Ottawa: Environics Research Group.

Espey and Good Company. 2003. *Perceptions of Quality Child Care Final Report.* Ottawa: Canadian Child Care Federation and Child Care Advocacy Association of Canada.

Finley, Honourable Diane. 2006. Interview, CBC News Sunday Night (Carole McNeil) (19 March). On file with author.

Friendly, M. 2001. 'Child Care and Canadian Federalism in the 1990s: Canary in a Coal Mine'. In *Our Children's Future: Child Care Policy in Canada,* ed. G. Cleveland and M. Krashinsky. Toronto: University of Toronto Press.

————and J. Beach. 2005. *Early Childhood Education and Care in Canada 2004.* Toronto: Childcare Resource and Research Unit, University of Toronto.

————, ———— and M. Turiano. 2002. *Early Childhood Education and Care in Canada 2001.* Toronto: Childcare Resource and Research Unit, University of Toronto.

————and S. Prentice. 2009. *About Canada: Childcare.* Winnipeg: Fernwood Publishing.

————and S. Prentice, forthcoming. 'Policy, Politics and Provision in Early Childhood Education and Care in Canada'. In *New Directions in Early Childhood Education and Care in Canada,* ed. N. Howe and L. Prochner. Toronto: University of Toronto Press.

————and L.A. White. 2008. 'From Multilateralism to Bilateralism to Unilateralism in Three Short Years: Child Care in Canadian Federalism 2003–2006'. In *Canadian Federalism: Performance, Effectiveness and Legitimacy.* 2nd ed. Eds. H. Bakvis and G. Skogstad. Toronto: Oxford University Press: 182–204.

Geddes, J. 2005. 'The Gathering Storm'. *Maclean's*

118, 27/28: 16–17.

Goelman, H., G. Doherty, D. Lero, A. LaGrange, and J. Tougas. 2000. *Caring and Learning Environments: Quality in Child Care Centres across Canada*. Guelph, Ont.: Centre for Families, Work and Well-Being, University of Guelph.

Gouvernement du Québec, Ministère de la Famille et des Aînés. 2007. *Meeting Early Childhood Needs: Québec's Educational Program for Childcare Services: Update 5*. At: http://www.MFA.gouv.qc.ca/fr/publication/Documents/programme_educatif_en.pdf.

Gouvernement du Québec, Secrétariat aux Affaires Intergouvernementales Canadiennes. 2010. Intergovernmental Agreements. At: http://www.saic.gouv.qc.ca/ententes_intergouvenementales/ententes_intergouvernementales_en.htm.

Government of British Columbia. 2010. Speech from the Throne (9 February). Victoria: The Government of British Columbia. Online: http://www.leg.bc.ca/39th2nd/2010_ThroneSpeech.pdf.

Government of Canada and Governments of the Provinces and Territories. 1999. *A Framework to Improve the Social Union for Canadians* (4 Feb.). At: www.socialunion.ca/news/020499_e.html.

Government of Prince Edward Island. 2010. *Preschool Excellence Initiative*. At: http://action.web.ca/home/crru/rsrcs_crru_full.shtml?x=129746.

Harper, S. 2009. 'Poverty'. In *House of Commons Debates* (Hansard) 40th Parl., 2nd Sess. (24 November). Online: http://www2.parl.gc.ca/HousePublications/Publication.aspx?DocId=4254820&Language=E&Mode=1&Parl=40&Ses=2#TOC-TS-1430.

Hausman, R., L.D. Tyson, and S. Zahidi. 2010. *The Global Gender Gap Report 2010*. Geneva: World Economic Forum.

Japel, C., R.E. Tremblay, and S. Côté. 2005. 'Quality Counts! Assessing the Quality of Daycare Services Based on the Quebec Longitudinal Study of Child Development'. *IRPP Choices* 11, 5.

Kaga, Y., J. Bennett, and P. Moss. 2010. *Caring and Learning Together: A Cross-National Study on the Integration of Early Childhood Care and Education within Education*. Paris: UNESCO.

Ladurantaye, S. 2010. 'Edleun Eager to Expand Childcare Reach Outside Alberta'. *Globe and Mail*, 20 September. At: http://www.theglobeandmail.com/report-on-business/your-business/start/franchising/edleun-eager-to-expand-childcare-reach-outside-alberta/article1731059/.

Laghi, B. 2005. 'East Coast Premiers Lobby for New Deal on Daycare Dollars', *Globe and Mail*, 29 Oct. At: action.web.ca/home/crru/rsrcs_crru_full.shtml?x_=82724.

Leblanc, D. 2005. 'Whoa, Baby! Chew on These Child-Care Plans', *Globe and Mail*, 6 Dec., A4.

Liberal Party of Canada. 1993. *Creating Opportunity: The Liberal Plan for Canada* (Red Book). Ottawa: Liberal Party of Canada.

———. 2004. *Moving Canada Forward: The Paul Martin Plan for Getting Things Done*. Ottawa: Liberal Party of Canada.

———. 2006. *Securing Canada's Success*. Ottawa: Liberal Party of Canada.

Livingstone, D.W., and D. Hart. 2005. *Public Attitudes towards Education in Ontario 2004: The 15th OISE/UT Survey*. Toronto: Ontario Institute for Studies in Education.

MacCharles, T. 2006. 'Child-care Battle Rages', *Toronto Star*, 4 May, A8.

MacIntosh, J. 2010. 'The Feds' Weak Case', *The Financial Post* (31 May).

McCain, M., and F. Mustard. 1999. *Reversing the Real Brain Drain: Early Years Study Final Report*. Toronto: Children's Secretariat of Ontario.

McRoberts, K. 1985. 'Unilateralism, Bilateralism and Multilateralism: Approaches to Canadian Federalism'. In *Intergovernmental Relations*, ed. R. Simeon. Toronto: University of Toronto Press.

Mahon, R. 2006. 'Main Features of the Early Learning and Child Care Bilateral Agreements'. At: b2c2.org/resources/index.php.

Michalski, J. 1999. *Values and Preferences for the 'Best Policy Mix' for Canadian Children*. CPRN Discussion Paper No. F/05. Ottawa: Canadian Policy Research Networks.

Mintrom, M. 1997. 'Policy Entrepreneurs and the Diffusion of Innovation', *American Journal of Political Science* 41: 738–70.

Noël, A. 1998. 'Is Decentralization Conservative? Federalism and the Contemporary Debate on the Canadian Welfare State'. In *Stretching the Federation: The Art of the State in Canada,* ed. R. Young. Kingston: Queen's Institute of Intergovernmental Relations.

———. 2000. 'General Study of the Framework Agreement'. In *The Canadian Social Union without Quebec: 8 Critical Analyses*, ed. A. Gagnon and H. Segal. Montreal: Institute for Research on Public Policy.

Organisation for Economic Co-operation and Development (OECD). 2004a. *OECD Thematic Review of Early Childhood Education and Care: Canada Country Note*. Paris.

———. 2004b. *OECD Thematic Review of Early Childhood Education and Care: France Country Note*. Paris.

———. 2006. *Starting Strong II: Early Childhood Education and Care*. Paris.

———. 2008. *Growing Unequal? Income Distribution and Poverty in OECD Countries*. Paris: OECD Directorate of Employment, Labour and Social Affairs.

Pascal, C. 2009. *With Our Best Future in Mind: Implementing Early Learning in Ontario*. Report to the Premier by the Special Advisor on Early Learning. Ontario: Government of Ontario.

Penn, H. 2010. *Do Child Care Markets Work?* Paper prepared as a keynote address at the First International ECCE Conference, Moscow, October 2010. Paris: UNESCO.

Prentice, S. 2006. 'Childcare, Co-Production, and the Third Sector in Canada', *Public Management Review* 8, 4: 521–36.

Shonkoff, J.P., and D.A. Phillips, eds. 2000. *From Neurons to Neighborhoods: The Science of Early Childhood Development*. Washington: National Academy Press.

Sokoloff, H. 2005. 'Gulf between Parties Is Size of a Small Child: Liberals, Tories Differ Distinctly on Daycare Options', *National Post*, 5 Dec., A8.

Statistics Canada/ Council of Ministers of Education, Canada. 2010. *Education Indicators in Canada: An International Perspective*. Cat. 81–604-X. Ottawa: Canadian Education Statistics Council.

Stewart, B. 2010. 'De-Funding: Another Critical Group Feels Ottawa's Ax.' CBC News (23 July). At: http://www.CBC.ca/canada/story/2010/07/23/f-vp-stewart.html#ixzz13mUWsX5X .

Timpson, A.M. 2001. *Driven Apart: Women's Employment Equality and Child Care in Canadian Public Policy*. Vancouver: University of British Columbia Press.

Timpson, A.M. 2002/2003. 'Trudeau, Women and the Mystic North', *London Journal of Canadian Studies* 18: 41–61.

UNICEF Innocenti Research Centre. 2008. *The Child Care Transition: A League Table of Early Childhood Education and Care in Economically Advanced Countries*. Report Card 8. Florence: The Centre.

United Nations Educational, Scientific, and Cultural Organization (UNESCO). 2006. *Strong Foundations: Early Childhood Care and Education*. Education for All Global Monitoring Report 2007. Paris.

White, L. 2002. 'The Child Care Agenda and the Social Union'. In *Canadian Federalism: Performance, Effectiveness, and Legitimacy*, ed. H. Bakvis and G. Skogstad. Toronto: Oxford University Press.

11 International Trade Policy and the Evolution of Canadian Federalism

Grace Skogstad

In the mid-1980s, exports accounted for about 25 per cent of Canada's GDP; today, they constitute 30 per cent.[1] The growing significance of exports is the outcome of commercial policies of the Canadian government. The implementation of the 1989 Canada-U.S. Free Trade Agreement (FTA), and the subsequent 1994 North American Free Trade Agreement (**NAFTA**), accelerated north–south trade with the United States and intensified Canada's dependence on the American market. In most years, in excess of 80 per cent of Canadian domestic exports go to the United States (Industry Canada, 2010).[2] While trade across provincial and territorial borders continues to be important, it is exceeded in value for all Canadian provinces by exports of goods and services to other countries. In addition to liberalizing trade agreements on the North American continent, Canadian governments have also sought access for Canadian industries and firms to other international markets. The Canadian government was a signatory to the multilateral General Agreement on Tariffs and Trade (**GATT**) at its origins in 1947 and is a member of its successor organization, the World Trade Organization (**WTO**). Moreover, Canadian governments continue to seek out bilateral and regional trade agreements with several countries.

These international trade and investment agreements, this chapter argues, are contributing to an evolution in the relationship between Canada's two orders of government. As the scope of the international commercial treaties that Canada signs widens—beyond matters of federal jurisdiction and into provincial jurisdictional matters—provincial governments are playing a larger role in Canada's international trade policy. Although the negotiation and ratification of international commercial agreements remain formally a matter of exclusive federal jurisdiction, in practice the two orders of government are working collaboratively and closely in the formulation of the Canadian negotiating position. Even while there are some outstanding issues respecting provinces' roles in international trade policy, the pattern is one of considerable intergovernmental co-operation and harmony: a model described here as de facto shared jurisdiction. The close intergovernmental collaboration also extends to the handling of trade disputes that arise from international trade agreements, even while it is the Government of Canada that is solely legally responsible for their resolution.

What explains the enlarged provincial role in international trade policy agreements? And, further, why are intergovernmental relations seemingly more cordial in international trade policy than they are in some of the other policy areas discussed elsewhere in this text? This chapter addresses these two questions as part of a larger discussion of the performance, effectiveness, and legitimacy of Canadian federalism in the area of international trade policy.

In answer to the first question, it argues that the increasingly active involvement of provinces in the formulation of Canadian international trade policy stems from Canada's constitution and judicial review of it. The 1937 ruling by the Judicial Committee of the Privy Council in *Attorney General for Canada v. Attorney General for Ontario* decreed that the federal government's right to negotiate and ratify international treaties does not extend to implementing provisions of international agreements whose subject matter falls within provincial jurisdiction. This judicial ruling remains in effect, and as long as it does so, the Canadian government has every incentive to obtain the input and consent of provinces and territories to provisions in trade agreements that affect their jurisdiction.

In answer to the second question, this chapter argues that four factors largely account for the relatively cordial intergovernmental relations in trade policy. They are, first, a rough consensus across governments, federal as well as provincial/territorial, that market-opening trade agreements provide economic benefits on the whole; second, the existence of formal and informal institutions that facilitate input into federal trade policy from provincial and territorial governments; third, the existence of 'trust ties' across officials of both orders of government; and fourth, institutionalized mechanisms of input from societal stakeholder groups. Evidence that intergovernmental relations are working well in international trade policy does not mean that there are not substantive matters of trade policy on which governments do not agree, nor does it mean that there are no outstanding issues related to the role of all provinces in international trade policy. Nor, yet again, does it obviate criticism in some quarters, including by non-governmental actors, of the processes for determining Canada's trade policy and the substance of that policy.

In documenting and evaluating the changing pattern of intergovernmental relations in international trade policy, this chapter is organized as follows. It begins with a brief discussion of the constitutional framework for international trade policy, and outlines different versions of a shared jurisdiction model of international trade policy that constitute a benchmark against which to gauge the change in Canadian intergovernmental relations over time in this policy sphere. The second section of the paper tracks the changing role of the provinces and territories in the negotiation of trade agreements and settlement of trade disputes. It notes an important further step along the path of shared jurisdiction with the negotiation of the Comprehensive Economic and Trade Agreement (CETA) with the European Union (EU). The third section of the paper appraises the performance and effectiveness of intergovernmental relations in international trade policy and considers the possible consequences of proposals to formalize and extend provinces' role. The fourth part of the chapter addresses the legitimacy of trade policy processes and substance from the perspective of non-governmental actors. The final section concludes the chapter and offers an explanation for why intergovernmental relations in trade policy have been relatively cordial to date.

International Trade Agreements and Canada's Constitution

The Constitution Act, 1867, gives the government of Canada alone the legal authority to conduct international relations. This exclusive authority includes representing the country in international institutions and signing international treaties like trade agreements. Trade and investment agreements require governments to curtail their own political authority—for example, giving up the right to give preference to domestic/local firms—in order to gain access to other markets or foreign investment. The government of Canada's exercise of its exclusive authority to negotiate and sign international trade agreements could therefore result in it binding not only its own political authority but also that of provincial/territorial governments. However, as noted above, this possibility has been significantly curtailed since 1937 when a judicial ruling divided the jurisdiction to implement international treaties between the two orders of government. While the government of Canada has the sole right to implement the provisions of international treaties that fall within its jurisdiction, this right does not extend to matters within provincial/territorial jurisdiction. The implications of divided jurisdiction over the implementation of international trade agreements have become greater over time as the substance of trade agreements themselves have changed.

The most important international trade agreement for Canada until the late twentieth century was GATT. After 1947, GATT promoted international trade by lowering tariffs and establishing rules for the conduct of trade across borders. These matters fell virtually exclusively within federal legal authority. Negotiating trade agreements became more complex, however, once tariffs were largely eliminated and GATT negotiations turned to potentially trade-distorting 'inside-the-border' regulatory and expenditure policies. Such measures were just as likely to be provincial as federal. The Tokyo Round of GATT negotiations (1973–9) covered a number of matters within provincial jurisdiction, such as agricultural subsidies, liquor board purchasing practices, and government procurement policies. Provinces possessed technical information needed by the government of Canada's trade negotiators, and they were brought into the process of formulating Canada's negotiating position (Winham, 1986). Until near the end of the Tokyo Round negotiations, however, their opportunities for input were irregular as were the briefings they received from federal negotiators.

The significance of divided jurisdiction when it comes to implementing international treaties became apparent in the mid-1980s when the European Community argued before a GATT tribunal that Canadian provincial liquor and wine distribution and marketing policies were inconsistent with Canada's GATT obligations. In its defense, the government of Canada stated that Canada's constitution prevented it from implementing GATT provisions with respect to practices of provincial liquor boards. GATT disagreed in a 1987 ruling, instructing the government of Canada to take 'all reasonable measures' to ensure regional and local governments and authorities adhered to the Agreement Canada had signed. It was only following protracted negotiations with all provinces that Ottawa persuaded all provinces to change their policies to meet their GATT obligations.

In the wake of the GATT ruling, and as international treaties expanded into provincial areas of jurisdiction, there were two conceivable paths that Canadian federalism could have taken. The first path—the route not taken—would have strengthened the government of Canada's authority at the expense of the provinces. This first path, which Ottawa apparently considered and then rejected with regard to the FTA (Issues of Constitutional Jurisdiction, 1988: 45), follows from the government of Canada's legal obligation to uphold the terms of international treaties. It requires Ottawa take all 'reasonable measures' under the GATT and 'all necessary measures' under the FTA/NAFTA. Pursuit of this path would have seen Ottawa negotiate, without provincial consultation and agreement, an international treaty that intruded into provincial jurisdiction, and then force provinces/territories to comply with it. Pursuit of this option would likely have resulted in a provincial challenge to the Supreme Court of Canada on the grounds that the federal action was inconsistent with the 1937 judicial ruling and Canada's constitution. Had the Supreme Court found that the federal intrusions into provincial areas of jurisdiction was warranted in order to implement international treaties,[3] the path of a centralized federation would have unfolded. As noted, such a scenario did not occur.

The second path—the route taken—was towards a de facto sharing of powers over international trade policy (Brown, 1991: 12). It respects the existing division of powers but gives provinces/territories a role in the negotiation of trade agreements and their implementation. This shared jurisdiction model takes a variety of forms, depending upon the extent of sub-national governments' involvement. One version is for the government of Canada to consult the provinces throughout a treaty negotiation and to obtain their a priori agreement for any treaty provisions that impact on their jurisdiction. However, the government of Canada remains the sole party at the negotiating table, the sole signatory to the international agreement, and the sole Canadian party to ratify the agreement. The provinces/territories are bound by the terms of the agreement that affect them, but the government of Canada remains solely responsible for ensuring that Canada (including the provinces/territories) meet those obligations.

Another version of the shared jurisdiction model also entails extensive consultation and provincial input into the formulation of Canada's negotiating position, but the Canadian government obligates only itself to enforce the agreement. Provinces have the latitude to bind themselves or not, and if they do sign the agreement, they are responsible if they breach its rules. This option has not been used for trade agreements, but it was used for the two parallel agreements to NAFTA: the North American Agreement on Environmental Co-operation (NAAEC) and the North American Agreement on Labour Co-operation (NAALC). Because the two agreements impacted far more on provincial jurisdiction than they did on federal, provinces were involved in the drafting of the Canadian proposals, had access to all the Mexican and American position papers on the NAAEC and NAALC, and were invited to the final stages of the negotiations in Washington in August 1993 (Kukucha, 2008: 182).

Yet other versions of the shared jurisdiction model expand further the role of provinces in international trade agreements. They include a formal role for provinces in negotiating, signing, and managing trade agreements that affect their jurisdiction, or, even more broadly, all international agreements. As the discussion below indicates, intergovernmental relations are evolving along the shared jurisdiction path, with an important step being taken since 2009 with the negotiation of the Comprehensive Economic and Trade Agreement with the European Union. The shift along this path comes with the intrusion of international agreements into more and more spheres of provincial jurisdiction.

Down the Shared Jurisdiction Path

A. Negotiating International Trade Agreements

The Conservative government's decision to negotiate the Canada–US Free Trade Agreement (FTA, effective January 1989) in the mid-1980s was driven by goals of securing better and more secure access to the American market for Canadian firms, including by eliminating barriers to trade in goods, services, and investment, and establishing formal mechanisms to settle trade disputes. Export markets are important to economic sectors like petroleum and natural gas, agriculture, forestry, electricity, mining, and motor vehicles. The provinces in which these economic sectors are concentrated thus welcome trade agreements that open other countries' markets to them. At the same time, other industries seek protection from foreign competition; provinces are likewise 'sensitive' to these industries—for example, cultural industries in the case of Quebec—especially when they are seen to be of strategic and/or political importance.

Not surprisingly, then, trade agreements can be contentious as the governments who negotiate them have to be balance their 'offensive' interests, where they can expect gains for their economy, with their 'defensive' interests, where there will be costs as industries fail under heightened competition. Indeed, the FTA was contentious, as the Canadian public squared off over its implications for Canadian sovereignty in the 1988 federal election campaign. The FTA met with opposition in Prince Edward Island, Manitoba, and Canada's largest provincial economy, Ontario. By contrast, provinces like Alberta, Saskatchewan and BC supported its opening of the American market to their energy and forestry products.

An important step towards a shared jurisdiction model of international trade policy was taken during the negotiation of the FTA when Ottawa recognized the necessity of an institutionalized forum for provincial input. It consulted and briefed the provinces through the Continuing Committee for Trade Negotiations (CCTN), and, in the latter stages of the bilateral negotiations, via first ministers' meetings. However, the government of Canada resisted a more extensive role for the provinces. It rejected a provincial proposal to establish an oversight committee of trade ministers co-chaired by a province and the federal government, and did not accede to provinces' request that they name a representative to participate directly in the negotiations (Ritchie, 1997: 142–8; Doern and Tomlin, 1991: ch. 6). Despite appreciable provincial consultation, the provinces were left out of the final, crucial stage of the bilateral negotiations. Prime Minister Mulroney never formally asked premiers for their concurrence with the negotiated package and the provinces thus never formally approved or rejected the FTA (Doern and Tomlin, 1991, Ritchie, 1997).

Nonetheless, the precedent of provincial consultation and briefing was established during the FTA negotiations. It has continued during the negotiation of NAFTA, the Uruguay Round of GATT (1986-1993) and Doha Round meetings of the WTO (2001-), the 1995-1998 OECD-led Multilateral Agreement on Investment (MAI), and the Free Trade Area of the Americas until the latter were suspended in 2003 (de Boer, 2002; Hale, 2004; Hocking, 2004; Kukucha, 2008). The primary mechanism throughout these negotiations was the Federal–Provincial–Territorial Committee on Trade, known as C-Trade. This committee has been chaired by a senior federal official in the Department of Foreign Affairs and International Trade, with its agenda accepted by all members. Quarterly meetings of C-Trade, or more frequently if negotiating circumstances dictate, have enabled provincial officials to be briefed and for information to be exchanged confidentially over a protected website. Federal and provincial ministers responsible for trade have met much less frequently (Dymond and Dawson, 2002: 8).

Through these institutionalized mechanisms, the government of Canada obtained provinces' agreement for provisions in NAFTA and the 1995 WTO agreements that affected their jurisdiction, and managed to exclude matters from the terms of WTO agreements on which provincial consensus and consent were not forthcoming. Throughout the eventually aborted MAI negotiations, provinces were 'consulted frequently and consistently', debriefed after every negotiating session, and copied on all reports. They also had access to all negotiating documents (DFAIT, 1998). This co-ordination was viewed as necessary because the MAI would have increased the exposure of provincial governments to challenges by foreign investors and governments.

Notwithstanding the above mechanisms of provincial input, some provinces—most notably, Quebec and Alberta—have repeatedly expressed their desire for a more formal and extended model of shared jurisdiction in international trade policy in order to protect their jurisdiction. In 2005, Canada's premiers, through the Council of the Federation (2005), proposed that provinces be given 'a significant and clear role in the development of Canada's international position on areas within provincial and territorial responsibility'. The Council requested 'a formal agreement' with the federal government 'to provide clarity, certainty and continuity' in their relationship with Ottawa regarding 'Canada's international activities that affect provincial and territorial jurisdictions, responsibilities and interests'.

While Liberal governments in Ottawa responded to such requests by pointing out that provinces/territories already had significant participation in international treaties, with the federal government consulting them when treaties affect areas of provincial jurisdiction, the Harper Conservative government has taken a different stance. After taking office in January 2006, and as part of its 'open federalism' agenda, Prime Minister Harper (2006) proposed 'establishing a formal mechanism for provincial input into the development of the Canadian position in international negotiations or organizations where provincial jurisdiction is affected'. Developments around the negotiation of a Comprehensive Economic and Trade Agreement (CETA) with the European Union since 2009 are putting to the test the Prime Minister's proposal.

Canada-EU Comprehensive Economic and Trade Agreement

A Canada-EU trade agreement has been strongly supported by the Canadian business community and, among premiers, championed particularly by Quebec Premier Jean Charest (Séguin, 2008; Benzie, 2008).[4] The EU market is the world's largest single common market, and more access to it would help to reduce Canadian exporters' dependence on the US market. While exports of goods (oil, gas, agricultural products, forestry products, minerals) continue to constitute the largest share of Canadian exports, the Canadian service sector is also seeking export opportunities. Accounting for between two-thirds and three-fifths of the economy in recent years (Foreign Affairs and International Trade, 2010), the service sector includes a diverse array of activities that are purchased by individuals, businesses and government. Among the most prominent services are those provided by the financial, information and communications, construction, computer, engineering, transportation, entertainment, tourism, education, and health sectors. While eliminating border tariffs to trade in goods continues to be an important part of current international trade negotiations, removing non-tariff and technical obstacles to trade and investment in services is also a large part. Among the latter are different regulations regarding the quality of product and service standards, as well as the qualifications of their providers.

Before the EU agreed to formal negotiations in May 2009, it wanted assurance that provinces and territories were committed to the process and would implement any concluded agreement (Taber and Séguin, 2009; Benzie 2008). The EU sought provincial/territorial commitment because several of its highest priorities in the negotiations fall in provincial jurisdiction and will require provincial concessions. An earlier attempt in 2005 to negotiate an EU-Canada commercial agreement had dissipated when provinces failed to be engaged. A high priority for the EU is obtaining the right for European companies to bid for provincial and municipal government contracts for goods and services. Many provincial governments give preference to local/ provincial residents and companies for the purchase of at least some goods and services.[5] Other EU goals that will require provincial concessions affect cultural industries, health, the environment, labour, and agriculture: matters that also fall exclusively within provincial areas of jurisdiction or are shared between them and Ottawa. The offensive issues for Canada and the provinces—where they hope to make gains—fall within both federal and provincial jurisdiction.[6]

The commitment that the EU demanded as a prerequisite to Canada-EU negotiations came formally from the Council of the Federation (2009). In early 2009, the Council issued a statement confirming not only provinces and territories' involvement (following negotiations with Ottawa on the form it would take) but also their willingness to 'take the necessary measures to ensure the implementation of any commitments they, as individual provinces and territories, undertake through the negotiating process'.

At that time, the sole province not to give its consent to the Council of the Federation's statement was Newfoundland and Labrador; its then premier Danny Williams refused to sanction the negotiations because of 'substantive issues with the content and process of CETA' (Council of the Federation, 2010). Its officials nonetheless closely monitored the negotiations until March 2011 when the province altered its position and announced that it would henceforth take 'a more active role in negotiations.' The shift from observer to active participant at the negotiating table, said the responsible Minister, was needed to allow Newfoundland and Labrador 'to continue to meaningfully shape the outcomes' of the negotiations and was warranted by the manner in which the province had been treated throughout the negotiating process. At the same time, the Minister stated that 'the Government of Newfoundland and Labrador will not support the final agreement unless it best serves the interests of the people of this province' (Government of Newfoundland and Labrador, 2011).

The fact that provincial matters are so integral to CETA has given provinces an unprecedented role in trade negotiations. Canada's Chief Trade Negotiator, Steve Verheul, described that 'unique' involvement to the House of Commons Standing Committee on International Trade on June 15, 2010:

> 'This [provincial] involvement includes participating in negotiating rooms on issues under their jurisdiction. We have had between 40 and 60 provincial and territorial representatives at each of the negotiating rounds, and we have been meeting them frequently... We also meet with them on the eve of every round [of negotiations] as well as at the close of each day of negotiations.' (Verheul, 2010a)

The novel step down the shared jurisdiction path, then, is that provinces and territories are present when Canada's negotiators discuss 'provincial tables'—procurement, services regulated at the provincial level, labour, environment, investment, state enterprises and monopoly coops—with their EU counterparts. Provinces/territories' presence does not include directly participating in negotiations; they speak only when (infrequently) asked to do so by the Canadian negotiator. On matters that fall exclusively within federal jurisdiction or that overlap with federal jurisdiction, provincial and territorial governments continue to have the same role as before: being consulted in advance of and after negotiations, but not having representatives in the room while these issues are being negotiated.

Provinces' greater involvement in the CETA negotiations also includes their presence in Europe for negotiating sessions, as well as playing host to European trade officials and political groups on their visits to Canada.

B. Resolving Trade Agreement Disputes

The shared jurisdiction model also characterizes the settling of trade disputes that arise over the terms of a trade agreement, and entail allegations that terms of agreements are not being upheld. Both the NAFTA and WTO agreements established mechanisms and procedures to resolve trade disputes among members. These dispute settlement procedures were a high priority for Canada because they are a means to ensure that a trade agreement's rules, rather than the economic or political power of a dominant trading partner, determine terms of trade. Although dispute settlement bodies are a crucial feature of managing commercial relations, they do not replace interstate diplomacy at the official and highest ministerial levels.

When it comes to settling international disputes, the Canadian constitution gives the government of Canada a privileged legal position vis-à-vis the provinces. It is the only Canadian government that can initiate dispute settlement procedures and name Canada's members to NAFTA panels. While private firms can initiate disputes under NAFTA's Chapter 11 on Investment, provincial governments cannot. The government of Canada also has the exclusive right to initiate a formal WTO complaint; neither provinces nor private parties can.

Despite its exclusive authority to manage international trade and investment disputes, the government of Canada has not chosen to exercise that authority unilaterally. Its consultative approach with the provinces (and affected industry) recognizes that most trade disputes have appreciable economic stakes for one or more provinces.

Moreover, when a provincial policy is targeted by a trade action, provinces will possess the information needed to rebut an unfair trade charge. Perhaps surprisingly, consultation with provinces also occurs when federal policies are in dispute (Skogstad, 2008a: 234).

The pattern of de facto shared jurisdiction around international trade disputes involves the two orders of government working closely to avoid disputes with trading partners and to settle trading tensions in advance of formal complaints. When such disputes escalate to formal complaints, the interaction across federal and provincial officials is continuous. The shared jurisdiction model has allowed provinces to participate as members of the Canadian delegation in international meetings and forums to resolve trade disputes that are of interest to them (Dymond and Dawson, 2002: 8). However, provincial delegates intervene only when asked to do so by the (federal) head of the Canadian delegation.

This extensive role for provinces in dispute settlement proceedings is paralleled by an equally appreciable role for representatives of the affected industry. As with the provinces, industry groups' involvement in formulating a trade challenge response is closely tied to their possession of expertise and acknowledges that industry groups bear the economic costs of borders closing to their products. Sometimes, as well, industry consultation and agreement are prerequisites to implementing an international agreement.

The imperative of a domestic consensus-building process creates the potential for what the German political scientist, Fritz Scharpf (1988), describes as a joint decision-making trap. This trap arises when unanimity is sought prior to decisions being taken, and manifests itself by decisions being prolonged and/or resulting in a sub-optimal outcome that reflects the interests of the most recalcitrant party. Is there any evidence that Canada's response to external trade challenges has been suboptimal because of the need to get the agreement of one or more provinces for how to deal with a trade dispute? To answer this question, the next section looks at two trade disputes that have been highly costly to Canada. The first is softwood lumber, where provincial measures and jurisdiction are overwhelmingly involved; the second is agricultural disputes, where both orders of government exercise legal authority. Investment disputes are also discussed because of their potential to generate intergovernmental frictions.

Softwood Lumber

The dispute over exports of Canadian softwood lumber to the United States is the largest by value and the longest-running of Canada's trade disputes with the United States. The United States is the major market for Canadian softwood lumber, absorbing two-thirds of sales. With the softwood lumber industries on either side of the border competing for the same—American—market, a rise in the Canadian share of the American market meets with quick opposition from the American lumber coalition. It alleges that provincial forest management practices in BC, Ontario, Alberta, and Quebec give Canadian producers access to cheaper timber than is available to them in the US. More specifically, the US coalition argues that provincial stumpage rates (the fees forest companies pay to log on Crown land) and restrictions on raw log exports are unfair subsidies that cause material harm to American lumber interests. It has sought duties on Canadian softwood lumber as a way to neutralize the effect of provinces' 'subsidies.'

The American coalition has had considerable success in impeding Canadian timber access to the American market. Since the early 1980s, it has successfully petitioned the American government to levy countervail duties on Canadian softwood lumber imports on four separate occasions.[7] In 2001, the coalition also persuaded the US to impose unprecedentedly large duties on Canadian softwood lumber imports, on the grounds that the Canadian products were not only subsidized by federal and provincial policies but also being 'dumped'; that is, sold below the cost of production or at prices lower than in Canada. The Canadian government, with the support of the provinces/territories and industry associations in BC, Ontario, and Quebec, challenged these duties under NAFTA and the WTO as inconsistent with US law and therefore illegal. Despite dispute settlement rulings in Canada's favour, the US government refused to remove the duties, although it did lower them.

Besides using existing legal remedies under the FTA/NAFTA to secure access for Canadian softwood lumber exports to the US, Canada also sought an outcome of 'managed trade'. Between 1986 and 1991, a Memorandum of Understanding (MOU) between the governments of Canada and the United States governed bilateral trade in softwood lumber. The MOU required Canada to impose a 15 per cent export tax on softwood lumber exports to the US. In 1996, Canada again agreed to restrict its access to the US softwood lumber market in order to stave off an American legal challenge to provincial forest management practices. That agreement lapsed, but in 2006, the Harper Conservative government agreed to conditions on Canadian access to the US market in return for the US lifting its remaining duties on Canadian softwood lumber imports. While this seven year agreement ended the costly litigation process, it did not end American allegations that Canadian provinces continue to illegally subsidize their lumber producers (McKenna, 2011). However, now these disputes are subject to binding arbitration at the London Court of International Arbitration.

Has the involvement of provinces in negotiations towards ending the disputes with the US impeded the resolution of these disputes? This question is difficult to answer. It is abundantly clear that the softwood lumber dispute originates in differences in Canadian provincial and American forest management practices, including their timber pricing policies. Were the disputed forest management practices federal practices and not provincial, the controversy would still exist. Still, the fact that there are several Canadian provinces whose policies are under attack and whose interests have to be reconciled probably does drag out the process of resolving trade conflicts. Negotiated access agreements require provinces and forest companies to agree on a formula (ordinarily, historic market share) by which to share the US market, as well as a means of curtailing exports—with an export tax or quotas—when the export ceiling is reached. Although Alberta, Quebec, and Ontario are all affected by American market access limitations, British Columbia has the most at stake. With about half of Canadian softwood lumber exports to the US, and with the sector significant to the provincial economy, BC's government and forestry companies have an effective veto over a negotiated agreement. On occasion, BC political leaders have acted unilaterally, and arguably in excess of their provincial authority, to press their interests directly to US trade officials.

Negotiated access agreements in 1986, 1996, and 2006 accommodated the demands of the British Columbia government and its dominant forest companies and forestry business and labour organizations. The dissatisfaction of the BC forestry sector with the 1986 MOU led the Canadian government to exercise the option to terminate it in 1991. The 1996 negotiated quota on Canadian exports to the US was proposed by the British Columbia forestry industry, and was not the option preferred by the Canadian government (Cashore, 1998: 27). The allocation of the export quota among the provinces was highly divisive, with British Columbia Premier Glen Clark complaining that Ottawa was favouring Ontario and Quebec at BC's expense. Over the duration of the agreement, the BC premier criticized its costs to the province's economy. The 2006 negotiated outcome again reflects the preferred position of British Columbia's government and lumber industry, which had earlier blocked an outcome negotiated by the federal Liberal government (LeGras, 2006). Still, the politics of domestic consensus-building span more than one province and more than one provincial forestry company and organization. The governments and forest companies and groups in Ontario and Quebec have to be on board as well (Howlett et al., 2006: A10).

Difficulties in securing agreement for the 2006 negotiated settlement reveal the important role that not only provinces but also private actors play in trade disputes. The 2006 accord required that forestry companies agree not to bring any further legal action against the US over softwood lumber exports. For several months after the accord was struck, and despite persistent industry opposition, the Harper government and its International Trade minister, David Emerson, formerly a Liberal minister of Industry who jumped to the Conservatives immediately after the 2006 election, departed from their Liberal predecessors in adopting a 'take or it leave it' attitude, even threatening to treat a vote on its implementing legislation as a vote of confidence in the government. By late summer, as the largest forest companies continued to indicate their disapproval with the deal, Emerson was forced to acknowledge the need for further modifications to the accord to ensure 'sufficient buy-in from industry' (Vieira, 2006). The agreement implemented in October 2006 contained other inducements to bring recalcitrant industry players on side.

Agricultural Trade Disputes

Agriculture, a matter of shared jurisdiction across the two orders of government, is another second area of prolonged bilateral trade disputes over access of Canadian products to the American market. These disputes have involved access of Canadian wheat, hogs, cattle, beef and pork to the US market as well as the access of American dairy products to the Canadian market. Federal and provincial officials have co-operated closely with one another and with organizations representing the affected agricultural sectors to resolve these disputes (Skogstad, 2008). Provincial officials were part of the Canadian team that defended Canadian dairy policies when they were challenged, partly successfully, at the WTO.

Intergovernmental tensions, as well as industry-government tensions, over how best to resolve disputes can sometimes arise. A case in point is the closing of the American border (and subsequently the Japanese and Korean) to Canadian cattle and beef, following the discovery in May 2003 of BSE (bovine spongiform encephalopathy or 'mad cow' disease) in an Alberta cow. At the time the American border closed, the Canadian livestock sector depended on the US market for 80 per cent of Canadian beef exports and almost 100 per cent of live cattle exports. The cattle industry is concentrated in Alberta, but virtually all provinces suffered economic losses as a result of export markets closing to Canadian beef and live cattle.

Reopening foreign markets, including the American market, required demonstrating to foreign consumers that Canada had put in place measures to mitigate the risk of BSE in the Canadian cattle herd and BSE-infected meat entering the food supply chain. But just what those measures should be was a matter of dispute. The Canadian government, referencing international standards, argued that only older animals at risk of contacting BSE should be tested. Alberta Premier Ralph Klein, responding to a view expressed by the cattle industry, urged the Canadian government to consider testing all slaughtered animals if it was needed to reopen the markets that had closed to Canada. The Alberta premier was rebuked by his own agriculture minister and the Canadian government, both of whom argued testing all animals was inconsistent with scientific international standards as well as the American approach. The Canadian government ultimately prevailed with its BSE risk mitigation strategy, working co-operatively with provincial governments and the industry to do so (Skogstad, 2008b: 195-201).

Investment

Trade disputes surrounding foreign companies' rights to invest in Canada are another potential source of intergovernmental disagreement. NAFTA prevents governments from discriminating in favour of local (domestic) investors and gives private investors assurance that their investment receives 'fair and equitable treatment,' including compensation in the event of government expropriation. Under Chapter 11 of NAFTA, a private investor has the right to bring binding arbitration against a foreign government that fails to ensure these rights. As with NAFTA provisions generally, it is the Canadian government that is responsible for upholding investors' rights, including the award of any compensation for unfair and inequitable treatment.

There have been several complaints under Chapter 11, and their growing number suggests they may soon be more important than those over government subsidies and dumping practices (as around softwood lumber). Some of these have involved the federal government. For example, in 1997, a Canadian government ban on the import and inter-provincial sale of MMT, a manganese-based additive used to increase octane levels in unleaded gasoline, was challenged by Ethyl Corporation, the US company that produces MMT. MMT had been prohibited in the US since 1974 and the Canadian government acted on the complaints of the automotive industry that MMT damaged vehicles' on-board diagnostic systems. Besides Ethyl Corporation, eight provinces also said they opposed the Canadian government's ban on inter-provincial sales of MMT. After four provinces successfully challenged the ban as contrary to the Agreement on Internal Trade, the government of Canada rescinded it and compensated Ethyl Corporation $13 million for lost profits and legal fees.

More recent disputes under Chapter 11 involve measures taken by a sub-national (provincial or municipal) government (Herman, 2010). The largest of these, in terms of compensation, was a federal government payment of $130 million to Abitibi-Bowater in

2010 for the company's loss of investment when the government of Newfoundland and Labrador expropriated a paper mill the company had closed down in late 2008. There is currently no mechanism whereby the federal government can recover costs from the provinces when it is provincial actions that cause significant legal obligations for the government of Canada. Prime Minister Harper did signal in August 2010 his government's interest in addressing this omission (Marotte and Ibbitson, 2010). If he or successor federal governments do seek to hold provinces and territories financial responsible for compensating investors whose rights have been violated by provincial actions, intergovernmental tensions are almost inevitable.

Performance and Effectiveness: Provinces' Role in International Trade Policy

The pattern of de facto shared jurisdiction in international trade policy documented above raises two questions. First, does it provide evidence that Canada is performing well, where performance is gauged by respect for core federal principles as well as the provision of forums in which governments can discuss, negotiate, and agree on policy outcomes? And second, is this pattern of intergovernmental relations also conducive to an effective international trade policy that allows Canada to meet international trade commitments and bargain hard for optimal outcomes?

Beginning with the first of these questions, there is evidence that intergovernmental relations in international trade policy do adhere to the core federal principle that governments at each level respect one another's authority and not act in a way that reduces it. Provinces are being consulted on matters that affect their jurisdiction. Nor is Ottawa trespassing into provincial jurisdiction in order to meet Canada's treaty enforcement obligations.

While provinces and territories do not appear to challenge the right of the federal government to be Canada's sole negotiator and sole representative in international trade negotiations,[8] they nonetheless seek further formalization of their role at all stages of trade policy. In 2010, provincial and territorial premiers, via their umbrella group, the Council of the Federation (2010), stated their intention to develop such a framework. Besides outlining a role for provinces in the negotiating process, the framework would also stipulate the means by which provinces and territories would formally signify their consent to agreements, as well as their role in the management of international agreements that affect their jurisdiction and in any institutional mechanism established to implement an agreement. And finally, the framework would specify arrangements to ensure information flows to provinces and territories.

With the formal framework still outstanding at the time of writing, it remains unclear both what form it will take and what the government of Canada's reaction to it will be. One important matter on which the provinces will themselves have to agree in devising their framework is whether their approval of an international treaty will require the consent of all provinces/territories or only a majority of them. A majority decision rule would have the advantage of preventing a collapse of trade talks because of lack of support from a minority of provinces/territories. A veto for all provinces rules out the possibility that no province, however, small, can have an agreement forced on them. In between these unilateral and majority decision rules are other possibilities, including a veto for a province on issues that affect its most important economic sectors.

Does a fuller role for provinces and territories in international trade policy yield a better substantive outcome in terms of trade agreements themselves? Are up to 25 Canadians in the negotiating room—versus one or two across the table—too unwieldy a number to devise a coherent trade position? Some think so. International trade lawyer, Lawrence Herman (2010), argues that by having provincial and territorial negotiators at the CETA negotiating table, 'Canada is risking trade negotiations with the Europeans by presenting a team that emphasizes, rather than diminishes, internal difference and divided interests.'

For others, the concern is not with provinces' impeding the ability of Canada to devise a coherent position that nets gains for the country as a whole. Rather, the worry is that not all provinces are equally equipped to participate meaningfully in international trade policy discussions. Christopher Kukucha (2004: 122–4; 2008) argues that it is only the larger provinces (Ontario, Quebec, Alberta, and, to a lesser extent, British Columbia) that have the human and financial resources to follow international trade policy matters closely. Even for these largest provinces, their lesser resources of expertise and personnel, compared to those of the Canadian government, require them to be selective in the issues on which they focus. On this view, smaller provinces, such as those in Atlantic Canada, lack the resources to follow trade issues closely. Still there remains the possibility for them to piggyback on the research and advocacy of larger provinces whose interests overlap with their own.

The CETA negotiations suggest that, notwithstanding gaps across provinces in the resources they are able to commit to trade negotiations, provinces and territories are generally up to the challenge of participating more fully in trade negotiations that affect matters of provincial jurisdiction. The challenges in terms of costs of human resources cannot be denied in a comprehensive trade negotiation, like CETA, that spans a large number of sectors and issues. All provinces and territories have faced additional costs in participating. For provinces and territories with smaller bureaucracies, sharing information and working collaboratively with others has been a way to overcome in-house gaps in information and experience. The provinces with the largest range of sectors under negotiation, Ontario and Quebec, are also those with the largest bureaucracies, although the very size of their bureaucracy can raise the costs of internal co-ordination on a trade strategy. The Agreement on Internal Trade has required the provinces and territories to develop their trade capacity. The three western provinces also have built up experience on internal trade issues in recent years. BC and Alberta have collaborated on the Trade, Investment and Labour Mobility Agreement (2009); BC, Alberta and Saskatchewan, on the New West Partnership Trade Agreement (2010).

In summary, the Canadian federal system does appear to be performing effectively when it comes to formulating an international trade policy that respects sub-national governments' jurisdiction. The outcome of the CETA negotiations, when it comes, will give us the best evidence to date of whether a shared jurisdiction model also works in terms of yielding an outcome that balances trading interests across provinces/territories and economic sectors.

Legitimizing International Trade Policy: Multi-Stakeholder Consultations and Legislatures

An effective, not to mention, a legitimate, trade policy also requires consultation with non-state actors. Accessing the knowledge and views of those with a direct stake in international trade agreements and of the public more generally are prerequisites to compliance with and support for these same agreements.

The federal government has developed formal structures to elicit the views of industry and sectoral groups directly affected by recent **market liberalizing** agreements. Fifteen Sectoral Advisory Groups on International Trade (SAGITs) were created during the FTA negotiations to consult with non-governmental actors and receive their input into trade policy. Since the early 2000s, the SAGITs have been supplemented with multi-stakeholder information and consultation sessions. Multi-stakeholder conferences organized by the federal Department of Foreign Affairs and International Trade, for example, were used to provide information and consultations on the aborted Free Trade Area of the Americas agreement (FTAA). They were supplemented by a dedicated multimedia Internet site and parliamentary hearings (Hocking, 2004). This federal strategy to build legitimacy within mobilized publics for Canada's international trade policy, receives high marks for 'process' and 'transparency' from observers (Dymond and Dawson, 2002: 15). It continues with the CETA negotiations, which have been described by Canada's chief trade negotiator as 'the most extensive and open process we've ever had in a trade negotiation. We consult regularly with industry and civil society after each round through teleconferences and have frequent meetings with stakeholders, on request' (Verheul, 2010b).

For their part, provincial governments' consultations with their publics have been described as less formalized and not extending beyond stakeholder industry groups (Kukucha, 2008: 138). The greater geographic proximity of industry groups to their provincial governments may explain the comparative weakness of formalized mechanisms for their input at the provincial level. In any event, at least some provinces are now using more formal mechanisms to elicit feedback from stakeholders on the CETA negotiations (cf. Ontario Ministry of Economic Development and Trade, 2010).[9]

While there is no good reason to suspect that provincial governments are any less responsive to mobilized sectoral interests than is the government of Canada, all governments have come under criticism for their failure to provide forums for the airing of broader public interests around trade and investment agreements. The Council of Canadians has been a major critic. It played an important role in helping to block the Multilateral Agreement on Investment and, by virtue of their protests in Seattle in late 1999, the delay of the launch of the Doha Round of the WTO. Their criticisms are substantive and procedural. Substantively, the Council of Canadians, along with the Trade Justice Network, believes trade agreements have more costs than benefits. That is, they undermine the independence and autonomy of governments in Canada and benefit corporate interests rather than Canadians as whole. Procedurally, they criticize the inadequate opportunities for the public to engage in debates around these agreements (Council of Canadians, 2010).

In terms of institutional mechanisms to solicit a broad array of viewpoints on international trade policy, parliamentary standing committees represent one opportunity. Their hearings enable groups representing economic and social interests to present their views on Canada's trade policies. Parliamentary committees, however, have only as much influence as cabinet ministers and first ministers (premiers, prime ministers) are prepared to give them. The negotiation and ratification of international agreements are prerogative rights of the Crown, vested in the cabinet and prime minister. There is no requirement for Parliament to give its prior approval to treaties, although its agreement must be sought for any changes to domestic law that are needed to implement treaty provisions. The situation is different in some provinces. Since 2002, the Quebec National Assembly must ratify any federal treaty that affects Quebec's areas of jurisdiction. An effort in 2005 by the Bloc Québécois to require a similar ratification process for the Canadian Parliament—and 'ensure real transparency' in treaty-making as well as making it 'more democratic' (Roy, 2005)—failed when it was rebutted by the Liberal government as not reflecting the 'reality' of ample opportunities for consultation of non-state interests in Canadian treaty-making.

Conclusion

Federalism has a discernible impact on the processes of formulating Canadian international trade policy. The constitutional division of legal authority to implement the provisions of international trade agreements has made it necessary for the government of Canada to engage in extensive consultation and consensus-building with provincial governments on its trade strategy. It also has several mechanisms to elicit the views of industry groups and, of late, individuals and groups representing broader social interests. These developments have led governments at the two orders along the path of shared jurisdiction when it comes to trade negotiations and trade dispute settlement.

The substance of Canadian trade policy is also different as a result of federalism. This statement applies particularly to matters within provincial jurisdiction, where the unwillingness of provinces to discuss these issues has left them out of trade and investment agreements (Kukucha, 2008). It is harder to gauge whether the substance of trade disputes is different as a result of federalism. In the case of softwood lumber, for example, provincial governments have been the primary interlocutor for forest industry firms and groups with the federal government. The BC Lumber Trade Council describes itself as 'joined at the hip with the BC government'; the Ontario Lumber Manufacturers Association says it relies on the Ontario government 'to put in our remarks as their own'; and the Quebec Forest Industry Council works closely with its provincial government.[10] That said, forestry companies and their trade associations have been powerful actors in their own right, and given their high economic stakes in the outcome of the dispute, it is not unreasonable to conclude that they would have exercised significant influence on international trade policy even were there no provincial governments to champion their cause. On agricultural trade disputes, provincial governments have also been intermediaries on the industry's behalf. Supply managed producers, in particular, have counted on the support of provincial governments (especially those in Quebec and Ontario) in the past to defend their interests. However, all federal governments—Liberal and Conservative—have also found it to be in their strategic and political interests to support policies that provide domestic protection for Canadian dairy producers. Federalism probably exacerbates the incoherence of Canadian agricultural trade policy; that is, it leads to a trade policy that is simultaneously liberal and protectionist in advocating that other countries open their markets for our export-oriented commodities even while Canada maintains restrictions on imports of supply-managed commodities. However, this position is not unique to Canada; the United States and the European Union have analogous incoherent trade-negotiating strategies.

Given the intergovernmental conflict that is so apparent in other policy areas, why have intergovernmental relations in trade policy been relatively free of conflict? One reason is the legal and political interdependence of the two orders of government. Neither order of government can realize its trade policy objectives without the co-operation and collaboration of the other. A second reason is that the technical nature of trade policy means that interactions occur primarily at the bureaucratic rather than the political level. At this level 'trust ties' and a mutual commitment to problem-solving around often highly technical issues tend to prevail (Dupré, 1985). These trust ties have been strengthened as the same individuals in the two orders of government have worked closely with one another on trade policy matters over several years. A third reason for the relatively harmonious pooling of political authority across governments is a shared interest in a liberal, rules-based trade strategy. All provincial economies depend on trade, even if some rely more than others on foreign markets to absorb surplus goods and services. Their support is consistent with polling data suggest that Canadians on the whole associate trade agreements with economic benefits (Mendelsohn et al., 2002). And yet a final, fourth reason, for relative harmony around international trade policy is that the industries that are directly affected by market opening agreements have been consulted extensively.

Still, relative harmony until now does not mean that intergovernmental tensions could not yet envelop trade policy, as they did with the negotiation of the FTA in the late 1980s. Intergovernmental conflict across the two orders of government is quite possible with the penetration of trade agreements deeper into provincial areas of jurisdiction. There is no guarantee that the shared jurisdiction model will extend beyond CETA. It is unclear whether provinces, for example, will play a similar role in the negotiation of a trade agreement with India. Unlike the EU, other countries seeking a trade agreement with Canada may not want provinces to play such an active role in trade negotiations. Even so, the significance of export markets for Canadian provinces will mean that their interest in shaping Canadian international trade policy is unlikely to abate. Indeed, if anything seems certain, it is that provinces and territories will expand their cross-border trade initiatives in North America and abroad. As they do so, a coherent international trade and investment policy for Canada will require more, not less, shared federalism.

Notes

I am grateful to the officials in the governments of Canada and several provinces who agreed to be interviewed as part of the research I undertook for this chapter.

1. Exports as a percentage of GDP peaked in 2000 at 45 per cent. They have since levelled off. The World Bank reported that Canadian exports of goods and services were 35% in 2008 but down to 28.7 per cent of GDP in 2009. See http://data.worldbank.org/indicator/NE.EXP.GNFS.ZS. Imports

of goods and services were slightly higher in 2009, at 30% but also down from an earlier peak of 34%. On imports see http://data.worldbank.org/indicator/NE.IMP.GNFS.ZS.

2. The figure was lower (75 per cent) in 2009, owing to a slowdown in the American economy.

3. Some analysts have speculated that the Supreme Court might have found such federal actions as consistent with federal legal authority under Section 91 for 'peace, order, and good government' (*R. v. Crown Zellerbach*, 1984) and/or 'the general regulation of trade' (*General Motors v. City National Leasing*, 1989).

4. On the business community, see statement of Roy MacLaren, 2008, co-chair of the Canada–Europe Roundtable for Business. A Joint Report produced by Canada and the EU outlined the mutual benefits that the two parties could expect to realize from a comprehensive agreement. See 'Joint Report on the EU-Canada Scoping Exercise March 5, 2009' on the website of Foreign Affairs and International Trade Canada: http://www.international.gc.ca/trade-agreements-accords-commerci-aux/assets/pdfs/Canada-EU Joint Report2009-03-05.pdf. On Quebec, Séguin (2008) reports 'For the past two years, [Quebec Premier] Mr. Charest has been pursuing a free trade agreement with Europe, working aggressively to eliminate resistance expressed by other provinces and territories.' See also Benzie (2008).

5. Canadian provinces and territories opened their construction contracts to American suppliers following negotiations under the US 2009 American Recovery and Reinvestment Act. The 'Buy American' provisions in the Act required all steel and manufactured goods purchased with stimulus funds under the Act to be made in the US or come from countries with an agreement with the US on procurement. Canada had no agreement that extended to procurement policies of Canadian provinces and territories. Following negotiations, Canadian suppliers secured the right to bid for American state and local public works projects. In return, the provinces/territories agreed to provide US suppliers with access to their construction contracts, including for a number of municipalities.

6. Among the subjects that fall into these offensive interests are tariffs on goods; animal and plant product safety standards; rules of origin, the temporary entry of labour, intellectual property rights and geographical indicators for food and other products, competition policy, telecommunications services, and dispute settlement mechanisms.

7. Under NAFTA and the WTO rules, countries are allowed to levy countervail duties on imports when they can demonstrate that (1) the enterprise or industry exporting the product has received a government financial contribution that confers a benefit (a subsidy), and (2) the subsidized import is causing material injury to an industry in the importing country. Canada successfully appealed the US's imposition of countervail duties in 1982.

8. This conclusion is based on interviews with provincial officials involved in the CETA negotiations.

9. This conclusion relies on information obtained in interviews with provincial officials in late 2010 and early 2011.

10. See testimonies of these groups to the House of Commons Standing Committee on International Trade, 31 May 2006.

References

Benzie, R., and S. Gordon. 2008. 'Brothers in arms; McGuinty and Charest throw down gauntlet in battle with Ottawa' *Toronto Star*, 3 June, A01.

Brown, D.M. 1991. 'The Evolving Role of the Provinces in Canadian Trade Policy'. In *Canadian Federalism: Meeting Global Economic Challenges*, ed. D.M. Brown and M.G. Smith. Kingston, Ont.: Institute of Intergovernmental Affairs, Queen's University.

Cashore, B. 1998. *An Examination of Why a Long-Term Resolution to the Canada–US Softwood Lumber Dispute Eludes Policy Makers*. Victoria: Canadian Forest Service, Pacific Forestry Centre.

Council of Canadians. 2010. 'Letter to the Minister of International Trade Re: CETA'. February 23. Downloaded July 1, 2010 at: http://www.canadians.org/trade/issues/EU/letter-van-loan-0210.html.

Council of the Federation. 2005. 'Council of the Federation Seeks Views of Federal Party Leaders', 19 Dec. At: <www.councilofthefederation.ca/newsroom/seekviews_dec19_05.html>.

Council of the Federation. 2009. Statement of the Council of the Federation - Support for the negotiation of a new and comprehensive economic agreement with the European Union. Ottawa. February 2. At: http://www.counciloft-hefederation.ca/pdfs/statement-EU-20Feb09.pf.

Council of the Federation. 2010. Strengthening International Trade and Relationships. Winnipeg. August 6.

Doern, G.B., and B.W. Tomlin. 1991. *Faith and Fear: The Free Trade Story.* Toronto: Stoddart.

Dupré, J.S. 1985. 'Reflections on the Workability of Executive Federalism'. In *Intergovernmental Relations,* ed. R. Simeon. Toronto: University of Toronto Press.

Dymond, W.A. 1999. 'The MAI: A Sad and Melancholy Tale'. In *Canada Among Nations 1999: A Big League Player?,* ed. F.O. Hampson, M. Hart, and M. Rudner. Toronto: Oxford University Press.

———— and L.R. Dawson. 2002. *The Consultation Process and Trade Policy Creation: Political Necessity or Bureaucratic Rent-Seeking.* Ottawa: Centre for Trade Policy and Law, Carleton University.

Foreign Affairs and International Trade. 2010. Trade in Services. See http://www.international.gc.ca/trade-agreements-accords-commerci-aux/services/Canada-ts.aspx?lang=en.

Harper, Prime Minister. 2006. 'Prime Minister Harper Outlines His Government's Priorities and Open Federalism Approach'. 20 April. At: http://www.conservative.ca/EN/1004/42251.

Herman, L. 2010. 'Buy American: We need only one voice at the table: This latest trade experience taught us that internal bickering doesn't make a deal', *The Globe and Mail,* 9 February, A25.

Hocking, B. 2004. 'Changing the Terms of Trade Policy Making: From the "Club" to the "Multistakeholder" Model', *World Trade Review* 3: 3–26.

House of Commons of Canada. 2004. Bill C-260. An Act respecting the negotiation, approval, tabling and publication of treaties. First reading, 3 Nov., First Session, Thirty-Eighth Parliament.

Howlett, K., R. Seguin, and P. Fong. 2006. 'Ontario–B.C. Alliance Influenced Outcome', *The Globe and Mail,* 28 Apr., A10.

Industry Canada. 2010. 'Trade Data Online', At: <www.ic.gc.castrategis.ic.gc./sc_mrkti/tdst/tdo/tdo.php#tag>.

'Issues of Constitutional Jurisdiction'. 1988. In *Canada: The State of the Federation 1987–88,* ed. P.M. Leslie and R.L. Watts. Kingston, Ont.: Institute of Intergovernmental Relations, Queen's University.

Kukucha, C. 2004. 'The Role of Provinces in Canadian Foreign Trade Policy: Multi-Level Governance and Sub-National Interests in the Twenty-first Century', *Policy and Society* 23, 3: 113–34.

Kukucha, C.J. 2008. *The Provinces and Canadian Foreign Trade Policy.* Vancouver: UBC Press.

Le Gras, G. 'Canada Provinces Still Split on Softwood: Minister', *Washington Post,* 28 February.

Marotte, B., and J. Ibbitson. 2010. 'Provinces must pay up in trade disputes: Harper; After footing $130-million Abitibi bill, Prime Minister says provinces will be on the hook for their own defeats', *The Globe and Mail,* 27 August, B3.

MacLaren, R. 2008. 'Free Trade Comment: Why a Canada-EU deal matters' *The Globe and Mail,* 15 October, A25.

McKenna, B. 2011. 'U.S. taking Canada to arbitration in softwood dispute', *The Globe and Mail,* 19 January, B5.

Mendelsohn, M., R. Wolfe, and A. Parkin. 2002. 'Globalization, Trade Policy and the Permissive Consensus in Canada', *Canadian Public Policy* 28, 3: 351-71.

O'Neil, P. 2009. 'Objections won't scuttle trade: EU; N.L. Premier Danny William opposes deal, but officials say there's enough Canadian support', *Edmonton Journal,* 24 February, E8.

Ontario Ministry of Economic Development and Trade. 2010. 'Ontario seeks your views on the Canada-EU Comprehensive Economic and Trade Agreement Negotiations'. Downloaded July 7 at: http://www.ontario.canada.com/ontcan//medt/en/about_eu_en.jsp.

Quebec, National Assembly. 2002. Bill 52: An Act to amend the Act respecting the Ministere des Relations internationales and other legislative provisions. Assented to 8 June. National Assembly, Second Session, Thirty-Sixth Legislature.

Ritchie, G. 1997. *Wrestling with the Elephant: The Inside Story of the Canada–U.S. Trade Wars.* Toronto: Macfarlane, Walter & Ross.

Roy, J.-Y. 2005. 'Private Members' Business: Hansard', House of Commons, 18 May. Ottawa: Parliament of Canada.

Scharpf, F. 1988. 'The Joint-Decision Trap: Lessons from German Federalism and European Integration', *Public Administration* 66, 3: 239–78.

Séguin, R. 2008. Sarkozy's visit to cement new ties with Quebec; Province courting EU with free-trade agreement as French President gets set for unprecedented speech at legislature next month', *The Globe and Mail*, 20 September, A4.

Skogstad, G. 2008a. 'Canadian Federalism, International Trade, and Regional Market Integration in an Era of Complex Sovereignty'. In *Canadian Federalism: Performance, Effectiveness and Legitimacy*, ed. H. Bakvis and G. Skogstad. Second edition. Toronto: Oxford University Press.

Skogstad, G. 2008b. *Internationalization and Canadian Agriculture: Policy and Governing Paradigms.* Toronto: University of Toronto Press.

Standing Committee on Foreign Affairs and International Trade. 1999. *Report: Implementation of the WTO Agreements and Dispute Settlement.* Ottawa: Parliament of Canada.

Statistics Canada. 1998. *Interprovincial Trade in Canada 1994–1996.* Catalogue no. 15-546-XIE. Ottawa: Statistics Canada.

Taber, J., and R. Séguin (2009) 'Harper talks free trade with European Union; Quebec takes seat at table saying provinces want to influence deal, but Nfld. opposes EU discussions due to seal-product ban', *The Globe and Mail*, 7 May, A4.

Verheul, S. 2010a. 'Testimony'. House of Commons. Standing Committee on International Trade. Thursday, 15 June.

Verheul, S. 2010b. 'Testimony.' House of Commons. Standing Committee on International Trade. Monday, 15 November.

Vieira, P. 2006. 'Lumber Deal Near Collapse. Support Lacking: Ottawa. Emerson Warns Lumber Leaders of "Consequences"', *Financial Post*, 1 Aug.

Winham, G.R. 1986. *International Trade and the Tokyo Round Negotiations.* Princeton: Princeton University Press.

Cases

Attorney General for Canada v. Attorney General for Ontario (Labour Conventions), [1937] A.C. 326.

General Motors of Canada Ltd. v. City National Leasing, [1989] 1 S.C.R. 641.

R. v. Crown Zellerbach Canada Ltd., [1988] 1 S.C.R. 401.

Websites

Department of Foreign Affairs and International Trade: www.international.gc.ca

12 Federalism and Economic Adjustment: Skills and Economic Development in the Face of Globalization and Crisis

Rodney Haddow

A decade ago, much discussion of the relationship between federalism and economic performance in Canada focused on the role of inter-provincial barriers in impeding free trade within the country. The two levels of government devoted considerable attention during the 1990s to an Agreement on Internal Trade (AIT). It was designed to reduce inter-provincial obstacles judged especially unacceptable when international trade agreements already had attenuated their use beyond our national borders (MacDonald, 2002). Potentially able to improve the efficiency of internal markets, the AIT nevertheless addressed only one aspect of the broader nexus of federalism and economic life in Canada. It touched only one limited respect in which political institutions can affect economic outcomes, or, to use terminology deployed in this discussion, of how governmental *hierarchies* affect *markets*. In this view, governmental hierarchies often burden or impede markets so that the best solution is for hierarchies to 'get out of the way', allowing markets, unshackled, to create prosperity.

The relationship between Canadian federalism and the nation's internal economic life is cast in broader terms in this chapter, which addresses the positive role federal and provincial governments—distinctive hierarchies, acting within the same territory—seek to play in stimulating markets. The chapter also examines how much these governmental activities foster local and regional *networks* among economic actors. It examines the interplay of hierarchies, markets, and networks in Canadian economic adjustment policy. The discussion will focus on two dimensions of economic adjustment: economic development and active labour market (or skills) policy. ('Economic adjustment' will be used here as a general term to refer to both economic development and **labour market training**.) The chapter concentrates on the contemporary period but also pays attention to the federal–provincial relationship in two earlier eras: from 1867 until World War II, and between the 1960s and the 1980s. In discussing recent developments, particular attention is paid to the period since Canada began to experience the impact of the global financial crisis in 2008. For reasons of space, the discussion of provincial policy concentrates on four jurisdictions: Ontario, Quebec, and one province each from the West (Alberta) and Atlantic Canada (Nova Scotia).

Throughout Canada's history, the intergovernmental relationship in economic development and labour market policy has been largely unco-ordinated and conflictual. Both levels of government are now very active in fostering economic adjustment, and the specific responsibilities of each level are often constitutionally ambiguous. But there is little effort to co-ordinate policies broadly. Despite this somewhat anarchic style, conflict nevertheless has abated in recent years. This trajectory is summarized in Table 12.1.

The concluding section relates this chapter's findings to the three federalism themes that are the focus of this volume: performance, effectiveness, and legitimacy. It argues that throughout the country's history, the federal–provincial relationship in the economic adjustment area has been less than ideal in each of these respects. Nevertheless, this relationship arguably has improved in recent years. There is little reason to conclude that Canada's economy would now be better served by alternative federalism arrangements.

Hierarchies, Markets, and Federal Policy in Canadian Economic History

It is now common to distinguish hierarchy from markets as a way of co-ordinating social activities (Williamson, 1987). Hierarchy relies on vertical control of subordinates by those assigned responsibility to direct their activities. Markets involve horizontal relations between actors whose interactions reflect self-interest and are regulated by prices. Much activity in the private economy clearly involves both kinds of co-ordination, as is the case, for example, with large corporations. The distinction nevertheless frequently is used to characterize the difference between *governments*, the most comprehensive and authoritative hierarchies in modern societies, and *private-sector economic actors* as a whole, whose interactions can often usefully be seen as driven by market incentives. Some market-oriented classical liberals envisage the possibility of markets operating in a relatively 'pure' form, largely unaffected by public hierarchies, or they conceive of this, at minimum, as an ideal to be striven for (Hayek, 1944). Scholarship on the history of market economies since the emergence of capitalism suggests, in contrast, that market activity is always supplemented by hierarchy, and that markets require the judicious use of public authority to be viable (Polanyi, 1944). Some governmental roles, termed *infrastructural*, are generic to all market economies. They include the protection of property through policing and the maintenance of a legal framework, provision of physical infrastructure, discouragement of market-inhibiting behaviour, and the dispensing of at least a minimal level of social protection. But comparative historical research has revealed that the precise nexus of hierarchy and markets varies considerably among capitalist societies. These differences reflect the distinctive conditions under which different nations began to develop capitalist economies, resulting in a variety that persists today (Gerschenkron, 1962; Hall and Soskice, 2001). In late-developing societies, governments play important roles, termed *interventions*, in addition to those listed above, by fostering indigenous business interests in the face of more advanced foreign rivals, assuring them access to cheap finance, subsidizing new technologies, protecting domestic markets at an early stage of development as a prelude to a later export-oriented approach to growth, and encouraging training.

In the United Kingdom, the first industrializer, governments made much less use of these interventionist tools than did governments in the later industrializers of Continental Europe and East Asia. In important respects, the state's role in Canada's early development reflected the pattern in the UK: neither federal nor provincial governments in the nineteenth century developed effective tools for intervention, such as funnelling financial resources to industry or encouraging technological advancement in domestic industries. Using its jurisdiction over tariffs and over more typically infrastructural tools such as transportation and immigration, the federal government nevertheless sought to foster industrialization after Confederation. In the wake of the 1879 National Policy, an industrial economy did emerge, but it was concentrated in southern Ontario, was technologically dependent on foreign, usually American, parent firms, and was largely confined to local markets, with the result that Canadian exports remained dominated by the raw materials sector. Consistent with the typical pattern in the Anglo democracies, labour market training also was not identified as an appropriate focus for much government intervention. The provinces played a more modest role in fostering economic development during the nineteenth century and, indeed, until after World War II. In both the Atlantic provinces (Bickerton, 1990) and the West (Fowke, 1957), the National Policy and subsequent federal initiatives occasioned considerable resentment. Ottawa's policies were seen there largely as tools to promote central Canadian interests. Yet it was in Ontario, paradoxically, that a provincial government launched significant economic development initiatives designed to correct for the perceived failings of federal policy (Nelles, 1974). For the most part, however, Ottawa was the dominant actor in the field until World War II and during the first two or three post-war decades. The complex interplay of federal and provincial authority that emerged later did not yet exist.

New Concerns, New Tools, and New Actors: Economic Adjustment in Post-War Canada

Canada experienced satisfactory economic growth during the quarter-century between the end of World War II and the early 1970s. In the context of General Agreement on Tariffs and Trade (GATT) agreements, elements of the old tariff-focused system of industrial protection in Canada eroded. By the 1960s, a concern nevertheless emerged that important problems had not been addressed. Observers advocated more interventionist means to address deficiencies in the supply of capital and labour in Canada. Attention was drawn to the continued technological backwardness and lack of export competitiveness of Canadian industries. Conjoined to nationalist objections to the predominance of foreign ownership in the manufacturing and resource sectors, Canadian industry's lack of competitiveness resulted in demands that Ottawa use stronger tools to foster domestic industry, including grants and loans to leading indigenous firms, research and development (R&D) assistance, restrictions on foreign ownership, and the use of public enterprises (Laux and Molot, 1988: 59). By the early 1980s, Ottawa had responded with many forms of intervention. However, these measures were never as comprehensive or as integrated as those that emerged earlier in the late industrializing nations (Howlett and Ramesh, 1992: 237–52). Because of persistent regional imbalances in the distribution of industry, there were also demands that more be done to support development outside of central Canada (termed **regional development** below). Ottawa's modest efforts to sponsor higher levels of industrial skills, a field until then largely left to the provinces, also came under attack, and proposals emerged to provide more public support for technical training in community colleges as well as on the job (Laux and Molot, 1988: 15).

Along with new concerns and new tools came new actors: the provinces became more involved in economic adjustment (Leslie, 1987: 173–5), hoping to rectify the perceived injustices they experienced under the old National Policy framework. In part, their enhanced standing reflected the nature of the new instruments themselves: unlike the tariff, transportation, and immigration powers that formed the core of Ottawa's post-Confederation National Policy, these new interventionist tools were within provincial as well as federal jurisdiction. The Constitution Act, 1867 is frequently judged to have granted the main economic powers to Ottawa. The latter did have the main economic role as it was understood in 1867, but it was mostly a negative role. Reflecting the classical liberal assumptions of the Constitution's drafters, government represented a potential burden on the economy and should restrict itself to those infrastructural activities needed to allow markets to function effectively: regulating banking and commerce, providing infrastructure, and, in the Canadian case, encouraging and regulating immigration. (The option of using tariffs, hopefully in keeping with British economic interests, was an exception to this liberal orthodoxy. Ottawa both acquired and used this power.) Consequently, the Constitution Act, 1867 was silent about industrial assistance, support for scientific research and R&D, and labour market training. Ottawa could claim a presence in these domains based on its extensive economic powers. But the provinces could do the same, based on listed responsibilities in section 92 of the Constitution Act: their jurisdiction over property and civil rights as well as education; their ownership of Crown land and the right to manage natural resources and receive royalties; and their power to collect direct taxes, today the most important source of government revenue, and to incorporate companies. In effect, the Constitution granted both levels of government the right to use the new tools of economic intervention. Table 12.1 outlines the historical patterns of this governmental intervention.

The new prominence of the provinces in economic development also had other causes. Construction of the post-war welfare state rapidly expanded provincial administrative and fiscal capacity, especially for the larger and more affluent provinces. Post-war social and cultural change ignited much stronger regional political identities in the West and, above all, in Quebec. The concentration of much growth in the resource sector enhanced provincial power. Ownership of their natural resources was also an enormous source of revenues and authority for them. Regionally based and provincially oriented elites also came to prominence in parts of the country in the post-war period. They stood in contradistinction to the federally oriented financial, commercial, and transportation interests based in central Canada that had supported and benefited from the National Policy economy (Stevenson, 2004).

The Variable Geometry of Post-War Federal–Provincial Economic Relations

Canada's Constitution therefore did little to specify the role of either jurisdiction or the relationship between them. Ottawa and the provinces assessed earlier federal development

Table 12.1 Nexus of Federalism and Economic Adjustment in Canada: Historical Patterns

Era	Most Distinctive Adjustment Tools for Market	Dominant Form of State Support	Jurisdiction	Intergovernmental Relationship
Pre-World War II	Tariffs; transport infrastructure; immigration	Infrastructure	Federal predominance	Federally led, with limited/occasional interaction of Ottawa and provinces
1960s–1980s	Grants & loans; state enterprise; ownership restrictions	Intervention	Federal and provincial	Unco-ordinated; strategic conflict
Post-1990	Science policy; R&D finance; agglomeration support	Facilitation via network enhancement	Federal and provincial	Unco-ordinated; less/reconfigured conflict

policies differently, and represented distinctive identities and interests. Interventionist policies, by their very nature, presupposed an enhanced role for the state and for its definition of 'national' economic interests. They also fostered interstate (federal–provincial, provincial–provincial) conflict when more than one government used interventionist measures separately, within the same territory. In view of these parameters, it is not surprising that little effective co-ordination emerged between federal and provincial economic development and **skills policies**. Ottawa's relationship to the provinces also varied across the country, reflecting the distinctive resource endowments of provinces and how much provincial objectives diverged from federal ones. Among the wealthier provinces, Ontario stood out as an exceptional case: until the late 1980s, it took only modest steps towards fostering indigenous industrial activity. It was content, observers argued, with the National Policy framework that had usually served its interests in the past and that continued to sustain its uniquely strong industrial base well into the 1980s (Courchene and Telmer, 1998: 11–12).

Beginning with the Quiet Revolution of the 1960s, Quebec developed an extensive set of interventionist tools—including public ownership and expansion of the hydroelectric sector and the use of state-guided investment funds to sponsor indigenous firms—that exceeded anything to be found elsewhere in Canada (Coleman, 1984: 91–129). Quebec's interventions represented a significant break with the Anglo-Saxon model of economic development and a partial step in the direction of the more directive and co-ordinated kinds of industrial development that typified late industrializers in Europe.[1] In the other three provinces discussed here, the core elements of this model were never threatened, and have reasserted their predominance in recent years (see below). Quebec firms frequently benefited from federal development assistance, and the two levels of government often co-operated on such measures. But the broader objectives and competing nationalisms informing each government's efforts meant that no strategic co-ordination was possible. In relation to regional development, Ottawa established itself as a significant dispenser of subsidies in poorer regions of Quebec. As the province developed its own policies for its less favoured regions, these typically operated as competitive rivals to those introduced by Ottawa.

Alberta's challenge to federal adjustment policy was equally pronounced, though based on different objections to federal policy and a distinctive vision of the state's economic role. Convinced that the post-1973 rise in energy prices would be of little long-term value unless the resulting bounty was used to diversify its economy, Alberta pursued diversification ambitiously during the next decade. It declined, however, to take on the kind of state-led developmental mentality that emerged in Quebec (Richards and Pratt, 1979). When world oil prices collapsed in the early 1980s, the diversification strategy, which had borne limited fruit, was substantially curtailed. The province nevertheless has subsequently remained a leader among the provinces, on a per capita basis, in the amount of financial assistance that it provides for industrial development.[2] Conflict with Ottawa was particularly palpable in Alberta, where federal energy policy was seen as favouring the short-term goal of providing cheap energy to central Canada and enhancing that region's National Policy-derived advantages at Alberta's expense. This tension reached its climax in the early 1980s when the Trudeau Liberals implemented the National Energy Program (NEP), the last of the major federal industrial policy initiatives launched two decades earlier (Clarkson, 2002).

Other provinces had equally strong objections to Ottawa's economic policies, but were less able to challenge them. In Nova Scotia, the province's ability to finance industrial interventions was far exceeded by Ottawa's. Provincial officials complained, to no avail, about Ottawa's failure to consult the province meaningfully before spending these sums on regional development, and about the expenditures' frequently fragmented and changeable objectives. Federal officials responded that provincial industrial spending also lacked an underlying logic, and seemingly was shaped by short-term political expediency. In Nova Scotia, as in all other provinces that received federal regional development funds (available today in every region), federal–provincial agreements have existed since the mid-1970s to co-ordinate development spending. But there is little evidence that these agreements attain this objective, as opposed to simply enumerating lists of goals and initiatives by the co-signing governments (Haddow, 2000).

Federal–provincial co-ordination was more extensive in the labour market training field than in economic development. But between the 1960s, when Ottawa first began to spend substantial funds on labour market training, and the mid-1980s, intergovernmental coordination resulted from the federal government largely conceding the right to provinces to decide how Ottawa's training money would be spent. The provinces typically used this authority to stabilize their community colleges. Provinces were much less successful in ensuring that federal funds benefited the intended recipients or the provincial economy. When this provincial failure led Ottawa to break with existing federal–provincial agreements in the mid-1980s, considerable federal–provincial conflict ensued. It was resolved only when Ottawa effectively transferred control over most of its training budget to the provinces in the mid-1990s (see below). Here, too, as with economic development, the prevailing pattern was one of poor co-ordination and competing strategic designs.

New Challenges and New Concepts: Globalization and the Network Economy

Canada's economy entered a period of rapid change in the 1980s. It experienced a combination of rapidly increasing openness to international trade and investment, abetted by major new international trade agreements in 1989, 1994, and 1995, slower economic growth, and chronic budgetary deficits for both federal and provincial governments. In 2008, it also experienced the impact of a sudden and dramatic global economic downturn. The new conjuncture was widely understood as an entirely new challenge for the Canadian economy. The new task was to survive economically in an environment where low-skill manufacturing jobs were threatened by competition from developing nations, investors could move funds more rapidly from one country to another, and governments had less capacity to finance intervention. The latter, moreover, increasingly ran afoul of international trade rules that prohibited governments from granting preferences to domestic firms over foreign ones, impeding foreign ownership, or subsidizing exports— tools used extensively during the post-war era.

Intervention has not been abandoned. Restrictions on foreign ownership are now less extensive, mostly confined to the airline, telecommunications, and media sectors. Tariff protection of domestic industries, the old National Policy standby, has largely ended. And the Auto Pact, a managed trade arrangement in the automotive sector, the backbone of Ontario's industrial economy, contravened the new trade regime and was eliminated. Industrial grants and subsidies also frequently run afoul of trade agreements. They are less available than in the past, and cannot be offered on a preferential basis to domestic firms. As Table 12.2 indicates, such grants and subsidies nevertheless remain important. Their use by Ottawa stagnated under the Mulroney Conservative administration between 1984 and 1993, and was curtailed severely by the subsequent Chrétien Liberal administration in its draconian deficit-reducing 1995 budget. Per capita federal spending on what Statistics Canada terms 'Resource Conservation and Industrial Development', our best available measure of industrial grants and loans, therefore declined precipitously in the late 1990s, while provincial spending declined more moderately. For both levels of government, however, the relatively economically buoyant and deficit-free years after 2000 saw a modest resurgence of spending. In 2009, government spending had returned to almost 80 per cent of its 1989 level in per capita, inflation-adjusted terms.

Table 12.2 Per Capita Spending in Constant (2002) Dollars on Resource Conservation and Industrial Development

	Federal	Provincial/Local	Total
1989	403.07	390.85	793.92
1994	323.68	358.48	682.16
1999	182.81	304.57	487.38
2004	294.71	337.55	632.26
2009	257.11	362.04	619.15

Source: Statistics Canada CANSIM database at http://cansim2.statcan.gc.ca, 3850001, seriesV156381 and V631862.

This new era of globalization, like its predecessor, nevertheless witnessed new concepts about how to promote growth. These new ideas suggested a need to depart from a primary reliance on the old interventionist tools. The new **endogenous growth theory** argued, contrary to classical economics, that a nation's long-term growth potential depended on its inherent capacity to generate innovative ways to improve productivity (Gilpin, 2001: 112–17). Economists also now speculate that the proximity of economic actors and the density of relationships among them are important in stimulating productivity-enhancing innovations (Krugman, 1995). In this **network economy theory**, networks are a crucial middle term between hierarchies and markets in understanding economies (Frances et al., 1991). Like markets, networks involve horizontal relations between voluntarily interacting actors. Unlike markets, they rely on 'untraded interdependencies', based on trust, shared knowledge, and face-to-face contact, without which market-based interactions would be impoverished.

The implications of these new ideas for government's role are not straightforward. The network concept confirmed the belief of market-oriented liberals that dynamic economies rely on unplanned, horizontal relationships, not government hierarchy. From this viewpoint, governments have even more reason than in the past to leave markets alone. But for others, the network concept justifies renewed state involvement, though of a different kind than had been practised earlier. It legitimizes government promotion of networks to enhance innovation. Such **innovation policy** measures include greater commitment to scientific research and its transfer to industry; more R&D, especially for firms in high-technology sectors; and the fostering of networks among firms, their suppliers and customers, research institutions, and sources of finance and advanced skills. While some argue that positive agglomeration effects can occur on a nationwide basis (in 'national systems of innovation'), the more common view is that geographic proximity is key: networks emerge in 'clusters', consisting of actors in a particular sector and city (Porter, 1991) or, more broadly, thrive in 'regional innovation systems' that include a number of interacting sectors within larger cities or sub-regions of a nation (Cooke, 1998). In this view, cities that are well-located and well-endowed with talented people are important units for stimulating economic prosperity and the innovations needed to create it (see also Jacobs, 1985). As such, cities may be more important than countries as a whole, or even large regions within them.

The policy instruments of use in fostering networks are available to both levels of government, like those of the preceding era. Both jurisdictions can fund research on new technologies, subsidize R&D, and encourage collaboration among proximate economic actors. Nevertheless, Ottawa has traditionally been more active than the provinces in sponsoring science research and its industrial dissemination (Niosi, 2000: 42–4). In recent years, moreover, the government of Canada appears to have expanded this commitment and refocused its economic adjustment spending initiatives to favour science and innovation-enhancing measures, partly at the expense of the older style of industrial subsidies. A glimpse, though partial and imperfect, of the extent of this shift is provided by Table 12.3, which reports government spending on scientific research organizations and on R&D assistance to non-governmental actors. (Some innovation-focused spending is also probably reported in table 12.2, alongside older kinds of intervention). Federal spending rose significantly during the early 1990s, weathered the late 1990s period of restraint relatively unscathed, and surged again after 2000. Provincial spending in this area, much lower than Ottawa's, nevertheless took off after 2000. In 2009, combined inflation-adjusted per capita federal and provincial spending on research support was almost double its level of 20 years earlier.

Federalism and the 'Network Economy' in the Twenty-first Century

Intergovernmental relations in the area of economic adjustment are no more co-ordinated today than they were in the past. There is still no forum within which Canadian governments can plan development measures jointly. Most initiatives are conceived with little prior intergovernmental discussion, although consultation is more common on implementation. Yet there is also less overt conflict between Ottawa and the provinces about the country's economic future, and the federal government's role in shaping it, than occurred between the 1960s and 1980s. Federal–provincial friction is greater in some regions than in others. But here, too, there has been change. In the post-NEP, free trade era, friction is much less pronounced with Alberta. It is greater with Ontario, which has belatedly discovered a need to husband its own economic fortunes and to query the value of federal policies in achieving this goal.

The provinces have expanded their research spending. For instance, they all now offer tax subsidies for R&D, although the extent of this generosity varies considerably (McKenzie, 2005). The Chrétien Liberal administration did little to promote innovation during its first term in power, but in its second, having conquered the deficit, it took significant steps in this direction. Stephen Harper's Conservative government has been less creative since coming to power in 2006, but has not curtailed the level of commitment made by the preceding administration. New measures under Chrétien included the launching of a Canada Foundation for Innovation, Genome Canada, and the Canada Research Chairs. Federal spending for existing arrangements, including the National Research Council, the Networks of Excellence, Technology Partnerships Canada, the Canadian Space Agency, and research in medicine, the natural sciences, and engineering, expanded considerably (Wolfe, 2002). Much of the new federal research funding went to the country's universities. Ottawa has shifted the focus of its spending on post-secondary education significantly since the mid-1990s. Broad block-grant transfers to the provinces to help them finance university operating expenses have been curtailed, while direct transfers to universities to bolster research have expanded considerably. As the data reported in Table 12.3 suggest, these initiatives continue to bolster federal research spending long after their launch in the late 1990s. The new spending is designed to increase Canada's perpetually low R&D levels and appears to have had some success, although Canadian firms remain R&D laggards compared to their competitors in most other affluent nations (De la Monthe, 2003: 177). Yet, according to critics, the additional funding did little to advance other aspects of the network concept, such as fostering stronger relationships among actors within innovative regions and clusters. Similarly, Ottawa failed to take the provincial governments into consideration as important partners in stimulating network-based innovation (Wolfe, 2002: 152). Ottawa's championing of the

Table 12.3 Per Capita Spending in Constant (2002) Dollars on Research Establishments

	Federal	Provincial/Local	Total
1989	48.07	11.97	60.04
1994	62.24	16.59	78.83
1999	54.96	8.15	63.11
2004	86.42	18.46	104.88
2009	96.52	16.30	112.82

Source: Statistics Canada CANSIM database at http://cansim2.statcan.gc.ca, 3850001, seriesV156359 and V631839.

new network-based growth agenda consequently has not been matched by any greater willingness to work co-operatively with the provinces.

Overall, the federal government's pursuit of its new agenda has occasioned less provincial resistance than did the preceding interventionist agenda. This is at least in part because of distinctive intrinsic features of these two agendas, not because Ottawa has involved the provinces more in its new one. During the interventionist years, the federal government and several provinces pursued equally ambitious, but fundamentally incompatible, strategies (Leslie, 1987: 8–22). This policy style led to conflict during the post-war high tide of interventionism. There is now much less room for states to see themselves as strategic 'players' pursuing comprehensive visions for the economies over which they exercise authority. Interventionist development tools are still very much in use, but globalization and the new growth concepts ensure that they are no longer deployed on behalf of comprehensive strategies. The new, network-focused growth agenda, in contrast, privileges localized dynamics, whose strength is supposed to depend on their internal vitality, not on their location in relation to broader national or provincial development goals. Political considerations nevertheless still influence greatly where Ottawa chooses to foster local activity. Observers frequently allege that provinces' desire to 'spread around' (within and between provinces) the opportunities created by the new economy often distorts Ottawa's selection of favoured projects.

Thus, Ottawa abandoned the pursuit of a strategic, national economic development policy (anchored, as it always was, on a determination to bolster a manufacturing economy concentrated in southern Ontario) after the Conservatives came to power in 1984 (Clarkson, 2002: 233–6). The subsequent 1989 Free Trade Agreement (FTA) provisions that effectively ruled out the regime of regulated exports, differential prices, and ownership restrictions, which had formed the core of the NEP, alleviated Alberta's main concerns about federal policy. The early 1980s collapse of Premier Lougheed's strategy of diversifying the province's economy by expanding its manufacturing base also meant that Alberta's own policies were less likely to be perceived in central Canada as a direct challenge to its established strength. Alberta has since turned its attention to encouraging the same kinds of science-based and innovative networks that have become the objective of federal policy (Taft, 1997: 112). To the extent that federal policy is now premised on facilitating place-specific innovation in a manner that no longer effectively privileges one region over others, it is not now, in principle, incompatible with the policies of any province, such as Alberta, that wishes to foster networks within its own borders.

During the 1980s, Quebec's development policies also departed somewhat from the particularly strategic interventionism that typified those of the Quiet Revolution, though they remain distinctive (Bernier and Garon, 2004: 210–15). In the late 1980s its Liberal government adopted the 'clusters' concept and the notion that localized networks are crucial for the province's future. An **industrial policy** designed to foster clusters was launched in 1991 and continued by the Parti Québécois government that came to power in 1994 (Bourque, 2000: 136–40). It has been updated several times since, most recently with a new innovation strategy in 2010. This policy involves much more government-sponsored formal co-ordination among actors than has ever succeeded in English Canada, and it is still complemented by more extensive use of state-sponsored investment funds, though these have become less active in pursuing nationalist goals. Its conception of how growth occurs nevertheless is relatively localized and disaggregated. This local focus represents a departure, albeit partial in Quebec's case, from the earlier tendency to conceive of the provincial economy as a strategic whole, in need of 'planning and thus an increased role for the provincial government', in order to achieve the key (Quebec) nationalist objectives of fostering a francophone-owned manufacturing base (Coleman, 1984: 116). Such a strategic stance is more likely to occasion conflict when it encounters distinctive strategies designed elsewhere.

Network economy thinking also underlies much recent development policy in Ontario. Rather than alleviating older conflicts, however, its influence has coincided with a discernible deterioration of the province's relationship with federal authorities regarding economic adjustment. In Ontario, unlike Alberta and Quebec, network economy thinking did not partly displace an earlier interventionist stance, but instead represented the province's first concerted engagement with development issues after several decades of relative quiescence. It also coincided with the emergence of serious doubts about whether federal policy is consistent with the province's economic interests. Ontario complains that it receives less than its fair share of federal regional development funds, and also does not receive its due in relation to the federal innovation outlays discussed above. The province opposed the FTA, and in the late 1980s formed private-sector panels to study how to sustain its manufacturing base, now perceived as threatened by economic globalization. The NDP administration of the early 1990s initiated programs designed to encourage innovation and collaboration among economic actors in various sectors. Unlike their Quebec counterparts, however, Ontario's network-promoting policies did not benefit from support across the partisan spectrum. Most NDP measures were terminated by the Harris Conservative government that came to power in 1995 (Wolfe and Gertler, 2001). The McGuinty Liberal administration, elected in 2003, has pursued a course partway between those of its NDP and Conservative predecessors—less interventionist than the former, but more activist than the latter. Like Quebec, it introduced a new innovation strategy in 2010.

Among the provinces examined here, Nova Scotia has experienced the least change. It is still disproportionately reliant on federal regional development funds, which have been reduced since the early 1990s (Haddow, 2001a: 254). Nova Scotia adopted network economy concepts to the extent of launching a series of Regional Development Authorities

(RDAs) across the province. Consisting of business and other leaders from the same locale, the RDAs are designed to foster potentially innovative interaction among these actors. However, the RDAs have almost no resources of their own, and rely on a shrinking supply of funds from existing provincial and federal programs to finance initiatives. The economic and demographic stagnation that characterizes much of Nova Scotia outside of Halifax presents RDAs with a Herculean task. As with other rural and thinly populated parts of Canada, most of these areas do not benefit from the creative dynamics that, according to network theorizing, occur in more densely populated and diverse cities and regions.

This pattern of federal–provincial relations was not altered by the economic crisis that began in 2008, though the downturn did for a time shift the focus of both federal and provincial policy partly away from innovation towards the short-term survival of mature industries.[3] As a comparison of the data for 2004 and 2009 in tables 12.2 and 12.3 indicates, this crisis meant that overall federal and provincial economic development outlays did not, at least immediately, fall during the recession in spite of the substantial deficits quickly experienced by all governments.

In Ontario, the crisis led to a massive joint initiative by Ottawa and the province in December 2008 to support Chrysler and General Motors, major employers in the province that were on the verge of bankruptcy. This step reflected an agreement that the two administrations had reached with the United States government to share the bail out costs. Ottawa's substantial financial commitment represented a departure in the auto sector, where it previously was reluctant to intervene. The crisis also contributed to Ottawa's decision in August 2009 to create FedDev, a federal economic development agency for Southern Ontario. Until then, this region had been alone in not hosting such an agency. Informed observers nevertheless still characterized the relationship between Ottawa and Ontario as ad hoc and unco-ordinated. FedDev's creation may have responded in part to pressure from the province, but its projects, like those elsewhere in Canada, are generally decided upon by Ottawa alone, though often after consultation with the province. The federal government also made it clear that it saw its involvement in the 2008 auto bailout as a temporary measure. Provincial officials expected to again be mainly responsible for assisting the industry once the car makers were stabilized. Ottawa renewed its participation in a joint federal–provincial innovation committee in 2008, after not attending for a number of years. But this forum is largely confined to information-sharing, not decision-making. In spite of the recent federal interventions, moreover, friction with Ontario did not abate during the crisis. Indeed, the province launched a research institute which was designed to show, again, that Ontario does not receive its fair share of federal funding, in this area as in others.

Ottawa's decision to support Ontario's auto sector caused resentment in other provinces, including Quebec. The latter province's request a decade earlier for assistance in preserving its one auto assembly plant had been turned down by the federal government. Quebec now complained that its forestry sector, also experiencing a severe crisis in 2008, was not receiving adequate consideration from Ottawa (Anonymous, 2009). In April 2009, the federal government responded by agreeing to a joint federal–Quebec initiative to help the province's forestry sector to become more innovative. This initiative was in addition to earlier federal measures for the sector that applied to all provinces, but from which Quebec was also able to benefit significantly because of forestry's considerable importance there. Here too, the broadly fragmented quality of previous federal–provincial relations regarding economic development did not change. Ottawa and Quebec maintain separate networks of private-sector regional development boards and offices across the province. Each network plans its own activities, though there is frequent co-operation on funding specific projects. Co-operation takes place on a case-by-case basis. Officials who work on specific projects often, for this reason, interact with their federal colleagues. In contrast, bureaucrats involved in overall policy-making for the province have much less contact with representatives from Ottawa, reflecting the fact that overall policy-making is done separately for the two levels of government.

Skills and the New Economy

The federal–provincial relationship regarding skills training has also evolved since the mid-1990s, but there is little evidence that the skills imparted in training programs are becoming more relevant for current economic needs, including those associated with the **new economy**. In the 1980s Ottawa had taken steps to enhance the quality of skills purchased with its training dollars. To do this, it effectively disengaged itself from provincial decision-making in determining how to allocate its funds. But in the wake of the narrow victory of the 'no' option in the 1995 Quebec sovereignty referendum, and of its own substantial deficit, Ottawa offered to devolve the administration of part of its training expenditures (the share that is funded from the Employment Insurance [EI] fund) to the provinces. Six provinces, including Quebec, Alberta, and Ontario (agreement with the latter was delayed until 2005), signed Labour Market Development Agreements (LMDAs) with Ottawa that accepted the 'full' federal offer. Called 'devolution', this allowed them to take over the administration of EI-financed programs previously delivered by Ottawa. The provinces would still have to meet certain federal conditions in spending the money, but these have little direct bearing on the content of the skills provided: provinces must ensure that a certain proportion of funded training recipients are, or recently were, EI recipients. They also commit themselves to meeting difficult-to-enforce targets regarding the proportion of trainees who return to work. The four other provinces signed more modest LMDAs. These agreements either allow the province to manage the funds jointly with Ottawa, which continues to administer them (called 'co-management'). In all provinces, the federal government nevertheless continues to administer non-EI-financed training programs of its own for three categories of people who have particular difficulties entering the labour force: youth, Aboriginal people, and the disabled. These changes shifted an important number of training recipients from federal to provincial administration, although in an uneven pattern (Bakvis, 2002). With respect to the substance of skills provided, however, federal and provincial programs remain largely disengaged, subject to policy objectives defined separately by each jurisdiction.

Moreover, the innovation-oriented economic development initiatives of Ottawa in the late 1990s have not been complemented by major steps to ensure that its remaining training measures address skill needs in innovative sectors. Indeed, the targeting of its main programs at the 'at-risk' groups mentioned above suggests that the centrepiece of federal skills policy today is equity rather than efficiency. Ottawa's lethargy in extending its innovation agenda to the skills area is partly explained by hesitation to reassert itself aggressively in a policy domain where it had so recently made significant concessions to the provinces. But it may also reflect a feature of the network economy perspective that has guided recent federal adjustment policy. Network thinking certainly assigns an important role to the supply of 'talent' in the success of innovative locales. Particular attention is paid to the attraction and retention of a 'creative class', i.e., professionals with advanced technology and entrepreneurial skills. In a labour market perceived to be increasingly global, there is a concern to attract the creative class as immigrants (Florida, 2004). Although Canadian immigration policy was adjusted in the mid-1990s to enhance the entry prospects of skilled workers and the well-educated (Green and Green, 2004: 127–8), some observers in high-technology industries argue that Canada must do more to attract this exclusive category of migrant (Haddow, 2001b: 15–16). In contrast, exponents of the network economy devote less attention to workers with less to offer to the 'new economy', and to the possibility that network-based growth may not be advantageous for them (Donald and Morrow, 2003). These less sought-after workers are deemed most likely to benefit from training in the more 'ordinary' vocational skills, provided in colleges or on the job, which is funded by the federal and provincial training measures discussed above.

Does Federalism Impede Economic Adjustment in Canada?

After 1945, the provinces actively pursued economic adjustment policies. The federal–provincial relationship in this area subsequently has manifested important continuities. It is mostly unco-ordinated, with each level of government typically pursuing its preferred policies after limited consultation with the other. Policies are strongly influenced by prevailing ideas about how best to promote growth. In the context of a diverse federation, such unco-ordinated policies occasion intergovernmental friction. The style of federalism in this domain comes closest to one of independent governments because of the piecemeal and inconsistent pattern of intergovernmental co-ordination. Jurisdiction is not 'watertight', however. Neither government can confidently exclude the other from the policy domain.

The nexus of federalism and adjustment policy nevertheless also experienced important discontinuities between the post-war period and the years since 1980. First, the ideas that now prevail about how to foster growth differ from earlier ones. After World War Two, strategic and interventionist approaches to economic adjustment became popular, although (with the partial exception of Quebec) within the comparatively limited scope permitted in the Anglo-Saxon economic model. Current policy is instead animated by a desire to facilitate innovative networks, which are likely to be found in the most urbanized, educated, and economically diverse locales and regions of the country. Variations in the pattern of policy change—for instance, the fact that Ottawa has altered the content of its economic development policies much more than its training ones—reflect the fact that the new growth agenda has distinctive implications for these different areas. While some of the instruments favoured earlier are still deployed now (especially industrial assistance), others have been curtailed or terminated, victims of a more globalized economy and of trade policy. In this new context there is less friction than before between federal and provincial policies. The retreat from policies centred on strategic 'grand designs' reduced conflict. The regional focus of federal–provincial tension, moreover, has changed in ways that were unlikely to be much affected, in the long run, by the economic downturn that began in 2008.

How should this pattern be evaluated in relation to the three federalism criteria—performance, effectiveness, and legitimacy—employed in this volume? Regarding performance, intergovernmental relations regarding economic adjustment have never been fully consistent with federalism principles. The ambiguity of jurisdictional responsibilities makes it difficult to assert that post-Confederation federal policies did not properly respect the jurisdictional autonomy of the provinces, because the written Constitution is of only limited help in identifying the provinces' responsibilities here. The National Policy, and much post-World War II federal policy after it, nevertheless was widely rejected outside central Canada as not reflecting the distinctive adjustment needs of the different regions. The absence of forums for intergovernmental bargaining meant that disaffected provincial governments lacked effective avenues for representing these concerns. In light of this earlier pattern, the performance of the federal system arguably has improved in the contemporary era, when federal adjustment policies are less subject to the accusation of regional bias, and when the dearth of formal mechanisms of federal–provincial co-ordination is less important. As will be suggested below, more elaborate intergovernmental machinery would probably generate more conflict, not less, in view of the distinctive development priorities of different regions. Canadian federalism is likely to perform best, regarding economic adjustment, when the need for formal intergovernmental negotiation and agreement is kept to a minimum.

To what extent does this intergovernmental pattern impede the effectiveness of economic adjustment in Canada, our second criterion? Would Canadians be better off economically, for instance, (1) if they lived in a unitary state, (2) if the provinces controlled all adjustment policies, or (3) if there were more extensive federal–provincial co-operation in this area? Quite likely, they would not. A substantial academic literature in the field of comparative political economy (CPE) now seeks to ascertain whether some of the institutional arrangements found in developed capitalist economies are better than others for promoting growth. But this scholarship gives us no reason for concluding that Canada would be better off with a fully centralized, decentralized, or co-ordinated policy regime. A standard distinction in the CPE literature, broached at the beginning of this chapter, is between the more **market-oriented political economies** that are typical of Anglo-Saxon nations, and an alternative model in Continental Europe and East Asia that involves either more non-market formal co-ordination among economic actors or more state intervention. Each model has distinctive strengths and weaknesses: the Anglo economies resolve adjustment problems best in an unco-ordinated, unplanned way. **Co-ordinative economies** are better at solving economic problems through co-operative interaction among economic interests. Neither model is clearly superior to the other in its long-term capacity to sustain economic growth (Hall and Soskice, 2001). Nevertheless, individual countries are much more dynamic economically than are others that conform to the same model. In effect, some countries do a better job of exploiting a model's particular strengths than do other countries that reflect the same model.

Canada's political economy more closely approximates the market-oriented model, and is best suited to non-planned economic adjustment. But its institutions feature idiosyncrasies that distinguish it from the Anglo-Saxon norm. A comparatively small population and extensive geography mean that the Canadian (federal and/or provincial) state has always been significantly involved in economic adjustment. Canada's federal Constitution ensures that these activities are divided between two jurisdictions. The country's internal diversity also entails that these multiple governmental actors face distinct challenges and favour different policies. The question, then, is the following: Is the style of policy-making described in this chapter the most effective, in light of an institutional endowment that creates a propensity for market-based adjustment, but that also has charged multiple and heterogeneous governments with a larger adjustment task than is typical in market-oriented settings?

A case can be made that it is, indeed, most suited to these parameters. Ottawa and the provinces are sufficiently heterogeneous in their goals that it is hard to argue that the country would be well served by centralizing adjustment policies controlled by Ottawa. The history of the post-Confederation National Policy suggests that centralized adjustment policy would likely be perceived as benefiting one region at the expense of others. What about full devolution of adjustment policy to the provinces? This scenario may hold some appeal for the larger and more affluent provinces, but not elsewhere. Even in richer provinces, moreover, governments continue to support a federal role in adjustment, presumably in recognition of the closeness of economic links between the provinces and the resulting value of sharing some important adjustment policies among them.[4]

In closing, it is worth noting that Canada's adjustment style may have two specific advantages with respect to policy effectiveness and legitimacy in the current globalization era. If network theorists are right, growth now occurs in a more localized, decentralized manner than in the past. A disaggregated, even relatively anarchic, approach to adjustment policy may be well suited to such an environment, presenting local economic actors with the opportunity to exploit links with many diverse government programs— an interactive style that is entirely consistent with the norm in dynamic economic networks. Further, federal–provincial conflict over adjustment, while a perennial feature of Canadian politics, has attenuated overall since the end of the post-war era of strategic intervention. Rather than representing a mortal challenge to its national integrity, as is often argued, globalization and the changes in federal and provincial adjustment policy styles that it encouraged may reduce the political-economic tensions that have plagued Canada's internal politics since its early history. In the past, these tensions often called into question the very legitimacy of our federal institutions for citizens and governments in many Canadian provinces.

Notes

1. This argument about Quebec's political economy is developed in Chapter 2 of Haddow and Klassen (2006).

2. See data reported by Statistics Canada for provincial spending on 'resource conservation and industrial development' since the 1980s; Statistics Canada, CANSIM II data series, table 3850001.

3. This paragraph and the next are based mainly on 10 interviews conducted by the author with economic development officials in Ontario and Quebec during the summer of 2010.

4. Some economists argue that the extent of trade among Canadian provinces is much greater than is reflected in official trade statistics; see Helliwell (2002). For an example of provincial premiers publicly endorsing a continued federal role in adjustment policy, in this case training, see Cordozo (2006).

References

Anonymous. 2009. 'Prime Minister Stephen Harper extends olive branch to absent Quebec premier,' *The Canadian Press*, January 30th.

Bakvis, H. 2002. 'Checkerboard Federalism? Labour Market Development Policy in Canada'. In *Canadian Federalism: Performance, Effectiveness, and Legitimacy*, ed. H. Bakvis and G. Skogstad. Toronto: Oxford University Press.

Bernier, L., and F. Garon. 2004. 'State-Owned Enterprises in Quebec'. In *Quebec: State and Society*, ed. A.-G. Gagnon. Peterborough, Ont.: Broadview.

Bickerton, J. 1990. *Nova Scotia, Ottawa, and the Politics of Regional Development*. Toronto: University of Toronto Press.

Bourque, G. 2000. *Le modèle québécois de développement*. Sainte-Foy, Que.: Presses de l'Université du Québec.

Clarkson, S. 2002. *Uncle Sam and Us*. Toronto: University of Toronto Press.

Coleman, W. 1984. *The Independence Movement in Quebec, 1945–1980*. Toronto: University of Toronto Press.

Cooke, P. 1998. 'Introduction: Origins of the Concept'. In *Regional Innovation Systems*, ed. H.J. Braczyk, P. Cooke, and M. Heidenreich. London: UCL Press.

Cordozo, A. 2006. 'Premiers Want a National Skills Strategy to Address Future Skills Needs', *The Hill Times*, 6 Mar.

Courchene, T., with C. Telmer. 1998. *From Heartland to North American Region State*. Toronto: Faculty of Management, University of Toronto.

De la Monthe, J. 2003. 'Ottawa's Imaginary Innovation Strategy: Progress or Drift?' In *How Ottawa Spends, 2003–2004*, ed. G.B. Doern. Toronto: Oxford University Press.

Donald, B., and D. Morrow. 2003. *Competing for Talent: Implications for Social and Cultural Policy in Canadian City-Regions*. Ottawa: Department of Canadian Heritage.

Florida, R. 2004. *The Flight of the Creative Class*. New York: Harper Business.

Fowke, V. 1957. *The National Policy and the Wheat Economy*. Toronto: University of Toronto Press.

Frances, J., R. Levacic, J. Mitchell, and G. Thompson. 1991. 'Introduction'. In *Markets, Hierarchies and Networks*, ed. G. Thompson, J. Frances, R. Levacic, and J. Mitchell. London: Sage.

Gerschenkron, A. 1962. *Economic Backwardness in Historical Perspective*. Cambridge, Mass.: Harvard University Press.

Gilpin, R. 2001. *Global Political Economy*. Princeton, NJ: Princeton University Press.

Green, A., and D. Green. 2004. 'The Goals of Canadian Immigration Policy: An Historical Perspective', *Canadian Journal of Urban Research* 13, 1: 102–40.

Haddow, R. 2000. 'Economic Development Policy: In Search of a Strategy'. In *The Savage Years: The Perils of Reinventing Government in Nova Scotia*, ed. P. Clancy, J. Bickerton, R. Haddow, and I. Stewart. Halifax: Formac.

———. 2001a. 'Regional Development Policy: A Nexus of Policy and Politics'. In *How Ottawa Spends, 2001–2002*, ed. L. Pal. Toronto: Oxford University Press.

———. 2001b. 'Report on the CSLS Roundtable on Creating a More Efficient Labour Market'. In *Reports and Proceedings from the CSLS Roundtable on Creating a More Efficient Labour Market*. Ottawa: Centre for the Study of Living Standards.

——— and T. Klassen. 2006. *Partisanship, Globalization and Canadian Labour Market Policy*. Toronto: University of Toronto Press.

Hall, P., and D. Soskice. 2001. 'An Introduction to Varieties of Capitalism'. In *Varieties of*

Capitalism, ed. P. Hall and D. Soskice. Oxford: Oxford University Press.

Hayak, F. 1944. *The Road to Serfdom*. Chicago: University of Chicago Press.

Helliwell, J. 2002. *Globalization and Well Being*. Vancouver: University of British Columbia Press.

Howlett, M., and M. Ramesh. 1992. *The Political Economy of Canada*. Toronto: McClelland & Stewart.

Jacobs, J. 1985. *Cities and the Wealth of Nations*. New York: Vintage Books, 1985.

Krugman, P. 1995. *Development, Geography, and Economic Theory*. Cambridge, Mass.: MIT Press.

Laux, J.K., and M. Mollot. 1988. *State Capitalism: Public Enterprise in Canada*. Ithaca, NY: Cornell University Press.

Leslie, P. 1987. *Federal State, National Economy*. Toronto: University of Toronto Press.

MacDonald, M.R. 2002. 'The Agreement on Internal Trade: Trade-offs for Economic Union and Federalism'. In *Canadian Federalism: Performance, Effectiveness, and Legitimacy*, ed. H. Bakvis and G. Skogstad. Toronto: Oxford University Press.

McKenzie, K. 2005. 'Tax Subsidies for R&D in Canadian Provinces', *Canadian Public Policy* 31, 1: 29–44.

Nelles, H.V. 1974. *The Politics of Development: Forests, Mines & Hydro-electric Power in Ontario, 1849–1941*. Toronto: MacMillan.

Niosi, J. 2000. *Canada's National System of Integration*. Montreal and Kingston: McGill–Queen's University Press.

Polanyi, K. 1944. *The Great Transformation*. Boston: Beacon Press.

Porter, M. 1991. *The Competitive Advantage of Nations*. New York: Free Press.

Richards, J., and L. Pratt. 1979. *Prairie Capitalism*. Toronto: McClelland & Stewart.

Stevenson, G. 2004. *Unfulfilled Union*, 4th edn. Montreal and Kingston: McGill–Queen's University Press.

Taft, K. 1997. *Shredding the Public Interest*. Edmonton: University of Alberta Press.

Williamson, O. 1987. *The Economic Institutions of Capitalism*. Oxford: Blackwell.

Wolfe, D. 2002. 'Innovation Policy for the Knowledge-Based Economy: From the Red Book to the White Paper'. In *How Ottawa Spends, 2002–2003*, ed. G.B. Doern. Toronto: Oxford University Press.

——— and M. Gertler. 2001. 'Globalization and Economic Restructuring in Ontario: From Industrial Heartland to Learning Region?', *European Planning Studies* 9, 5: 575–92.

13 Federalism and Canadian Climate Change Policy

Mark Winfield and Douglas Macdonald

The efficient and effective co-ordination of federal and provincial government activity is essential in the field of environmental policy. Pollution crosses borders, and Canadian courts have established that the regulation of harmful emissions lies within the jurisdictional competence of both orders of government. In this chapter we examine the processes by which the two orders of government co-ordinate their environmental policy-making. In particular we examine the institutions and processes used to develop and implement 'national' policy, defined as the sum of federal and provincial efforts, whether co-ordinated or not.

The substantive focus of the chapter is on national climate change policy, specifically as it deals with climate change mitigation, meaning the need to reduce greenhouse gas (**GHG**) emission levels relative to their current levels to prevent 'dangerous' climate change as identified by the United Nations Intergovernmental Panel on Climate Change (**IPCC**). The temporal focus is on the evolution of Canadian climate change policy since the January 2006 election of the Conservative government led by Prime Minister Stephen Harper. The chapter examines the approaches being taken with respect to emissions from the large industrial sources ('large final emitters', or **LFEs**) that account for more than half of Canada's total emissions of GHGs. Initiatives with respect to transportation emissions (which account for approximately one quarter of Canada's GHG emissions), buildings (10 per cent of emissions), agriculture (7.5 per cent of emissions) and individual citizens are also considered where they are relevant to the analysis. The upstream oil and gas industry, electricity generation sector, and road freight transportation have been the key areas of GHG emissions growth in Canada since 1990 (Environment Canada, 2010a).

Climate change presents some particularly difficult challenges for the system of intergovernmental relations and national policy formulation in Canada. Canada's provinces and territories represent profoundly different regional economies and energy mixes. In Alberta and Saskatchewan, the extraction and export of fossil fuels are foundations of the provincial economy. Other provinces, like Quebec, BC, and Manitoba, with abundant hydroelectric resources see a potential for 'low-carbon' energy exports, while an energy-consuming province like Ontario, notwithstanding the shift in its employment base from manufacturing to services, is concerned about the implications of climate change policies for its energy-intensive manufacturing sector. These contradictory interests with respect to climate change have made formulating coherent national strategies extremely challenging.

Canadian climate change policy is subject to two major external influences, the global policy framework provided through the 1992 United Nations Framework Convention on Climate Change (UNFCCC) and the 1997 Kyoto Protocol, as well as the perceived need to harmonize Canadian initiatives with American policies. The latter consideration is driven by Canada's high level of economic dependence on exports to the US, with 80 per cent of Canadian exports going south of the border.

This chapter has three objectives with respect to Canadian climate change policy. First, it seeks to address the research questions set out for the volume by its editors, specifically

1) How well is the system of federal–provincial intergovernmental relations functioning with respect to the climate change issue in terms of its effectiveness (i.e., ability to broker different interests to allow agreement to be reached), efficiency, transparency, accountability?
2) How effective are the policy outcomes and decisions generated by that system in terms of addressing the climate change problem?
3) How do relevant audiences evaluate the legitimacy both of the system and of the outcomes it generates?

Secondly, the chapter provides explanations for why the traditional structures for federal–provincial environmental policy co-ordination have evolved into a system that is now bi-national and bifurcated. The federal government has explicitly tied its approach to climate change to that of the US federal government, while several provinces, notably BC, Ontario, Quebec, and Manitoba, are grounding their climate change polices in regionally based sub-national initiatives with US states. These disparate paths of the federal government and a majority of the provinces represent a major departure from the norms of national policy formulation in Canada. Finally, the chapter reflects on potential future paths for the development and implementation of an effective and legitimate national climate change policy for Canada.

National Climate Change Policy-Making

Canadian national climate change policy formulation and implementation has moved through four distinct phases since 1990.

1990–2002: Multilateralism

Climate change policy-making at the national level in Canada began in 1990, when the government of Brian Mulroney adopted the goal of stabilizing Canadian greenhouse gas emissions, two years before that same goal was agreed to by the international community in the United Nations Framework Convention on Climate Change (UNFCCC) at the Rio Conference in 1992. Starting in 1993, joint meetings of the federal, provincial and territorial environment and energy ministers (JMM) became the major institutional vehicle for federal–provincial co-ordination of climate policy. The JMM process led to the first national climate change plan in 1995. Unfortunately the plan was nothing more than a lowest-common-denominator description of what provinces were willing to commit to—essentially nothing more than asking the sources within their borders to reduce emissions voluntarily, absent any legal or financial incentives put in place by the state.

Leading up to the Kyoto Conference of the Parties to the UNFCCC, using the JMM process, the federal and provincial environment and energy ministers agreed in November 1997 that the Canadian international position should retain the goal of stabilization, with a new deadline of 2010 instead of 2000. Shortly afterwards, Prime Minister Chrétien responded to external pressure from other heads of state (Bernstein, 2002; Harrison, 2007) and personally intervened in the policy process. On 3 December, the opening day of the Kyoto meeting, Canadian representatives were instructed to state that Canada would commit to a target 3 per cent below 1990 levels (at the end of the Kyoto meeting, that target had been changed to a 6 per cent reduction commitment), effectively abandoning the consensus that had emerged through the JMM. In departing from the decision resulting from the federal–provincial process and substituting his own, Prime Minister Chrétien and his cabinet considerably damaged the credibility of the multilateral process among the provinces (confidential interviews).

Eventually a revitalized JMM process led to an October 2000 National Implementation Strategy and Business Plan, but like its 1995 predecessor, the plan set out no specific targets for each province or for any given economic sector and continued to rely primarily on appeals for voluntary action. At the federal level, voluntary action was to be induced by government spending for technological development and the implementation of specific emission-reduction projects. However, during 2002 the JMM process fractured completely in the face of the stresses associated with ratification of the Kyoto Protocol, with the federal government pressing for sector-specific targets and the use of more coercive instruments, as opposed to staying the course with a voluntary regime, while Alberta pushed for a much softer approach.

2002–6: Federal Unilateralism and Bilateral Engagement with Provinces

With the collapse of the intergovernmental process, the federal government started down the path of unilateral policy development and implementation. The Chrétien government released its own climate change plan in November (Canada, 2002) and proceeded, over provincial objections, to hold a ratification vote on the Kyoto Protocol in the House of Commons on 10 December. Five days later, the federal Minister of Natural Resources released an open letter to the Canadian Association of Petroleum Producers, setting out commitments made during secret negotiations between the federal government and industries that fall. The oil and gas sector was limited to reducing emissions by no more than 15 per cent, measured on an intensity basis, and all industrial sectors would be subsidized for all reduction costs greater than $15 per tonne of carbon dioxide equivalent (Natural Resources Canada, 2002).

By 2003 there were no longer any institutional mechanisms in place for the multilateral co-ordination of climate policy. Between 2003 and 2006 the only co-ordination was a federal effort to negotiate bilateral agreements with the provinces and territories. The effort was backed with offers of substantial federal funding. By the fall of 2006, the government of Canada had entered into six such agreements: Nunavut, 2003; PEI, 2003; Manitoba,

2004; Newfoundland, 2004; Ontario, 2004; and Saskatchewan, 2005 (Manson, 2006). Alberta took unilateral action of its own, adopting in 2002 a climate change plan with provincial targets significantly weaker than the Canadian national target under Kyoto, and announcing it would enact climate change legislation of its own, in part to forestall federal regulation within its borders.

Although the bilateral agreements contained virtually no specific commitments for either party, they did provide the framework for shared-cost funding of specific projects, backed initially by a $250 million partnership fund, with the potential to increase to $2–$3 billion in the 2005 federal budget (Canada, 2005: 189). The more serious intent of the federal government, now led by former Chrétien finance minister Paul Martin, was also demonstrated by the December 2005 addition of the six Kyoto GHGs to the list of 'toxic' substances under the *Canadian Environmental Protection Act* (**CEPA**), providing the federal government with the legislative authority to regulate their emissions. Official notice of pending emissions regulations for LFEs was issued at the same time (Canada, 2005a).

2006–8: Kyoto Abandonment and the Emergence of Sub-national Initiatives

The third period in Canadian climate policy ran from the arrival of the minority Stephen Harper Conservative government in January 2006 to the fall of 2008. During that time, climate policy moved in two different directions. The federal government, motivated primarily by ideology (Harrison, 2007), sought in 2006 to weaken the climate policy being implemented by the Liberal government it replaced, by abandoning the Kyoto objective of reducing emissions to 6 per cent below 1990s levels, cutting climate policy spending, changing the base-line against which reductions are measured from 1992 to 2006 (thus seeking roughly similar cuts from a level more than 25 per cent higher) and moving further into the future the time-table for implementation of industry regulation. Then, in 2006, in the face of increasing public concern about the environment and particularly climate change, it proposed a program for industry regulation, albeit with weaker targets than those of the preceding Liberal government, under the auspices of a *Clean Air Act*, amending CEPA. Faced with Parliamentary opposition, the government abandoned that approach and instead proposed a 'Regulatory Framework for Air Emissions (April 2007)' to be implemented through the existing CEPA, embodying emission reduction targets comparable or (as the government claimed) more stringent than those proposed by the Liberal government. On the surface the government's approach appeared to be a return to unilateralism. Yet provincial objections were initially surprisingly muted, perhaps because there was a tacit understanding that the much weaker federal requirements were not likely to be vigorously applied. This understanding, which may also explain the lack of provincial objections to federal regulation in 2003, was reinforced by the federal government's willingness to enter into 'equivalency' agreements with the provinces under CEPA, providing that the federal regulations would not apply in those provinces. By spring 2011, the federal government had yet to actually implement any regulations under the plan.

While the federal government was variously weakening, strengthening and then ultimately putting its climate policy on hold, some provinces began for the first time to put in place potentially effective measures (Pembina Institute, 2009). In June 2006 Quebec launched a comprehensive *2006–2012 Action Plan* for climate change that included a tax on refineries, new tailpipe emission standards, alternative energy targets and reduction targets for various industrial sectors. Ontario announced its *Go-Green* climate change plan in June 2007. Its centrepiece, an earlier commitment to phase out coal-fired electricity generation, was supplemented by major investments in public transit and a cap-and-trade system for other large industrial sources. British Columbia undertook a major repositioning on the climate change issue, moving from being part of the 'blocking' coalition led by Alberta to being a leader on climate change policy. As part of its June 2008 *Climate Change Action Plan*, BC imposed a $15 tonne carbon tax (scheduled to rise to $30/tonne by 2012) on fossil fuels, effective 1 July 2008. The province subsequently announced complementary energy and transit plans, and committed to developing a cap-and-trade system for industrial emissions.

Although with very weak standards, Alberta had earlier, in 2002, adopted climate change legislation and then in 2007 imposed regulatory requirements on the intensity of industrial GHG emissions. While the Quebec, Ontario and BC actions represented genuine changes in policy, the earlier Alberta action was explicitly designed to forestall federal regulation of Alberta GHG sources. The Alberta Environment Minister Lorne Taylor said on November 11, 2002: 'Alberta will introduce legislation giving it complete authority to implement climate change policies and block any attempt by the federal government to impose the Kyoto Protocol treaty in the province' (*National Post*, cited in Houle, 2009: 13).

In addition to these individual initiatives, a number of collaborative initiatives on climate change began to emerge among sub-national governments from 2006 onwards. The provinces attempted to work out a common approach to climate change through a succession of Council of the Federation meetings (May and August 2007) and a January 2008 Premiers' Forum on Climate Change. The primary result of these efforts, however, was to make more apparent the extent of provincial differences. Alberta Premier Stelmach publicly declared 'mission accomplished' after derailing an Ontario-led effort to establish a national cap-and-trade system among the provinces (Benzie and Gordon, 2007). The effort to work together in a national policy process, despite the significant differences in interest that had characterized the provinces' behaviour during the multilateral phase of Canadian climate change policy formulation, collapsed completely. The provinces are now deeply divided into two camps: Ontario, Quebec, Manitoba and BC in one camp; Alberta and, after the arrival of the Saskatchewan Party government in 2008, Saskatchewan, in the other.

Sub-national groupings of US states were also taking action independently of their federal government, with more initial success than their Canadian counterparts. The Western Climate Initiative (**WCI**), which emerged in February 2007, was initially a partnership between the states of California, Arizona, New Mexico, Oregon and Washington. It was focused on the development of a common, regional GHG emission reduction target (ultimately a 15 per cent reduction from 2005 levels by 2020) and the creation of a regional cap-and-trade system for GHGs. The initiative took on a transboundary aspect with BC's decision to join in April 2007, followed by Manitoba in June. Quebec and Ontario became WCI partners in April and July of the following year, respectively. Ontario also announced its intent to join a second regional initiative, the Regional Greenhouse Gas Initiative, among North-eastern American states[1] in March 2007. A Midwestern Greenhouse Gas Reduction initiative has also emerged among the

Midwestern states (http://www.midwesternaccord.org/), with Manitoba as a member and Ontario as an observer.[2]

2008: The 'Green shift', Obama and Sub-national Transnational Multilateralism

The beginning of the fourth period in Canadian climate change policy was defined by two electoral events in the fall of 2008. The October 14 Canadian federal election, which was marked by the defeat of Liberal leader Stéphane Dion's ambitious 'Green shift'—an ecological fiscal reform proposal of a carbon tax and offsetting reductions in personal and corporate income taxes—initially suggested that the Harper government had successfully managed its effective withdrawal from the Kyoto commitment, although the Conservatives had still obtained nothing more than a minority government. The US election on 4 November resulted in a new administration under President Barack Obama and strong democratic majorities in both houses of the US Congress. Obama came to office in part on the basis of a *Climate and Energy Plan* centred on a cap-and-trade system that aimed for an 80 per cent reduction in GHG emissions from 1990 levels by 2050. The plan also included $150 billion in investments in clean energy and green job creation, along with more specific proposals to boost building energy efficiency, build a smart electricity grid, and encourage public transportation.[3]

The day after President Obama was elected, the federal Ministers of the Environment and Foreign Affairs announced that Canada would propose to the US negotiation of a new treaty, intended to address both climate change and North American energy security. The response from the new US administration was lukewarm at best and the only outcome of Obama's visit to Ottawa in February, 2009 was a 'Clean Energy Dialogue' consisting of periodic meetings of US and Canadian officials (Hale, 2010). Rather than a treaty with Canada, the US administration was focused on the adoption of a 'stimulus' package in response to the economic crisis of the fall of 2008; it included extensive funding for energy efficiency, renewable energy, and public transit (West, 2009).

The details of US climate change policy, effectively delegated by the administration to the US Congress, saw the adoption of a *Clean Energy and Security Act* by the House of Representatives in June 2009. In addition to establishing targets of a 3 per cent absolute reduction in GHG emissions relative to 2005 by 2012, 17 per cent by 2020, and 83 per cent by 2050, the bill included provisions for 'border tax adjustments' (i.e., carbon tariffs) on imports to the United States if no binding international agreement or equivalent domestic policies were in place in the country of export by 2020 (Pew, 2010). With the *Clean Energy and Security Act* delayed in the US Senate, in December 2009 the administration opened the possibility of regulating GHG emissions under the US federal *Clean Air Act* without congressional action through an 'endangerment' finding under the act with respect to GHGs (Reguly, 2009a). The finding effectively permits the US federal government to regulate GHGs like other air pollutants under the Act, although the timetable upon which such action might occur remains uncertain at best. In the 2 November 2010 mid-term elections, Republicans gained control of the House of Representatives, making climate legislation extremely unlikely. Nevertheless, President Obama said he still planned to act on the issue and, beginning 1 January 2011, EPA started to introduce climate change regulations.

Despite its efforts to lower expectations on the outcome of the upcoming December 2009 Copenhagen UNFCCC Conference of the Parties (**CoP**) (McCarthy, 2009), the Harper government found itself under increasing international pressure to strengthen its commitments to action on climate change (Smith, 2009). Unlike the situation leading into the Kyoto negotiations, these pressures had no impact on the Canadian government's negotiating position. The Canadian government's position was helped in part by the fact that the US was very late in putting its position on the table, and ultimately only committed to 17 per cent reduction in emissions relative to 2005 by 2020 (Woods, 2009).

The Copenhagen CoP did not result in a new binding agreement; the 'Copenhagen Accord' was an agreement amongst the US, China, and a limited number of other countries, which was only 'noted' by the formal CoP. Nevertheless, the Canadian federal government adopted a policy of 'continentalization' of Canada's GHG emission targets, presenting in January, 2010 a new reduction target of 17 per cent reduction by 2020 relative to 2005, in order to ensure policy was 'completely aligned' with the US target and 'subject to adjustment to remain consistent' (Government of Canada, 2010). Federal environment minister Jim Prentice noted that 'It is absolutely counter-productive and utterly pointless for Canada and Canadian businesses to strike out on their own, to set and to pursue targets that will ultimately create barriers to trade and put us at a competitive disadvantage' (Government of Canada, 2010).

Moreover, the implementation schedules for Canadian emission controls on LFEs were tied to the pace of action in US (McCarthy and Galloway, 2010). The federal government's one area of significant action, the adoption of more stringent vehicle fuel economy standards, was entirely driven by the need to harmonize standards with those being adopted by the Obama administration in the 2009 bailout of the North American automobile industry (Keenan and McCarty, 2010). The measure was effectively the first product of the Canadian federal government's new approach of moving in lockstep with its US counterpart.

Surprisingly, however, with respect to another LFE sector, electricity, the government has said it will act independently of the US. On 23 June 2010, Environment Canada announced plans to regulate emissions from coal-fired electricity plants once the existing fleet of facilities reaches the end of its economic life in approximately 2025, despite the absence of any comparable US regulatory initiative (Environment Canada, 2010c). Thus current federal policy seems to be aligned with US policy for some LFE sectors and not for others; there is no clear statement of the criteria used to decide which are aligned and which are not.

The fourth period story at the sub-national level was, at least initially, more hopeful. Ontario, Quebec, and BC all adopted cap-and-trade legislation for GHG emissions in anticipation of the development of a continental cap-and-trade system under the auspices of the WCI (Pembina, 2009). Manitoba committed to adopting similar legislation (Manitoba, 2009). All four provinces continued to implement other aspects of their climate change plans (Pembina, 2009). Ontario, for example, adopted a regulation requiring the phase out of its coal-fired power plants by the end of 2014 (Ontario, 2007). Saskatchewan and BC have publicly stated they plan to sign 'equivalency agreements' with the federal government (Saskatchewan, 2009; Environment Canada, 2010d). In neither case is the agreement a codification of co-ordinated policy developed by the jurisdictions. Instead, it is exactly the opposite: an institutional locking in of provincial unilateralism, by means of a guarantee given by the federal government that it will not regulate within their borders.

The WCI, which was emerging as the dominant North American sub-national initiative on GHG emissions, initially made good progress on the design of its cap-and-trade and offset systems. Montana and Utah became partners, and six other states (Alaska, Colorado, Idaho, Nevada, Wyoming and Kansas), several Canadian provinces (Nova Scotia, Saskatchewan, and the Yukon Territory), and a number of Mexican states became observers. However, by the middle of 2009 the initiative ran into difficulties in some key US states. The Washington, Oregon and Arizona legislatures rejected cap-and-trade legislation to implement the WCI initiative (Barringer, 2010). Although on 2 November, 2010, California rejected a ballot proposition to suspend that state's climate legislation, the fate of the WCI is now uncertain. This development has major implications for the Canadian provinces, as the WCI was the foundation of provincial level initiatives on LFEs.

Explaining the Evolution of Canadian National Climate Change Policy-making

The evolution of the Canadian national process from multilateral and bilateral policy-making within Canadian borders (albeit always with a keen concern for US policy) to a process completely and explicitly aligned with US policy at both jurisdictional levels has been driven by a number of factors. On the US side, in the absence of action by the George W. Bush administration, some states, led by California, started to act independently. They were driven by various concerns about the impacts of climate change, potential economic opportunities, strong policy capacity around energy and environmental issues, and political opportunity in light of growing public concern over the environment in general and the climate change issue in particular. Competitiveness considerations motivated activist states to draw in as many others as possible, including Canadian provinces in their economic regions (Rabe, 2004; 2009; Macdonald and VanNijnatten, 2010). Although state officials in bodies like the WCI recognized from the start that their policies would eventually need to be harmonized with US federal policy, state initiatives have remained in place because the new Obama administration has given less priority to climate change than health care and other issues, stalling the possibility of action by the US federal government.

Provincial participation in the emergent sub-national initiatives has been propelled by a mix of factors as well. They include the need to create markets large enough for cap-and-trade systems to be viable, competitiveness concerns in terms of ensuring that other jurisdictions within their regions are subject to a regulatory regime for GHG emissions as well, and finally concerns over access to the US market in the face of Canadian federal inaction. Access concerns arose because the climate change legislation introduced in the US Congress, like the McCain-Lieberman *Climate Stewardship and Innovation Act*, included trade-related measures against exports from jurisdictions with less stringent climate change policies. Other factors particular to each province also explain provincial action: in BC, for example, the personal views of the Premier combined with electoral calculations, and in Ontario concern over distributional impacts of the Harper government's approach to the issue (Urquhart, 2007).

Performance of the Current National Policy-making System

As can be seen by the foregoing account, the process for developing and implementing national Canadian climate policy has evolved considerably since the early 1990s. This section evaluates the performance of the current policy-making system in place since the election of President Obama in November 2008, using the criteria for performance evaluation set out by the editors in the Introduction to this text. It first describes the current system, primarily by distinguishing it from the traditional system for developing federal–provincial national environmental policy; second, it evaluates that system, using the criteria of consistency with federal principles, workability, and ability to generate consensus; third, briefly explains why, in our view, the current system has come into being; and, finally, it provides suggestions for fixing what we see as a dysfunctional system in the conclusion of the chapter.

A number of analysts have described the establishment and evolution of traditional environmental federalism (Harrison, 1996, 2002). The corner-stone is the courts' ruling that both levels of government share constitutional jurisdiction for regulating pollution. More specifically there is a strong consensus among legal scholars that the federal government has the constitutional authority to regulate the emissions of GHGs under CEPA (Hogg, 2008), as well as to levy a carbon tax if it chooses to do so (Chalifour, 2009). Since both levels of government have moved to exercise that authority with respect to pollution, the need to co-ordinate their policy-making has been apparent since the early 1970s. Two major institutional forms have been used.

The first is multilateral policy development by committees of federal and provincial officials, operating under the auspices of the Canadian Council of Ministers of the Environment (**CCME**). That process became formalized in the 1990s, with federal–provincial negotiation of the 1998 Harmonization Accord. The Accord is a system for consensual discussion, characterized by lowest-common-denominator decisions that, the courts have ruled, have no legal force. Implementation of those decisions is completely at the discretion of the participating jurisdictions, with no binding requirements to even report to the CCME or any other body on actions taken (Winfield and Macdonald, 2008).

The other major institutional form of federal–provincial policy co-ordination is bilateral negotiations and agreements. A number of these agreements were signed in the mid-1970s and then again in the 1980s, following multilateral federal–provincial development of the 1985 national acid rain program. As noted earlier, following the breakdown of the JMM process, the Martin government began to pursue bilateral agreements for the co-ordination of federal and provincial climate change policy.

The multilateral and bilateral systems are still functioning with respect to environmental issues other than climate change. National climate change policy-making, however, has moved into a very different institutional form. The most notable feature is that the Canadian federal–provincial process is now embedded within the US process at two levels, federal and sub-national. However, there is no institutionalized connection between the two levels. While, for instance, state and provincial officials engaged in development of WCI policy exchange information regularly with their counterparts in both Washington and Ottawa, there are no written agreements or regular meetings that include federal officials from the two countries and relevant state and provincial officials. There is no one organizational mechanism to co-ordinate all policy activity amongst governments in the two countries and at both levels. Nor, within Canada, is there institutionalized co-ordination between the two levels; there is no mechanism for discussions among the WCI, Midwestern Greenhouse Gas Accord, New England–Atlantic associations, and the Canadian federal government.

Within the US, it is accepted by all policy makers that federal–state institutional co-ordination will emerge if and when Washington enacts climate legislation. As has happened before, it is likely federal law will be influenced in its design by state-level policy, but will pre-empt state legislation (Rabe, 2009). There is no similar acceptance of the need for federal–provincial co-ordination within Canada. As noted, Alberta has enacted climate-change law precisely to prevent federal regulation. The Saskatchewan 2009 agreement in principle to negotiate an equivalency agreement has the same purpose. The Canadian federal government may have the constitutional and legal authority to ensure uniformity, but unlike its American counterpart, some key provinces question the legitimacy of its exercise of that authority with regard to climate change. The Canadian government simply does not have, in practice, the same power to ensure uniformity as its American counterpart.

In addition to a lack of institutionalization between the two levels of government, there is a similar lack of institutionalization between the two countries at each level. To address pollution, the US and Canadian governments have signed treaties, such as the 1972 Great Lakes Water Quality Agreement and the 1991 Air Quality Accord, which are given force by domestic legislation in each country. As noted, the Government of Canada proposed to the US a comparable climate treaty in the fall of 2008, but was rebuffed. This means that, currently, the only institutional basis for policy co-operation by the two federal governments is a 2002 Joint Statement of Intent to engage in bilateral efforts to address climate change and the comparable 2009 Clean Energy Dialogue. Nor does sub-national cross-border collaboration rest on a secure institutional footing. Being sub-national governments, provinces and states cannot enter into agreements comparable to those between sovereign states. The fragility of even the most advanced of the sub-national initiatives, the WCI, has been highlighted by the objections of some state legislatures to the participation of their executive branches in the effort, emphasizing the potential limits of executive federalism under the separation of powers system on which the US federal and state governments are based.

Within Canada, policy co-ordination is either cursory or, amongst some provinces, takes place only within the context of the cross-border, sub-national arrangements like the WCI. The Council of the Federation, which includes all provinces (but not the federal government), has been unable to agree on climate policy, due to the veto-state actions of Alberta, noted above. The Harper government has routinely referred to 'consulting with the provinces' as it has introduced federal policy, and on 25 November 2009 all environment ministers met to discuss Canada's position at the upcoming Copenhagen Conference of Parties (Environment Canada, 2009). That meeting is the only time all ministers have met since the Harper government was elected in January, 2006. Clearly one meeting was not enough to establish accord, given the provincial criticisms of federal policy, referred to below.

Otherwise, federal and provincial governments are simply proceeding to develop their own climate-change policy with no attempt to consult or co-ordinate action with other Canadian governments. There may have been informal discussion but none of the major steps taken to date by the Harper government (the 2006 Clean Air Act; 2007 Turning the Corner plan; 2008 proposal for a Canada–US treaty) has been preceded by formal, publicly visible discussion with the provinces. On 10 June 2009, then Environment Minister Prentice announced his government was developing plans for offsets to be used in a national trading system. He acknowledged provinces were also developing trading plans and said simply: 'The initiative I am announcing today will complement those efforts, not supplant or duplicate them' (Prentice, 2009). How they would complement one another, absent mechanisms for co-ordination, was not discussed. Targets in the climate change plans of Nova Scotia (2009), Ontario (2007) and BC (2008) were set without any consideration of the extent to which they contributed to achieving an overall Canadian target (confidential interviews). Alberta set a very different target from that of the country as a whole in 2002, at the demise of the federal–provincial process.

To summarize, the current national climate policy is characterized by three features: it is embedded in US systems and policy leadership is coming from that country; it lacks a strong institutional structure; and it consists primarily of unilateral, rather than co-ordinated action. To the extent co-ordination is being achieved, it is through the new system of cross-border, sub-national negotiation. In the following section, we evaluate and explain the policy outcomes generated by that system. Here we do the same for the system itself.

The first criterion of performance is 'consistency with federal principles', defined as both providing jurisdictional autonomy within the constitutionally-recognized sphere of action and as balancing that diversity with national unity. It would seem that the first criterion is being met. Both Alberta and Saskatchewan have acted to ward off federal regulation within their borders, but they must have been given enough private assurances that that will not happen, since neither has made public complaint. The Harper government, reacting to such things as BC policy leadership which far exceeds its own, has consistently said provinces are free to develop their own policy. Federal criticism of Quebec motor vehicle regulation was dropped after both governments harmonized their standards by adopting those negotiated by California and Washington. Autonomy certainly exists; national unity, on the other hand, does not.

The second performance criterion is 'workability', defined as providing forums in which governments can work together, even if only to exchange information. This criterion is not met. The Council of the Federation is such a potential forum, but since it has not generated any policy decisions it can hardly be said to be working. Since the demise of the 1992–2002 multilateral process, there has been no organizational body bringing all governments together on a regular basis.

Thirdly, performance is measured by 'capacity to produce results' in terms of overcoming conflicts and reaching agreement. Again, this criterion is not met. The fundamental conflict in Canadian climate-change policy is between the carbon provinces—Alberta and Saskatchewan—and those who, for a variety of reasons, are prepared to take more substantial action to reduce emissions. The current system precludes any possibility of bridging that divide, because the provinces involved have moved into separate institutional forums: autonomous action and the WCI. Since they no longer meet to discuss common policy, the two camps cannot possibly reach agreement.

Policy Outcomes

The outcomes of Canadian national climate change policy-making, both in the original multilateral form and the more recent US-embedded form, can only be described as failures. Federal and provincial officials devoted considerable time and energy to development of national policy through the JMM process in place from 1992 to 2002. The most significant policy outcome was the Voluntary Climate Registry (VCR)/EcoGESte program, which was widely regarded as an abject failure in terms of producing GHG emission reductions from the LFEs; in providing an appearance of action, it provided an excuse for inaction (Bramley, 2002). It was, however, the only policy option available in 1995, not only because of the Alberta veto but also because no other federal or provincial government was willing to consider law-based regulation.

The federal government began to consider regulatory options prior to collapse of the program in 2002, but did not adopt the recognized method of inducing firm behaviour change through voluntary programs: that is, threatening regulation if the program is ineffective. Instead, the federal government simply abandoned the program (Macdonald, Houle and Patterson, forthcoming). Nor yet did the federal government engage in the diplomacy needed for the JMM process to bridge the emerging provincial divide. Instead, it set aside the federal–provincial agreed position for Canada to take into the 1997 Kyoto negotiations. Then in 2002 it opted for unilateral, direct federal regulation with no real effort to negotiate with Alberta, and ignoring the unanimous provincial request that the process be moved up from ministers to First Ministers prior to ratification. Throughout this period, the federal government was unable to resolve the internal conflict between Environment Canada and Natural Resources Canada. The failure of the JMM process to generate meaningful policy options was perhaps pre-ordained, given sharply diverging provincial interests, but it was also due to inept federal leadership.

The 2003–6 period of federal unilateralism and bilateral engagement with the provinces may have laid the groundwork for the substantive action in the future, particularly through the addition of the Kyoto GHGs to Schedule 1 of CEPA, but the actual policy outputs were limited to the series of bilateral agreements between the federal government and some provinces and territories. Although the specific provincial commitments contained in the agreements were vague, the federal funding which flowed through the agreements does seem to have facilitated some provincial level initiatives. Ontario, for example, has indicated that it used the funding it received to support its phase-out of coal-fired electricity (Ontario, 2007a).

Other than action by some provinces, the overall substantive result has been a near total failure to reduce greenhouse gas emissions since Canadian governments first began to commit to action on climate change in the early 1990s. Rather, there was a steady increase in GHG emissions between 1990 and 2003. As shown in Figure 13.1 emissions then levelled off from 2003 onwards, declining 0.8 per cent between 2003 and 2008 (Environment Canada, 2010a). However, the fluctuations in emissions since 2003 have

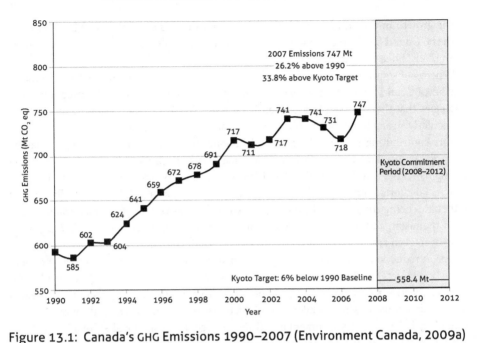

Figure 13.1: Canada's GHG Emissions 1990–2007 (Environment Canada, 2009a)

Source: Environment Canada. 2009a. `Canada's 2007 Greenhouse Gas Inventory: A Summary of Trends' accessed at http://www.ec.gc.ca/Publications/default.asp?lang=En&xml=F62F0CF4-5254-45F2-9365-B01BE0576174 October 25, 2010. Reproduced with the permission of the Minister of Public Works and Government Services Canada, 2011.

been attributed by Environment Canada to changes in the mix of sources used for electricity production (coal use varied with the availability of hydro and nuclear generation); changing emissions from fossil fuel production (as a result of the level of petroleum extraction activities); and varying demand for heating fuels for winters. Large increases in areas such as Transportation and Mining and Oil and Gas Extraction were offset by declines in emissions from manufacturing (Environment Canada, 2010a). None of the reductions could be attributed to any federal or national action on climate change.

Evaluations of the federal government's current climate change strategy are negative. The conclusion of the Commissioner for Environment and Sustainable Development and the National Round Table on the Environment and Economy, as mandated by the *Kyoto Protocol Implementation Act, 2007* (a Liberal private member's bill passed in the context of the minority parliament), is that not only has the federal government abandoned the Kyoto target, but the emission reductions from its current and proposed measures are likely 'overestimated' (NRTEE, 2009) and are unlikely to be adequate to meet even the government's reduced emission reduction targets (CESD, 2009). The federal government's own 2010 report filed under the *Kyoto Protocol Implementation Act* indicated that earlier reports had overstated the likely emission reductions flowing from some of the government's existing and proposed measures between 2010–12 by a factor of ten (Environment Canada, 2009, 2010b). The current federal government has failed to make any effort to develop a national policy that would address, in particular, the situation in Alberta and now Saskatchewan with respect to the upstream oil and gas sector, which is the key driver of the growth in Canada's emissions. At the same time it is using the need for alignment with the United States to defer action on LFES, even though regulations for the sector have been ready since the end of 2005.

Where substantive action has occurred, it has been at the provincial level. Ontario, Quebec, BC, and Manitoba have been making progress towards the implementation of the strategies that they adopted independently between 2006 and 2008. Movement has been particularly strong in relation to transportation and electricity (Pembina, 2009). One of the factors contributing to the stabilization of national GHG emissions, for example, may be Ontario's reduced reliance on coal-fired electricity, with the province's coal-fired generation falling by 73 per cent between 2003 and 2009 (OCAA, 2010; see also ECO, 2010). However, provincial efforts with respect to cap-and-trade systems for LFEs have been stalled by the difficulties being encountered by the WCI, on whose framework the provincial strategies had been premised, and more general uncertainty regarding future US climate change policy. Moreover, even among the more active provinces, significant gaps remain between the GHG emission reduction measures that they have planned or have in place and their emission reduction targets (on BC see Pembina, 2009, on Ontario see ECO, 2009). More broadly, absent an effective national regime, those provinces that are the key drivers of the increases in Canada's emissions may undermine reductions in emissions achieved by others. The Canadian federal, intergovernmental and the emergent transnational sub-national initiatives have yet to demonstrate any capacity to deal with that problem.

Legitimacy of the Current National Policy-making System and Its Outcomes

This section examines the appropriateness of governing arrangements and their outcomes in the eyes of the major Canadian climate-change policy constituencies. The latter are participating governments themselves, opposition parties in the House of Commons, relevant industrial sectors, environmentalists, and Canadian citizens. We also give our own evaluation of the legitimacy of the current system and its outcomes in terms of two criteria: the ability to meet Canadian international commitments and democratic accountability.

Their actions indicate that participating governments view the evolution of the process toward US embeddedness as completely legitimate. At the federal level, the current system is not a sharp break from the past. Since 1992, with the sole exception of Kyoto ratification in 2002 (which is explained by exceptional circumstances, such as Prime Minister Chrétien's desire for a 'legacy' issue) successive Canadian federal governments have worked to ensure that Canadian policy, both at the international and domestic levels, did not deviate markedly from that of the US. What is different about the current era is that this harmonization is much more explicitly stated, both in the failed attempt by the Harper government to achieve a climate-change treaty and in the repeated references to the need for harmonization by the Environment Minister. That change is explained by the change in the US administration. During the Clinton and George W. Bush administrations, when it is clear there would be little US federal leadership, there was no need for explicit harmonization, since it could be provided implicitly by a comparable Canadian go-slow approach. With the election of an activist President in 2008, however, and the concurrent threat of impediments to trade due to lower Canadian standards, the Canadian federal government, driven like its predecessors by the imperative of maintaining access to the US market, had no choice but to *explicitly* adopt a policy of harmonization (Macdonald and VanNijnatten, 2010). The Harper government uses the criterion of a 'balance' between economy and environment and the need for 'long-term' solutions to legitimize its policy actions to date (Prentice, 2009).

Canadian provinces participating in the New England/Atlantic, Midwestern and WCI cross-border arrangements (all but Alberta and Saskatchewan) obviously see those forums as legitimate. Until 2002, they worked to co-ordinate their policy by participating in the Canadian federal–provincial process and now they are co-ordinating instead with US states. Alberta and Saskatchewan participated in the Canadian process, but Alberta did so with the objective not of co-ordination but instead of ensuring that the process did not impose what it saw as unacceptable costs on the oil and gas industry (Macdonald, 2009). Now they are working to achieve that same objective of policy autonomy by staying out of the cross-border processes. Neither provincial government has stated it views the processes as illegitimate. In terms of current federal government policy decisions, however, some provinces do have reservations respecting legitimacy. At Copenhagen, Ontario and Quebec took the extraordinary step of criticizing federal policy, calling for a 'tougher position' (Reguly, 2009b).

Similarly, federal opposition parties seem to accept the legitimacy of Canada–US joint policy, but have questioned the legitimacy of the Harper government's abandonment of Canada's Kyoto commitment. They have taken a number of unsuccessful actions in the House of Commons to force the Harper government to accept the Kyoto objective of a reduction of emissions to 6 per cent below 1990 levels. The 2006 Clean Air Act was sent to a special committee of the House, where it was significantly strengthened by the opposition majority on the committee, but was never brought back to the House by the government. An opposition private member's bill requiring the government to implement a plan that would reach the Kyoto target was adopted in the House and then effectively ignored by the government. (A court action by environmentalists requiring the government to comply with the House decision was unsuccessful.) Opposition parties measure the legitimacy of the Canadian government's climate change policy by Canada's failure to comply with the international regime to which it is a party, rather than viewing these international treaties as an abandonment of Canadian sovereignty

Canadian industry, as represented by associations such as the Canadian Council of Chief Executives (CCCE) or the Canadian Association of Petroleum Producers (CAPP), is not at all troubled by closer co-ordination of policy with that of the US. Given its fundamental objective of ensuring access to the US market, this is hardly surprising. During the Kyoto ratification debate of 2002, relevant business actors argued Canada should abandon the Kyoto regime and instead align its policy with that of the US (Macdonald, 2007). Now that the federal government has explicitly followed that advice, industry, of course, offers no criticism. The major business pre-occupation is with attacks on the legitimacy of oil sands' critiques from environmentalists inside Canada; they fear it may influence border access, in the US. In response, CAPP has initiated a 'dialogue with Canadians' which includes an advertising campaign, industry representatives' speeches, media relations, energy literacy initiatives and other elements (CAPP, undated).

Environmentalists, like other Canadian policy actors, have not argued that ceding policy-making authority to the US is in any way illegitimate. Instead, they have generally welcomed cross-border initiatives like the WCI, since they are associated with at least some policy movement in provinces like BC. Instead, their critique focuses upon both the failure of the Harper government to develop effective policy and the entire oil sands project itself. Indeed the government was awarded the dubious honour of being labelled 'Fossil of the Year' by environmental non-governmental organizations (ENGOs) following the Copenhagen negotiations. Data on Canadian citizens' support for policy action on the environment show it reached an all-time high in 2007 and then declined significantly with the recession of 2008. Despite this, the environment continued to be identified in national public opinion polls as the third most important issue facing Canada up to the May 2011 federal election (Nanos, 2011), although it did not prevent the Harper government from obtaining majority in that election.

In summary, the evolution of the national climate policy process, from the traditional form of federal–provincial environmental policy-making in the 1990s to the current, very different, process, has not raised legitimacy concerns amongst the relevant constituencies. Instead, various actors have questioned the legitimacy of the abandonment of Canada's international obligation as a member of the Kyoto regime and criticized the ineffectiveness of current federal government policy and the oil sands development project itself.

Conclusion

Canadian national climate change policy is now made through weakly institutionalized Canada–US co-ordination at the national and sub-national levels, with almost no co-ordination between those two levels. The two Canadian governments with highest per capita emissions and therefore the most to lose from effective national policy, Alberta and Saskatchewan, stand apart from this new, two-country, two-level system and instead are implementing unilateral policy. Given these provinces' current objectives, their policies will undercut all other Canadian mitigation efforts. There is no formal, institutionalized federal–provincial process for making national policy. Canadian federalism is no longer working in this particular issue area. For a number of reasons, most notably the veto-state role consistently played by Alberta and the absence of a committed leader state at the federal or provincial level, Canadian intergovernmental relations have been unable to generate effective policy. From the 1960s on, Canadian federalism was strong enough to meet the challenge posed by Québécois nationalist aspirations, but it has since been unable to meet the subsequent challenge of reducing GHG emissions in a continentally integrated economy.

That said, the new process is generating better policy outcomes than did the traditional climate policy process up to 2006, particularly at the provincial level. The Harper government at least moved to impose new vehicle efficiency regulations because of its policy of US alignment. More broadly, the inaction on the part of the US administration has provided the justification for continued inaction on the part of the Canadian federal government, and some provinces are acting in part due to US sub-national leadership.

The current situation is nonetheless ultimately unacceptable. Canada has failed utterly to produce an effective national policy response despite what is now an overwhelming scientific and economic consensus regarding the urgency of action on the climate change problem, and that delay only raises the impacts and costs of both mitigation and adaptation. Canada's economic interests are poorly served by simply moving lockstep with the US federal government. In early 2011, the likelihood of major action at the federal level in the US is at best uncertain, and even if a federal regime were to emerge, its design would respond to economic concerns in the US, not Canada. The emergence of trans-border sub-national initiatives on climate change is a major new development in North American federalism. Initiatives such as the WCI are becoming major forums for climate change policy development, but as recent events have demonstrated, they are inherently unstable. Moreover, these initiatives are only coalitions of the willing, within which the jurisdictions who account for the bulk of the growth in Canada's GHG emissions have declined to participate.

What can be done? In the short term, there is really no option other than continuation of the development of the sub-national, cross-border initiatives. At present, they represent the only game in town and are actively engaging with the technical and policy challenges that must be addressed. Ultimately, however, the Canadian federal government must show policy leadership, first by setting policy goals commensurate with the scale of the threat posed by climate change and, secondly, in clearly demonstrating it is willing to use the full range of regulatory, fiscal, and other policy tools available to it in order to achieve those goals. Such a display of a willingness to act unilaterally, in the face of resistance from some provinces, is the best way to re-engage with the provinces. Although objecting, those provinces will at least come to the table to engage in federal–provincial negotiation. Ideally, that would lead to a renewed multilateral policy-making process. If it does not, the federal government will have to act alone, using federal law and other policy instruments.

So far, the political and economic incentives needed for the federal government and provinces to engage with the level of seriousness and commitment required have been absent. The one thing that has prompted responses from all of the provinces and the federal government, and that might provide such incentives, has been threat of the loss of market access for exports. This may be what will compel even the carbon provinces either to accept a federal regulatory and policy regime, developed through intergovernmental negotiation, or even imposed to some degree unilaterally by the federal government, or to implement more effective regimes in co-ordination with the federal government and the other provinces themselves.

Some sort of 'border adjustment' will likely form part of any national GHG emission reduction regime that eventually emerges in the US. However, in light of the recent failure of congressional action on climate change and the difficulties now facing the Obama administration, when such a regime will emerge is now at best an open question. A climate change framework at the international level that includes trade-related measures seems even more remote. The absence of these external drivers, and the urgent need to prevent what the IPCC has termed 'dangerous' climate change, makes leadership from the Canadian federal government even more imperative.

Notes

1. The signatories to the December 2009 RGGI Memorandum of Agreement are Connecticut, Delaware, Maine, Maryland, Massachusetts, New Hampshire, New Jersey, New York, Rhode Island, and Vermont.
2. The State members are Iowa, Illinois, Kansas, Michigan, Minnesota, and Wisconsin. Indiana, Ohio and South Dakota are observers.
3. See http://www.barackobama.com/issues/newenergy/index.php.

References

Barringer, F. 2010. 'Cap-and-trade is Dead. Long Live Cap-and-trade'. Retrieved from *New York Times* Blogs, 28 July.

Benzie, R., and S. Gordon. 2007. 'McGuinty Shows bitterness in climate-change rebuff; Fails to seal premiers on pact to cut green-house gas; Alberta's Stelmach crows "mission accomplished"'. *The Toronto Star*, 11 August.

Bernstein, S., 2002. 'International Institutions and the framing of Domestic Policies: The Kyoto Protocol and Canada's Response to Climate Change', *Policy Sciences*, 35:203–36.

Bramley, M., 2002. *The Case for Kyoto: The Failure of Voluntary Corporate Action*. Drayton Valley: Pembina Institute.

Burke, B., and M. Ferguson. 2010. 'Going Alone or Moving Together: Canadian and American Middle Tier Strategies on Climate Change'. *Publius: The Journal of Federalism*, 40, 3: 436–59.

Canada. 2002. *Climate Change Plan for Canada: Achieving our Commitments Together*. http://publications.gc.ca/collections/Collection/En56-183-2002E.pdf

Canada. 2005. *2005 Budget Plan*. Ottawa: Department of Finance.

Canada. 2005. *Moving Forward on Climate Change: A Plan for Honouring our Kyoto Commitment*.

Canadian Association of Petroleum Producers (undated). 'Earning our Voice'. http://www.capp.ca/canadaIndustry/oilSands/Dialogue-Resources/Pages/JointheConversation.aspx#wXJON0n6qf9k, accessed 12 December 2011.

Chalifour, N.J. 2010. 'Chapter 10. The Constitutional Authority to Levy Carbon Taxes'. In *Canada: The State of the Federation 2009: Carbon Pricing and Environmental Federalism*, ed. T.J. Courchene and J.R. Allan.

Montreal and Kingston: McGill–Queen's University Press.

Climate Progress. 2010, July 16. 'Big Oil Showdown in California: Proposition 23 puts clean energy in danger', accessed at http://climateprogress.org/2010/07/16/california-proposition-23-clean-energy-climate-ab3/

Commissioner for Environment and Sustainable Development (CESD). 2009. 'Kyoto Protocol Implementation Act', *2009 Spring Report* online http://www.oag-bvg.gc.ca/internet/English/parl_cesd_200905_02_e_32512.html

Environment Canada, 2009. 'A Climate Change Plan for the Purposes of the *Kyoto Protocol Implementation Act*'. Ottawa, May. http://www.ec.gc.ca/doc/ed-es/KPIA2009/tdm-toc_eng.htm, accessed 7 June 2010.

Environment Canada. 2009a. 'Canada's 2007 Greenhouse Gas Inventory: A Summary of Trends', accessed at http://www.ec.gc.ca/Publications/default.asp?lang=En&xml=F62F0CF4-5254-45F2-9365-B01BE0576174 October 25, 2010.

Environment Canada. 2010a. 'A Summary of Trends 1990–2008', http://www.ec.gc.ca/ges-ghg/default.asp?lang=En&n=0590640B-1 accessed 1 June, 2010.

Environment Canada. 2010b. 'A Climate Change Plan for the Purposes of the *Kyoto Protocol Implementation Act*'. Ottawa: Environment Canada, May. http://www.climatechange.gc.ca/Content/4/0/4/4044AEA7-3ED0-4897-A73E-D11C62D954FD/KPIA_2010.pdf.

Environment Canada. 2010c. News Release 'Government of Canada to Regulate Emissions from Electricity Sector'. 23 June, 2010.

Environment Canada. 2010d. News Release 'Canada and British Columbia Sign Agreement to Address Climate Change'. 6 April, 2010.

Environmental Commissioner of Ontario. 2009. *Finding a Vision for Change: Annual Greenhouse Gas Progress Report 2008/09*. Toronto: December.

Environmental Commissioner of Ontario. 2010. *Broadening Ontario's Climate Change Policy Agenda: Annual Greenhouse Gas Progress Report 2010*. Toronto: May.

Government of Canada. 2010. 'Canada Lists Emissions Target under the Copenhagen Accord' February 1, http://www.climatechange.gc.ca/default.asp?lang=En&XML=D5E39C3A-C958-4876-8222-E3541F7B9C8D.

Hale, G.E. 2010. 'Canada–US Relations in the Obama Era: Warming or Greening?' In *How Ottawa Spends: 2010–2011*, ed. G.B. Doern and C. Stoney. Montreal and Kingston: McGill-Queens University Press.

Harrison, K. 1996. *Passing the Buck: Federalism and Canadian Environmental Policy*. Vancouver: UBC Press.

————. 2002. 'Federal–provincial Relations and the Environment: Unilateralism, Collaboration, and Rationalization'. In *Canadian Environmental Policy: Context and Cases*, ed. D.L. VanNijnatten and R. Boardman. Toronto: Oxford University Press.

————. 'The Road not Taken: Climate Change Policy in Canada and the United States'. *Global Environmental Politics*, 7, 4: 92–117.

Hogg, P. 2008. *A Question of Parliamentary Power: Criminal Law and the Control of Greenhouse Gas Emissions*. Toronto: CD Howe Institute.

Houle, D. 2009. 'Alberta climate change policy in the Canada–US context'. Paper presented at the 2009 Annual Meeting of the American Political Science Association. Toronto.

Keenan, G., and S. McCarthy. 2010. 'Ottawa puts hefty price on emission standards', *The Globe and Mail*, 25 May.

Macdonald, D. 2009. 'The failure of Canadian climate change policy: veto power, absent leadership and institutional weakness'. In *Canadian Environmental Policy: Prospects for Leadership and Innovation*, ed. D.L. VanNijnatten and R. Boardman. Toronto: Oxford University Press.

————. 2007. *Business and Environmental Politics in Canada*. Peterborough: Broadview.

Macdonald, D., and D.L. VanNijnatten. 2010. 'Canadian Climate Policy and the North American Influence'. In *Borders and Bridges:*

Canada's Policy Relations in North America, ed. M. Gattinger and G. Hale. Don Mills: Oxford University Press.

Macdonald, D., D. Houle, and C. Patterson. Forthcoming. 'L'utilisation du volontarisme afin de côntroler de gaz à effet de serre du secteur industriel: une comparaison des programmes ÉcoGESte et VCR'. In *L'experience des ententes volontaires dans les secteurs industriel au Québec*, ed. Jean Crête. Québec: Les Presses de l'Université Laval.

Manitoba. 2009. 'Premier commits Manitoba to move towards cap-and-trade legislation', News Release, December 15, http://www.gov.mb.ca/chc/press/top/2009/12/2009-12-15-111900-7325.html accessed 1 June, 2010.

Manson, A. 2006. Director General, Domestic Climate Change Policy, Environment Canada, personal communication with Douglas Macdonald, 31 Jan.

McCarthy, S., B. Curry, and G. Keenan. 2008. 'Ottawa moves to emulate US on new fuel mileage standards', *The Globe and Mail*, 17 January.

McCarthy, S. 2009. 'Ottawa dashes hopes for treaty in Copenhagen', *The Globe and Mail*, 23 October.

McCarthy, S., and Galloway, G. 2010. 'Ottawa stalls on oil and gas emission rules', *The Globe and Mail*, 16 April.

Nanos. 2011. 'Final Issue Trendline', 1 May. http://www.nanosresearch.com/election2011/20110501-IssueE.pdf

National Round Table on the Environment and Economy (NRTEE). 2009. 'Response of the National Round Table on the Environment and the Economy to its Obligations under the *Kyoto Protocol Implementation Act*' July 2009, http://nrtee-trnee.ca/eng/publications/KPIA-2009/Index-KPIA-NRTEE-Response-2009-eng.php

Natural Resources Canada. 2002. 'Government of Canada Responds to Industry Concerns about Climate Change', accompanying release of letter from the Hon. Herb Dhaliwal, Minister to Jr. John Dielwart, Chairman, Canadian Association of Petroleum Producers, 18 December.

Ontario. 2007a. *2007 Ontario Budget*. Toronto: Ministry of Finance.

Ontario Clean Air Alliance (OCAA). 2010. 'Finishing the Coal Phase Out' Toronto, OCAA March. http://www.cleanairalliance.org/files/

active/0/phaseout%20progress%202010.pdf accessed 1 June, 2010.

Pembina Institute. 2009. *Highlights of Provincial Greenhouse Gas Reduction Plans.* Drayton Valley, AB: The Pembina Institute.

Pew. 2010. Climate Policy Memo, Pew Centre on Climate Change, http://www.pewclimate.org/federal/policy-solutions/climate-policy-memo

Prentice, J., Minister of Environment. 2009. 'Notes for an address by the Honourable Jim Prentice, P.C., Q.C., M.P. Minister of the Environment on Canada's climate change plan'. June 4. http://www.ec.gc.ca/default.asp?lang=En&n=6F2DE1CA-1&news=400A4566-DA85-4A0C-B9F4-BABE2DF555C7

Rabe, B.G. 2009. 'Second-Generation Climate Policies in the States: Proliferation, Diffusion, and Regionalization'. In *Changing Climates in North American Politics: Institutions, Policymaking, and Multilevel Governance*, ed. H. Selin and S.D. VanDeveer. Cambridge, Mass.: MIT Press.

———. 2004. *Statehouse and Greenhouse: The Emerging Politics of American Climate Change Policy.* Washington: Brookings Institution Press.

Reguly, E. 2009a. 'US outlines dual path to cutting greenhouse gases', *The Globe and Mail*, 20 December.

Reguly, E. 2009b. 'Ontario, Quebec assail federal emissions targets', *The Globe and Mail*, 14 December.

Saskatchewan, Government of. 2009. News Release: 'Saskatchewan Takes Real Action to Reduce Greenhouse Gas Emissions'. 11 May, http://www.google.ca/#hl=en&source=hp&biw=1276&bih=831&q=Saskatchewan+Takes+Real+Action+to+Reduce+Greenhouse+Gas+Emissions+2009&btnG=Google+Search&aq=f&aqi=&aql=&oq=Saskatchewan+Takes+Real+Action+to+Reduce+Greenhouse+Gas+Emissions+2009&fp=5c4cf627214e10d6

Smith, J. 2009. 'UN Chief prods Canada on lagging climate plans', *The Toronto Star*, 28 November.

Urquhart, I. 2007. 'Don't look to premiers for leadership', *The Toronto Star*, 10 August.

Valiante, M. 2002. 'Legal Foundations of Environmental Policy: Underlining Our Values in a Shifting Landscape'. In *Canadian Environmental Policy: Context and Cases*, ed. D.L. VanNijnatten and R. Boardman. Toronto: Oxford University Press.

West, L. 2009. 'U.S. Economic Stimulus Package Includes Billions for Energy and the Environment' About.com, N.D., http://environment.about.com/od/environmentallawpolicy/a/econ_stimulus.htm.

Winfield, M., and D. Macdonald. 2008. 'The Harmonization Accord and Climate Change Policy: Two Case Studies in Federal–provincial Environmental Policy'. In *Canadian Federalism: Performance, Effectiveness, and Legitimacy*, second edition, ed. H. Bakvis and G. Skogstad. Don Mills: Oxford University Press.

Woods, A. 2009. 'Ottawa takes heat on climate', *The Toronto Star*, 26 November.

14 Remaking Immigration: Asymmetric Decentralization and Canadian Federalism

Keith G. Banting

Canadian federal institutions leave a deep imprint on the policy structures of the country. Government programs in sector after sector have been shaped by the institutional configuration of one of the most decentralized federations among contemporary democracies, and by the intergovernmental diplomacy through which the multiple governments manage their interdependence. For much of the postwar era, immigration stood as an exception to this pattern. The federal government dominated the process from the selection of newcomers through their settlement, integration, and eventual naturalization as new citizens. In recent decades, however, the sector has been transformed by a rapid decentralization, with provincial authorities now exercising a substantial role in the selection and settlement of immigrants. More intriguingly, this decentralizing process has been highly uneven, with some provinces playing a much larger role than others, producing a highly asymmetric pattern of intergovernmental relations. This process has not been guided by a comprehensive blueprint of the new policy regime. Rather, the transformation has proceeded through a series of incremental adjustments, usually in the form of bilateral political deals between the federal government and individual provinces. These changes have been layered on top of each other, with limited reference to any comprehensive federal–provincial rationale or to their cumulative impact. The result is one of the most complex immigration systems in the world, and a set of intergovernmental relations characterized by pervasive **asymmetry** rather than a common conception of federalism.

Decentralization is hardly new in Canada. Nor is asymmetry unknown, either in Canada or in other federations. In the Canadian case, Quebec has long played a larger role than other provinces in many policy sectors, exercising powers considered essential to maintaining a distinct society. As we shall see, immigration is one of those sectors. But the immigration sector is also marked by an unusual level of asymmetry in relations between the federal government and other provinces, with no obvious policy rationale for the complex patterns that have emerged.

This chapter traces the evolution of Canadian federalism in immigration and immigrant integration, and provides a preliminary assessment of the consequences. The final section pulls the threads of the discussion together and reflects on the implications of the Canadian federalism.

Federalism And The Integration Continuum

Canada maintains one of the largest immigration programs relative to the size of its population among OECD countries. Figure 14.1 tracks the trend in overall admissions of **permanent residents** from 1984 to 2009, capturing a sustained rise over the period. Figure 14.2 tracks the equally dramatic rise in temporary residents: foreign workers, foreign students, and refugee claimants. Not surprisingly, the selection and integration of this large and diverse flow of newcomers are a constant preoccupation in Canada, and the challenges the country faces are managed through an increasingly complex federal system.

The constitution sets out the bare bones of the division of power over immigration and integration. Jurisdiction over immigration is concurrent. Section 95 of the Constitution Act 1867 bestows authority to make laws related to immigration on both the central government and the provinces, with the proviso of federal paramountcy: any provincial law related to immigration 'shall have an effect in and for the Province as long as and as far as it is not repugnant to any Act of the Parliament of Canada'. At the other end of the continuum, Section 91(25) grants exclusive authority over **naturalization** to the federal government. The constitution is silent, however, about the intervening phases of the continuum. Immigrant settlement and integration were not distinct concerns of governments in the mid-nineteenth century, when the constitution was drafted. The general division of authority over relevant programs prevails as a result, and the longer-term integration of immigrants depends heavily on provincial policies and programs, such as labour market policy, education, and social services.

These spare constitutional provisions give only a partial view of intergovernmental relations in this sector. They have been supplemented with a complex array of political

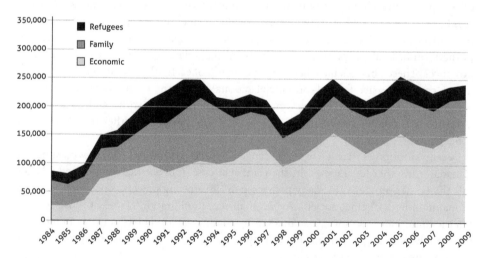

Figure 14.1 Composition of Immigrant Inflow by Category of Permanent Resident, 1984–2009.

Source: Based on data in Citizenship and Immigration Canada (2010). Reproduced with the permission of the Minister of Public Works and Government Services Canada, 2011.

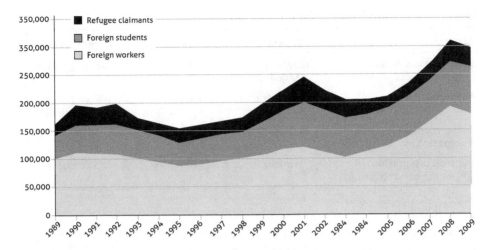

Figure 14.2 Temporary Residents Entering Canada Each Year, Principal Categories, 1989–2009.

Source: Based on data in Citizenship and Immigration Canada (2010). Reproduced with the permission of the Minister of Public Works and Government Services Canada, 2011.

agreements that have been layered on top of each other through intergovernmental bargaining over the years. Although full meetings of federal–provincial–territorial ministers began again in 2002, after a hiatus of over a century, the critical bargaining tends to proceed on a bilateral basis between the central government and individual provinces. The result is considerable asymmetry, with Quebec having carved out a distinct role in the sector several decades ago and with significant variation creeping into the role of other provinces as well. In addition, intergovernmental relationships have been changing rapidly in this sector, with significant decentralization in several phases of the process having occurred in the last few years. As a result, Canada has established the most complex immigration/integration regime of any federation in the OECD.

The process of immigrant integration can be thought of as a continuum which begins with the selection and admission of immigrants and proceeds through their initial settlement and their eventual integration into the economic, social and political mainstream of the country. The federal–provincial balance differs significantly across distinct components of the continuum. Table 14.1 provides an overview of the intergovernmental balance in each phase of the integration continuum and the following sections set out the details.

Selection and Admission

Prior to the establishment of the Canadian federation in 1867, each of the separate colonies in British North America had been preoccupied with immigration. The decision to grant concurrent powers to both levels of the new federation was therefore understandable, and an intergovernmental conference on immigration the year following Confederation produced Canada's first federal–provincial agreement. However, provincial interest began to wane as early as an intergovernmental conference in 1874, and provincial inactivity persisted into the decades following the Second World War.

Table 14.1 Federalism and the Integration Continuum

Stage	Federal	Quebec	Other Provinces
Selection and Admission	Traditionally dominant	Substantial	Growing rapidly
Settlement	Asymmetric responsibility	Exclusive responsibility	Asymmetric responsibility
Socio-economic integration	Secondary	Primary	Primary
Political integration (including naturalization)	Primary	Secondary	Secondary

Federal predominance came under challenge beginning in the 1960s. Not surprisingly, the push for decentralization started in Quebec, where immigration has always held a particular sensitivity. Within the province, Quebecers of French-Canadian ancestry represent a strong majority; within the larger Canadian and North American contexts, however, they are a minority and are concerned about the future of their language and culture. Historically, immigration was often seen as a threat to that culture, especially during the postwar era when immigrants tended to assimilate to the English-speaking community in the province. In those years, analyses of public attitudes found that Quebecers of French-Canadian descent were more opposed to immigration and less comfortable with ethnic and cultural pluralism than other Canadians (Berry, Kalin, and Taylor, 1976; Lambert and Curtis, 1982, 1983). Opposition to immigration began to ease later in the century, as the birth rate in Quebec declined and the francophone share of the population of the country as a whole began to shrink (Gidengil et al., 2004). Nonetheless, the sensitivity of the issues remained.

The Quebec government engages these sensitivities with growing determination. Beginning in 1972, the province adopted a series of increasingly powerful language and education laws to steer immigrants into the francophone community. These policies were controversial when they were enacted, with Quebec nationalists and immigrant communities mobilizing massively on opposing sides. But the primacy of French as the language of the public realm has become a central pillar of the provincial policy regime. In addition, the Quebec government sought to take greater control of immigration policy, establishing its own ministry of immigration in 1968 and pressing the federal government to cede a larger role to the province.

The federal response was shaped by the intense constitutional battles which dominated Canadian politics in the last decades of the twentieth century. The federal government tried to forestall Quebec's separation and the breakup of the country by recognizing and accommodating Quebec's distinctiveness within the federation. Starting in 1971, the federal government signed a succession of agreements with Quebec to accommodate the province's aspirations. The 1978 Cullen-Couture Agreement gave Quebec effective control over the selection of economic immigrants. In 1987, a proposal for constitutional reform known as the Meech Lake Accord included a provision to entrench the terms of the Cullen-Couture Agreement and to transfer responsibility for all settlement services to the province. When the constitutional Accord failed to be ratified, the federal government concluded a separate Canada–Quebec immigration agreement in 1991, implementing the Accord's approach.

The province utilized its expanded autonomy to establish its own approach to immigrant selection. It implemented its own version of the points system, which differs somewhat from the federal approach, especially in giving greater weight to French-language skills. In principle, authority over policies concerning other categories of immigrants—**family class** and refugees—remained in federal hands, but the selection of refugees is carried out jointly by the federal government and Quebec. The federal government remains responsible for the final admission of all immigrants and screens provincial nominees for security and health concerns. Nevertheless, the critical first step in the selection process had shifted to provincial hands.[1]

Quebec exceptionalism did not persist. As is often the case in Canada, an initiative which Quebec sought as recognition of its distinctiveness triggered a broader decentralization. Initially, it was the federal government pressing for decentralization, as it was uncomfortable with asymmetry and did not want Quebec to be the only province with an immigration agreement. Other provinces responded cautiously. In contrast to Quebec, the cultural imperative was less compelling; they tended to see immigration as a politically sensitive and potentially expensive program which they were content to leave to the federal government. As a result, initial immigration agreements were principally geared towards information sharing and consultation (Vineberg, forthcoming).

By the late 1990s, however, provincial interest in more substantial agreements was growing. The concentration of immigrants in Ontario, British Columbia and Quebec led other provinces to demand their 'fair share'.[2] Because of the mobility provision of the Canadian Charter of Rights and Freedoms, immigrants cannot be compelled to settle in specific parts of the country. But a provincial role in selection and settlement might still have steering effects. The Liberal government of the day wished to avoid replicating the Canada–Quebec approach, which would have eliminated the federal role in selection of economic migrants, and it responded tentatively in 1995 by introducing the Provincial Nominee Program (PNP). Under this program, provinces were authorized to identify a number of economic migrants to meet specific regional economic needs. As in the Quebec agreement, the federal government issues the final acceptance; but provincial programs are not bound by the federal points system or language requirements, and their selection criteria vary in important ways. Manitoba and Saskatchewan were the first to take up the offer, establishing PNPs in 1998. By 2007, all other provinces (except Quebec) and two of the three northern territories had signed on.

The initial intention was that the PNP would be small, and there were only 477 admissions in the first year. However, provincial enthusiasm for the program grew. In 2003, the federal government lifted the cap on the number of provincial nominations for Manitoba and, in the words of a senior Manitoba official, the program expanded 'well beyond our wildest expectations' (Clément, 2003: 199). In 2008, the Conservative federal government removed all caps on provincial nominations. In part this was a reflection of the Conservatives' more decentralist orientation to federalism. More importantly, expanding the PNP system also helped circumvent a massive backlog in the Federal Skilled Workers Program, which was generating long delays in obtaining visas. The intergovernmental

Table 14.2 Target Levels for Economic Immigration, 2011

Category	Low (000s)	High (000s)
Federal economic class	74.0	80.4
Provincial economic class		
Quebec economic class	34.6	35.9
Provincial nominees	42.0	45.0
Total economic class	150.6	161.3

Note: principal applicants plus spouses and dependants

Source: Citizenship and Immigration Canada, *Annual Report to Parliament* (Ottawa, 2010), Table 1.
Reproduced with the permission of the Minister of Public Works and Government Services Canada, 2011.

agreements governing PNPs require the federal governments to process provincial nominees first, contributing to shorter wait times (Citizenship and Immigration Canada, 2010: 63).

The number of provincial nominations soared. With a cap on the total level of admissions but no cap on the PNP program, PNP selections necessarily grew at the expense of the federal program. In 2009, the Auditor General worried that the PNP could quickly squeeze out the federal economic program almost completely (Auditor General of Canada, 2009: Chapter 2: 12). In introducing its immigration plan for 2011, the federal government announced that, once again, 'the admission range for federal economic immigration has been reduced to permit further growth in the Provincial Nominee Program' (Citizenship and Immigration Canada, 2010b: 8). But the minister also indicated that the PNP intake would be stabilized at the 2011 target. At that level, provincial selections, including under the Quebec economic class, would broadly equal the number being admitted under the federal program (see Table 14.2). However the re-imposition of the cap caught provinces that had developed their programs and has resulted in a disproportionate distribution of provincial nominees across provinces. When provinces complained, the federal minister pushed back: 'we can't have 10 provinces arbitrarily settling their own goals, because ultimately there's one pipeline for immigration . . . and that runs through the Government of Canada' (Maher, 2010). He did promised the provinces some flexibility in implementing the targets for 2011, but the uneven distribution across provinces persists.

In summary, the process of selecting economic migrants has undergone a major decentralization. The federal government still controls important levers over immigration, including the overall levels of admissions and final admissions. It also maintains a significant steering capacity and could effectively ask the provinces for more policy uniformity and reporting in the deployment of their respective PNPs. So far, it has not done so, and provinces remain significant, autonomous players in the selection process.

Settlement and Socio-economic Integration

The story is much the same in the realm of socio-economic integration. However, the relationships here need to be considered in two dimensions: settlement programs provided to newcomers in their first years in the country, and programs relevant to longer-term integration. The intergovernmental relations in the two dimensions differ considerably.

Settlement: Canada has developed a comprehensive set of programs, with a particular focus on the pre-naturalization phase. The federal government remains the largest funder of such programming, and it supports a variety of reception and adjustment services, language instruction at the basic and enhanced levels, and programs that link newcomers with Canadian volunteers who act as hosts and informal counsellors. Outside of Quebec, Canada provides the majority of these services through third parties, including immigrant service provider organizations (SPOs), multicultural/ethnic organizations, educational institutions, or partners in the private sector (Biles, 2008: 141). Settlement programs have traditionally been available only to permanent residents. Temporary workers, international students, refugee claimants awaiting disposition of their claim, and immigrants who have become citizens are ineligible. This limitation has become more problematic as the number of temporary residents has increased. These newcomers and their families are not eligible for federally funded language training or other supports, although some provinces have stepped in to provide services in certain cases.

The intergovernmental trajectory in settlement programs parallels that in selection. Once again, Quebec led. As part of the 1991 Canada–Quebec immigration agreement, the federal government withdrew from all settlement services in the province and provided a financial transfer to the province to support its new responsibilities. In the aftermath of the failed effort at constitutional reform, the federal government was especially anxious for a deal, and the terms of the final financial settlement were extremely generous (Seidle, 2010: Table 1). In contrast to agreements with other provinces, the transfer is technically a 'grant' rather than a 'contribution', which triggers no reporting or accountability obligations. The province is not even required to spend the money exclusively on settlement programs and does not do so, dispersing some of the funding to mainstream ministries. Moreover, the transfer to Quebec rises automatically with general federal spending levels and is guaranteed never to decline.

Devolution to other provinces soon followed, although on more limited and less generous terms. The precipitating factors were a fiscal crisis and budgetary restraint. The federal government was faced with severe fiscal pressures in the mid-1990s and became increasingly annoyed that the provinces were not helping to finance settlement programs. It therefore sought to off-load responsibility for the delivery of settlement programming onto provinces. Two provinces were open to the idea, but not on the financial terms initially on offer. The federal government had to up the ante, ironically by virtually the full amount it had hoped to save through devolution (Vineberg, forthcoming). In 1999, Manitoba and British Columbia assumed comprehensive responsibility for settlement services, although their deals with the federal government differed from the Quebec agreement in being contribution agreements which require reporting to the federal government. During the 2000s, the federal government began to have second thoughts about extending full devolution to other provinces and signed more limited deals with Alberta and Ontario, which did not want full devolution at that point. In its 2010 budget, Ontario announced that it wished to pursue full devolution, but the federal government rejected the idea. The federal minister told the press, 'We weren't prepared to rush into that kind of arrangement' (Media Q, 2010).

As a result, the field of settlement services is currently characterized by considerable asymmetry, with four types of intergovernmental relationships:

- comprehensive provincial control (Quebec): full provincial autonomy; secure financial transfer from the federal government; no requirement to report to the federal government;
- devolved model (British Columbia and Manitoba): provincial delivery of services; federal discretion over funding levels; provincial report to the federal government;
- co-management model (Alberta): federal and provincial officials jointly select projects to be funded and decide which will be funded and delivered by each level of government; and
- consultation model (other provinces): federal government consults with provinces but retains final decision-making over programs, which it delivers through its own regional offices in conjunction with local non-profit organizations.

Perhaps the most striking feature of this pattern is that the federal government has a very different relationship with each of the three major immigrant-receiving provinces, Ontario, Quebec, and British Columbia. This variegated pattern reflects the accumulation of bilateral political agreements rather than a multilateral approach to intergovernmental relations. Moreover, in contrast to some other policy areas, there was no commitment to offer the terms of later deals to provinces who settled earlier. The resulting asymmetry defies any coherent policy rationale.

Longer-term Integration: The process of long term integration into the mainstream can take many years, and the process is influenced by the general public services which were not designed specifically with immigrants in mind. As we have seen, a key problem in recent years has been the slowing economic incorporation of highly educated newcomers. In this context, credential recognition, supplementary training programs, and income support are important to newcomers. All of these responsibilities fall primarily in provincial hands.

For skilled immigrants trained in regulated professions, the recognition of their qualifications by occupational regulatory bodies is critical. These bodies are accountable to provincial governments and their assessment, recognition, and licensing practices, including their use of standards and accountability frameworks, vary from province to province. The federal government has established a Foreign Credentials Referral Office but, given the limits of its jurisdiction, it cannot actually conduct credential assessment. It provides advice to immigrants and intending immigrants, and develops tools for employers to assist them in assessing and recognizing the qualifications of foreign trained individuals (Alboim and McIsaac, 2007).

Training programs, which can be important to even skilled immigrants, also now fall under provincial jurisdiction. The federal government provides financial support for provincial programs through federal–provincial Labour Market Development Agreements (LMDAs), a decentralizing initiative launched in the aftermath of the Quebec referendum in 1995. However, eligibility for LMDA-supported training is limited to individuals who are eligible for federal Employment Insurance benefits and therefore excludes immigrants who are new market entrants. In 2007, the federal government announced a separate transfer to provinces to support labour market programs for people who are not eligible for training under the Employment Insurance program, but immigrants were not specified as a particular target group and no funds were specifically earmarked for them.

If immigrants become unemployed and need income support, their primary source of support is provincial social assistance. In part, this reflects the limitations of the federal Employment Insurance program: at the national level, only about 40 per cent of the unemployed actually receive Employment Insurance benefits. This pattern is accentuated for immigrants by the regional nature of the program. Coverage rates are dramatically lower in areas where the percentage of immigrants is higher. In Toronto, where almost one in two residents is an immigrant, only 22.3 per cent of unemployed people were receiving unemployment benefits in 2004 (Battle, 2006). In effect, the federal government has largely opted out of income stabilization in the half of the country where most immigrants live. When times get tough in these regions, immigrants must increasingly turn to provincial social assistance programs.

Finally, for young immigrants and children of immigrants born in Canada—the second generation—the educational system is the primary instrument of integration. Education is the most sacred of provincial jurisdictions, and the federal government has virtually no role at the primary and secondary levels. At the post-secondary level, the federal government is a partner in the student loan program and supports research. But it is provincial decisions that shape the overall scope and quality of the system. Education of the second generation is one success story that has not dimmed. As we saw earlier, Canada has a strong comparative advantage in educating immigrant and minority students.

The cumulative trend is clear: settlement and socio-economic integration have also witnessed asymmetrical decentralization in recent years.

Political Integration

In contrast with immigrant admission and socio-economic integration, the process of political integration is dominated by the federal government. The three key instruments of identity formation and political integration are multiculturalism policy, the Charter of Rights and Freedoms, and naturalization.

The multiculturalism approach to immigrant integration was initially a federal initiative, introduced in a statement by the prime minister in 1971 and codified by a subsequent federal government in the Canadian Multiculturalism Act (1988). The formal program of multicultural grants is relatively small, but the approach permeates a wider range of federal departments and agencies. Moreover, versions of the policy have been adopted by provincial and municipal governments, and by businesses and civil society organizations (Garcea, 2006).

The Canadian version of multiculturalism has sought to recognize and accommodate cultural differences, and to encourage active participation in the Canadian mainstream. The core goals of federal multiculturalism, as laid out in 1971, were: recognition and accommodation of cultural diversity, removing barriers to participation, promoting interchange among groups, and promoting acquisition of the official languages. The Canadian approach has thus been integrationist: it has sought to shift the terms on which integration proceeds, but the ultimate goal has been integration into the wider society (Kymlicka, 1998; Ley, 2010). Changes in the federal program over the years have reinforced the integrative intent. Starting in the late 1970s, participation and interethnic exchange increasingly received the lion's share of funding under the federal program. Irene Bloemraad's (2006) comparison of the political integration of immigrants in Canada and the United States illuminates the program's impact. Multicultural funding has enabled immigrant groups to participate more quickly and more effectively in mainstream Canadian political institutions by facilitating the self-organization of the community, creating new cadres of community leaders who are familiar with Canadian institutions and practices, and creating new mechanisms of consultation and participation.

In addition to this organizational impact, multiculturalism has helped nurture a more inclusive sense of national identity, one more capable of accommodating the diverse diversity of contemporary Canada. The adoption of the policies of bilingualism and multiculturalism in the 1960s and 1970s represented a state-led redefinition of national identity, an effort to de-centre the historic conception of the country as a British society and to build an identity more reflective of Canada's cultural complexity. The adoption of a new flag, one without ethnic references, was a symbol of this wider transition. In addition to promoting a conception of Canada more open to newcomers, multicultural norms have sought to shape the identity of the historic population. As Harell (2009) observes, multiculturalism has helped to 'normalize' diversity, especially for younger generations. Over the decades, Canadians have developed a multicultural conception of their identity, a definition of the country as a diverse community. In many countries, individuals with the strongest sense of national identity are most opposed to immigration. In Canada, those with the strongest sense of Canadian identity embrace immigration and immigrants more warmly than their less nationalist neighbours (Johnston, Banting, Kymlicka, and Soroka, 2010).

A second instrument of political integration is the Charter of Rights and Freedoms, which was entrenched in the constitution in 1982. Despite the embrace of diversity in political discourse, discrimination remains part of lived reality on the ground, and the Charter takes on particular importance. Section 2 of the Charter establishes a set of fundamental freedoms, including a guarantee of freedom of religion which has been important in protecting members of minority religions. In addition, Section 15 forbids 'discrimination based on race, national or ethnic origin, colour, religion, sex or mental or physical disability'. The reach of Charter jurisprudence extends through elaborate human rights machinery, including federal and provincial human rights commissions. In addition, the Charter plays a role in political debates. It has contributed to a new rights-conscious culture, in which Canadians increasingly see themselves as a community of people holding the same rights and freedoms, irrespective of where they live, the language they speak or where they were born. In the immigration field, the Charter is an instrument for 'Canadianizing' newcomers, inviting them to see the federal government as a source of their protection from discrimination and to identify with the pan-Canadian political community (Gagnon, 2009).

The Charter both reinforces and limits the multicultural approach to integration. Section 27 of the Charter states that it will be 'interpreted in a manner consistent with the preservation and enhancement of the multicultural heritage of Canadians'. But the commitment to individual rights embedded in the Charter also stands as a counterweight to the multicultural strategy. The liberal democratic principles enshrined in the Charter circumscribe the range of cultural traditions deemed legitimate, ensuring that accommodation of difference does not justify discrimination or deny basic equalities, such as the equality of women. As Eliadis (2007: 151) observes, 'when multiculturalism is unhinged from equality, it tends to career off in unpleasant and increasingly unacceptable directions'.[3] Whenever a claim advanced in the name of multiculturalism is framed as being in conflict with individual or equality rights, the Charter values tend to trump, as was illustrated by the controversy in Ontario over a proposal for a Sharia tribunal to arbitrate family and inheritance issues (Boyd, 2007).

The final tool in the federal arsenal is naturalization. The federal government, with exclusive authority over the granting of citizenship, has chosen an accelerated approach, with immigrants becoming eligible for naturalization after three years in the country. They must take a citizenship test to demonstrate understanding of Canadian democracy, history, and geography, as well as their basic ability to communicate in either English or French. The pass rate on the test has traditionally been very high, and the rate of naturalization of newcomers is among the highest in the world. According to a 2005 study, 84 per cent of eligible immigrants were Canadian citizens in 2001; in contrast, the rate was 40 per cent in the United States and lower still in many European states (Tran, Kustec, and Chui, 2005). The introduction of a new citizenship guide and a more demanding test in March 2010 led to a drop in the pass rate. The test was revised in October to ease the rules, although the rate remains somewhat lower than in the past (Beeby, 2010).

The federal approach to political integration has been contested. Each instrument of federal action—multiculturalism, the Charter of Rights and Freedoms, and naturalization—has proven controversial in Quebec. Quebec's provincial government has developed its own approach to diversity, known as interculturalism, which encourages newcomers to develop a sense of belonging to the Quebec political community (Gagnon and Iacovino, 2007; Labelle and Rocher, 2004). While federal language legislation and the Canadian Charter promote the choice of two official languages, English and French, the Quebec model defines French as the language of public life in the province. Quebec's provincial language laws have also come into conflict with the federal language regime, including the language provisions of the federal Charter of Rights.

Immigrants to Quebec are thus swept up into two nation-building projects, two conceptions of the community they are encouraged to join. The Quebec government encourages minorities to join its national project of building a distinct society in Quebec. The federal government emphasizes attachment to the pan-Canadian community, and the granting of citizenship as a symbolic affirmation of its vision of Canada. The study guide which the federal government gives to immigrants preparing for the citizenship test, the ceremonies at which citizenship is formally awarded, and the oath of loyalty which newcomers take are all celebrations of Canada, replete with Canadian flags and symbols, have prompted Quebec nationalists to suggest that the Quebec government give an official status to Quebec citizenship. In effect, 'two identity-making processes that are in conflict with each other are operating simultaneously towards ends that are at odds with each other' (Labelle and Rocher, 2004: 275; see also Labelle and Rocher, 2009; Gagnon, 2007: 122). These dynamics have no parallel in other provinces.

The imprint of federalism thus pervades the integration continuum. An uneven decentralizing process has transformed the admission and integration of immigrants to Canada. Only the final stage of immigration policy, political integration, is dominated by the federal government. In three decades, Canada has moved from a highly centralized process to a decentralized asymmetrical world.

Impacts

Does any of this matter? Are the patterns of immigration policy and integration programs different than they would be in a more centralized institutional setting? Does the level of asymmetry matter, and if so in what ways? This section explores these questions, examining the implications of institutional changes with respect to immigration policies for responsiveness, equity, coherence, accountability, the larger federal balance, and immigrant integration.

Responsiveness to Regional Diversity

The promise of decentralization is greater policy responsiveness to local conditions and greater scope for experimentation. Is the promise realized in practice?

In the case of selection, decentralization has clearly allowed some provinces to tailor policy to local conditions. Most obviously, the Canada–Quebec accord has allowed Quebec to introduce a distinctive version of the points system, which gives greater weight to applicants who speak French. The federal government, which is committed to treating French and English equally, would have greater difficulty doing this. Insofar as greater autonomy for Quebec is required for Canadian unity, immigration policy has undoubtedly contributed to the survival of the country as a single state,

The PNP initiative in Manitoba is also widely seen as successful. It has allowed the province to change the occupational mix of new arrivals, shifting the balance from the knowledge workers favoured by the federal program towards semi-skilled trades, such as industrial butchers, truck drivers, and welders. Manitoba has also succeeded in dispersing immigrants to smaller communities outside of the Winnipeg metropolitan area. Most importantly, the retention rate for PNP selectees was above 70 per cent after five years; in comparison, the retention rate for federal economic immigrants who came to Manitoba in the same period dropped to 60 per cent after one year and continued to decline thereafter (Carter, Pandey, and Townsend, 2010; for a more critical view, see Lewis, 2010). The Manitoba PNP helps explain the increase in the proportion of immigrants in the prairie provinces noted earlier in Table 14.3.

This pattern of success has not been universal. Other small provinces that traditionally receive few immigrants, such as those in Atlantic Canada, have not been as active or as effective in managing their programs. At the extreme, important elements of the program in Prince Edward Island were suspended amid controversies about conflicts of interest and financial improprieties, and vigorous demands in the provincial legislature for an independent inquiry (CBC, 2009).

The asymmetric decentralization of settlement programs has also offered opportunities to three provinces to strike out in new directions. The federal administration of settlement programs has often been criticized for its inability to adapt national policies to diverse localities, and the non-profit organizations delivering settlement services in Manitoba reported an improvement when the provincial government assumed responsibility for

Table 14.3 Distribution of New Permanent Residents, by Region, 2000 and 2008

Region	2000 %	2008 %
Atlantic provinces	1.3	2.7
Quebec	14.3	19.6
Ontario	58.7	42.4
Prairie provinces	9.1	18.8
British Columbia	16.5	16.4

Source: Citizenship and Immigration Canada, *Annual Report to Parliament* (Ottawa, 2010). Reproduced with the permission of the Minister of Public Works and Government Services Canada, 2011.

services (Leo and August, 2009). However, there are no guarantees here. A parallel study of British Columbia found that community organizations were systematically shut out of the policy process, and that part of the initial federal financial transfer for settlement services was redirected elsewhere in the provincial budget. The extent of engagement and consultation with local communities, service providers, and municipalities clearly depends less on the level of jurisdiction than on the ideological orientation of the government involved. In the words of the analyst who studied both provinces: 'in multi-level governance there are no straight lines, and no one dimensional solutions' (Leo and Enns, 2009: 95).

Equity

Does asymmetric decentralization help or hurt immigrants? According to some commentators, the diversity of selection systems inevitably reduces equity, as applicants with the same attributes are likely to receive different treatment depending on the door on which they knock (Alboim, 2009). However, multiple doors also increase the range of opportunities for people wishing to come to Canada. Truck drivers as well as engineers now have a chance, if they know where to knock. The biggest problem may be that the complexity of the system places a premium on sophisticated knowledge of the various pathways into the country, making applicants increasingly dependent on a thriving industry of immigration lawyers and consultants who advise them. While most of these experts are undoubtedly highly professional, there have been complaints of exploitation of sometimes desperate applicants.

Does asymmetric federalism benefit or hurt immigrants after they have arrived? The level and quality of reception settlement services certainly vary across the country. However, whether these variations are greater than differences in the quality of provincial education and social services available to the general population is an important question on which we lack clear evidence. Certainly, local immigrant groups are not well placed politically to challenge the provision of inadequate services compared to those in other provinces, and much therefore depends on the attitudes of the provincial governments. But as long as provinces continue to compete for immigrants, differences in the support they provide are unlikely to be dramatic.

There is a larger point here. In some societies, federal institutions might leave minorities vulnerable to discrimination at the hands of local majorities. In Canada, however, support for immigration does not vary significantly across the regions, and decentralization is less likely to expose immigrants to pockets of deep hostility. Moreover, while history records many cases of racial discrimination at both levels of government, the Charter of Rights now provides stronger protection from majorities at both the national and provincial levels. There is greater uneasiness about the cultural challenges posed by immigration in Quebec than in the rest of the country, and a recurring series of frictions have emerged there. But immigrants to Quebec do not report discrimination more often than elsewhere in the country. Indeed, in a survey conducted by Statistics Canada, racial-minority immigrants in Quebec were slightly less likely to report discrimination than their counterparts elsewhere; and second-generation racial minority respondents reported roughly the same level of discrimination as their counterparts in the rest of Canada (Banting and Soroka, forthcoming).

Equity can also be considered from the perspective of provincial governments. Decentralization was driven in part by a concern for 'fairness' for different regions, and the PNPs are contributing to a 'fairer' distribution of immigrants across the country. But the asymmetric nature of the decentralization also generates conflict. For example, inequalities in federal funding for settlement have been a problem. The 1991 Canada–Quebec agreement provided Quebec with vastly more funding per immigrant than provinces carrying much larger burdens such as Ontario and British Columbia. Ontario only agreed to establish a PNP, which Ottawa wanted, if the federal government devoted a 'fairer' share of its settlement funding to immigrants in the province, and sorting out that inequity required a significant additional injection of new federal funds (Seidle, 2010). But the federal government did not actually meet the spending levels specified in the Canada–Ontario Immigration Agreement and then announced cuts in funding for settlement services in the province in 2011, something that it cannot do in Quebec. In addition, the federal refusal to offer Ontario the same devolved model as BC and Manitoba has sparked anger. Overall, the scorecard is mixed. Decentralization does not seem to be exposing immigrants to greater risks, but asymmetry is not serving the cause of interprovincial equity.

Policy Coherence

While there seem to be gains in terms of responsiveness, asymmetric decentralization has produced a very complicated immigration system. The lack of a common policy framework for economic immigration has generated diverse pathways to entering Canada. In the words of one commentator, 'potential immigrants to Canada are confronted with the Quebec immigration program, nine provincial nominee programs, and two territorial programs, each with their [sic] own sub-component, selection criteria, fees, application processes, and timelines' (Alboim, 2008). The Auditor General of Canada has also underscored the emergence of 'more than 50 different categories, each with its own selection approach and criteria' (Auditor General of Canada, 2009: Chapter 2: 25; Seidle, 2010: fn. 19).

Elements of policy incoherence are inevitable. Fragmentation creates openings for venue-shopping, with prospective immigrants switching from government to government looking for the entry point most favourable to them. Indeed, people refused permission by the federal immigration department are sometimes advised to apply to a province instead. Such problems emerged in the early days of the Manitoba PNP when the federal government stiffened its own entry requirements in 2002. As a result, 'Manitoba was flooded with applicants seeking a back door into the country' (Leo and August, 2009: 501-2). Moreover, given the right of inter-provincial mobility once in the country, some provinces act as a backdoor into others, eroding the apparent benefits of a provincial role in selection. Although Manitoba has succeeded in retaining PNP arrivals, inter-provincial mobility is generally higher among recent immigrants than among the general population, including among those admitted to Canada under the Provincial Nominee Program (Okonny-Myers, 2010; Citizenship and Immigration Canada, 2010a: Table 3-7).

The Auditor General of Canada (2009: 26-7) is clearly uncomfortable with the variable geometry of the current system, and has recommended that the PNPs be formally evaluated. The federal government committed itself to carry out such a review in 2010–11.

Accountability

It is hard to believe the new regime has increased accountability of those responsible for immigration policy to legislatures and to citizens. Analysts of intergovernmental relations in Canada have long argued that accountability is enhanced when each level of government is exclusively responsible for its own programs, and that complex intergovernmental arrangements obscure responsibility and weaken the ability of citizens to hold governments to account.

In the postwar era, immigration was managed by one government and the public knew whom to reward or blame. Since then, immigration has fallen into the netherworld of asymmetric intergovernmentalism. Canadians can be forgiven for being confused. Who is responsible for monitoring and evaluating the immigration system? Who is in charge of fixing problems? At the moment, the answer to both questions is everyone and no-one.

In effect, a mismatch has emerged between the division of responsibilities in Canadian federalism and the mechanisms of accountability in Canadian democracy. In centralized policy sectors, the federal government is accountable to Parliament and answerable to the Canadian electorate as a whole. In fully decentralized policy sectors, provincial governments are responsible to their legislatures and electorates, and co-ordination, if needed, is pursued through inter-provincial committees. But in a highly asymmetric sector, like immigration, neither of these systems is likely to function as effectively as it would do with a single government in charge.

Nation Building / Province Building

Much of the history of Canadian federalism in the last half century can be written in terms of ongoing struggles between nation-building and province-building. Both levels of government have sought to strengthen their relationships with citizens and civil society, a dynamic best illustrated by social policy. For the central government, social policy has been seen as an instrument of territorial integration, part of the social glue holding together a vast country subject to powerful centrifugal tendencies. National social programs create a network of relations between citizens and central government throughout the country, helping to define the boundaries of the national political community and enhancing the legitimacy of the federal state. However, provincial governments, especially the Quebec government, have also seen social policy as an instrument for building a distinctive community at the regional level, one reflecting the linguistic and cultural dynamics of *québécois* society. For both levels of government, therefore, social policy has been an instrument not only of social justice but also of statecraft, to be deployed in the competitive processes of nation-building (Banting, 2005).

A similar dynamic is at work in the immigration field. Which level of government admits new immigrants and supports their settlement and integration is undoubtedly important to their long-term conception of the political community they are joining. Which level of government engages with civil society organizations to deliver settlement services matters to the overall pattern of linkages between state and society. As immigrant selection is decentralized, the federal government fades a little more from the lives of future citizens; as settlement programs are decentralized, hundreds of lines of contact between the central government and civil society are cut. For example, in 2008, the federal government had contribution agreements with over 300 local civil society organizations that deliver local settlement services (Biles, 2008: 166). But such federal–local links are severed in provinces with full devolution agreements. Not only does the federal government receive less feedback about the experience of immigrants on the ground, it becomes more distant, less engaged in the economic and social realities of the country, and less likely to be understood and trusted by local communities.

There is, of course, a political dimension to this intergovernmental struggle. Both federal and provincial politicians seeking votes in immigrant communities are finely attuned to the advantages of settlement services. Such programs come replete with opportunities for politicians to visit events organized by local immigrant organizations, and present cheques to support the integration services they provide. In recent years, the federal Conservative government has assiduously courted immigrant votes, especially in Ontario, and the home page of the federal department, Citizenship and Immigration Canada, carried a large box suggesting that local organizations 'Invite the Minister' to their events. [4] Such considerations could not have been lost on federal politicians when they rejected Ontario's request to devolve responsibility for the settlement services used by the largest concentration of immigrants in the country during the year preceding the 2011 election. Provincial politicians in regions with devolved programs are undoubtedly also conscious of the political dimensions of such linkages with civil society.

Levels of Integration

Does any of this matter to the integration of immigrants to Canada? Are there significant regional variations in the economic, social, and political integration of newcomers? If so, can such regional differences be attributed to the federal nature of the policy regime? This final question is the most challenging. Untangling the influence of differences in provincial programs from all of the other factors that influence integration is an analytically difficult task. Nevertheless, the question is important since, as we saw at the outset, Canada is having greater difficulty integrating its newcomers than it had in the past.

Differences in integration levels across the English-speaking regions of the country are small, and there is no evidence as yet that decentralization has led to strikingly different levels of success. In the case of Manitoba, for example, PNP selectees had an initial economic advantage. Although they were much less likely to hold university degrees, their earnings were very similar to the earnings of the more highly educated immigrants admitted under the Federal Skilled Workers program in their year of arrival. But in the years after landing, immigrants with university degrees saw more rapid earnings growth, offsetting the initial PNP advantage. More generally across the country, Federal Skilled Workers earned more than those admitted under provincial nominee programs (Carter, Pandey, and Townsend, 2010: Figure 3-2, 29). The social and political integration of immigrants also proceeds in similar ways across the English-speaking regions. Bilodeau et al. (2010) compare the attitudes of immigrants and the native-born on questions which normally produce sharp differences across the regions of the country, such as whether people trust the federal government or believe that their province is treated fairly in the federation. Their findings suggest that immigrants tend to embrace the views prevailing in the province where they settled.

This lack of obvious differences across the rest of the country should not be surprising. In part, the decentralizing trend is too recent to have left much of a mark on integration patterns. In addition, powerful factors that shape the inclusion of newcomers into Canadian life are undoubtedly to be found in the day-to-day lived experience of newcomers as they confront their new surroundings. Public programs are likely to have a more modest impact.

The big difference is between Quebec and the rest of Canada. While economic integration has weakened in all parts of the country, it has weakened more in Quebec (Boudarbat and Boulet, 2007; Chicha and Charest, 2008; Nadeau and Secklin, 2010). One reason for the difference is that the mix of immigrants into Quebec is weighed a bit more heavily to refugees than in other provinces. But analysts also point to the importance that Quebec immigration policy gives to the ability to speak French. The global pool of potential immigrants who speak French is smaller than the English-speaking pool, and immigrants to Quebec tend to have lower skill levels than in the rest of the country. In effect, 'in choosing its immigrants, Quebec must compromise between immigrants' linguistic skills and the other skills that they bring with them' (Nadeau and Secklin, 2010: 279). However, these differences seem inherent in the nature of Canadian dualism, and the larger linguistic politics of Canada, rather than the details of Quebec's immigration policies. Had immigrants heading for Quebec been selected according to federal criteria, they might have fared even less well in the Quebec labour market (ibid.: Figure 5).

Differences also appear in social and political integration of immigrants in Quebec. In contrast to the rest of the country, immigrants to Quebec are less likely to embrace the identities and loyalties of the native-born population in the province, expressing greater support for the federal government than do their neighbours (Bilodeau et al., 2010). Differences emerge in the second generation of visible minority groups as well. The sense of 'belonging' of second-generation visible minority groups is markedly lower in Quebec than in the rest of the country (Banting and Soroka, forthcoming). As in the case of economic integration, it seems difficult to attribute these patterns of inclusion to the minor differences in settlement programs that exists between Quebec and the rest of the country. Rather, they reflect the distinctive nature of identity politics in the province.

Conclusions

In the space of two decades, Canada has moved from a centralized immigration regime to a decentralized, asymmetrical world. Some provincial governments are now powerful actors in immigrant selection and settlement. The result is one of the more complex immigration systems in the world, and intergovernmental relations characterized by asymmetry rather than a common conception of federalism.

How does this complex intergovernmental system fare when evaluated according to the criteria of performance, effectiveness and legitimacy adopted in this book? Coming to a single evaluation is difficult since the federal–provincial balance in the immigration sector varies so much across the country. Evaluations about an asymmetric system tend to be asymmetric themselves, with the mix of positives and negatives varying from region to region.

Take, for example, performance in light of traditional federal principles. Given the **concurrent jurisdiction** over immigration in section 95 of the constitution, the highly centralized regime that had emerged in the first half of the twentieth century was anomalous, and the recent decentralization has moved federal–provincial relations closer to the norm in other domestic policy sectors. After a hiatus of 100 years, federal and provincial ministers now meet to discuss immigration policy. Moreover, in three provinces, the provincial government delivers settlement services to newcomers in much the same way it delivers general health and social services to residents generally. But this is not the case in other provinces. The asymmetric nature of the transition also leaves this sector in a strange federalism limbo.

Assessing the effectiveness of the programs that have emerged is equally complicated. Much depends on whether one favours responsiveness to regional interests or overall policy coherence. In the case of settlement services, there is little evidence that asymmetric decentralization raises deep concerns about the warmth of the welcome Canada offers to immigrants or to the success of their integration into Canadian life. But the provincial role in selecting immigrants - unparalleled in other federations - poses the trade-off more directly. On the one hand, decentralization allows provinces to adjust the flow of newcomers in light of their cultures and economies. On the other hand, it is no longer possible to give a clear statement of the criteria for admission to Canada, and it is not surprising that the Auditor General of Canada has raised questions about the consequences of so many different doors into the country. There would seem to be a clear case for closer federal–provincial co-ordination in establishing meta-rules to govern the process.

The biggest challenges concern the final criterion of legitimacy. The fairness and legitimacy of intergovernmental relations can be assessed from three perspectives: fairness to citizens, and in this case to immigrants; the implications for the quality of Canadian democracy; and the equitable treatment of regions. The evolving federal balance is probably not deeply unfair to newcomers. Admittedly, the variation between provinces in selection and settlement services means that immigrants in similar circumstances are treated differently. But multiple entry points increases the opportunities for those wishing to come to the country; and the variation in settlement services is probably not much greater than the variation in the core health and social services available to the general population. As long as provinces continue to compete for immigrants, differences in provincial support are unlikely to violate Canadian conceptions of equity.

In contrast, it is hard to claim that asymmetric decentralization has enhanced the vibrancy of Canadian democracy. Decision-making has retreated into closed intergovernmental meetings. In theory, decentralization should create greater potential for openness, allowing local communities and civil society organizations to participate more actively in policy development. As we have seen, however, there are no guarantees this will happen in practice. More importantly, the complexities of asymmetry make the system opaque, obscuring lines of accountability and making it more difficult for voters to know who to hold accountable. Indeed, it is now difficult to envision a coherent national debate about the selection criteria for economic immigrants or settlement policy, since who is responsible varies so much across the country.

Finally, when legitimacy is viewed in inter-regional terms, the conclusions are again asymmetric. Quebec autonomy in immigration has a clear policy rationale: it has helped the province preserve a distinct, French-speaking society in North America, and has undoubtedly helped preserve Canada as a single state. But the wider asymmetry across the rest of the country lacks such a rationale and has exacerbated tensions. Devolution may have contributed to a somewhat 'fairer' distribution of immigrants across the country, making some provincial governments happier. But asymmetrical political deal-making about money and authority over settlement services has increased provincial anger elsewhere. The regional winners and losers may have been reshuffled, but it is hard to say that Canada is inter-regionally fairer as a result.

Given this decidedly mixed scorecard, the lack of public debate about asymmetric decentralization is striking. While immigration policy seizes centre stage in countries around the world, public debate in Canada largely ignores the sweeping transitions taking place. A few researchers and analysts comment from time to time, but wider engagement is rare. In part, this reflects the Canadian public's unusually supportive attitudes towards immigration (Banting, 2010). In part, it reflects the low-visibility, stealth-like instruments used to change policy. Ministerial instructions and closed negotiations rather than high-profile legislative changes have been the order of the day. But the lack of debate undoubtedly also reflects the diffuse and variegated nature of power over immigration policy in Canada.

Notes

1. For a comparison of the points systems used for economic immigrants by the federal and Quebec governments, see Citizenship and Immigration Canada (2010a).
2. Manitoba had been demanding its 'fair share' of immigrants since 1969. See Hawkins (1988: 180).
3. Besides Eliadis (2007), see Smith (2009).
4. http://www.cic.gc.ca/english/department/minister/index.asp#invite. Downloaded 12 March 2011.

References

Alboim, N. 2009. *Adjusting the Balance: Fixing Canada's Economic Immigration Policies*. Toronto: Maytree.

Alboim, N. and E. McIsaac. 2007. 'Making the

Connections: Ottawa's Role in Immigrant Employment', *IRPP* 13, 3. Montreal: Institute for Research on Public Policy.

Auditor General of Canada. 2009. 'Selecting

Foreign Workers Under the Immigration
Program', Report of the Auditor General of
Canada to the House of Commons. Ottawa.

Banting, K. 2005. 'Canada: Nation-Building in
a Federal Welfare State'. In *Federalism and
the Welfare State: New World and European
Experiences*, ed. H. Obinger, S. Leibfried and
F.G. Castles. Cambridge: Cambridge University
Press.

Banting, K. 2010. 'Is There a Progressive's
Dilemma in Canada? Immigration,
Multiculturalism and the Welfare State',
Canadian Journal of Political Science 43, 4:
797–820.

Banting, K. and S. Soroka. Forthcoming.
'Minority nationalism and Immigrant
Integration in Canada', *Nations and Nationalism.*

Battle, K., M. Mendelson and S. Torjman. 2006.
*Towards a New Architecture for Canada's Adult
Benefits*. Ottawa: Caledon Institute of Social
Policy.

Beeby, D. 2010. 'Massive failure rates follow new,
tougher Canadian citizenship tests', *The Star*,
29 November.

Berry, J., R. Kalin and D. Taylor. 1976.
Multiculturalism and Ethnic Attitudes in Canada.
Ottawa: Supply and Services Canada.

Biles, J. 2008. 'Integration Policies in English-
Speaking Canada'. In *Immigration and
Integration in Canada in the Twenty-first Century*,
ed. J. Biles, M. Burstein and J. Frideres.
Montreal: McGill–Queen's University Press.

Bilodeau, A., S. White and N. Nevitte. 2010. 'The
Development of Dual Loyalties: Immigrants'
Integration to Canadian Regional Dynamics',
Canadian Journal of Political Science 43, 3:
515–44.

Bloemraad, I. 2006. *Becoming a Citizen:
Incorporating Immigrants and Refugees in the
United States and Canada*. Berkeley: University
of California Press.

Boudarbat, B. and M. Boule. 2007. 'Détérioration
des salaires des nouveaux immigrants
au Québec par rapport à l'Ontario et à la
Colombie-Britannique', *Choix* 13,7. Montreal:
Institute for Research on Public Policy.

Boyd, M. 2007. 'Religion-Based Alternative
Dispute Resolution: A Challenge to
Multiculturalism'. In *Belonging: Diversity,
Recognition and Shared Citizenship in Canada*,
ed. K. Banting, T. Courchene and L. Seidle.

Montreal: McGill–Queen's University Press.

Canadian Broadcasting Corporation (CBC). 2009.
'Inquiry into immigrant investor program
needed: NDP', 4 November http://www.cbc.ca/
canada/prince-edward-island/2009/11/04/pei-
pnpo-inquiry-ndp-584.html.

Carter, T., M. Pandey and J. Townsend. 2010. *The
Manitoba Provincial Nominee Program: Attraction,
Integration and Retention of Immigrants*. IRPP
Study No. 10. Montreal: Institute for Research
on Public Policy.

Chicha, M-T. and É. Charest. 2008. 'L'intégration
des immigrés sur le marché du travail à
Montréal', *Choix*, 14, 2. Montreal: Institute for
Research on Public Policy.

Citizenship and Immigration Canada. 2010. *Facts
and Figures. Immigration Overview, Permanent
and Temporary Residents 2009*. Ottawa: Minister
of Public Works and Government Services
Canada.

Citizenship and Immigration Canada. 2010a.
Evaluation of the Federal Skilled Worker Program.
Ottawa.

Citizenship and Immigration Canada, 2010b.
Annual Report to Parliament. Ottawa.

Clément, G. 2003. 'The Manitoba Experience'. In
Canadian Immigration Policy for the 21st Century,
ed. C. Beach, A. Green and J. Reitz. Montreal:
McGill–Queen's University Press.

Eliadis, P. 2007. 'Diversity and Equality: The Vital
Connection'. In *Belonging: Diversity, Recognition
and Shared Citizenship in Canada*, ed., K.
Banting, T. Courchene and L. Seidle. Montreal:
McGill–Queen's University Press.

Gagnon, A.-G. 2007. 'Immigration in a
Multicultural Context'. In *Federalism,
Citizenship, and Quebec: Debating
Multiculturalism*, ed. A.-G. Gagnon and R.
Iacovino. Toronto: University of Toronto Press.

Gagnon, A.-G. 2009. 'Immigration in a
Multicultural Context: From Laissez-faire to
an Institutional Framework in Quebec'. In
*Immigration and Self-Government of Minority
Nations*, ed. R. Zapata-Barrero. Brussels: P.I.E.
Peter Lang.

Gagnon, A.-G. and R. Iacovino. 2007.
*Federalism, Citizenship, and Quebec: Debating
Multiculturalism*. Toronto: University of Toronto
Press.

Garcea, J. 2006. 'Provincial Multiculturalism
Politics in Canada, 1974–2004: A Policy

Analysis', *Canadian Ethnic Studies* 38, 3: 1–20.

Gidengil. E. et al. 2004. 'Language and Cultural Insecurity'. In *Québec: State and Society*, 3 ed. A.-G. Gagnon. Peterborough: Broadview Press.

Harell, A. 2009. 'Minority–Majority Relations in Canada: The Rights Regime and the Adoption of Multicultural Values'. Paper presented at the Canadian Political Science Association Annual Meeting, Ottawa.

Hawkins, F. 1988. *Canada and Immigration: Public Policy and Public Concern*, 2nd ed. Montreal: McGill–Queen's University Press.

Johnston, R., K. Banting, W. Kymlicka and S. Soroka. 2010. 'National Identity and Support for the Welfare State', *Canadian Journal of Political Science* 43, 2: 349–77.

Kymlicka, W. 1998. *Finding Our Way: Rethinking Ethnocultural Relations in Canada*. Toronto: Oxford University Press.

Labelle, M. and F. Rocher. 2004. 'Debating Citizenship in Canada: The Collide of Two Nation-Building Projects'. In *From Subjects to Citizens: A Hundred Years of Citizenship in Australia and Canada*, ed. P. Boyer. Ottawa: University of Ottawa Press.

Labelle, M. and F. Rocher. 2009. 'Immigration, Integration and Citizenship Policies in Canada and Quebec: Tug of War between Competing Societal Projects'. In *Immigration and Self-Government of Minority Nations*, ed. R. Zapata-Barrero. Brussels: P.I.E. Peter Lang.

Lambert, R. and J. Curtis. 1982. 'The French and English Canadian Language Communities and Multicultural Attitudes', *Canadian Ethnic Studies* 16: 30–46.

Lambert, R. and J. Curtis. 1983. 'Opposition to Multiculturalism among Québécois and English-Canadians', *Canadian Review of Sociology and Anthropology* 20: 193–206.

Leo, C. and M. August. 2009. 'The Multilevel Governance of Immigration and Settlement: Making Deep Federalism Work', *Canadian Journal of Political Science* 42, 2: 491–510.

Leo, C. and J. Enns. 2009. 'Multi-Level Governance and Ideological Rigidity: The Failure of Deep Federalism', *Canadian Journal of Political Science* 42, 1: 95.

Lewis, N. 2010. 'A Decade Later: Assessing Successes and Challenges in Manitoba's Provincial Immigrant Nominee Program', *Canadian Public Policy* 36, 2: 241–64.

Ley, D. 2010. 'Multiculturalism: a Canadian Defence'. In *The Multicultural Backlash: European discourses, policies and practices*, ed., S. Vertovec and S. Wessendorf. London: Routledge.

Maher, S. 2010. 'N.S. faces uphill battle on immigration', *The Chronicle-Herald*, 9 December.

Media Q. 2010. 'After-caucus media scrum with Minister Jason Kenny'. Transcript prepared for Citizenship and Immigration. Ottawa. 5 May.

Nadeau, S. and A. Secklin, 2010. 'The Immigrant Wage Gap in Canada: Quebec and the Rest of Canada', *Canadian Public Policy* 36, 3: 265–85.

Okonny-Myers, I. 2010. 'The Interprovincial Mobility of Immigrants in Canada'. Ottawa: Citizenship and Immigration.

Seidle, L. 2010. *The Canada-Ontario Immigration Agreement: Assessment and Options for Renewal*. Toronto: Mowat Centre for Policy Innovation, University of Toronto.

Smith, M. 2009. 'Diversity and Canadian Political Development', *Canadian Journal of Political Science* 42, 4: 831–954.

Tran, K., S. Kustec and T. Chui. 2005. 'Becoming Canadian: Intent, Process and Outcome', *Canadian Social Trends* 76, Catalogue No. 11-008. Ottawa: Statistics Canada.

Vineberg, R. Forthcoming. 'History of Federal–provincial Relations in Immigration and Integration'. In *Immigration and Inclusion of Newcomers and Minorities Across Canada*, ed. J. Biles, M. Burstein, J. Frideres, E. Tolley and R. Vineberg. Montreal: McGill–Queen's University Press.

Part III

Re-imagining the Federation

Questions for Critical Thought

1. What are the emerging models of aboriginal governance? Are these emerging models likely to change relationships across the two orders of government—for example, by requiring them to co-operate more closely, or by easing or increasing tensions across them?

2. Is a new order of municipal government—to add to the two orders of federal and provincial governments—necessary and/or politically feasible?

3. Under what circumstances are non-governmental organizations likely to have a more active role in the intergovernmental process? Does an enlarged role for non-governmental actors make Canadian federalism and intergovernmental relations more democratic? Could it hamper consensus-building and so impair the effective functioning of the federal system?

4. What accounts for why Canadian federalism has looked very different—in terms of its degree of centralization or decentralization, for example—at different points in time?

5. Is the changing character of Canadian federalism over time a good or a bad thing—as measured by criteria of its performance, effectiveness and legitimacy? Is it the case that at times the Canadian federation has done better in terms of these criteria? Will it do better in the future and what would be required to bring this about?

15 Canadian Federalism and the Emerging Mosaic of Aboriginal Multilevel Governance

Martin Papillon

In the past forty years, Aboriginal peoples[1] have mounted a fundamental challenge to the institutions of Canadian federalism. They have adopted the language of recognition and national self-determination to reassert their political status and to question the legitimacy and authority of Canadian governments over their lands and communities. Following the analytical framework proposed in this volume, this chapter discusses and assesses the performance, effectiveness, and legitimacy of Canadian federalism in light of these challenges. How, and to what extent, have the institutions and processes of Canadian federalism responded to Aboriginal claims for greater recognition and political autonomy? Fifteen years ago the Royal Commission on Aboriginal Peoples proposed a fundamental reconfiguration of Aboriginal–state relations in which **First Nations**, **Inuit** and **Métis** governments would form a **third order of government** in the federation. Are current dynamics conducive to such development?

There are significant obstacles to the recognition of Aboriginal governing institutions as coequal partners in the federation with provinces and the federal government. Deeply embedded assumptions about state sovereignty, as well as institutions and practices inherited from colonial policies, have proven highly resistant to change. Moreover, the diversity in socio-economic and demographic conditions of Aboriginal communities, not to mention the particularities of each nation's historical relationship with the Canadian state, complicates the picture for advocates of an Aboriginal order of government.

That being said, significant changes have taken place over the past few decades in the dynamics of Aboriginal, federal, provincial, and territorial relations. In addition to the constitutional recognition of Aboriginal and treaty rights, new treaties and self-government agreements have proven to be a significant platform from which some Aboriginal nations and communities have rebuilt their governing capacities. Less visible but nonetheless significant changes have also taken place in the dynamics of policy-making and policy implementation between Aboriginal organizations and governments and their federal, provincial, and territorial counterparts. These changes have led to the development of a complex and highly diverse mosaic of multilevel governance relations. It is increasingly through such multilevel exercises that Aboriginal organizations and governments are asserting their authority and legitimacy, and reconfiguring the landscape of Canadian federalism. The extent to which this process of incremental changes is conducive to larger shifts in the structure of Canadian federalism over the long run is, however, a matter of debate.

Aboriginal Peoples and Canadian Federalism: Facing the Legacy of Colonialism

Aboriginal peoples are the descendants of the populations that lived in what is now North America prior to the arrival of European settlers. Like all colonized societies, Aboriginal peoples in Canada are facing a state that was imposed upon them by external powers. The now dominant society simply imposed its conception of sovereignty and claimed exclusive jurisdiction over the territory. In the process, Aboriginal peoples, who initially engaged in nation-to-nation treaty relations with the Crown, were absorbed into the dominant political order without their consent. This process of 'internal colonization' is now well documented, from the initial stage of diplomatic alliances and treaty making to the processes of land confiscation, cultural assimilation, and dismantlement of traditional forms of government (RCAP, 1996, vol. 1). Indigenous societies became 'domesticated' and 'dependent' nations, as Chief Justice John Marshall of the United States Supreme Court famously stated. The Aboriginal self-determination movement now challenges this forced domestication. Indigenous peoples around the world seek to reassert their status as distinct political entities with a unique relationship with the state and the majority population.[2] In Canada as elsewhere, there remain a number of challenges in addressing the legacy of colonialism.

A Multi-faced Reality

Aboriginal people represent approximately 3.8 per cent of the Canadian population. They are highly diverse: of the 1,172,790 individuals who identified with an Aboriginal group in the 2006 census, 60 per cent identified as North American Indians (First Nations), 33 per cent as Métis, and 4 per cent as Inuit.[3] In addition, there are between 40 and 60 distinct Aboriginal nations in Canada today, according to the Royal Commission on Aboriginal Peoples (RCAP, 1996, vol. 2), each with its own traditions, history, language, and sense of collective identity. To further complicate things, 54 per cent of the Aboriginal population now lives in urban areas.[4] As Figure 15.1 suggests, Aboriginal people form a significant proportion of the population in the northern territories, Saskatchewan, and Manitoba.

Aboriginal people also face important social and economic challenges, largely as a result of past policies designed to accelerate their assimilation into the Canadian mainstream. As the comparative data in Table 15.1 indicate, while improving in certain areas, the Aboriginal population's socio-economic conditions are still significantly worse than those of the average Canadian. The average income of Aboriginal families is 28 per cent lower than that of non-Aboriginal Canadians. Fifty-five per cent of Aboriginal individuals living in cities live in poverty, compared to 24 per cent for all Canadians. These conditions are compounded by demographic trends; the Aboriginal population is younger and growing faster than the Canadian average. A chronic housing crisis and a lack of basic infrastructure, such as sewage and drinking water, also negatively affect the living conditions of the Aboriginal population in many remote areas.

Aboriginal peoples also vary considerably in their status and institutional relationships with the Canadian state. For one, while all Aboriginal peoples were recognized as having the same rights under the Constitution Act, 1982, it is important to recognize that not all have a treaty-based relationship with the Crown. The result is significant variations in the

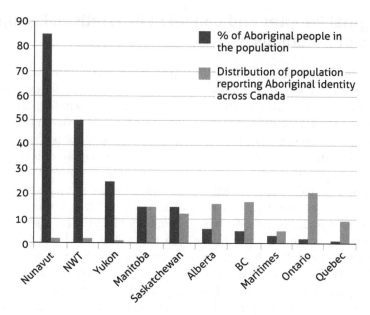

Figure 15.1 Geographic Distribution of the Aboriginal Population

Source: Statistics Canada, *Aboriginal Peoples in Canada in 2006: Inuit, Metis, and First Nations, 2006 Census*, 97-558-XIE2006001, January 2008

land and governance regime of each nation. In addition, while most First Nations come under the regime of the federal Indian Act, Inuit and Métis do not. The federal government also distinguishes between First Nations who are considered 'status' Indians, and thus entitled to certain benefits under the Act, and **non-status Indians**, who fall outside the Act and live mostly in urban areas. These legal distinctions, despite their somewhat arbitrary nature, tend to reinforce political divisions amongst Aboriginal peoples.

Table 15.1 Socio-Economic Conditions of the Aboriginal Population of Canada

	Aboriginal Population	Canadian Population
Median age	27	40
Employment rate	53.7%	63.7%
Low-income families	21.7%	11.1%
No high school diploma (15 and over)	44%	23%
Crowded housing	11.3%	2.9%
Single-parent families	32% on reserve	16%
	46% in urban areas	
Life expectancy at birth	Men: 68.9	Men: 76.3
	Women: 76.3	Women: 81.5

Sources: Statistics Canada (2008); INAC (2010a)

These differences in conditions, status, and entitlements have significant repercussions for Aboriginal peoples and their relationship with Canadian federalism. Clearly, there is not one single Aboriginal reality to be addressed with a single set of solutions. This reality is further compounded by the fact that Aboriginal peoples do not necessarily all share the same conception of their relationship with the Canadian state. While some simply reject Canadian sovereignty over their traditional lands, others, especially the Inuit and Métis, have historically been less reluctant to accept the authority of the Canadian Constitution. Aboriginal populations living in urban settings also often have very different viewpoints and interests than those living in remote areas, where control over the land and natural resources is a key element of ongoing conflicts with the state. Within each community there are also often conflicting views between 'traditionalists', who seek to reassert traditional lifestyle, values, and governing practices, and those who focus on the modernization of socio-economic and political structures as a key element of the project of autonomy.[5]

The Constraining Nature of Canadian Federalism

In addition to their diverse realities, Aboriginal people also face significant challenges related to the institutions of Canadian federalism. Although the Royal Proclamation of 1763 recognized the status of Aboriginal nations as distinct political entities, no Aboriginal representatives were invited to the Charlottetown and Quebec conferences of 1864, where the foundations of the Canadian federation were established. As a result, they never consented, explicitly or implicitly, to the division of authority over the land and peoples that resulted from the Constitution Act, 1867. Instead, they effectively became an object of federal jurisdiction according to section 91(24) of the Act, which confers on the federal Parliament the power to legislate over 'Indians and Land reserved for Indians'. The institutions of Canadian federalism thus have very little, if any, legitimacy from an Aboriginal perspective. The initial exclusion of Aboriginal peoples from those institutions created a number of constraints that still limit their political aspirations in the Canadian context.

Most significantly, while authority in a federation is divided between orders of governments, the doctrine of state sovereignty is still deeply entrenched in the British-inspired Canadian parliamentary system. There is no space in the Canadian federation for the expression of political authority outside the two constitutionally recognized orders of government.[6] As a result, from a strictly positivist constitutional perspective, Aboriginal governments' authority can only be delegated from the federal and provincial Parliaments. Aboriginal peoples, supported by many legal scholars and Aboriginal rights advocates, reject this conception of sovereignty and argue instead that they have an **inherent right to self-government**, that is a right that emanates not from the Constitution, but from their historical presence—as politically organized peoples—on the land (Macklem, 2001; Borrows, 2002). As we will see in the second part of this chapter, a limited definition of the inherent Aboriginal right to self-government has been accepted by the federal government and most provinces, but its implementation in practice still faces significant institutional resistance.

Without formal status as federal partners, Aboriginal peoples and their governments[7] also have no statutory voice in the shared institutions of 'intrastate federalism', such as the federal Parliament, the Cabinet, or the Supreme Court, other than what their demographic weight calls for. They also have had historically only limited access to the important mechanisms of 'interstate federalism' associated with the growing web of intergovernmental processes and institutions that characterize the Canadian federation.

The division of powers in the Canadian federation has also contributed to what are often tense relations between Aboriginal peoples and provinces (Long and Boldt, 1988). Especially relevant in the Canadian context is provincial authority over public lands and natural resources. Provinces have naturally sought to maximize local economic development, mainly through natural resource extraction, often without much regard for Aboriginal rights and interests. Highly visible conflicts over hydroelectric developments, forestry and fisheries, or over developments on public lands for which the title is still contested by an Aboriginal group, regularly make headlines in Canadian media and contribute to divisions and a high degree of mistrust between the Aboriginal population and non-Aboriginal Canadians.[8]

Finally, Aboriginal people have also long been, and continue to be, victims of the competitive nature of Canadian federalism, especially with regards to the provision of social programs and services. Paradoxically, the issue here is not so much who *can*, but rather who *must* exercise its legislative authority. Again, the conflict revolves around the interpretation of section 91(24) of the Constitution Act, 1867. As we have seen, the federal government initially interpreted its responsibilities restrictively and excluded Inuit, Métis, and non-status Indians from the Indian Act regime. But even for those covered by the Indian Act, the federal government has on numerous occasions sought to transfer its responsibilities for the provision of services to provinces.[9] The latter, though reluctant to allow federal interventions in their areas of jurisdiction, have always insisted on the federal government's responsibility for the provision of social programs to the Aboriginal population. As a result, a significant number of Aboriginal individuals, especially off-reserve Indians and Métis, have fallen into a jurisdictional gap and for a long time were simply ignored by both orders of government. Even today federal and provincial authorities tend to interpret their respective responsibilities in relation to Aboriginal people more or less liberally depending on the interests at stake. Jurisdictional uncertainties add to an already complex policy challenge in developing long-term, co-ordinated solutions to Aboriginal socio-economic conditions (Noel and Larocque, 2009).

We can thus conclude that in addition to lacking legitimacy as a result of Aboriginal people's exclusion at the time of the creation of the federation, Canadian federalism has not been a particularly effective conduit for addressing the legacy of colonialism. Nor has it historically performed well as a unifying system of governance. In fact, the institutions and processes of Canadian federalism have exacerbated conflicts with Aboriginal people and have contributed significantly to the reproduction of the system of exclusion inherited from the colonial period. Reconciling the Canadian federal system with Aboriginal claims to self-determination is thus not a simple task.

A Renewed Federal Partnership?

Although the institutions of Canadian federalism in many ways constitute an obstacle for Aboriginal people, Canada's 'federal condition' can also open the door to significant opportunities. Canadians are familiar with the idea of coexistence in a diverse, even divided, political community. The ongoing debate over the accommodation of Quebec nationalism has opened avenues for Aboriginal people towards a greater recognition of their political status, as the definition of what constitutes Canada as a political community is constantly questioned in public discourse as well as in intellectual circles.

The redefinition of Canadian federalism in order to recognize the political status of Aboriginal nations has been the object of many theoretical reflections in recent years. While some have argued that Aboriginal peoples could form a province, the small size, territorial dispersion, and diversity of Aboriginal communities make such a proposal impractical.[10] The most widely discussed model consists instead of recognizing Aboriginal governments as a third order of government, with a distinct sphere of authority within the existing federation. This is the model proposed by the Royal Commission on Aboriginal Peoples (RCAP). According to the Commission, the foundation of this third order rests on the recognition of the inherent right to self-government as an existing right under section 35(1) of the Constitution Act, 1982. As a previously self-governing political community, each Aboriginal nation should be entitled to control a series of 'core' jurisdictions and to negotiate a new division of responsibilities with the federal and provincial governments through treaties or other forms of agreement (RCAP, 1996, vol.2: 215).

As an alternative to incorporating Aboriginal governments *within* the existing federation as a third order, some argue in favour of a renewal of the existing treaty-based relationship *outside* the institutions of Canadian federalism (Ladner, 2003). In this perspective, Aboriginal nations are and have always been sovereign entities on their own, independent of the Canadian Constitution, and treaties establish bilateral confederal relations with Canada in the same way that international treaties are the constitutive basis of the European Union. Proponents of this alternative argue that early treaties between Aboriginal nations and the Crown, which are still valid today, created a bilateral relationship of self-rule and shared rule between co-existing and coequal partners. According to Sakej Henderson (1994), this '**treaty federalism**' should be reinstated as the basis of a renewed, postcolonial partnership between Aboriginal nations and the Canadian state. Building on a similar perspective, James Tully (1995) argues that Canada should be conceived as a double confederation: the treaty-based partnership between Aboriginal peoples and the Crown, and the newer federal–provincial federation.[11]

While the RCAP and treaty federalism models offer inspiring theoretical models for reconfiguring Canadian federalism in light of Aboriginal claims, they nonetheless pose numerous practical challenges. Most significantly, it is not clear how Aboriginal peoples would be represented in the shared institutions of a two-level federal system, or even in a third-order model. Should all nations, no matter their size, have equal representation, or should representation be more proportional? How would shared decisions be made? Moreover, as Alan Cairns (2000: 191) argues in his critique of the RCAP model, it is not self-evident how one can reconcile a treaty-based, nation-to-nation association with a substantive conception of shared citizenship, a necessary condition to foster a sense of solidarity and co-operation across communities that are bound to live together in a common territory. Finally, these models, which both assume some degree of fiscal autonomy for Aboriginal governments, may not be suitable for all Aboriginal nations or communities, as most are highly dependent on fiscal transfers from the federal government, especially those with limited land bases or access to resources. As history shows, equality in principle means little without some balance in resources. These obstacles are not insurmountable, but they illustrate the challenges of moving from theoretical constructs to more concrete institutional reforms.

The Changing Relationship between Aboriginal Peoples and Canadian Federalism

So, where are we today? Moving away from theoretical considerations and looking at recent developments, it is safe to say that the relationship between Aboriginal peoples and the institutions of Canadian federalism has changed in the last few decades. From the now infamous 1969 White Paper on Indian Policy, which sought to do away with the differentiated status of Aboriginal peoples, to the constitutional recognition of Aboriginal and treaty rights and the negotiation of treaties and self-government agreements in Quebec, Yukon, British Columbia, and elsewhere, the shifts are remarkable. That being said, the existing framework of Canadian federalism continues to be more of a constraint on than a vehicle for Aboriginal aspirations. The recognition of Aboriginal governments as a third order of government, or of a parallel treaty-based federal structure, remains more theoretical than real, and the representation of Aboriginal peoples in shared federal institutions remains problematic. Interestingly, it is perhaps outside the traditional institutions of the federation, in emerging dynamics of multilevel governance between Aboriginal, federal, and provincial governments, that the changes with the greatest significance for Canadian federalism are taking place.

Recognition through the Courts

With only limited access to the traditional institutions of Canadian federalism, Aboriginal peoples, like other minorities in Canada, have used the courts and the language of rights to assert their claims for recognition. As a result, the courts have played a central role in redefining the legal framework of Aboriginal peoples' relationship with the Canadian federation. The 1973 Calder decision, in which the Supreme Court recognized for the first time the possibility that an Aboriginal title resulting from prior occupation of the land could have legal force in contemporary Canada, created a significant hole in the doctrine of unmediated Crown sovereignty. It opened the constitutional door for one of the most significant developments in Aboriginal–state relations since Confederation: the recognition of Aboriginal and treaty rights in section 35(1) of the Constitution Act, 1982.

A significant Aboriginal rights jurisprudence has developed since 1982 in which the Supreme Court confirmed the substantial nature of Aboriginal constitutional rights and limited the power of governments to infringe on these rights without a compelling reason.[12] The Court effectively created a legal space, albeit a limited one, for Aboriginal peoples to assert their presence in the political landscape of the Canadian federation. Although the Supreme Court never said so explicitly, it is increasingly accepted that section 35 rights include the inherent right to self-government. The failed Charlottetown Accord of 1992, to which all first ministers agreed, contained a disposition to that effect, and the federal government reiterated its support for such interpretation of section 35 in a policy statement in 1995.[13]

The Supreme Court has adhered to a relatively restrictive interpretation in its few decisions where governance rights under section 35 have been discussed. As for other Aboriginal rights, the Court has limited governance rights to activities, customs, or traditions 'integral to the distinctive culture of Aboriginal peoples' and has insisted on the need to reconcile these rights with federal and provincial constitutional authority. This interpretation has prompted commentators to suggest that the Aboriginal rights recognized under section 35 are 'frozen in time', as they concern traditional practices and do not constitute a basis for the development of modern governance structure and a renewed political relationship with the state (Asch, 2002; McNeil, 2004).

Beyond questions of definition, there are inherent limits to what the courts can do in redefining the status and role of Aboriginal governments. The interpretation of Aboriginal rights by the Supreme Court, however liberal it may be, will remain constrained by the parameters of the Canadian Constitution, from which it derives its own authority. Though important in establishing a more level playing field and interpreting negotiated agreements, tribunals can neither create new institutions of governance nor completely replace the political process in redefining the constitutional foundations of our relationships. In fact, the Supreme Court has recognized its limited role in this respect a number of times.[14] Given the lack of legitimacy of existing institutions, the redefinition of the relationship between Aboriginal peoples and the Canadian federation should ideally stem from negotiations between mutually consenting parties. The federal government and the provinces have recognized the need for a negotiated response, at least in principle.

Modern Treaties

The re-emergence of treaties as a key institutional mechanism for negotiating and redefining the relationship between Aboriginal peoples and the Canadian federation is certainly one of the most significant constitutional developments of the past thirty years in Canada. There are, however, many disagreements regarding the meaning of 'modern treaties'. For the federal government, as well as for the provinces involved in negotiations, the objective of treaties is not to renegotiate the configuration of state sovereignty but rather to confirm its legality and legitimacy in light of the Canadian Constitution. The stated objective of the federal land claims policy, under which modern treaties are negotiated, is 'to obtain certainty respecting ownership and use of lands and resources' (INAC, 2010b: 2). To ensure certainty, the federal government requires the surrender of all existing and possibly existing land rights on the territory covered by the agreement in exchange for the rights and benefits defined in the settlement. This approach, under which Aboriginal rights outside those defined in the agreement are 'extinguished', has been the object of criticism from numerous quarters, including the United Nations.[15] Not surprisingly, the understanding of treaties that informs this process is fundamentally at odds with Aboriginal conceptions of the treaty process as establishing a political relationship between coequal partners, sharing responsibility for stewardship of the land.

Despite these important limits, and the extremely slow and frustrating nature of the process, land claim negotiations have been an important vehicle for Aboriginal peoples to redefine their relationship with the federal and provincial governments. Following its 'inherent right' policy of 1995, the federal government now accepts the negotiation of self-government arrangements as an integral part of land claim settlements, thus creating constitutionally protected and distinct governance structures for a growing number of Aboriginal nations and communities.[16]

The Nisga'a Final Agreement, signed in 1998 after 25 years of mobilization and negotiations, is worth noting in this context. The agreement provides for ownership and
self-governing control of approximately 2,000 km² of land in the Nass Valley in British
Columbia, including surface and subsurface resources. The agreement establishes law-
making authority—within the limits of the Canadian Constitution—for the Nisga'a
Lisims Government and four Village Governments, as well as three urban locals, which
provide a voice for Nisga'a citizens who do not live in the Nass Valley. The Nisga'a Lisims
Government has paramount legislative authority over the management of community
lands, citizenship, and local matters. However, the treaty includes important limitations
on Nisga'a authority even in areas where Nisga'a laws are paramount. The Nisga'a government cannot make laws that run contrary to the general interests of the federal and provincial governments, and must operate within the framework of the Canadian Constitution,
including the Charter of Rights. In a number of other areas, such as education, transport,
and environmental regulation, Nisga'a authority is concurrent with federal and provincial
jurisdictions. In most cases, Nisga'a laws prevail only if they meet or exceed federal and
provincial requirements.[17] A similar system of paramount and concurrent jurisdictions
was established under the Council of Yukon Indians Umbrella Agreement of 1993, under
which Yukon First Nations have been negotiating specific self-government agreements.

Another important milestone was achieved with the Nunavut Land Claims Agreement.
Signed in 1992, it led to the creation of the Nunavut territory in 1999 and the establishment of a public government controlled by a majority of Inuit. The new territory covers
almost 2 million km². The Inuit themselves are recognized as having collective title to
351,000 km² of land (of which about 10 per cent include sub-surface mineral rights), as
well as a share of resource royalties and participation in co-management bodies in a number of areas involving land development and environmental issues.[18] The Government
of Nunavut is a public government and follows the Canadian parliamentary model. It is
formed by a cabinet of nine ministers, responsible to a legislature of 19 members elected
by the population of the territory. Like the other two territories, Nunavut does not have
the constitutional status of a province. Its authority is delegated though federal legislation
and, most significantly, unlike a province it does not have jurisdiction over Crown lands
and resources. Its authority is nevertheless significant in most areas where provinces
normally have jurisdiction and, like the other territories, it has full status in the various
federal–provincial intergovernmental mechanisms. Although it is a public government,
the Nunavut government promotes the interests, culture, and traditions of Inuit. It has
also tried since its creation to adopt a working philosophy that corresponds to Inuit approaches to governance, through a policy known as Inuit Qaujimajatuqangit, aimed at
shaping the public service according to Inuit values.

Modern treaties and self-government agreements constitute an important development in Canada's constitutional landscape. Aboriginal nations like the Nisga'a or the
Inuit in Nunavut are recognized as legitimate political entities, sharing in practice some
governmental authority with the federal and provincial orders of governments. On the
other hand, treaty-based self-government agreements certainly do not constitute a radical realignment of the distribution of sovereignty and democratic legitimacy in the federation. Self-governing Aboriginal nations still struggle to have their status and place
properly recognized in the institutions and processes of Canadian federalism. In many

ways, these developments seem to take place in spite of our federal system rather than in conjunction with it.

Participation in the Intrastate and Interstate Institutions of Canadian Federalism

As was noted earlier, a central element compounding the lack of legitimacy of Canadian federalism for Aboriginal peoples has been their exclusion, as political entities, from its institutions and processes. Although there have been many discussions of reforming the institutions of 'intrastate' and 'interstate' federalism so as to make them more inclusive for Aboriginal peoples, success has been limited. For now, proposals to reform the electoral system and the structure of representation in the federal Parliament to increase Aboriginal representation remain only theoretical. Although there are Aboriginal Members of Parliament and Senators, their influence on the overall balance of power is limited to their demographic weight. The Royal Commission on Electoral Reform and Party Financing proposed the establishment of special Aboriginal electoral districts to enhance Aboriginal representation in the House of Commons (RCER, 1991). The RCAP (1996, vol. 2) also proposed the creation of an additional Aboriginal House of Representatives, and the Charlottetown Accord contained guarantees for enhanced Aboriginal representation in a reformed Senate. Not surprisingly, such reforms have met with skepticism amongst advocates of individual equality and status-blind representation in parliamentary institutions, but they are also perceived with suspicion by some Aboriginal peoples themselves, especially those defending a treaty-based, nation-to-nation conception of the relationship (Schouls, 1996). From that perspective, greater participation of Aboriginal citizens as individuals in Canadian institutions is associated with institutional assimilation, and helps to legitimize unilateral Canadian sovereignty (Alfred, 2005).

Interestingly, it is perhaps in the institutions and processes of interstate federalism that Aboriginal peoples have made the most significant headway. National Aboriginal organizations have gained access to the various intergovernmental forums through which Canadian governments co-ordinate their policies. The main national Aboriginal organizations are the Assembly of First Nations (AFN), which represents mostly on-reserve First Nations; the Congress of Aboriginal Peoples (CAP), representing non-status Indians; the Métis National Council (MNC); the Inuit Tapiriit Kanatami (ITK); the Native Women's Association of Canada (NWAC); and two more organizations representing Inuit and Métis women respectively. The participation of Aboriginal organizations in the mechanisms of Canadian intergovernmental relations is a legacy of the constitutional negotiations of the 1980s and early 1990s. Between 1983 and 1987, these national organizations were directly involved in the intergovernmental negotiations dedicated to the definition of Aboriginal rights under section 35(2) of the Constitution Act, 1982. Despite its ultimate failure, this process allowed the organizations involved to gain legitimacy and significant experience in dealing with the intricacies of intergovernmental negotiations (Brock, 1991). The outcry produced by their exclusion from the Quebec-driven Meech Lake process contributed to their return as full, and high-profile, participants during the 'Canada round' that led to the Charlottetown Accord in 1992.

Many assumed that the inclusion of Aboriginal national leaders in constitutional talks created a precedent that would be difficult to reverse. With the demise of mega-constitutional negotiations, however, Aboriginal organizations lost their leverage and today their participation in the various mechanisms of intergovernmental relations—at the first minister, ministerial, or administrative level—remains contingent on the nature of the issues being debated and the discretion of federal and provincial governments. For example, despite intense lobbying by the Assembly of First Nations, Aboriginal organizations were excluded from the Social Union Framework Agreement negotiations in the late 1990s. They were, however, included in the implementation process following the Agreement though consultations at the administrative level (Dacks, 2001).

In 2004 and 2005, Aboriginal organizations were also invited to participate in the development of joint initiatives with the provinces and the federal government on a variety of policy issues. This multilevel consultation process led to the Kelowna Accord, an intergovernmental agreement on a five-year plan to foster socio-economic development in Aboriginal communities.[19] In a succession of events indicative of the limited institutional and political weight associated with such agreements, the newly elected Conservative government of Stephen Harper promptly withdrew federal support for the Kelowna Accord. The Harper government did eventually implement some of the measures contained in the Accord, but the funding commitments and the implementation model involving provincial and Aboriginal partners were set aside for good. The Conservative government has so far shied away from further multilateral policy negotiations with Aboriginal organizations, preferring a more classic approach to policy development and implementation.

Interestingly, Aboriginal organizations have had more success with provinces in recent years. In the aftermath of Kelowna, an inter-provincial Aboriginal Affairs Working Group was established to facilitate co-ordination with Aboriginal organizations on social and economic issues. Aboriginal organizations are also now routinely invited to a one-day session with Premiers in advance of the annual meeting of the Council of the Federation. Of course, these processes remain purely consultative. In fact, the demise of the Kelowna Accord and subsequent events suggest the status of Aboriginal representatives in executive federalism will remain largely ad hoc and contingent on the federal–provincial agenda for the foreseeable future. Except for Nunavut, the Aboriginal presence in intergovernmental forums is unlikely to become institutionalized. There are very few incentives for the federal and provincial governments to encourage greater Aboriginal participation in a process that is already complex and difficult to manage with fourteen governments. The prospect of further institutionalization also raises the question of who would determine which organizations, or Aboriginal governing institutions, have the legitimacy to take part in intergovernmental processes.

Beyond the Existing Institutions of Federalism: Changing Relations of Governance

The developments discussed thus far concern fairly high-profile aspects of the changing dynamics between Aboriginal peoples and Canadian federalism. In parallel with constitutional debates and the negotiation of treaties and self-government agreements, some fundamental, though less visible, changes in the relationship between Aboriginal organizations and governments (band councils and others) and their federal and provincial counterparts are also taking place in the dynamics of everyday governance. In the past twenty years, the federal government and its provincial counterparts have undertaken a

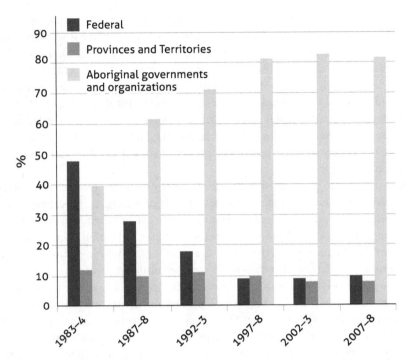

Figure 15.2 Who Administers Federal Funds for Aboriginal Programming (percent)

Data source: Indian and Northern Affairs Canada.

significant decentralization of programs and services to Aboriginal governments and or-ganizations. The process of decentralization started as early as the 1960s, with the trans-fer of school administration to some First Nations. But it was only in the 1980s that it became a systematic element of federal policy, as Aboriginal claims for greater autonomy coincided with the rise of the neo-liberal agenda promoting a scaled-down, more flexible state and a greater role for communities in their socio-economic development.

As Figure 15.2 suggests, the transfer of budget for program management to Aboriginal governing authorities rapidly increased in the mid-1980s. The result was a significant shift in the role of both Aboriginal governments and Indian and Northern Affairs Canada (INAC), the main federal department responsible for Aboriginal programs. In 1983, INAC directly managed close to 50 per cent of programs directed towards Aboriginal peoples. This proportion is now reduced to 8 per cent. In addition to local infrastructures, First Nations band councils and tribal councils, as well as local and regional Inuit govern-ments, are now largely responsible for the administration of social services, education, training, economic development, and housing services in communities.

This redefinition of the federal approach to Aboriginal governance is largely consistent with broader changes in the dynamics of governance in most industrialized countries (Pierre and Peters, 2000). As in many other service-oriented policy areas, instead of run-ning programs directly, the federal government increasingly works in partnership with Aboriginal organizations and governments in the regulation, management, and delivery of services. A number of government programs developed in the wake of *Gathering Strength*, the 1998 federal action plan designed in response to the report of the Royal Commission on Aboriginal Peoples, follow this 'partnership' approach (INAC, 1997). More recently, the Harper government's Economic Action Plan was implemented largely through partnerships with local Aboriginal organizations and governments (INAC, 2010c). A number of bilateral and trilateral agreements in specific policy fields are also reshaping Aboriginal governance. For example, in July 2006 a trilateral agreement between the federal government, the government of British Columbia, and the First Nations Education Steering Committee of that province proposed the transfer of some legislative authority to First Nations in education matters.[20]

What is the impact of administrative decentralization and governance through partnerships? While this new approach increases the role of Aboriginal governments in the administration of programs, it does not change their legal and constitutional status, nor does it change the division of powers and authority in the federation. With some exceptions, these decentralization agreements are mostly administrative in nature. Very few are enacted through legislation. They can thus be revoked unilaterally, or drastically reduced, without much warning. Administrative decentralization may in fact increase the dependent and hierarchical relationship between Aboriginal authorities and federal and provincial governments, since the capacity of Aboriginal governments to deliver services to their communities is entirely dependent on such programs. Moreover, the minister of Indian Affairs is still responsible to Parliament for the funds allocated through those agreements. As a result, the transfer of responsibilities is accompanied by an increased emphasis on accounting and reporting mechanisms, which, as the Auditor General noted in a recent report, has become a significant administrative burden for Aboriginal governments.[21] In sum, critics of decentralization may well be correct when they argue that it represents little more than a new way for Canadian governments to maintain a form of 'control at distance' on Aboriginal communities (Neu and Therrien, 2003).

That being said, one should not underestimate the long-term political impact of administrative transfers on the role and legitimacy of Aboriginal governments. For one, even if they do not formally transfer any jurisdiction, these agreements considerably increase the relevance of Aboriginal governments in the daily life of communities. They are, in effect, becoming the sole governmental presence in those communities. Second, despite tight fiscal controls, administrative decentralization leaves a certain leeway for Aboriginal governments in the implementation of programs. In a decentralized governance context, the relationship between the policy objectives defined at one level and the implementation process at another needs to be relatively loose, so that the agents responsible for implementation can adapt programs to their specific context (Pierre and Peters, 2000). The administration of decentralized programs targeted at Aboriginal economic development or training, for example, involves a substantial degree of policy choice in defining priorities at the community level. In addition to the development of policy capacity, this margin of autonomy for Aboriginal governments can also reinforce their democratic legitimacy in communities where they have long been considered little more than state agents. Decentralized program administration fosters political debates and deliberation in communities that, for most of the last century, have been governed from above and shut out of any substantial democratic debates regarding their own development. In other words, it may well force Aboriginal governments to be more responsive to the priorities, values, and culture of their communities.

This decentralized approach to governance is also significantly altering the nature of the relationship between Aboriginal governments and their provincial counterparts. Administrative decentralization, just like formal self-government arrangements, increases the need for co-ordination and consultation between governments that have historically operated in parallel. In fact, the growing role of provinces in Aboriginal policy may be one of the most misunderstood consequences of this new model of decentralized governance. Ongoing discussions are necessary in order to negotiate the various administrative agreements, establish financial needs, and evaluate services, but also to co-ordinate federal or provincial objectives with Aboriginal ones, and define future priorities. For example, the transfer of federal education responsibilities to band councils or Aboriginal-led school boards creates a need to co-ordinate with provincial governments in order to ensure the recognition of diplomas and facilitate Aboriginal students' access to post-secondary education. The transfer of responsibilities over public security involves similar trilateral relations to ensure co-ordination and co-operation between Aboriginal, federal, and provincial police corps. As a result, Aboriginal governments have significantly developed their intergovernmental capacities in the past decade. Many Aboriginal governments now have a team of professional civil servants whose expertise is not in running programs but in policy analysis, fiscal relations, and the negotiation of intergovernmental agreements.

The capacity of Aboriginal governments to influence the outcome of intergovernmental negotiations over administrative agreements varies considerably depending on their demographic and geographic situation, their resources, and, of course, the nature of their institutions of governance. Aboriginal nations with a treaty-based self-government agreement have significantly more leverage and resources to engage in government-to-government relations. Even within the Indian Act framework, not all Aboriginal governments are equal in their capacity to engage in intergovernmental relations. Those with a strong tradition of political affirmation and an effective governmental structure logically fare better. The Kahnawake Mohawks, for example, have unilaterally asserted their authority in a number of policy areas, such as education, policing, gambling, and other commercial activities, as well as trade of good and services, and then used intergovernmental forums with the federal and Quebec governments to negotiate the recognition of their authority in exchange for a greater co-ordination and harmonization in the implementation of policies.

Conclusion: An Emerging Mosaic of Multilevel Governance Relations

The relationship between Aboriginal peoples and Canadian federalism remains uncertain and tentative. The initial exclusion of Aboriginal peoples from the federal compact still looms large today, affecting not only the legitimacy but also the performance and effectiveness of the institutions and processes of Canadian federalism as they try to address the difficult colonial legacy. Although Canadians are often perceived to be more supportive of Aboriginal rights than their Australian or American counterparts, this support has not led to a radical reconfiguration of Canadian federalism along the lines proposed by the RCAP and proponents of treaty federalism. Multiple factors work against such a significant reform of Canadian federalism, most significantly the institutional resilience of existing practices and conceptions of state sovereignty and governmental authority. The profound diversity, demographic situation, and socio-economic conditions of Aboriginal peoples also compound these difficulties. So does the fiscal dependency of Aboriginal governments on their federal and provincial counterparts.

That being said, significant shifts have taken place in the constitutional framework and institutions of Canadian federalism. As we have seen, these shifts remain very much a work in progress. The extent and meaning of Aboriginal rights are still being defined though the courts as well as through public and academic debates. Despite recent developments in treaty negotiations, federal and provincial authorities still impose significant limits on both the process and the substance of agreements. The status of the self-governing structures slowly emerging from such processes varies considerably from one agreement to the other, and their viability largely depends on the willingness of both federal and provincial authorities to put resources and goodwill into implementing each agreement. In this respect, Canadian federalism has performed rather poorly, as the specific responsibilities and obligations of the federal and provincial governments often remain unclear. The participation of Aboriginal organizations in mechanisms of executive federalism raises a new set of issues in terms of legitimacy and accountability, as their status in such processes remains largely ad hoc and uncertain. The rejection of the Kelowna Accord also raises concerns regarding the effectiveness of intergovernmental mechanisms in addressing pressing social and economic issues in Aboriginal communities that cut across the boundaries of federal and provincial jurisdictions.

As I have suggested, it is perhaps in the emerging dynamics of multilevel governance in the negotiation of policy implementation that Aboriginal, federal, and provincial relations have changed most significantly. This change may not affect the constitutional status of Aboriginal peoples, but Aboriginal governments now play a growing role in the development and implementation of policies, and as a result consolidate their capacity and legitimacy both within the communities and in their relations with federal and provincial authorities. Aboriginal governance is now increasingly being played out in multiple venues. If the federal government has kept the upper hand with its constitutional authority and fiscal capacity, provinces now play an increasing role as a result of their involvement in treaty negotiations and in the process of administrative devolution to Aboriginal governments and organizations. Aboriginal governments have been increasingly proactive in developing their intergovernmental capacity, and engage with their federal and provincial counterparts in policy negotiations. In other words, Aboriginal governance is less and less a unidirectional, top-down affair and is increasingly becoming a multilevel, trilateral reality.

This emerging trilateral, multilevel governance regime is far from uniform, as the context, status, needs, and expectations, as well as the political clout, of Aboriginal nations vary considerably. Different self-government agreements, land bases, and provincial positions in relation to Aboriginal peoples also affect the nature and dynamics of multilevel governance. It is perhaps more accurate to talk of a mosaic of multilevel governance relations between Aboriginal nations and their federal and provincial counterparts, each with its own institutional framework and evolving dynamics. While it does not create a formal third order of governments or a parallel treaty-based federal structure, this emerging multilevel mosaic offers what can, in effect, be defined as an alternative way for Aboriginal peoples to reshape their relationship with Canadian federalism. In this perspective, change is not coming from above, through formal constitutional processes, but rather from below, through the consolidation of Aboriginal governments' capacity and legitimacy in exercises of governance. Only time will tell whether this changing dynamic can eventually lead to a more efficient and legitimate relationship between the Canadian federation and Aboriginal peoples.

Notes

The author would like to acknowledge the helpful comments of Peter Russell and the editors of this volume on earlier drafts of this chapter. Some sections were also inspired by an earlier text by the author, 'Vers un fédéralisme postcolonial? La difficile redéfinition des rapports entre l'État canadien et les peuples autochtones', published in *Le Fédéralisme canadien contemporain. Fondements, traditions, institutions*, ed. Alain-G. Gagnon (Montreal: Presses de l'Université de Montréal).

1. Following the practice in the Canadian literature, the term 'Aboriginal peoples' in this text refers to Métis and Inuit peoples as well as First Nations (still often referred to as Indians). Distinctions among the three are made when necessary.
2. For a normative defence of Aboriginal self-determination, see for example Tully (2000), Macklem (2001) and, in the international context, Anaya (2004).
3. The data in this section are from Statistics Canada (2008) and INAC (2010a).
4. Of major Canadian cities, Winnipeg has the largest Aboriginal population, with 68,300 persons, accounting for 10 per cent of its population.
5. The debate between 'traditionalists' and 'modernists' is reflected in the academic literature, especially amongst Indigenous scholars. See Alfred (2005) and Newhouse (2000) for an interesting contrast.
6. According to the oft-repeated doctrine established by the Judicial Committee of the Privy Council, 'whatever belongs to self-government in Canada belongs either to the Dominion or to the provinces, within the limits of the British North America Act'. *A.G. Ontario* (1912).
7. Aboriginal governments vary considerably in form and size, as well as in degree of responsibility and legitimacy within communities. Elected band councils are the most common form of government for First Nations. Formally, they exercise delegated authority under the Indian Act, although many play a much greater political role. Bands have also aggregated themselves into national or regional tribal councils. Other Aboriginal governments were created though federal or provincial legislation pursuant to self-government agreements and exercise powers accordingly. In some cases, self-governing structures reproduce the ethnic-based council system, but Inuit in Nunavut and elsewhere, for example, have opted for public forms of local and regional governments. For an overview, see Belanger et al. (2008).
8. There is no space here for an exhaustive list of recent conflicts, but one can think of the 1990 Oka crisis in Quebec, the 1995 standoff at Ipperwash Provincial Park and the 2006 land dispute in Caledonia, Ontario, as examples of land disputes that turned sour. Conflicts over the fisheries in the Maritimes and British Columbia are examples of disputes over natural resources.
9. The infamous *White Paper on Indian Policy* of 1969 notably proposed such a transfer.
10. The obvious exception here is Nunavut, where Inuit form a majority on a significant territory that could well become self-sustainable given its extensive natural resources.

11. Abele and Prince (2006) discuss in greater details the conceptual foundations of treaty federalism and the differences with the model proposed by the RCAP.

12. Landmark decisions, such as *Sparrow* (1990), *Van der Peet* (1996), *Delgamuukw* (1997) and *Marshall* (1999), amongst others, have defined the extent and content of Aboriginal and treaty rights. For critical analyses, see amongst others Borrows (2002) and Macklem (2001).

13. Both the Charlottetown Accord and the 1995 policy statement made it clear, however, that such a right was to be exercised within the existing boundaries of the Canadian Constitution.

14. For example, in *Delgamuukw* (1997), former Chief Justice Lamer called for a negotiated solution to conflicts over resource extraction and land development.

15. See *Concluding Observations of the Human Rights Committee: Canada*. United Nations, cpr/c/can/co/5, November 2005.

16. At the time of writing, 22 final agreements had been ratified since the first 'modern treaty', the *James Bay and Northern Quebec Agreement* in 1975. This includes ten specific agreements with Yukon First Nations negotiated under the *Council for Yukon Indians Umbrella Agreement* of 1993. See INAC (2010b) for an overview of existing agreements.

17. For various viewpoints on the *Nisga'a Final Agreement*, see the special issue of *BC Studies* (no. 120, Winter 1998–9).

18. For a discussion of the Agreement and its impact on Inuit governance and culture, see Henderson (2007).

19. The five major national organizations were directly involved in defining the agenda of the meeting and in the administrative process that laid the ground for the agreement. For more details on the Kelowna summit, see www.scics.gc.ca/cinfo05/800044004_e.pdf (accessed 29 October 2010).

20. For an overview see http://www.fnesc.ca/jurisdiction/index.php (accessed 7 October 2010).

21. The Auditor General (2002) estimates that band councils are required to produce an average of 202 reports to various federal agencies each year under the most common of existing funding arrangements.

References

Abele, F. and M. Prince. 2006. 'Four Pathways to Aboriginal Self-Government in Canada', *American Review of Canadian Studies*, 36: 568–95.

Alfred, T. 2005. *Wasáse: Indigenous Pathways of Action and Freedom*. Peterborough, ON: Broadview Press.

Anaya, J. 2004. *Indigenous Peoples and International Law*. Oxford: Oxford University Press.

Asch, M. 2002. 'From Tierra Nullius to Affirmation: Reconciling Aboriginal Rights with the Canadian Constitution', *Canadian Journal of Law and Society* 17, 2: 23–39.

Auditor General (Canada). 2002. *Streamlining First Nations Reporting to Federal Organizations*, Auditor General's December 2002 Report, Chapter 1. Ottawa: Minister of Supply and Services.

Bélanger, Y. (ed.). 2008. *Aboriginal Self-Government in Canada, Current Trends and Issues*, 3rd ed. Saskatoon: Purich Publishing.

Borrows, J. 2002. *Recovering Canada: the Resurgence of Indigenous Law*. Toronto:

University of Toronto Press.

Brock, K. 1991. 'The Politics of Aboriginal Self-Government: A Canadian Paradox', *Canadian Public Administration* 34, 2: 272–85.

Cairns, A. 2000. *Citizens Plus: Aboriginal Peoples and the State*. Vancouver: University of British Columbia Press.

Dacks, G. 2001. 'The Social Union Framework Agreement and the Role of Aboriginal Peoples in Canadian Federalism', *The American Review of Canadian Studies* 31, 2: 301–15.

Henderson, A. 2007. *Nunavut. Rethinking Political Culture*. Vancouver: UBC Press.

Henderson, S. 1994. 'Empowering Treaty Federalism', *Saskatchewan Law Review* 58, 2: 242–71.

Ladner, K. 2003. 'Treaty Federalism: An Indigenous Vision of Canadian Federalisms'. In *New Trends in Canadian Federalism*, 2nd edn, ed. F. Rocher and M. Smith. Peterborough: Broadview Press.

Indian and Northern Affairs Canada (INAC). 1997.

Gathering Strength: Canada's Aboriginal Action Plan. Ottawa: Minister of Supply and Services.

Indian and Northern Affairs Canada (INAC). 2010a. *Financial Overview 2010.* Ottawa: Minister of Public Works and Government Services Canada. Available at: www.ainc-inac.gc.ca/ai/arp/fin/index-eng.asp. (accessed 30 October, 2010).

Indian and Northern Affairs Canada (INAC). 2010b. *General Briefing Note on Canada's Self–Government and Land Claims Policies and the Status of Negotiations.* Available at: www.ainc-inac.gc.ca/al/ldc/ccl/pubs/gbn/gbn-eng.asp. (accessed 30 October 2010).

Indian and Northern Affairs Canada (INAC). 2010c. *2008–2009 Estimates. Report on Plans and Priorities.* Ottawa: Treasury Board of Canada Secretariat. Available at: www.tbs-sct.gc.ca/rpp/2009-2010/inst/ian/ian00-eng.asp. (accessed 30 October 2010).

Long, J., and M. Boldt. 1988. *Governments in Conflict? Provinces and Indian Nations in Canada.* Toronto: University of Toronto Press.

Macklem, P. 2001. *Indigenous difference and the Constitution of Canada.* Toronto: University of Toronto Press.

McNeil, K. 2004. *The Inherent Right of Self-government: Emerging Directions for Legal Research.* Report prepared for the First Nations Governance Centre.

Neu, D., and R. Therrien. 2003. *Accounting for Genocide: Canada's Bureaucratic Assault on Aboriginal People.* London: Zed Press.

Newhouse, D. 2000. 'Modern Aboriginal Economies. Capitalism with a Red Face'. *Journal of Aboriginal Economic Development,* 2, 1: 55–61.

Noel, A. and F. Larocque. 2009. Aboriginal Peoples and Poverty in Canada: Can Provincial Governments Make a Difference? Annual Meeting of the International Sociological Association's Research Committee 19 (RC19), Montreal, 20 August 2009.

Pierre J. and G. Peters. 2000. *Governance, Politics and the State.* New York: Oxford University Press.

Royal Commission on Aboriginal Peoples (RCAP). 1996. *Report of the Royal Commission on Aboriginal Peoples,* 5 vols. Ottawa: Communication Group Publishing.

Royal Commission on Electoral Reform and Party Financing (RCER). 1991. *Reforming Electoral Democracy.* Ottawa: Supply and Services Canada.

Schouls, T. 1996. 'Aboriginal Peoples and Electoral Reform in Canada: Differentiated Representation versus Voter Equality', *Canadian Journal of Political Science* 29, 4: 729–49.

Statistics Canada. 2008. *Aboriginal Peoples in Canada in 2006: Inuit, Métis and First Nations, 2006 Census.* Cat. No. 97-558-XIE. Ottawa: Statistics Canada.

Tully, J. 1995. *Strange Multiplicity: Constitutionalism in an Age of Diversity.* Cambridge: Cambridge University Press.

———. 2000. 'The Struggles of Indigenous Peoples for and of Freedom'. In *Political Theory and the Rights of Indigenous Peoples,* ed. D. Ivison, P. Patton, and W. Sanders. Cambridge: Cambridge University Press.

———. 2001. 'Reconsidering the BC Treaty Process'. In *Speaking Truth to Power: A Treaty Forum,* ed. Law Commission of Canada. Ottawa: Minister of Public Works and Government Services Canada.

Turpel, M. E. 1993. 'The Charlottetown Discord and Aboriginal Peoples' Struggle for Fundamental Political Change'. In *The Charlottetown Accord, the Referendum, and the Future of Canada,* ed. K. McRoberts and P. Monahan. Toronto: University of Toronto Press.

Cases

Attorney General for Ontario v. Attorney General for Canada (Reference Appeal), [1912] A.C. 571.

Delgamuukw v. British Columbia, [1997] 3 *S.C.R. 1010.*

R. v. *Pamajewon,* [1996] 2 S.C.R. 821, [1996] 4 C.N.L.R. 164.

R. v. *Marshall,* [1999] 3 S.C.R. 456.

R. v. *Sparrow,* [1990] 1 S.C.R. 1075.

R. v. *Van der Peet,* [1996] 2 S.C.R. 507.

16 **The Urban Agenda**

Andrew Sancton

All three levels of government have been profoundly important to Canadian cities for many decades. This situation is unlikely to change anytime soon. Our cities, this chapter will argue, would be better served if our elected politicians at all three levels focused their attention on working together within their own spheres of jurisdiction to tackle the real urban problems, rather than involving themselves excessively in attempts to rearrange their various roles and responsibilities. In any event, neither Rob Ford nor Naheed Nenshi—two quite different individuals surprisingly elected in 2010 as mayors of Toronto and Calgary respectively—appear to have any desire to re-open old debates about formally enhancing municipal responsibilities.

Municipalities have not often been thought of as being part of the Canadian federal system. The first section of this chapter, by contrasting the role of municipalities in American and Canadian federalism, explains why this has been so. In the early 2000s there was much discussion about why municipalities merit more attention from the federal government, but the second section of this chapter demonstrates that federal involvement with municipalities is nothing new. The third section outlines the various approaches to A '**new deal for cities**' that were articulated a decade ago. The next briefly outlines how the Harper government has approached cities and why its abandonment of the 'new deal' has provoked virtually no opposition. The concluding section addresses some of the underlying reasons why, despite the growing importance of cities in Canada, their municipal governments are unlikely ever to become full partners in the Canadian federation. The conclusion also links the urban agenda to the themes of this book: the performance, effectiveness, and legitimacy of the Canadian federal system.

Municipalities and the Canadian Federation

Municipalities, together with local special-purpose bodies, comprise the Canadian system of local government. The words 'local' and 'government' are both crucial to understanding the nature of municipalities. In the Canadian context, 'local' means any specified territory that is smaller than the province in which it is located. In most cases, the territories of local governments are much smaller, often including only the built-up areas of small villages.

The term 'government' is more problematic. Everyone accepts that such central institutions as parliaments and ministries are part of 'government'. But what about incorporated companies that are similar to privately owned companies in all respects except that they are owned by the government? This question is answered in different countries—and often even within the same country—in different ways. If such definitional issues are difficult at the central level, they are even more so at the local level, in part because, for English-language countries at least, the historical origins of what we now know as 'local government' are just as closely connected to private corporations as to government.

In English constitutional theory, the government always acts in the name of the monarch. The institutions that today we label as 'local governments' began as municipal corporations. Such corporations were essentially private: Parliament vested a self-perpetuating governing body with the authority to establish certain public institutions (such as marketplaces), to pay for them through specified levies, and to make appropriate regulations to facilitate their operation. Whatever authority they possessed derived from Parliament, but they did not act in the name of the monarch. To this day in Britain (and Canada), the central government is Her Majesty's government and all its actions are carried out in her name. Local governments in Britain are now very much public governmental institutions, but they still possess a corporate legal form and they still do not act on behalf of the monarch. Local governments in North America have followed a similar evolutionary pattern (Hartog, 1983).

Even when municipal corporations and their successors are clearly defined in law as public and democratic institutions, it is still sometimes difficult to know what aspects of their operations form part of the government. This problem of defining what municipal governments do has become especially obvious in recent years as the tenets of New Public Management have become more popular and local governments have become increasingly involved in various forms of partnerships with each other and with private enterprise. Some observers have labelled such arrangements as 'governance' because they are much looser and more flexible than the rigid hierarchies and defined accountabilities usually associated with traditional departments of government. Governance arrangements are often extremely difficult to classify as either public or private.

Nevertheless, bearing in mind the definition of 'local' that has already been discussed, it is possible to list the following core characteristics of local governments:

- they are distinct legal entities rather than administrative subdivisions of some other entity;
- they are controlled by a governing body most of whose members are local citizens;
- they have some form of legally defined access to public funds or to publicly regulated fees;
- they have some degree of decision-making autonomy with respect to at least one aspect of public policy within their defined territory; and
- apart from the governing body itself, they have no other forms of membership; all eligible residents of the defined territory are automatically under their jurisdiction with respect to their defined responsibility.

This is a broad approach to the definition of 'local government'. It allows us to include institutions that are much more specialized than municipalities, whose distinguishing characteristics are that the members of their governing bodies are usually popularly elected and that they are at least partially responsible for a wide range of public services, everything from garbage collection to recreational programs for children. Special-purpose bodies, on the other hand, often have appointed governing bodies and are always responsible only for a particular public function or set of closely related functions.

Among all the world's liberal democracies, one could probably find that almost any conceivable function of government is somewhere carried out, at least in part, by a local government. There can be no theory about which level of government is—or should be—involved in any particular function. There are, however, theories about which level of government—central or local—is likely to be more effective in setting broad, enforceable policies with respect to particular functions. For example, it is generally acknowledged that income-support policies are best set at the federal or provincial level (Peterson, 1981). Doing so forces upper-income residents of rich municipalities to contribute to the cost of such policies even if their own areas contain few poor people. Similarly, it makes sense that central governments would create rules about environmental protection. Otherwise, particular municipalities could simply pass on their pollution to their neighbours through prevailing winds and river flows. But there is no strong reason why, subject to central control, local governments could not be responsible for delivering or enforcing such centrally made policies.

At the other end of the spectrum are government functions that seem especially amenable to autonomous local decision-making. An example might be the provision of public open spaces (often the site of civic ceremonies and outside special events) and decorative urban parks. It is hard to imagine any reason why a central (provincial) government would have any interest in such matters. Nevertheless, chances are that somewhere, sometime, there has been a central-government program that, under certain conditions, has provided funds to local authorities to help improve the quality of urban life or promote local economic development by subsidizing the cost of providing urban public spaces.

A vast range of public services and regulatory regimes are often the responsibility of local governments. Disputes about which level of government should do what with respect to a particular function are common and are part of the everyday give-and-take of democratic politics. Sometimes proponents of a particular view can advance good technical reasons for their position. Usually, however, participants in these debates are trying to promote a particular policy outcome rather than being concerned in the abstract about what government is better suited to the task at hand. In any event, there appears to be a strong view among Canadians that municipal governments are and should be especially concerned with matters relating to the regulation and servicing of property: zoning, local roads, sewers, water supply, and parks, for example (Lorimer, 1972).

Under both the American and Canadian federal constitutions, municipal institutions come under the formal jurisdiction of states and provinces. But in the United States the federal system is commonly conceptualized as a partnership between the federal government, on the one hand, and 'state and local' governments, on the other. There are at least two interconnected reasons why 'provincial and local' is not a common term in Canadian political discourse.

First, unlike American states, Canadian provinces do not have their own distinct written constitutions (Cameron, 1980). In the constitutions of the various American states, local government receives at least some form of constitutional recognition and protection. In many states, the municipal governments of the larger cities are guaranteed a form of 'home rule', which prevents the state legislature from changing local municipal boundaries, functions, and structures without some form of local consent. In this context, the term 'state and local' makes perfect sense: in any particular state, the basic structures of both the state government and the various local governments are established under the authority of the same state constitution. In Canada, on the other hand, the provincial legislatures established by the Constitution of Canada can alter all aspects of a province's governmental structure except for the office of lieutenant-governor. Canadian municipalities thus have no established form of constitutional protection whatever. They have not been recognized as being in any sense equal to provincial governments.

The second reason why we seldom use the term 'provincial and local' in Canada is that our federation is in part held together by the notion that provincial governments collectively possess at least equal political status with the federal government. This notion is itself closely connected to the recognition that the Quebec National Assembly has a special responsibility to advance and protect Quebec's distinct French-speaking character. Anyone in Canada who in any way equates a municipal council with the Quebec National Assembly is, at a minimum, using highly controversial political language. If Quebec's legislature cannot be considered in any way like a municipal council, neither can the legislature of any other province.

Previous Urban Agendas

Canada's first 'urban agenda' was advanced by the Unionist government of Sir Robert Borden in the aftermath of World War I. In late 1918, following the return of Canadian soldiers, housing became a major national issue. Under the authority of the War Measures Act, the federal government loaned $25 million to the provinces for 25 years at 5 per cent interest. The money was to be granted mainly to municipalities willing to construct new housing for sale at cost, but limited-dividend housing societies and lot owners building houses for their own personal occupancy could also benefit. Other relevant federal restrictions were that land should be purchased 'without regard to speculative value'; not more than 10 per cent of the cost of any house should derive from the cost of the land; 10 per cent of all land purchased should be reserved for playgrounds; water and sewage should be supplied before construction; and all houses should meet specified minimum standards of construction (Canada, 1919: 55). Ontario responded in April 1919 with the passage of the Ontario Housing Act, which outlined the conditions under which municipalities could gain access to the federal funds (Sancton and Montgomery, 1994: 765). Significantly, the federal conditions laid down in 1918 for providing funds to municipalities were tougher and more detailed than any conditions in place today. In this sense there was more federal involvement in urban policy then than there is today.

The next federal initiative did not emerge until the Great Depression. In 1935 Parliament approved the Dominion Housing Act authorizing the federal government to share up to a

quarter of the value of individual mortgage loans with approved lenders and to set housing standards as a condition for federal involvement. In 1937 amendments were approved
to allow for federal participation in loans for home improvements and in 1938 the Act was
replaced by the National Housing Act, which also provided for federal loans to builders
of low-rental family housing. Such loans were never taken up because they required that
provinces or municipalities limit taxes on such properties and guarantee operating losses
(Axworthy, 1972: 30).

In another attempt to ease unemployment, Parliament in 1938 approved the Municipal
Improvements Assistance Act, which provided low-interest loans to municipalities to
reinvest in their physical infrastructure. Writing about this legislation in 1975, David
Bettison commented that

> [t]he constitutional problem of financial responsibility for local authorities was met by having
> the provincial governments approve each local authority's project and also guarantee to the
> Dominion the repayment of the loan and amortization charges to the municipality. . . . The
> maximum limit of federal funds was fixed at $30 million and the distribution among muni-
> cipalities was to be determined by the ratio of a municipality's 1931 census population to the
> population of the dominion at that date. (Bettison, 1975: 67–8)

During World War II, the federal government allocated space, administered rent controls, and directly provided housing to employees of war-related industries. Such obvious
involvement in matters under direct provincial jurisdiction could not survive the end
of the war. Parliament approved more housing legislation in both 1944 and 1945. The
1944 Act provided that the federal government could pay 50 per cent of municipal costs
of what was soon to be called 'slum clearance'. The 1945 Act established the Central
Mortgage and Housing Corporation (CMHC) as a Crown corporation to administer the
federal government's involvement in housing. Its expenses were covered by its income
from loans and from the provision of mortgage insurance to private lenders.

After 1949 amendments allowed the federal government to cover up to 75 per cent
of the costs of low-rental public housing. Demands that the federal government use its
superior financial resources to end the shame of urban slums and overcrowding were
similar to today's claims that only the federal government is able to finance the massive expenditures to solve our cities' infrastructure deficits. Perhaps the major difference is that large-scale public housing projects were more controversial. Nevertheless,
the federal Liberals under Prime Ministers King and St Laurent were clearly supportive.
Together with Premier Duplessis of Quebec, they built during the mid-1950s the massive Habitations Jeanne-Mance in downtown Montreal over the strong objections of first-
term mayor Jean Drapeau (Black, 1977: 401–2), who did not believe that any level of
government should own housing, especially large apartment buildings that he felt were
unsuitable for families. Sponsorship of 'urban renewal' placed the federal government at
the heart of some of the great urban conflicts of the late 1950s and 1960s (Fraser, 1972).

At the same time the federal government, after provincial approval, continued to make
direct loans to municipalities for infrastructure improvement. This practice was further institutionalized and expanded in 1963 when the Pearson government sponsored
the Municipal Development and Loan Board Act. Premier Lesage of Quebec objected

strenuously but the federal government proceeded anyway. The Act stayed in force until 1968 (Bettison, 1975: 150–2).

Opposition to urban renewal was sparked more by displaced residents than by the kind of ideological or moral concerns advanced by Mayor Drapeau in Montreal. In any event, by the mid-1960s urban issues were squarely on the national agenda, in part because American cities were literally being torched by urban protestors but also because no one knew how middle-class Canadian adult baby boomers were going to be housed. Shortly after taking office as prime minister in 1968, Pierre Elliott Trudeau agreed to let his deputy prime minister, Paul Hellyer, chair a federal Task Force on Housing and Urban Development. The Hellyer Task Force is surely the high-water mark for apparent federal interest in urban affairs. Its members toured the country (shepherded by Hellyer's executive assistant, Lloyd Axworthy) hearing deputations from all kinds of groups about issues deeply within provincial and municipal jurisdiction. The Task Force did not hesitate to make recommendations that directly intruded into spheres of provincial jurisdiction. Some examples are:

- municipalities or regional governments, as a matter of continuing policy, should acquire, service, and sell all or a substantial portion of the land required for urban growth within their boundaries
- the federal government should make direct loans to municipalities or regional governments to assist in assembling and servicing land for urban growth (Canada, 1969: 43)
- the federal government should make loans to municipalities to acquire dispersed existing housing for use by low-income groups (ibid., 57)
- since urban planning can be done effectively only on a regional basis, the provinces should establish a system of regional governments, equipped with adequate powers for each major area (ibid., 63)
- the federal government, in co-operation with a provincial government, should seriously consider the construction of a 'new city' as a pilot project where proposed urban solutions could be tested in an actual environment (ibid., 75).

The report was made public in late January 1969. In late April Hellyer resigned from the cabinet because Prime Minister Trudeau refused to take any action on it, even on recommendations that were clearly within federal jurisdiction (Axworthy, 1972: 240). Instead, in 1971 the federal government created the Ministry of State for Urban Affairs, an agency with no direct administrative responsibilities but with a mandate to co-ordinate federal government activities in Canada's cities. The various problems of the Urban Affairs ministry have been well documented (Cameron, 1974; Feldman and Milch, 1981; Stoney and Graham, 2009). A sympathetic account by a former senior official listed the following well-known urban projects as having been 'studied, proposed, and shepherded' by the ministry:

- the Waterfront Development in Halifax
- the Civic Centre and City Square in St John's, Newfoundland
- the Vieux-Port in Montreal
- Harbourfront in Toronto

- the cancellation of Transport Canada's plan for an international airport in Pickering
- the Trizec complex in Winnipeg
- the Rideau Canal waterway in Ontario
- Granville Island in Vancouver
- the Lachine Canal redevelopment in Quebec
- the railroad relocation projects in Regina (Saumier, 1987: 44).

Even allowing for some self-congratulatory hyperbole and recognizing that most of these projects took place on federally owned lands, this is remarkable evidence of direct federal involvement in the shaping of Canadian cities. Nevertheless, the ministry was abolished as a symbolic cost-cutting measure. By this time, it had many enemies, but no friends (Feldman and Milch, 1981: 259).

One of the ministry's major innovations—not seen before or since—was its sponsorship of national tri-level conferences. Ironically, the very creation of the ministry probably slowed a planning process for such conferences that had been underway for some time. The ministry's existence caused provincial politicians to hesitate, fearing new federal jurisdictional incursions. National tri-level conferences were held in 1972 and 1973. A third was scheduled for 1976 but was cancelled by provincial ministers of municipal affairs. Then, as now, municipalities were pushing for new tax sources and saw the tri-level conference as the ideal forum to make their case. They were not successful. Regional and local tri-level conferences were also held and led to some real results, Winnipeg probably being the best example (Feldman and Graham, 1979: 29–58).

Urban issues did not reappear on the federal agenda until the 1990s (Young and McCarthy, 2009). However, on the basis of apparently unrelated federal initiatives involving urban land and infrastructure, housing, and security, Caroline Andrew wrote in the early 1990s that 'one could claim' federal influence on major urban centres 'was more profound in the 1980s than in previous periods' (Andrew, 1994: 430). The famous 'Red Book', containing the Liberal platform for the federal election of 1993, committed a government led by Jean Chrétien to spend $6 billion over two years, in co-operation with provinces and municipalities, to upgrade transportation and local services. The promise was the culmination of 10 years of lobbying by the Federation of Canadian Municipalities (FCM) to obtain federal funding for the municipal 'infrastructure deficit' (Andrew and Morrison, 1995: 108). After winning office, the new government quickly negotiated infrastructure agreements with each of the provinces and territories, specifying how much was to be spent and on what kinds of projects. The FCM was mildly concerned that in some provinces not all the money went to municipal projects and some media outlets focused on a few seemingly frivolous expenditures (ibid., 133). Generally, however, the program was a political success for the government and was consequently renewed in one form or another until the end of Chrétien's prime ministership in 2003.

A New Deal for Cities?

By the late 1990s the FCM was lobbying for more than just increased money for municipal infrastructure. It started to advance a much broader 'urban agenda' aimed at enhancing the role of municipalities within the Canadian federal system (Chenier, 2009). In responding to the FCM's agenda, Liberal finance minister Paul Martin found a way openly to distinguish his policies for Canada from those of his party rival, Prime Minister Jean Chrétien. The campaign for infrastructure funds involved a relatively specialized and technical set of issues that was mainly restricted to political insiders. But the campaign for a new urban agenda was designed to capture public attention in a much more dramatic and politically effective way. Cities featured on the national political agenda in the late 1960s and early 1970s because there was a real fear that they would be subject to the same cycles of decay, violence, and territorial inequalities that American cities had been experiencing. Now the concern was that cities are crucial for global economic competitiveness and that Canadian cities might not have whatever it takes to be successful, especially in relation to American cities. In the 1960s American cities were the horrible example; in the early 2000s their renewed economic dynamism was seen as a threat to Canadian complacency.

Concern about the state of Canadian cities has came from banks (TD Bank Financial Group, 2002), think-tanks (especially the Canadian Policy Research Networks, e.g., Bradford, 2005), academics (Young and Leuprecht, 2006), consultants (Berridge, 2002), and from research sponsored directly by the FCM itself (Federation of Canadian Municipalities, 2005). Most of the concern was about money. There were at least four different variants of this concern:

1. There has been insufficient societal investment in urban infrastructure, including infrastructure associated with such vital urban institutions as hospitals, universities, research institutes, museums, and other cultural facilities.
2. The Canadian tax system extracts more than is appropriate from urban areas to redistribute and invest in small towns and rural areas.
3. Compared with other advanced industrialized countries, the national government makes very limited contributions to the capital and operating budgets of urban municipalities.
4. Urban municipalities have insufficient capacity to raise money themselves because they are generally restricted to taxes on real property and user charges.

The federal government, even if it wanted to, could not fix all of these problems because of the important role of the provinces. In particular, it could do nothing about the fourth concern. What follows is a discussion of some of the issues that were been raised about potential federal involvement.

Infrastructure

The FCM has been very successful in pressing the case for increased federal funding of municipal infrastructure. Its original claim that there was a $60 billion 'infrastructure deficit' is often cited as justification for such funding. However, since the financial crisis and the beginning of the recession in 2008, federal funding for infrastructure has been justified much more on the basis that it stimulates the economy than that the federal government has any special obligation to help erase an 'infrastructure deficit'. The 'Building Canada Fund' predates the financial crisis and remains specifically targeted to municipalities. It is supposed to provide $8.8 billion of federal funds from 2007–14 (Canada, 2010a). All such funding requires provincial approval for each individual project.

Infrastructure subsidies are rarely criticized (but see Mintz and Roberts, 2004). At least one particular issue, however, merits further consideration: federal spending on water purification plants. Such spending subsidizes the provision of drinking water. But most policy analysts, representing a wide spectrum of ideological views, seem to agree that individual consumers should be paying the full cost of the water they consume. In his *Report of the Walkerton Inquiry*, Mr. Justice O'Connor wrote: 'As a general principle, municipalities should plan to raise adequate resources for their local water systems, barring exceptional circumstances'. O'Connor discusses briefly how such 'exceptional circumstances' might be defined, and it is clear that the availability of federal infrastructure funds is not one of them (Ontario, 2002: 312). In any event, the federal government continues to subsidize the capital costs of new municipal infrastructure for drinking water while stating that 'Investments in water infrastructure, supported by improved metering and effective pricing, will help reduce water consumption and protect fresh water supplies' (2010b).

Urban versus Rural

The original argument here—most articulately advanced by Joe Berridge (2002: 15–17)—was that Canada's federal and provincial legislatures pay far more attention to rural issues than is warranted by the size of the rural population. He presented data showing that more big cities are under-represented in the House of Commons and that there are more references in debate to rural problems than to urban ones. The argument is that an 'urban agenda' is needed to counteract the inherent anti-urban bias within the normal political process. Whatever one thinks about this argument, it is clear that the government led by Prime Minister Paul Martin (2003–6) ultimately did not accept it. The original idea for a 'New Deal for Cities' emerged from the policy process as the 'New Deal for Communities', a notable semantic shift.

Berridge's concern about urban representation in the House of Commons is justified. The main problem is that the less populous provinces and territories—which almost by definition are more rural—are overrepresented in the House of Commons. There is still a bias *within* each province's membership in the House of Commons in favour of rural areas, but this has decreased markedly over the last few decades (Courtney, 2001). A constitutional amendment would be necessary to remove the special protection of smaller provinces and open the door to fairer representation of urban voters. The Conservative federal government has introduced legislation (Bill C-12 in 2010) that would significantly increase representation for Ontario, British Columbia, and Alberta in the House of Commons while protecting the seat count of smaller provinces'. The federal Parliament can act alone to make this change, as long as it does not produce a scheme in which a province ends up with fewer MPs than senators. Despite their alleged attachment to cities, the Liberal Party in government never addressed this issue of urban under-representation. If the Conservative government proceeds with its own legislation, it could well end up doing more for the political strength of voters in the city-regions of Toronto, Vancouver, Calgary, Edmonton, and Ottawa than anything accomplished by the Liberals.

Federal Financial Support

In 2004, the federal government decided to refund to municipalities all of the money they spend on GST for the purchase of goods and services. Between 2007 and 2014 this is supposed to provide Canadian municipalities with $5.8 billion that they otherwise would not have had (Canada, 2010a). It is highly unlikely that Canadian municipalities will ever again be required to pay any portion of the GST. Consequently it is unlikely that municipalities will continue to view their exemption as a form of federal financial assistance. Nevertheless, the fact that they obtained the exemption remains a significant victory. A subsequent campaign, led by Mayor David Miller of Toronto, failed to convince the federal government to transfer to municipalities a portion of the GST equal to one per cent of the value of the goods and services on which it was levied.

In its 2005 budget, the Liberal government promised that municipalities would begin receiving a share of the federal tax on gasoline, such that by 2010 they would be receiving five cents per litre (the federal tax, exclusive of the GST, is 10 cents per litre). The money is being channelled to the municipalities in accordance with the terms of federal–provincial agreements and is allocated to provinces on a per capita basis. The Ontario government allowed the federal government to negotiate directly with the Association of Municipalities of Ontario and the City of Toronto; Ontario is the only province that is not a party to one of the agreements. The funds are to be used 'to support environmentally sustainable infrastructure projects such as public transit, water and wastewater treatment, community energy systems and the handling of solid waste' (Canada 2005). For municipalities under 500,000 in population, the funds could also be used for roads.

Finally, the 2005 budget added $300 million to the $200 million already committed to Green Municipal Funds administered by the FCM. These funds 'provide grants, low-interest loans and innovative financing to increase investment in infrastructure projects that deliver cleaner air, water, and soil, and climate protection' (ibid.).

Apart from the GST relief, the new federal funding does not have a direct impact on municipal operating budgets. In theory, most of the funding is supposed to be for capital expenditures that municipalities would not otherwise have incurred. In reality, however, the federal government is unable to enforce such a requirement. The federal money clearly substitutes for at least some planned municipal capital expenditure. In some cases, it causes municipal capital spending plans to be accelerated. Such funding is aimed at improving the quality of life in Canadian communities, not at reducing municipal tax rates. To some extent, however, the new funding reduces total borrowing in the future and therefore will eventually serve to reduce borrowing costs that otherwise would have had to be absorbed through the local property tax. But federal funding of this kind did not solve the municipal fiscal problems about which big-city mayors were complaining.

New Sources of Revenue

The concern of big-city mayors has been that they are excessively reliant on the property tax. Unlike many of their American counterparts, Canadian central-city municipalities receive no income tax revenues from suburban commuters and no sales tax revenue from tourists. In comprehensive visions of a 'new deal' for Canadian cities, this problem would be addressed. There is no shortage of consultants' reports calling for wide-ranging changes in the fiscal system such that Canadian city governments would be net gainers (Slack, 2004). The fact is, however, that the federal government can do little or nothing to grant cities new taxation authority. In theory, Ottawa could share more tax revenue with municipalities, following the model worked out with the gasoline tax. Or it could lower the rates for certain taxes after extracting ironclad guarantees from provinces that they would legislate to allow municipalities to move into the fiscal territory from which the federal government withdrew. But neither prospect was ever very likely. The provinces claimed, with considerable justification, that fixing their 'fiscal imbalance' with Ottawa was the immediate priority, not some elaborate scheme to have the federal government come to the aid of municipalities. The road to new sources of revenue for Canadian municipalities runs through provincial capitals, not Ottawa. In the past, Mayor Miller of Toronto was one of the most fervent advocates for new municipal sources of revenue, and he convinced the Ontario government to give his city modest new taxation authority. However, the city's new mayor, Rob Ford, stated in his 2010 campaign that Toronto had a spending problem, not a revenue problem, and that he would act to repeal the new taxes on land transfers and vehicle registrations that his predecessor had championed.

In addition to lobbying for money, the FCM and big-city mayors argued that they deserved 'a voice at the national table'. In its 2005 budget, the Liberal government responded with soothing words:

> The government is consistently seeking new ways to involve Canada's municipal governments in the decision-making process on national issues that directly affect their interests. The proposed new Department of Infrastructure and Communities will be the Government of Canada's primary contact for municipal issues. In addition, the Minister of Finance has formally met with municipal decision-makers as part of his pre-budget consultations and is committed to do so again for future budgets. The Government will continue to seek further opportunities for dialogue with municipal leaders, while respecting provincial and territorial jurisdiction. (Canada, 2005)

Such words were hardly a clarion call for a new form of tri-level Canadian federalism. But Canadians were never to learn what, if anything, they meant. Within a few months, the government lost the confidence of the House of Commons, and early in 2006 it lost the ensuing election.

'Open Federalism' and the Urban Agenda

In *Stand Up for Canada*, its platform for the 2006 election, the Conservative Party of Canada included a separate section entitled 'Stand Up for Our Communities'. Under 'Improving Canada's National Infrastructure' the Conservatives stated:

> Infrastructure is a crucial investment in our economic productivity and quality of life. Suburban commuters should not have to sit on gridlocked highways. Truckers carrying cargo vital to Canada's economy should not have to dodge potholes for much of the year. The Liberals have committed to funding municipal infrastructure, but roads, highways, and

border crossings never seem to keep up. A Conservative government will have a better approach to fixing Canada's infrastructure deficit. (Conservative Party, 2005: 36)

The Conservatives went on to promise that they would maintain municipal funding committed to by the Liberals and that they would '[e]xpand the New Deal to allow all cities and communities, including cities with more than 500,000 people, to use gas transfer dollars to build and repair roads and bridges to improve road safety and fight traffic congestion' (ibid., 38). They also promised to '[g]ive public transit riders a federal tax credit to cover the cost of their monthly transit passes' (ibid., 39). Both promises have been implemented. For infrastructure, it is clear that the main thrust of their policy is to make it easier for municipalities to use federal funds for roads, a policy aimed obviously more at their suburban political supporters than at residents of the inner cities. The Conservatives' political connection to suburbia has important implications for analyzing the role of cities in Canadian federalism, a subject to be addressed in the next and concluding section of this chapter.

More important than the Conservatives' particular promise about communities is their general approach to relations with the provinces. In their election platform the Conservatives referred to their approach as 'Open Federalism' (ibid., 42). Once elected, Prime Minister Harper developed the concept in somewhat greater detail during a speech in Montreal in April 2006. Although not referring to anything related to the 'urban agenda', he stated that

[o]pen federalism means respecting areas of provincial jurisdiction. Open federalism means limiting the use of the federal spending power, which the federal Liberals abused—much to the dismay of all hard-working, tax-paying Canadians. (Canada, 2006b)

This was the first indication that the Conservatives would not be expanding 'the urban agenda'. The second was that Prime Minister Harper did not appoint a separate minister for infrastructure and communities. Instead, the minister of Transport adds these responsibilities to an already large portfolio.

As with all federal governments, many policies and actions of the Harper government—'especially those relating to large infrastructure projects—are having profound impacts on the quality of life in Canadian cities. But the Harper government has never attempted to proclaim its own distinct 'urban agenda'. Federal involvement in Canadian cities will inevitably continue and evolve but, for all practical purposes, the days of the federal 'urban agenda' are over. More significantly, perhaps, it appears that municipalities are no longer much interested in a federal 'urban agenda' either. The fact that Rob Ford, now the mayor of Canada's largest city, has no interest in engaging the federal government is only the most dramatic indication of this fact.

Cities and Federalism

The important issues about the relevance of cities for Canadian federalism do not relate to the details of federal funding for particular municipal projects or exactly how the federal government organizes itself to manage its involvement in city issues. What is important is the possibility that the increasing significance of cities for our economic and social life will lead to profound changes in the structure of our federation. Anyone reading the work of such varied authors as Jane Jacobs (1984), Kenichi Ohmae (1995), Neal Peirce (1993), and Tom Courchene (2005) might think it will. Even the well-known Canadian historian Michael Bliss has recently wondered about the country evolving 'into a league of provinces, and perhaps a sprinkling of **city-states**, [emphasis added] some of these jurisdictions effectively independent' (Bliss, 2006). Alan Broadbent (2008) has devoted an entire book to making the case that Toronto, Montreal and Vancouver need to attain the same status as provinces so as 'to make Canada strong'.

Speculating in this way has its value. But it is time to subject such thinking to some serious analysis before we all get carried away with futuristic fantasies—or romantic nostalgia for the Italian city-states of the fifteenth century. Can cities somehow become as important as provinces? Will some even secede from provinces and effectively become provinces themselves? If not, then we need not be concerned that the growing economic importance of cities will somehow change the nature of Canadian federalism.

My argument (Sancton, 2008) is that, in Canada and other Western liberal democracies, cities will not become like provinces; they will not become independent units of government. In short, they will generally *not* become city-states. This kind of self-government requires a territory delimited by official boundaries. For cities, unlike sovereign states and provinces, the boundaries will never be static, will never be acceptable to all, and will always be contested. Boundaries fatally limit the capacity of cities to be self-governing.

It should be apparent already that, in using the word 'cities', I am *not* referring to central-city municipalities that carry the name of their 'city-region'. This distinction is the source of much confusion and difficulty. There *are* examples of populous city-regions comprising only one municipality but, for fast-growing city-regions at least, the boundaries of such a municipality will always be problematic. The much more common pattern, especially in North America, is for city-regions to comprise dozens, or even hundreds, of municipalities. Making central-city municipalities—and perhaps also their surrounding suburbs—more autonomous does nothing except reify existing boundaries that are invariably seen as arbitrary, outdated, discriminatory, and irrelevant; but to focus on the economic and social reality of a city means focusing on the city-region as a whole—and determining its territorial extent for the purposes of self-government is not a practical proposition.

Arguing that cities cannot be self-governing might seem unnecessary. A much more common concern is that cities are hardly self-governing at all, and need release from the dead hand of central regulation. I am highly sympathetic to such a concern, but have become worried about the implications—and confusions—relating to many of the arguments (and inflated rhetoric) about more autonomy for cities. They take us down a path that, in my view, can ultimately be damaging for cities, if for no other reason than that they divert valuable resources to fruitless undertakings, much like searching for the end of a rainbow.

Residents of some Canadian cities (Calgary, Winnipeg, Regina, Saskatoon, and Halifax, for example) can point out that their municipalities actually do include almost all the residents of their respective city-regions, as such regions are defined by Statistics Canada.

But the fastest growing of these cities is Calgary and it is clearly facing territorial problems (Ghitter and Smart, 2009). For decades it has continually annexed contiguous land so as to ensure a steady stream of new developable land (Foran, 2009). But the City of Calgary is also surrounded by non-contiguous *urban* municipalities. Such places as Airdrie, Crossfield, Cochrane, Chestermere, and Okotoks are growing even faster than Calgary itself. The more Calgary grows, the more these places will grow and the more they will become integrated into the urban area focused on Calgary as the central city. The strategic choice that the City of Calgary faces is whether it will work co-operatively with these urban governments or whether its ultimate objective will be to absorb them as part of a continuing commitment to a rigid model of continuing annexation.

All the great, growing cities of the world eventually expand in such a way that their influence starts to impinge on neighbouring communities that were once quite distinct. But no central governments in the Western world, as a matter of consistent, ongoing policy, provide for central cities to absorb systematically their urban-based municipal neighbours. Even Ontario, one of the most interventionist jurisdictions with respect to municipal boundaries and structures, has not followed such a policy for Toronto; hence the continued existence of Mississauga (Urbaniak, 2009), with a current population of close to 700,000.

Toronto is Canada's most likely candidate for city-state status. Precisely because the city does have a large territory, a substantial population, and significant fiscal resources, it is at least possible to imagine a disgruntled, charismatic mayor convincing his or her constituents that secession from Ontario would be a good idea. In financial terms, city taxpayers would probably be better off than they are now. The city's population would make it the third largest province in Canada, behind the rest of Ontario and Quebec.

The main problem with such a plan is that it would bifurcate the Toronto city-region. The city's boundaries run through densely populated areas. Turning them into provincial boundaries would surely create more problems than it would solve. Deciding on the 'real' boundaries of the Toronto city-region is a nightmare. Even Statistics Canada (Canada, 2006c) is unsure. It now refers to an area it calls the 'Extended Golden Horseshoe', which includes 6.7 million people (59 per cent of Ontario's population), stretching from Barrie to Niagara Falls and from Kitchener to Clarington.

In Alberta, Statistics Canada uses a similar area it calls the 'Calgary–Edmonton Corridor', with a population of 2.15 million that constitutes 72 per cent of the province's population. In British Columbia there is the 'Lower Mainland and Southern Vancouver Island', with a population of 2.7 million or 69 per cent of the province's population.

Rather than wasting time worrying about the emergence of city-states, it is time to recognize that the provinces containing our largest city-regions have in fact become dependent on these urban centres. These provinces contain vast, sparsely populated territories, but their political centres of gravity are increasingly located in Canada's largest cities. Large or small, these provinces require within them multi-functional units of local government to make decisions about local issues and services. The municipalities that include the territories of our central cities especially merit our careful attention and scrutiny because the cumulative impact of their many seemingly small decisions will determine much about the quality of our urban life. Meanwhile, the federal government will continue to make crucial decisions about such matters as fiscal policy, immigration

(Good, 2009), and criminal law that will have much to do with the general pattern of our urban lives. Provincial governments will continue to make big decisions about health, education, and social services—as well as strategic infrastructure investments for city-regions and their hinterlands.

The 'urban agenda' of the late 1990s and early 2000s began as a concern about the state of our largest city-regions. But these places contain dozens of municipalities, even after the controversial municipal amalgamations in Toronto and Montreal. Many of the toughest policy choices for the future relate not to our central-city municipalities but to the municipalities on the edges of our city-regions. The mayors of our central cities should have a voice in these decisions, but they cannot claim to represent people who do not elect them. No one argues that only our largest central-city municipalities should have a place at the table in Canadian federalism. Such an arrangement would not be fair to the majority of Canadians who live outside these municipalities. But to argue that our city-regions should have such a place leads to even more problems. In this case no one even knows how such an objective would be accomplished. Such is the dilemma of attempting to integrate our city governments into the decision-making processes of Canadian federalism.

Assessing how the Canadian federal system responds to urban problems and issues is a complicated task. The complications arise primarily from the fact that, for politicians at least, 'urban problems' are either defined primarily by municipalities or are seen as being mainly within their jurisdiction. As we have seen in the first section of this chapter, however, municipalities are not formally part of the federal system, even though municipal leaders conducted a sustained campaign over many years to gain some form of enhanced recognition. Many big-city mayors past and present would no doubt argue that the Canadian federal system cannot possibly be rated highly on criteria relating to performance, effectiveness, and legitimacy unless they are fully included as part of the process. In short, some mayors have been just as interested in changing the definition of federalism (with respect to cities at least) as they are with making traditional two-level federalism work better in addressing urban problems. Others have been less interested in formal definitional issues but still insist that urban problems cannot be effectively addressed by the federal system unless mayors are 'at the table' and able to participate in decision-making as political equals to representatives of the federal and provincial governments.

But all such demands cause problems for most provincial governments—especially the government of Quebec—because they open the possibility that a province will not be seen as speaking with one voice. The provinces' worst fear is that on some issues the federal government will be able to ignore them altogether as it makes direct deals with their municipalities. If provinces resist municipal demands for more direct involvement with the federal government and if the federal government accepts this provincial resistance, how are we to assess the result? From a traditional perspective, the system appears to be performing well because the federal government is respecting provincial jurisdiction. But from the perspective of many big-city mayors, such an outcome would be an illustration of everything that is wrong with Canadian federalism. I have already argued that adjusting the processes of Canadian federalism to include formally the municipal representatives of large cities is not as easy as some the proponents suggest. But, by any conceivable measure, we have not gone far down that road, and are unlikely even to continue the journey while the Harper government is in office.

So let us assume instead, with respect to urban problems, that Canadian federalism involves only the federal and provincial levels of government, with each having an obligation at least to take account of the expressed wishes of municipal representatives, especially of big-city mayors who are directly elected by more voters than any leader in federal and provincial politics. Even with this assumption, assessments remain difficult, primarily because the nature of the most acute urban problems varies from place to place. Even within the same city, there can be wide disagreement about the nature of the most pressing issues. For example, in Toronto some might point to homelessness, others to the appalling way in which the downtown is cut off from the lakefront, the city's most desirable natural asset. Both issues involve the federal and provincial governments, but the relevant governmental programs and actors are dramatically different in each case.

Even allowing for all these qualifications, there can be little doubt that Canadian cities have experienced hard times in recent years. This, after all, was one of the main reasons why the 'urban agenda' of the 1990s and early 2000s emerged in the first place. Accustomed to seeing their cities as safer, cleaner, and more vibrant, Canadians who travelled to American cities and who observed what was happening to them gradually became aware that, as conditions in American cities were improving, they seemed to be declining in many Canadian ones, most notably Toronto. At least some of the difference seemed to be accounted for by the injection of massive amounts of American federal dollars for new urban infrastructure, funds that were simply not available in Canada. These funds flowed in the United States without any significant debate about which level of government should be doing what.

On the basis of apparent popular perceptions about the health of Canadian cities in recent years, Canadian federalism cannot be ranked highly in terms of performance, effectiveness, or legitimacy. Perhaps attitudes will soon change, however, as Canadians begin to experience the results of the recent increased federal funding for urban infrastructure. But cities need more than new capital investment. Improvements in the day-to-day public services so important for the quality of urban life will depend at least partly on efforts to improve the fiscal balance between the federal governments and the provinces. The needs of cities for better public facilities and services must be kept on the Canadian political agenda. But these needs can be met without restructuring the Canadian federal system.

References

Andrew, C. 1994. 'Federal Urban Activity: Intergovernmental Relations in an Age of Restraint'. In *The Changing Canadian Metropolis: A Public Policy Perspective*, vol. 2, ed. F. Frisken. Toronto: Canadian Urban Institute.

———and J. Morrison. 1995. 'Canada Infrastructure Works: Between Picks and Shovels and the Information Highway'. In *How Ottawa Spends 1995–96: Mid-Life Crises*, ed. S.D. Phillips. Ottawa: Carleton University Press.

Axworthy, N.L. 1972. 'The Task Force on Housing and Urban Development: A Study in Democratic Decision-Making', Ph.D. thesis, Princeton University.

Berridge, J. 2002. *Cities in the New Canada*. TD Forum on Canada's Standard of Living. Oct.

Bettison, D. 1975. *The Politics of Canadian Urban Development*. Edmonton: University of Alberta Press.

Black, C. 1977. *Duplessis*. Toronto: McClelland & Stewart.

Bliss, M. 2006. 'Has Canada Failed?', *Literary Review of Canada* 14, 2: 3–5.

Bradford, N. 2005. *Place-Based Public Policy:*

Towards a New Urban and Community Agenda for Canada. Research Report F/51. Ottawa: Canadian Policy Research Networks, Mar.

Broadbent, A. 2008. *Urban Nation: Why we Need to Give Power back to the Cities to Keep Canada Strong*. Toronto: HarperCollins.

Cameron, D.M. 1974. 'Urban Policy'. In *Issues in Canadian Public Policy*, ed. G.B. Doern and V.S. Wilson. Toronto: Macmillan of Canada.

———. 1980. 'Provincial Responsibilities for Municipal Government', *Canadian Public Administration* 23, 2: 222–35.

Canada. 1919. Commission of Conservation. *Conservation of Life* 5–1 (Jan.). Ottawa: King's Printer.

———. 1969. *Report of the Task Force on Housing and Urban Development*. Ottawa: Queen's Printer.

——— Department of Finance. 2005. *Budget 2005: A New Deal for Canada's Communities*. 23 Feb.

———. 2006b. Office of the Prime Minister. 'Prime Minister Harper Outlines His Government's Priorities and Open Federalism Approach'. At: www.pm.gc.ca/eng/media. asp?category='2&id=1119.

———. 2006c. 'Thematic Maps'. Statistics Canada. At: geodepot.statcan.ca/Diss/Maps/ThematicMaps/index_e.cfm.

———. 2010a. Infrastructure Canada, 'Building Canada Plan—Funding Allocations'. http://www.buildingcanada-chantierscanada.gc.ca/plandocs/index-fig01-eng.html.

———. 2010b. Infrastructure Canada, 'Building Canada—Modern Infrastructure for a strong Canada'. http://www.buildingcanada-chantier-scanada.gc.ca/plandocs/booklet-livret/booklet-livret08-eng.html#drinkingwater.

Chenier, J.A. 2009. 'The Evolving Role of the Federation of Canadian Municipalities', *Canadian Public Administration* 52, 3: 395–416.

Conservative Party of Canada. 2005. *Stand Up for Canada: Conservative Party of Canada Federal Election Platform 2006*. At: www.conservative. ca/media/20060113-Platform.pdf.

Courchene, T.J. 2005. *Citistates and the State of Cities: Political-Economy and Fiscal-Federalism Dimensions*. IRPP Working Paper Series, 2005-03. Montreal: Institute for Research on Public Policy, June.

Courtney, J.C. 2001. *Commissioned Ridings:*

Designing Canada's Electoral Districts. Montreal and Kingston: McGill–Queen's University Press.

Federation of Canadian Municipalities. 2005. Big City Mayors' Caucus. *Cities: Partners in National Prosperity*, 2 June.

Feldman, E.J., and J. Milch. 1981. 'Coordination or Control: The Life and Death of the Ministry of State for Urban Affairs'. In *Politics and Government of Urban Canada: Selected Readings*, 4th edn, ed. L.D. Feldman. Toronto: Methuen.

Feldman, L.D., and K.A. Graham. 1979. *Bargaining for Cities: Municipalities and Intergovernmental Relations, An Assessment*. Montreal: Institute for Research on Public Policy.

Foran, M. 2009. *Expansive Discourses: Urban Sprawl in Calgary, 1945–1978*. Edmonton: AU Press.

Fraser, G. 1972. *Fighting Back: Urban Renewal in Trefann Court*. Toronto: Hakkert.

Ghitter, G., and A. Smart. 2009. 'Mad Cows, Regional Governance, and Urban Sprawl: Path Dependence and Unintended Consequences in the Calgary Region', *Urban Affairs Review* 44. 5: 617–45.

Good, K.R. 2009. *Municipalities and Muticulturalism: The Politics of Immigration in Toronto and Vancouver*. Toronto: University of Toronto Press.

Hartog, H. 1983. *Public Property and Private Power: The Corporation of the City of New York in American Law, 1730–1870*. Chapel Hill: University of North Carolina Press

Jacobs, J. 1984. *Cities and the Wealth of Nations: Principles of Economic Life*. New York: Random House.

Lorimer, J. 1972. *A Citizen's Guide to City Politics*. Toronto: Lorimer.

Mintz, J.M., and T. Roberts. 2004. 'Holes in the Road to Consensus: The Infrastructure Deficit—How Much and Why?' C.D. Howe Institute e-brief, 13 Dec.

Ohmae, K. 1995. *The End of the Nation State: The Rise of Regional Economies*. New York: Free Press.

Ontario. 2002. *Report of the Walkerton Inquiry. Part Two: A Strategy for Safe Drinking Water*. Toronto: Queen's Printer.

Peirce, N.R., and C.W. Johnson, with J.S. Hall. 1993. *Citistates: How Urban America Can*

Prosper in a Competitive World. Washington: Seven Locks Press.

Peterson, P.E. 1981. *City Limits*. Chicago: University of Chicago Press.

Sancton, A. 2008. *The Limits of Boundaries: Why City-regions Cannot be Self-governing*. Montreal and Kingston: McGill–Queen's University Press.

Sancton, A., and B. Montgomery. 1994. 'Municipal Government and Residential Land Development: A Comparative Study of London, Ontario in the 1920s and 1980s'. In *The Changing Canadian Metropolis: A Public Policy Perspective*, vol. 2, ed. F. Frisken. Toronto: Canadian Urban Institute, 777–98.

Saumier, A. 1987. 'MSUA and the Regionalization of Federal Urban Programs'. In *The Ministry of State for Urban Affairs: A Courageous Experiment in Public Administration*, ed. H.P. Oberlander and A.L. Fallick. Vancouver: Centre for Human Settlements, University of British Columbia.

Slack, E. 2004. *Revenue Sharing Options for Canada's Hub Cities*. A Report prepared for the Meeting of the Hub City Mayors, 17–18 Sept.

Stoney, C., and K.A.H. Graham. 2010. 'Federal–municipal Relations in Canada: The Changing Organizational Landscape', *Canadian Public Administration* 52, 3: 371–94.

TD Bank Financial Group. 2002. TD Economics. *A Choice between Investing in Canada's Cities or Disinvesting in Canada's Future*. Special Report. 22 Apr.

Urbaniak, T. 2009. *Her Worship: Hazel McCallion and the Development of Mississauga*. Toronto: University of Toronto Press.

Young, R., and C. Leuprecht, eds. 2006. *Canada: The State of the Federation 2004: Municipal–Federal–Provincial Relations in Canada*. Montreal and Kingston: Institute of Intergovernmental Relations and McGill–Queen's University Press.

Young, R., and K. McCarthy. 2009. 'Why do Municipal Issues Rise on the Federal Policy Agenda in Canada?' *Canadian Public Administration* 52, 3: 347–70.

17 Democratizing Executive Federalism: The Role of Non-Governmental Actors in Intergovernmental Agreements

Julie M. Simmons

In July of 2008, Lawrence Cannon, then federal Minister of Transport, Infrastructure and Communities, Jim Flaherty, the federal Minister of Finance, George Smitherman, then Ontario Deputy Premier and Minister of Energy and Infrastructure, and Dwight Duncan, the Ontario Minister of Finance, held a press conference where they announced the signing of the Building Canada Infrastructure Framework Agreement. This $6 billion agreement represented the joining of the two orders of government to fund infrastructure projects in the province until 2014. Building Canada is a federal program that is part of a larger $33 billion federal economic action plan which, at the press conference, Minister Flaherty dubbed 'the largest single federal investment in public infrastructure since World War Two' (Government of Canada, 2008).

This agreement, like other similar infrastructure agreements between the federal government and other provinces, is a classic outcome of executive federalism. Executive federalism can perform well as a forum for negotiating and reaching agreement between two equal orders of government. It can achieve swift results because of the discretionary power enjoyed by prime ministers, premiers, and their cabinets, in the Canadian institutions of government. While intergovernmental negotiations can be tedious and cumbersome, they can also be breathtakingly efficient, as in this case. But the better executive federalism performs in this regard, the more closely its *effectiveness* at *resolving* policy problems should be scrutinized. However, as many of the other chapters in this volume suggest, determining whether policy problems have been effectively resolved often is contingent upon the preferred policy outcomes of the evaluator. Accordingly, this chapter focuses on a greater extent on the *legitimacy* of executive federalism.

Executive federalism adds complexity to the functioning of democracy in Canada. The more substantive the policy outcomes of intergovernmental agreements are, the more immediate is the question of executive federalism's legitimacy. When executive federalism yields high-profile agreements, we are reminded of its imperfect fit with the idea that policy should result from transparent and public deliberation in elected forums of decision-making. Executives, such as the ministers in the example above, can commit to plans, programs, and the expenditure of tax dollars without any prior discussion or agreement to these commitments in the House of Commons or any provincial legislature. A casual observer of this press conference might ask, 'Is any of this $6 billion "new money" or has it all been announced previously in the federal and provincial budgets?'

Since meetings among executives are very rarely public, unlike debates in the House of Commons or provincial legislatures, one is also left wondering how the ministers arrived at the figure of $6 billion. Added to these questions about transparency are issues of participation: Who will decide what projects are to be funded under this Ontario-Canada agreement? How will such projects affect the priorities of the provincial and municipal governments of Ontario that have already been established through processes involving local elected governments and community actors? A third set of questions is related to the issue of accountability. When the two orders of government co-operate, yielding successful intergovernmental agreements, how do citizens determine who to hold accountable for policy developments? In this case, how are citizens to unravel who is responsible for government activity or inactivity on various infrastructure projects? Put another way, if one community gets a new cultural arts centre funded through this program, and a community in a neighbouring federal riding does not, is it the fault of the local government or should citizens hold their federal or provincial representatives accountable?

This chapter explores why this debate about the democratic character of executive federalism is unresolved, identifying the narratives about democracy, effective governance, and identity that currently underlie arguments about the role of non-governmental actors in intergovernmental deliberations. It investigates the complex relationship between **representative democracy** and participatory democracy: the former, a system in which elected representatives and their officials alone make decisions; the latter, a system in which citizens deliberate with elected and unelected government actors. The chapter identifies three models of democracy—representative, consultative, and deliberative—that differ in terms of the role that non-governmental actors (unelected individual citizens, or representatives of groups whose members share an interest or identity) have in policy-making with an intergovernmental dimension. The chapter provides examples of these three models drawn from intergovernmental negotiations and agreements. It concludes that the principles and rationales guiding interaction with non-governmental actors in particular policy sectors and within individual governments have a tendency to spill over into intergovernmental decision-making. Nevertheless, non-governmental participation in intergovernmental relations tends to be mitigated by the principles of representative democracy. These principles underpin executive federalism and the forces of elite accommodation found there. It is challenging to reconcile participatory democracy with representative democracy in policy-making in general. It is even more challenging in an intergovernmental decision-making process and in the current era when 'expert' advice has more currency than citizen perspectives. As a result, over the last decade or so, governments have shifted from involving citizens in the development of intergovernmental agreements to calling upon them to monitor their implementation.

The Debatable Democratic Deficit of Intergovernmental Relations

Concerns about a **democratic deficit** stem from questions about (a) the impact of intergovernmental relations on responsible government and (b) who can best represent the interests of Canadians—elected representatives, citizens, 'stakeholders', or 'policy experts'.

Executives of majority governments can enter into intergovernmental agreements assured, by virtue of party discipline, that their home legislature will have confidence in their actions. Further, intergovernmental agreements rarely require legislative change, and thus rarely become the subject of debate in any legislative forum. One consequence is low public awareness of policy developments. When intergovernmental meetings take place, they may or may not result in carefully crafted communiqués, and even these may leave rather unclear what headway ministers have made. Even when such communiqués are decipherable, they are unlikely to garner the same degree of media attention as would a debate within a legislature. Data suggest that Canadians continue to find it difficult to trace which elected executives—federal or provincial—are responsible for which policy developments (Cutler, 2008; Anderson, 2008; Cutler and Mendelsohn, 2005).

During the constitutional negotiations of the 1980s and 1990s, the legitimacy of executive federalism became intertwined with broader concerns about representative government itself. On matters of constitutional change, considerable consensus suggests that, in a post-Charter era, rights-bearing Canadians will not accept the idea of democracy being reduced to indirect representation through their elected premier and prime minister meeting behind closed doors (Banting, 1997; Stein, 1993; Brock, 1995; Simeon and Cameron, 2002). The Meech Lake Accord, a carefully crafted consensus among first ministers, failed to be ratified in every provincial legislature, in part because groups of citizens sharing common identities or interests were critical of its content and the closed process through which it had been negotiated. The results of the federal government's 1991 Citizens' Forum on Canada's Future (the Spicer Commission) confirmed that these views were widespread among Canadians. In a marked departure from traditional executive federalism, first ministers involved citizens in the ratification of the Charlottetown Accord through a referendum. What the failure of the Charlottetown Accord suggested about the possibilities for citizen involvement in future constitutional change has been open to debate. For Atkinson (1994), the lesson was that the 'aggregative' process of bargaining and coalition-building among grassroots interests was as vulnerable to stalemate as the 'integrative' process of achieving consensus through deliberation and debate among elites. Similarly, Lusztig (1994) forecast that constitutional change would ultimately fail if the masses in a divided society were part of the legitimization process. More optimistic accounts have suggested that the problem lay not in the fact that non-governmental actors were included in the Charlottetown process, but in the manner of their inclusion (Chambers, 1998). The key is to create spaces for deliberation for non-elites that are integrative (non-majoritarian) (Mendelsohn, 2000). Regardless of the variation in these interpretations, the last two episodes of mega-constitutional politics revealed that, at least when it comes to constitutional change, representative government is insufficiently democratic to meet citizen expectations.

There are other narratives in the contemporary debate about the adequacy of representative democracy that affect the debate about the legitimacy of executive federalism. A disturbing number of Canadians perceive government to be unresponsive to them, either because the bureaucracy is too rule-bound or because politicians can't be trusted. Thomas (2009: 215) cites one *Globe and Mail* poll from 2007 in which politicians shared last place with car salesmen in a ranking of trustworthiness of different occupations. Mebs Kanji (2002: 74) warns that if mistrust continues to rise or the public's confidence in governmental institutions continues to decline, it 'may eventually detract from the public's overall support for the system of representative government'. Declining voter turnout in Canadian elections (Kanji and Bilodeau, 2006; Reza Nakhaie, 2006) suggests some degree of discontent with politicians and/or the political system. At the same time, Canadians' participation in protest politics—for example, signing a petition, boycotting a product, or attending a lawful demonstration—is higher than ever, and stands out in an international comparison of advanced industrialized democracies (Gidengil et al., 2004).

This citizen interest in alternative participation in the political process has led many theorists to focus on the policy-making process itself, rather than its outcomes, as a measure of democratic legitimacy.[1] The most common narrative maintains that providing citizens with a formalized role in the policy-making process would be beneficial for democracy. Public participation is thought to allow individuals to share views (something the act of voting does not accommodate); enable participants to explore a wider option of alternatives; produce decisions that are more likely to be in the public interest; create the perception of the final decision as legitimate; and enhance citizen understanding through the consideration of others' views (Abelson et al., 2003: 241–2). Proponents of this kind of citizen involvement in public policy argue that if representative democracy were supplemented with public deliberation, individual citizens might be more likely to revise their opinions in the light of discussion with others (Chambers, 2003). Of particular importance to advocates of deliberative democracy is its link to the recognition of difference. The objective is not to achieve accommodation of one's own interests but rather to explore alternative perspectives. Particular care is given to ensure that those who are affected by a policy have an opportunity to participate as equals in the deliberation, even if they might otherwise not have the means, information, or expertise to participate (Johnson, 2007). Indeed, local, provincial, and federal governments have experimented with these forms of public participation.[2] However, resources of time and finances are required to facilitate the participation of a wide array of interests and identities in a policy-making process, and sometimes such a process is incompatible with government timelines and expectations of efficiency. Moreover, the greater the number of participants and the diversity of the perspectives they share, the more challenging it is to make the process meaningful for the participants.

Always present in any discussion of intergovernmental relations in Canada are two alternative conceptions of who best represents Canadians: the federal government or provincial governments as a whole. The question of who represents Canadians is all the more complex when non-governmental actors, representing themselves or a particular identity or interest, or policy 'experts' outside the public service are part of the process. Should only those with something at 'stake' be involved in a policy process? If so, who determines whether an individual is a 'stakeholder'? When expert opinion is at variance with the views and interests of citizens affected by a policy, how should governments respond?

Given the resources needed for meaningful citizen involvement, many view elected representatives as the most legitimate actors to represent Canadians in policy-making. Reflecting on the role of non-governmental actors in intergovernmental relations, Hugh Thorburn (1989: 177) cautions that democracy is not necessarily enhanced by a decision-making process in which there is no guarantee that 'all groups' or even 'groups representing all' can or will participate. Similarly, Jennifer Smith (2004: 105) reminds us that

interest group lobbying of ministers and government officials involved in intergovernmental deliberations 'has a behind the scenes quality that precludes widespread and
informed public debate about whatever is at issue'.

In addition, some scholars have raised questions about how governments use non-
governmental input. Éric Montpetit (2006) worries that the federal government might
engage stakeholders or citizens as a way of making decision-making processes that exclude provincial governments appear more legitimate. Especially in the case of executive
federalism, where the legitimacy of executives making extra-parliamentary decisions has
traditionally hinged on their accountability to their respective elected legislatures, graft-
ing opportunities for non-governmental participation onto intergovernmental forums
may do less to strengthen democracy than would a focus on revitalizing deliberation
among elected representatives within individual legislatures. As Hartley and Skogstad
(2005: 324) argue, 'where accountability of public officials to their citizens is at a premium, retaining this democratic value turns one in the direction of reforms to strengthen
the representational and deliberative character of parliamentary institutions.' For Laforest
and Phillips (2007), however, parliamentary reform by itself will not reverse the decline
in public trust and confidence in political institutions; interest groups and voluntary
associations as well as citizens need to play a role in a variety of deliberative processes.

Another narrative contributing to the debate about the legitimacy of executive federalism stems from the paradigm of the **New Public Management**. Beginning in the 1980s,
the adequacy of the expertise within the public sector was contested. Public servants
were encouraged to see themselves as service providers whose mandate was to be more
responsive to citizen needs. Based on a market model of customer satisfaction, better
public policy is thought to result from consultation with those—variously referred to as
customers, clients, or stakeholders and citizens—who will use the policy or service that
government seeks to develop. As the federal Deputy Ministers' Task Force on Service
Delivery Models defined it in 1996, Citizen-Centred Service 'incorporates citizens' concerns at every stage of the service design and delivery process; that is, citizens' needs
become the organizing principle around which the public interest is determined and
service delivery is planned' (cited in Marson, 2008: 239). Since the 1990s, 'horizontal
management' has called upon public servants to focus on process as much as on policy
substance, with careful attention to identifying problems and solutions through networking consensus with other government departments, but also with non-governmental
stakeholders (Aucoin and Savoie, 2009). These imperatives are present in perspectives of
the appropriate role for non-governmental actors in intergovernmental relations as well.
For example, Harvey Lazar (2006: 42) argues that adjustments to the 'intergovernmental
dimension of the social union' require the involvement of 'people found in the sector
ministries of provincial and federal governments and among the interest and stakeholder
groups whose members are most affected'.

Whether the new administrative practices of responsiveness to and partnership with cli-
ents/citizens actually strengthen democracy or lead to better policies is a matter of debate
(Pierre, 1998). Encouraging public servants to be accountable to the interests they serve
seems to undermine the idea that public servants are accountable to the Crown. The more
the nature of government interaction with non-governmental actors shifts from responsiveness to collaboration, with non-governmental actors playing a role as decision-makers

alongside the elected and permanent executive, the more important it becomes to ask who non-governmental actors represent and to whom they are accountable. However, the important point here is that, together with the distinctly Canadian experience of popular sovereignty and constitutional reform, these narratives about the adequacy of representative government and what constitutes a legitimate process of decision-making in general inform the debate about the legitimacy of executive federalism in particular.

In the last decade, however, a number of factors have muted the debate about the appropriate role of non-governmental actors in intergovernmental relations or made less likely a role for citizens in these relations. Within Ottawa, power is concentrated in the Prime Minister's Office (PMO), with limited discretion afforded to individual ministers and departments (Savoie, 2010). This context of **New Political Governance** (Aucoin, forthcoming), in which political leaders take greater control of the state machinery, is ill suited to the bottom-up approach to identifying policy problems and solutions and the consensus building that undergirds horizontal management. If the PMO is reticent to share agenda-setting with other central agencies and line departments, it is unlikely to share agenda-setting and policy development with non-governmental actors in the conduct of its intergovernmental negotiations with provinces.

During this same period, particularly in Ottawa, governments have increasingly relied on the participation of non-governmental experts, as opposed to citizens, in policy development, privileging 'scientific' outcome-based evidence over experiential knowledge of citizens (Laforest and Phillips, 2007). Another measure of the influence of non-governmental experts, as opposed to citizens, in the policy process is that a majority of Cabinet documents are now produced by consultants, rather than by public servants (Savoie, 2010). Grace Skogstad (2003) reminds us that so-called 'expert' advice is not a democratic source of legitimacy. If adopted by federal and provincial governments in their intergovernmental negotiations, reliance on experts does not represent a deepening of the democratic experience for citizens.

Prime Minister Stephen Harper's campaign of 'Open Federalism' intends to return to a more classical interpretation of the constitution with minimal overlap of federal and provincial areas of responsibility and also does not mesh well with an expanded role for citizens and advocacy organizations in intergovernmental relations. Two components of 'Open Federalism' are 'respecting provincial jurisdiction' and 'keeping the federal government's spending power within bounds' (Government of Canada, 2006). As a result, ministers of various policy areas may still annually meet with their provincial counterparts, but major intergovernmental initiatives are not negotiated at these meetings in the same way they were under Prime Minister Chrétien. Another aspect of Open Federalism is 'taking advantage of the experience and expertise that the provinces and territories can contribute to the national dialogue', which, in practice, means elevating provinces and territories well above non-governmental actors in intergovernmental policy development. One example of this shift is the Treasury Board Policy on Transfer Payments introduced in 2008 which distinguishes between 'collaborative agreements' involving the federal and provincial governments and those involving the federal government and other third parties (delivering services for example) (Nugent and Simmons, no date).

Finally, in the last decade, the federal government and provinces, to varying degrees, have implemented 'performance management' strategies, aimed at measuring the results (outcomes) of policies and taking action based on these results.³ This is a departure from the previous focus on measuring inputs (funds devoted to a program, for example) or outputs (number of people benefiting from a program, for example) (Simmons, 2010). In the intergovernmental sphere, performance management has also made an impact, with many intergovernmental agreements emphasizing that governments will regularly report results to citizens.

Many of the intergovernmental agreements discussed elsewhere in this volume embody this approach and span policy fields from early childhood development to municipal infrastructure. The approach was particularly palatable to all governments following dramatic cuts to federal fiscal transfers to the provinces in the mid 1990s. As Chapter 7 in this book outlines, following these cuts, many provinces were not prepared to answer to the federal government for how they spent federal funds, as had been the case with traditional conditional grants. With both federal and provincial governments agreeing to be accountable directly to constituents through reporting results, provincial and federal governments were on equal footing, rather than one order of government answering to the other.

This new performance management approach to accountability in intergovernmental relations has been criticized on a number of fronts, including that citizens lack the inclination or expertise to interpret government performance reports and have limited means to take action in light of the results. These concerns aside, in the last 10 years, provincial and federal governments have chosen to formally involve citizens in the implementation phase of the policy process to a far greater extent than in the policy development phase. But calling upon citizens to monitor government compliance with intergovernmental agreements does not have the same democratic implications as does involving them in the process of making those agreements.

Before exploring specific examples of non-governmental involvement in intergovernmental negotiations, the next section identifies dimensions of participation that correspond to the narratives discussed above.

Dimensions of Participation

In order to distinguish different forms of non-governmental participation in intergovernmental relations, it is useful to think of three models of democracy and two sites at which intergovernmental actors can be part of intergovernmental relations. The two sites of involvement in intergovernmental relations are, first, at the level of individual governments, whether federal or provincial; and second, within intergovernmental forums. The models of democracy differ according to the activity in which government and non-governmental actors partake, the nature of the non-governmental actors involved, and who ultimately makes the policy decision. Although the models of democracy may share some characteristics, they differ from one another in at least one regard.

Underlying the first model, **representative democracy**, is the idea that elected representatives have sufficient legitimacy to represent the views of citizens. Accordingly, there is no *formal* role for non-governmental actors. Although various interests in society may organize in groups to lobby federal or provincial governments, or even an intergovernmental forum, government actors do not seek to engage non-governmental actors, and ultimately decision-making authority resides with elected officials.

In contrast, **consultative democracy** parallels New Public Management's emphasis on government responsiveness to citizens. Government actors seek advice from the citizens who will be most affected by a government decision, or seek to explain to them why the government's plan is the best possible course of action. The non-governmental participants are commonly referred to as clients or stakeholders. Although government actors may meet repeatedly with non-governmental actors, iterative consultation does not necessarily occur. Interaction may also take the form of one-way consultation, with government actors listening to the views of clients or stakeholders or, alternatively, governments telling clients and stakeholders why a particular decision has been made. Governments may engage in two-way consultation, asking for input from non-governmental actors but also sharing information with them. Governments may also conduct three-way consultation, exchanging information and ideas with non-governmental actors, but also facilitating a dialogue among the non-governmental actors. The significant point is that government actors remain the final decision-makers in the consultative democracy model. However, because responsiveness to citizens, or at least its appearance, is a primary goal, consultative democracy often involves governments 'reporting back' on how non-governmental actors' participation affected the final policy outcome. Explaining this link to participants enhances the latter's sense of how they affected the real process of decision-making.

Deliberative democracy, as distinguished from representative democracy and consultative democracy,[4] seeks not a confrontation of pre-determined interests, but rather an exchange of reasons for espousing a position (Weinstock and Kahane, 2010: 1). The goal of the exercise is not to pursue one's own interests at the expense of the accommodation of others, or even to achieve an outcome that accommodates all interests. Rather, it is to explore why interests differ and to engage in reflection and persuasion, with participants potentially revising their own arguments in light of the exchange.[5] The outcome is not a reflection of which interests are better organized or financed, but rather a reflection of the best argument. With this purpose in mind, interaction is necessarily multidirectional: participants have multiple opportunities to meet with one another, ideally without time limitations on the exercise, and particular care is taken to ensure that members of identity groups who might not otherwise have the means to mobilize are given the resources they need to be informed participants in the process. This last measure is more substantial than governments issuing an open invitation for the public to comment on an ongoing development. It is also different from government actors choosing groups that they perceive to represent the spectrum of stakeholders affected by a policy decision or, alternatively, that they believe to be sufficiently informed to participate, as often occurs with consultative democracy. Although deliberative democracy includes the possibility for elected officials to share the authority to make decisions with non-governmental actors, the more likely outcome is for the process of engagement to inform the final decision of governments in a way that is clear to the participants. The reasons that government officials use to justify their actions should be made public. It is unrealistic for all participants to assume that policy outcomes will accommodate their specific perspectives; however, non-governmental participation that parallels real decision-making, as opposed to being part of it, runs the risk of feeding public cynicism.

Table 17.1 Roles for Non-Governmental Actors in Select Intergovernmental Relations

Site of Participation	Representative	Consultative	Deliberative
Intergovernmental	• (1) Martin Bilateral Agreements	• (4) Strengthening Ontario's Future and our Country's Fiscal Arrangement • (6) A Vision for Canada's Forests: 2008 and Beyond	• (2) Advisory Panel of the Council of the Federation (inter-provincial) • (5) Canada Forest Accord and National Forest Strategy(2003–2008)
Individual Government		• (3) Expert Panel on Equalization and Territorial Formula Financing	

In mapping the existence of representative democracy, consultation, and deliberative democracy, this chapter distinguishes between activities that individual governments initiate and those attached to specific intergovernmental forums of ministers. This distinction is important because there are long-standing arguments about how the site of participation affects the effectiveness and legitimacy of intergovernmental decision-making. On the one hand, excluding non-governmental actors from the intergovernmental site of decision-making is thought to limit the influence of non-governmental actors on the decision-making process and outcome. It can be disillusioning to be part of a meaningful process of public participation with one's provincial government or with the federal government, only to be informed that the results of that public deliberation just couldn't be accommodated at the intergovernmental table. As Richard Simeon (2006 [1972]: 282) observes, when the concerns that non-governmental groups have brought to individual governments are 'less central than status or ideological goals of governments, they will be the first to be jettisoned in the conference room'. At the same time, however, engaging non-governmental actors in intergovernmental forums may reduce the effectiveness of those forums in terms of their ability to produce new or revised policy.

With these models of democracy and sites of participation in mind, it is possible to distinguish among different roles for non-governmental actors in select cases of intergovernmental activity.[6] These differences are summarized in Table 17.1 and discussed in regard to the fiscal imbalance debate, the Canada Forest Accord and National Forest Strategy 2003–2008, and A Vision for Canada's Forests: 2008 and Beyond. As the fiscal imbalance debate involves premiers and ministers of finance involved in high-profile 'power politics', we might expect to see fewer opportunities for consultation and deliberative democracy. The forestry agreements make for a useful comparison because they were negotiated out of the spotlight of media attention, with significantly lower stakes at play, and within a sector with considerable experience with engagement of nongovernmental actors in policy development. We might expect these negotiations to be more amenable to non-traditional forms of citizen participation.

The Fiscal Imbalance Debate

When the Conservatives won the federal election in 2006, Prime Minster Harper joined an ongoing debate between Ottawa and the provinces over a 'fiscal imbalance' in the revenue generating powers of the two orders of government. Provinces argued that there was a vertical fiscal imbalance because they had insufficient ability to finance areas of provincial policy jurisdiction like health care, education and social services, while the federal government had more ability to finance areas of federal jurisdiction than it actually required. Another related debate involved horizontal imbalance, or differences in the revenue-generating capacity of provinces. This debate began in the early 2000s and culminated in the 2007 Federal budget. Throughout this period there was evidence of traditional closed-door executive federalism but also three distinct models of engagement with non-governmental actors.

(1) Martin Bilateral Agreements

In early 2005, then Prime Minister Paul Martin brokered two high-profile intergovernmental deals involving two different regions of the country. In February, Martin made five-year agreements on offshore resource revenues with the premiers of Nova Scotia and Newfoundland and Labrador worth $830 million and $2.6 billion respectively. Four months later, he responded to Ontario Premier Dalton McGuinty's campaign for Ontario's 'Fair Share', announcing that an additional $5.75 billion in federal dollars would be transferred to that province over five years. In both instances, the agreements were the result of a series of exchanges dating back several months, if not years, between high-level officials and first ministers of the two orders of government. These exchanges were sometimes well publicized, particularly when there was significant disagreement between the two sides. Most infamously, the government of Newfoundland and Labrador temporarily removed the Canadian flag from provincial buildings in late 2004 to signal its frustration with the federal government. The actual agreements received mixed reviews from academics, think-tanks and the media (e.g., Plourde, 2006; Feehan, 2009). The focus of these reviews was on both process and substance with many observers concerned about the ad hoc, bilateral nature of the negotiations (especially the Ontario deal) and calling for a more principled, rules-based approach to federal–provincial fiscal arrangements. A broader discussion involving all premiers seemed preferable, in light of the financial impact of these agreements on the functioning of the federation as a whole. Despite the sometimes public nature of these negotiations, the federal–provincial exchanges leading to these agreements reflect traditional executive federalism, and no experimentation with consultation or deliberative democracy.

(2) Advisory Panel of the Council of the Federation

In 2005 the premiers collectively agreed, through the Council of the Federation, to establish an 'independent panel' to investigate the vertical and fiscal balance and make recommendations to the premiers on how to address any imbalances. Although the Advisory Panel consisted of just five people with academic, public sector, and business expertise, the Panel's engagement of individual citizens reflects some of the characteristics of deliberative democracy. The panel asked Canadian Policy Research Networks, a think tank, to lead a dialogue with Canadians. A total of 93 randomly selected Canadians participated in five day-long regional sessions held in major city centres. Twenty-one of the regional participants 'reflecting a diversity of backgrounds and perspectives' then participated in a national dialogue process (Advisory Panel on Fiscal Imbalance, 2006: 109). At the regional conferences, participants discussed four different alternative federal–provincial fiscal arrangements.

The executive summary of the citizens' dialogue reveals that it was oriented to exploring differences among participants, having them reflect on each others' views, and attempting to establish a set of shared understandings. These features are hallmarks of the participatory deliberative democracy model:

> Participants discussed the four approaches to sharing funds, identifying what they liked and disliked about each approach and why. They agreed on their common ground and differences, probed tensions among competing values and determined the tradeoffs that they were prepared to make. Through this process they identified the values and principles that they want to see guide the sharing of funds in Canada. (ibid., 109–10)

In addition to citizens, the panel engaged 20 'experts'—former elected and unelected public servants, academics, and individuals affiliated with several think tanks—in a three-day round table. However, because the results of this round table are not part of the report, how the round table informed the report is less clear. Three observations can be made about this process. First, government officials—elected or unelected—were several degrees removed from this engagement with citizens. Second, as the Advisory Panel report is informed by several sources of information, it is only possible to loosely trace the results of the dialogue with Canadians to the recommendations of the Advisory Panel. Third, given the premiers' very different perspectives on how to resolve the issue of fiscal imbalance, and their varied reaction to the Advisory Panel report (Stevenson, 2009), it is difficult to see how it informed their collective negotiating position with the federal government.

(3) Expert Panel on Equalization and Territorial Formula Financing

The federal government also engaged non-governmental actors in establishing its position on fiscal imbalance. In March 2005, the Martin Liberal government created a five-person Expert Panel on Equalization and Territorial Formula Financing (2006a). Like the Council of the Federation's Advisory Panel, this Expert Panel did not work in isolation. It invited email submissions in reaction to a 'Key Issues' paper posted on its website, and also held five regional round tables and a round table of academics. Unlike the Advisory Panel's engagement of *citizens*, these round tables provided 'additional opportunities for academics, government officials, business representatives, and other interested parties to meet with the Expert Panel' (Expert Panel, 2006b). Although the summaries of the round-table discussions imply some variation in their format, they also suggest that the emphasis was on participants stating their views with rapporteurs submitting their impressions of the key themes and areas of disagreement among participants. This process differs from one in which participants engage in self-reflection and identify shared principles and points of disagreement. One summary of a regional round table states that

> [t]he roundtable did not drive for consensus, and thus some caution must be exercised in applying the conclusions that follow to the entire group of participants; no votes were called and opposing points of view may not always have been expressed. It should also be noted that the opinions that were expressed were, in many cases, just that—opinions. (Gibbins, 2005)

Unlike the participation process associated with the provincial advisory panel, in which regional exercises informed a national exercise, with some repeat participants, the participation process associated with the federal government's Expert Panel provided snapshots of regional opinions at one point in time. Of the three forms of democracy, this process most closely resembles consultative democracy. Many of the Expert Panel's recommendations were adopted in the federal 2007 budget, entitled 'Restoring Fiscal Balance for a Stronger Federation', demonstrating a clear link between the report and the government's policy.

(4) Strengthening Ontario's Future and Our Country's Fiscal Arrangement

A similar form of consultative democracy was evident in the actions of the Ontario government on the issue of fiscal imbalance.[7] It hosted a one-day summit on 'strengthening Ontario's future and our country's fiscal arrangement' for over 200 'leaders, stakeholders, and citizens to share their views'. The participants 'represented all of the province's regions, political orientations, and sectors, including business, healthcare, education, agriculture, municipal governments, community groups and the academic world' (Ontario, 2006b). This inclusiveness was consistent with a model of participatory deliberative democracy. However, the day's activities were more reminiscent of the consultative democracy model. After Premier McGuinty outlined his vision for fiscal arrangements and participants heard from a 'panel of experts', participants, guided by a discussion paper, engaged in small discussion group activities. The summary of the discussions was to 'help shape Ontario's position as we proceed with discussion with the federal government and other provinces and territories in the months ahead' (Bountrogianni, 2006).

These three examples of governmental efforts to bring non-governmental actors into the fiscal imbalance debate yield three observations. First, these exercises took place in the early stages of negotiations on concrete options between the two orders of government. Much of the federal–provincial activity still lay ahead. Second, the consultations were nevertheless a departure from the traditional approach of first ministers to their negotiations as evidenced in the Martin bilateral agreements. Even though the fiscal balance is among the more difficult policy topics for citizens to comprehend, more Canadians became aware of equalization as a result of these processes of engagement (and the published reports that followed) than would otherwise have been the case. More Canadians could contemplate the merits of various federal–provincial fiscal arrangements than in the past. Third, the three fiscal imbalance exercises reflected, to varying degrees, appeals to popular and **expert authority** to legitimize the substance of the reports. The extent to which appealing to expert authority, as opposed to **popular authority**, is democratic is discussed further in the conclusion of this chapter.

(5) Canada Forest Accord and National Forest Strategy 2003–2008

An example of intergovernmental decision-making that further resembles deliberative democracy is the activity of the National Forest Strategy Coalition (NFSC), under the rubric of the Canadian Council of Forest Ministers (CCFM). Since the CCFM was established in 1985 it has overseen three National Forest Strategies, each of which establishes a vision for a sustainable forest in Canada. The 1998–2003 strategy listed strategic priorities for guiding the policies and actions of Canada's forest community and over 100 separate 'commitments to action' reflecting these priorities. The National Forest Strategy for 2003–8 resulted from a process initiated by the NFSC, composed of the 42 signatories to the Canada Forest Accord, a companion document to the 1998–2003 strategy. These 42 signatories included the federal Minister of Natural Resources and the ministers from each of the provinces and the territories (with the exception of Quebec), as well as industry organizations, conservation and Aboriginal groups, and professional associations. The 2003–8 strategy has the backing of 63 signatories to the Canada Forest Accord for 2003–8. These agreements are distinctive from other intergovernmental agreements not just because non-governmental actors are signatories to them but also because of the scope of the deliberative processes used to establish them.

The 2003–8 strategy was the result of a development process that began in 2001 with an NFSC working group establishing and evaluating six different approaches to involving the 'forest community' in developing a new strategy. Ultimately the Coalition settled on an approach whereby it widely distributed copies of a Consultation Workbook in anticipation of six regional workshops held across the country in 2002. Completed workbooks and an independent evaluation of the previous National Forest Strategy informed the discussion at these regional workshops. Based on the feedback at the regional workshops and the completed workbooks, the Coalition created a 'What You Said' document, and a Vision and Issues paper that informed the first draft of the new strategy. 'Engaged Canadians' were then invited to comment on this draft. In early 2003 a national workshop, which brought together 'a limited group of forest experts and leaders representing a wide array of Canadians at the national level' to review the draft in detail, resulted in a second draft of the strategy. It was posted on the Coalition's website for public comment and also distributed to 'engaged Canadians' (NFSC and CCFM, 2002). The final draft of the strategy was presented at the Ninth National Forest Congress in May 2003.

The strategy is described as a consensus document (NFSC, 2006), which, rather than 'satisfying everyone on all matters . . . focus[es] on a compelling vision and strong objectives to face priorities across our nation's forest' (NFSC and CCFM, 2002). As such, together with the broadly inclusive and deliberative process by which it was created, it is closer to participatory deliberative democracy than consultative democracy. Inasmuch as the signatories include non-governmental actors, it is certainly a departure from representative democracy. But like its 1992 and 1998 predecessors, the 2003–8 National Forest Strategy was a voluntary agreement. Each of the eight strategic themes outlined in the Strategy was to be supported by a team of governments and forest community organizations, with team members identifying which aspects of the strategic themes they would work towards achieving. There has been little, if any, link between the deliberative process and substantive policy outcomes, given that the major industry representative involved in the development of the Strategy—the Forest Products Association of Canada—did not sign the Accord and participating governments,[8] taken as a whole, were even less enthusiastic about the National Forest Strategy Coalition than they had been in the past. The Sierra Club, one of the main environmental voices in the development phase, consequently disassociated from the Coalition in 2006.

(6) A Vision for Canada's Forests: 2008 and Beyond

The Canadian Council of Forest Ministers retreated to a more traditional form of consultation with the successor to the Canada Forest Accord and National Forest Strategy 2003–2008. Entitled 'A Vision for Canada's Forests: 2008 and Beyond', it represents a consensus among the forest ministers in Canada, and not among a broader coalition of the forest community. This fourteen-page, 'intentionally non-prescriptive' document (Canadian Council of Forest Ministers, 2008) is intended to guide forest policy for 10 years and is in contrast to the much more detailed, prescriptive and lengthy five-year forest strategies. To devise the Vision, the CCFM significantly relied on self-selecting non-governmental participants to comment on documents drafted by the CCFM (as opposed to a multi-stakeholder coalition). First the CCFM released a Discussion Paper in June of 2007 which proposed a vision for Canada's forests, posting it on the CCFM website and those of the participating governments. Paper copies were also mailed to 'key organizations', with a 25 per cent response rate. In total, 33 responses were received and summarized in a 'What Was Heard' report. The CCFM then released a draft Vision in December of 2008, allowing for a 45 day review period. During that time, the CCFM also hosted one national workshop. Although it is not clear how many individuals participated in the workshop, the CCFM received feedback from what it describes as 'a diverse group of interested parties including: Aboriginal academics, non-governmental organizations . . . and industry representatives from the traditional forest sector, but also new sectors that have potential to be part of the value chain' (Canadian Council of Forest Ministers, 2008). This list does not mention environmental groups, suggesting that the spectrum of participants could have been broader. A summary of the consultation was made public virtually at the same time as the CCFM released the final Vision. But ultimately, because the vision reads as a description of forestry policy in Canada, rather than a guide for future concrete policy-making, there is no link between the consultative process and substantive policy change. A skeptic might be inclined to conclude that the Forestry Ministers had a predetermined agenda to create a vision that did not hem in industry but which was granted legitimacy by the consultation exercises.

Conclusions

This review of some of the ways in which non-governmental actors participate in intergovernmental relations reveals how the narratives of stakeholder participation, responsiveness to citizens/clients, citizen deliberation, and expert advice that have surfaced in policy-making circles have also appeared in the intergovernmental realm. Of the cases examined here, the most developed forms of non-governmental participation are not solely the purview of low-profile, low-stakes negotiations in policy sectors with a track record of engaging non-governmental actors. Even first ministers have initiated round-table discussions and indirectly engaged citizens in deliberative democratic exercises. Whether these initiatives enhance the legitimacy of intergovernmental relations depends on one's view of ideal democratic practices and whether there is indeed a democratic deficit to be addressed. But assessment also depends on the performance and effectiveness of executives. Are governments or intergovernmental forums that choose to engage non-governmental actors making headway on the policy issues around which non-governmental participation has been centred? If the answer is no, then even those in favour of participatory democracy would be disappointed.

The cases examined here reveal just how complex it is to marry non-governmental participation with intergovernmental decision-making. When attempting to reconcile forms of non-governmental participation with intergovernmental forums premised on the responsible government model, patterns of elite accommodation are difficult to avoid. Whether led by first ministers or by ministers in a sector such as forestry, where officials are well acquainted with the participation of non-governmental actors in policy making, there seems to be a trade-off between enhancing legitimacy through non-governmental participation, on the one hand, and performance and effectiveness, on the other.

The performance, effectiveness, and legitimacy of executive federalism were high in the case of the fiscal imbalance because, in the end, the federal government adopted a new regime for equalization that is rules-based, and received input from academics, think tanks, citizens, and provinces. At the same time, the more deliberative the nature of the engagement of non-governmental actors, the more the legitimacy of executive federalism hinges on a direct line between the outcome of deliberations and the policy outcome. In the fiscal imbalance case, the premiers were significantly removed from the deliberative process the Advisory Panel initiated, and how their viewpoints on fiscal imbalance were informed by the deliberative process is impossible to trace. Thus, we could interpret the legitimacy of executive federalism as low in this case.

In the Canada Forest Accord and National Forest Strategy 2003–2008, the role for non-governmental actors resembled deliberative democracy. However, despite high performance (the successful creation of an agreement), the effectiveness of this voluntary agreement in modifying existing forestry practices was questionable at best. The Vision for Canada's Forests: 2008 and Beyond again represents high performance for executive federalism: forest ministers reached agreement. But, the effectiveness of this vision on forestry policy is even more dubious than in the case of the Accord and Strategy. Thus, there is a certain artificiality about the consultation associated with the Vision and, in turn, executive federalism seems to lack legitimacy.

Should individual governments engage non-governmental actors, or should engagement take place at the intergovernmental level? On the one hand, engagement at the intergovernmental level carries the risk of further hampering effective outcomes. Such was the case with the Canada-Wide Accord and National Forest Strategy 2003–2008. The intergovernmental decision-making process is already cumbersome and mutual agreement on solutions by executives is difficult. On the other hand, if non-governmental actors are not engaged within intergovernmental forums, their concerns may be more easily sacrificed, intentionally or unintentionally, by governments in quest of a solution that meets their own preferences. For example, one of the key preferences expressed by citizens in the CPRN exercise commissioned by the Council of the Federation's Advisory

Panel was that federal and provincial governments return to conditional grants with one level of government accountable to the other (Maxwell, MacKinnon, Watling, 2007). Yet, this preference was in sharp contrast to provincial government rhetoric of the previous ten years. It is not surprising that premiers, acting collectively through the Council of the Federation, did not act on the CPRN-expressed citizen preference. The cases examined here reveal that the activity of elite accommodation—which is deeply embedded in intergovernmental relations—can reduce non-governmental actors' sense of political efficacy, irrespective of where the opportunity for participation is located.

The cases considered here do not settle the debate of who most legitimately represents Canadians, or which site of non-governmental participation (intergovernmental or individual governments) is more democratic. In his study of transportation policy in Canada in the 1970s, Richard Schultz (1976) stressed that a government might publicly engage a constituency of interests to bolster the legitimacy of its position vis-à-vis other parties to the negotiation. More recently, Éric Montpetit (2006: 98) has argued that the federal government can use citizen engagement to justify bypassing negotiations with provincial governments. At the core of these observations is the question of who—the federal government, non-governmental groups and individual citizens, or provincial governments—can best speak for Canadians. When elected executives, federal or provincial, invite non-governmental actors to participate in intergovernmental forums, they are in effect conceding their own inability to adequately represent the interests of Canadians.

The cases reveal that individual governments' decisions to engage non-governmental actors in their own jurisdiction or to invite non-governmental actors to participate in intergovernmental forums are not informed exclusively by their answer to the question 'Who best represents Canadians?' but are also guided by a variety of practical and strategic considerations. In the case of fiscal imbalance, both orders of government used non-governmental actors in strategic ways. Should governments use non-governmental participation to advance their strategic interests this way? The potential downside is that just as scenes involving some actors in a film end up on the editing room floor for reasons other than the quality of the actors' work, the perspectives of non-governmental actors may not be reflected in a final federal–provincial agreement. When non-governmental participation is used strategically, the sense of political efficacy of non-governmental actors is most threatened—and likely, as well, their trust in public officials.

These cases also point to the uneasy relationship between expert advice and citizen advice as well as the difference between collaborating with non-governmental actors in service delivery and participatory deliberative democracy. It is not surprising that with an issue as complex as fiscal imbalance, executives found ways to combine expert authority with citizen participation. But how to reconcile conflicts between these sources and the preferences of executives remains a challenge.

Finally, the case of the Canada Forest Accord and National Forest Strategy demonstrates that impulses towards deliberative democracy are not the same as impulses towards collaboration with non-governmental actors in the delivery of service or the realization of policy outcomes. Deliberative democracy is seemingly a good fit for the development of a voluntary agreement. But when the non-governmental actors involved in the process seek to influence the actions of governments, the policy outcome of a voluntary agreement again threatens citizens' sense of political efficacy.

Is executive federalism incompatible with meaningful non-governmental actor participation? In intergovernmental forums, the legitimacy of ministers and first ministers has traditionally been derived from their status as elected representatives responsible to a legislature for their actions. At the same time, intergovernmental forums typically make trade-offs to reach a mutually accommodating outcome. But the only way to determine whether it is possible to reconcile non-governmental actor participation with executive federalism is to continue experimenting with roles for non-governmental actors in intergovernmental deliberations. Nonetheless, in the current intergovernmental climate of Open Federalism, New Political Governance, and preference for 'expert' analysis, we should limit our expectations that such experimentation will take place.

Notes

1. Alternatively, this distinction is characterized by Scharpf (2000) as one between 'input' legitimacy and 'output' legitimacy. His framework is applied to the Canadian context by Skogstad (2003) and Montpetit (2006). Steve Patten's analysis of Canada's institutions of policy-making reflects the shift to input legitimacy. Patten (2001: 225) takes as a starting point the idea that 'in public affairs and policy-making, democratic legitimacy depends on the nature and quality of public deliberation and the decision processes associated with such deliberation.' Similarly, Lorne Sossin (2010: 277) calls for 'democratic administration' in Canada, asserting that 'democracy is ultimately not about outcomes but about the process of reaching outcomes.'

2. Laforest and Phillips (2007) overview some major initiatives dating back to the Berger Inquiry into the Mackenzie Valley pipeline in the mid-1970s.

3. Performance management is part of a broader expansion of accountability initiatives. A summary of the impact of these accountability initiatives is found in Thomas (2008).

4. Representatives elected by citizens can themselves deliberate, engaging in conversation that allows them to reflect on the positions of others; however, here I assume, as most deliberative democratic theorists do, that deliberative democracy involves a role for citizens (Kahane et al., 2010).

5. Some who advocate deliberative practices involving non-governmental actors suggest that government actors may not necessarily convene such processes (Phillips and Orsini, 2002; Stein et al., 1999). However, in their consideration of the contribution of the National Action Committee on the Status of Women to the debate on assisted reproductive technology in Canada, Montpetit et al. find that deliberation in autonomous public spheres can have limited effect on policy-making. They rightly point out that 'deliberation among citizens, in an inclusive public sphere distinctive from the state, makes discourses, not decisions' (Montpetit et al., 2004: 138).

6. The list of cases of non-governmental participation examined here is not exhaustive; rather, the cases have been selected to demonstrate a spectrum of approaches.

7. Ontario is one of the provinces to engage citizens on this topic. For example, the Quebec Government in 2001 appointed a Commission on Fiscal Imbalance which, as part of its research sponsored a public opinion survey across Canada.

8. Alberta joined Quebec in declining to sign the 2003–8 Accord.

References

Abelson, J., P.-G. Forest, J. Eyles, P. Smith, E. Martin, and F.-P. Gauvin. 2003. 'Deliberations about Deliberative Methods: Issues in the Design and Evaluation of Public Participation Processes', *Social Science and Medicine* 57: 240–51.

Advisory Panel on Fiscal Imbalance. 2006. *Reconciling the Irreconcilable: Addressing Canada's Fiscal Imbalance*. Ottawa: Council of the Federation.

Anderson, C.D. 2008. 'Economic voting, Multilevel Governance and Information in Canada.' *Canadian Journal of Political Science* 41, 2: 329–354.

Atkinson, M. 1994. 'What Kind of Democracy Do Canadians Want?' *Canadian Journal of Political Science* 27, 4: 717–45.

Aucoin, P. Forthcoming. 'New Political Governance in Westminster Systems: Impartial Public Administration and Management Performance at Risk.' *Governance*.

Aucoin, P., and D.J. Savoie. 2009. 'The Politics–Administration Dichotomy; Democracy versus Bureaucracy?'. In *The Evolving Physiology of Government: Canadian Public Administration in Transition*, eds. O.P. Dwivedi, T. Mau and B. Sheldrick. Ottawa: University of Ottawa Press.

Banting, K. 1997. 'The Past Speaks to the Future: Lessons from the Postwar Social Union'. In *Canada: the State of the Federation 1997: Non-Constitutional Renewal*, ed. H. Lazar. Montreal and Kingston: McGill–Queen's University Press.

Bountrogianni, M. 2006. Preface to the print version of Ontario, *Report on Outcomes: A Strong Ontario for a Strong Canada: A Summit On Strengthening Ontario's Future and Our Country's Fiscal Arrangements*. Toronto: Government of Ontario.

Brock, K.L. 1995. 'The End of Executive Federalism?' In *New Trends in Canadian Federalism*, ed. F. Rocher and M. Smith. Peterborough, Ont.: Broadview Press.

Canadian Council of Forest Ministers. 2008. *A Vision for Canada's Forests: 2008 and Beyond.*

Chambers, S. 1998. 'Contract or Conversation? Theoretical Lessons from the Canadian Constitutional Crisis', *Politics and Society* 26, 1: 143–72.

———. 2003. 'Deliberative Democratic Theory', *Annual Review of Political Science* 6: 307–26.

Cutler, F. 2008. 'Whodunnit? Voters and Responsibility in Canadian Federalism'. *Canadian Journal of Political Science* 41, 3: 627–54.

Cutler, F., and M. Mendelsohn. 2005. 'Unnatural Loyalties or Native Collaborationists? The Governance and Citizens of Canadian Federalism'. In *Insiders and Outsiders: Alan Cairns and the Reshaping of Canadian Citizenship*, ed. G. Kernerman and P. Resnick. Vancouver: University of British Columbia Press.

Expert Panel on Equalization and Territorial Formula Financing. 2006a. *Achieving a National Purpose: Putting Equalization Back on Track*. Ottawa: Department of Finance. At: www.eqtff-pfft.ca/epreports/EQ_Report_e.pdf.

———. 2006b. Consultation Activity Report. At: www.eqtff-pfft.ca/english/consultationcalendar.asp.

Federal–Provincial–Territorial Ministers Responsible for Social Services. 2005. 'Federal–Provincial–Territorial Social Services Ministers Reach Consensus on Early Learning and Child Care', *News Release*, 11 Feb.

Feehan, J.P. 2009. 'Equalization 2007: Natural Resources, the Cap and the Offset Payment Agreements'. In *Canada the State of the Federation 2006/07: Transitions: Fiscal and Political Federalism in an Era of Change*, ed. J. R. Allan, T.J. Courchene and C. Leuprecht. Montreal and Kingston: McGill–Queen's University Press.

Gibbins, R. 2005. 'Roundtable on Equalization and Territorial Formula Financing', *Summary Report*. At: www.eqtff-pfft.ca/english/documents/FinalReport-Calgary.pdf.

Government of Canada. 2008. 'Canada and Ontario Sign $6.2-Billion Building Canada Infrastructure Agreement', *News Release*. At: http://www.buildingcanada-chantierscanada.gc.ca/media/news-nouvelles/news-nouvelles-eng.html.

———. 2006. 'Prime Minister Promotes Open Federalism', *News Release*. At: http://pm.gc.ca/eng/media.asp?id=1123.

Gow, I. 2009. 'Evolution of Disciplinary Approaches and Paradigms in the Study of Public Administration in Canada'. In *The Evolving Physiology of Government: Canadian Public Administration in Transition*, eds. O.P. Dwivedi, T. Mau and B. Sheldrick. Ottawa: University of Ottawa Press.

Hartley, S., and G. Skogstad. 2005. 'Regulating Genetically Modified Crops and Foods in Canada and the United Kingdom: Democratising Risk Regulation', *Canadian Public Administration* 48, 3: 305–27.

Johnson, G.F. 2007. 'The discourse of democracy in Canadian nuclear waste management policy', *Policy Sciences* 40: 79–99.

Kahane, D., D. Weinstock, D. Leydet, and M. Williams. 2010. eds. *Deliberative Democracy in Practice*. Vancouver: UBC Press.

Kanji, M. 2002. 'Political Discontent, Human Capital and Representative Governance in Canada'. In *Value Change and Governance in Canada*, ed. N. Nevitte. Toronto: University of Toronto Press.

Kanji, M., and A. Bilodeau. 2006. 'Value Diversity and Support for Electoral Reform in Canada', *PS: Political Science & Politics* 39, 4: 829–36.

Laforest, R., and S. Phillips. 'Citizen Engagement: Rewiring the Policy Process'. In *Critical Policy Studies*, ed. M. Orsini and M. Smith. Vancouver: UBC Press.

Lazar, H. 2006. 'The Intergovernmental Dimensions of the Social Union: A Sectoral Analysis', *Canadian Public Administration* 49, 1: 23–45.

Lusztig, M. 1994. 'Constitutional Paralysis: Why Canadian Constitutional Initiatives Are Doomed to Fail', *Canadian Journal of Political Science* 27, 4: 747–71.

Marson, B. 2008. 'Citizen-Centred Service in Canada: From Research to Results'. In *Professionalism & Public Service: Essays in Honour of Kenneth Kernaghan*, ed. D. Siegel and K. Rasmussen. Toronto: University of Toronto Press.

Maxwell, J., M.P. MacKinnon, and J. Watling. 2007. *Taking Fiscal Federalism to the People*. CPRN Research Report. Ottawa: CPRN.

Mendelsohn, M. 2000. 'Public Brokerage: Constitutional Reform and the Accommodation of Mass Publics', *Canadian Journal of Political Science* 33, 2: 245–72.

Monpetit, É. 2006. 'Declining Legitimacy and Canadian Federalism: An Examination of Policy-Making in Agriculture and Biomedicine'. In *Continuity and Change in Canadian Politics: Essays in Honour of David E. Smith*, ed. H.M. Michelmann and C. de Clercy. Toronto: University of Toronto Press.

———F. Scala, and I. Fortier. 2004. 'The Paradox of Deliberative Democracy: The National Action Committee on the Status of Women and Canada's Policy on Reproductive Technology', *Policy Sciences* 37: 137–57.

National Forest Strategy Coalition (NFSC). 2004. *Implementing the National Forest Strategy. A Sustainable Forest: The Canadian Commitment*. Implementation Approach for the National Forest Strategy (2003–2008). At: nfsc.forest.ca/background/implementation2003_e.html#implementation.

———. 2006. National Forest Strategy. At: nfsc.forest.ca/strategy_e.htm.

———and Canadian Council of Forest Ministers (NSFC and CCFM). 2002. *Consultation Workbook To Help Define a Vision and Identify Key Issues for the Next National Forest Strategy 2003–2008 for All Canadians*. At: nfsc.forest.ca/background/workbook.html.

Nugent, A., and J.M. Simmons. No date. 'Panacea or Peril? Intergovernmental Accountability and the Auditor General'. Mimeo.

Ontario. 2006a. *Discussion Paper for: A Strong Ontario for a Strong Canada: A Summit on Strengthening Ontario's Future and Our Country's Fiscal Arrangements*. At: www.strongontario.ca/english/summit/DiscussionPaper.pdf.

———. 2006b. *Report on Outcomes: A Strong Ontario for a Strong Canada: A Summit on Strengthening Ontario's Future and Our Country's Fiscal Arrangements*. At: www.strongontario.ca/english/summit/Outcomes.pdf.

Patten, S. 2001. 'Democratizing the Institutions of Policy-making: Democratic Consultation and Participatory Administration', *Journal of Canadian Studies* 35, 4: 221–39.

Phillips, S.D., and M. Orsini. 2002. 'Mapping the Links: Citizen Involvement in Policy Processes', *CPRN Discussion Paper* F(21).

Pierre, J. 1998. 'Public Consultation and Citizen Participation: Dilemmas of Policy Advice'. In *Taking Stock: Assessing Public Sector Reforms*, ed. B.G. Peters and D.M. Savoie. Montreal and Kingston: McGill–Queen's University Press.

Plourde, A. 2006. 'Offshore Energy Revenues and Equalization: Having your Cake and Eating It Too?'. In *How Ottawa Spends 2006–2007; In From the Cold: The Tory Rise and the Liberal Demise*, ed. G.B. Doern. Montreal and Kingston: McGill–Queen's University Press.

Savoie, D.J. 2003. *Breaking the Bargain: Public Servants, Ministers and Parliament*. Toronto: University of Toronto Press.

Savoie, D.J. 2010. *Power: Where is It?* Montreal and Kingston: McGill–Queen's University Press.

Scharpf. F.W. 1988. 'The Joint-Decision Trap: Lessons from German Federalism and European Integration', *Public Administration* 66, 3: 239–78.

——. 2000. 'Interdependence and Democratic Legitimation'. In *Disaffected Democracies: What's Troubling the Trilateral Countries?*, ed. S.J. Pharr and R.D. Putnam. Princeton, NJ: Princeton University Press.

Schultz, R. 1977. 'Interest Groups and Intergovernmental Negotiations: Caught in the Vise of Federalism'. In *Federalism and Political Community: Essays in Honour of Donald Smiley*, ed. D.P. Shugarman and R. Whitaker. Peterborough, Ont.: Broadview Press.

Simeon, R. 2006 [1972]. *Federal–Provincial Diplomacy: The Making of Recent Policy in Canada*. Toronto: University of Toronto Press.

——and D. Cameron, 2002. 'Intergovernmental Relations and Democracy: An Oxymoron If There Ever Was One?' In *Canadian Federalism: Performance, Effectiveness, and Legitimacy*, ed. H. Bakvis and G. Skogstad. Toronto: Oxford University Press.

Simmons, J.M. 2010. 'Desperate Measures: Why Performance Measurement Just Doesn't Measure Up'. In *Approaching Public Administration: Core Debates and Emerging Issues*, ed. R. Leone and F. Ohemeng. Toronto: Emond Montgomery Publications Limited.

Skogstad, G. 2003. 'Who Governs? Who Should Govern? Political Authority and Legitimacy in Canada in the Twenty-First Century', *Canadian Journal of Political Science* 36, 5: 955–73.

Smith, J. 2004. *Federalism*. Vancouver: University of British Columbia Press.

Sossin, L. 2010. 'Democratic Administration'. In *The Handbook of Canadian Public Administration Second Edition,* ed. C. Dunn. Toronto: Oxford University Press.

Stein, M. 1993. 'Tensions in the Canadian Constitutional Process: Elite Negotiations, Referendums and Interest Group Consultation, 1980–1992'. In *Canada: The State of the Federation 1993*, ed. R.L. Watts and D.M. Brown. Kingston: Institute of Intergovernmental Relations.

Stein, J.G., D.R. Cameron, and R. Simeon, with A. Alexandroff. 1999. 'Citizen Engagement in Conflict Resolution: Lessons for Canada in International Experience'. In *The Referendum Papers: Essays on Secession and National Unity*, ed. D.R. Cameron. Toronto: University of Toronto Press.

Stevenson, G. 'Fiscal Federalism and the Burden of History'. In *Canada the State of the Federation 2006/07: Transitions: Fiscal and Political Federalism in an Era of Change*, ed. J. R. Allan, T. J. Courchene and C. Leuprecht. Montreal and Kingston: McGill–Queen's University Press.

Thomas, P.G. 2009. 'Trust, Leadership and Accountability in Canada's Public Sector'. In *The Evolving Physiology of Government: Canadian Public Administration in Transition*, ed. O.P. Dwivedi, T. Mau and B. Sheldrick. Ottawa: University of Ottawa Press.

Thomas, P.G. 2008. 'The Swirling Meanings and Practices of Accountability in Canadian Government'. In *Professionalism & Public Service: Essays in Honour of Kenneth Kernaghan*, ed. D. Siegel and K. Rasmussen. Toronto: University of Toronto Press.

Thorburn, H.G. 1989. 'Federalism, Pluralism and the Canadian Community'. In *Federalism and Political Community: Essays in Honour of Donald Smiley*, ed. D.P. Shugarman and R. Whitaker. Peterborough, Ont.: Broadview Press.

Weinstock, D., and D. Kahane. 2010. 'Introduction'. In *Deliberative Democracy in Practice*, ed. D. Kahane, D. Weinstock, D. Leydet and M. Williams. Vancouver: UBC Press.

18 Conclusion: Taking Stock of Canadian Federalism

Grace Skogstad and Herman Bakvis

The essays in this volume have documented the complexity of Canadian federalism, revealing the multiple faces of Canadian federalism: in a single policy field over time and across policy fields at a given point in time. Appraisals of the performance, effectiveness, and legitimacy of Canadian federalism thus likewise depend, as several authors have noted, not only on our evaluative criteria, but also on the point in time at which we are evaluating Canadian federalism. In this concluding chapter, we summarize what we have learned about the relationship between different models of Canadian federalism, on the one hand, and its performance, effectiveness and legitimacy, on the other. We close the chapter by highlighting a number of factors that are likely to affect future possible paths of Canadian federalism.

The Faces of Contemporary Federalism

The multiple faces of Canadian federalism are revealed in Table 18.1. While authors of chapters in this text have sometimes used other names to describe models of federalism, the six models identified in Table 18.1 are generally in wide usage. They are: first, an independent governments model in which the two orders of government work independently on policy matters within their assigned jurisdictions; second, a unilateral shared-cost model in which the autonomous activity of one order of government (invariably the government of Canada) imposes conditions on the other and/or distorts its priorities (Lazar, 2006); third, a collaborative shared-cost model in which both orders of government contribute to the costs of social programs via transfer payments or tax points; fourth, a collaborative regulatory model in which governments co-ordinate their rules and regulations, for example, on how markets can function; fifth, a joint-decision model in which formal rules of intergovernmental agreement require a super-majority, or even unanimity, for a decision to be taken; and sixth, asymmetrical federalism, in which one constituent unit (province) has a different status than other units in the federal system, either constitutionally or by virtue of special administrative arrangements. As has become clear throughout this text, these various models of intergovernmental relations reflect the *practice* of federalism—that is, governments' behaviour—as distinct from what the Canadian constitution stipulates.

Table 18.1 identifies programs and policy areas discussed in this volume that illustrate the different models of intergovernmental relations. Other policy arenas not examined in this text could be added. For example, to the 'independent governments' column could be added defense and international diplomacy at the federal level, and education (primary through secondary) at the provincial level. Similarly, the asymmetrical federalism column could also include labour-market training, the participation of Quebec and New Brunswick in La Francophonie, and Quebec's representing itself at UNESCO.

Table 18.1 highlights a number of features of intergovernmental relations in Canada. First is the persistence of the arm's-length 'independent governments' model. This model appears to be more prominent since the Harper Conservatives took office in 2006, as evidenced, for example, by the entry of subject matters like early childhood education and care into this column, as compared to its pre-2006 collaborative federalism status. Second is the prevalence of collaborative federalism, a model whose emergence was noted in the first edition of *Canadian Federalism* (2002). An interesting new variant of the collaborative regulatory model is its functioning at the sub-national level. For example, some but not all provinces collaborate on climate change policy without participation from the federal government.

Third is the importance of asymmetrical federalism. It undoubtedly owes much to Quebec's political leaders and its intellectual elite, who have long championed asymmetry as an essential feature of a well-performing federation (Laforest, 2010). Although de jure recognition of Quebec's special status is the ultimate goal, Quebec's federalist premiers and its intellectual elite have also pressed hard for de facto asymmetry with substantial decentralization of intergovernmental administrative arrangements. Quebec continues to benefit from the success of that effort with respect to the federal government's spending power in the province. The Health Care Accord signed in September 2004, as Antonia Maioni has observed, explicitly recognized asymmetrical federalism as 'an essential part of the fundamental logic of federalism'. But de facto asymmetry is not confined to Quebec. As Keith Banting documents in Chapter 14, although Quebec was the first province to carve out a distinct role for itself in immigration in the early 1970s, since then several other provinces have struck bilateral deals with the government of Canada in immigration policy. As a result, 'pervasive asymmetry' across provinces characterizes Canadian immigration selection and settlement. Fiscal federalism (Chapter 7) also reveals asymmetry. Nova Scotia and Newfoundland and Labrador bargained successfully in 2004 for their natural resource revenues to be excluded from calculation of their equalization payments.

More generally, when efforts at establishing multilateral agreements including all provincial/territorial governments break down, the alternative of bilateral agreements (in climate change and child care under the Martin government) is likely to widen the scope for asymmetrical federalism. The examples of asymmetry extend to other policy areas not investigated here, including programs to support farm incomes across Canada.

The fourth feature of Table 18.1 is variation in models of federalism not only across policy spheres at a given point in time, but also within a single policy sphere *over time*. For example, health care policy has shifted from a model of unilateral shared-cost federalism to collaborative shared-cost federalism; child care and early childhood education, from one of collaborative federalism to independent governments (as noted above); social assistance, from collaborative shared-cost federalism to unilateral shared-cost federalism;

Table 18.1 Models of Federalism and Programs/Policy Fields

Independent Governments	Collaborative Shared-cost	Unilateral Shared-cost	Collaborative Regulatory	Joint-Decision	Asymmetrical
(Un)employment insurance	Health care (1960s–mid-1980s; 2004–)	Health care (1986–late 1990s)	International trade policy	Contributory pension plans (CPP/QPP)	CPP/QPP
Immigration (pre-1971)	Social Assistance (1966 CAP)	Social assistance (since 1995)	Income tax collection*		Health care (2004)
Old-age income security (OAS/GIS)	Child benefits (1970–2005)**				Immigration (since 1971)
ECEC (2006–)	Post-secondary education (as part of EPF)				Income tax collection
Economic development			Climate change (1992–2002)		Revenue-resource sharing (2004)
Labour Market Training (Skills) Policy					
Climate change (2002–)					
Equalization					
Cities					
Aboriginal peoples					

* Except for corporate income taxes in Quebec, Ontario, and Alberta, and personal income taxes in Quebec

** Early Childhood Development Agreement, Multilateral Framework Agreement

and climate change policy, from collaboration (or multilateralism, to use Winfield and Macdonald's term) to federal unilateralism and bilateral engagement, and now to provincial and national governments independently co-ordinating their policies with those of American states.

What determines the form that intergovernmental relations take in a given policy area? And, as a corollary question, why does the pattern of relations vary so much over time? Four factors in combination are especially important to explain the model of federalism and the pattern of intergovernmental relations. They are first, the nature of constitutional jurisdiction; second, the history of intergovernmental relations in the sector concerned; third, the ideas and interests of the executives at both levels; and fourth, the broader international context within which Canadian politics unfolds.

Canada's constitution, as interpreted by the courts, is consequential to the pattern of intergovernmental relations that arises in a policy sector. The constitution's impact is felt not only in its assignment of jurisdictional authority (including fiscal) but also, as David Cameron observes in Chapter 3, in shaping understandings of relations between parties to Confederation. The 'independent governments' model of federalism reflects instances in which the Constitution has unambiguously assigned exclusive jurisdiction to one order of government, for example, cities to the provinces, and unemployment insurance to the federal government. The 'joint decision' and 'collaborative federalism' models are found in areas where both orders of government have been assigned jurisdiction in whole (pensions, immigration) or in part (international trade) for a subject matter, so that neither can achieve its goals without collaborating with the other.

Both federal and provincial governments share jurisdiction over contributory pensions; their goal of a co-ordinated pension plan across the country has led them to accept a joint decision-making model of federalism, as Keith Banting documents in Chapter 8. The decentralized asymmetry in immigration policy that Keith Banting documents in Chapter 14 also occurs in an area of shared constitutional jurisdiction (albeit, unlike pensions, immigration is a matter where the government of Canada is paramount). Divided jurisdiction over international trade has led to collaboration in policy-making. While the government of Canada has the exclusive legal authority to negotiate and ratify international treaties, the provinces alone have the legal authority to implement the provisions in those treaties that fall under the matters assigned to them. The failure of the government of Canada to elicit provincial support for terms of international trade agreements that fall under provincial jurisdiction would impair its subsequent ability to honour those agreements. To avoid this outcome, as Chapter 11 documents, a collaborative or de facto shared jurisdiction model of federalism has evolved in international trade policy. To take yet another example, while the constitution is silent on 'the environment', the courts' ruling that both levels of government share constitutional jurisdiction for regulating pollution creates strong incentives for governments to co-ordinate their policy-making. One example is the 1998 Environmental Harmonization Accord.

Canada's constitution also affects models of federalism by its imbalanced assignment of legal powers relative to fiscal capacities across the orders of government. Jurisdictional powers under the constitution do not always line up with the financial resources needed to act on them. The vertical fiscal imbalance between Ottawa and the provinces/territories, and the horizontal fiscal imbalance (across richer and poorer provinces) have not only justified fiscal federalism (as Doug Brown explains in Chapter 7), but also shared-cost federalism, both unilateral and collaborative. These jurisdictional imbalances have played a major role in the emergence of the federal spending power and the subsequent transformation of virtually every area of social policy into a potential case of shared-cost jurisdiction.

Still, it is important not to make too much of constitutional jurisdiction; it is not an accurate guide to who does what. Three other broad factors are needed to account for these variations in patterns of intergovernmental relations across policy fields and in the same policy area over time. The first of these is the history of intergovernmental relations—what might be called policy legacies—in the sector concerned. Although there is flux over time in the model of intergovernmental relations prevailing in a given policy sector (health is a good example)—so that the model at time t_2 varies from that at time t_1—there is also little doubt that some models are products of historical patterns. The joint-decision model associated with the Canada and Quebec pension plans is a good example. These plans were implemented in the mid-1960s with rules requiring substantial agreement but not complete unanimity for any program changes.

A second important set of factors that affect patterns of intergovernmental relations over time is the ideas and policy goals of the executives at both levels. As Richard Simeon and Amy Nugent pointed out in Chapter 4, intergovernmental relations in Canada have not been well institutionalized, with the result that government elites have usually had the latitude to abandon past models (for example, co-ordinated shared-cost federalism) and pursue their own strategies and preferences. Three examples of how the policy and partisan goals of first ministers shape models of federalism are early childhood education and care (ECEC), federal policies towards cities, and climate change. An ECEC policy was a high priority for Prime Minister Paul Martin, whose government used its fiscal resources to forge multilateral and bilateral agreements with the provinces to advance it; in contrast, Prime Minister Stephen Harper, with different partisan interests and a different set of priorities, abandoned Martin's effort and virtually retreated from intergovernmental relations in this policy area. When it comes to cities, whereas Paul Martin enunciated an 'urban agenda', Stephen Harper had not by early 2012 proclaimed a distinct 'urban agenda'.

Climate change policy is the third example (Chapter 13). The Liberal Chrétien government often acted unilaterally in its goal of establishing Canadian targets for the reduction of greenhouse gas emissions under the Kyoto Protocol in 1997. The Harper Conservative government has disavowed a global approach to reducing greenhouse gases and explicitly tied its approach to climate change to that of the US federal government. Several provinces, notably BC, Ontario, Quebec and Manitoba are also following this bi-national approach, grounding their climate change polices in regionally based sub-national initiatives with US states.

These examples reinforce how patterns of Canadian federalism can be significantly reshaped by the ideas and partisan goals of first ministers. The second edition of *Canadian Federalism* (2008: 382, 384) observed the 'prevalence' of collaborative federalism and described it as 'the favoured approach in contexts of policy interdependence'. However, Prime Minister Stephen Harper's avowed commitment to Open Federalism—that is, to restricting federal intervention to federal areas of jurisdiction and not using the federal spending power in areas of provincial jurisdiction—has stemmed the tide of collaborative federalism to some degree and meant a return to watertight compartments in terms of federal/provincial jurisdictional responsibilities.

At the same time, the Harper government has not been averse to unilateralism. Its proposal to create a national securities regulator has the potential to undermine section 91(13) (provincial jurisdiction over property and civil rights). The proposal is supported by only one province (Ontario) and opposed by most of the others, including Quebec and Alberta.

A final factor that helps to account for the shifting patterns of federalism models is the broader international context. Current features of this context are the integration of Canada's economy into competitive regional and global markets, and Canada's membership in international organizations whose rules prescribe appropriate conduct for states and best practices in specific policy domains.

These internationalizing features are having some effect on intergovernmental relations, but the effects are uneven, giving rise to models of both collaborative federalism and independent governments. The goal of market opening and integration is encouraging greater intergovernmental collaboration in international trade policy, as treaties to promote this goal trespass further and further into provincial areas of jurisdiction. A different effect is witnessed in economic development policy. Haddow argues in Chapter 12 that international ideas about best practices in terms of promoting economic growth are more consequential and the content of these ideas is leading to an independent governments' model of federalism in economic development policies. Whereas membership in international organizations to promote climate change mitigation initially shifted Canada under Prime Minister Chrétien toward a collaborative model of federalism, that model broke down when the Prime Minister acted unilaterally to raise Canadian targets and provinces refused to come on board with these targets. Canada has been in breach of the international Kyoto Protocol treaty and in late 2011 the Harper Conservative government gave notice of its intention to withdraw formally from it. As noted, the integration of the Canadian economy into the American is the bigger driver of Canada's continental climate change policy. The Conservative government's one area of significant action on climate change policy, the adoption of more stringent vehicle fuel economy standards, was driven entirely by the need to harmonize standards with those being adopted by the Obama administration in the 2009 bailout of the North American automobile.

The impacts of the international context on Canadian federalism are usually experienced in conjunction with other factors noted above, and most especially the ideas and goals of political executives including, especially, first ministers. The contrast between Prime Minister Martin and Prime Minister Harper when it comes to the influence of prevailing international ideas about best practices for early childhood education and care is instructive. Paul Martin was persuaded by these ideas and took significant steps to establish federal–provincial publicly funded ECEC programs; upon his election, Stephen Harper abandoned these programs and opted for a child care policy more consistent with his conservative belief that child care is a private responsibility.

How Is Canadian Federalism Faring?

The criteria by which to appraise Canadian federalism throughout this text have been its performance, effectiveness, and legitimacy. In terms of performance, the relevant questions of the various models of Canadian federalism—and Canadian federalism as a whole—have been the following. Is there a balance between shared and self-rule—between vesting the central government with sufficient power to unite the country on common purposes and entrusting provincial leaders with the authority to express the values of their distinct political communities? Do institutional forums provide a setting for discussion and negotiation between governments and facilitate agreement, or at least understanding, on major issues in a manner that respects the positions of both levels of government? Or, alternatively, are governments at the two orders competitive and adversarial to the point of being dysfunctional? In terms of effectiveness, the relevant question has been whether the institutions of Canadian federalism are enabling problems to be addressed in a timely, effective, and efficient fashion. And in terms of legitimacy, the question has been whether the governing arrangements and policy outcomes associated with the various models of federalism are perceived as appropriate and acceptable by Canadian citizens and policy stakeholders.

Assessing federalism's performance, effectiveness, and legitimacy is admittedly a challenging and subjective exercise; assessments inevitably vary depending upon the perspective of the assessor. Appraising the federation as a whole within these criteria is arguably even more difficult, yet such holistic views of Canadian federalism are of fundamental importance insofar as they permeate policy-making in various policy arenas and affect the stability of the system as a whole. We begin with some appraisals of federalism as a whole before turning to the evaluations in various policy domains.

For many Quebec citizens and many, perhaps most, of the Québécois political elite, the Canadian federal experience is, in David Cameron's words (Chapter 3), 'deeply flawed, a story of continuing failure so far as Quebec is concerned'. This negative judgment of the failure to respect federal principles is based, among other things, on Ottawa's aggressive use of its spending power in areas of provincial jurisdiction, and the passage of the 1982 Constitution, to which Quebec is subject but not a consenting party. In Cameron's view, however, the Canadian federal system has performed fairly effectively over the years in relation to Quebec, providing the framework within which French Canada has survived, changed, and now flourishes. In his words, 'French-speaking Canadians have been able to use their majority status in Quebec to shape the provincial government and public policy very substantially to suit their needs, and Quebec as a federal actor has been able to profoundly influence the character and operation of Canadian federalism.' Nonetheless, Cameron recognizes that the Canadian federation suffers a problem of legitimacy in Quebec, where a significant portion of the population believe the 1982 Constitution is illegitimate in that it lacks the consent of the Quebec people. This weak legitimacy can also be attributed to an overwhelming tendency for Quebec elites to emphasize federalism as a system of self-rule—and a means to preserve and promote Quebec's distinct identity—and to underplay federal systems as also entailing shared rule and the promotion of values of solidarity and interdependence (Laforest, 2010).

Besides many Québécois, Aboriginal peoples also view Canadian federalism negatively. As Martin Papillon (Chapter 15) observes, the initial exclusion of Aboriginal peoples as parties to Confederation has had a deleterious impact on their perceived legitimacy of Canadian federalism. It has also impaired the performance and effectiveness of the institutions and processes of Canadian federalism when it comes to serving the needs of Aboriginal peoples. Aboriginal peoples have 'no statutory voice' in the institutions of intrastate federalism (Parliament) and they have only limited access to the institutions of executive federalism. While federal and provincial governments accept in principle the inherent right of Aboriginal peoples to self-government and have taken important shifts toward redefining the extent and meaning of aboriginal rights, it is Papillion's conclusion that much more remains to be done before intergovernmental mechanisms are effective sites for addressing the pressing social and economic issues in aboriginal communities that cut across federal and provincial jurisdiction.

Yet a final, largely negative, overview of Canadian federalism is provided by Simeon and Nugent (Chapter 4). While they acknowledge instances of co-operation and collaboration, they stress that 'the overall dynamic of intergovernmental relations is competitive and adversarial, despite frequent promises of co-operation'. The competitive dynamic tends to emphasize turf protection, the claiming of personal credit, and avoidance of blame, and in so doing, impairs effective problem-solving. In their view, the preoccupation of federal and provincial policy-makers with federal–provincial relations diverts their attention from larger questions, including those of Canada's economic and political roles in the world.

Table 18.2 provides a report card of the performance, effectiveness, and legitimacy of Canadian federalism and intergovernmental relations, as based on the various assessments presented by chapter authors. There are several points to keep in mind in reading the table.

First, as noted above, assessments of Canadian federalism are subjective; different appraisers are likely to arrive at different assessments. One example is fiscal federalism. Brown's (Chapter 7) assessment of the performance of fiscal federalism is positive, crediting the transfer of tax points, the removal of conditions on grant programs, and the maintenance of equalization payments with enabling provinces to maintain their autonomy. Yet this assessment is at odds, as Brown notes, with the damning critique of fiscal federalism by the expert advisory panel to the Council of the Federation, the forum representing provincial governments. In the view of the advisory panel, the processes of fiscal federalism are deeply flawed: lacking principles or rules, and with agreements subject to change or termination by Ottawa. Another example is cities. Sancton (Chapter 16) notes that big-city mayors tend to judge the federal system, from which they are largely excluded, more negatively than do provinces, whose judgment of Ottawa depends primarily on its respect for provincial jurisdiction. And yet a third example is social assistance. Benefits have eroded since the abolition of the Canada Assistance Plan in 1995 with much tougher conditions in place to receive social assistance. For conservatives, this outcome is likely to be viewed as an indicator of more effective policy-making insofar as its shifts possible recipients of social assistance into the labour market; in contrast, liberals and social democrats will view it more negatively.

Second, federal institutions and processes are not the only influences affecting the processes and outcomes of policy debates, and their independent effect is thus extremely difficult, perhaps impossible, to isolate. Simeon and Nugent (Chapter 4) have shown how deeply the democratic deficit in intergovernmental relations is rooted in the executive dominance of parliamentary government. The scores in Table 18.2 on *process legitimacy* may therefore be as much an indictment of the executive dominance inherent in the Westminster parliamentary system as they are of patterns of intergovernmental relations.

Third, the table records a composite score even while chapter authors have very often drawn a more nuanced picture that captures how different publics and political actors

Table 18.2 Policy Areas: Performance, Effectiveness, and Legitimacy

Policy Area	Performance		Effectiveness		Process Legitimacy		Output Legitimacy	
	2008	2011	2008	2011	2008	2011	2008	2011
Fiscal federalism	Fair	Good	Good	Fair	Fair	Fair	Fair	Fair
Canada Pension Plan/Quebec Pension Plan	Good	Good	Good	Fair	Good	Good	Good	Fair
Social assistance	Fair	Fair	Fair	Poor	Fair	Good	Fair	Fair
Employment Insurance		Fair		Poor		Good		Poor
Health care	Poor	Fair	Fair	Fair	Fair	Fair	Fair	Fair
Early Childhood Education and Care	Poor	Poor	Poor	Poor	Poor	Poor	Poor	Poor
Immigration		Good		Fair		Poor		Fair
International trade	Good	Good	Good	Good	Good	Good	Good	Good
Economic development	Good	Good	Good	Good	Fair	Fair	Good	Good
Climate change	Poor	Poor	Poor	Poor	Poor	Poor	Poor	Poor
Environmental Regulatory Harmonization (other than climate change)	Good	Good	Fair	Fair	Fair	Fair	Fair	Fair
Cities	Good	Fair	Fair	Fair	Poor	Poor	Fair	Fair
Aboriginal peoples	Fair	Poor	Poor	Poor	Fair	Poor	Poor	Poor

view the federalism model that dominates in a sector. For example, stakeholders who prefer national standards and common policies across the country are likely to score the performance of asymmetrical federalism as lower than those who put a premium on policy outcomes that allow for inter-provincial variation.

Fourth, the effectiveness of intergovernmental relations in one policy area may be dependent upon developments in an ancillary area. A good example is social assistance and employment insurance. Both respond to the same clientele: the unemployed. Yet, there is no mechanism for integrating them, and people are caught in gaps and contradictions between the two programs. Only some sort of intergovernmental process could repair what many describe as a broken system, and one which results in one of the weakest levels of income support for the unemployed in OECD countries.

Federalism's performance, effectiveness, and legitimacy across two periods of time are given in Table 18.2, contrasting the scores of the authors in this edition with those given with scores given in the second edition of *Canadian Federalism* published in 2008. (Immigration was not discussed in the second edition of *Canadian Federalism*; accordingly, only 2011 scores are given.) In terms of performance, a score of 'good' indicates that constitutional jurisdiction and the federal balance are respected, and that intergovernmental processes are workable in facilitating the consultation, negotiation, and co-ordination necessary to produce results over time. A score of 'fair' is awarded when some, but not all, of these conditions are met. A score of 'poor' is recorded where intergovernmental relations tend to break down, be riddled with acrimony and distrust, or non-existent when intergovernmental co-ordination is needed for resolution of problems. By way of example, climate change policy receives a score of 'poor' for performance because, although the independent governments' model is consistent with federal principles, there are no forums in which governments can work together, and without these forums, no capacity to produce results that would overcome inter-provincial conflicts and reach agreement.

In terms of policy effectiveness, a score of 'good' means that the policies produced through intergovernmental institutions and processes generally do address substantive problems in a timely and cost-effective fashion; allow for asymmetry as warranted; provide scope for policy innovation and adjustment to changing circumstances; and allow Canada to meet its international commitments. A score of 'fair' means that only a minority of these goals are achieved. Immigration (Chapter 14), for example, is scored as 'fair' on policy effectiveness because while asymmetric decentralization increases the opportunities for those wishing to enter Canada, it also results in these newcomers being treated differently once in the country. A score of 'poor' indicates both policy failure and failure to meet most of the above criteria. Some instances of policy failure are straightforward, such as the steady increase in greenhouse gas emissions since Canadian governments first began to commit to action on climate change in the early 1990s. In other cases, evaluations of Canadian federalism's policy effectiveness is gauged vis-à-vis what professional experts say are effective policies to address a problem. For example, ECEC policies since 2006 receive a poor rating because these policies—giving parents cash through targeted vouchers and tax breaks—are inconsistent with OECD best practices of how to ensure that child care and early childhood education are blended in quality programs that are accessible to families (OECD, 2006).

Output legitimacy scores are closely related to policy effectiveness scores with one important difference: output legitimacy gets at *perceptions* of the appropriateness of outcomes. It is possible for policy effectiveness and output legitimacy scores to diverge because policies can be effective in addressing problems or meeting international commitments but still not reflect the preferences and values of some political communities. For example, while the Canadian and provincial governments view as legitimate Canadian governments' alignment with American climate change policies, and federal opposition parties and environmentalists agree this development is better than no action at all, the latter two groups still question the legitimacy of the Harper government's abandonment of Canada's Kyoto commitment. A score of 'good' on output legitimacy indicates that the policy outcomes of intergovernmental relations receive the approbation of a broad constituency; 'fair' means that some but not all stakeholders/citizens view policy outcomes as appropriate; and 'poor' means that the outcomes are opposed by virtually all significant members of the policy/political community.

Finally, ratings on process legitimacy reflect the degree to which policy-making processes conform to citizens' expectations regarding adherence to democratic norms of accountability and representation. In Table 18.2 a 'good' ranking indicates respect for democratic norms of accountability to citizens, transparency to public scrutiny, and opportunities for citizen input. A score of 'fair' means that some but not all of these democratic criteria are met; for example, there may have been some opportunities for citizen/stakeholder input, but processes have generally been non-transparent and accountability weak. A 'poor' rating on procedural legitimacy means that none of these democratic criteria has been met.

Across all policy areas, the scores assigned by authors in this collection for the performance, effectiveness, and legitimacy of Canadian federalism are much more likely to be 'fair' or 'poor' rather than 'good'. *These ratings signal a diminution in the performance, effectiveness and legitimacy of federalism since 2008.* How can we account for the discrepancy of evaluations of federalism's performance, effectiveness and legitimacy across policy areas? And what relationship, if any, do these ratings have with the model of federalism in play in any given policy area?

Beginning with the second question, it is helpful to consider what distinguishes policy domains where ratings of 'good' predominate as compared to those characterized by 'poor' ratings: international trade policy, as an instance of the former, and climate change, early childhood education and care, and aboriginal policies as examples of the latter. The reasons for federalism's poor record on aboriginal policy have been described earlier in this chapter, so the discussion here turns to the other policy areas. International trade has been described as an example of collaborative federalism, in which the consultative processes appear to work well and in conformity with jurisdictional assignments. In most instances, the positions taken by Canada in international trade forums have had the support of provincial governments. And the end results appear to enjoy legitimacy in the eyes of both levels of government as well as among economic groups most directly affected by the outcomes of these agreements. In contrast, climate change and early childhood education and care (ECEC) are both examples of policy arenas in which the operative model is currently one of independent government across the two orders. From the perspective of the authors of the chapters investigating climate change and ECEC policies, the absence of intergovernmental relations is a major obstacle to more effective performance, policy-making, and greater legitimacy of outcomes and processes. Outstanding problems and better policies in these areas simply cannot be achieved, in their view, without intergovernmental consultation and co-ordination.

Still, elsewhere the independent governments/classical federalism model is equated with better assessments of Canadian federalism. Economic development is a case in point. The federal–provincial relationship in the area of economic adjustment policies is largely unco-ordinated, with no forum within which Canadian governments can plan development measures jointly, and each level of government typically pursuing its preferred policies after limited consultation with the other. This pattern of intergovernmental relations has historically created intergovernmental conflict; the government of Canada's National Policy was controversial, pitting region against region, as Garth Stevenson has elaborated in Chapter 2. As Rod Haddow documents in Chapter 12, conflict is far more muted today as ideas that promote market-based adjustment have made formal mechanisms of federal–provincial co-ordination less important. In his view, because of the distinctive economic development priorities of different regions, more elaborate intergovernmental machinery would probably generate more conflict, not less.

If any lessons can be drawn about federalism models from the cases examined here, they are that federalism's performance, effectiveness, and legitimacy are promoted when three conditions apply. First, the federal government is not in a position to engage in unilateral action. Second, the collaborative model is operating to address policy matters that transcend provincial borders and is underpinned by decision rules that require consensus though not outright unanimity; and, third, failure to reach a consensus is likely to have negative consequences for both governments and their respective bases of electoral support.

Health care demonstrates both how unilateral federal action can jeopardize the functioning of Canadian federalism as well as how these same governments can have strong incentives to collaborate on matters of high salience to the electorate. Health care has often been described as a dysfunctional area of federalism, characterized for several years by tension between governments, blame avoidance, and absence of innovation. Ottawa's extensive use of its spending power has come with conditions that have limited provinces' ability to restructure their health-care plans to incorporate private as well as public care. Still, the incentives for intergovernmental collaboration will remain high as long as most Canadians place a high value on a publicly funded single-payer system that provides reasonably high-quality care with a very high level of accessibility at costs far below those of the US system.

If it is desirable to limit federal unilateralism and promote intergovernmental collaboration, the Canada Pension Plan/Quebec Pension Plan nonetheless provides a cautionary tale. The joint-decision model here creates a high threshold for federal and provincial agreement on changes to these contributory pensions, thus earning high marks for 'performance'. However, change to these programs has been constrained by the requirement for the federal government plus two-thirds of the provinces representing two-thirds of Canada's population to agree to all changes. To the degree that programs need to change to take account of altered circumstances, a high threshold of intergovernmental agreement for joint-decision making models weakens their effectiveness. Nor is it clear that a joint-decision making rule that demands the agreement of more governments than does the general amending formula in Canada's constitution is legitimate.

The implications for the performance of the Canadian federation of increasing decentralized asymmetrical federalism are also ambivalent. On the one hand, there can be little doubt that de facto asymmetry, by providing Quebec in particular with the flexibility to tailor national programs to its distinct needs and aspirations, has contributed to Canadian unity. On the other hand, decentralized asymmetry weakens the bonds that unite Canadians as a whole (Brock, 2008). The 'pervasive asymmetry' that now characterizes Canadian policies with respect to the selection and settlement of immigrants, argues

Banting (Chapter 14), is weakening the presence of the government of Canada in new Canadians' lives. In his words, as immigration settlement programs are decentralized, 'the federal government fades a little more from the lives of future citizens' and the federal government 'becomes more distant, less engaged in the economic and social realities of the country, and less likely to be understood and trusted by local communities'.

Before leaving this discussion of how federalism is working, it may be helpful to reflect further on the role of non-state actors in intergovernmental processes and the degree to which their involvement affects the functioning of federalism on our three main dimensions. One of the prevailing themes in the literature on Canadian federalism is the limited involvement of citizens/non-state actors in interstate federalism. Richard Simeon (2006 [1972]), in his classic study of the negotiations surrounding the Canada/Quebec Pension Plan, refers to the 'freezing out' of organized interests when governments perceive the stakes to be high. From one perspective, the exclusion of organized interests in such cases is not necessarily 'anti-democratic': as Simeon and Nugent, as well as Julie Simmons (Chapter 17) remind us, executive federalism is ultimately still rooted in representative democracy. As long as the executives who are party to intergovernmental relations represent the best interests of their citizens and answer to them regularly through their elected legislatures and periodically via elections, then one could argue that democracy is served.

And yet it is clear that citizens, especially those with a clear stake in a particular policy outcome, seek something more: their own participation in intergovernmental processes, greater transparency in intergovernmental negotiations and deal-making, and more reporting back on the agreements so brokered. Governments appear to agree—to some extent. The array of 'fair' and 'good' entries in the 'process legitimacy' column of Table 18.2 suggests that federalism and intergovernmental relations are doing better than critics like Simeon would suggest. Advocacy groups have certainly taken part in policy formulation under the independent governments' model. Current thinking in economic development, for example, emphasizes 'networks' of state and non-state economic actors as essential to economic growth.

Nor are citizens, at least in organized groups, uniformly excluded from intergovernmental processes. In certain domains, for example, international trade policy, organized interests are much more intimately involved in the intergovernmental process than many might have thought.

More generally, the competitive dynamic in federalism gives governments incentives to engage in what Simmons (Chapter 17) calls 'consultative democracy'. In health care, one of the most rancorous of federal–provincial arenas, Maioni observes in Chapter 9 that the creation of the Romanow commission provided an opportunity for 'an extraordinary exercise in participatory democracy'.

Still, Simmons argues that it is difficult to marry non-governmental participation with intergovernmental decision-making. In her view, there is a trade-off between enhancing legitimacy through non-governmental participation, on the one hand, and performance and effectiveness on the other. Intergovernmental forums typically make trade-offs to reach a mutually accommodating outcome and when such trade-offs are at variance with the outcomes reached through engagement of non-governmental actors, the latter will question their legitimacy. Evidence that non-governmental groups are likely to be more involved in discussions around voluntary agreements also raises doubts about their role in contributing to effective policy-making. Simmons concludes that not only does Canada's pattern of interstate federalism offer few opportunities for citizens to engage in deliberative and repeated exchanges with state actors in intergovernmental forums, over the last decade or so, governments have shifted from involving citizens in the development of intergovernmental agreements, to calling upon them to monitor their implementation.

Looking Ahead

Where is Canadian federalism headed? Will it continue to follow its current path of multiple models of federalism, or will one of these emerge as more prominent? In addition, is it possible that there will be major institutional and constitutional reforms in Canadian federalism? Previous editions of *Canadian Federalism* (2002, 2008) responded to these questions by suggesting some possible alternate scenarios. We take the same approach here. To gauge the plausibility of different scenarios, we begin by outlining the economic, political, and international context of Canadian federalism that we expect to be more or less feasible in the years ahead.

First, in terms of the Canadian economy, as a result of the 2008–9 recession, both federal and provincial governments have moved from a context of budgetary surpluses in the 2000s to one of budgetary deficits. In the past, tackling deficits has pitted governments at the two orders against one another. The inherent competitive dynamic of Canadian federalism would suggest it will do so again. At the same time, structural changes in the Canadian economy are causing a shift in economic power westward, especially to Alberta. How governments in the rest of Canada—especially in Ontario, which is the major loser in this restructured economy—react to this situation will determine whether the tenor of intergovernmental relations is competitive or collaborative. It will also affect the legitimacy of different models of federalism and, particularly, the support of residents in provinces like Ontario for a strong central government with capacities to redistribute wealth across the country. At the very least, the structural reconfiguration of Canada's economy will put pressure on equalization, a core component of fiscal federalism.

There is a real prospect that regionalism will resume as a factor in Canadian federalism, despite its virtual demise with the ending of the National Policy (Chapter 2, Garth Stevenson). Not only equalization but also climate change policies pit provinces that produce fossil fuels (Alberta and Saskatchewan) against those that do not.

Second, the political context is clearly the most difficult to predict. In 2004, 2006, and 2008, Canadians elected minority governments in Ottawa. Despite its minority status from early 2006 to May 2011, the Conservative government was able to put its imprint on Canadian federalism in a number of areas. As noted, it cancelled the child care and early childhood education agreement that the Martin government had negotiated with the provinces. It also withdrew from the 2005 Kelowna Accord negotiated with First Nations. From 2006 onward, the Harper government presented a somewhat contradictory face on federalism. On the one hand, it promoted an 'open federalism' of Ottawa refraining from intervening in provincial jurisdiction. On the other hand, it engaged in unilateralism, such as its proposed national securities regulator initiative.

Having secured a majority in the May 2011 election, the Conservative government may now pursue its agenda more vigorously. It may pursue further decentralization in the federation and retreat from an interventionist federal government role. How the Conservative government deals with the negotiations on the health care accord, negotiated by the Martin Liberal government in 2004 and set to expire in 2014, will reveal its commitment to open federalism, support for universal health care and belief in an appropriate role for the private sector.

The most profound impact of the current Conservative majority government may well be in the area of senate reform. Its proposals for elected Senators who serve fixed terms have already been strongly opposed by Canada's two largest provinces. Ontario's premier has indicated that he would prefer to see the Senate abolished. In Premier McGuinty's view, Ontario does not need elected senators to represent its interests in Ottawa; the current system of interstate representation is more than adequate. Quebec's government has already referred Ottawa's proposals to its supreme court. A major federal–provincial confrontation thus looms over the Conservative government's proposed institutional change. Should Stephen Harper ultimately succeed in having his vision of a reformed senate realized, he would introduce a strong element of intrastate federalism, hitherto largely absent in Canadian federalism. The consequences would no doubt be transformative for the Canadian federation.

The implications for Canadian federalism of the changed status of the opposition parties following the May 2011 general election are also difficult to predict. The NDP has replaced the Liberal Party as the official opposition, the Bloc Québécois has virtually disappeared from the House of Commons, and the Liberals have been relegated to third place. With more than half its caucus from Quebec, the NDP faces the challenge of representing Quebec's interests in the House of Commons and reconciling Quebec's interests with those of other Canadians. On the issue of Medicare, for example, will the NDP urge the Conservative government to use its spending power to strengthen provisions of the Canada Health Act that ban extra-billing? Or will it argue that Ottawa needs to respect the jurisdiction of the provinces generally, and Quebec in particular, and refrain from using the spending power to achieve its objectives? In the past it was a reasonably straightforward proposition to predict that the Liberals would be the more interventionist party. In the case of the NDP, however, its recent elevation to the status of official opposition, its Quebec base, and its undoubted goal to displace permanently both the Liberals and the Bloc make it difficult to predict the party's stance on federal–provincial issues.

An additional unknown in the political context is Quebec. David Cameron (Chapter 3) suggests that there is a good prospect that the Parti Québécois will be the victor in the next election in the province. If so, its formal commitment to sovereignty for Quebec will force the issue of Quebec sovereignty back onto the Canadian federalism table. Alternatively, the re-election of the Quebec Liberal Party or the election of a third party that is not committed to sovereignty will mean a continuation of aggressive Quebec actions to advance Quebec's standing in the federation but largely through modifications to existing public policies. The outcome of the May 2011 general election gives both the PQ and the Quebec Liberal Party cause to rethink their strategies vis-à-vis both the Quebec electorate and Ottawa. Moreover, Quebec's highly volatile electorate may create opportunities for third parties in Quebec to attract support away from both the PQ and the Liberal provincial Party.

Third, turning to the international context, there can be little doubt that Canada's embeddedness in an internationalized political economy will continue. Canada's dominant economic sectors depend on accessing foreign markets in order to be profitable. This structural dependence gives governments strong incentives to continue to pursue agreements that liberalize trade in goods and service as well as in investments. This goal suggests more, not less, intergovernmental collaboration. But that collaboration need not necessarily be across the two orders of government. It could be provinces voluntarily coordinating their policies with their American counterpart, for example. Such internal inter-provincial and bi-national (Canadian and American) collaboration would build on initiatives underway in labour market and climate change policies.

Fourth, if history is a guide, we should expect considerable continuity in the institutions of Canadian governance. As Simeon and Nugent (Chapter 4) have argued, the formal parliamentary and federal institutions have shown themselves to be 'remarkably resistant to change'. The possible exception is the Senate. The Harper government's Senate reform initiative may prove that organizations do not last forever—at least not in their earlier form.

Fifth, insofar as most Canadians live in cities, it is reasonable to expect that their problems, including immigration as well as better public facilities and services, emerge higher on the political agendas of federal and provincial governments. In the view of Andrew Sancton (Chapter 16), responding to these policy problems does not require a restructuring of the roles and responsibilities of governments at the two orders but rather politicians at the municipal, provincial, and federal levels working together within their own spheres of jurisdiction to tackle these issues.

Based on this reading of the context of Canadian federalism in the years ahead, we posit three distinct scenarios. The first envisions the continuation of multiple models of federalism across different policy spheres and evolution of Canadian federalism through a 'muddling through' approach. There is continuity in Canada's Constitution and political institutions: that is, no formal changes in the division of powers; no constitutional recognition of Quebec's specificity; and no changes in the role, composition, or function of the Senate. Incremental adjustments do not appreciably alter the existing balance of power between the two orders of government; both orders of government are important. Both the government of Canada and the provincial governments continue to be important actors in their own right. Competitive and co-operative elements co-exist and the informal pattern of asymmetry continues. In response to the imbalances in federal–provincial and inter-provincial revenues, the government of Canada adjusts the equalization formula but not in a significant way. Urban problems are addressed, as Sancton suggests (Chapter 16), by the two senior orders of government working together within their own spheres of jurisdiction. In the second edition of *Canadian Federalism* we found this scenario to be quite plausible. We are less confident of its likelihood in light of the election of a Conservative majority government and its subsequent initiative to reform the senate.

In the second scenario, provincial governments become more ascendant in either an independent governments or collaborative model of federalism. The differences of policy goals across provinces that arise from their disparate regional economies weaken support for nation-wide policies, including equalization payments, and more taxation powers are transferred to provinces. To the degree that the collaborative federalism model persists, it is more likely to characterize voluntarily co-operation among provinces in the pursuit of shared goals. The devolution of Canadian federalism proceeds without constitutional change. This scenario does not rule out intergovernmental co-operation—for example, to address urban problems or in the matter of international trade policy. This scenario is more plausible than it was earlier, with the elevation of the Conservative government to majority status in May 2011.

Under a third scenario, the devolution of Canadian federalism is accomplished by major formal institutional changes, most likely to the Canadian Senate, and possibly even constitutional changes. (It is a matter of debate, though, whether a reformed elected senate will necessarily have devolutionary effects.) This scenario could be triggered by the Parti Québécois taking control of the government in Quebec at a time when—as now, with the current Conservative government—the government of Canada has very limited representation in Quebec. If this scenario unfolds, among the important matters of constitutional debate is certain to be formal constitutional recognition of Quebec's distinct status and recognition of First Nations as a third order of government. Since a Conservative majority government is already in place, with Senate reform at the top of its agenda, and an unpopular Liberal provincial government will soon be facing re-election, this third scenario is at least as plausible as the second one.

Predictions of major institutional or constitutional changes in the past, however, have typically been confounded. If something more than the status quo seems necessary to improve the performance, effectiveness, and legitimacy of the federal system, what can be done short of constitutional and major structural changes in the federation? Two reforms could be made within the existing institutional framework.

One reform is to institutionalize the rules of the game of intergovernmental relations. Simeon and Nugent (Chapter 4) believe that the absence of rules and norms regarding matters such as the convening of first ministers' conferences, voting procedures, and alterations to intergovernmental agreements exacerbates conflict in the system. Federalism appears to work better where agreements incorporate explicit rules for amendments to programs as circumstances change. In the interest of enhancing the standing of the federal system on the three dimensions, governments could—and should—make a much greater effort to incorporate decision rules governing amendments to federal–provincial agreements, whether in the area of fiscal federalism or of climate change. Such rules would ideally go beyond the simple right of a government to terminate an agreement after giving notice. As an example of the institutionalization of intergovernmental relations, the Council of the Federation represents a step in the right direction.

A second change would be to embrace more fully various mechanisms of consultative democracy: that is, to bring non-state actors into intergovernmental discussions. As Simmons observes in Chapter 17, such linkages have the potential to improve both governments' and non-governmental actors' understanding of issues, and thereby to enhance both the legitimacy and effectiveness of policy outcomes.

The full weight of effective and legitimate governing should *not* be put on the institutions and processes of Canadian federalism. Indeed, if it is democratic government that

Canadians seek, then analysts suggest that there are other institutions besides federalism on which we might more profitably focus our attention (Lane and Ersson, 2005; Norris, 2005). A prime example is the electoral system, which could be reformed to secure a fairer translation of votes into seats (Norris, 2005). The issue of electoral system reform has been on the agenda of several provincial governments in recent years and some provinces are serving as laboratories for innovation in the electoral system. Unfortunately most of these experiments have come to naught. Governments need to take electoral reform more seriously if the consequences for representative democracy—and by extension, for Canadian federalism—are to be significant.

To conclude, there is room within the existing constitutional framework to reform the practices and norms of executive federalism as well as those of the parliamentary system whose functioning bears so significantly on intergovernmental relations. Whether the political will exists, either among the elites who inhabit the world of executive federalism or within civil society, and what conditions might help foster such political will, are important questions. They deserve the consideration of Canadians, their political leaders, and, not least, those who study the country's federal system.

References

Bakvis, H., and G. Skogstad. 2008. *Canadian Federalism: Performance, Effectiveness, and Legitimacy.* 2nd ed. Toronto: Oxford University Press.

Brock, K.L. 2008. 'The Politics of Asymmetrical Federalism: Reconsidering the Role and Responsibilities of Ottawa', *Canadian Public Policy* 34 (2): 143–61.

Council of the Federation, Advisory Panel on Fiscal Imbalance. 2006. *Reconciling the Irreconcilable.* Available online at: www.councilofthefederation.ca.

Laforest, G. 2010. 'The Meaning of Canadian Federalism in Québec: Critical Reflections', *REAF*, 11: 10–55.

Lane, J.-E, and S. Ersson. 2005. 'The Riddle of Federalism: Does Federalism Impact on Democracy?' *Democratization* 12, 2: 163–82.

Lazar, H. 2006. 'The Intergovernmental Dimensions of the Social Union: A Sectoral Analysis', *Canadian Public Administration* 49, 1: 23–45.

Norris, P. 2005. 'Stable Democracy and Good Governance in Divided Societies: Do Powersharing Institutions Work?' Faculty Research Working Paper RWP05-014. John F. Kennedy School of Government, Harvard University.

Simeon, R. 2006 [1972]. *Federal–Provincial Diplomacy: The Making of Recent Policy in Canada.* Toronto: University of Toronto Press.

Glossary

Accessibility requires reasonable access unimpeded by financial or other barriers to medically necessary hospital and physician services for residents, and reasonable compensation for both physicians and hospitals.

Asymmetry exists when the division of power between the federal and provincial government in a particular policy sector differs among the provinces, with some provinces exercising wider powers than others. Asymmetry stands in contrast to symmetrical relationships, in which all provinces exercise the same power and authority.

Auto Pact an agreement between Canada and the United States in 1965 which allowed Chrysler, Ford and General Motors to import vehicles and parts into Canada duty-free provided they would assemble a certain proportion of their vehicles in Canada. It greatly increased employment and production in Canada but was terminated by NAFTA.

Bilateralism the state of intergovernmental governance in which the federal government collaborates with individual provincial governments (McRoberts, 1985: 71).

Bill 101 The Charter of the French Language, also known as Bill 101, was passed by the Quebec National Assembly in 1997. This highly controversial legislation, one of the earliest initiatives of the first Parti Québécois government, was the subject of several court cases. It made French the official language of Quebec. Its purpose, as stated in the Preamble to the bill, was 'to make French the language of government and the law, as well as the normal and everyday language of work, instruction, communication, commerce and business.'

Block grant refers to an intergovernmental transfer of funds in which the amount of the grant is unrelated to actual expenditure levels by the receiving government. An example is the Canada Health Transfer, which is determined by the federal government and is not directly related to actual provincial expenditures on health care.

Brokerage Party Many students of party politics argue that, unlike their European counterparts, Canada's two main federal parties, the Liberal Party of Canada and the Conservative Party of Canada (formerly the Progressive Conservative Party), lack well defined ideological programs that guide either their electoral behaviour or their policy making once they are in power. Instead, they have acted historically as 'brokers' of ideas and interests, seeking to forge broad-based electoral coalitions bringing together voters from different social classes, religious groups, and regions. These parties have appealed to voters primarily on the basis of leadership, style, and patronage and have exhibited a large degree of ideological flexibility. In some formulations, brokerage parties are labelled 'omnibus parties.'

Bundesrat the upper house of the German federal Parliament, consisting of delegations appointed by the governments of the states. Its consent is required for most legislation, and its partisan composition depends on the outcome of elections in the states.

CCME (Canadian Council of Ministers of the Environment) consists of the federal, provincial and territorial ministers of the environment.

CEPA (Canadian Environmental Protection Act) the principal federal environmental statute. It authorizes the federal government to regulate emissions of 'toxic' substances, including GHGs .

City-state a major urban area having a government that is a sovereign country (Singapore), or that has special authority within a sovereign country (Hong Kong has its own currency within China), or that is a constituent unit of a federation (Berlin, Hamburg, and Bremen within Germany).

Clarity Act   The federal Clarity Act (2000) followed up on the 1998 Supreme Court Secession Reference opinion, insofar as the role and responsibilities of the federal government and Parliament were concerned. It provided that the federal government would not enter into negotiations with a province on the basis of a referendum on secession unless the House of Commons determined that the referendum question was clear and a clear majority of the population of the province had voted in favour.

Classical federalism   a federal system in which both orders of government act independently and each remains within its own constitutionally assigned jurisdiction; no attempt is made to consult or co-ordinate activities with the other order.

Collaborative federalism   the dynamic of governments at the two orders working together non-hierarchically to co-determine public policies for Canadians.

Competitive federalism   the dynamic of governments at the two orders competing with one another to gain credit for policy successes and avoid blame for policy problems.

Comprehensiveness   requires that all medically necessary services provided by hospitals and doctors be insured.

Concurrent jurisdiction   refers to a sector in which both the federal government and the provincial governments have the constitutional authority to legislate. In Canada, agricultural policy, immigration and pensions are areas of concurrent jurisdiction. Concurrent jurisdiction is normally accompanied by an assignment of paramouncty, which specifies which government's legislation prevails in cases of conflict.

Conditional grants or transfers   are payments made, usually on an annual or quarterly basis, from one government to another for a specified purpose and according to conditions normally established by legislation. *Unconditional grants or transfers* are payments made, usually on an annual or quarterly basis, from one government to another for general purposes, without specific conditions.

Conscription Crisis—World War I   The first Conscription Crisis broke out in 1917, when Prime Minister Borden passed legislation implementing compulsory military service in Canada to assist in the recruitment of troops to fight in Europe. The measure bitterly divided the country along language and ethnic lines, with most French Canadians opposed and most English Canadians in favour, and its effects were felt long after the war was over.

Conscription Crisis—World War II   Acutely aware of the divisive impact of conscription in the previous war, Prime Minister Mackenzie King pledged that there would be no conscription for overseas military service. In response to strong public pressure from English Canada, King held a plebiscite seeking to be released from the pledge. It passed, but 73 per cent of Quebec voters voted against the proposal, and over 80 per cent of voters in the other provinces voted in favour. King prevaricated as long as he could, but ultimately passed legislation formally authorizing conscription if necessary. Few conscripts were called up before the war's end, but the conflict sowed division once again between French and English Canadians.

Consultative democracy   a form of democracy in which actors are consulted in the policy making process, but representatives of the government (elected or unelected) ultimately make decisions.

Contributory pension   refers to a pension plan in which eligibility for benefit and the level of benefit are determined by contributions made during employment by the individual and his or her employers. The Canada Pension Plan is a contributory pension. (See also 'Social insurance program'.)

Co-operative federalism   the dynamic of federal and provincial governments co-operating to undertake initiatives on behalf of Canadians. The golden age of co-operative federalism was the 1950s and early 1960s when the two governments created national social programs.

Co-ordinative economy   a term used to characterize economies, especially in Continental Europe and East Asia, in which firms typically co-ordinate extensively with each other to develop new products and financing, and with their workers for industrial relations and skills development.

CoP   Conference of the Parties: meetings of all countries that have ratified an international agreement and where decisions are made about the implementation of agreements, possible amendments, and future work under the agreement.

Cost-shared grants   are funds transferred to specific programs on the condition that they be matched by the receiving government according to a specified formula (e.g., 50–50).

Council of the Federation   a formal association of provincial and territorial premiers (and their ministers) whose objective is to promote co-operation and co-ordinated responses to federal initiatives.

Deindexation   refers to the removal of an automatic increase in benefit levels to compensate for the effects of inflation.

Deliberative democracy   a form of democracy that is an exchange of equals resulting in an outcome reflecting the best argument. Participants are encouraged to reflect on and revise their own arguments in the process. While government actors might share decision-making authority with non-governmental participants, government actors must provide public justification for their decisions.

Democratic deficit   a perceived deficiency in the democratic legitimacy of an arrangement, institution or organization. The deficit is measured as the difference between how that arrangement, institution or organization works in practice and how it is supposed to work in theory.

Durham Report   Lord Durham's *Report on the Affairs of British North America*, reporting on the 1837 Rebellions in Lower and Upper and Canada, was completed in January 1839. Outside Canada, it is regarded as one of the great state papers of the nineteenth-century British Empire, outlining the way in which the principles of English liberalism could be reconciled with the bonds of empire. Inside Canada, the *Report* is best known for its severe comments on French Canadians and their society, and for its recommendation to consolidate Upper and Lower Canada in a united province, which, with the immigration of British colonists, would, Durham hoped, lead to the assimilation of the French Canadians of British North America into the English-speaking world.

Early Childhood Education and Care (ECEC)   the OECD (2006, annex A) defines early childhood education and care as non-parental care and education programs in a variety of settings, including public and private child care centres, preschools, kindergartens, family day care homes, and childminders. For further definition of terms, see OECD (2006: 227–30).

Endogenous growth theory   argues that the ability of an economy to grow depends largely on its internal capacity to support innovation, rather apply technology from outside.

Equalization   is a federal government program designed to bring the fiscal capacity of the poorer provinces closer to a national average so that they can fully meet their constitutional and program spending obligations. See also *horizontal fiscal balance*.

Executive federalism   a system in which relations between governments are carried out largely through the senior executives of federal, provincial and territorial governments.

Expert authority   the idea that those with superior knowledge should decide issues that affect the broader population.

Family class   immigrants who are closely related to a person already resident in Canada. Normally, family members who wish to immigrate to Canada must be sponsored by their relative in the country.

Federalism deficit   an aspect of the 'democratic deficit', it refers to the failure of the institutions and practices of intergovernmental relations to meet democratic expectations.

First Nations   the majority of Aboriginal peoples in Canada. There are approximately 40 to 60 historic nations in Canada, divided into nearly 700 bands. They are still sometimes referred to as 'Indians'.

First-Past-the-Post Electoral System   Also known as the single-member, simple plurality electoral system, this 'winner-take-all' form of voting is the electoral system currently in use for federal and provincial elections in Canada, as well as for national elections in such countries as the United States and the United Kingdom. At election time, voters cast their ballots for a single candidate in a given riding or constituency; the candidate receiving the most votes in the riding wins. If more than two candidates are running in a riding, it is possible, and indeed likely, that the winning candidate will receive only a plurality of the votes, not a majority.

Fiscal capacity   is the ability of a government (federal or provincial) to raise revenues within its jurisdiction. Each government's fiscal capacity depends on the level and nature of economic activity, as well as the amount of wealth and its distribution within its borders.

GATT   General Agreement on Tariffs and Trade, created in 1947 as a set of trading rules that promoted fairer and freer trade across countries.

GHG (Greenhouse Gas)   substances believed to contribute to global climate change. Six GHGs are identified under the Kyoto Protocol and listed as 'toxic' substances for the purposes of CEPA: carbon dioxide (CO_2); methane (CH_4); nitrous oxide (N_2O); hydrofluorocarbons (HFCs); perfluorocarbons (PFCs); sulphur hexafluoride (SF_6).

Government Party   In his book, *The Government Party: Organizing and financing the Liberal Party of Canada, 1930–58*, published in 1977, Reginald Whitaker argued that by the 1950s the Liberal Party of Canada had in many respects merged with the federal government apparatus. The Conservatives, by contrast, were seemingly condemned to near-permanent opposition status, at least until the brief Diefenbaker interregnum (1957–63). For much of the twentieth century, the Liberals were, for a variety of reasons, the 'natural party of government' in Canada.

Hinterland   the dependent and usually exploited region in an unequal relationship between two regions.

Horizontal fiscal balance or imbalance   refers to the relative fiscal positions among the provinces (states, etc.) in a federation. Imbalances reflect the differing fiscal capacities of these units to carry out similar constitutional and program spending responsibilities. Balance is achieved by redistributing fiscal resources to the poorer provinces. This is done in Canada through the equalization program.

Income-tested   refers to a benefit program in which the size of the payment declines as the other income of the recipient increases. An example is the Guaranteed Income Supplement received by low- and middle-income elderly Canadians.

Industrial policy   a general term, more common several decades ago, when most such programs focused on the manufacturing sector, to characterize government programs that promote economic activity.

Inherent right to self-government   the right of Aboriginal peoples to govern themselves, based on their historical presence as distinctly constituted nations prior to the establishment of Crown sovereignty in what is now Canada.

Innovation policy   Programs widely pursued by federal and provincial governments in Canada to promote firms' introducing new technology-rich products and novel ways of producing them.

Intergovernmental Canada   refers to the interdependencies and interactions among federal and provincial governments in Canadian policy and policy-making.

Interstate Federalism   See 'Interstate versus Intrastate Federalism' below.

Interstate versus Intrastate Federalism   Alan Cairns and Donald Smiley have distinguished between two basic methods of accommodating regional (or sub-national) interests in a federal system. The institutions of **interstate federalism**, such as First Ministers' conferences, allow the two levels of government to meet face-to-face, whereas the institutions of **intrastate federalism**, such as the Senate (as it was originally designed), Cabinet and cabinet committees, afford the provinces a voice within the central government itself.

Inuit   Aboriginal people living in the Circumpolar North. In Canada, they mostly live in Nunavut, where they form a majority, in Nunavik (northern Quebec), and in Labrador. Inuit were excluded from the Indian Act.

IPCC (Intergovernmental Panel on Climate Change)   United Nations body established under the UNFCCC to co-ordinate and interpret scientific research on climate change.

JMM (Joint Ministers' Meetings)   meetings of the federal, provincial and territorial ministers of the environment and of energy.

Joint-decision federalism   a mode of intergovernmental relations in which decisions require governments at both orders to agree, either unanimously or by a super-majority

Labour market training   education that is vocational or work-related, rather than a 'liberal' university-level arts or science program education.

Legislative federalism   refers to formal provisions for elected legislatures to play a role in intergovernmental relations

LFEs (Large Final Emitters)   major industrial sources of GHG emissions like coal-fired power plants, oil sands operations and cement plants.

Manitoba Schools Crisis   In 1890, Manitoba abolished French as an official language in the province, and withdrew public funding for separate denominational schools, thereby effectively ending the English Protestant and French Catholic school systems. These measures removed the protections of the Manitoba Act of 1870, which had brought Manitoba into Confederation. They deeply offended the French, Catholic minority in the province and outraged opinion in Quebec, but Manitoba's actions were ultimately upheld by the highest court (then the British Judicial Committee of the Privy Council).

Maritime Rights Movement   a non-partisan organization formed after the First World War that lobbied for measures to help the economies of New Brunswick, Nova Scotia, and Prince Edward Island, which were lagging behind the rest of the country. Its influence led to the appointment of a Royal Commission in 1926 that recommended reducing freight rates in the region and increasing subsidies to the Maritime provinces.

Market liberalization   the opening of domestic borders to competition from foreign goods and services by reducing or remov-ing tariffs and other measures that restrict imports.

Market-oriented political economy   a term used to characterize economies, espe-cially those of English-speaking countries, in which firms typically have a largely competi-tive and arm's length relationship with each other and with their workers.

Métis   the descendants of early unions be-tween Europeans settlers (mostly French) and First Nations people. They are not governed under the Indian Act.

Metropolis   the dominant region in an unequal relationship between regions; the op-posite of hinterland.

Multilateralism   the state of intergovern-mental governance in which the federal gov-ernment acts jointly with most or all provincial governments (McRoberts, 1985: 71).

NAFTA (North American Free Trade Agreement)   effective January 1994, is an agreement among Canada, Mexico, and the United States designed to foster trade and investment by progressively eliminating tariffs and reducing other barriers to trade and investment. (More information about NAFTA can be found at: www.dfait-maeci.gc.ca/nafta-alena/over-e.asp.)

National Energy Program   a program announced by the Trudeau government in 1980 to reduce foreign ownership in the petroleum industry, to give the federal govern-ment a larger share of the revenue from that industry, and to encourage exploration for oil and gas on the continental shelf and the northern territories. It was bitterly resented in western Canada, particularly in Alberta.

National Policy   the policy of economic development on which John A. Macdonald campaigned in the election of 1878 and which his government began to implement a year later. It included high protective tariffs, construction of a transcontinental railway, and distributing federally owned land to encourage settlement on the prairies—all policies copied from those of the Republican Party in the United States.

Naturalization   refers to the process of officially granting citizenship. In Canada, the federal government has authority over the granting of citizenship.

Network economy theory   posits that economic growth and innovation in the modern information economy depend to an important degree on networking, or inter-connection, among firms in leading sectors.

New Deal for Cities   a set of proposals ad-vanced in the early 2000s designed to enhance the position of major urban municipalities within the Canadian federal system; as the 'New Deal for Cities and Communities', its scope was extended to all municipalities to reflect commitments made by the Liberal government led by Prime Minister Paul Martin (2003–06), especially in the 2005 federal budget.

New economy   a term used to character-ize recent trends in developed economies that depend to an important extent on information technologies and the skills of highly trained workers.

New Political Governance a counterpoint to New Public Management characterized by the reassertion of elected leaders' control of the state apparatus. In Canada it is associated with the concentration of power in the Prime Minister's office and the expectation that public servants demonstrate enthusiasm for the government's agenda beyond traditional expectations of loyal implementation of the government's program.

New Public Management a style of public sector management that borrows heavily from private-sector principles and includes values like customer service, entrepreneurship, responsiveness and flexibility.

No-lateralism the state of intergovernmental governance in which intergovernmental relations continue at the bureaucratic level but there are few new or renewed initiatives at the first ministers' level.

Non-status Indians members of First Nations communities, often living in urban areas, who are not covered by the Indian Act.

Open federalism the Harper Conservative government's philosophy of intergovernmental governance which seeks to 'place formal limits on the use of the federal spending power for new shared-cost programs in areas of exclusive provincial jurisdiction' (Canada, House of Commons, 2007, p. 8) and to adhere to a decentralized vision of the federation that strictly interprets the division of jurisdiction to allow for provincial autonomy in areas that are perceived to be within provincial jurisdiction.

Opt out refers to the provision which allows a province to withdraw from a federal–provincial shared-cost program but still receive an equivalent payment from the federal government.

Pareto Optimum a concept developed by Italian political economist Vilfredo Pareto meaning a distribution of resources or benefits among a group such that no one's situation can be improved without detrimental effects on the situation of someone else.

Patriation reference When Prime Minister Trudeau initially attempted to unilaterally present a package of amendments to the UK Parliament, several provinces challenged the legality of his tactic. The Supreme Court consolidated these challenges in the *Patriation Reference.* It ruled that while constitutional conventions obliged the federal government to consult the provinces and obtain a 'substantial degree' of consent before proceeding with amendment, there was nothing strictly illegal about the federal government proceeding unilaterally.

Permanent residents are people who are not Canadian citizens but have been granted permission to live and work in the country without any time limit on their stay. Permanent residents hold many of the same rights as citizens, but they cannot vote, stand for elected office, hold a Canadian passport, or join the armed forces. Permanent residents may apply for Canadian citizenship after three years in the country.

Popular authority the idea that 'the people', irrespective of their level of expertise, should decide issues that directly concern them.

Portability requires that coverage be maintained when a resident moves or travels within Canada or travels outside the country (coverage outside Canada is restricted to the coverage the resident has in his/her own province).

Prorogation The Governor-General, on the advice of the Prime Minister, ends a session of Parliament by means of prorogation. All government bills, if they have not yet received Royal Assent at the time of prorogation, 'die', and must be reintroduced as new bills in the subsequent parliamentary session.

Public administration   requires that the administration of the insurance plan of a province be carried out on a non-profit basis by a public authority.

Quasi-Party System   a concept developed by Canadian political theorist C.B. Macpherson in his book *Democracy in Alberta*. Rather than a competitive party system there is only one dominant party, owing to the absence of class conflict within the society and its conflict with an external metropolis.

Quebec Veto reference   Following the Patriation Reference's finding that a constitutional amendment required substantial provincial consent, the government of Quebec questioned whether such consent could be said to exist without the agreement of that province. The Supreme Court ruled that Quebec did not have a veto over constitutional change, and that the agreement of the other provinces met the conventional threshold for consent to constitutional change.

Reciprocity   Canadian term for a limited free trade agreement between Canada and the United States, particularly applying to natural products. Reciprocity existed between 1854 and 1866. The Liberals proposed similar agreements in 1891, when they were in opposition, and in 1911 when they were the government, but suffered electoral defeat on both occasions.

Reform Party   Founded in the fall of 1987 with the slogan, 'The West Wants In', the Reform Party of Canada was an important expression of western alienation from the federal party system, the ideological vehicle of a potent form of right-wing populism, and one of the most successful minor parties in the country's political history. Under the leadership of Preston Manning, Reform won 52 seats in the 1993 general election and 60 seats in 1997, making it the Official Opposition. The party

effectively disbanded in 2000, transforming itself into the Canadian Reform Conservative Alliance (better known as the Canadian Alliance) with a new leader, Stockwell Day.

Riel Rebellions   The Métis leader, Louis Riel, led two rebellions in what became Manitoba and Saskatchewan, opposing the settlement of the Prairies by English-speaking easterners and the displacement of Aboriginal peoples. The Red River Rebellion occurred in 1869, and the North West Rebellion took place in 1885.

Regional development policies   programs designed to stimulate economic growth in a specific region of the country or province, usually one with higher than average unemployment.

Representative democracy   a form of democracy including an assembly elected by citizens.

Secession reference   Following the 1995 sovereignty referendum in Quebec, the government of Canada referred three questions on the legality of a unilateral declaration of independence to the Supreme Court. The court ruled that a unilateral declaration had no legal grounding in either domestic or international law, and should a clear majority of residents in a province vote to secede from Canada on the basis of a clear referendum question, the federal government and the other provinces had an obligation to negotiate secession. The federal government based its 2000 Clarity Act on the ruling.

Sectionalism   the American term for a political sentiment leading to conflict between regions, of which the Civil War was the most dramatic example. Canadians use the term regionalism to describe the same phenomenon, but in the United States regionalism refers only to co-operative relations among neighbouring states.

Selectivist   refers to programs which provide income or services to needy individuals only. Selectivist programs are contrasted with universal programs which provide benefits to all individuals. An example of a selectivist program is social assistance.

Skills policies   training programs designed to enhance the vocational or work-related aptitudes of workers.

Social assistance   Often referred to as 'welfare', this is a benefit provided to individuals without adequate income from all other sources. In Canada, social assistance is provided by provincial governments (in Ontario with the assistance of municipalities).

Social insurance program   is a contributory program in which eligibility for benefit and the level of benefit depend on contributions made during employment by the individual and his or her employers. Leading examples are Employment Insurance and the Canada Pension Plan. (See also 'Contributory pension'.)

Sovereignty-Association   The central plank in the Parti Québécois platform under René Lévesque was sovereignty-association, a scheme that called for the independence of Quebec, linked to a negotiated political and economic association with the rest of Canada.

Supreme Court Reference on Secession   In response to the question of whether Quebec had the right to unilaterally declare its independence, the Supreme Court of Canada found that Quebec possessed no such right, either in international or Canadian law. But it also said that, in the event that a clear majority of provincial voters in response to a clear question favoured independence, there would be a constitutional obligation on the part of the rest of Canada to negotiate with Quebec.

Tax allocation   refers to the division of tax revenues among the jurisdictions in which they have been generated.

Tax base   refers to the part of the economy that is explicitly covered by the tax in question.

Tax expenditure   is spending in the form of foregone government revenues, usually as a specific tax credit or deduction. Tax expenditures are not usually shown in budget documents as expenditures as such.

Tax harmonization   refers to the effort to make tax structure and its implementation similar across the provinces, to ensure that individuals and firms can move freely and do business in all parts of the federation (i.e., the economic union). Harmonized tax structures need not be identical, but key features such as tax base will be identical or very similar.

'Tax on tax'   is the system in which provincial tax payable is expressed as a percentage of the federal tax payable, levied on the identical tax base, and using the same tax rates and brackets. A separate provincial 'tax on income' implies separate tax rates and brackets (and possibly tax base) for the provincial share.

Tax point   See 'tax room'

Tax rate   is the percentage of income or business transaction payable as tax. *Tax brackets* divide total incomes in order to tax higher income at a higher rate. For example, federal personal income tax in 1999–2001 had five different income brackets. Bracket creep occurs when inflation, rather than a real salary increase, pushes a taxpayer into a higher tax bracket.

Tax room   provides—usually through a transfer of percentage points of tax share—'room' for the provinces to collect a greater share of a given tax base, while the federal share is correspondingly reduced.

Third order of government   the recognition of Aboriginal governing authorities as a legally distinct order of government within the Canadian Constitution.

TILMA   acronym for Trade, Investment and Labour Mobility Agreement, meaning specifically the agreement between Alberta and British Columbia signed in 2009.

Treaty federalism   federal association between sovereign Aboriginal nations and the Canadian state based on the negotiation of agreements amongst equal partners that have a status equivalent to international treaties.

Tremblay Report   Quebec Premier Maurice Duplessis created the Royal Commission of Inquiry on Constitutional Problems in 1953 in response to what he saw as the centralizing approach of the federal Rowell-Sirois Report and the Massey Commission. Headed by Justice Thomas Tremblay, the report elaborated a powerful, philosophically grounded view of traditional French Canadian culture, and advanced a classical understanding of federalism in which each order of government (but particularly the federal government) would confine itself scrupulously to its own sphere of jurisdiction.

UNFCCC (United Nations Framework Convention on Climate Change)   an international treaty produced at the United Nations Conference on Environment and Development (UNCED) in 1992. The treaty provides an overall framework for addressing climate change. In 1997 the Kyoto Protocol was adopted under the convention. The protocol commits certain countries (including Canada) to specific GHG emission reduction targets.

Unilateral federalism   the dynamic of one order of government (usually the federal) imposing its views and priorities on the other (usually the provincial), by attaching conditions to its fiscal transfers.

Unilateralism   the state of intergovernmental governance in which each level of government acts independently of the other (McRoberts, 1985: 71).

Universality   Requires that all residents of the province be entitled to public health insurance coverage.

Vertical fiscal gap   refers to a situation in which the central government's revenues exceed its expenditure needs and the provinces' revenues do not exceed theirs. In most federations the central government reduces the gap by transferring some of its surplus to the provinces.

Vertical fiscal imbalance   occurs when the *vertical fiscal gap* is not sufficiently reduced by transfer payments from the federal government, and provinces claim a chronic inability to meet their expenditure responsibilities with their own revenues.

Veto points   refer to a decision-making system in which the approval of a number of politically independent agents or agencies is required, thereby giving each of those agents or agencies the ability to block or 'veto' proposals for change.

WCI (Western Climate Initiative)   an initiative of a number of US states and Canadian provinces to adopt joint policies to reduce their GHG emissions.

WTO (World Trade Organization)   replaced the GATT in 1995 as a forum for the negotiation and enforcement of multilateral trade agreements to liberalize trade. (See its website: www.wto.org.)

Index